Hegel

Religion, Economics, and the Politics of Spirit
1770–1807

IDEAS IN CONTEXT

Edited by Richard Rorty, J. B. Schneewind, Quentin Skinner,
and Wolf Lepenies

The books in this series will discuss the emergence of intellectual traditions and of related new disciplines. The procedures, aims, and vocabularies that were generated will be set in the context of the alternatives available within the contemporary frameworks of ideas and institutions. Through detailed studies of the evolution of such traditions, and their modification by different audiences, it is hoped that a new picture will form of the development of ideas in their concrete contexts. By this means, artificial distinctions among the history of philosophy, of the various sciences, of society and politics, and of literature may be seen to dissolve.

Titles published in the series:

Richard Rorty, J. B. Schneewind, Quentin Skinner (eds.), *Philosophy in History*
J. G. A. Pocock, *Virtue, Commerce, and History*
M. M. Goldsmith, *Private Vices, Public Benefits*
Laurence Dickey, *Hegel: Religion, Economics, and the Politics of Spirit, 1770–1807*

Forthcoming titles include:

Keith Baker, *Approaching the French Revolution: Essays on the Political Culture of the Old Regime*
Martin Dzelzainis, *The Ideological Origins of the English Revolution*
Mark Goldie, *The Tory Ideology: Politics and Ideas in Restoration England*
Ian Hacking, *The Taming of Chance*
Lynn S. Joy, *Gassendi the Atomist*
Lorenz Kruger (ed.), *Probability in Science to 1930*
Edmund Leites (ed.), *Conscience and Casuistry in Early Modern Europe*
Wolf Lepenies, *The Three Cultures*
David Lieberman, *The Province of Legislation Determined*
Noel Malcolm, *Hobbes and Voluntarism*
Nicolai Rubinstein, *Essays in Renaissance Political Theory*
Quentin Skinner, *Ambrogio Lorenzetti*
Quentin Skinner, *Studies in Early Modern Intellectual History*
Margo Todd, *Christian Humanism and the Puritan Social Order*

This series is published with the support of the Exxon Education Foundation.

Hegel

Religion, Economics, and the
Politics of Spirit
1770–1807

LAURENCE DICKEY

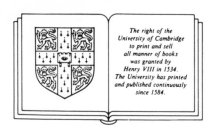

The right of the
University of Cambridge
to print and sell
all manner of books
was granted by
Henry VIII in 1534.
The University has printed
and published continuously
since 1584.

CAMBRIDGE UNIVERSITY PRESS

Cambridge

New York   Port Chester   Melbourne   Sydney

Published by the Press Syndicate of the University of Cambridge
The Pitt Building, Trumpington Street, Cambridge CB2 1RP
40 West 20th Street, New York, NY 10011, USA
10 Stamford Road, Oakleigh, Melbourne 3166, Australia

First published 1987
First paperback edition 1989

Printed in the United States of America

Library of Congress Cataloging-in-Publication Data
Dickey, Laurence Winant.
Hegel: religion, economics, and the politics of spirit, 1770–1807.
(Ideas in context)
Bibliography: p.
Includes index.
1. Hegel, Georg Wilhelm Friedrich, 1770–1831.
I. Title.   II. Series.
B2948.D6   1987   193   87-711

ISBN 0-521-33035-1 hard covers
ISBN 0-521-38912-7 paperback

British Library Cataloging in Publication available

Contents

Preface

This study of Hegel began as a Ph.D. thesis in intellectual history at the University of California, in 1974. At the time, I thought my research project had a manageable focus: All I wished to do was make some historical sense of Hegel's intellectual development prior to the completion of the *Phenomenology* in 1806. Very quickly, however, I realized how naive my initial expectation had been; I discovered that a historical study of Hegel's development required a highly complex and elaborate explanatory structure. There was, I learned, much truth to Weber's distinction between *aktuelle Verstehen* ("direct" or "observational understanding") and *erklärendes Verstehen* ("explanatory understanding").[1] Or, to put it another way, I realized there was a difference between a philosophical explanation of the historical development of Hegel's thought and a historical explanation of his philosophy as a process of development.[2]

Of course, one could argue in commonsensical fashion that the best way to understand any thinker is to read him, but when it comes to Hegel that is not an altogether satisfactory procedure. For not all thinkers can be understood with equal ease, and this caveat is especially true of Hegel not only because of the density and complexity of his thought but also because he came out of a German and European cultural tradition that has become quite foreign to the twentieth-century Western mind. Thus, a beginning student is likely to find Hegel's thought almost incomprehensible on first reading.

Indeed, Hegel is a thinker who needs to be read with a discerning commentary alongside – better yet, with several such commentaries alongside. But here a problem arises: that of the interpretative diversity of Hegelian scholarship. Hegel, after all, was a genius, and he was protean. In addition, he was a "reader" – he read widely and in several subject areas. Consequently, his work has attracted the attention of scholars with a variety of intellectual interests. The result, as William Wallace noted long before the twentieth-century "takeoff" in Hegel studies, has been that "interpreters of his system have contradicted each other, almost as variously as the several commentators on the Bible."[3] This means, in turn, that an engagement with the principal works of Hegelian scholarship leaves one with the impression that Hegel's thought can have one meaning, and also several other different meanings all at once; and this impression encourages one to discount the possibility of ever discovering any particular historical coherence in his thought.

In view of this diversity of interpretation, one might well wonder if anything at all new can be said about Hegel's thought. Of late, scholars have proposed to meet this hermeneutical challenge with the battle cry – "back to the text." This, however, strikes me as an altogether inappropriate strategy for gaining new insight into the coherence of Hegel's thought. For the argument that informs this approach presumes the "innocence" of a text and its meaning can be understood quite apart from considerations of historical context.[4] The key assumptions in this strategy are that a thinker's work is an autonomous and self-contained object of inquiry whose meaning, if it is a "classic," is "timeless," and that, as a classic, it embodies a closed system of inner meaning which requires no outer references to be understood. According to this view, works of genius are of perennial relevance and only need to be read "line by line" and "over and over again" before they reveal the "essential meaning" of a thinker's thought.[5]

For the purpose of developing a truly historical perspective on Hegel's work much of the force of this argument is of dubious value, first, because it diverts attention from the historical question of Hegel's relationship to his world and, second, because it completely avoids the matter of the existing interpretative diversity of Hegelian scholarship.[6] For the meaning of what Hegel "said" in any (or all) of his works has been construed in several different ways by a number of diligent, resourceful, and very talented interpreters. And that is not only because each generation of scholars is bound to rewrite history for itself but also because, as Paul Ricoeur has noted, a thinker's work is "like a cube or volume in space"; it presents itself in several different "reliefs," each of which offers a viewer a different perspective on the whole of which it is but a part.[7]

If this is true, and I think it is, then the meaning of Hegel's work is not self-evident, and to insist that it is, and that the matter of the interpretative diversity of Hegelian scholarship can be resolved by returning to Hegel's texts and by tightening up the rigor of the "logical analysis" of the ideas presented in them, is simply presumptuous and will lead to more controverted interpretation rather than to clarification of Hegel's meaning.

In keeping with these convictions, I have chosen to approach Hegel in another way. My guiding methodological assumption is that to explain the coherence of Hegel's thought as a developmental sequence we need to begin by giving a historical account of what he was writing about when his thought can be said to have begun to develop. And that means we need to know something about his origins.

Very often the point of departure for a discussion of a thinker's origins is biography. For reasons that are explained in the Introduction to this study, I have elected not to pursue that strategy. Suffice it to say an examination of Hegel's biography (as biography) does not help us explain much about what he was thinking and writing about in the late 1780s and 1790s – when he was a schoolboy living in the Duchy of Württemberg. Instead, I approach the problem of Hegel's origins by offering what Clifford Geertz would call a "thick description" of the world in which he lived.[8] That world was the Protestant culture of "Old-Württemberg" in the eighteenth century. Indeed, it is Hegel's experience of that culture – of its assumptions, preoccupations, and problems – that constitutes the point of departure for this study of Hegel's thought as a process of development.[9]

In Part I of this study I try to locate Hegel within this *context*. I do so in three different yet related ways. First, I emphasize that the Duchy of Württemberg was unique among "the Germanys" in the eighteenth century.[10] Second, I make the rather obvious point that this *setting* impinged on Hegel in varying ways.[11] So, rather than undertake a discussion of the history of all that existed in Old-Württemberg (i.e., *histoire totale*), I try to pinpoint what aspects of that *culture* were crucial conditioners of the young Hegel's thought.[12] Thus, in Chapters 1, 2, and 3, I examine the culture of Old-Württemberg in terms of two of its main traditions – namely, the religious tradition of "down-to-earth" Pietism and the political tradition of the "Good Old Law." By so doing, I establish *a* cultural context within which Hegel can be placed.[13] Finally, I try to show that the interplay between the two traditions defined what Kenneth Burke would call the "circumference" of the young Hegel's thought.[14] Fundamental to this endeavor is the attempt to show that Protestant civil piety, a religiopolitical concept that was formed by the interplay between the two traditions, became a "core concept" in the development of Hegel's thought.[15]

In Part II I slightly shift the focus of Hegel's relation to the Protestant culture of Old-Württemberg. Thus, in Chapter 4 I emphasize how Hegel's writings of the 1790s revolved around the concept of Protestant civil piety. Indeed, in this chapter I show how the "spins" Hegel gave to his concepts of *Volksreligion* and *Sittlichkeit* reflected his abiding concern with the ideal of Protestant civil piety.[16]

Saying that much of what Hegel wrote in the 1790s can be explained
in terms of his Württemberg origins would seem to imply that this
is synecdochic study in intellectual history.[17] As such, the arguments
of Parts I and II would seem to be susceptible to the charge of over-
contextualization.[18] It could be claimed, for example, that I have allowed
the context to "overwhelm" the thinker and, by so doing, have done an
injustice to Hegel's "genius."[19] Obviously, I think that this line of
criticism is unfair, for it misses the *historical* point of the problem of
Hegel's Württemberg origins.[20] The fact is that Hegel was a "representative" Württemberg thinker until some time in the 1790s.[21] He was not
born a genius and probably only began to think like one when he started
to reflect on the matter of the relationship between Protestant civil piety
and the emergent socioeconomic and political forces he came to learn
about in studies he undertook after having left Württemberg in 1793. It
is at this point, I think, that Hegel becomes Hegel and his genius begins
to reveal itself over time and independent of his Württemberg origins.

In Part III, therefore, the conceptual thrust of my narrative changes
radically. That is because, as Hegel begins to relate his conception of
Protestant civil piety to what R. D. Cumming would call his "other
studies," it is no longer possible to discuss his development unilinearly –
as moving in a single direction and in terms of a sequence that begins in
the culture of Old-Württemberg.[22] Previously, Hegel had allowed his core
concept, Protestant civil piety, to shape other concepts in its image. From
1794 on, however, Hegel had to square Protestant civil piety with what
he was learning from his other studies – that is, from what he was reading
about "political economy," "sociological realism," and history in his
Scottish sources (e.g., Ferguson, Smith, and Steuart).

In Chapters 5 through 8 I try to explain the adjustments Hegel made
in his thinking in order to reconcile his religiopolitical conception of
Protestant civil piety with those socioeconomic and historical studies.[23]
Very briefly, the adjustments were of several kinds and unfolded more or
less over the ten-year period 1794 to 1804. Up to, say, 1794, the idea of
Protestant civil piety possessed something like absolute value for Hegel.
Indeed, as a framework for experience it governed much of his behavior
and expectations, to the extent that it could be said to have constituted his
"second nature."[24] There was, however, very little room within that
framework for economic influences – which is to say that Protestant civil
piety could function as an unquestioned cultural ideal for Hegel only as
long as he remained ignorant of economics.

All that changed sometime in the mid-1790s, when Hegel "discovered
the economy." At that time his reading of the Scots convinced him that
Protestant civil piety could not function as a motivational and cultural
ideal as long as it failed to take account of the economy and the way it

shaped the dynamic of modern social life. To this end, I explain in Chapters 6 and 7 how adjustments Hegel made in his conception of *Sittlichkeit* reflected a larger effort to restate the doctrine of Protestant civil piety in a language and form that met the requirements of late eighteenth-century Scottish thought.

Here, it is important to note three things. First, throughout this period Hegel continues to talk about *Sittlichkeit* as a collective ethical idea. Second, although *Sittlichkeit* remains a constant concern in his thought during these years, the nature of that concern changes markedly after his discovery of economics. Whereas before 1794 Hegel had regarded *Sittlichkeit* as a universal prescription for all kinds of contemporary historical problems, he treats it after that date as an ideal that itself needs to be situated within a historically specific constellation of socioeconomic forces. Finally, we need to note that Hegel's decision to shift the conceptual context in which *Sittlichkeit* has been located does not necessarily entail abandonment of Protestant civil piety as a religiopolitical ideal. What happens is not so much the displacement of one theory of collective life by another as the relocation of *Sittlichkeit* in another context, one that had been articulated *on the level of theory* by the Scots. Hegel's problem, therefore, was not so much how to preserve the ideal of *Sittlichkeit* against the forces of the world depicted by the Scots as how to insinuate and ensure the persistence of *Sittlichkeit* in the kind of world they had described. Or, to put it differently, Hegel's problem was how to turn the arguments of the Scottish Enlightenment to the advantage of the religiopolitical ideal of Protestant civil piety.

Understanding the texts in which this shift in the context of *Sittlichkeit* occurs is complicated by two other problems. That Hegel accepted the main thrust of Scottish thought cannot be gainsaid. But there can also be no doubt that he had reservations about how the Scots viewed the triangular relation among economy, society, and politics. Specifically, the Scots had persuaded Hegel of the need for "objectivity" in the study of society; but within that framework Hegel resisted their tendency to treat man as a *social* being whose nature was essentially *economic*. So, while he admired the Scots for both their socioeconomic objectivism and their materialistic sense of history, he aimed from the start at altering the "modality" of their arguments, especially those that celebrated the naturalism and materialism of collective life.[25]

That this was Hegel's intention is clear from the ambiguity he deliberately built into his concept of *Sittlichkeit*.[26] Indeed, historically to appreciate Hegel's thought as a process of development depends in large part on understanding the way he synonymizes and then desynonymizes the terms "natural" and "*Sittlichkeit*" in his writings after 1800. In his Scottish mode, Hegel is quite willing to synonymize the two – that is, to discuss the economy, its social implications, and the ethical life of the collectivity in terms of *natürliche Sittlichkeit*. In this mode, Hegel means to be objective, historical, contemporary, and so on. But the "modality" of what he writes about *natürliche Sittlichkeit* is governed by a hidden agenda, by a larger conceptual purpose, namely, to draw attention to the conceptual need to desynonymize the two terms. Here Hegel's argument is that if the collectivity were ever to have the quality of a truly ethical life, it would have to create *within* the realm of objective experience itself a sphere of action designed to promote the realization of "true *Sittlichkeit*." And although Hegel discusses this sphere in the conditional mode, there can be no doubt it was associated in his mind with *Sittlichkeit* qua the religiopolitical ideal of Protestant civil piety.[27]

When, therefore, Hegel begins to adjust his conception of *Sittlichkeit* to what he has learned from his Scottish studies, he simultaneously begins to develop not only a critique of the substance of those studies but an argument for the reconstitution of Protestant civil piety as well. There is, in other words, a "triple transition" taking place in Hegel's thought from 1794 on. First, he is shifting the discussion of *Sittlichkeit* to a more "objective" context; second, he is criticizing *certain aspects* of the ethical life that obtain within that context; and, finally, he is manipulating that criticism so that it will lead to the reconstitution of true *Sittlichkeit* from a point of view *internal* to the "new" objective context itself.[28]

In many respects, the story of Hegel's development between 1794 and 1804 pivots on the way he attempts to negotiate this triple transition. For that reason, it is important to hold each of the three "moments" of transition separate. To do otherwise, to collapse each moment into a larger "moment" of objective experience, would be to overlook Hegel's realism and deprive his thought of much of its complexity and conceptual dynamic. Indeed, to do so would be to blur the distinctions Hegel made between the economic, social, and political dimensions of objective experience; and it is precisely Hegel's sense of those distinctions and their relations with one another that explains why his thought developed the way it did after 1794.

Finally, in the Epilogue to this study, I offer some reflections on how the *Phenomenology* in general and the concept of "absolute *Geist*" in particular stand relative to the triple transition Hegel had tried to negotiate between 1794 and 1804. Here I attempt to show that this triple transition was not so much background to the *Phenomenology* as the mold in which that great book was cast. Even so, it is very difficult to decide whether the *Phenomenology* constitutes a fourth moment of transition in Hegel's thought or a variation on the thrust and meaning of the arguments he had made while fleshing out the substance of the third transition. Clarification of much of the confusion about Hegel as thinker,

I argue, depends on understanding what issues are involved in resolving that complex matter.

One last preliminary word, I think, is in order here. Because of my contextual commitments I have had to discuss a good deal of material that will strike the reader, at least initially, as not immediately relevant to the Hegel of conventional scholarship. This is especially true of Part I, where I have had to go back in time to the early Christian era in order to make clear the theological issues that exercised German Protestants in the eighteenth century. This procedure of "gearing up" in fifteen hundred years of Christian history to talk about Hegel is, I think, absolutely necessary if we are to avoid repeating the many errors past scholars have made in this vital area of Hegel scholarship. Moreover, what I have discovered in going over this history myself is that there were resources within the Christian tradition that Hegel drew upon to reconcile his religious commitments with his socioeconomic studies. A truly historical study of Hegel, therefore, must at some point gesture in the direction of this material. To do that conscientiously, in a way that does not simply reiterate conventional wisdom, requires working through the material carefully and in a manner that allows the reader to understand why the argument unfolds as it does. Part I of this study is designed to serve that pedagogical purpose. But so as not to overencumber the narrative, I have addressed a number of important issues of interpretation in the notes to the chapters that constitute Part I.

Acknowledgments

Finally, after so many years, I have the opportunity publicly to acknowledge the many institutional, professional, and personal debts I have accumulated while preparing this manuscript for publication. Early on, while working on this project as a graduate student, I received substantial institutional support from the University of California at Berkeley. I was privileged to attend that great public university both as an undergraduate and as a graduate student, and I was astonished that the university in general and the history department in particular always found ways to fund research and writing while I was a student there. Concurrently, I received generous support for dissertation work from the Council for European Studies (1974), from the German Academic Exchange Service (1974–75), and from the Mabel McLeod Lewis Memorial Fund of Stanford University (1978–79).

Subsequently, while preparing the manuscript of this book, I substantially rewrote the dissertation and, in the process, incurred many new institutional debts. To acknowledge them I should like to thank the Council for Research in the Social Sciences at Columbia University for supporting my work during the summers of 1981 and 1983; and the Spencer Foundation of Teachers College, Columbia University, for a summer grant in 1982. Above all, I owe a special debt of gratitude to the Institute for Advanced Study at Princeton. While a member of the Institute's School of Social Science in 1983–84, I had the time, under the most favorable conditions, to write what amounts to Parts II and III of this study. I am deeply grateful, therefore, to the faculty of the School of Social Science, especially to Wolf Lepenies, for having invited me for the year. It was, for me, a most rewarding experience.

During both stages of the work I did on this manuscript, I received unwavering support and encouragement from two of my teachers – William J. Bouwsma and Martin E. Malia. All I can say about them is that, were it not for their examples and for the confidence they showed in me, this study would never have been completed. For personal as well as professional reasons, therefore, I dedicate this book to them.

I also feel a more general obligation to those who have read particular sections of this manuscript and have suggested ways to improve them. So, to Peter Brown, Julian Franklin, George Kelly, Majorie Reeves, Melvin Richter, and Quentin Skinner — thank you for your comments and for saving me from some embarrassing scholarly blunders. In addition, I wish to offer particular acknowledgments here to Reinhard Bendix, Hans Rosenberg, and Quentin Skinner. During my years at Berkeley, Bendix and Rosenberg were exceptionally generous to me with their time and with their extraordinary knowledge of German history. I am most appreciative of that. More recently, Quentin Skinner not only has extended many kindnesses to me but also has gone out of his way to encourage me in the Hegel project. And thank you, Quentin, for suggesting that Cambridge University Press might be interested in a study of this sort.

My indebtedness to colleagues and friends at Columbia University is at least as great. Were it not for their patience, advice, and pleasant company, I surely would have tried to rush this study into print. In particular, I owe special debts to Marc Raeff and Wim Smit for reading and commenting on large parts of the manuscript and for their constant goodwill. I would also like to thank J. Malcolm Bean, Michael Rosenthal, and Isser Woloch for general support and encouragement while I was bringing this project to term. And to the late Stephen Koss I wish to extend belated thanks for the many considerations he rendered me while we were colleagues at Columbia University.

Finally, I am grateful to Jacqueline Philpott and Dorothy Shannon for expert typing and editorial work during the time when I was preparing this manuscript. To Jacqueline, in particular, I am obliged for many things besides, not the least of which was a very special companionship that sustained me when I despaired of scholarship.

Introduction
Hegel in a Protestant cultural context

Any number of students of Hegel's thought have noted that he grew up in a Protestant culture.[1] Few of these students, however, have thought it necessary to explain how different one Protestant culture could be from another among the congeries of states that comprised "the Germanys" in the eighteenth century.[2] That, I think, is because most scholars have rather uncritically accepted the argument that Hegel's idealism is "the last great expression" of a German cultural tradition that has its religious roots in Protestant "inwardness" and its political roots in subordination of the individual to state authority.[3]

In this introductory chapter, I wish to show how misleading this view is as a point of departure for the study of Hegel's thought. Although in some general sense Hegel's origins were indeed German Protestant, they were rooted more specifically in a Protestant culture that, because it was ruled by a Catholic duke, could neither counsel nor countenance the values that governed the relation between religion and politics elsewhere in Germany. On the contrary, for most of the eighteenth century the Protestant culture of Old-Württemberg was governed by an ideal of civil piety that required extensive political vigilance vis-à-vis an absolutizing and catholicizing duke.[4] It is the dynamics of this particular Protestant culture, not some "global" German one, that we need to reflect upon if we are to understand Hegel's origins.[5] The argument of this chapter moves toward that end.

1. The "old man" as schoolboy

The first twenty-four years of Hegel's life have posed something of a problem for students of his thought. Most of his biographers have duly noted the paucity of evidence and information that have come down to us from these, his "schoolboy years" – a period that runs, say, from Hegel's entry into the lower division of the Stuttgart Gymnasium Illustre in 1777 to the completion of his studies at the University of Tübingen in 1793.[6] Part of the gap in our knowledge about these early years is directly attributable to Hegel himself. A man of protean intellectual interests, always ready to talk or write on any subject, Hegel unfortunately never deigned to discuss or write about his own origins, intellectual or otherwise.

Moreover, there is little in the way of commentary from contemporaries to corroborate suspicions about the goings-on of these years.[7] Like his equally famous co-Württemberger Schiller, Hegel left little personal information: we have only a few anecdotes and vague recollections from a sister, Christiane, to help fill the gaps in the record.[8] We do, of course, possess a collection of documents in Hegel's hand that date from this period.[9] This body of evidence includes some sporadic entries that – in the manner of schoolboys of the period – Hegel made in a *Tagebuch* (diary) between June 1785 and January 1787;[10] several essays and some materials that were prepared for classroom presentation between 1785 and 1793; and numerous excerpts from academic journals and books that Hegel apparently had read during these years and wanted to preserve for future scholastic references.[11] But for the most part this evidence is fragmentary, thematically disjointed, and not easily related to the problem scholars have posited as central to an understanding of Hegel's "mature" philosophical outlook.

With only these sources to draw upon, scholars have been reluctant to read too much intellectual significance into the schoolboy period.[12] The available evidence, it has been pointed out, simply will not support any broad generalizations about the formation of Hegel's early intellectual outlook.[13] Still, when pressed – as scholars invariably are – to explain the importance of this period for Hegel's intellectual development, his biographers have elected to approach the period in terms of Hegel's personality and its relation to his "method" of thought.

To this end, Hegel's biographers have remarked – almost to a man – upon the "objective" character of the schoolboy documents.[14] Karl Rosenkranz, Hegel's first biographer, was quick to note the careful, measured, and modest intellectual quality of these early academic exercises. Since then, Hegelian scholarship has elaborated on Rosenkranz's observation and used it to substantiate the claim that from an early age Hegel was inclined toward a life of scholarship.[15] How else explain the unpretentious, thoroughly controlled, and almost detached academic quality of the essays; the meticulousness manifest in the organization, indexing, and cross-referencing of the excerpted material; the attention lavished on books assiduously secured for the "private" library of a boy of eight?

Furthermore, Hegel scholars are at one in maintaining that while these early schoolboy exercises do not presage the originality and genius of later years, they do manifest concerns that are studiously precocious – at the very least they are not those of a "typical" schoolboy (then or now).[16] After all, as Christiane has told us, Hegel was a model student.[17] In fact, he was valedictorian of the class that graduated from the Stuttgart Gymnasium in 1788, an honor that earned him an all-important third-place ranking in the "promotion" that entered the University of Tübingen in the fall of the same year.[18] And it certainly was no accident that Hegel's *Kommilitonen* (schoolmates) made light of his diligence, reliability, and respect for traditional *Bürger* values and standards of behavior by tagging him with the nickname "the old man," the same nickname contemporaries gave to J. J. Moser, who, during Hegel's youth, was the epitome of "Old-Württemberg" values.[19]

This biographical preoccupation with Hegel's early propensity for scholarship and his "overly normal" personality has prompted several scholars to add a speculative broad brush stroke to the imperfect character sketch that has come down to us from the schoolboy period.[20] For these scholars, a deeper significance may be drawn from study of the labored and self-conscious academic "works" of these years. According to this view, Hegel in his youth was not a homogeneous or original thinker, as were his Tübingen companions Schelling and Hölderlin.[21] Compared with the intuitive genius of these two thinkers, Hegel's was a reflective intelligence. For that reason, Hegelian scholarship has hypothesized that Hegel's objectivity was part of an effort to try to compensate intellectually for a personal deficiency – for a lack of imagination that was reflected in a natural disposition toward "boyish pendantry."[22]

To support this conjecture, these scholars note how Hegel was academically mature beyond his years. They note how he liked to pass time with older men (when possible, with his teachers), walking and discussing intellectual issues,[23] and how he showed respect for the integrity and authority of traditional ideas and values as well as for the claims of new ones. Above all, however, they point to Hegel's patience, which stood in marked contrast to the impulsiveness and daring of Schelling and Hölderlin. The long and tedious hours Hegel spent excerpting material on subjects that interested him demanded a patience, perseverance, and discipline of mind that was highly unusual for a boy his age. He was old beyond his years, as it were. Moreover, his willingness to think through problems from every conceivable point of view – indeed, his entire manner of thought – gave every indication of a scholar in the making. These traits did not always endear Hegel to his more impetuous and playful classmates, however; for whatever the subject, whatever the consensus, the old man could find a way to complicate the simplest matter. Thus, at Tübingen, his fellows bestowed upon him and his overly cautious academic ways the title of *"lumen obscurum."*[24]

Hegel, then, was a slow developer; and he had a plodding intellectual style to match – which meant that the "reflective" and "objective" cast of his mind compelled him to develop a high tolerance of the opinions of others. Only after broad exposure to, and thorough immersion in, the problems that exercised his youthful intelligence did Hegel think it proper to venture an intellectual determination of his own. Thus, scholars have argued, the content of the schoolboy exercises is more a "notional" than a "real" expression of his early intellectual views: it is indicative of the *direction* of his interests, not of his opinions per se.[25] And since Hegel did not give "real" assent to these ideas, it is impossible to reduce them to a consistent intellectual position. Hence, they reason, the hard core of Hegel's youthful intellectual convictions lies less in the content than in the form of these early writings – in the spirit of inquiry that animates them, and in the systematic and scholarly way Hegel set about the task of framing intellectual problems and faithfully representing the opinions of others. Their conclusion: if there is any hidden long-range significance to be gleaned from these documents, it is to be found in what Hegel's method tells us about his personality.

Hegel's intellectual openness, his sense for the nuances of problems, and his tolerance of the ideas of others meant that he often began an intellectual endeavor by acquiescing in the say-so of others. But rather than raise questions about his originality, Hegel's dependence on the work of others has invited scholarly speculation about what sources were crucial to his early development. After all, since as a youth Hegel was allegedly a passive borrower of ideas of other thinkers, it would seem to follow that an acquaintance with his reading may cast light on the issue of his intellectual development.

This concern with Hegel's literary experience – which has been greatly enhanced by the availability of the excerpted material – is of a piece with two important developments in twentieth-century Hegelian scholarship: the study of the intellectual influences on his thought during its formative years and the study of the chronology of his writings. Actually, an overview of the *raison d'être* behind each historiographical development suggests the following convergence of scholarly interest. Because Hegel was a reflective thinker who arrived at his intellectual determinations slowly, it is possible to explain his development in terms of the assimilation of the thought of certain key thinkers, for far from setting his own terms of intellectual debate, Hegel generally followed the leads of others. As a matter of course, Hegel read widely and in scattered sources. But we know by his own admission that he found the work of Kant, Fichte, and Schelling most stimulating. Taking Hegel at his word about his admitted sources, many scholars have held that the emergent and evolving thought patterns of German idealism were crucial to his development.[26] As they argue the point, Hegel fell under the successive influences of Kant,

Fichte, and Schelling before bringing the *Entwicklungsgeschichte* of German idealism to its culmination, and its close, in his own work. The assumption of these studies is clear: Hegel's development from the schoolboy years, through young manhood, and down to the *Phenomenology*, recapitulated the philosophical movement of German idealism as a whole. In that respect, these studies hold that the coherence of Hegel's development is intellectually best understood in terms of an "idealist in the making."

Studies of the chronology of Hegel's writings have led to similar conclusions.[27] According to these studies, the most obvious changes in Hegel's thought during these early years occurred after his reading of something new in the writings of Kant, Fichte, and Schelling. Beginning with his encounters with problems in the philosophy of Kant while at Berne (1794–1796), Hegel allegedly moved from one philosophical system to another – from Kant's to Fichte's and from Fichte's to Schelling's – before, finally, moving from Schelling's to one of his own making. Again, the argument is that Hegel's development is best understood internally – as a series of changes rooted in the systematic, philosophical correction of the method of one idealist's thought by another. Thus, here too the tie between Hegel's development and the successive historical stages in the unfolding of German idealism is preserved.

Needless to say, the studies that have demonstrated the correspondence between the major turns in the pattern of Hegel's biobibliographical development and the ingress of Kant's, Fichte's, and Schelling's ideas into his thought fit in rather well with the tendency to emphasize the methodological significance of his schoolboy personality. Ostensibly, Hegel's propensity for objectivity made him susceptible to the influence of Kant, Fichte, and Schelling, the dominant thinkers of the period, and the combined impact of their influence was reflected in the course of his philosophical development into a full-fledged idealist. Even more important, though, this convergence of historiographical interest makes it possible to read the "method" of the schoolboy period into the early works and to argue that the continuity of development between the two periods constitutes the essence of a coherent intellectual outlook: namely, that which expressed itself in the idealism of the "young Hegel." And from this it follows that the "logic" of Hegel's development is the same as that of German idealism, and is best apprehended systematically, as the gradual application, refinement, and extension of the methodological principles of philosophical idealism to all areas of human experience.

2. The ideal of Protestant civil piety in Old-Württemberg

That, of course, is an assumption we intend to question here. Despite its neatness, much about this approach to Hegel's thought is inadequate.

First of all, and aside from the overall tautological character of the Hegel – German idealism connection, the approach is inadequate on methodological grounds because it tends to reduce intellectual history to intellectual biography; and, as I have already observed, intellectual history involves (or should involve) more than that. It is not enough, I think, for the intellectual historian to proceed in a descriptive fashion – to know, in this case, what Hegel "said" on this or that matter, and when; what he read, and when he read it; which authors stimulated him and which did not; and where he stood in relation to the broader intellectual currents of the age. Standing on the shoulders of giants, Hegelian scholarship can today set its sights higher – that is, it can put its findings at the service of broader historiographical problems. Hence, our approach to Hegel will be expository, argumentative, and historical, and will be designed to show what is central and what is peripheral to Hegel's thought, and why he borrowed from certain thinkers rather than others. In short, our approach will try to establish a "criteria of relevance" for Hegel's borrowings by relating the problems he confronted in his early work to the cultural context in which he lived.[28]

This brings us to a second reason the "idealist in the making" approach to Hegel is inadequate. It lacks a proper sense of historical context, of how circumstances of time (the late *Aufklärung*) and place (Old-Württemberg) shaped Hegel's thought.[29] Admittedly, much can be learned about Hegel from a study of the Kant–Fichte–Schelling philosophical sequence. But Hegel was not born an idealist. Nor was he born a Kantian, or even a philosopher. Though he was a cautious and careful scholar, systematic, philosophical thought was something he learned over the years. Indeed, as a youth, he hardly possessed anything like a clearly delineated method of thought and exposition. In fact, during these years Hegel was eclectically casting about to discover and establish his own intellectual identity.[30] In this quest, however, it was the culture of Old-Württemberg, not the principles of German idealism, that furnished what Lucien Febvre would have called the "mental equipment" of his mind.[31]

To this end, we should remember that although Hegel is known primarily as a philosopher, he was basically a theologian *manqué*. He was trained in theology at Tübingen, and at a time when the university was polarized over the moral and religious implications of Kant's philosophy.[32] While the "Old Tübingen" school of theology, which was led by Professors Flatt and Storr, was attempting to use the skeptical dimension of Kantianism to preserve a belief in biblical supernaturalism, a younger generation of enthusiasts among the student body saw in Kant's work the means to free mankind from both religious superstition and the clutches of the very orthodox church that supported it. As a consequence, Hegel's chief intellectual concern in the 1790s was not so much with

philosophy as with theology. And that concern put Hegel in the main-
stream more of declining eighteenth-century than of emergent nineteenth-
century patterns of thought. So, if Hegel was early on a practitioner of
methodological procedures that allow us to characterize him as a
nineteenth-century idealist in the making, we must remember that it was
toward resolution of the religious problems of Old-Württemberg that he
directed these procedures. And by making these problems his own, Hegel
became ipso facto a representative of much that concerned the "last
generation" of Old-Württembergers.[33]

Indeed, Hegel was born and raised in Old-Württemberg and had been
nourished on its traditions; and in the eighteenth century that meant a
great deal in terms of one's intellectual outlook. In the eighteenth century, to claim Old-Württemberg "origins" was to assert much more than
one's *place* of birth. As Rürup has noted, Old-Württemberg connoted
more than a *Heimat* (homeland): it stood for a tradition and way of life as
well.[34] To put it simply, Old-Württemberg was a culture as much as a
geopolitical expression, and to be raised there meant to be born into a
climate of opinion that sustained and made intelligible the attitudes,
values, and prejudices of a group of Protestants who, for political as well
as religious reasons, thought about public life very differently than
Protestants elsewhere in Germany.[35] For the most part these attitudes and
values were articulated in a "structure of signification" that had
"meaning-imparting" significance for the culture as a whole.[36] That
structure, or "meaning complex," expressed itself in what I have called
Protestant civil piety, a cultural ideal that was crucial to the "social
construction of reality" in Old-Württemberg. This ideal gave focus and
direction to the language, beliefs, shared traditions, and common activities of collective life, especially in the cities, where the possibility for
political involvement in the affairs of Württemberg was greatest.[37]

As a meaning complex, however, Protestant civil piety had both a
religious and a political dimension; and each dimension existed as an
independent tradition in the culture of Old-Württemberg. One of these
traditions originated in the religious thought of Württemberg's "down-
to-earth" pietists and was closely associated with their related conceptions
of *praxis pietatis* and eschatological fulfillment in history.[38] The other
tradition embraced the "Good Old Law" school of political thought and
represented the convictions of the Protestant "patriots" who dominated
the Estates of Württemberg and prided themselves on resisting their
Catholic duke's attempted encroachments on the rights of the Protestant
collectivity.[39]

And yet, the ideal of Protestant civil piety was founded less on a
conscious theory of how religion and politics should interact than on a
tacit assumption, one that was the result of what Berger and Luckmann

would call a "process of habitualization."[40] The assumption was that one
of the basic functions of religion was to make men better by improving
the ethical quality of civil life. With time this belief in the civil value
of religion became part of the general stock of Old-Württemberg's
knowledge about itself.[41] For the most part, however, this knowledge
was part of the "pretheoretical lives" of Württemberg Protestants; that is,
the knowledge was sharply patterned and had "meaning-imparting" force
for them without being integrated into a single, consciously articulated
system of cultural value.[42] So, while the ideal of Protestant civil piety
undoubtely had its roots in religion, it also had a civil–political function.
As such, it possessed many of the characteristics of what Frye might call a
"myth" of collective religious concern.[43]

     In Part I, I detail what circumstances coalesced to make the interplay
between religion and politics, down-to-earth Pietism and the Good Old
Law, possible in Old-Württemberg. Suffice it to say here that the pietist
doctrine of *praxis pietatis* had activist political implications and the Good
Old Law, insofar as it safeguarded Protestant religious rights, had an
obvious religious edge. Indeed, in Württemberg religion existed very
much to reinforce politics; likewise, politics was very often seen as an
extension of the individual's religious personality. Our point, then, is
that in the culture of Old-Württemberg in the eighteenth century religious and political impulses achieved a relative degree of "meaningful
relatedness."[44] That was because religion was concerned with something
more than individual salvation; it was one of the sanctioning agents of
civil piety as well.

     Viewed in this way, public and private were interwoven in the culture
of Old-Württemberg to the extent that they became part of the same
equation of identity; of a *polis-ecclesia*, as one writer has perceptively
termed it.[45] Individual personalities, to be sure, combined these impulses
in various ways and in different proportions. J. A. Bengel, the father of
down-to-earth Pietism in Württemberg, was more religiously minded
than J. J. Moser, the main eighteenth-century spokesman for the Good
Old Law; Moser, in turn, was more politically minded than Bengel.[46] But
for much of the eighteenth century Württemberg managed to maintain
something of a balance between the impulses, with the result that man's
political obligation to civil society took on religious significance and his
religious commitments political importance.

     Scholars have been slow, however, to recognize the importance of
Protestant civil piety as a formative influence on Hegel's thought. There
are, I think, conceptual and historical reasons for this. The conceptual
reason has to do with the way twentieth-century scholarship has approached
the role religion played in the intellectual history of early modern
Europe.[47] To that end, the modern conception of religion is premised on a

clear separation of church and state, of religion and politics.[48] This separation – which flies in the face of classical theoretical positions articulated in Durkheim's and Weber's sociologies of religion – invariably forces us to look in history for the sharp distinctions implied in present usage of the term. Moreover, the separation obliges us to regard any blurring of the lines between religion and politics as the result of "misplaced sacredness" (i.e., idolatry), of ideology (i.e., the use of religion to legitimate certain kinds of secular interests), or of the persistence of a cultural "residue" that is soon to be superseded because it is part of a transition period of historical development.[49]

This separation of religion and politics reinforces a second assumption implicit in the modern conception of religion: namely, the identification of religion with the church. Indeed, the modern conception of religion equates it almost exclusively with "church religion," with its "visible" or "objective" institutional manifestations.[50] This equation is all the more important because it reaffirms the separation of religion and politics. By equating religion with the church and juxtaposing that equation with the doctrine of the separation of church and state, this conception makes religion a matter of private rather than public experience. Altogether, then, the separation of church and state; the identification of religion with its most visible institutional manifestation, the church; and the association of religion with the private rather than the public realm of experience add to the difficulty of seeing any authentic or autonomous religious impulse in the public life of societies of the past.

Finally, and this is especially relevant to the study of religion in a Protestant culture, the modern association of Protestantism, Lutheranism, and Pietism with "inwardness," "individualism," and "subjectivism," on the one hand, and with submission to outer political authority on the other, overlooks the fact that there was a strong, antiauthoritarian, civil impulse within the Lutheran religious tradition itself, especially in Old-Württemberg.[51] And, as we shall see, the failure to appreciate the impulse toward "Protestant civil piety" in the culture of Old-Württemberg lies behind much of the confusion over the religious and political aspects of Hegel's thought.

There are signs, however, that the modern conception of religion is changing; and our conception of the role of religion in early modern European history is also changing. Since the 1960s a revolution in the sociology of religion has occurred, for sociologists of religion have become ever more receptive to the theoretical insights of Weber and Durkheim, both of whom linked religion to many aspects of social life other than the church.[52] As a result, it is no longer anathema to speak of religion as integral to man's conception of nature, the state, or human history.

More specifically, this revolution has led to a new awareness of the civil

impulse in certain forms of Christian thought and of the "invisible" ways
in which Christianity shaped man's sense of the reasonable, the useful and
practical, the ethical, and the educational in the cultures of early modern
Europe and eighteenth-century America. Here the argument is that in
certain of these cultures (e.g., England during the Civil War and America
in the eighteenth century) the political dimension of human experience
was invested with ultimate religious significance.[53] Hence, in these
cultures participation in politics had a soteriological aspect; that is,
political participation was deemed an important vehicle both in man's
transcendence of himself and in humanity's salvation. Thus students of
"civil religion" in America maintain that while today we distinguish
between the religious, the political, the ethical, and the educational,
many societies of the past did not. To that end, the sociologist Robert
Bellah suggests that the concept "civil religion" allows us to talk about
relations and clusters of problems that, while not part of our conceptual
world, were doubtless part of the conceptual world of the past.[54] Civil
religion, in short, is a designation scholars are currently using to point to
the overlooked interpenetration of religious and political modes of
thought and value in public life of past societies in general and Protestant
cultures in the seventeenth and eighteenth centuries in particular.

The possibility of talking about the existence of a reciprocal relationship between religion and politics makes the idea of civil religion conceptually relevant to this study.[55] What makes it historically relevant
to this study is the fact that the ideal of Protestant civil piety was very
much a product of just such a reciprocal relationship. Thus when I talk in
this study about Protestant civil piety in Old-Württemberg I am referring
to what may be regarded as a quite specific historical form of civil
religion.

Another reason scholars have failed to give serious attention to the idea
of Protestant civil piety is historical and is linked to the persistent notion
that Lutheranism in general and Pietism in particular were reactionary
and mystical religious movements centrally preoccupied to recover an
"authentic" Christian faith by returning to a form of religious piety that
required no worldly mediation.[56] Pietism, for example, is usually discussed in terms of a religious "revivalism" that gave expression to the
inherent Lutheran penchant for religious subjectivism and otherworldly
intellectual orientations.[57] Proceeding from this conception, it has been
assumed that Pietism was indifferent or antithetical to the concrete and
progressive aspects of eighteenth-century secular culture. Thus it is easy
to see how scholars could simply ignore Pietism as an agent of progress
and practical action in eighteenth-century thought.

Recent studies, however, have proved that assumption false, especially
in Old-Württemberg.[58] Indeed, for Württemberg's "down-to-earth"

pietists the reality of the eighteenth century called for "religious reform" as much as for "religious revival."[59] And religious reform entailed engaging the world, not retreating from it. Thus, Pietism was anything but disinterested in secular culture. What is more, it had to be, for in order to give substantive meaning to its opposition to the stasis of orthodoxy, Pietism had to encourage a vigorous program of *praxis pietatis*. As we shall see, the doctrine of *praxis pietatis* put the pietists in the vanguard of many of the progressive movements of the age. To anticipate the argument of Part I just a bit, Pietism offered a powerful stimulus to, and vital support for, the followers of the Good Old Law in the Estates. The acute sense of ethical urgency and need for social regeneration that was so essential to Pietism's doctrine of *praxis pietatis* combined nicely with the "civil virtues" upon which the *Altrechtlern* (Old Lawyers) based their legal traditionalism and opposition to princely despotism. Indeed, when the pietists began to envisage social discipline and public watchfulness as *extensions* of religious piety they not only were assuming a posture of this-worldly asceticism but were expressing the "political formula" of the Estates as well.

Down-to-earth Pietism, however, was not just a religious expression of that formula, for in addition to legitimizing the Estates it served a genuine religious purpose: it helped meet the theological crisis precipitated by the decline of orthodox Lutheranism and by the concomitant rise of separatism. Caught between reactionary orthodoxists and revivalist separatists, and confronted with the asocial and antisocial inclinations of these two polar tendencies in German Lutheranism, down-to-earth Pietism set forth in the doctrine of *praxis pietatis* a religious ideal that recalled men to civil activism and, in the process, made Lutheranism socially and politically relevant to secular behavior, an achievement neither orthodoxy nor separatism could manage. The result: the generation of a relatively new Protestant conception of *homo religiosus* and his relation to civil society and salvation.[60]

For this reason, the culture of Hegel's homeland does not fit into modern historiographical schemes that presuppose a ready-made distinction between reactionary-religious and progressive-secular ways of relating to the world. As several commentators have pointed out, Old-Württemberg was not a land of "either-or"; rather it was a land of "both-and" – that is, circumstances in Old-Württemberg precluded the separation of sacred from secular.[61] Indeed, for Württembergers religious salvation and secular socialization were part of one and the same civil experience. That experience, in turn, was constantly informed by the need for political vigilance vis-à-vis the duke. Consequently, withdrawal from, or passive indifference to, the world of civil experience was never really an institutional possibility for Protestants in Old-Württemberg.

Rather, they were obliged to view civil life as a "legitimate field of action" and as a place of "Christian opportunity."[62] That was a reformist conception of the world that Hegel ascribed to for most of his life.

3. Christian reform: Accommodationism, teleology, and the economy of salvation

In large part, then, the study of Hegel's thought must begin with his internalization of the basic religious and political impulses that "clustered" historically around the Old-Württemberg ideal of Protestant civil piety.[63] But for a fuller explanation of what Hegel was "talking about" in the writings of the 1790s, we cannot stop there. As unique as the culture of Old-Württemberg was as a field for Protestant activism, its ideal of Protestant civil piety drew much support from a relatively new Protestant conception of *homo religiosus* that was just beginning to emerge in the religious thought of the *Aufklärung*.[64]

Indeed, the Württembergers' attempt to make Protestantism both ethically and politically relevant to civil affairs drew them to a mode of hereditary Christian wisdom around which a "tradition of discourse" had already developed.[65] Familiarity with the dynamics of this tradition, I think, constitutes another important referential dimension of Hegel's cultural context.[66] In this tradition it was understood that for political action to be moral it had to be grounded in Christianity and that in order to motivate men to be good Christians Christianity had to be politically and ethically relevant to civil existence. This meant, of course, that to stay "relevant" Christianity had repeatedly to reform itself; that is, it historically had to accommodate itself to the world. Many spokesmen of the *Aufklärung* were looking for precisely this kind of "accommodationism" when they began to rethink the character of *homo religiosus*.[67] Implicit in the idea of accommodationism was a theological anthropology that squared with their emergent sense of *homo religiosus* as an ethically active participant in civil affairs.[68]

This tradition – which, following Gerhard Ladner, I should like to designate as the tradition of "Christian reform" – took ethical and eschatological elements from widely divergent sources in the history of Christian thought and formed from them an anthropology of fallen and restored man that allowed for – indeed, demanded – man's participation in civil life as well as in his own salvation.[69] The thrust of the tradition was to show that through ethical activism man could transform the world in accordance with God's wishes[70] and, by so doing, make significant "progress" not only toward transcending his own fallen nature, but toward establishing the Kingdom of God *on earth* as well.[71] It was the theologically optimistic anthropology of this tradition, with its obvious ethico–eschatological–synergistic implications, that one encounters again and again among "progressive" eighteenth-century German Protestant thinkers. Hence, its importance for our purposes here.

Clearly, it is not easy to attach a label to this tradition, but Ladner's conception of Christian reform, I think, provides a framework for explaining many parallels between Hegel's thought and basic religious tendencies not only in the *Aufklärung* but in the history of Christian thought as well. I cannot, of course, claim to have mastered all the complexities of this tradition, let alone the scholarship upon which it is based. But there is, I think, a certain "logic" to the idea of Christian reform that allows for a summary statement of the conceptual relations around which Ladner develops the idea of Christian reform both as a tradition and as a mode of religious discourse.

To begin this summary, we need to remember that the Alexandrian Fathers (especially Clement and Origen), who figure so prominently in Ladner's book, were committed to building a bridge between the religious doctrines of Christianity and the teachings of Greek philosophy.[72] In this the two Fathers were very much part of an Alexandrian syncretistic theological tradition that began with Philo's attempt to present the wisdom of the Sacred Hebrew Scriptures to Alexandrians through the medium of Greek philosophy.[73] Like Philo, the Fathers endeavored to do this by stressing the connection between Genesis 1:26 and key passages in Plato's *Republic* and *Theaetetus*.[74] Decisive in this was the relation they drew between the "image-likeness to God" reference in Genesis (i.e., what Ladner calls "Christian divine-human resemblance ideology") and the "assimilation to God" (i.e., *homoiosis*) references in Plato.[75] Since the term *homoiosis* was used in the Septuagint to translate "likeness," the implication seemed to be that part of man's religious obligation to God involved striving during his life for ethical perfection.[76] If this were true, then man had to possess a capacity for virtue, even for a virtuous life.[77] From that reading, the Alexandrians concluded that man could not be ethically indifferent (as many gnostic cults were then claiming he should be) to what goes on in the world.

What is more, the Alexandrians insisted that the pursuit of virtue in this world had to be voluntary[78] – that is, the Alexandrians conceived of *homo religiosus* as possessing something of a "plastic" nature: he had, as Pelagius would later put it, "a capacity for either direction," a capacity for either virtue or sin.[79] For that reason, the Alexandrians held man responsible for his actions in this world and expected him to shape the conditions of his existence, as much as possible, in accordance with the religious imperative of *homoiosis*.

The result of this Platonic–Christian convergence was, as Ladner well understands, a theological anthropology in which man, because he had been created in the image likeness of God, was expected over time gradually to form himself (or restore himself) to the ideal for his Maker.[80] By so doing, the Alexandrians argued, man not only would be assimilating to God, as far as this were possible,[81] but he also would be participating in his own salvation. Needless to say, this kind of voluntarism, ethical activism, and moderate synergism appealed enormously to the *Aufklärer*.[82]

This theological anthropology has three important implications for the conception of Christian reform. First of all, implicit in the idea of *homoiosis* is the idea that part of the salvation process involves ceaseless striving after perfection.[83] Though man was a sinner, he still possessed, according to the Alexandrians, a capacity for virtue that could be developed by practice.[84] So, while the capacity for virtue was a gift of the Creator, who had made man in His own image, the responsibility for developing the capacity was man's.[85] This is very clear in Origen, who, while discussing the need for man to reform himself to a likeness of God, wrote:

> that man received the honor of God's *image* in his first creation, . . . means that the perfection of God's *likeness* was reserved for him at the consummation. The purpose of this was that man should acquire it for himself by his own earnest efforts to imitate God, so that, while the possibility of attaining perfection was given him in the beginning through the honor of the "image," he should in the end through the accomplishment of these works obtain for himself the perfect "likeness."[86]

From this it should be clear that for Origen and Clement *homoiosis* had three related meanings. It existed as a potential within the "God-seeking soul"; as a process in time whose meaning was measured in terms of striving after "relative perfection"; and as the *end* of *homo religiosus* himself.[87] As Ladner summed it up, *homoiosis* "was given to man at the time of creation as a disposition still to be fulfilled."[88] It had, in short, a teleological dimension in it.

Second, if the Alexandrians' notion of striving after ethical perfection tends to blur the distinction between salvation and *homoiosis*, their emphasis on salvation as a *process* tended to make the *pursuit* of perfection rather than its *attainment* the measure of a Christian life. "Approximation" to God's likeness, not the "deification" of man, was what they were counseling. To put it another way, the focus on process permitted the Alexandrians to envisage *homo religiosus* less in terms of what he had been in the past or was in the present than in terms of what he could *hope* to become in the future. What was divine in man for them, then, was his potential – his capacity for growth and self-transcendence.[89]

This point needs to be emphasized. In the final analysis acceptance of *homoiosis* as a theoteleological concept compelled the Alexandrians to develop a theological anthropology that had two other important dimensions: one that linked man's educability to redemption in history; and another that explained human salvation in terms of a theology of history that had itself been shaped by pedagogic considerations.[90] As we shall see in Parts I and II of this study, these three related conceptions are essential to the late eighteenth-century Protestant revision of the orthodox Lutheran conception of *homo religiosus*. Indeed, a good deal of what Lessing, Kant, Schiller, and Hegel say about human nature, collective existence, history, and God is structurally similar to the reformist position the Alexandrians had taken on these issues much earlier.

Take, for example, the well-known tendency toward accommodationism in late eighteenth-century Protestant thought.[91] One of the earliest Christian advocates of the accommodationist doctrine was Clement.[92] As he saw it, accommodationism was absolutely essential to Christianity. Without that doctrine it would be impossible to uphold the integrity of Scripture. That is, one could not argue for the unity of the Old Testament and the New without first establishing some mode of continuity between the two. Here is where accommodationism was crucial to Clement's purposes. Against those who wished to separate the God of the Jews from the God of the Christians Clement argued the accommodationist position – for a theology of history that claimed God had arranged for human salvation to unfold sequentially and according to a logic that was gradually revealed to man through a series of covenants God made with him.[93] As Clement put it, "God was known by the Greeks in a Gentile way, by the Jews Judaically, and in a new and spiritual way by [Christians]."[94]

To explain why God had acted this way, Clement had to elaborate further. In that context, he proceeded to argue that God's covenants with the Greeks, Jews, and Christians differed because those peoples varied in terms of their capacities to perceive and act upon God's plan for the redemption of the human race. Overall, Clement continued, that plan was designed gradually to draw humanity toward salvation by means of a series of educational experiences, each of which was meant to increase man's capacity to understand what it meant for him to have been created in the image and likeness of God. Like any good "husbandman" (i.e., teacher), God was mindful of the proper time to sow the seeds of virtue and of the proper time to reap them.[95] So he dealt with the Jews through the agency of the law; with the Greeks through the agency of philosophy; and with Christians through the agency of the Gospel. In that sense, each covenant was an expression of the educational "economy" with which God approached the cultivation of His creation.[96] That is, although each covenant was presented as a dispensation given by God to a particular people at a specific moment in time, the series of covenants was itself designed to bring man to, and culminate in, a fully mature Christian consciousness.

From this, Clement concluded that history was the medium through which the wisdom of the divine economy worked to realize its pedagogic intention with regard to human salvation. The measure of that intention was registered on man in the form of his increasing consciousness of his own religious nature – of what it meant to fulfill his *telos* as *homo religiosus*.[97] We know, moreover, that Clement believed that the dispensation God had given Christians had been fully expressed in the *gnosis*, the wisdom, of the New Testament.[98] That wisdom, which patristic thought associated with the economy of the Incarnation itself, was to guide man toward realization of his *telos* as a Christian. But Clement also realized that that wisdom could only be actualized in the world through the active and voluntary agency of man himself.[99] For Clement, therefore, the covenant God had made with Christians required *homo religiosus* to become an active participant in the salvation process.[100] When Clement arrived at that point the theoteleological notion of *homoiosis* and the covenantal conception of the course of history combined to form a theology of history – that of the divine economy – that had activist (i.e., Pelagian) implications.[101]

This brings us to the final implication of the Alexandrians' theological anthropology. The stress they placed on *homoiosis* as a process of ethical self-realization in history had important consequences for the way future Christians would view eschatological fulfillment.[102] Indeed, among the Alexandrians there was a close connection between the impulse toward ethical activism and a certain form of eschatological renewal. That is to say, the idea of *homoiosis* as a process of ethical perfectionism worked best in conjunction with an eschatological conception that stressed the possibility of *terrestrial immanence* of the Kingdom of God.[103] Very simply, much of the motivational logic of Christian reform hinged on two related beliefs: that the pursuit of ethical perfectionism *prepared* the way for the realization of the Kingdom of God on earth and that the possibility of such a realization ensured the pursuit of ethical perfection.[104]

From this brief sketch, we can see that the idea of Christian reform presupposes three things about *homo religiosus*: (1) he must possess a capacity for *homoiosis* after the Fall; (2) he must be actively committed to the pursuit of "relative perfection" in time; and (3) he must conceive of the *end* of that perfection in terms of eschatological fulfillment of the Kingdom of God on earth. As we shall see, these three conceptions figured prominently in the thought of Lessing, Kant, Schiller, and Hegel. Yet, even before them, among the early Württemberg pietists, these conceptions had been used to challenge the theological anthropology of orthodox Lutheranism. That anthropology, of course, had been heavily influenced by Augustine's ethical and eschatological teachings. It cannot be surprising to learn, therefore, that when the *Aufklärer* began to contest orthodox anthropology they drew on anti-Augustinian ethical and eschatological sources.[105] In the remainder of this chapter and in the next one I examine the Pelagian and Joachimite tendencies in *Aufklärer* thought from this vantage point.

4. Christian reform in the *Aufklärung*: The pelagianizing tendencies

Students of the European Enlightenment have been rather slow to appreciate the full intellectual and historical significance of the impulse toward Christian reform in eighteenth-century German thought. The reason is rooted in a particularly one-sided view of the internal dynamic and alignment of intellectual forces in Europe during the eighteenth century. This view has recently been restated and eloquently defended by Peter Gay.[106] According to Gay, the Enlightenment of the *philosophes* involved a struggle against the fanaticism, bigotry, and superstition of Christianity and its churches.[107] In this, Gay agrees with Paul Hazard, who has argued that the aim of the Enlightenment was to "overthrow" the Cross and utterly to destroy "the religious interpretation of life."[108]

For the *philosophes*, Gay maintains, this amounted to a life-and-death struggle "between two irreconcilable patterns of life, thought and feeling,"[109] a struggle that among other antitheses pitted modern pagans against Christians, scientific criticism against religious faith, reason against unreason, and an anthropological view of the human condition against a theological one.[110] "As the Enlightenment saw it," writes Gay, "the world was, and had always been divided between ascetic, superstitious enemies of the flesh, and men who affirmed life, the body, knowledge, and generosity; between mythmakers and realists, priests and philosophers."[111] Human history, the *philosophes* felt, was living proof of this, and it was their purpose – as enlightened philosphers of history – to show how the "Dark Ages" of the past were governed by the evils of priestcraft and the obscurantist mentality of the Christian churches. Conversely, it was their avowed duty to show how ages of "light and learning" were associated with cultural epochs in which reason held sway over men's minds.[112]

Thus, Gay argues that from very early on the *philosophes* sought to secure their independence from religion by setting their "classical" heritage over and against their "Christian" one; that is, they wished to use the ancients' power of criticism to emancipate themselves from the fetters of what at the time was called – when politely put – "positive" or "organized" religion.[113] As a result, Gay declares, a "tide of atheism"

swept the eighteenth century,[114] and the course of its development was
reflected in the progressive radicalization of the religious views of three
generations of *philosophes*.[115] Throughout the century, he claims, the
philosophes became more skeptical and vocal in their criticism of religion,
moving from the Christian skepticism of Bayle, to the deism of Voltaire
and the English moral philosophers, and finally to the outright atheism
and materialism of Hume, Gibbon, and Holbach. And, for Gay, this
radicalization was only a reflection of an escalating historical process
leading away from Christianity and toward "modernity."

The *philosophes*, so runs the argument, put "Christianity on Trial" and
religion on the defensive in the eighteenth century,[116] with the result that
the Enlightenment presented man with a difficult, but nevertheless clear,
choice between a classico-secular and politically involved view of man and
his relation to the world on the one hand, and a Christian-religious and
apolitical or antipolitical view on the other hand. Opting for the latter
meant to remain tied to "medieval" forms of thought and to live in the
"City of Darkness"; opting for the former meant just as clearly to pursue
"modernity" and to live in the "City of Light."

Here, in distilled form, we encounter one of the intellectual canons of
Enlightenment historiography, as well as the rationale behind the familiar
and persistent notion that the Enlightenment was basically secular and
antireligious in its inspiration and character.[117] The problem, however,
is that application of this thesis to the European Enlightenment makes
the *philosophes'* "party of humanity" so exclusive that only a few French
thinkers qualify for membership (and there is even some doubt about
whether the members of the d'Holbach circle would qualify).[118] On this
reading most German thinkers, those who tried to reconcile the ways of
God with the ways of man through synergism, theodicy, or some related
form of Christian activism, were excluded from the "family." And not
belonging to the "little flock" made them fair game – as Pangloss in
Candide discovered – for the barbs and lampoons of the *philosophes*, who
tolerated no equivocation on this issue.[119]

The attempt to understand German thought in the eighteenth century with these categories, then, is fraught with difficulty; and Gay is
well aware (as his critics are) of the problem the *Aufklärung* poses for
his thesis of a "single" European Enlightenment.[120] It would seem to
follow that because German thought was slow to throw off the religious
yoke of Christianity, it did not conform to the pattern of the Western
Enlightenment.[121] Indeed, by all accounts there is little evidence
to suggest that the *Aufklärer* engaged in anything like a "war on
Christianity" in the eighteenth century.[122] Moreover, *Aufklärung* thought
does not exhibit any inclination to posit a negative and inverse conception
of the relation between Christian religious and classico-secular modes of

thought and value. On the contrary, among eighteenth-century German Protestants classical learning was generally employed to support Christianity, not to discredit or destroy it.[123] And this is not unusual – for at least since the Alexandrians many Christians, including the illustrious Augustine himself, had found a positive affirmation of their religious faith in classical literature and philosophy.[124] Really, it all depends on how one reads the classics: the *Aufklärer* read them one way, the *philosophes* another.[125]

What is more, there was no necessary opposition for the *Aufklärer* between the *vita contemplativa* and the *vita activa*. As they well knew there had been many moments in the history of Christianity when the pursuit of religious "wisdom" extended to the *vita activa-politica*.[126] Finally, it is simply a mistake to assume that because the *Aufklärer* attacked orthodox Lutheranism, they did so as conscious members of, or unconsciously on behalf of, a secular opposition. As students of the "secularization" process have made clear, this argument confuses the facts of religious decline and religious reform with secularization.[127]

On these grounds, then, there is no inherent opposition between Christian and classical modes of thought and value among the *Aufklärer*. Far better, therefore to view them as "Christian reformers" whose allegiances oscillated less between religious and secular values than between two poles of Christian value that may roughly be labeled "biblical" and "classical."[128] This distinction, I think, is of enormous heuristic value, for it allows us to appreciate *Aufklärer* fascination with two key figures in the history of Christian thought – Augustine and Pelagius.

In the remainder of this chapter I shall refer to the complex of values that is associated with the biblical conception of Christianity as theocentric and Augustinian and the complex of values that is associated with the classical conception of Christianity as egocentric and Pelagian.[129] I am fully aware of the difficulty of using these heavily loaded ideological and polemical terms. Modern scholarship, for example, has conclusively demonstrated "the many-sided and elusive character of Augustinianism."[130] Indeed, the religious views of the "historic Augustine" had many dimensions. And much that has passed for Augustinianism was, surely, peripheral to the central purposes of Augustine himself. But however ambiguous Augustine was on some issues, he expressed himself clearly on others, though often within a polemical context that invited exaggeration. Indeed, when it came to questions of affirming the inherent corruption of human nature or the doctrines of original sin and gratuitous grace, Augustine minced few words. Thus, I equate theocentric religion with Augustinianism simply because Augustine was for eighteenth-century German Protestants the archexemplar of this religious frame of mind.[131]

Pelagianism, on the other hand, has become a catch-all phrase for any manner of deviation from Augustinianism. Traditionally, Pelagianism has been taken to refer to lines of "heretical" theological development that include various versions of Hellenized Christianity – Neoplatonic Christianity, Christian Humanism, and Christian Stoicism – and various forms of theological rationalism. At best, it is understood as a via media between Augustinianism and Stoicism; at worst, as outright "Godlessness."[132] Whatever the case, the assumption is, as one commentator has put it, that the "inheritance of Pelagius was fully classical" and deeply imbued with the "ethical ideals of paganism."[133]

The use of these two terms is further complicated by the fact that they do not always involve a direct link to the historical figures of Pelagius and Augustine. It is well known, for example, that Pelagius was an eclectic, unsystematic thinker;[134] that he was concerned less with the subtleties of Christian theology than with the moral perfection of the individual believer and the theological defense of Christian asceticism;[135] that it was the radical and politically astute Caelestius who carried the flag for Pelagianism as rational theology in Africa in its early years[136] and the "propagandist–journalist" Julian who years later systematized Pelagius' views into a coherent theological doctrine;[137] that Rufinus of Syria was the initial source of the religious opposition to the doctrine of original sin;[138] that Pelagius, through the "most ingenious disingenuousness," escaped condemnation in 415 in Palestine by in effect denouncing "Pelagianism";[139] that until 1926 Pelagius' commentaries on Paul's Epistles were thought to be the work of the very orthodox Jerome;[140] that the theology of the so-called "Semi-Pelagians" is less a general endorsement of Pelagianism than an ad hoc rejection of Augustine's views on original sin and predestination (otherwise, it is very Augustinian);[141] and that since 1926 it has become quite evident that Pelagius was not a "special" heretic and deserved, therefore, to be both "rehabilitated" and "reevaluated" as a *Christian* thinker.[142]

On Augustine's side of the dichotomy, the ideas that have come to be associated with "Augustinianism" express only a part, albeit a fundamental part, of the famous bishop's religious thought. For the most part, what is commonly meant by Augustinianism (at least after the Renaissance) refers to the practical authoritarianism of Augustine's later writings – to his anti-Pelagian tracts and vitriolic exchanges with Julian.[143] Written under the pressure of Pelagian "heretics," of probing and oftentimes critical inquiries from ascetically minded Gallican monks, and of "old age,"[144] as well as under the inspiration of religious convictions he had formed in the aftermath of the conversion he recorded in the *Confessions*,[145] these writings reveal the desire of one who wanted desperately to exorcise the classico-Pelagian spirit of ethical perfectionism from Western Christendom, even if it meant adopting an anti-intellectual position, resorting to the manipulation of the "hoary stereotypes of public opinion," and playing on the "element of invisible, unconscious guilt" in men in order to impress on them the disastrous consequences of the Fall for being human.[146]

These extreme views, and the aggressive behavior that went along with them, stood in sharp contrast to the Augustine who, for a while, dedicated himself to fashioning Platonism in Christian form. To that end, Pelagius and Julian delighted in quoting telling passages from Augustine's early works on free will and from his diatribes against Manichaeism to support their own claims about man's essential incorruptibility;[147] and they relished quoting from a letter Augustine wrote in 413 in which he acknowledged Pelagius' orthodoxy.[148] Indeed, in their eyes Augustine had once been, as A. J. Smith has put it, "a thoroughgoing Pelagian."[149] And so, in light of the "Pelagian" strain in Augustine's thought, it is not inappropriate to distinguish between the hardheaded, rigid, and dogmatic thought forms of Augustinianism and the more complex and nuanced religious thought of the "historic" Augustine. For as Gilson has observed, "the history of Augustinianism is by no means the history of the thought of St. Augustine."[150]

Yet, despite the limitations and element of distortion inherent in the use of the terms, Augustinianism and Pelagianism have value for the historian.[151] If we accept these two *isms* as *terminis technicis* for fixed theocentric and egocentric conceptions of religous fellowship and salvation (and for the anthropological implications associated with each), it becomes obvious that whenever and wherever one observes manifest tension between Augustinian and Pelagian religious and ethical principles within the same thinker or the same cultural milieu, this tension is a symptom of a culture's reassessment of its understanding of the meaning of *homo religiosus*.[152]

The *Aufklärung*, I think, is no exception to his rule. Far from being a purely doctrinal dispute among Protestant theologians with differing views of Christianity, the debate between orthodox Lutherans and the *Aufklärer* over the relative merits of Augustinianism and Pelagianism involved differing views of how Protestants should respond to the new, secular exigencies of the eighteenth century. In this connection, the *Aufklärers'* efforts to enlist the Alexandrian Fathers and Erasmus (instead of Luther) in support of their cause and to rehabilitate Pelagius at the expense of the authority of Augustine and his "African" conception of Christianity are suggestive both of a shift of theological interest among German Protestants and of a desire on the part of some Protestants to assume a posture of Christian reform toward the problems of the world.[153]

Indeed, the renewed interest in Pelagianism (as a *type* of Christian thought) represented a comprehensive cultural response to deep and changing needs within German society. In that context, the shift from Augustinianism to Pelagianism during the *Aufklärung* may be taken as an indication of an increasing willingness among German Protestants both to make men more responsible, in a preparatory way, for their own salvation and to encourage them in their capacity as Christians to take their civil environment seriously.[154] For it was that environment, and the "habits" it fostered in men, that they thought was the source of evil in human existence. Thus, one of the remarkable paradoxes of the *Aufklärung*: the more "humanized" it became in an individualistic religious sense, the more environmentalist it became in its approach to the ethical life of the collectivity in a secular sense.[155]

There were, of course, concrete historical reasons for the different responses of the *philosophes* and *Aufklärer* to the classical and Christian ideological components in the Western cultural tradition.[156] In France, the institutional situation of the Catholic church and the demise of a tradition of religious dissent after the Edict of Nantes, as well as the existence of newly emergent social conditions that were capable of supporting intellectual life independent of the encumbrances of the old patronage system, encouraged the *philosophes* to frame the struggle against their Christian adversaries (and supporters at court) in the most extreme terms. As Leslie Stephen perceived, "In Catholic France a rigid and unbending system was confronted by a thoroughgoing skepticism."[157] Consequently, the conflict between Christian and classical values was represented in France as an "either–or" proposition: "Shall Europe be Christian, or shall it not?" is the way Hazard felicitously put it.[158] Under these conditions, to be a classicist was to be a "realist," particularly in ethical and political matters, and an "unbeliever," if not an outright atheist, in religious matters. It also meant to be politically engaged. In this context, then, a realist could brook no compromise with Christianity. No halfway solutions were possible.

Yet, as has been noted, this was not the situation in Germany during the *Aufklärung*. In Germany, realism proved compatible with the *Aufklärers'* Pelagianizing tendencies.[159] Indeed, the *Aufklärer* were not disposed to force a decision between either of the two symbolic cities; man owed an allegiance to both, and it was the task of the *Aufklärung*, they thought, to provide a framework for that mediation.[160] Hence, they rejected much of the dogmatic of Lutheran orthodoxy because it failed to promote ethical activism. Conversely, they rejected the radical subjectivism of separatism because it was anti-intellectual as well as anti-social. And when confronted with the utilitarianism and thoroughgoing secularism of the *philosophes*, they rejected that too, and for basic religious reasons. In this field of choice, then, what the *Aufklärer* recommended involved neither a retreat to the entrenched position of orthodoxy, a call for religious revivalism, nor a movement toward secularism. Rather, what they recommended was a program of religious renewal and social regeneration based on the modest blend of activism and reasonableness that was characteristic of the tradition of Christian reform.[161]

At any rate, the conflict between religious and secular culture was more clear-cut in the salons of France than in the world of the Protestant German universities.[162] Indeed, there had always been a strong classical impulse in German theological studies. Philip Melanchthon had seen to that when, in the sixteenth century, in his capacity as Luther's agent, he had masterminded the incorporation of the new humanistic learning, and especially of Aristotle, into the curriculum of the rapidly proliferating Protestant universities.[163] To be sure, Melanchthon's "pedagogical solution" to the problem of what role the teachings of Renaissance humanism would play in the reformatory-religious values of German Protestants was to integrate Protestantism and rationalistic humanism into a framework of "confessional humanism," to make "the new learning" the "handmaid" of Protestant theology.[164] But by putting the *studia humanitatis* at the service of the *studia divinitatis*, Melanchthon also prepared the way for the institutionalization of classical learning in German universities. From that institutional base, it was hoped that the new learning would act as a moderating force between the dogmatic excesses of overly orthodox Lutherans on the one hand and sectarians on the other.

Of course, the currency of such learning angered many Lutherans. The so-called *Gnesio-Lutheraner* (genuine Lutherans) were especially outspoken in their opposition to Melanchthon.[165] But so long as Melanchthon enjoyed the support of Luther, the potential for factionalism within "historic Lutheranism" was greatly diminished. After Luther's death in 1546, however, the *Gnesio-Lutheraner* set their sights on purging Lutheranism of "Philippist" deviations; that is, of its Calvinist tendencies. By the 1580s, the *Gnesio-Lutheraner* had consolidated their position against the Philippists and made short shrift of their "Crypto-Calvinist" doctrines by promulgating the very orthodox Formula of Concord in 1580. Instead of the moderate synergism of Melanchthon's confessional humanism, "orthodox Lutheranism" came to be identified with the dogmatic certainty of what H. von Sybrik has called "confessional absolutism."[166]

Still, the new learning and the synergism that went along with it survived, even if in attenuated "scholastic" form in the German universities. Despite its emasculated condition, it remained an endemic cultural force in Germany throughout the seventeenth century,[167] long after the influence of the social group that had been its "carrier" in the sixteenth century had waned. And so it was that classical learning lived on in German universities until the early eighteenth century, when the combined effects of the scientific revolution, the rise of French culture, and changes that came in the wake of the Thirty Years' War undermined orthodoxy and, in the process, freed classical learning from its narrow, scholastic confines.

This classical revival, of course, was only one of several intellectual impulses unleashed by, or which overlapped, the decline of orthodoxy. And many of these impulses originated outside the university system.[168] Leibniz's criticism of the quality of learning in the universities is well known.[169] So, too, is his concern to establish "academies" as the new learning centers for the promotion of culture. At the same time, the demands for trained administrators of newly emerging "bureaucratic states" like Prussia enhanced the prestige of the law faculty, relative to that of the theological faculty. As Germany developed an "infrastructure" sufficient to support intellectual life outside the universities, "moral weeklies" offered an alternative forum for the discussion of ethico-religious issues. By the time of Hegel's birth, this cultural efflorescence was on the verge of crystallizing into a hard-core intellectual eclecticism, the kind of eclecticism we conventionally associate with the diverse cultural trends of the *deutsche Bewegung*.

Yet, even among these new and diverse impulses, the flashpoint of intellectual interest remained religious. During the period dating roughly from 1748 to 1774 (what I shall call the *Aufklärung* proper) the issue of man's nature – his condition, his potentialities, his morality, his relation to God, and his ultimate destiny – was the subject of extensive and intensive literary, philosophical, and theological debate.[170] To be sure, during the *Aufklärung* "anthropology" and "theology" were inextricably connected, with the result that all intellectual problems of the period were fused with religious ones, much as they had been in the ages of the Alexandrian Fathers and of Augustine and Pelagius.[171]

Indeed, *Aufklärung* debates over theology were, for the most part, debates over human anthropology, and anthropology was a subject that evoked great interest in the wider cultural context – among classicists, neologian theologians, writers of the *Sturm und Drang*, and nascent idealists and neohumanists. While neologian pastors like Jerusalem, Sack, and Spalding and their academic counterparts Ernesti, Michaelis, and Semler found it impossible to discuss divinity without making reference to humanity, philosophers like Leibniz, Wolff, and Kant and poets like Klopstock could not discuss humanity except in terms of its relation to divinity.[172]

Thus, unlike the scholastic wrangles of the seventeenth century, which had had a limited audience, the theological disputes of the *Aufklärung* had wider resonances. They were not merely quarrels over esoteric religious doctrine. Rather, they were implicit acknowledgments that the orthodox Lutheran conception of *homo religiosus* was slowly being transformed under the joint pressure of changing religious conceptions and new and emergent social conditions. Hence, theological anthropology and the opportunity for Christian reform began to coalesce in *Aufklärung* thought.

It was in this context that the *Aufklärer* resolved to contest orthodox Lutheranism's conception of *homo religiosus*, and especially its doctrine of original sin. In this, they quickly found themselves confronting the authority of Augustine. At that point, of course, the dynamic of the situation was simplified: it had been rehearsed many times in the history of Christianity. While orthodox Lutherans fell back on the dogmas of Augustinianism to defend themselves against critics, the *Aufklärer* were launching increasingly sharp attacks on the "black-biled" Augustine and on the integrity of his "African" conception of Christianity.[173] Concomitantly, while the *Aufklärer* were making serious efforts to rehabilitate Pelagius and other "heretics" who had taken exception to positions associated with the theology of the bishop of Hippo, orthodox Lutherans were decrying the Pelagianism of the *Aufklärer*.[174]

Matched, as they were, against Augustine, the *Aufklärer* articulated views that had an authority of their own as alternatives to Augustinianism. Thus, the opportunity for the ingress into, and recovery of, Pelagianism, synergism, and Joachimism in *Aufklärer* thought. And as *Aufklärer* opposition to original sin intensified, and as Pelagian tendencies began to reveal themselves in their action as well as thought, the *Aufklärung* itself began to move away from a theocentric and toward an egocentric conception of *homo religiosus*. Thus, the *Aufklärung* may be taken as marking a chronological divide between two different epochs of German Protestantism.[175] In this the *Aufklärers'* Pelagianizing tendencies, which were put in the service of Christian reform, were decisive in tipping the balance from one toward the other.[176]

Still, there is very little that is really "new" about the religious thought of the *Aufklärung*. Even its anthropology was "revolutionary" only within a thoroughly traditional pattern of Christian theology. The *Aufklärer*, moreover, did not see themselves as innovators in matters of theology. On the contrary, they saw themselves as defenders of an ancient form of Christian wisdom. In their thinking, dogmatism inhibited action and the exploitation of the Christian opportunities of the present.[177] To be sure, much that has been identified as unique to the *Aufklärung* has been postdated by scholars. The fact is that *Aufklärung* religious thought consisted of a reversion to a tradition of religious thought, that of Christian reform, that had found cogent expression in the views of the Alexandrian Fathers, Pelagius, and Joachim. Thus, as eighteenth-century exponents of this tradition, the *Aufklärer* were the bearers of only a *relatively* new way of thinking about *homo religiosus*.

At this point, I think, it behooves us to take a closer look at the theological anthropology that informed orthodox Lutheranism's conception of *homo religiosus*. Throughout the seventeenth century orthodox anthropology had been biblical, theocentric, and Augustinian in its orientation toward human existence. Man was depicted as totally dependent on an utterly transcendent and inscrutable God for salvation. Nothing man could do in the way of "works" could justify him in the eyes of his Maker. Nor was there any ethicoreligious point in trying to "prepare" for salvation. Accordingly, orthodoxy envisaged man as servile, abject, depraved, and incapable of participation in his own salvation. He was, after all, a "sinner," and that was the core of his religious personality.

This conception of *homo religiosus* was contested by many *Aufklärer*. They were, as was just noted, not original in this. The view of theocentric religion, whether in Augustinian or Lutheran form, had been opposed often enough in the past: by Pelagians of various sorts, by Renaissance humanists, and by any number of groups of Protestants in the religious history of early modern Europe. Nevertheless, two aspects of orthodox anthropology particularly exercised the *Aufklärer*, whatever their own internal differences. First, they objected to the aloofness and remoteness of the God of orthodoxy. The idea of a transcendent deity, who was detached from men in their daily lives and indifferent to how they behaved in society, flew in the face of the *Aufklärers'* interest in developing a Christian ethic that would be relevant to civil existence.[178] And second, they denied the orthodox dogma of original sin and the anthropological implications that followed from it, implications that offered little encouragement to men to take active responsibility for their lives and civil existence.[179] For these two reasons, the theology of the *Aufklärung* has been described as Semi-Pelagian.[180]

This does not mean that the *Aufklärer* were trying to replace a religious doctrine that stressed man's complete dependence on God with a secular doctrine that emphasized free will and self-salvation. As was noted earlier, the *Aufklärer* were by and large Christian reformers – which meant that they tried to offer "Christian" alternatives to orthodoxy. To the doctrines of a transcendent God, original sin, and gratuitous grace they opposed conceptions of a God who was immanent in the world; of a man who was ethically responsible in a religious sense for his actions in this world; and of a salvation process that required human participation to complete itself. Viewed in this way, the *Aufklärer* could be said to have been searching for what their detractors called "a compromise theology," a theology that was voluntarist in a religious sense, activist in an ethical sense, civil in a human sense, and moderately synergist in a soteriological sense.[181]

Characterizing the theology of the *Aufklärung* as Pelagianizing and synergizing and the *Aufklärer* themselves as Christian reformers enables us to appreciate some of the internal coherence of *Aufklärung* religious thought. Here again, the fifth-century "contest" between Augustine and Pelagius is illuminating. As Harnack, Brown, and Bonner have remarked, there are few crises in the history of Christianity that allow us to observe so clearly the basic value polarities inherent in Christian thought.[182] Stated baldly, what was at stake in this contest was whether a theocentric or egocentric conception of salvation best expressed the nature of the religious relationship between man and God. In a narrow theological sense, and in a set of shorthand equations (which are by no means exhaustive), the contest was over whether "grace" or "nature," "faith" or "works," "gratuitous" or "merited" grace, or a "revelational" or "demonstrational" type of religion would govern the doctrine of the Western church. And, as we have already suggested, these basic theological antitheses generated diametrically opposed conceptions of *homo religiosus*. So, when the *Aufklärer* set out to rehabilitate Pelagius, much more was at issue for them than the orthodoxy of a heretic; the concern with Pelagius expressed a desire to read a new set of distinctive religious potentialities into their conception of man. These potentialities, I think, constitute the religious core from which the coherence of *Aufklärung* thought may be derived.[183]

The best way to see that coherence is to examine the differences between Augustine's and Pelagius' conceptions of man after the Fall and then draw out the implications for several different areas of thought, each of which was vital to the *Aufklärung*.[184] To begin with, the direction of the development of Augustine's religious thought suggests that he increasingly came to revere the prerogatives of Divine initiative in human salvation. Man's redemption, he felt, depended on an utterly transcendent God's gifts to man. God, he claimed, reached down to man and communicated to him through the media of revelations, divinely inspired prophets, and the inscrutable mystery of "gratuitous grace." Just as clearly, Pelagius' religious conceptions were dominated by man and took their starting point in ordinary human life. What he emphasized was man's capacity ethically to respond to the Divine initiative, in whatever form it assumed. As respondent, man was judged capable of rising toward God and of realizing an ever-increasing likeness to God in the conduct of his own life. Augustine, in short, held to "theocentric religion" – salvation was wholly a question of God's gracious condescension to man – while Pelagius subscribed to "egocentric" religion – man participated in his own salvation by trying to raise himself up to the Divine.

Here, obviously, Pelagius is quite the synergist and owes much to the theology of the Alexandrian Fathers.[185] Like them, he regarded salvation as a "cooperative" endeavor between man and God.[186] Through the "general grace" of the Creation, Pelagius maintained, man had been created free, which meant he possessed a free moral will, born of reason and of his knowledge of good and evil.[187] Pelagius assumed, moreover, that because man had been given the "capacity for either direction," for virtue or vice, he could – in theory – lead and aspire to a sinless life.[188] Sin, for Pelagius, was always a matter of choice – and wrong choices were simply the consequence of an undisciplined will, faulty judgment, or a combination of the two.[189] In that respect, a sinless life was a very real possibility for the man who maintained proper symmetry between his will and his intellect.[190] For Pelagius, therefore, man's capacity for sinlessness (*posse non peccare*) was the essence of the endowment of the grace of the Creation.[191] "In the beginning," he wrote, "God set man and left him in his own counsel."[192] From that point on he would be held responsible for his actions and expected to conduct himself as if he truly were "a god," but not as if he were "God."[193] Pelagius asserted, in short, a doctrine of *homoiosis*: he believed, in other words, that "God helps those who help themselves."[194]

But what of the Fall? Did man forfeit his *posse non peccare* because of Adam's transgression? For Pelagius, as for the Fathers, the answer to this question was an emphatic "No!"[195] Yet this negative reply did not mean, conversely, that man could achieve salvation through his own powers.[196] As the researches of T. Bohlin have shown, Pelagius' view of salvation was always "dialectical."[197] By dialectical, Bohlin means that for man to participate in salvation he must bring himself into communication with God through the agency of the *logos*. Man's experience of the *logos*, then, makes possible a dia-logos, a communication, with God. Thus, the dialectic Bohlin sees in Pelagius' thought is really a metaphor for a communicative structure that requires man to participate in his own salvation. Even while making allowances for human input into the soteriological process, Pelagius always held that Divine assistance was required for human salvation – in the beginning with the Creation and in the end with the last Judgment. So, in the matter of grace, nature, and salvation, Pelagius, like the Fathers, advocated a theology of moderate synergism.

More specifically, Pelagius believed that Christian perfection was predicated on moral progress; in turn, moral progress was based on a belief in man's innate capacity for virtue and in his educability. Indeed, as Pelagius saw it, the idea of moral process was inherent in the three covenants that God had given to man. There had been a natural one under Adam; a lawful one under Moses; and one of grace under Christ.[198] Each covenant, Pelagius argued, corresponded to a stage in the progressive education of mankind. Simply put, during "the time of nature" man, in his "natural innocence," had turned away from God, violated the original covenant, subverted the order of the cosmos, experienced God's wrath, and hence came to sense what consequences would follow from arrogant, rebellious, and deviant behavior. Then, during "the time of law," man was forced like a disobedient child to live according to the prescriptions of the Law. Finally, with the Incarnation, man came "face to face" with the *Idea* of Christianity, with Christ, the model of Christian perfection in whom, to speak with Hegel, humanity and divinity are at one in the "concrete universal."

As the embodiment of Christianity, Christ was the model to be imitated. That meant, for Pelagius, that with the Incarnation mankind had "come of age" and entered a stage of spiritual development in which it was expected to respond fully and self-consciously to Christ's example and moral teachings.[199] The gift of the Incarnation was one of knowledge, not complete redemption. Man had progressed beyond "childhood" to become the "adopted son" of God. "There is no more pressing admonition," Pelagius would have remarked, "than this, that we should be called sons of God."[200] And to be a "son" in late antiquity meant at once to be an "autonomous person" and the carrier of a "family" ideal.[201]

On the basis of this tripartite theology of history Pelagius argued that on at least two occasions after the Fall man had manifested an ability to respond – on his own initiative – to the providential plan as it was revealed to him by God's agents, Moses and Jesus. From this, Pelagius concluded that by the nature of his original endowment man always possessed the capacity for *homoiosis*. For that reason, sinfulness for Pelagius was like a habit: it was *external* to man and circumstantial, not an irreversible legacy of the Fall.[202] Hence, he reasoned, sinful behavior could be reversed, just as bad habits could be changed. "Conversions," in other words, were always possible for Pelagius. In fact, the overall thrust of Pelagius' theology was to convince man of the ever-present possibility of moral reform and spiritual progress, and the efficacy of strenuous individual effort for salvation. As Brown has noted, "Pelagius...wrote for men who want to make a change for the better."[203]

At any rate, in all of this Pelagius was in full accord with the Alexandrian Fathers' attitude toward sin, free will, grace, and predestination. Confronted with the Good, and with good examples, men would *gradually* come to know the Good. To actually do the Good, however, required a commitment and contribution from them: a voluntary assertion of the will to perfect themselves as Christians.[204] As Bohlin has noted, Pelagius was "no determinist" – and that is precisely why he was an environmentalist.[205] So, in addition to a synergistic conception of man's relation to God, Pelagius also possessed – and this is decisive – a soteriological sense that made collective action and civil existence crucial for human salvation.[206]

Consequently, Pelagianism and egocentric religion encourage a form of practical, community activism, preach a "service ethic," and try, above all, to turn political participation into an aspect and extension of *praxis pietatis* and the expansion of the Christian personality. And to ensure that this ethic of "freedom in" and "freedom through" the community is passed on from one generation to the next, Christians who are inclined toward Pelagianism generally take an active interest in promoting a kind of civil awareness within the educational system that borders on the patriotic.[207] Looked at in this way, it is hardly surprising to find a rediscovery of the virtues of citizenship and a renewal of interest in ethico-political activism evolving simultaneously with Pelagianism. There is, of course, a very thin line between a politics that has been Christianized and a Christianity that has been politicized. On a theoretical level, then, Pelagianism raises the problem of civil religion, and civil religion the problem of Pelagianism.[208] And on those terms both are relevant to the problem of Protestant civil piety in Old-Württemberg in the eighteenth century.

Augustine contradicted Pelagius' views at almost every point. To Pelagius' view of Christianity, with all its egocentric resonances, Augustine opposed a religious faith that was theocentric and based on the notion of a transcendent God upon whom man is completely dependent for salvation; to Pelagius' assertion that "in the beginning God set man and left him in his own counsel," Augustine countered with Jeremiah 10:23: "I know, O Lord, that the way of man is not in his power; nor is it for him to walk and direct his own steps";[209] to "free will" he opposed "original sin"; to man's religious eros for God, God's agape for man; to the image of "sons," that of "children"; to God as a moral ideal, the ideal of a transcendent deity; and to "merited grace," a combination of "prevenient" and "gratuitous" grace.

At the deepest level, Pelagius and Augustine were at variance over the consequences of the Fall for human nature. Following Paul and Ambrose, Augustine contended that "Adam was created by God, but when he consented to the devil he was born of the devil, and all whom he begot were like himself."[210] With the Fall, man had irretrievably lost his potential for divinity. By "turning away from God," man had forfeited forever his *posse non peccare*. And because he no longer shared in the divine essence, he had been deprived of access to the providential order, with the result that his knowledge of good and evil was irrevocably impaired. His intelligence, therefore, was suspect, and not of sufficient scope or sophistication to serve as a vehicle of salvation. To think otherwise was evidence of "being puffed up," of succumbing to the kind of *hybris* for which Augustine scored Pelagius.[211]

In fact, in its corrupted condition, man's intelligence was his peril and his temptation, for it deceived him into attributing to himself what was God's, into "worshipping and serving the creature more than the Creator."[212] This, for Augustine, was the natural consequence of Pela-

gianism, and Augustine would have no part of it. Grace, for him, could
never be solicited. Grace was given freely, gratuitously, by God; therefore, it was not a reward for things "well done."[213] It was not within
man's power to command, participate in, or expect grace: that was God's
prerogative; and the ultimate test of faith was to persevere in one's faith
without any guarantee of salvation. The mystery of grace was, as God
was, inscrutable. For that reason Augustine put faith at the very "heart"
of his theology and tied it to man's affective faculty.

As might be expected, Augustine and Pelagius also held differing
conceptions of sin. Although Augustine concurred with Pelagius and the
Alexandrians that the "law of sin" was rooted in "habit," he rejected their
contention that sin was a force of habit *external* to man.[214] Rather, he
envisaged sin as a "deeply insidious" force that had insinuated its way into
man's *internal* being. Reflecting in the *Confessions* upon his own conversion, Augustine recalled how the "iron bondage of his own will" to the
things of "this world" had prevented him from turning to God of his own
free will.[215] "Inveterate evil," he wrote, "had more power over me than
the novelty of good."[216] Based on this recollection, Augustine fulminated
against Pelagius' facile and excessively optimistic view of human motivation. Right and wrong, Augustine noted, were seldom matters of
"choice" and correct judgment. Man, he insisted, possessed "conflicting
wills," not a single one. Sin, therefore, was not external to the personality: it was inherent in it, and a *condition* of human existence. Hence, it
could not be eradicated, as Pelagius claimed, through adherence to a
personal ascetic code, the provision of a "good environment," exposure to
"good examples," or "education."[217] There was, in short, no escape from
sin for Augustine, and there was, certainly, no such thing as moral
progress or human perfectibility. In one way or another those contentions
flew in the face of everything Pelagius and the Alexandrian Fathers
believed in.[218]

Here we glimpse one of the decisive issues in the perennial struggle
within Christianity between its Augustinian and Pelagian tendencies. In
denying the ideal of Pelagian perfectibility – that is, in denying that
through a combination of individual self-control (i.e., asceticism) and
environmentalism (i.e., education and "creative politics") men could
make moral progress in the world – Augustine was also questioning the
value of educaton as a remedy for the "absolute flaws" that he believed
inhered in fallen man.[219] Indeed, for Augustine education was useless as a
tool of religious liberation and moral uplift; worse, it was "diabolical,"[220]
for it "puffed" men up, taught them to be "pleased" with themselves, and
made them think apotheosis by way of culture was possible for the learned
(in the short run) and perhaps for humanity in the long run.[221] As
Augustine noted, "We can deform the image of God in us, but we cannot

reform it."[222] Only Christ, Augustine maintained, could do that. Hence, his enmity for Christian educators who presumptuously told men "to be like God."[223]

It is precisely this kind of "education" and its appeal to the "pride" of a "better I" within us that is vital to the religious thought of some of the *Aufklärer*, most of the German neohumanists, and Hegel.[224] (It is, I shall try to show, at the heart of the interrelation among his conceptions of *Geist, Sittlichkeit*, and *Bildung*.) What Augustine and orthodox Lutherans condemned as a manifestation of creaturely "pride," they saw as necessary "preparation" for collective salvation.[225] Lessing saw this clearly when he wrote that "Education is revelation coming to the individual man; and revelation is education which has come, and is still coming, to the human race."[226] As such, education was the secular expression of an ongoing communication between man and God about the *process* of human salvation in time.[227]

Again, we encounter one of the great paradoxes of the *Aufklärung*, one that many students of Hegel's thought have yet to understand: namely, that during the late eighteenth century many German Protestants saw in education – in *Bildung* – a way both to reform *homo religiosus* and to re-generate civil life. Put another way, they made the matter of collective salvation turn upon their ability to persuade their fellows that pride in education and a commitment to self-perfection within the framework of civil life were signs of religious grace.[228]

Hegel, I think, was very much concerned to cultivate this kind of pride in man. Given the Württembergers' concern with Protestant civil piety and the *Aufklärers'* concern with *homo religiosus*, I doubt that he did so unintentionally. If this is true, and I shall show that it is, then we might regard Hegel as a thinker who believed that religious renewal was only possible if Christians committed themselves to a certain kind of civil activism.[229] It is this religiously informed commitment to civil activism, which was so much a part of the culture of Old-Württemberg, that I wish to discuss in Part I of this study. Granted, this procedure will delay somewhat our consideration of Hegel as a thinker. But to appreciate fully the language and conceptual structures Hegel used in the 1790s, we have to do some "contextualizing"; that is, we have to go backward into the culture of Old-Württemberg before we can go forward into the texts of Hegel's youth.

PART I

◁══════════════════════════════════════▷

Hegel's Württemberg
"Civil Millenarianism" and the two faces of Protestant civil piety

Every religion has some political opinion linked to it by affinity.

The spirit of man...will regulate political society and the City of God in uniform fashion; it will...seek to harmonize earth with heaven.

For the Americans the idea of Christianity and liberty are so completely mingled that it is almost impossible to get them to conceive of the one without the other.

...preachers in America are continually coming down to earth. Indeed they... are forever pointing out how religious beliefs favor freedom and public order, and it is often difficult to be sure...whether the main object of religion is to procure eternal felicity in the next world or prosperity in this.

Alexis de Tocqueville

The purpose of Part I of this study is to identify the religious and political threads of meaning that eighteenth-century Württemberg Protestants wove into a seamless web that had "meaning creating significance" for the culture of Old-Württemberg as a whole. The argument will be that this "web of signification" can be talked about in terms of the ideal of Protestant civil piety and that that ideal constituted the conceptual axis upon which discussion of religious and political matters in Old-Württemberg turned for most of the eighteenth century.[1]

As has been noted, Württembergers borrowed from the theological anthropology of the *Aufklärer* to articulate this religiopolitical conception. There were, to be sure, many striking affinities between the Pelagianizing tendencies that were inherent in the *Aufklärers'* conception of *homo religiosus* and the requirements for citizenship that were implicit in the Württembergers' ideal of civil piety. But just as important to the Württembergers' enunciation of this ideal was a tradition of Christian eschatology – one we have designated as Joachimism[2] – that gave coherence to the ideal and provided the rationale for the interplay between its religious and political components. It is this tradition – the way it fed into the culture of Old-Württemberg through the figure of J. A. Bengel and the way it subsequently shaped political values and expectations – that I wish to make the point of departure for the next three chapters.

Christian eschatology, of course, has never presented itself as a uniform and homogeneous tradition.[3] From the very beginning, it has been available in several versions, each of which has been animated by different concerns and has held different implications for a Christian's attitude toward, and action in, the world. It should not surprise us, therefore, to find the rehabilitation of Pelagius dovetailing with the endorsement of an eschatological tradition – Joachimism – that encourages ethical activism in the world.[4] More to the point, we should be aware that Joachimism, like Pelagianism, initially offered itself to the world as an alternative to the perceived ethical "defeatism" of Augustinianism – that is, what draws Pelagianism and Joachimism together is the kind of optimistic theological anthropology that we have argued was characteristic of the religious thought of the Alexandrians and the *Aufklärer*.[5] Indeed, as one scholar has noted, the issues that accompanied the emergence of Joachimism in the thirteenth century are "more than reminiscent of the old Pelagian–Augustinian debate."[6]

In the three chapters that follow, I shall try to show how the Old-Württemberg traditions of down-to-earth Pietism and the Good Old Law interacted in ways that suggest a Joachimite eschatological and Pelagian ethical convergence. However, I do not mean to offer this convergence as an explanation for what happened in eighteenth-century Württemberg. What made the interplay between eschatology and ethics, Joachimism and Pelagianism, down-to-earth Pietism and the Good Old Law, possible was a specific historical situation that developed in Württemberg early in the eighteenth century.

What happened was that in 1733 a Catholic duke, Karl Alexander, who had absolutist political ambitions, ascended the throne in Württemberg, thereby precipitating a crisis in the religious and political loyalties of the state's predominantly Protestant population.[7] From that moment on, it was impossible for Württemberg Protestants to look to their duke as a "godly prince" whom God had appointed to oversee Württemberg's fulfillment of the promise of the Reformation.[8] Prior to 1733 it had been understood that the duke was a symbol who linked the sacred and the secular together in a single Christian commonwealth. There was, of course, nothing particularly Protestant or German about this conception of kingship. From Eusebius in the fourth century to Foxe in the sixteenth century, Christians had used the device of deification of a political leader to invest their respective societies with the aura of a "godly polity."[9]

Increasingly, however, this religious conception of kingship came to be discussed in terms of Christian eschatological expectations. This is especially true of the period in European history that runs from the thirteenth to the seventeenth centuries, when something that Majorie Reeves has called "political Joachimism" fired the eschatological imagination of any number of Catholic and Protestant thinkers.[10] As she has argued, throughout this period a "need was felt to seek an alternative agent to the papacy in the work of [religious] renewal."[11] And, as she has shown, the eschatological tradition of Joachimism,[12] in conjunction with the ancient political tradition of the "Last World Emperor,"[13] provided both the framework for this kind of renewal and the incentive for this kind of activism. At a minimum, political Joachimism endowed the ruler with the responsibility for defending Christians against Antichrist; at a maximum it assigned him (or her, as was the case in Foxe's England) the task of being the "Savior Emperor" who would lead the people of a particular nation to redemption.[14]

Clearly, the political–religious situation in Württemberg after 1733 called for an adjustment in this very conventional conception of how Christians should relate to things political. The problem of Württembergers, obviously, was twofold: to detach the idea of religious endowment from the duke and to attach it to themselves as a Protestant people.[15]

This adjustment, I think, had extremely important implications for how Württemberg Protestants viewed the world, especially the political world, in the eighteenth century. First of all, the adjustment encouraged them to depict the duke as the embodiment of "political Antichrist," as an "Antichrist-tyrant."[16] Throughout the sixteenth and seventeenth centuries, the apocalyptic expectations of Württemberg Protestants had focused on an Antichrist that was external to Old-Württemberg itself. To this end, Catholic armies, whether from Spain or France, were envisaged as Antichrist's military agents in the world. The accession of 1733, however, forced Württembergers to reconsider their conception of Antichrist. Clearly Antichrist now meant to use Karl Alexander, the new Catholic political leader of a Protestant people, to subvert Christianity and to reverse the gains of the Reformation. Antichrist, therefore, was no longer just an external military threat to Württemberg Protestants; he was an internal political one as well.[17] Hence, it remained for the people of Württemberg to resist this subversion.

So conceived, Württemberg Protestants could define themselves in two ways: religiously, as a Christian people struggling against Antichrist; and politically, as a people seeking to preserve Protestant "liberty" against the spiritual, military, and authoritarian political forces of Catholic tyranny.[18] Thus, if Württemberg Protestants appear to be antipolitical because they insisted on separating themselves from political affairs, it must be remembered that they did so not because of the attractions of Lutheran "inwardness" or spiritual individualism, but because of a very practical need for Protestant solidarity vis-à-vis Antichrist. To put it another way, in Württemberg the politics of Protestantism was not so much anti-political as "counterpolity" oriented.[19]

If one aspect of the Württembergers' adjustment to the development of 1733 entailed using the rhetoric of Christian eschatology to depict the duke as Antichrist, another aspect of the adjustment involved having to present themselves as a "millennial people."[20] Application of the Antichrist–Christian eschatological categories to the situation in Württemberg after 1733 not only rendered the godly polity into two warring groups but also channeled millennial values and responsibilities toward the people qua society and away from the prince qua state.[21] From this shift it followed that the preservation of Protestant "liberty" was a "sacred" cause of the people[22] and that Württemberg Protestants had been "chosen" by God to ensure its perpetuation.[23] Did not the presence of Antichrist among them mean that they were being asked to assume a collective sense of their election as a Protestant people? If Protestant princes could act as God's agents of redemption in the world, why not also a Protestant people?

What is more, was not the purpose of the struggle with Antichrist – indeed, the purpose of the Reformation itself – to extend Christ's word, expand Christian liberty, and, by so doing, ensure "progress" toward the reconstitution of the "godly polity" on earth?[24] Were not the tribulations suffered under Antichrist in the present an assurance of salvation tomorrow? In short, by resisting Antichrist in the present, could not Württemberg Protestants see themselves as cooperating with God to advance His purposes *within* history?[25]

This kind of thinking, of course, implied that what Luther had begun in 1517 needed to be carried further. He indeed had inaugurated and led the movement toward realization of the spiritual liberty of the First Reformation; but that Reformation, it was argued, needed to be followed by a second one, one that would oversee the institutionalization of that liberty.[26]

Viewed in this way, one could say that the eschatological categories Württemberg Protestants used to explain the religio-political situation in 1733 had two different aspects. First, eschatology served as a vehicle for Protestant socialization.[27] In this sense the Württembergers' idea of the Protestant *ecclesia* was quite social in an antipolitical sense. And yet, by casting themselves as a millennial people Württembergers were obliged to accept responsibility for social affairs in a way that was prepolitical.[28] Their millenarian expectations demanded the gradual development of a fuller conception of what it meant for a Protestant to be a citizen. Indeed, since this conception of citizenship was inextricably tied to the millennial role they had set for themselves, the requirement of citizenship necessarily had a futuristic and conditional dimension built into it. In this context, the Protestant sense of *ecclesia* was more expansive, more truly "civil" (in the pre-Hegelian sense of the term), for it meant, eventually, to embrace the political as well as the social dimension of collective life.[29]

On the surface, these two modes of eschatological thinking seem contradictory. But they are not. When taken together they urge Württembergers to separate themselves from the state in the present in order to secure a position from which they can cultivate a Protestant politics for the future. Withdrawal from the state, in other words, was an historically specific act, not an absolute one; or, to speak with Kenneth Burke, it was an "incipient act," meant less to be a once-and-for-all "substitute" for politics than a preparation for the qualitatively different politics of the future.[30]

Here, in the idea of "civil millennialism," we see quite clearly the two faces of Protestant civil piety in Old-Württemberg.[31] On the one hand, as a response to the presence of Antichrist among them, Württembergers are thoroughly defensive and traditionalist in their support of the Protestant status quo (hence, the legal traditionalism of the Good Old Law); on the other hand, as a millennial people, they are civil activists and "progressivists" (hence, the "evolutionary eschatology" of down-to-earth Pietism). In the first case, civil millennialism translates into a conservative, social collectivism; in the second case, into a progressive, political collectivism.

It is this juxtaposition of tradition and innovation, of conservative social and progressive political elements, that I think explains much about the culture of Old-Württemberg in the eighteenth century. And if there was ambiguity in this juxtaposition it was nevertheless very convenient for binding conservative and progressive Württembergers together in one people. It would be a mistake, however, to regard this mode of eschatological expectation as new.[32] According to Reeves it was the "mood" of simultaneous apprehension and hope that Joachim gave expression to with his eschatological categories.[33] How, and under what circumstance, Joachimism became relevant to Württemberg will, then, figure prominently in Chapters 1 and 2.

Doubtless other nonreligious factors conditioned political attitudes in Old-Württemberg; but the fact that for most of the eighteenth century the duke of Protestant Württemberg was a Catholic with absolutist political intentions says much about the force that welded pietists and *Altrechtlern* into "oppositional men" whose sense of the civil was eschatologically conditioned.

In the culture of Old-Württemberg, therefore, it is not a question of religion versus politics, but of the cooperation of both at once. And

Joachimite eschatology did much to sanctify that alliance. Of course, the combination of religion and politics in Protestant civil piety makes it hard for the modern sensibility to appreciate the different faces of the culture of Old-Württemberg, but it is precisely this convergence that explains the potency and force of religion in the lives of Württembergers, who thought of themselves simultaneously as pious Protestants and virtuous citizens. This conviction lay at the heart of the culture of Old-Württemberg and its ideal of Protestant civil piety in the eighteenth century. Bengel and Moser stand at the beginning and Hegel at the end of this tradition in the eighteenth century, and it will be our task in Chapters 1 to 3 to explain the coherence and dynamic of the tradition as it worked its way toward, and culminated in, Hegel's writings of the 1790s.[34]

Before turning to these chapters, a brief word is in order on how Part I has been organized. In these three chapters the organizing principle has been chronological rather than thematic. I chose this procedure because the major religious and political developments in the culture of Old-Württemberg in the eighteenth century suggest this kind of weighting. In that sense, historical circumstances rather than any preconception on my part about the relation between religion and politics dictated the order of the chapters. The fact is that in Old-Württemberg the timing of events was such that there was a shift in the focus of intellectual life from religious to political matters over the course of the eighteenth century. Obviously, I think that an appreciation of this shift of emphasis makes Hegel's way of thinking more understandable.

Yet, for all that, the order of the chapters is not designed to imply a logical sequence of cause and effect. As Geertz has recognized, "all cultural performances are not religious performances, and the line between those that are and artistic, or even political, ones is often not so easy to draw in practice, for, like social forms, symbolic forms can serve multiple purposes."[35] Delineating that difference, however, is not really our problem, because from the outset our interest has been with the interplay between religion and politics; thus, it is not our intention to try to establish a one-way relationship between them. As Peter Berger has argued, "In looking at any particular historical situation of religion it is very largely a matter of convenience. . .as to which of the two spheres one begins with. Depending on the starting point, one may then be able to show how a particular theoretical constellation [e.g., Pietism] results from a certain practical infrastructure [e.g., political exigencies], or conversely how a particular social structure is the result of certain movements in the realm of [religious] ideas."[36]

From that standpoint, if the inquiry of Part I ends with a discussion of politics it is not meant to imply that Pietism was the cause of the Good Old Law political outlook. Rather, it is our claim that the religious and political themes discussed in these three chapters run parallel in time and exist simultaneously in the culture of Old-Württemberg. To put the matter in Tocquevillean terms, it is our claim that certain "affinities" are discernible between the religious conceptions of Pietism and the modes of thought and behavior we have associated with the *Alte Recht* political situation.[37] As a result of our analysis of this affinity, we hope to show "the manner and general direction" of Pietism's influence on politics in Old-Württemberg.[38]

We are, then, interested in ascertaining how the religious attitudes of pietists, especially toward eschatology, oriented or influenced the political conceptions of the *Altrechtlern*. Again, our concern is not with causality. As Parsons has observed of Weber's work, "It is rather that, in addition to the other forces working in that direction, it [religion] is sufficient to throw the total balance [in a culture] in favor of the one possible outcome rather than the other."[39] Thus, one might say that it is our contention that pietists were "idea-prone" in certain political directions and that in Old-Württemberg their religious beliefs were often the starting point for calculations of political responsibility.[40]

With regard to the relationship between Chapters 1, 2, and 3, one might say that in Chapters 1 and 2 we discuss the motives and meaning of the religious values embodied in Pietism, and in Chapter 3 we relate those values to political beliefs and conduct. Chapter 3, in other words, may be seen both as a discussion of "applied religion" and as a politico-institutional analogue to the religious discussion of Chapters 1 and 2.

1

The religious culture of Old-Württemberg

I. Christian eschatology and "down-to-earth" Pietism

Only recently have scholars begun to recognize the value of Christian eschatological speculation as a resource for studying the intellectual history of early modern Europe.[1] Indeed, it has become quite evident that very often the eschatological imagination figured prominently in debates over the purposes and directions of cultural life during this period of Western history. As E. von Dobschütz noted long ago, the key to exploitation of Christian eschatology as a source of historical evidence lies in envisaging it as a "living force" in the lives of past cultures.[2] In that respect, the study of eschatology has important implications for how these cultures went about the task of what sociologists of religion today call the "social construction of reality."[3]

As we have noted, though, Christian eschatology has appeared in several different modes that differ markedly in terms of the urgency they assign to action relative to speculation about the Last Things.[4] That is to say, differences in eschatology quite often arise out of a concern about the means rather than the end of eschatological fulfillment.[5] To that end, scholars have distinguished, to name just a few sets of antitheses, thoroughgoing from futurist; inaugurated from consequent; realized from unrealized; revolutionary from evolutionary; existential from apocalyptic; and transmuted from sublimated eschatologies.[6] More to the point of our purposes here, students of eschatology have learned to distinguish between "traditional–conservative," "progressive evolutionary," and "progressive revolutionary" eschatologies.[7] Obviously, therefore, there are many ways of talking about eschatology; but the points to remember are that certain eschatological schemes are more action oriented than others and that the dynamics of certain historical situations are more appropriate for some eschatological modes than for others.[8]

Despite the profusion of eschatological labels, there is a way to make

40

sense of the various tendencies in Christian eschatology. It seems to me that modern scholarship has identified three basic modes of eschatological expectation that have existed side by side in Christianity since the days of the early Church.[9] First, there are the two eschatological tendencies of the so-called Synoptic Gospels: namely, the "thoroughgoing" tendency that is associated with Schweitzer's work and the "futurist" tendency that any number of commentators have discussed.[10] According to thoroughgoing eschatology the central message of the Gospels lay in the notion that the Parousia, the Millennium, and the Coming of the Kingdom of God were impending rather than remote events. On this reading, Jesus' allusions to an imminent earthly Kingdom were interpreted as a way to summon men to prepare for the glorious Coming by repenting their sins. Indeed, since thoroughgoing eschatology held that the Kingdom was already at hand, it was concerned less with celebrating the temporal fulfillment of eschatology (which it took for granted) than with stressing the moral implications that should follow from the "fact" that the Kingdom of God was "drawing near."

Here we observe the use of thoroughgoing eschatology as a way to promote a penitential and dynamic right-angled view of Christian conversion.[11] This view, as it was embodied in the preachings of John the Baptist and Jesus, required men to change their values and attitudes radically before they could call themselves followers of Christ. Paradoxical as it may seem, thoroughgoing eschatology expects every Christian to act as if the Kingdom of God that is "not yet" fully realized were an already accomplished historical fact.[12] Assured of the outcome of history, thoroughgoing eschatology required men to repent their sins and to change their values in order to achieve a condition of internal religious readiness for the arrival of the final eschatological moment. Thus, the appeal of thoroughgoing eschatology sprang not so much from the specter of the end of time as from an inexorable logic that demanded a change in value and the acceptance of a religious ethic of repentance as a condition of the end of time.[13]

There was, however, another way to read the eschatological message of the Synoptic Gospels — a "futurist" one at that; and it was futurist in the same way that the eschatology of Jewish apocalyptic had been: it conceived of the Parousia, the Millennium, and the Coming Kingdom as events that would take place in an indefinite future beyond historical time.[14] In this — perhaps the most familiar scheme of Christian eschatological interpretation — the religious consummation in the Kingdom of God promised by the Synoptic Gospels is other-worldly and beyond historical time; that is, it is projected so far into the future that it deprives eschatology of its temporal relevance and, thereby, emasculates it of its revolutionary and ethical activist potentialities. With the decisive events of religious consummation postponed indefinitely, futurist eschatology exhorted Christians to await the Coming of the Kingdom quietly and patiently. In the meantime, it was enough for Christians to endure the trials and tribulations of life in this world in quiet resignation, secure in the confidence that deliverance into the Kingdom eventually would be granted to them.[15]

From the standpoint of ethico-religious activism, this line of eschatological interpretation obviously was not conducive to arousing the discontents of oppressed religious minorities. Nothing about futurist eschatology suggests an intention to incite anyone to revolt against either religious or secular authorities. In a word, as the core of a religious doctrine, futurist eschatology posed no threat to the status quo. Indeed, if anything, futurist eschatology was patently quietistic. It could be used (as ideology) to assuage the political and religious frustrations of oppressed minorities or developed (as doctrine) to console the membership of persecuted and faction-ridden religious groups who, like the Jews of the Diaspora or the members of the early Christian church, used it to instill unity among themselves.

It is worth observing, moreover, that futurist eschatology was not likely to raise disturbing questions about the province of church authority in matters of salvation.[16] Unlike thoroughgoing eschatology, which, historically, has repeatedly questioned the efficacy of ceremonialism and sacramental piety as means of salvation (in both the Catholic and Protestant churches), futurist eschatology reinforced the claims and aims of ecclesiasticism.[17] Because futurist eschatology delayed religious consummation to a far distant future and, in effect, took it out of this world, it added considerable luster to the sanctity and mystery of the sacraments and to the church's claim that, as sole custodian of the sacraments of grace, it had an indispensable role in the administration of salvation.

As was noted earlier, thoroughgoing and futurist eschatology coexisted in the thought forms of the early Christian Church. But toward the end of the first century of our era these two eschatological tendencies had to make way for a third tendency – one that is expressed in the Fourth Gospel and took account, in Bultmann's words, "of the embarrassment into which the Christian community was brought by the nonappearance of the Parousia."[18] Indeed, the unexpected delay in the arrival of the Kingdom of God demanded a change in Christian eschatology – more, obviously, in its thoroughgoing than in its futurist variant.

In this context, one of the main theological problems of the early Church was to explain the discrepancy between the claims of thoroughgoing eschatology (that the final dénouement was right around the corner and that the Kingdom would arrive in "the twinkling of an eye") and the facts of history.[19] Some religious sense simply had to be made of the so-called "historical interim" that was stretching out like a blank page after the Incarnation.[20]

It is in this context that the Fourth Gospel becomes relevant to modern scholarship's understanding of Christian eschatology. And here C. H. Dodd's distinction between realized and unrealized eschatology becomes very illuminating.[21] For Dodd, thoroughgoing eschatology had misstated what the Gospel had meant when it claimed that "time was fulfilled" and the Kingdom of God realized in Christ's life.[22] According to Dodd, the Gospel never meant to imply that Christianity would only be fulfilled with the Second Coming.[23] The *literal* end to history, Dodd argued, had nothing to do with Christian eschatology, for the fulfillment of that eschatology had already been "realized" in the Incarnation.[24] By that Dodd meant not only that "the whole purpose of God in history" was "made manifest" in Christ's life but also that everything of true religious value in Christianity had been realized in time.[25]

Given this perspective, Dodd was obliged to contend "that nothing more [of religious value] could happen in history [after the Incarnation], because the eternal meaning which gives reality to history" was "now exhausted."[26] With the Incarnation "the *eschaton*" had truly "entered history," revealing once and for all the "hidden rule of God."[27] That meant, in turn, that "the Age to Come" had come in Christ's life and that the "Gospel of primitive Christianity" was "a Gospel of realized eschatology."[28]

In defending this thesis, Dodd was forced to acknowledge that his conception of realized eschatology referred to the realization of religious value in time but not necessarily in history.[29] For Christians, therefore, much remained to be realized after the Incarnation in the way of action, self-perfection, and the institutionalization of Christ's message in the world. According to Dodd, this is what concerned the author of the Fourth Gospel. The Fourth Gospel was meant to address the "unrealized" aspect of Christian eschatology. Activism, not mysticism, was essential to its message, as it presented the Incarnation less as the end of history than as the beginning of Christian fulfillment in a life of active piety.[30] Better, therefore, to speak (as Dodd has admitted) of "realized" eschatology in terms of "inauguration" than of finality, and of "unrealized" eschatology as a challenge to, and an imperative of, Christian life.[31]

Two aspects of Dodd's work are decisive for this study. First, the eschatology of the Fourth Gospel must be understood as a mix of thoroughgoing and futurist elements. But its futurist aspect must be envisaged as simply nonhistorical in an immediate sense rather than as nonterrestrial in an other-worldly sense. Second, the Fourth Gospel's eschatology combines axiology and teleology.[32] On the one hand, Christians are drawn to Christ as the symbol of fulfilled life (i.e., axiology). On the other hand, they must take it upon themselves to fulfill those values in history (i.e., make it their *telos*). This interplay between axiology and teleology, of course, is crucial to what was said earlier about Christian reform, for the Fourth Gospel makes voluntarism, activism, and synergism essential to eschatological fulfillment.[33] This explains, I think, how the Alexandrian Fathers could assimilate *homoiosis*, as the self-realizing *telos* of *Homo religiosus*, into what has been called "evolutionary eschatology" in general, and into covenant theology and Joachimism in particular.[34]

Having made these basic conceptual points about the study of Christian eschatology I might point out that the sixteenth, seventeenth, and eighteenth centuries constituted an age of apocalyptic expectation. There is ample evidence in many recent studies of the intellectual history of Western Europe and America to confirm this view.[35] In all these studies, moreover, there is a noticeable movement away from the idea that eschatology must serve the ideological purposes of either reactionary conservatives or revolutionary fanatics.[36] Indeed, instead of approaching eschatology at the extremes several of these studies have noted how eschatology could serve the interests of moderate reformers as well.[37]

Still, it is precisely among this group of respectable establishment gradualists that the tension between pessimism and optimism, crisis and expectation, apprehension about the present and hope for the future, is most obvious. That, of course, was because evolutionary eschatology offered its proponents no opportunity for other-worldly escapism.[38] For them, the other world was in the future of this world, and it was their responsibility to cooperate with God in making the future actual in the present.[39] The tension itself, however, was nicely balanced in that despair about the present was motivation to anticipate and prepare for the promise of the future.[40]

The mood created by these kinds of juxtapositions is, as Grundmann, Bouwsma, Reeves, and Bloomfield have noted, typical of the late medieval prophetic tradition in general and of Joachimism in particular;[41] it should not be surprising to find much interest in Joachimism among respectable Christian reformers.[42] Perhaps more important, though, is a point Tuveson has made about the relation between this mood and the Reformation as an event in history itself. The fact that the Reformation occurred at all could be interpreted as a sign both of despair over the corruption of the church in the present and of a hope for its reform in the future. In this sense, the Joachimite eschatology is fundamental both to the "mood" of the Reformation and to the way the reformers tried to give coherence to what they were doing.[43] Hence, Joachimism's importance to the intellectual history of Protestant Europe and America in the period between the Reformation and the French Revolution.[44]

1. From "realized" to "evolutionary" eschatology

As an event in history, the Reformation compelled Protestants to reinterpret the meaning of scripture, to rethink church history, and to devise a new theology of history to explain what had happened to Christian Europe in the sixteenth century.[45] Foxe's *Actes and Monuments* is archetypal here, for it tells us much about the direction Protestant thought was taking along those lines in Europe from about 1550 on.[46] Very simply, the strategy of that book (in its various editions) was threefold: to charge the Roman church with having become too worldly and, hence, with having succumbed to the designs of Antichrist in its policies; to depict several late medieval critics of the church's increasing worldliness as martyrs who, in calling for reform of the church, had anticipated what would take place in the sixteenth century; and to present the Reformation itself as an act of Christian liberation from false prophets within the church.

In this scheme, the fourteenth-century Englishman John Wyclif loomed quite large for, according to Foxe, he had initiated "the war of the elect against Antichrist" and, by so doing, had prepared the way for a "general reformation" of European Christianity in the sixteenth century.[47] As William Haller has remarked, "Foxe was...certain...that Wyclif begot Huss, Huss begot Luther and Luther begot truth."[48] It is interesting, moreover, that in his criticism of the Roman church, Wyclif had availed himself of several recent developments within the tradition of late medieval prophecy.[49] In this, as Reeves and Bloomfield have pointed out, he found the eschatological works of some "Joachimites" most helpful.[50] Wyclif didn't invoke just any eschatology to criticize the church; he invoked one that had recently emerged as prominent in the late medieval reform movement.[51] Not for nothing, then, had Ernest Renan, while writing about Joachim in 1866, puzzled over why the Reformation had not started in the twelfth century when Joachim began to advance his "proto-Protestant" eschatological critiques of popery.[52]

Within this context, in which Joachimism's expectations about the Last Things were made to serve the polemical purposes of reformers, Augustinian eschatology was considered to be the principal obstacle to church reform.[53] To set the background here, we need to remember that Augustine's conception of God's relation to the church in history was not easy to enlist into the ranks of a movement bent on the reform of men and the institutions that governed their lives in this world. Augustine, after all, had been a declared enemy of perfectionism and progress in Christian history.[54] What is more, much of his eschatology and the sacramentalism that accompanied it had consciously been designed to combat the ethical activism and perfectionism implicit in earlier forms of Christian eschatological thinking.[55] The result, as Pocock has well understood, was to divert attention from the diachronic to the synchronic presentation of God's relation to men; instead of human salvation being brought about by a succession of acts...in time, it appeared rather in terms of...actions of pure grace... which...were usually thought of as institutionalized in the...church.[56]

Would-be reformers, therefore, had to contend with the authority of Augustianian eschatology before reform of the medieval church could be attempted. The note Protestants took of Joachim and Joachimism needs to be understood in the context of that reform impulse.

To appreciate fully the role Joachimism played in Protestant criticisms of the Roman church requires some discussion of the various eschatological modes of early Christianity.

As members of a persecuted church it was natural for early Christians to apply the prophecies of the Book of Revelations to the Roman Empire.[57] Rome was, as R. Markus has put it, "the Beast to whom the Dragon" had "entrusted his world-wide authority."[58] That image of Rome changed, however, in the fourth century with the Christianization of the Empire. And the man whose work testified to that change was Eusebius of Caesarea, the man to whom Foxe had likened himself in *Actes and Monuments*.[59]

As the "first Christian historian," Eusebius offered the first official account of the new relationship between the Empire and the Church.[60] As he explained it, Christianity and Rome had providentially been destined to cooperate in a joint endeavor aimed at the gradual Christianization of the world. It "was not by mere human accident," Eusebius declared, that Christ's birth had coincided with the reign of Augustus.[61] Indeed, the simultaneous appearance of Christ and Augustus had prefigured the convergence of Christian monotheism and Roman worldly hegemony that Eusebius argued had been signaled by Constantine's conversion.[62] In Constantine's conversion, then, Eusebius perceived God's purposes working themselves out in history.[63] As Cranz has told us, Eusebius described Constantine as a concrete example of "the Logos' mediation between God and man" in history.[64] As the "first Christian Roman Emperor," Constantine was an ideal Christian as well as an ideal emperor.[65] With him, the *tempora christiana* had finally arrived. For that reason, there was no need to hesitate about linking the religious fortunes of Christianity with the political fortunes of the Empire or with the personality of the emperor.[66] The Empire had clearly been created as an instrument of Christian progress and thus had been meant to play a part in the redemption of mankind in history.[67]

If there was absolutism in Eusebius' deification of Constantine and theological imperialism implicit in the mission he assigned Christianity in the Empire, there was also much room for ethical activism in his theology of history, in what Mommsen has called his "full-fledged Christian idea of progress."[68] For in Eusebius' rendering of Christian history the Incarnation is less the *end* of a sequence of divine dispensations coming from God to man than the *beginning* of a *process* that leads to man's realization in his own life of the values symbolized in Jesus' life. To be sure, the individual's encounter with Christ was still the decisive experience, but for Eusebius the individual's assimilation of that experience made him responsible for the realization of the *eschaton* in history.

So conceived, eschatology began to lose the sense of something that happened to man and to gain the sense of something that he must pursue for himself.[69] That, in turn, made eschatology anthropologically and ethically relevant to how Christians were to live in this world. Swallowed up in anthropology, eschatology was shaped in Eusebius' hands to the needs of men in the historical interim — to the needs of Roman men in a Christian empire whose task was to Christianize the world. In this form, obviously, the weighting of Eusebius' eschatological preferences was toward activism. Indeed, Eusebius was not as interested in eschatology per se as in the way it could be a motive for Christian activism within the Empire. No longer were Christians limited to discussing salvation only in terms of man's receptivity to divine initiative; henceforth, they could argue that salvation required human input as well. Given that perspective and all the emphasis Eusebius placed on what man must *do* in order to be a Christian, it should not be hard to see how the Alexandrians' notion of *homoiosis* as the self-realizing *telos* of *homo religiosus* persisted in Eusebius' thought in the form of the ethical imperatives of evolutionary eschatology.[70] To put it more abstractly, it should be easy to see how interpretation of the Incarnation in terms of the teleology of inaugurated eschatology rather than of the axiology of realized eschatology was a point of theological convergence for Eusebius and the Alexandrian Fathers.[71]

Augustinian eschatology took shape against this background of Eusebius' absorption of *homoiosis* into his theology of Christian progress in history. Like many other prominent theologians of the late fourth century, Augustine initially had enthused with Eusebius about the promise betokened by the advent of the Christian empire.[72] But in the last decade of the fourth century, well before the sack of Rome in 410 and the soon-to-follow contest with Pelagius, Augustine had been disturbed by the religious implications of *Reichstheologie* and the claim that the Roman Empire was a vehicle of Christian salvation.[73]

Several things about the Alexandrian–Eusebius eschatological line disturbed him.[74] First, the appeal to action as the basis of religious conviction posed a threat to organized religion, to the church's claim that it was the sole vehicle of human salvation.[75] With the accent on action, the rituals and dogmas of the church could be envisaged as nothing more than the outward signs of religious certainty. Hence, they could be regarded as merely sense symbols with which to aid and stimulate the individual to active holiness.

Second, and as Augustine well knew, this kind of religious activism could with one short step (though largely because of Augustine it took hundreds of years to make) give currency to "ascetic," "elitist," and perfectionist attitudes toward religious salvation.[76] Indeed, he feared that once ethical rigorism and activism were introduced to religious consciousness, the question of salvation would tend to evolve into a question of how to develop a planned and methodical soteriological program. This, Augustine felt, lay behind Eusebius' efforts to depict the Roman Empire as an instrument for the ethical transformation of the world. That commitment, in turn, led to what Augustine contended was a fatal confusion, for there was a very thin line between religious works that had a civil content and civil works that were undertaken to promote certitude of one's own salvation.

Given these concerns, Augustine became convinced that any linkage between the Roman Empire and Christian salvation was destructive of the religious identity of every Christian. What is more, it was in violation of the meaning of Scripture as he had come to understand it after 393.[77] What troubled Augustine was precisely what charged Eusebian optimism: once religious salvation and the world, Christian piety and political virtue, were aligned, there was no way to distinguish Christians from pagans or to check the religious pretensions of the latter. Therefore, from whichever end he approached the problem of extricating Christianity from the politico-religious complex of Eusebius' *Reichstheologie*, Augustine would be forced to develop a distinctive Christian (i.e., Augustinian) perspective on the relation between religion and politics in human experience.

Paradoxically, the historical entanglement of Christianity and the Roman Empire in the late fourth century dictated that Augustine approach the problem of Christian identity from two vantage points. First he had to depoliticize religion, which in the ancient world meant removing Christian piety from public life – hence, Augustine's eventual clash with Pelagius. And second he had to detheologize politics, which in the ancient world meant removing the Empire from the soteriological process – hence, his objections to Eusebius.[78] That both these objectives could be accomplished by positing ultimate religious values beyond time, in a "heavenly city" that transcended any "earthly city," goes far to explain the dynamic of Augustine's thought. And that dynamic emerges most clearly, I think, in Augustinian eschatology, the orthodox Christian answer to the claims of evolutionary eschatology in whatever form.[79]

Since we are already familiar with how Augustine depoliticized religion, what follows focuses on his efforts to detheologize politics and, hence, his conflict with Eusebius. To detheologize politics Augustine first had to set limits to the religious claims of the Empire and the emperor. He did this by developing a "dualist theory of society" that recognized the value of the *res publica* for *human existence* but denied its religious value.[80] For this reason, the emperor could not command the religious allegiance of Christians on the basis of his political authority. Following Paul, Augustine conceded secular authority a certain amount of legitimacy in temporal affairs. But fearful as he was of the consequences of an emperor cult in the church, he maintained that the first citizen of the *res publica* was only a member of the *ecclesia*, not its head. Whatever the merits of this argument, this development in Augustine's thought clearly distinguishes his position from that of Eusebius, who, obviously, paid greater court to the emperor.[81] Where Eusebius had been optimistic about the prospect of the connection between Christianity and the emperor, Augustine was, if not pessimistic, at least studiously "neutral" (or "agnostic") about such a prospect during his "middle period" and openly hostile to it during his "late period."[82]

More specifically, Augustine allowed practical control of the machinery of government to the authorities of the "earthly city." They were responsible for pursuing peace, maintaining the material well-being of society, and, above all, repressing evil in men.[83] Concomitant with these responsibilities, Augustine granted secular authorities a monopoly of coercive power. Like Paul, who in Romans exhorted Christians to render "all their dues" to Caesar so he could "execute wrath upon him that doest evil," but also like the classical Greek philosophers, who saw the *polis* as a check on the "instinctive affections" of man, Augustine proclaimed the *res publica* the vehicle of "order" *par excellence*.[84] Still, Augustine made this concession to secular authorities less because he esteemed them than because he believed that their exercise of coercive power was in accordance with the *res publica's* inferior status as a worldly institution. Thus, while the *res publica* was deemed fundamental to the defense of a religious society against its enemies (both inside and outside), it was not recognized as essential to the salvation of the Christian.[85]

To be sure, the priority Augustine gave to "order" in his thought was not, as Cranz has reminded us, unique to him. As any reader of Aristotle's *Politics* knows, the preservation of order was one of the central purposes of the *polis* in classical political thought. But beyond this the *polis* had a creative ethico-educational function to fulfill in classical political thought: it was the agent that directed men toward virtue and set them in motion toward moral perfection. In a word, it defined the *telos* of being human.[86]

Like the *ecclesia* in Christian thought, the *polis* in classical thought was a vehicle of salvation. Translated into the language of practical politics, the *polis* was supposed to mediate between the forces of "order" and "progress" in human affairs; it was supposed to mediate, that is, between tradition and innovation in civil experience.[87] In this connection, the *polis* was envisaged as an agent of collective education and ethical activism. As such, the *polis* commanded a loyalty that, when measured on a vertical scale of values, placed it above the individual but below God. The *polis*, therefore, represented a realm of experience that man and mankind had *to go through* in order to achieve salvation. In terms of our previous discussion of Alexandrian theology and Pelagian ethics, the *polis* is a "moment" in the process whereby man assimilates to God.[88]

Needless to say, this willingness to posit the *polis* as an instrument of ethical perfection, education, and "creative politics," which is certainly present in the thought of the Alexandrian Fathers, Pelagius, and Eusebius, is wholly absent in Augustinian thought.[89] As we have seen, Augustine repudiated this kind of perfectionism, with the result that there is little incentive in Augustinian anthropology for man to engage the world and to try to transform it through reformist activity.

Quite naturally, Augustine's antipathy for perfectionism carried over to his eschatology. And, as Cranz has brilliantly shown, it is in the *Ad Simplicianum* that that eschatology was first developed.[90] Augustine wrote *Ad Simplicianum* after a period of intense biblical studies between 393 and 396. These studies, Cranz argues, persuaded Augustine to abandon the notion of history as a soteriological drama in which God gradually led man toward redemption. A close reading of the promises and threats of the Bible had convinced Augustine that the claims of current "Christian" views of history did not square with the radical contrast the Bible drew between sin and salvation, the profane and the sacred. As Augustine's thinking became more biblically oriented, he began to see that the idea of gradual and regular progress toward Christian perfection and salvation on earth was wholly illusory.[91] The general lesson of the Gospel and the particular lesson of history, Augustine pointed out, was not that of moral progress, but that of death and resurrection, of men dying and being reborn in Christ. For Augustine, then, this meant that the importance of history for Christianity emerged more in a series of "crises" than in an "evolutionary pattern." There was Adam's crisis before the law, the Jews crisis under the law, and the Christian's crisis under the grace of Jesus Christ. This, Augustine felt, was the key to Christian faith, and he made that faith the basis of the religious and eschatological views expressed in the *Ad Simplicianum*.

To understand what that faith consisted in we need only look at the interpretation of history that informs the *Ad Simplicianum*. Having abandoned the pretensions of evolutionary eschatology, Augustine developed a view of history that, while drawing upon the traditional scheme of six ages, profoundly altered the scheme's meaning for history.[92] This was accomplished by, in effect, reducing the six-age scheme of history to one with only two terms of temporal reference: one focused on the *praparatio evangelica* of the world of the Old Testament and the other focused on the teachings of the New Testament. As Augustine now saw it, the Incarnation was the last term in a series of events that announced the end of history in axiological terms.[93] Accordingly, pre-Christian history was history for Augustine only insofar as it prognosticated the coming of Christ and the fulfillment of Christian values. In this way, Augustine argued, the Incarnation represented the coincidence of all times in one *kairotic* moment in which all "time was fulfilled." With the Incarnation, all that God had meant to communicate to man was revealed: hence, Augustine's development of a two-term view of history in which the five ages of Old Testament history were telescoped into one period – the prehistory of Christianity.[94]

This two-term scheme of history should give us pause, for the radical contrast of "old" and "new" suggests the theological emphases of "realized eschatology." Indeed, realized eschatology stresses the monumental, once-and-for-all character of the Incarnation – and that, most certainly, was inherent in Augustine's position from 396 on. Unlike Eusebius, who had emphasized the "unrealized," teleological aspects of the meaning of the Incarnation for Christianity, Augustine insisted that all that was of value in Christianity had been fully realized in Christ's life. From there, Augustine went on to argue that post-Incarnation history was neither a field of Christian opportunity, a vehicle of Christian self-realization, nor a medium for man's participation in his own redemption. Rather, it was a realm of human fragmentation *par excellence*: a realm of dispersion, dissipation, and degeneration.[95]

According to Augustine, therefore, history had no intrinsic value for Christians. It was a mere excursus with only chronological, not theological, meaning.[96] It was clear to Augustine that the "promise" of the Old Testament had been "fulfilled" in the New, and that mankind's spiritual development had been meant to cease with the Incarnation. And since the Apostolic church embodied that spirit, all that remained for a Christian to do was to join the church and partake of its sacraments. The church, not the Roman Empire, had been designated the "institution of salvation" in this world.[97]

Thus did Augustine allow eschatology to be swallowed by a sacramentalism that mediated between what had already been realized in time and what some day would be realized by men beyond time. On either count, salvation had little to do with history as a process (i.e., evolutionary eschatology) or with the self-realizing teleology of *homo religiosus* (i.e., *homoiosis*). Quite simply, Augustine had made eschatology a function of organized religion. It was to remain that way until Joachim and his followers recovered the principles of evolutionary eschatology and put them at the service of the late medieval religious movement that aimed at the reform of a church that could be said to have organized itself around "realized" eschatology.[98]

During the late Middle Ages, then, would-be Christian reformers knew that before any reform of the church could be initiated Christians would have to be convinced that reform itself was not only feasible but religiously significant as well.[99] Indeed, reformers realized that reform depended very much on finding a way for drawing God – whom Augustine had presented as utterly transcendent – back into history where He could be enlisted in the service of reform.[100] In this context, eschatology presented itself to them as a device for doing just that, with the result that we find many late medieval reformers, including Joachim, adopting modes of eschatological argumentation that were clearly Johannine and evolutionary in that they emphasized the teleological rather than the axiological dimension of the Incarnation.[101]

In the late twelfth century, Joachim of Fiore – a Calabrian abbot and member of the reform-minded Cistercian religious order – assumed a leading role in this shift of eschatological emphasis.[102] Obviously, neither the whole of Joachim's thought nor his *Sitz im Leben* can be taken up in detail here. Suffice it to say that a brief overview of his trinitarian periodization of history and its theological implications helps explain much about his influence on the Reformation. And although there is much about later Joachimism's development of this trinitarian view of history that Joachim would have disavowed, his name was generally attached to the "anthologies" of trinitarian eschatological writings that were circulated with such notoriety from the thirteenth until well into the sixteenth century.[103]

During the last two decades of the twelfth century much was happening that could spark the eschatological imagination of a late medieval church reformer. Signs of the time were everywhere, warning the church to end its corrupt practices or risk succumbing to Antichrist immediately. Islam was rising; Saracens were encroaching upon the borders of Christendom; the Crusades were floundering; there was ethical inertia throughout the church, and even in Joachim's own Cistercian order; all these signs, Joachim believed, signaled an imminent crisis for Christianity. Hence, Joachim's pessimism. Hence, his attempt to use eschatology to point up the corruptions of the medieval church and to draw attention to its vulnerability in face of the perennial challenge of Antichrist.

But if there was much to be pessimistic about in this situation, there were also reasons for optimism. For, as Joachim himself has told us, it was made clear to him (in a moment of divine illumination) that the tribulations of the present were to be interpreted as annunciatory of a triumphant, Christian future.[104] "What was revealed to Joachim," Löwith has observed, "was both the historical and mystical significance of the symbols and figures of the Old and New Testaments, converging in a total picture of the history of salvation from beginning to end."[105] As Joachim interpreted this convergence, it prefigured the emergence of a new age of spiritual perfection that was to follow immediately on the present one.[106] Joachim put it this way:

The signs as described in the gospel show clearly the dismay and ruin of the century which is now running down and must perish. Hence I believe that it will not be in vain *to submit to the vigilance of the believers*, through this work which *divine economy* has made known to my unworthy person in order to awaken...them, if possible, by a new kind of exegesis.[107]

Hence, Joachim's optimism. Hence, his belief that slumbering Christians could be awakened to activism and reform by eschatological expectancy, by the prospect of the imminent arrival of a new religious age *in history*.[108]

This claim about the coming of a new age in history, then, involved a "new kind of exegesis"; and at the heart of that exegesis was an evolutionary eschatology that grew out of a trinitarian view of history.[109] Specifically, Joachim offered an exegesis of Scripture that held that mankind's spiritual evolution was not meant – as Augustine had claimed – to cease with the Incarnation, with the foundation of the Apostolic church, or with the subsequent development of the sacraments. Furthermore, Joachim made it clear that this evolutionary process had not been meant to cease with the end of Christ's life. The trinitarian doctrine, after all, spoke of a series of religious dispensations that God deigned to make known to man, gradually, in keeping with the wisdom of the "divine economy." Each of these dispensations, Joachim pointed out, had a definite historical setting and, by implication, referred to a different stage in the evolving religious consciousness of man: there was the dispensation of the law under the sign of the Father and the Old Testament; that of the Gospel and the church under the sign of the Son and the New Testament; and, finally, the dispensation – to come in 1260 – of a new order of religious men under the sign of the Holy Spirit.[110]

This mode of exegesis had much to recommend it, for it allowed Joachim to treat each historical stage as well as each stage's particular form of religious dispensation as part of a broader and unified pattern of evolving Christian consciousness in history. Each epoch and dispensation, therefore, possessed religious significance only insofar as it participated in the evolution of the divine purpose in history. Yet Joachim's theology

of history accorded history as such its own distinctive structure of development and recognized the relative autonomy and integrity of each stage and
dispensation in the evolutionary process.[111] No stage, Joachim felt, could
be singled out as the epitome of normative Christianity. It was enough, he
thought, to explain that this or that form of religious consciousness was
bonum et necessarim in suo temporare, that is, in accordance with the program
of the "divine economy" and natural to man at a certain stage of his
religious evolution. Thus, Joachim was able to be sharply critical of the
present shortcomings of Christianity without having to renounce his
Christian faith, for the prospect of the "coming Age" held out the
possibility of a new Christian dispensation that simply operated under
another sign than that which had hitherto been provided by the
church.[112]

To Joachim's way of thinking, therefore, man's redemption in and
through history unfolded organically like a tree that from its trunk bears
branches that themselves bear fruit.[113] Each has grown from the same
seed, yet each is distinct. Christian wisdom, too, unfolded organically for
Joachim. As mankind passed from infancy, to youth, and on to maturity,
so the history of Christian wisdom moved for him from "clarity to
clarity"[114] – from its innocence (before the law), to its infancy (under the
law), to its youth (under grace), and to its maturity (under the Holy
Spirit).[115]

It is precisely this conception of spiritual growth in time and of man's
gradually expanding religious consciousness in history that Joachim, like
the Alexandrians before him, meant to express with the idea of divine
economy. The theology of the divine economy holds that God reveals
himself to men economically; that is, in a way that is consistent with the
meaning of the Trinity and yet that makes that meaning dependent upon
man's capacity to receive and act upon the ever-more sophisticated forms
of religious communication that are symbolized in the three figures of
the Trinity itself. So conceived, the process of successive, trinitarian
revelation becomes tied to the evolving religious consciousness of men
in history. As the successive revelations of law, grace, and spiritual perfection were made known to man, so man moved through successive
stages of Christian wisdom – from *pistis* to *gnosis*, from the letter to the
spirit, from the visible to the invisible.[116] In that respect, Joachim's
economy of salvation argument synchronized very well with the
Alexandrians' conceptions of the covenant and of *homoiosis* as the self-
realizing *telos* of *homo religiosus*.[117] Assimilation to God as a teleological
process and the evolution of religious consciousness in history as an
eschatological process have become one in Joachim's theology of history
and in the reform movement of the late Middle Ages. And with the
emergence of that theology of history we witness a late medieval recovery
of a theological anthropology that at its core was anti-Augustinian.[118]

Though Joachim was not a systematic thinker, there is a discernible pattern in his eschatologically inspired exegesis of the Bible.[119] The pattern, as has been suggested, has some obvious affinities with the synergism of the Alexandrian Fathers. There were, for example, the tendencies to minimize the consequences of the Fall for the salvation of man and to regard the Incarnation as the beginning of a process whereby Christians were expected to strive after spiritual progress in history. Moreover, by locating the third age *in* history rather than beyond it, Joachim made it possible for others to read an aspect of Pelagian perfectionism into the eschatological imperative of the larger theological pattern. And there can be no question but that like Eusebius he meant to make history a field of opportunity for Christian activism.

The point of Joachim's efforts, of course, had been to expand man's sense of the role he might play in the salvation process.[120] In doing this, however, Joachim also gave history religious significance, making it a vehicle of salvation that, according to the economy of salvation argument, was on the verge of carrying Christians into a new age of ultimate religious fulfillment. If that were so, truly "heretical" consequences could follow from Joachim's "trinitarian eschatology."[121] If the idea of an imminent third age were pushed to its logical conclusion – and by the 1250s that was what was being done[122] – questions would certainly be raised about the soteriological efficacy of the sacraments administered by the church.[123]

The "logic" of the argument was simple: if a third age were to emerge, the papal church, as *the* institution of grace during the second religious age, was not meant to have the final word in soteriological matters in the third. Just as the New Testament had succeeded the Old, so the Eternal Gospel would succeed the New.[124] The church could be viewed as a "passing stage in the development of the history of salvation"[125] and could be expected "to yield to the coming church of the Spirit" in the matter of salvation.[126] More to the point, it would be required to relinquish its authority to a new order of religious men who were being persecuted in the present for having anticipated the coming of the new age.[127]

Here the revolutionary consequences of Joachimism begin to emerge and to run beyond Joachim's reformist program. What has happened is that a relationship has been established between the idea of the providentially planned obsolescence of the church and the idea of persecution as testimony of one's election, of one's having been chosen by the Holy Spirit to announce the coming of the new age.[128] The greater the "persecution," the more certainty one could have about his "mission"; the more one was condemned for "novelty," the surer one could be of the correctness of his "anticipations."

Several interesting points arise out of this persecution–election connection and some of them go far to explain the particular nature of Joachim's appeal to sixteenth-century Protestants.

Earlier we noted that the dispensation of the third age was associated in Joachim's mind with a new order of religious men.[129] Through this order something that he called *intelligentia spiritualis* – full understanding of what was required of *homo religiosus* in the third age – was to reveal itself to all mankind. Joachim, we know, claimed that he had received the gift of *intelligentia spiritualis* during his moment of inspiration.[130] Here we need to be careful, for by this Joachim meant something quite different from the ecstasy of mystical illumination.[131] Traditionally, the gift of prophecy had been understood to arise from an individual's direct communication with God.[132] As Reeves (and others) has noted, though, Joachim was not an "esoteric mystic" who, on the basis of being a "privileged soul," claimed to be able to divine the future.[133] Rather, Joachim made a more modest claim for his gift of *intelligentia spiritualis*: namely, that it was the gift to study and meditate upon the two books of Scripture, and from them to draw spiritual understanding of the quality of Christian life in the coming Age. Hard study and meticulous exegesis, therefore, were essential to Joachim's prophetic gift, a gift available to anyone who made exegesis a scholarly vocation.[134] No, Joachim was more an exegete than a prophet,[135] more a "sober" scholar than a "revolutionary fanatic."[136] And the combination of scholarship, of exegesis and prophecy, of mysticism and science, as it were, accounts in large part for Joachim's appeal to scholarly and respectable sixteenth- and seventeenth-century Protestants.

Endowed with the elixir of *intelligentia spiritualis* Joachim made a vocation of scriptural exegesis. At the same time, however, he seemed to be making *gnosis* rather than *pistis* the measure of a Christian life. Again, we need to look closely at Joachim's position to see that this is not the case.

There are several reasons for saying this. First, Joachim insisted that the results of his exegesis had to be submitted "to the vigilance" of all Christians.[137] If Christians were to be awakened by his method of exegesis, it would have to be because they saw the contemporary relevance of Joachim's message and chose, voluntarily, to respond to it. In that sense, Joachim was what some today would call a prophet of "interactionism."[138] Second, the voluntarist aspect of Joachim's message was linked to his conception of the third age as one in which the religious goal of an "associated life" would be fully realized.[139] Christians could not be forced to enter the third age; they had to do so collectively and voluntarily or not at all.[140] Hence, there is little sense in Joachim of his being associated with an "esoteric sect" within which the future age to come is fulfilled within the membership of the sect itself.[141]

Related to these two points is an all-important third one that makes the transition from the second to the third age of history contingent upon the interplay between the *gnosis* of the few and the *pistis* of the many.[142] It was precisely because Joachim realized that this interplay would take time to develop that he placed the beginning of the third age at a date in the future (1260) that would give the next generation of his Calabrian disciples time to educate and prepare Christians for the coming age.[143] For this reason, he expected the exegete to exhibit the kind of patience vis-à-vis his audience that had been implicit in the economy God had displayed in the series of successive revelations through which He had gradually made Himself known to man.[144] There is, in short, a very real educational component in Joachim's method of exegesis; what is more, it reveals itself not only in the process of exegesis but also in the didactic purposes to which the results of that exegesis are meant to be put.

Finally, by presenting the gift of *intelligentia spiritualis* as something that becomes manifest *through* rather than *in* the life of the exegete, Joachim made it clear that he envisaged his own task in historically specific rather than cosmic universal terms.[145] That is, he was very careful to explain his gift as unique to his vocation and to his time and place in history and not as peculiar to his own religious personality.[146] Though his *gnosis* separated him from other Christians, the purpose of that *gnosis* was to help "the general body of Christian people" make the transition to the third religious age of history.[147] So circumscribed, Joachim's gift of *intelligentia spiritualis* does not easily translate into a sense of gnostic election or moral superiority.[148] In Joachim's extremely historical evolutionary eschatology, every Christian is equally as close to the coming religious age as any other. So, if there is elitism in Joachim's gnosis, the gnosis itself is set in a very "democratic" framework.

2. Joachimism and Protestantism: The godly prince and the Radical Reformation

Clarification of the ideas that are the driving forces within covenant theology and evolutionary eschatology in general and in Joachim's trinitarian view of history in particular enables us more precisely to appreciate how and why eschatology came to influence Protestant thought during the Reformation, a Reformation that, as an ongoing process, had several phases to it and lasted for about one hundred years.[149] As the phases changed, so too did the needs of Protestants, and the use to which Joachimism was put changed accordingly. Along these lines delineation of the long-term pattern of development leads directly to Old-Württemberg in the early seventeenth century and to an understanding of the way Joachimism was used there to give expression to the ideal of Protestant civil piety.

How, then, was Joachimism used by Protestants in the sixteenth century? First of all, and most obviously, Protestants used Joachim as a "major weapon" in their "attack on the Roman Church."[150] As a prophetic witness to Roman corruption, Joachim was cited again and again by antipapal writers as an authority who had clearly perceived the relationship between the church and Antichrist.[151] Throughout the century, from Osiander's depiction in 1527 of Luther as chastiser of the church to the publication of Flacius' collection of medieval prophetic texts in 1597, Joachim was a key source in the "Protestant polemic against the papacy."[152] In this context, Reeves has claimed that John Bale's exploitation of Joachim in a 1544 publication was typical of the initial usage among Protestants. Citing Joachim as a precursor of Protestant reform, Bale wrote, "The church of Rome shall be destroyed in the third state, as the synagogue of the Jews was destroyed in the second state. And a spiritual church shall from then forth succeed to the end of the world."[153]

Based on this kind of evidence, Reeves has concluded that Joachimism was used in an "entirely negative sense" during the initial phase of the Reformation.[154] In that phase, Joachimism was used primarily to prove two things: that "the Roman church equals Babylon," and that the pattern of Christian history was such that it pointed to Protestantism as the culmination of a long historical development.[155] And yet, if these were the main religious uses to which Protestants initially put Joachimism, such an application had political implications as well. That was because the argument about the Reformation as the climacteric of Christian history required the military support of Protestant princes to sustain it in reality. Consequently, when the religious negativism of Joachimism was filtered through reality it emerged in the form of a Protestant political dependence on "godly princes" for the preservation of the Reformation. Hence, the "conservative" political implications of Joachimism in the early years of the Reformation.[156]

Mention of the relationship between Joachimism and the idea of the "godly prince" raises larger questions about the politics of Protestants in the sixteenth century. Here the conventional distinction between the magisterial and radical Reformation becomes relevant to our discussion. If Joachimism leads in the direction of the godly prince it also points toward a "godly people" argument.[157] Both lines of development can be explained, I think, in terms of the political dynamic of what Reeves has identified as "later Joachimism."[158]

As Reeves has told us, application of Joachimism to political problems developed independently of Joachim almost fifty years after his death.[159] It was probably in the 1240s, with the publication of the earliest and most famous pseudo-Joachimist text, the *Commentary on Jeremiah,* that the "second," explicitly political, phase of Joachimism began.[160] The timing and content of the publication are not hard to explain. Apparently, as the fateful year of 1260 approached, a group of Italian Joachimists felt compelled to "restate" Joachim's trinitarian view of history so that the future could be cast in the mold of a "rejuvenated Roman Church" under the guidance of an "Angelic Pope."[161] What was specifically political about the text was that it singled out the German house of Hohenstaufen as the residence of Antichrist and "the source of all evil" in the world.[162]

"German political Joachimism," Reeves argues, began as a "counterblast" to this "Italian propaganda."[163] Two aspects of the Germans' use of Joachim are interesting here. First, this counterblast originated in Old-Württemberg, coming from the leader of a group in Swabia who recast Joachim's trinitarian view of history so that it seemed to point to Frederick II and "his seed," not an "Angelic Pope," as the redeemers of history.[164] Second, the Hohenstaufen were presented both as chastisers of the Church in the present and as the renewers of the Christian spirit in the future.[165] As such, they, and not a group of exegetes, were to guide Christians through the transition from the second to the third religious age of history. Clearly, political figures could be incorporated into Joachimism to advance God's religious purposes in history.[166]

Once this identification was made, there was no limit to the political figures who could use Joachimism to endow themselves with a sense of religious mission. As Reeves has meticulously shown, throughout the fourteenth and fifteenth centuries French and German groups repeatedly appealed to Joachimism in their respective searches for a "Second Charlemagne" and a "Third Frederick."[167] And as Reeves has also perceived, these types of religio-political associations carried over to the sixteenth century, when Charles V and Luther's protector, Frederick of Saxony, were designated the respective carriers of Catholic and Protestant hopes of renewal in history.[168] Thus, when Protestants invoked the image of the godly prince to justify their dependence on him, they were doing more than responding to the political exigencies of the moment; they were giving political expression to one of the basic tendencies of Joachimism as well.

If one line of political Joachimism culminated in a view of the godly prince as the agent of what Tyndale once called "a full and godly reformation,"[169] the other line expressed itself among various groups of "radicals" who had gradually become disillusioned with the speed with which these princes were fulfilling their function as agents of the Reformation.[170] Indeed, from Müntzer, through Knox, to early seventeenth-century English Puritans, we witness a clear shift in how Protestants gave focus to their religio-political expectations.[171] Specifically – and the pattern of Knox's development is archetypal here – we witness a move away from the idea that "godly rule" was meant to be the exclusive preserve of the godly prince.[172] As the century moved forward, radical groups more and more charged godly princes with "tarrying with the Reformation" and with impeding its overall progress.[173] To reestablish Protestant momentum, they argued, "godly people" had to assume a much more active role in reformatory religious processes. They had to seize the initiative, as it were, and take the responsibility for bringing about a "full reformation" themselves.[174]

This shift in understanding of who was responsible for overseeing fulfillment of the religious values of the Reformation explains the appeal of another aspect of Joachimism to certain groups of sixteenth-century Protestants. With the shift of agency from godly prince to godly people the ideas of election, of new orders of spiritual man, and of the people as a congregation of the holy organized independent of the prince began to figure more prominently in the minds of Protestant activists.[175] Many of these ideas, of course, were very old – they go back at least to Montanus – but they had been associated with Joachimism for the past few centuries. Indeed, since the 1250s, when the Franciscan spirituals had tried to endow their own order with the elixir of *intelligentia spiritualis*,[176] radicals of various sorts had, in Reeves' words, appealed to this dimension of Joachimism to "underline their own sense of mission."[177]

In truth, this form of Joachimism was not political in any conventional sense.[178] The exclusiveness of election tended to militate against truly political involvements. But as the century moved on, the political character of the radical Reformation began to change; with time it became less exclusive and more collectivist in a populist sense. Given that dynamic, it developed a more reformist and constitutionalist conception of what role a godly people should play in the Reformation.

For that reason, it would be misleading to associate the radical Reformation only with the politics of extremist groups – say, exclusively with the politics of sanits out of office.[179] To be sure, the Anabaptists were radicals in an extremist sense, and Knox was certainly not a constitutionalist. But as Skinner and Walzer have well understood, there were groups of constitutionalists, especially among the Huguenots, within the radical Reformation as well.[180] Still, while the politics of these groups differed markedly from those of revolutionaries and anarchists,[181] their activism was informed by similar considerations: namely, by a refusal to accept the godly prince as the agent of the Reformation and by a sense of urgency about the need for a "Second Reformation," for what Milton had called a "reforming of the Reformation itself."[182]

Here, of course, the negativism and expectationism of Joachimism were being used by Protestants to challenge the religiopolitical orthodoxy *of their own* Reformation. As they saw it, the church's acquiescence in things religious to the godly prince had resulted in the domestication of the sense of ethico-eschatological urgency that had initially charged the Reformation.[183] That sense of urgency, they argued, had to be restored, even if it meant raising disturbing questions about the politics of Protestant orthodoxy. In what remains of this chapter, I wish to show how the religious history of Old-Württemberg, from Andreae to Bengel, is best understood within the context of a reformist call for a Second Reformation.[184] By doing that, I hope to show how the call for such a Reformation entailed a commitment to the kind of Protestant civil piety we discussed earlier.

3. Studion and Andreae: Joachimism and the Second Reformation in Old-Württemberg

Many of the rather general points I have just made about the politics and social uses of Joachimism in the sixteenth century can be illustrated by looking at two important figures in the cultural history of Old-Württemberg in the early seventeenth century: Simon Studion and J. V. Andreae. Both were familiar with Joachimism and employed aspects of it in their work;[185] and Andreae, who has been described as "the single most important influence on the church history of the Württemberg territory for over two hundred years," is illuminating for much else besides.[186] Both, moreover, were involved in a late sixteenth- and early seventeeth-century movement of religious reform that was European in scope and that may be discussed in terms of what we have called the Protestant call for a Second Reformation.

During the so-called "age of religious wars," numerous socioeconomic and political dislocations in Europe made the development of a more activist and worldly oriented theology a religious imperative for many Protestants. As elsewhere in Protestant Europe, reform-minded Lutherans were involved in this kind of endeavor toward the end of the sixteenth century.[187] The problem was how to promote ethical activism and civil engagement in the face of the opposition of an "orthodox" creed that had become increasingly dogmatic and ethically indifferent to the world over the course of the sixteenth century.[188] What scholars today characterize as "confessional orthodoxy" had imposed a formalism and rigidity upon Lutheranism and, by so doing, had deprived Lutherans of any incentive to action.[189] Granted, the events that had culminated in the Formula of Concord in 1580 seemed to assuage factionalism within Lutheranism and to hold out the promise of Lutheran solidarity vis-à-vis Catholicism and the other Protestant churches; but the price of accord had been the reduction of Lutheranism to a series of sterile precepts as "Scholastic" and as scornful of the dignity of man as any previously known under Catholicism.[190] Hence, the need for a Second Reformation.

In the face of orthodox dogmatics and inertia, J. Arndt's (1555–1621) publication in 1606 of *True Christianity* marks a major turning point in Lutheran thought. From that time on reform-minded Lutherans, from Andreae to Spener and Bengel, could cite a Lutheran source in support of their own commitments to a doctrine of *praxis pietatis*.[191] As one student of Arndt had noted, he made "the doctrine of the Word" the point of departure for the "ethical doctrine" of the deed.[192]

According to Arndt, orthodox Lutheranism had recently become more concerned with upholding "right doctrine" than with promoting "right action" – with compelling Lutherans to "believe much" rather than to "do much."[193] "What," Arndt asked repeatedly throughout *True Christianity*, "is Christian faith without a Christian life?"[194] What has happened, he wondered, to the Lutheran commitment to the "work of reform"?[195] Where is the "expectation" of "deliverance" that excited hopes for the future and, by so doing, gave urgency to action in the present?[196] How was it that ritual, ceremony, and dogmatic wranglings had come to replace the practice of piety as the measure of a Christian life?[197]

In answering these questions, Arndt made it clear that his principal concern was not to challenge Luther's doctrine of justification by faith but rather to insist that sanctification by works was an explicit expression of that implicit faith.[198] With this shift of emphasis toward sanctification, *praxis pietatis*, and works, we can begin to see ethical activism and synergism trying to assert themselves once again in Lutheranism.[199] And, as we have come to realize, there is a good deal of the doctrine of *homoiosis* in synergism of whatever sort.[200]

There are, to be sure, several strategically crucial references in *True Christianity* to what we earlier noted Ladner had called the "assimilation ideology" of the Alexandrian Fathers;[201] to wit, the title of the first chapter of Book One is "Of the Image of God in Man." From, that starting point Arndt pursues a line of argument with which we are quite familiar. According to Arndt the purpose of a Christian life is to restore to its full brilliance "upon earth" the "image of God" that had been tarnished by the Fall.[202] Predictably, Arndt proceeds from that point to argue that man possessed after the Fall that all-important "spark" that would permit him (with God's help) to recover his lost "glory."[203] More to the point, Arndt specifically linked Plato's notion of *homoiosis* to the idea of Christ by making the latter the model of an ethical ideal whose light guides Christians from "glory to glory."[204] The explicit association of Plato with a theology of sanctification suggests that Arndt approached the idea of a Christian life in terms of the self-realizing teleology of *homo religiosus*.[205] And indeed he did. How else explain his likening Christianity to the "*process*" by which a child *grows* into a man?[206] How else explain his concern with "Christian progress"[207] – with the series of "gradual sanctifications" that are essential to the completion of a Christian life?[208] How else explain his counsel that a Christian does "not all at once grow up into a perfect man; but remains a child for some time, who must be continually nourished and nurtured by the virtue and power of the divine Spirit, and so brought every day *more and more into a conformity* with the Lord Jesus Christ"?[209] And finally, there is the conventional cautionary remark, warning man to "take heed" that "you do not, therefore think, as if man were made equal with God in holiness"[210] – Which is to say, Arndt's doctrine is one of approximationism and of gradual "assimilation to God" rather than one in which the "deification of man" takes place through some mystical "identification" with God.[211]

As might have been expected, the arguments of *True Christianity* were immediately criticized by many orthodox Lutherans.[212] Arndt was charged with "synergism" and with being a "Pelagian."[213] Whatever the charge, it was Arndt's call for activism, not the labels his opponents attached to him, that attracted reform-minded Lutherans to *True Christianity*. And that was because Arndt's activism and his call for continuous reformation opened the future to religious hope, a precious commodity during the Age of Religious Wars.[214]

Mention of opening the future to the idea of religious hope brings us back to covenant theology, evolutionary eschatology, and Joachimism and to the figure of Simon Studion (1543–1608), who used a scheme of evolutionary eschatology to give impetus to activism and urgency to his own call for a "general reformation."[215]

Unfortunately, not much is known about Studion. We do know this Old-Württemberg schoolteacher was a conspicuous figure in three very important aspects of early seventeenth-century Protestant culture. To be specific, he was involved in introducing (or reintroducing) Joachimism to Old-Württemberg;[216] in the effort to form a "Protestant union" in Europe that, in Yates' words, was "formed to counteract the Catholic League" that was taking shape in France in the 1580s;[217] and, most important of all, in providing the Rosicrucian movement with an eschatological framework that gave coherence to its call for a "general reformation" of contemporary Lutheran piety.[218] All three of Studion's involvements were expressed in an unpublished manuscript he left us, the *Naometria*, and the "clustering" of these involvements in one manuscript suggests à la Weber that it may well serve as a focus for understanding what constituted meaningful historical action in Old-Württemberg at the start of the seventeenth century.

First, the matter of Studion and Joachim.[219] Just how Studion came to know of Joachim is not clear. In the sixteenth century Joachim would have been available to him in so many sources that it is difficult to pinpoint exactly which ones registered on him most.[220] We can be certain, though, that Studion knew of Joachim, because he mentions him in the *Naometria*[221] and because Andreae specifically linked the *Naometria* with Joachim's prophecies.[222] Moreover, Studion would have been drawn to Joachimism because it expressed exactly the "mood" of the time:[223] despair over Catholic resurgence in Europe and over the flagging of will among Lutherans themselves and optimism that a series of events, specifically to come in 1604, 1612, and 1620, would bring an end to Antichrist's rule and produce a "general reformation" in Europe.

Studion articulated these prophecies, and elaborated on the events surrounding the key dates in them, in the *Naometria*. But he did so in a way that reveals both his debt to what we have called "political Joachimism" and his involvement in the formation of a Union that was to protect Protestants in Europe from a resurgent Catholicism[224] [through the Union, Protestants were to overcome Antichrist (1612) and complete the general reformation (1620) that had been announced (1604) by the completion of the *Naometria* itself].[225]

In this context, the work of Frances Yates is most instructive. It shows that Studion's *Naometria* expected the Duke of Württemberg, Frederick I, to play a leading role not only in the formation of the Protestant Union but in the overthrow of Antichrist and the initiation of the general reformation as well.[226] The duke was, as it were, to assume the role of the savior–emperor who had been prominent in the eschatological imagination of Württembergers since the days of Frederick II, the Holy Roman emperor.[227] Needless to say, Frederick, who has been described as "somewhat lightheaded," indulged Studion in all this, with the result that the *Naometria* was allowed to circulate in manuscript at court and at the University of Tübingen.[228]

With that sanction and exposure, the *Naometria* became an important resource for negative Protestant concerns about the present and positive concerns about the future.[229] So received, the *Naometria* did two things: it attempted to allay this fear of Antichrist in the present by invoking an Erastianism that smacked of political Joachimism and it offered the hope of a "general reformation" in the future in which the whole of society was to participate. Given its two faces, one conservative and political and the other progressive and social, the *Naometria* offered "a pattern of two's and three's" that exactly fitted the mood of early seventeenth-century Württemberg Protestants, who wavered uncertainly between Erastian religio-political and radical religio-social convictions.[230]

There is one final dimension of the *Naometria* that deserves attention; it, too, as Peuckert has argued, can be related to Joachimism. What I have in mind is the prominent position the *Naometria* had in the emergence, early in the seventeenth century, of the Rosicrucian movement.[231] Much evidence suggests a direct link between the two. First of all, there is the use of the "rose-cross" symbol in the *Naometria*, a prefiguration of the symbol used in the publications of the movements' two basic manifestos – the so-called *Fama* of 1614 and the *Confessio* of 1615.[232] Second of all, there is the significance of the date 1604 for Studion and the Rosicrucians. For both it represents the moment when the "general reformation" of Europe is to begin.[233] Finally, and most important of all, there is the matter of Studion's and the Rosicrucians' involvement in an organized society of spiritual men whose task it was to oversee the beginning of the general reformation.[234] In the *Naometria*, Studion speaks of the formation in 1586 of such an order – the "militia Crucifera Evanglica" – and implies that its purpose was to prepare men for the coming general reformation.[235] We know, moreover, that the Rosicrucian manifestos that were published in 1614 and 1615 were circulating in the 1590s in Tübingen among a close circle of friends (including Andreae), all of whom have been linked to "Naometrianism" and to the Rosicrucian movement.[236]

What this suggests – and Peuckert has argued strongly for this interpretation – is the presence of Joachimism among a group of Württemberg Protestants who defined their order's task in terms of the kind of mission Joachim had assigned to those possesed of *intelligentia spiritualis*.[237] That, undoubtedly, is how Studion and the Rosicrucians conceived themselves. They were, as Yates has noted, committed to an "illuminism" that had an inward spiritual and outward reformist face.[238] With regard to the latter, they wished to apply "the advances in knowledge" made by "Renaissance science" to the organization of society;[239] with regard to the former, they wished to reveal "to man new possibilities in himself, teaching him [à la Arndt] to understand his own dignity and worth and the part [à la Joachim–Studion] he is called upon to play in the divine scheme."[240]

Adherence to that optimistic self-conception, however, suggests a sense of urgency, activism, and election that is more an aspect of Joachim's pattern of threes than twos. In addition, it suggests a concern more with educating and preparing men for the reformation that is to come than with rallying them around a "godly prince" who will protect them against Antichrist.[241] Quite clearly, Studion was more involved with the Erastian thrust of the latter than with the more radical thrust of the former. We must turn to J. V. Andreae (1596–1654) to see the consequences of the shift from the one to the other, from Joachimism in the service of political twos to Joachimism in the service of social threes.

Andreae was involved in all aspects of this variegated movement among reform-minded Lutherans. For example, he knew of Joachim, mentioning that what Joachim had had to say about the coming of the third religious age in his own time would prove more relevant to the situation of Protestants in the seventeenth century;[242] he revered Arndt and dedicated

Christianopolis (1619) to him because he felt *True Christianity* had given full expression to the idea of *praxis pietatis*;[243] he moved in the Tübingen circle around Studion and, while not indulging in the circle's penchant for prophetic predictionism, did join it in pushing for continuous reformation (he advocated, to that end, the formation of voluntary societies both for disseminating scientific knowledge and for spearheading efforts at social reform and Christian fellowship);[244] he wrote *Christianopolis* with the express purpose of emphasizing the importance of education in the training of youth and of preparing it for the general reformation that would usher in a Christian community that, in Yates' words, while "socially" organized "on a pietistic plan" still would be possessed of a "scientific" culture;[245] and he organized *Christianopolis* around many of the collective ideals he had observed during his so-called "Genevan experience" in 1611.[246] Suffice it to say Andreae was a socially concerned Lutheran activist with marked interests in making "civil" reform and the teachings of science part of the process of "gradual sanctification."[247]

Ironically, the devastation suffered by Württemberg during the Thirty Years' War added historical point to Andreae's concern with continuous reformation.[248] Indeed, the havoc of war gave new urgency to the call for social activism and socio-religious reform; and between 1618 and 1650, and especially between 1639 and 1650 when he was court preacher in Stuttgart, Andreae was in a position to see that that sense of urgency became part of the Church of Württemberg's orientation toward the world.[249]

Two aspects of Andreae's leadership warrant elaboration. First, his efforts at preserving the church entailed changing its "mission," entailed making it an agent of social regeneration. Given Andreae's convictions and the circumstances of the war, this cannot be regarded as an unexpected development. Indeed, for him it was axiomatic that the central truths of Christianity, Protestantism, and the Reformation were not meant to remain locked up in the church.[250] Rather, through the practice of piety, these truths were to become part of the civil life of a Protestant people. What Arndt had said about Christ's relationship to man, Andreae felt could also be said about the church's relationship to society: as agents of renewal they both inaugurated an activism that worked "from the inside out."[251] Put another way, there is an obvious parallelism between Arndt's notion of "gradual sanctification" and Andreae's conception of social regeneration: both require human participation (i.e., "works") to realize themselves fully as religious processes.[252]

Andreae had first given shape to these kinds of civil, activist concerns in 1619, in his famous tract *Christianopolis*. Written under the influence of a variety of confessional sources, *Christianopolis* was designed to shake the theology of orthodox Lutheranism out of its lethargy, ethical complacency, and narrow confessional biases.[253] Specifically, Andreae wanted to revitalize the church and expand the range and deepen the responsibility of its civil commitments. To this end, he framed *Christianopolis* in terms that suggested, subtly, a contrast between the ethical intensity and civil activism of the Reformed church in Geneva and the lack of ethical discipline and civil awareness of his own Lutheran church.

Convinced that important lessons could be drawn from such a juxtaposition, he used the city of Christianopolis – an imaginary utopia cast in the image of More's and Campanella's earlier utopias – to convey his impression of how Geneva had achieved "a harmony of faith and morals" in civil life that could and should be emulated in the Lutheran church.[254] More specifically, Andreae's purpose was to impress upon the Lutheran mind that the education of youth was the key to the present regeneration and future well-being of the Christian religion and polity.[255] Hence, his concern in *Christianopolis* and in the reconstruction of the Württemberg church was to encourage reform of education and religious instruction and through those efforts to convince Lutherans that civil activism was a natural extension and expression of Christian piety.[256]

I am not suggesting that Andreae's "Genevan experience" was the cause of his interest in "civil activism." There were, as was suggested earlier, many other contemporary sources for Andreae's view, including the practical piety of his own mother.[257] Rather, the impulse behind this view must be sought in the problems of ethical inertia that Andreae linked to the need for a Second Reformation, problems that demanded reform initiatives for which Calvinists, Rosicrucians, and even some Catholics had already developed strategies and programs.[258] Without those problems these ethical, educational, and civil reform initiatives could have "influenced" few Lutherans.[259] So it is not so much a question of whether Andreae was a Calvinist, a Rosicrucian, a proto-Pietist, or – as German scholarship would prefer to see him – an orthodox reformer, as it is a question of the willingness of European Protestants to meet the challenge of a European problem with reform programs that did not develop along narrow confessional lines.

If the impulse to "civil piety" was part of Andreae's legacy to the Church of Württemberg, a second aspect of that legacy grew out of his attitude toward political authority.[260] We know that since the Peace of Augsburg in 1555 the doctrine *cuius regio, cius religio* (he who rules the land determines the religion) had given enormous impetus to Erastianism throughout Germany. By the early seventeenth century, however, many reform-minded German Lutherans had become impatient with that arrangement. To them it seemed that the mingling of politics and religion, of what Andreae called "Law and Gospel," had put a brake on the Reformation.[261] Reflecting in *Christianopolis* on how Luther had subordinated "submissiveness" to activism during the Reformation, Andreae ventured the proposition that "this very drama may be played again in our own day."[262] Continuing, Andreae noted that "whether we look at the churches, the courts, or the universities," there is everywhere no lack "of unscrupulous ambition, greed, gluttony, license, jealousy, idleness, and other mastering vices at which Christ violently shuddered, but in which we chiefly delight."[263] Summing up the argument in *Christianopolis*, Andreae concluded that Lutheranism had "sold its Christian liberty to Antichrist [i.e., to the 'orthodox' church], its natural liberty to tyranny [i.e., to the 'godly prince' of Erastianism], and its human liberty to sophistry [i.e., to Lutheran scholasticism at the universities]."[264]

Remedying this situation, therefore, required another reformation, one that would be conducted independent of state authority and would aim at reform of society through the agencies of the church, voluntary associations of Christian families, and the universities. To impress upon the people the urgency of reform, Andreae framed the German experience of the Thirty Years' War in terms of an eschatological challenge.[265] In sermon after sermon he urged Württembergers to see the war as a "necessary evil" sent by God to test the faithful and to prod them into action.[266] Antichrist had invaded their institutions (i.e., for a period in the 1630s Catholic Austria controlled Württemberg), and it therefore remained for them, as a Protestant people, to take responsibility for their own religious lives. With "one and the same effort," Andreae concluded, Württemberg Protestants could "preserve the safety of the republic" (i.e., Protestantism's conservative face) and ensure that "the children which we bear" now will, in the future, look to "earth" as much as "heaven" for their fulfillment (Protestantism's progressive face).[267]

Obviously, Andreae's related commitments to education and social activism on the one hand and to the separation of religion from politics (i.e., his Anti-Erastianism) on the other, pushed him and the Church of Württemberg in the direction of a civil piety that was shaped to the needs of reform-minded Protestants in the middle of the seventeenth century. This was, however, a civil piety that was working "outward" and "upward" from society toward the state, not "inward" and "downward" from the state toward society.[268] Through ever-widening circles of participation that sense of piety and mutual assistance was to spread from the individual (who had been reborn in Christ), through the family, to voluntary networks of families that, when taken together, comprised the fellowship of a Protestant people.[269] That was a conception of the dynamic of Protestant piety that was to dominate the culture of Old-Württemberg down to Hegel's day.

4. German Pietism and the Second Reformation:
"Dying into life" as the telos of *homo religiosus*

From what has just been said, there can be little doubt but that when Andreae began calling for a Second Reformation he meant to give a civil face to Lutheran piety. Nor can there be any doubt about the impetus the Thirty Years' War gave to that call. But the circumstances of the war itself forced Lutheran reformers to postpone attempts to initiate reform until the second half of the seventeenth century.[270] At that time, a real opportunity for reform presented itself, and the German pietists then began to reiterate the call for a Second Reformation.[271]

Spener (1635–1705), the father of German Pietism and a man who repeatedly acknowledged his religious debts to Arndt and Andreae,[272] put it exactly when he remarked, "I have never been of the opinion, and am not so now, that the Reformation of Luther was brought to completion as one might hope."[273] Much, he argued, remained to be done.[274] With Arndt he wished both "to withdraw minds of students and preachers from an inordinately controversial and polemical theology which has well-nigh assumed the form of an earlier scholastic theology" and "to guide them...to the actual practice of faith and godliness."[275] And, with Andreae, he wished to separate religion from politics because Protestant princes had succumbed to "an irresponsible caesaropapism" by subordinating religion to political interest.[276] As for the leaders of the church, who might be expected to convene a council for reform, Spener remarked that "If we wait for them..., we shall die before our wish is realized, and reform will always be postponed...to the uncertain future."[277] Better, he conjectured, for "godly people" (i.e., Christian ministers) to take the message of reform "to the people of God" so that "earnest" Christians can get on with the work of reformation.[278] As Spener was wont to remark, "it is by no means enough to have knowledge of the Christian faith, for Christianity consists rather of practice."[279]

We would go far afield if we fully elaborated the development of the line of Lutheran piety that runs from Arndt and Andreae to Spener, a line that is to be identified with an ongoing concern for the idea of a Second Reformation.[280] Nevertheless, a few general remarks are in order because this type of piety culminates in German Pietism and in the kind of concerns that pervaded the religious culture of Old-Württemberg in the eighteenth century.

With regard to German Pietism, it is best to begin by distinguishing the *pietists*, who wished for reform within the church, from the *separatists*, who advocated withdrawal from the church as a means of religious regeneration.[281] Granted, initially the word "Pietism" was a general term of abuse that was indiscriminately attached to the activities of both groups.[282] But gradually, and especially in Old-Württemberg during the early eighteenth century, the distinction between pietists and separatists was drawn and made a part of eighteenth-century ecclesiastical histories of the Württemberg church.[283] Indeed, among Württemberg Protestants something like a "church-type" and "sect-type" differentiation was employed to distinguish pietists from separatists.[284] The former were regarded as reformers, the latter as enthusiasts; the former were to be tolerated, even accommodated; the latter were not.[285]

Next, it should be remembered that in its day Pietism appealed to German Protestants because it appeared to be a practical and progressive extension of the Lutheran tradition.[286] This fact is often overlooked by scholars, because they tend to see Pietism only as a *theological* reaction against orthodoxy and not as an effort aimed at its *practical* extension.[287] The reason for this oversight, I think, lies in a failure to appreciate the *historical* position of Pietism relative to orthodox theology. The problem for Pietism was that as a religion of simple faith, it had to assert itself against an orthodox tradition that claimed on Luther's authority to be the religion of simple faith par excellence. No doubt this put a considerable restraint on Pietism's critical, theological horizon because in theory much of that horizon had already been preempted theologically by orthodoxy. For Pietism to attack orthodoxy directly on theological grounds, then, would have been self-defeating. So, instead of posturing self-righteously as the "true" heirs and authoritative interpreters of Luther – that is, instead of using Luther to impugn Lutheranism – the pietists expeditiously cast the problem of their relation to orthodoxy less in terms of doctrinal differences than in terms of the difference between the *theory* and the *practice* of piety.[288]

This shift had the effect of permitting Pietism to have an appeal of its own without abandoning the Lutheran tradition. It could enunciate a practical philosophy of life that was shaped to the contemporary need of personal and social regeneration and, at the same time, claim to be perfectly Lutheran. Thus, from an historical standpoint, Pietism was neither a mere "reaction" to orthodoxy nor an ideology of transition between orthodoxy and Enlightenment. Rather, it was a movement of religious reform that transformed theological problems into problems of practical piety. As Spener rather pointedly put it, "the reality of our religion consists not of words but of deeds."[289]

Related to this last point is another, one that was a consequence of Pietism's initial desire to make sanctification rather than justification the focus of a religious life.[290] None of the leading spokesmen of German Pietism was a systematic theologian. As one of Spener's translators has noted, Spener was "primarily a reformer of Christian life, not a reformer of

Christian thought."[291] To have been otherwise would have forced Spener to engage in the kind of disputations and strident polemics that he thought had distracted orthodoxy from its central purpose.[292] By focusing on how to discipline, shape, and direct "the will" rather than on how to command allegiance to a set of religious precepts through imposition, the pietists wished to shift the terms of theological debate among Lutherans from questions about dogmatics to ones about *praxis pietatis*.[293] As a result, the "mystical epistemology" of Lutheran orthodoxy, which Eugene Rice has characterized as "skepticism" rescued by "grace,"[294] gave way to an epistemology that, while equally as skeptical about some things, made human "will" responsible, in part, for the salvation process.[295] And that emphasis, no doubt, made the pietists look quite Pelagian and synergistic in their theological anthropology.[296]

Still if the pietists were skeptical about the soteriological efficacy of the teachings of Lutheran scholasticism, they were not anti-intellectual – for a very good reason. As we have already noted, it was not easy for Pietism to generate support for reform of orthodoxy without appearing to align themselves with the separatists. Indeed, the practical religious alternative to the impasse at which the wrangling theologians of orthodoxy had arrived seemed to be separatism – either that or the kind of thorough-going secularism for which few pietists held any brief. Yet the separatists were not inclined to try to solve or even address the question of how to regenerate the world. That kind of indifference to what the pietists perceived as the critical religious problem of the age made separatism anathema to them. They wanted to engage the world and transform it, not stand passively by as it sank to ever-deeper levels of depravity.[297]

As a result, the pietists were in the awkward position of having to advocate a third or in-between religious position, different from both orthodoxy and separatism but likely – as modern scholarship has proved – to be confused with first one and then the other. Theirs was the ambiguous position of the "middle group" in a time of turbulence, of the reformer in a time of polarization. Separatists accused them of not going far enough in their religious commitments; conversely, orthodox Lutherans scored them for going too far. Occupying an intermediate position, in short, made Pietism liable to misunderstanding by all the contending parties – a dilemma that was soon translated into the charge of "Pelagian" leanings. But the pietists insisted on, and persisted in, prescribing moderate reformism as the proper antidote both to the ethical sterility of orthodoxy and to the "enthusiasm" and antisocial penchant of separatism.

It is in the context of the pietists' conflict with the separatists that their all-important interest in education as an agency of civil piety needs to be understood.[298] We have already seen how the confrontation with orthodoxy led Pietism toward "the will" as the key to religious renewal.

This enabled them to explain the problem of continuity within the Lutheran tradition in terms of a shift in Lutheran interest from thought to action, from dogmatics to *praxis pietatis* This shift did not entail any anti-intellectualism on the part of the pietists. If the "intellectualism" of Lutheran scholasticism provoked the pietists in the short run, it was from the anti-intellectual subjectivism of the separatists that they wished to dissociate themselves in the long run. To do this, they had to make salvation a gradual, collective, and historical process, and that is precisely what their conception of education allowed them to do.

The key to the pietists' understanding of education lies in their conception of the pastorate as a religio-pedagogical agent of civil reform.[299] After the Thirty Years' War, and continuing on into the Wars of Louis XIV, there had been a sustained and noticeable decline in both public morality and the quality of the Lutheran pastorate. Pietism saw a connection between the two developments. As Spener put it, "When you see that the people are undisciplined, you must realize that no doubt their priests are not holy."[300] Given this observation, Spener concluded that "we preachers. . . need reformation as much as any estate can ever need it."[301] Francke, Spener's associate and successor as leader of the pietist movement, was just as adamant, maintaining that "True godliness is best imparted to tender youth by the godly example of the teacher himself."[302]

What Spener and Francke have done here, of course, is to identify the pastorate as the agent both of religious corruption in the present and of religious reform in the future. Spener made the argument this way:

Since ministers must bear the greatest burden in all these things which pertain to a reform of the church, and since their shortcomings do correspondingly great harm, it is of the utmost importance that the office of the ministry be occupied by men who, above all, are themselves true Christians and, then, have the divine wisdom to guide others carefully on the way of the Lord. It is therefore important, indeed necessary, for the reform of the church that only such persons be called who may be suited. . . . Not the least among the reasons for the defect in the church are the mistakes which occur in the calling of ministers.[303]

Having identified the problem, Spener proceeded to offer an institutional remedy for it:

. . . if such suitable persons are to be called to the ministry they must be available and hence they must be trained in our schools and universities. May God graciously grant that everything necessary thereunto may be diligently observed by the professors of theology and that they may assist in seeing to it that the unchristian academic life. . . may by vigorous measures be suppressed and reformed. Then the schools would, as they ought, really be recognized from the outward life of the students to be nurseries of the church for all estates and as workshops of the Holy Spirit.[304]

Within the universities, however, Spener singled out "professors of theology" as vital to the entire reform effort.[305] Professors, Spener wrote,

...could themselves accomplish a great deal here by their example (indeed, without them a real reform is hardly to be hoped for) if they would conduct themselves as men who have *died unto the world*, in everything would seek not their own glory but that of their God and the salvation of those entrusted to them, and would accommodate all their studies, writing of books, lessons, lectures, disputations, and other activities to this end. Then the students would have a living example according to which they might regulate their life, for we are so fashioned that examples are as effective for us as teachings, and sometimes more effective.[306]

In this way, students of theology, who are themselves to become "examples to the flock," will receive the "guidance" they need to enter "the calling" of the pastorate.[307]

It is hardly an overstatement, then, to say that for pietists the education of the pastorate in the universities was essential to their endeavor to regenerate society. Throughout Germany, wherever Pietism penetrated, an effort was made to impress upon teachers and pastors alike the full range of their vocational responsibilities — toward the needy, the community, and especially the young.[308] In his own way, Andreae had anticipated this development in *Christianopolis*. There, he had written about the compelling power of teaching by example; about making the idea of the "calling" the point of legitimation between the preacher and the people; and about "youth" being "the most valuable asset" of the "republic" in the present and of the reformer who has his eye on religious regeneration in the future.[309] Taking their cues from Andreae, the pietists reiterated his arguments, pointing out again and again how Christian education consisted in the appreciation of the interconnection of "religion, justice and learning" in communal life.[310] Properly informed, youth would be the natural ally of the reformer — in his struggle against popery and Caesaropapism, tyranny, and scholastic dogmatism. If youth could be won to the cause of *praxis pietatis* and moral reform, societal and religious regeneration would follow as a matter of course.

For Pietism, then, youth was the "life blood" of the reform movement, the object of the movement's pedagogic efforts, and the force behind its program of religious renewal.[311] Through the young, the moral possibilities of the present could be seized and turned to the advantage of the future. For Pietism, in other words, youth was the phenomenal and temporal expression of the *telos* through which *homo religiosus* worked to fulfill the *eschaton* in history.[312] Youth was expected to respond to good examples (i.e., the pietists were, like the Pelagians, environmentalists) and to be willing to sacrifice its own interests for those of the collectivity.

To this end, Spener celebrated "denial of self" as "the first practical principle of Christianity";[313] and one could not better fulfill that principle than by service to the community through the practice of piety in one's vocation.[314] This is what Arndt and Spener meant by the phrase "dying unto life" – *praxis pietatis* was offered not just as a correction to orthodox inertia, but also as the agency of transition from the individual to the collectivity and from the crises of the present to the hope of the future.[315]

Indeed, one of the distinctive marks of the pietists' views on education lay in their association of it with *praxis pietatis*, vocational activity, and with what Arndt called the process of "gradual sanctification." Such associations, however, were perfectly consistent with their profiles as reformers and with the "middling" position they occupied between orthodoxy and separatism. Against orthodoxy they could exalt the imperative of *praxis pietatis*; against separatism, the importance of education and service as essential to sanctification. It is worth observing, moreover, that the intermediate position assumed by Pietism between orthodoxy and separatism reflected its belief that the spiritual welfare of man depended on the interplay between education and will. Like the Alexandrian Fathers, whom Spener and Bengel often quoted, the pietists here were advancing a view of man and salvation that pointed toward religious activism and cooperative grace. But instead of invoking some godly prince as the agent of communication between man and God, the pietists assigned that role to the pastorate and, above all, to those who had made the teaching of the pastorate their calling.[316] From that standpoint, education was for Pietism the secular equivalent of grace, in that through a series of pedagogic transmissions it created in the collectivity the will to try to assimilate to God.[317]

Lessing, it seems to me, understood what was at issue here very well. With the pedagogical teachings of Clement and Joachim clearly in mind, Lessing maintained that education had become the device (i.e., the new dispensation) God used to reveal His purposes to man in history.[318] Education was now the tool of the divine economy, and the goal of that economy was to create in man the will and reason to persevere in the pursuit of *homoiosis*, in the pursuit of the ceaseless moral reform of himself to the image and likeness of God.

In this, however, Lessing was simply elaborating views that had been commonplace earlier among the pietists. Indeed, in Spener's *Pia Desideria* (1675) we find the essence of Lessing's argument already articulated. For example, while trying to explain why religious reform was imperative, Spener made an argument with which we are quite familiar, if only because it repeats the Alexandrian and Joachimite position on the telos of *homo religiosus*. Spener wrote:

First, we are not forbidden to seek perfection, but we are urged on toward it. And how desirable it would be if we were to achieve it! Second, I cheerfully concede that here in this life we shall not manage that, for the farther a godly Christian advances, the more he will see that he lacks, and so he will never be farther removed from the illusion of perfection than when he tries hardest to reach it.[319]

Or again:

...even if we shall never in this life achieve such a degree of perfection that nothing could or should be added, we are nevertheless under obligation to achieve some degree of perfection.[320]

This, obviously, is a doctrine of "assimilationism," not "deification."[321] And as we know from Joachim, assimilationism requires patience, nurturance, and time. Spener knew that, too; with one eye on orthodoxy and the other on separatism he wrote:

Let us not abandon all hope before we have set our hands to the task [i.e., the argument against orthodoxy]. Let us not lay down our rod and staff if we do not have the desired success at once [i.e., the argument against separatist "enthusiasts"].... Our fruit...must be borne in patience, and the fruit in others will be *cultivated by us with perseverance*.... *Seeds are there...do your part in watering them, and ears will sprout and in time* become ripe.[322]

With this kind of moderation to recommend it, the pietists' conception of education provided an antidote to the inertia of orthodoxy and the impatience of separatism.[323] Through education, divine providence worked with economy gradually to move man toward salvation that, in order to be realized, obliged him to make assimilation to God the telos of his life. There is a sense of perfectionism here, but it is not something that is realized immediately, nor by an elect group outside the church. "We may say," wrote Spener, "that the injunctions to become more and more perfect apply to the whole church."[324] Spener, I think, could say that because the emphasis he put on education as an agent of religious regeneration had made gradual sanctification accessible to all. From this it followed that the collectivity itself would become the embodiment of election.[325]

In this framework, the pietists' conception of *praxis pietatis* becomes part of the theology of the divine economy.[326] Ethical activism and a certain mode of eschatological speculation have become one, with the result that gradual sanctification (Arndt), civil regeneration (Andreae), and Pietism's commitment to a Second Reformation (Spener) may be construed as different aspects of one and the same call for religious reform. Indeed, between Arndt and Andreae, Spener and Francke, spiritual regeneration began to be perceived by German Protestants as a "process" with discernible individual, collective, and historical dimensions to it. Yet there was nothing deterministic about the stages in the soteriological sequence; they could be hastened or retarded depending on how men *acted*, as individuals and in groups.[327] Regeneration, in short, had an aspect of self-realizing teleology about it, and we know that that aspect very often presented itself to reform-minded Christians in the form of evolutionary eschatology.[328] That is the form it assumed in Old-Württemberg in the eighteenth century in the thought of J. A. Bengel, who, we shall argue, brought *praxis pietatis* and evolutionary eschatology together into one coherent theological framework.

The religious culture of
Old-Württemberg

II. J. A. Bengel and the theology of
the divine economy

The historical coherence of much of what was stated in the last chapter can
be illustrated by the career and thought of J. A. Bengel (1687–1752).[1]
At the same time, elaboration of Bengel's religious views, especially those
that relate to what we shall call his theology of the divine economy, is
indispensable to understanding the way in which religious and political
conceptions dovetailed in the culture of Old-Württemberg in the eighteenth century.[2] That means, of course, that this chapter is transitional in
that it uses the focus on Bengel to connect the ethicoeschatological
argument of Chapter 1 with the political narrative of Chapter 3.

1. Bengel: The eschatological mood

The date of Bengel's birth – June 24, 1687 – fell within a year of two
significant events in the annals of Old-Württemberg: the beginning of the
War of the League of Augsburg in 1688 and the Württemberg
Consistory's issuance in the same year of the *Instruction wegen des Ordinis
Studiorum* (henceforth *Instruction*).[3] Bengel was, in both his personal and
his professional outlook, very much a product of both events. In the first
case, Louis XIV's decision to press his claim for French possession of the
Rhine Palatinate led not only to its destruction but eventually to the
devastation of Württemberg as well.[4] Indeed, Jan. 2, 1689, saw a French
army under General Melac standing before Stuttgart, menacing the
capital city as well as the rest of the land with its incendiary military
tactics.[5]

Clearly, the havoc the French played in Württemberg intermittently
for the next five years hampered the land's efforts to effect a recovery from
the ravages of the Thirty Years' War.[6] Still, the new French incursion was
only one of several sources of general anxiety with which Württembergers
had to contend late in the seventeenth century. In the east, the Turks were

exerting renewed pressures on the frontiers of Christian Europe. Con-
currently, German Protestants felt threatened from the west. Like many
English Protestants, they were quick to link Louis' revocation of the Edict
of Nantes, French military expansion, and the possibility of a Roman
Catholic succession in England with a resurgent Catholicism in Europe.
In fact, as Hazard has noted, 1685 was the "high-water mark" of the
Counter-Reformation in Europe.[7] Small wonder that in Württemberg, a
Protestant enclave in an otherwise Catholic region of southwest Germany,
many of the deepest anxieties of the age found expression and some psy-
chological satisfaction in eschatological and apocalyptic images.

In the imagination of Württemberg Protestants, the Thirty Years'
War, the "Turkish peril," "Popish plots" in Western Europe, numerous
conversions of Protestant princes to Catholicism, and the general turmoil
of the present were challenges devised by God to test the faith of Protestant people.[8] Indeed, in their minds a capacity to endure evil and suffering was felt to be a religio-educational experience, a "trial" of one's faith,
as Bengel put it during these years.[9] Spener, surely, anticipated the
attitudes of many Württembergers on this score when he remarked:

> . . . I count afflictions a blessing, for through them God has preserved many of his
> own and has to some extent averted the harm that would have resulted if people
> had been driven to deeper despair by uninterrupted external prosperity.[10]

In Württemberg, in other words, persecution in the present attested to
one's election in the future — which meant that Württembergers saw
themselves in a covenant with God that obliged them to advance His
purposes in history.[11] With the "signs of the time" everywhere, it was
easy for a Württemberg Protestant like Bengel to see Antichrist and his
agents "at the door" and to measure experience in eschatological terms.[12]
By the same token, it was just as easy to offer eschatological modes of
thought and action as remedies for the current dangers. Thus, circumstances did much to put Bengel in an "eschatological mood" with which
we are quite familiar by now: foreboding about the present fostered
exuberant expectations about the future.[13] In the first case the mood was
deeply pessimistic, in the second case, cautiously optimistic in that
eschatology was put at the service of *praxis pietatis*, social regeneration,
and the gradual historical redemption of a Protestant people.[14]

The year 1688 was a watershed in the history of Old-Württemberg in
yet another sense. In issuing the *Instruction* the Consistory ordered a
gradual reform of the curriculum of the Stuttgart *Gymnasium* and, more
importantly, of the program of studies for theological candidates in the
Stift at the University of Tübingen.[15] More significantly still, these
reforms bore all the marks of Andreae's and Spener's influence.[16] At the
same time, the successful promulgation of the *Instruction* pointed to some

slippage in the position of orthodox Lutheranism among church and university authorities.[17] The vulnerability of orthodoxy, in turn, seemed to bespeak opportunities for consideration of future reform proposals, a prospect that at once added vigor to the lobbying efforts of the reformers but still kept them within established institutional channels.

At bottom, what was at stake in the debates over the *Instruction* was whether the dogmatic principles of orthodox theology (represented by the Tübingen faculty) or the need for social and moral regeneration (represented by the Consistory) would take precedence in the religious affairs of Württemberg Protestants.[18] Granted, at the time the *Instruction* was viewed more as a retreat from orthodoxy than as an advance toward Pietism. But on several crucial issues the pietist input was decisive.[19]

First of all, the *Instruction* recommended a change in *what was read* in the program of religious studies. Henceforth, theological students were expected to read and appreciate the writings of the "Lutheran Fathers of Pietism" (e.g., Arndt, Andreae, and Spener), such natural-law thinkers as Grotius and Pufendorf, and "Fathers" like Clement – all of whom the Consistory argued offered a practical corrective to the lifeless, scholastic formulas of orthodoxy.[20]

Second, the *Instruction* insisted on a change in *the manner* in which religious material was read.[21] The *Instruction* made it perfectly clear that mastery of the philological–historical method of exegesis rather than of orthodox dogmatics should be the purpose of a theological education. In this, the *Instruction* showed keen interest in the exegetical techniques of the Reformed Churches;[22] and this interest, we shall see, was a prelude to the kind of critical New Testament studies we find Bengel engaged in during the 1720s, 1730s, and 1740s.[23] Concurrently, the study of history was to be expanded, because the new exegetical emphasis made, à la Joachim, the interpretation of history an act of both scholarly and religious vocation.[24]

Within fifteen years of these changes, and of Bengel's birth, Spener's followers in Württemberg had secured a position for Pietism in the Church of Württemberg.[25] This was accomplished largely by two men – Consistory Director J. G. Kulpis, a close friend of Spener's, and J. A. Hochstetter, whom Francke once called the "Schwabian Spener." Through their efforts, the *Instruction* became the expression and vehicle of down-to-earth Pietism in Old-Württemberg.[26] Thereafter, and for a long time to come, Württemberg Protestants were convinced that a Christian education should consist in equal measures of what the *Instruction* called *praxi Christianism* and *Bildung*[27] – which is to say, practical piety (*Frommigkeit*) and academic learning (*Gelehrtsamkeit*) were to give rise to a Christian character in which the scholastic stigma of learning at the expense of life (*Lehre ohne Leben*) could be avoided.[28]

Overall, then, the moment of Bengel's birth was propitious, for he was intimately involved in weaving eschatological and ethical strands of the Christian heritage into a pattern of reform for the present and future. In fact, Bengel's life mission was to be scholar and prophet of the interwoven motivation of eschatology and ethics in eighteenth-century Protestant theology. And this effort to reconcile the two in the framework of the theology of the divine economy puts Bengel in the tradition of evolutionary eschatology qua covenant theology and marks him as a proponent of Christian reform.

2. Bengel: The eschatological motivation

J. A. Bengel was born into a family that proudly traced its origins back to the Reformation.[29] On his mother's side of the family, Bengel could claim to be a descendant of the great Christian humanist and Württemberg church reformer Johann Brenz, who had undertaken to reconcile the divergent religious views of Luther and Melanchthon in Württemberg in the middle of the sixteenth century. In addition, Bengel's mother's great-grandfather was Matthias Hafenreffer (1561–1619), chancellor of the University of Tübingen, author of the standard history of Christian dogma in the seventeenth century, and friend and educator of Andreae.[30] On his father's side, the ancestral line led back to Johann Bengel, who had studied theology at Tübingen in the late 1540s. Like Brenz, Johann Bengel was a religious reformer and numbered among his closest friends Brenz's fellow religious reformer, Erhard Schnept. For generations thereafter both sides of the family had served the church and the state with honor and, in the case of the family of Bengel's mother, with some distinction. The family, in short, belonged to the *Ehrbarkeit*, if not to the levels that actually shaped policy in the Estates.[31]

Not a great deal is known about Bengel's father, Albrecht Bengel (1650–1693). What we do know, however, suggests an unusually dedicated servant of the Church of Württemberg.[32] Public service and *praxis pietatis* defined for Albrecht the proper concerns of the Church, and he lived according to those convictions. Born in the middle of the seventeenth century, Albrecht Bengel reached maturity at a time when Spenerian religious seeds were being sown in Württemberg. And, in that connection, Albrecht moved in a religious circle in the 1660s and 1670s that was animated by the Arndt–Andreae–Spener line of Lutheran piety and that was dedicated to *praxis pietatis* and to the renovation of the battered Church of Württemberg. Albrecht Bengel was, therefore, a member of the first generation of pietists in Old-Württemberg.

But if Bengel's father was rather untypical in his zeal for *praxis pietatis*, he at least indulged in the same kind of eschatological fantasies as his fellow Protestants. Like them – and some of his diary entries confirm this – he felt Antichrist was on the move everywhere.[33] It was only natural that he should feel this way. After all, during the 1680s he witnessed more than his share of death and suffering.[34] Besides having to deal with his personal loss of his first three children to infantile infirmities, his duties as *Seelsorger* in the town of Winnenden obliged him to attend the sick and dying. In 1692, he recorded in his diary that he had seen hundreds die that year, either from disease or from cumulative attritions of the recent French invasion. "Indefatigable" was a word contemporaries invoked to describe the labors of Albrecht Bengel in 1692 and 1693. But this was an epithet filled with irony, for it was invariably the theme of the eulogies citizens of Winnenden gave after Albrecht's death in 1693. Constantly on the go and in daily contact with the sick, he himself soon came down with fever early in 1693 and died shortly thereafter from ensuing complications.

The suddenness of his father's death made a powerful impression on Johann Albrecht Bengel, who had been given his name by his father in 1687, presumably as a reminder of an impeccable religious ancestry extending back to his two sixteenth-century namesakes, Johann Brenz and Johann Bengel. Later, while reflecting upon his youth, Johann would dwell on the religious dedication and public service of his father.[35] He remembered him fondly and revered his example. Yet, at the same time, as Bengel later recalled, he was stunned by his father's death. In retrospect, Bengel recalled entreating God to spare his father's life and, after his father had succumbed, he remembered importuning God to restore him to life. Coming to grips with his father's death, therefore, was hard for Bengel. Why had his father been taken from him so early? What purpose could his premature death serve? Why had his prayers gone unanswered? Was he to blame? Had he been negligent in his religious duties and observances? Or was it rather that God was remote and indifferent to the mundane affairs of the world?

These were agonizing personal questions for a young man of Bengel's ilk. But they also had broader historical resonances. For these questions, coming as they did on the heels of the Thirty Years' War and simultaneously with a new French incursion into Württemberg – which saw French troops in 1693 burn Bengel's hometown, Winnenden, and the family home with it – served to focus Bengel's attention on one of the great religious problems of the late seventeenth century: the origin of evil and the purpose of human suffering in the divine plan for the salvation of the human race.[36]

With the "riddle of theodicy" before him, Bengel decided at an early age that the deep hurt of his father's death had been divinely ordained. Like Spener, he came to feel that personal tragedy was a "necessary evil,"

was God's way of testing him, His way of asking him to prove his mettle
as a Christian and of ascertaining whether he had strength enough to
practice the vocation of *Gottesgelehrten*. To be sure, this was a transparent,
personal rationalization of the ways of God to man. Nevertheless, it was a
rationalization with deep historical significance, for just this kind of
thinking was in vogue in Winnenden in the late seventeenth century. It
was, for example, alive there in 1696, in the motto that the first pastor of
the city (a Magistrate Hegel) chose to inscribe over the door of the home
the city had rebuilt for him after the holocaust of 1693 – "The greater the
misery, the closer the Lord."[37]

Bengel eventually fell back on this way of thinking, and the eschatological mood and motivation that went along with it, to explain his
personal sorrow. Indeed, from early on Bengel's religious ideals seemed to
be shaped by the contradiction between dire apocalyptic forecasts for the
present and ethical hope for the future. Like Joachim, and like many
contemporary pietists, Bengel decided to affirm and live with the contradiction instead of forcing himself to make an either-or decision about it.[38]
Thus, the tension between divine determinism and man's ethical
responsibility, which had been a growing force in Protestant Germany
throughout the seventeenth century, and certainly since the Thirty Years'
War, found a point of equilibrium in Bengel's religious outlook. Whether
this outlook was a consequence of personal indecision or of strength is
impossible to say. What is clear, though, is that it was an outlook with
biographical and historical rather than logical coherence. Or, to put the
experience in terms of its "manifest and latent" functions, Bengel's
reaction to his father's death was not to surrender to self-pity but to
prepare ever more earnestly for a religious career and a life of *praxis pietatis*.
If God had taken his father, it was for a reason; and that reason, Bengel
felt, would be revealed to him later in life. For now, it was enough to
pursue his religious calling with renewed dedication. In the event that
he would be called upon later to act as an instrument of divine providence,
it was best to prepare for that eventuality now. So Bengel threw himself
into preparation for what we have already seen Spener describe as the
Godly calling of the Lutheran pastorate.

3. Bengel, Spener, and Coccejus: Between orthodoxy and separatism

In any event, Albrecht Bengel's death, and the subsequent disruption of
the family concord by the French intrusion into Winnenden, left Bengel,
his brother and sister, and his widowed mother in dire straits. To ease
some of the economic pressure on the family and to ensure a good education for her son, Bengel's mother sent him in the summer of 1693 to

Marbach, to live with the family of David Wendelin Spindler (1650–?), a former schoolmate of her husband who had taught briefly in the Winnenden Latin school during Johann's first year of schooling.[39]

Unfortunately, Spindler is a rather shadowy figure in Bengel's life, but what is known about him suggests a religious "enthusiast" with strong separatist inclinations.[40] Apparently he was a teacher of some talent. His qualities soon came to the attention of the Consistory in Stuttgart, with the result that he was called in 1699 to fill a position in the Stuttgart *Gymnasium*.[41] Thus, we are able to place Bengel at the age of 12 in Stuttgart during a period when the future of the Protestant church in Württemberg was being decided by the triangular interplay among orthodox, pietist, and separatist religious forces in the capital city.

Although a lack of hard evidence makes it difficult to conjecture about Bengel's relationship with Spindler – the most notable of which is the almost total absence of Spindler from the pages of Bengel's recollections[42] – our present state of knowledge does permit a few inferences about the general lines of Bengel's development during the years he lived with Spindler (1693–1702).

As we indicated above, evidence suggests that in the 1690s, Spindler was becoming increasingly involved with Pietism, and with what then was called its separatist wing.[43] While doubts have been raised about Spindler's separatist activities before his call to Stuttgart, there is no reason to doubt his extensive separatist involvements after 1699.[44] After Spindler had spent only three years in Stuttgart, it was clear – at least to the Consistory – that he was one of the key figures in the separatist movement in Württemberg. Rumors of late-night meetings in the Spindler house circulated in the community and alarmed a deacon, who complained to the Consistory, thus eventuating a series of inquiries – in 1702, 1703, 1705, 1707, and 1710 – into Spindler's religious attitudes (toward Boehme and Arnold), his educational views, and his separatist sympathies.[45] Though Spindler was a pious man and not inclined toward violence, the excesses of a few separatists in Stuttgart in 1710 determined his fate with the Consistory. In 1710 he was relieved of his teaching position "because of his separatist opinions and conduct."[46] Unable any longer to earn a livelihood, he left Stuttgart the following year to pursue as unknown end.

If Bengel's subsequent religious activity is indicative of his attitude toward separatism, there is not much basis for supposing any susceptibility on his part to Spindler's religious views. That was because Bengel's early exposure to separatist doctrine was offset by an even more extensive exposure to those pietists who pursued a more reformist line of development.[47] Besides the example of his father, there were three good reasons for Bengel's attraction to Pietism and its moderation: Spener's influence on religious life in Württemberg in the 1690s, the educational orientation of the Stuttgart *Gymnasium*, and the concern with Coccejanism (i.e., federal theology) that was developing at Tübingen during Bengel's years of study there (1703–1713). This combination, we shall see, not only drew Bengel away from separatism and toward Pietism but also ensured that evolutionary eschatology (whether in the form of the expectationism of Joachim or Coccejanism) would be a resource for "reform" from within the Church of Württemberg rather than for a "revivalism" outside of it.[48]

That Spener's teachings lent themselves to moderation and reformism should be obvious from what was said in the last chapter. And his impact on Old-Württemberg is well documented. Since Spener's trip to Stuttgart and Tübingen in the 1660s, Württemberg pietists had labored to create an audience and gain a hearing for his religious views in Württemberg.[49] By 1698 – just a year before Bengel arrived in Stuttgart with the Spindlers – followers of Spener's, who were in constant correspondence with him, held several key positions in the institutional bodies that shaped church policy in Württemberg. In the Consistory and Synod, the councils that regulated church and university life in Württemberg, prelate J. A. Hochstetter (1640–1720) exercised a decisive influence. J. G. von Kulpis (d. 1698), a legal adviser to the prince on foreign affairs, was in his capacity as director of the Consistory from 1694 to 1698 inclined toward Spener's views. And his successor, Consistory Director Ruhle, has also been identified as an associate of Spener. At the University of Tübingen, *Stift* supervisor C. Wölfflin (1625–1688) and *Stift* superintendent B. Raith had prepared the way for the entry of Spenerian religious views. Later, A. A. Hochstetter (1668–1717), the son of J. A. Hochstetter, and C. Reuchlin (1660–1707), two of Bengel's teachers at Tübingen, continued in the early eighteenth century to elucidate pietist doctrine. Finally, at the duke's court, Pietism had – besides that of Kulpis and Ruhle – the support of J. R. Hedinger, who, as court preacher and member of the Consistory, used his influence after 1698 to discourage efforts by orthodox Lutherans to lump Pietism and separatism together.[50]

With this kind of support, it was relatively easy for Spener's views to penetrate Württemberg. Besides Andreae's legacy, there were simply too many disillusioned Lutherans who were willing to work for reform and reconstruction of the Württemberg Church. So, in 1694, while the theological faculties at Leipzig and Wittenberg were spearheading an assault on Spenerian Pietism throughout Germany, Württemberg authorities avoided any direct confrontation with the reformers by prohibiting the religious activities of "enthusiasts" but not those of the reform-minded pietists.[51] After promulgating this policy, the Consistory received Spener's thanks, for at no point did the 1694 "Edict Against

Pietism" find anything objectionable or heretical in the work of Spener or, in principle, in the formation of *collegia pietatis*, though reservations were expressed about the practical possibility of abuses.[52]

Indeed, the Edict of 1694 testified to the existence of a consensus of mutual toleration between reform-minded elements of orthodoxy and Pietism. So long as Pietism was willing to work for reform from within the established Church, allowances would be made both for dissent and for some modification of doctrine – which meant that *praxis pietatis* would be given a more vital role in matters of Christian salvation. Henceforth, there would be many opportunities to test the staying power of the new consensus. And as the Edicts of 1703, 1704, 1706, and 1707 showed, on each such occasion the same accord and resolution were reached. Pietists might conduct conventicles, separatists could not; Spener should be read, Boehme and Arnold could not.[53]

To be sure, the increasing strength of the separatist movement between 1694 and 1710 put some strains on the reconciliation. The debate in the Consistory over the formation of conventicles within the *Stift*, which took place between 1703 and 1707, was only one of several potentially divisive issues. But despite an occasional divergence of views, the chief representatives of orthodoxy – J. W. Jaeger – and of Pietism – J. A. Hochstetter, Hedinger, and Reuchlin – agreed once again to limit their strictures "against Pietism" to separatist activity.[54]

It was in this religious atmosphere that Bengel lived, and this atmosphere encouraged him to assimilate the religious views of Pietism rather than separatism. However, another circumstance of Bengel's youth inclined him toward the moderation of Pietism: the nature of his education in the Stuttgart *Gymnasium*. Under the influence of the school's rector, J. G. Essich, Bengel was confirmed in the belief that *Lehre ohne Leben* could never provide an adequate basis for Christianity.[55] Like Andreae, Essich believed that a Christian education should aim at the cultivation of Christian character, and that that character should consist of a balance of personal piety, learning, and service to the community. Moreover, the statutes that governed the *Gymnasium*, which were part of the *Instruction* of 1688, and which Essich drew up under the auspices of Kulpis, emphasized à la Spener the absolutely crucial role the teacher should play in developing an efficacious program of Christian education.

The teacher, Essich felt, set the example for youth – as he went, so went the young. Thus, Essich made sure that the *Gymnasium*'s teachers were of the highest quality, both in their command of the curriculum and in the conduct of their own lives. In stressing the exemplary aspect of the teaching vocation Essich was not alone, for besides Spener, Hedinger, Reuchlin, and, later, Bengel, all voiced the same opinion: true *Bildung* was composed of active piety and learning, and it was the duty of schools to orchestrate that harmony, a harmony that struck a responsive chord among those who found orthodoxy ethically stagnant and separatism anti-intellectual.[56]

The third force that pushed Bengel in the direction of Pietism was a current in the theological outlook of the University of Tübingen.[57] When Bengel entered the university in 1703 as a candidate for a degree in theology, the views of Pietism were already represented in the theological and philosophical faculties. Reuchlin had been professor of theology there since 1699, and A. A. Hochstetter, before becoming a professor of theology in 1705, had been a member of the philosophical faculty.[58] Both these men, we noted earlier, were fully committed to advancing the case for *praxis pietatis*. And Bengel very quickly fell under their influence. But just as important to Bengel's development as a religious thinker was his association with J. W. Jaeger (1647–1720), former prelate of Maulbronn, honorary professor of theology at Tübingen (1695–1704), and since 1704, first professor of theology and chancellor of the university.[59] From Jaeger Bengel learned – in the form of Coccejanism – the nuanced ways and meaning of evolutionary eschatology qua the "contractual" school of federal theology.[60]

Jaeger's theological views are difficult to fit into the conventional categories of the Lutheran tradition.[61] He had in the 1690s more or less broken with orthodoxy but refused to put his talents to work for Pietism. He agitated for ecclesiastical reform without wanting to break with Lutheran scholasticism and for *praxis pietatis* without endorsing Pietism. In addition, he developed some key insights into the tradition of mystical theology and used them piecemeal to enhance his theology of history. An admirer of Spener, he disdained many of his followers and warned of the dangerous implications of the Spenerian doctrine. At the same time, he was versed in federal theology and stressed the compatibility of its eschatological outlook with the program of *praxis pietatis*.[62] Though he was not a pietist, his advocacy of federal theology constituted a significant break in the ranks of orthodox Lutheranism as well as a concession to the ethical and civil activism of Pietism.

Still, much of Jaeger's apparent eclecticism can be explained by the fact that he was professor of *Kontroverstheologie* at the university[63] – that is, he was a specialist in defending orthodoxy in polemical exchanges with theologians of other Christian churches. For that reason, Jaeger read in, assimilated, and readily exposed his students to much material drawn from the various religious traditions. Moreover, he skillfully used the disputation – as Spener meant to use the conventicle – as a forum for the growth and understanding of better religious instruction.[64]

Like Spener, Jaeger was no supporter of a cloistered virtue. As he saw it, Christian truth would ultimately emerge from the struggle of religious ideas in disputation. If the purpose of the conventicle was – in Spener's words – to "open wide to the erring the gates to a knowledge of the truth," then the disputation served to make diversity of doctrinal opinion the instrument of religious knowledge itself.[65] In both cases the axiom was the same: "Not only should we know what is true in order to follow it, but we should also know what is false in order to oppose it."[66] Again, the words are Spener's, but they apply just as much to Jaeger, and express an almost Erasmian conception of the virtue of free religious discussion. As a result, Jaeger was cast, despite his orthodoxy, in the role of a moderate spokesman for religious toleration. And, as a corollary of this, Jaeger and his students tried through historical studies to recover, assimilate, and put into effective use in the present the true religious insights of the past, whatever their doctrinal implications. And so it was that Bengel, who was one of Jaeger's students from 1705 to 1712, became well acquainted with the major traditions of Christian thought as well as with the controversial doctrines of heretics.[67]

From this standpoint, it has been suggested – in a rather roundabout way by Heinz Liebing – that Jaeger's eclecticism, toleration, and avid and sustained interest in the dogmatic history of the Christian churches were characteristic expressions of the university's predilection for "federal theology" between the ages of "Orthodoxy and *Aufklärung*."[68] For our purposes, however, it is instructive that Emanuel Hirsch has ascribed many of the same characteristics and the same transitional status to Pietism.[69] According to Hirsch, it was Pietism, not federal theology, that acted as the innovative force and agent of ideological transition between Orthodoxy and *Aufklärung*. This divergence of views presents us with an intriguing historical possibility: namely, that the convergence of Pietism and federal theology, of Spener's notion of *praxis pietatis* and Coccejus' eschatology, may be explained on the level of religious ideas in terms of the reformism that is so central to evolutionary eschatology in whatever historical form.[70] Certainly Bengel's background points in this direction and suggests that his own theology of the divine economy, which was developed to avoid having to choose between orthodoxy and separatism, may have an ethico-eschatological dynamic similar to that of the tradition of Christian reform we have been elaborating.

4. Bengel as exegete: The "contractual" school of federal theology

The historical grounds and intellectual conditions for the convergence of federal theology and Pietism had already been well prepared, then, when Bengel enrolled at Tübingen in 1703. But this convergence would have been long delayed had it not been for Jaeger. Like many of his contemporaries, Jaeger was disturbed by the proliferation of divergent Christian doctrines at the end of the seventeenth century.[71] Even more bothersome to him was the seeming incapacity of the Tübingen theological faculty to clarify the confusion. As befuddled as its students were by current debates, the faculty had proved incapable of guiding students through the increasingly arcane complex of contemporary dogmatics.

Since the *Instruction* of 1688, the Consistory also had been alarmed by the lack of focus and direction in the theological *Studium* at Tübingen.[72] This dissatisfaction was further intensified in 1699, when a report submitted to the Consistory at the conclusion of a visitation to Tübingen noted the tentativeness and impreciseness of the faculty on the matter of what Lutheranism should consist in. To remedy this situation, the Consistory advised the university to prepare a new *Kompendium* of dogmatics that could be used to give new direction to the studies of theological candidates. The old *Kompendium* of M. Hafenreffer's, which had been canonical since 1600, was overly "scholastic" and hence obsolete in terms of contemporary needs. After much haggling between the university and the Consistory, the task of preparing a new *Kompendium* eventually fell to Jaeger, who produced in 1702 his *Compendium Theologiae Positivae*, a text that remained authoritative in Württemberg until the decade of Hegel's birth.[73]

This work, like Jaeger's later ecclesiastical history of the seventeenth century, was an eclectic mixture of orthodox, rationalistic, mystical, and pietistic theological views cast in a framework of federal theology.[74] Without directly broaching the issue of the ethical sterility of orthodoxy, Jaeger raised the issue indirectly by introducing Lutherans to federal theology and its heightened sense of the ethical responsibilities of *homo religiosus*.[75]

Unfortunately, the origins of federal theology in Württemberg are somewhat obscure. We know names and places, but not much else. According to Jaeger himself, C. Wolfflin, whom we noted earlier was one of Spener's initial supporters at Tübingen, was the first theologian to take up the study of federal theology.[76] Apparently he became familiar with federal theology in the 1760s through the writings of Coccejus, who is generally acknowledged as its most authoritative spokesman.[77] At any rate, from that time on, Coccejanism and federal theology became indistinguishable in Württemberg and, through Jaeger's work and teaching, the stock of many minds at Tübingen.[78]

Despite the fact that it was a doctrine of the Reformed church of the Netherlands, federal theology appealed to reform-minded Lutherans – whether orthodox or pietist – because it gave simultaneous expression to their whole range of contemporary historical experience and expectation: it explained the crises of the immediate past in terms of apocalyptic; it addressed the problem of regeneration in the present in terms of *praxis pietatis*; and it held out promise for the future by eschatologically linking *praxis pietatis* to the coming of the Kingdom of God. Dedicated as they were to preserving a "middling" position between orthodoxy and separatism, the reformers, orthodox and pietist alike, seized upon federal theology because they believed it was a legitimate extension of orthodoxy.[79] From their vantage point, federal theology justified a doctrine of *praxis pietatis* and offered a solution to the problem of how to arouse man to ethical action without precipitating a rupture within Lutheranism. In a word, federal theology enabled them to bridge the gap between God and man and, in true synergist fashion, enabled them to make man's ethical behavior part of the soteriological drama. As we noted earlier, Pietism looked upon itself as a balance of piety, civil service, and learning, and federal theology represented for it the fullest expression of the theological and anthropological implications of that balance.

The responses to Jaeger's *Kompendium* were predictable.[80] Chancellor of the University Müller expressed the objections of orthodoxy when he criticized the encroachments federal theology seemed to make on God's prerogatives in matters of salvation. Conversely, J. A. Hochstetter voiced the position of Pietism when he conjectured that the *Kompendium* would profit from a more explicit and positive treatment of *Theologia moralis*.

At any rate, the inclusion of tenets of federal theology in the *Kompendium* was Jaeger's way of meeting Pietism's demands for reform of orthodoxy without abandoning orthodox dogmatics completely. The terms and conditions of salvation were still initiated and determined by divine fiat, but salvation itself, at least in the "interim," was now bound up with *praxis pietatis* and man's self-directed activity. With an eye on mounting separatist pressure, Jaeger drew on the religious conceptions of orthodoxy and Pietism and, in the process, laid the consensual basis for an alliance for those Lutherans who sought a "middling position" between orthodoxy and separatism.[81]

By all accounts Bengel had a stimulating and highly rewarding intellectual relationship with Jaeger.[82] In keeping with the spirit of tolerance and freedom of inquiry, Jaeger allowed his students much leeway in their studies. And Bengel was no exception. He worked closely with Jaeger while the latter was compiling information for his ecclesiastical history, which appeared in two volumes in 1709 and 1717.[83] And he benefited considerably from the difficult disputations Jaeger arranged for him. Above all, however, what Bengel learned from Jaeger was how to understand and appreciate the basic theological structure and ethico-anthropological implications of federal theology.

For evidence of this one need only examine the kind of biblical exegesis Bengel developed after leaving Tübingen in 1713. Having secured a teaching position at the newly constituted cloister school at Denkendorf, Bengel concerned himself for the next twenty-eight years (1713–1741) with biblical studies and with meeting the pedagogic needs of the students who eventually formed the nucleus of the "school of Bengel" in Old-Württemberg.[84]

When Bengel departed Tübingen, he did so with a firm intellectual grasp of the principles of federal theology and an earnest devotion to Pietism. But for all the inroads it had made at Tübingen one obstacle remained to be overcome before Pietism could become an effective reform movement outside the university. Promotion of the religious beliefs that were associated with the doctrine of *praxis pietatis* required biblical justification – which in the contemporary context meant that Bengel à la Joachim and Coccejus would have to develop new principles of exegesis, principles that would provide impetus for religious reform by showing how the case for the practice of piety was presented in, and instrumental to, the Bible's religious message.[85]

Bengel's manner of exegesis had much in common with that of Joachim and Coccejus: all three depicted exegesis as a scholarly vocation in order to place the exegete in a position to point others on the way toward eschatological fulfillment in this world.[86] We have already commented on Joachim's exegetical strategy and its relation to the ethical activism of evolutionary eschatology; we need now to identify the terms in which federal theologians in general and Coccejus in particular put exegesis at the service of remarkably similar ends. Granted, the terminology of Coccejanism is quite different from that of Joachimism; but, as we shall see, the dynamic in both is the same in that there is a concerted effort to move Christianity away from a "realized" and toward an "evolutionary" mode of eschatological expectation.[87]

Simply stated, Coccejus' exegetical mode was synergistic: it drew attention to the Bible's depiction of salvation as a *process* in which man and God participated in an ongoing communication about the terms of human redemption in history.[88] This communication, or "dialogue," Coccejus argued, manifested itself in a series of covenants between God and man in history, each of which represented a moment of divine condescension to man's historically circumscribed ability to participate in his own salvation.[89] Before the Fall, Coccejus conjectured, the agreement took the form of a "covenant of works."[90] The distinctive characteristic of this covenant was that it depended on man's use of his "natural" faculties in order to be fulfilled.[91] Hence, the interrelatedness in Coccejus' mind of the ideas of a covenant of works and a "covenant of nature."[92]

According to Coccejus, however, Adam's disobedience "abrogated" the terms of this agreement: the Fall, as it were, irreparably impaired man's faculties and rendered him incapable of fulfilling the original covenant of works.[93] Thus, the need for a new covenant, one that Coccejus discussed in terms of a "covenant of grace."[94] For many Calvinists, this covenant was totally gratuitous, given by God to man as a sign of His "absolute goodness."[95] It was embodied in the sacrifice of Jesus Christ and required only "receptive faith" to become redemptive of human life.[96]

To this point there is little to suggest a difference between Coccejus' mode of exegesis and that of the main line of development of covenant theology within Calvinism in general.[97] But when it came to explaining how the covenant of grace operated within the framework of the divine–human relationship as it was mediated in, by, and through Christ, Calvinists tended to divide into "strict" and "moderate" groups, with the result that covenant theology itself developed in two very different directions.

To appreciate what is at issue here we need to make a basic distinction between the strict Calvinists, who regarded the covenant of grace as an "absolute testament" or "promise" of God's agape for man, and those of more "moderate" persuasion who regarded it as a "conditional contract" in which God required men *to do* certain things before the terms of the covenant could be fully met.[98] Among the former, who are sometimes grouped in what has been called the "Genevan" school of covenant theology, the claim was that the covenant of grace was a "free gift" given by God to man in the form of a promise (i.e., the Old Testament prophecy) that had been *fully realized* in Christ's life, death, and Resurrection (i.e., the story of the New Testament).[99] Here the covenant of grace is equated with the gift of the Incarnation itself, and all men had to do to enter into that covenant was to accept Christ as their savior.[100] And since acceptance of Christ was a "gift" of the covenant itself, faith alone was deemed sufficient for salvation, for through it man was "brought into" the covenant without having himself to "perform" any tasks.[101] That was so, of course, because all the conditions of redemption were "already fulfilled" for man "by Jesus Christ." Thus, strict Calvinists approached covenant theology almost totally from the "grace" side of the agreement – which meant that there was very little that was "reciprocal," "mutual," "conditional," or "contractual" about man's relation to God in their understanding of it.[102] As Coccejus put it, this was a "one-way" rather than a "two-way" interpretation of covenant theology; and, as we shall see shortly, it was not one he could abide.[103]

Were this all strict Calvinists had said about the covenant of grace there would have been little to distinguish their position from that of the Anti-nomians. But in their exegesis of the Bible strict Calvinists went to great lengths to finesse the problems raised by the Antinomians. In the process, however, they undercut their own position somewhat, and thereby opened the way for moderate Calvinists like Coccejus to read aspects of conditionality into covenant theology.[104] Since it is that aspect of Coccejus' work that Bengel puts at the center of his mode of biblical exegesis, it is worth looking at more closely.

Among strict Calvinists, it had been common since Calvin to divide the covenant of grace into two "economies" or "modes of administration."[105] There was the promise of the Old Testament (made through Abraham to the Jews) and the fulfillment of the New Testament (made through Jesus Christ to all mankind).[106] Obviously, as Schrenk and McGiffert have well understood, this involved imposing a "Christian pattern of meaning on the Judaic sources."[107] That is, the exegetical strategy of the two economies argument was, in McGiffert's words, to sever "Abraham's grace from the covenant of works by emphasizing Abraham's faithfulness − his justification by faith alone."[108] Yet the argument also conveniently countered the Antinomian claim that Abraham and Mosaic law were both part of the covenant of works and, hence, really had nothing to do with the covenant of grace or with Christianity. In this context, the two economies of grace argument ensured continuity of development between the Old Testament and the New in the same way that "accommodationism" had for Clement. The continuity, in turn, permitted strict Calvinists to treat aspects of Old Testament legalism as part of the covenant of grace; and that was something they very much needed in order to cope with their Antinomian critics.[109]

The immediate result of this exegetical maneuver was to neutralize the Antinomians − the covenant of grace did not abolish the law so much as make it a consequence of the pursuit of Christian liberty and righteousness.[110] Still, however careful strict Calvinists were to differentiate law as a sanction for works and law as a rule of faith,[111] their mode of exegesis − which, in McGiffert's words, embraced "an Old Testament form of covenant that seemed often to prescribe correct behavior, good works and perfect holiness as the conditions of divine favor"[112] − made it possible for moderate Calvinists to put the conditional aspects of covenant theology at the service of ethical activism.

Given that shift, a moderate Calvinist exegete like Coccejus, who refused to acquiesce in the predestinarianism of "scholastic Calvinism," could use the two economies argument as the basis for the kind of reformism that made *doing* rather than *believing* the standard for a truly Christian life.[113] Instead of stressing the covenant as a means by which man was passively brought into covenant with Christ, Coccejus emphasized how the "newness of life" that man received from Christ not only liberated him in a soteriological sense, but also allowed him to make Christian liberty the measure of collective life in a sociological sense.[114] That, of course, was a conception that dovetailed very nicely with the tradition of Lutheran piety that ran from Arndt to Spener, a tradition that conceived of the regeneration of fallen man as a *process* that worked from inside out rather than from outside in.

With this shift of emphasis, moderate Calvinists tended to articulate the views of the so-called "Zurich school" of covenant theology.[115] According to this school, for a covenant truly to be binding it had to be a two-way proposition.[116] God, of course, initiated the covenant by offering grace to man through the sacrifice of Jesus Christ. He was, as Coccejus put it, the "stipulator," who in Roman law lay down the condition of a "contract."[117] In this context, man was the respondent, the "astipulator," who either "kept" the terms of the contract or did not.[118] Keeping the contract, through, did not mean in any sense that God and man were equal. Nor did the decision to keep the covenant imply that its terms had been arrived at by way of negotiation. It meant, rather, that the covenant between the two was "mutual" in the sense that it required action from both parties.[119]

There are, then, aspects of conditionalism and voluntarism within the "contract" school of covenant theology; and for our purposes here that is decisive, because it means that moderate Calvinists like Coccejus envisaged grace less as something that automatically "moved" man toward salvation than as something that "enabled" him to move freely in that direction himself.[120] Accordingly, God can be said here to be dispensing grace by "indirection," for He is not commanding obedience based on His authority so much as giving man the potential to restore *himself* to his original "likeness" with God.[121] Viewed in this way, covenant theology qua contract theory certainly becomes Pelagian and synergist; indeed, it is conditional and "performance" oriented.[122] In terms of our earlier discussion of *homoiosis*, covenant theology in this form may be said to have tilted toward an "egocentric" religious conception of man and a "teleological" conception of religious salvation. To put it slightly differently, in the hands of the federal school of moderate Calvinists, covenant theology fast became a vehicle for preparationism, assimilationism, and moderate synergism. And, as we have learned, those kinds of emphases are indicative of a shift in exegetical key from realized to evolutionary eschatology.[123]

If this is true, then we might expect to find moderate Calvinists pushing à la some of Joachim's heirs for the expansion of the covenant of grace from a "two-term" to a "three-term" sequence.[124] There would be, first of all, the economy of the Old Testament, expressed in what McGiffert has called Abraham's gift of "foresight" (i.e., *pistis*).[125] Next would come the economy of the New Testament, manifest in the gift of "hindsight" (i.e., gnosis) through which every Christian comes to "see" Christ as a "mirror of his own life."[126] Finally – and here eschatology becomes relevant once again to our story – there would be a third economy that would be triggered when men begin to translate the gnosis of being redeeemed in Christ into a practical program of active piety that would ensure the realization of the Kingdom of God on earth in the not-too-distant future.[127]

Certainly Coccejus is moving in this direction. He is ambiguous, however, as to whether the third economy emerges within the second economy of the covenant of grace itself or emerges therein in anticipation of a totally new age of collective redemption.[128] What is clear, though, is that this mode of exegesis had enormous value as an instrument for encouraging "earnest" Christians to try to "glory" in God through *praxis pietatis*.[129] "Theology is practical," Coccejus had claimed; it was a declaration whose meaning was lost neither on Spener nor on Bengel – on the "down-to-earth" pietists, that is.[130]

From what has just been said about the ethical dynamic of the contract version of covenant theology (i.e., of federal theology qua Coccejanism and moderate Calvinism) it should be easy to see why pietists in general and Bengel in particular were drawn to it as a mode of biblical exegesis.[131] It fitted exactly with the argument for "gradual sanctification" that had been developing among reform-minded German Lutherans since Arndt. What Arndt and Spener had said about the relation of sanctification to justification was conceptually similar to what Coccejus had said about the relation of two-way contracts to one-way testaments. Indeed, in both cases grace was to be understood as a conditional matter in which justification by faith entailed a voluntarist commitment to sanctification by works.

There is much in Bengel's work that permits us to characterize his mode of exegesis in these terms. Take, for example, the exegetical mode Bengel used in the *Gnomon*, a book published in 1742 that represented the fruits of a lifetime of reflection on the meaning of the New Testament and its scholarship.[132] First, we notice in the Preface that Bengel was quite concerned to dissociate himself from the separatists, whom he regarded as irresponsible in their interpretations of the Bible.[133] Since the Reformation the exegetical mode of separatism had expressed itself in what Haller has called an extreme "religious individualism."[134] The argument had been that every believer possessed the capacity to discern for himself the meaning of Scripture. The feeling was that religious sincerity, not knowledge of Scripture, was the only condition necessary for apprehension of the divine word. All that was required to understand the Bible, the separatists asserted, was the "inner light" of faith, and that was a gift every Christian, regardless of his learning or social standing, could acquire. In effect, that meant that faith could dispense with learning, religion could be separated from reason, *pistis* from *gnosis*, grace from nature, and religion from education. Carried to its logical conclusion, the separatists' rendering of the Protestant doctrine of *sola fide* seemed to point toward a radical religious subjectivism of an anti-intellectual sort. That is, it pointed toward the kind of separatist doctrine that tried to turn anti-intellectualism into a theological virtue.[135]

Bengel, like Joachim and Coccejus, would have none of this, and to combat it – to prevent separatists from reading whatever content they wished into the Bible – Bengel proudly announced that biblical exegesis was a scholarly vocation. (This, of course, was also perfectly in keeping with the "vocational" focus Spener had given to his understanding of the Lutheran pastorate.) To that end, he told readers of the *Gnomon* – very much as Joachim and Coccejus had told their readers – he had been called by God to become a *Schriftstheologue*.[136]

Just what Bengel meant by calling himself this is revealed in the exegetical mode of the *Gnomon* itself. There we see Bengel attempt to balance his scholarly and activist commitments within a theological framework that tries to avoid the pitfalls of orthodox inertia and separatist anti-intellectualism. To achieve this balance, Bengel began by accepting as an article of faith that the Bible truly represents God's word.[137] But he also held that what was written in the Bible had been composed by human hands, and that in its transmission over the centuries the text had been altered – sometimes through conscious design, sometimes through simple errors of transcription.[138]

In this context, Bengel set two tasks for himself.[139] First, the written text had to be corrected and purged of its human accretions, interpolations, errors of omission and commission in transcription, and so on. He wished, as it were, to settle once and for all the issue of an "unaltered" biblical text.[140] Many of the conflicting interpretations of the Bible, Bengel felt, had their origins in these differing variants of the text. Thus, he reasoned, a standard edition of the New Testament would militate against the proliferation of "rankly abundant discrepancies" that had so alarmed Jaeger.[141] To this end, he published in 1734 his own critical edition of the Greek New Testament.

Second, Bengel sought to establish a consensual basis for biblical exegesis by clarifying the "meaning" of the text. This brings us to a crucial aspect of Bengel's work, for in the *Gnomon* he did this by putting philology and *studium chronologieum* at the service of textual exegesis.[142] In doing so he recalls the exegetical techniques of the Reformed church in general and of Coccejus in particular. This was because Bengel knew full well that the standardization of text would resolve only some of the issues that divided exegetes. Even an authoritative text could not alter the fact that "the force" of some words and sentences held different meanings for different men.[143] To deal with the ambiguity of language, Bengel distinguished – as Coccejus had – between the *sensus grammaticus* and the *sensus realis* (or *sensus spiritualis*) of what was written in the Bible.[144] While in the first case the task was to establish "the full force of words and sentences" by placing them in their proper grammatical context, in the second case it was to discover "the original signification of the words" by placing them in their proper historico-cultural context.[145]

Given these objectives, Bengel had to ask such questions as: When and where were the various parts of Holy Scripture composed? Who composed them? What were the cultural traditions out of which the authors of the Bible came? What does an understanding of the stylistic conventions then in use tell us about the composition of the text and about the intentions of their authors? For whom were these texts written? Needless to say, by asking these questions Bengel did much to historicize and relativize the meaning of the Bible, and those were developments that he recognized would undoubtedly lend themselves to the subjectivist mode of separatists exegesis. To avoid that Bengel had to find a way to make *praxis pietatis* a collective rather than an individual endeavor[146] – that is, he had to find a way to sociologize the contractualism of covenant theology.[147]

5. The sociology of the divine economy

Here the economy of salvation argument that Zwingli and Calvin had developed versus the Antinomians offered interesting possibilities, especially if one were disposed, as Bengel certainly was, to use its conditional aspect to promote ethical activism, social regeneration, religious recollectivization, and the collective salvation of a covenanted people.[148] To this end, Bengel wasted no time in telling the readers of the *Gnomon* what his mode of exegesis was all about. In the first sentence Bengel associated himself with the two economies argument. He wrote:

The word of the living God, which formed the rule of faith and practice to the primitive patriarchs, was committed to writing in the age of Moses, to whom the other prophets were successively added. . . . The Scriptures, therefore, of the Old and New Testaments, form a . . . *system* of Divine testimonies . . . they exhibit one entire and perfect body.[149]

In keeping with the thrust of this argument, Bengel conceded that these testimonies had been "accommodated to the then existing state of things."[150] As he noted later in the preface, in His testimonies to man God "accommodates Himself to the grossness of our perceptions"[151] For that reason, he argued, "the whole style of Scripture is full of condescension."[152] And yet it was perfectly obvious to Bengel that the message of each testament was the same; namely, for man "to perform" what God had asked of him in Scripture – that is, while Bengel used the two economies argument in his mode of exegesis, he did so in a way that stressed its conditional aspect.[153] What is more, he maintained that the overriding message of Scripture was one that had "gradually" increased in "clearness and explicitness" from "the time of Moses down to that of the Apostles."[154]

The economy of salvation argument was a mode of exegesis that, we have seen, had roots in Clement and Joachim as well as among Calvinist covenant theologians.[155] And from the very beginning the argument had been historically oriented in ways that consistently encouraged ethical activism among Christians.[156] God revealed Himself to man slowly and in forms congenial to human nature at different stages of its development. For that reason, it was argued, what it meant to be a Christian was constantly changing. Bengel accepted this without equivocation. It was, obviously, useful in dealing with orthodox intransigence. But Bengel also used the theology of the divine economy to argue against antisocial separatists. He did this by claiming that the "order" in which the divine economy revealed itself had anticipated the present need not only for activism but for collectivism as well.[157] And that combination, as we shall see, had profound implications for political conceptions in Württemberg right down to Hegel's day.

A good example of how Bengel accomplished this can be seen in the *Gnomon*'s running commentary on the seeming biblical antithesis between the religious teachings of James and Paul.[158] Traditionally, Lutheranism had treated the doctrines of the two apostles as expressions of polar antitheses within Christianity. In their terminology, the teachings of the former stressed sanctification by works, those of the latter justification *sola fide*. Throughout the *Gnomon* – and, above all, in his commentary on Romans, Galatians, and James – Bengel indicated that he believed James and Paul presented complementary rather than antithetical tendencies within Christianity.[159] What made their teachings appear contradictory, he argued, was the way in which the two men tailored the Gospel message to fit the differing needs of their audiences.[160] James, Bengel pointed out, was concerned with overcoming Jewish resistance to Christianity. Over against unconverted Jews James set "works" as a vehicle available to anyone who wished to participate in the soteriological drama.[161]

Conversely, Paul very often addressed a Gentile audience; his purpose was to convince it of the insufficiency of the legalism and intellectualism of ancient religions. Thus, he emphasized the necessity of justification through Jesus Christ.[162] Thus, in his teachings he accented faith rather than good works and justification rather than sanctification. Because the apostles appealed to different audiences, they stressed different aspects of the Gospel message – a message that, for Bengel, was a composite of faith and works, of justification and sanctification, within a larger syndrome of what he often referred to as "spiritual maturity."[163]

In elaborating this line, Bengel was taking a bold step. Luther, after all, had dismissed arguments for sanctification outright and had even once described the Book of James as "an epistle of straw."[164] But many Protestants, Lutheran reformers and pietists as well as moderate Calvinists, had made the case for a measure of sanctification in matters of salvation, and Bengel followed them in much of his discussion of James and Paul.[165] For this reason, his exegetical strategy for explaining what the two apostles said was designed to rehabilitate James within two wider theological contexts: one wished to show that Christianity was "to be estimated, not merely from Divine worship, but also from the daily mode of life [i.e., *praxis pietatis*]";[166] and another tried to use the conditional aspects of the covenant of grace to channel that activism in the direction of religious recollectivization.[167]

To make this argument, Bengel began by making it very clear whom he was writing against in his exegesis of James. As he presented it, the main obstacles to the rehabilitation of James were those "degenerate disciples of Luther" who, "like Cyclopians, have for their banner faith *only*" and "seek to avoid practice, by sheltering themselves under the pretense of faith."[168] These "pretended Christians," Bengel wrote, used Paul to justify their views but had, in fact, "employed his words . . . in a sense opposite to that intended" by him.[169] And since this distortion of Paul lay behind their criticism of James, it followed for Bengel that they had also misconstrued what James had said.[170]

To correct this imbalance, Bengel set out to demonstrate that James and Paul were not so different after all. As he wrote:

It must not, however, be supposed that they are at variance with each other. . . . We ought rather to receive . . . the doctrine of each as apostolical. . . . They both wrote the truth, . . . but in different ways, as those who had to deal with different kinds of men.[171]

"Living faith," which Bengel associated with a faith that has come alive through works, was for him the common concern of James and Paul.[172] Just as Paul had "strenuously urged works" on those who were "abusing the doctrine of faith" in his own day,[173] so James recognized "the inward and peculiar power of faith" – which is to say, he understood that works were the "active principle of faith."[174] If there was a difference between the two, Bengel argued, it lay in the fact that while Paul was interested in conversion as a form of justification, James was interested in "the state resulting from" that conversion, the state "when a man continues in the righteousness which is of faith, and makes *progress* in that which is of works."[175]

From this it should be clear that Bengel's exegesis of James aimed at providing biblical justification for the doctrine of *praxis pietatis*. But in order to give that doctrine the particular dynamic he wished, Bengel linked it to the economy of grace argument as it had been developed among covenant theologians of the contractual school. He did this by drawing Abraham, the key figure in much of covenant theology and a key figure in Hegel's early theological writings, into his discussion of James and Paul.[176]

Abraham enters the exegesis of James at a crucial point, just after Bengel has shown that James and Paul agreed that faith and works were necessarily complements to each other in a fully Christian life. According to Bengel, Paul "brings forward Abraham" as a believer, as one who has entered into the covenant of grace through "faith only."[177] James, however, approaches Abraham from what we have identified as the contractual point of view, for he emphasizes what Abraham did in the way of works, in the way of preparatory activity, *in the interim* between his entry into the covenant with God and his moment of sacrifice.[178]

In this context, Bengel offers an interpretation of Abraham that is extremely revealing. He writes that "the vigour of faith, which produces works, is increased, excited, and strengthened by the very act of producing them. . . ."[179] He then declares that through works faith derives a sense of its own perfection – which is to say that "Faith is made perfect, that is, shown to be true, by works."[180] This, Bengel felt, was the lesson the story of Abraham had for Christianity. Abraham undoubtedly "returned" from his "sacrifice much more perfect in faith than he had gone to it."[181] And that was because in the interim between the initiation of the covenant and the actual sacrifice Abraham had fulfilled in his life activity the terms of his contract with God. In so doing, Bengel reasoned, Abraham had had his faith transformed: from passive acquiescence it had moved toward a conscious pattern of *praxis pietatis*. He had, as it were, voluntarily and consciously fulfilled in his life the conditions of his covenant with God. As a result, he may be said not only to have perfected his faith but also to have participated in his own salvation.[182]

If the contractual dimension of Bengel's interpretation of Abraham sounds synergist that is because it most assuredly is. And many other arguments in the *Gnomon* confirm this judgment. For example, Bengel's discussion of Abraham is careful to delineate three different moments in the process of his redemption.[183] There is the moment of the original covenant, Abraham's *believing;* that of the progressive unfolding of the covenant, Abraham's *doing* and, finally, that of its culmination, the moment when Abraham's doing was translated into the knowledge that the terms of the covenant had been fully realized, Abraham's *spiritual maturity*.[184] And to underline the point that Abraham had made "progress" in his "faith," Bengel likened the original covenant to the moment when "morning dawns, when man receives faith, and. . .sleep is shaken off."[185] That moment, Bengel continued, is followed by another, when man must "rise, walk and do his work, lest sleep should again steal over him."[186]

The point of all this for Bengel is to show that the "exhortations of the Gospel always aim at *Higher and Higher Degrees* of perfection";[187] hence, the Bible presupposes "the oldness of the condition in which we now are, compared with those newer things, which ought to follow, and which correspond *to the nearness of salvation*."[188] Citing Paul, Bengel claims that "the course of the Christian, once begun, therefore proceeds onward continually, and comes *nearer and nearer to the goal* [of spiritual perfection]."[189] He insists, however, that this perfectionism be understood in two ways: first, as part of "striving" to assimilate to God even though "identification" with God would never take place;[190] and second, as a "trial of faith" in which the patience and humility of every Christian is tested.[191] Put another way, Bengel allows perfectionism and patience to check each other in a way that yields an "adult" or "mature" conception of Christian wisdom.[192] In that respect, Bengel presents perfectionism as an integral part of what drives "faith" toward ethical action and as part of an eschatological "hope" that draws action out of faith.[193]

In all of this, Bengel's theology of the divine economy appears to have been cast in the form of an evolution eschatology qua covenant theology. From a soteriological point of view, man is allowed to participate more and more in the process of human redemption as history unfolds.[194] There is, however, an aspect of this theology that deserves more attention because it provides a striking example of just how down-to-earth this Württemberg pietist could be when he wished to be so. What I have in mind is the way Bengel translated the theology of the divine economy from the language of soteriology into that of a sociology of Christian fellowship.[195]

To understand how he accomplished this, we need to look closely at the language of the theology of the divine economy itself.[196] Earlier we noted how the economy of salvation was tied to the idea of progressive revelation in history and how among Christian reformers both of these ideas served pedagogic purposes. Economy and instruction, indeed, seemed to flow together in a conception of God as a good Husbandman who knew how to "cultivate" that which was His.[197] In Coccejus, the moderate Calvinist, and Bengel, the down-to-earth pietist, the language of the theology of the divine economy is also commercial and legalistic.[198] We hear talk, therefore, about contracts, account books, debtors and creditors, and so on. Indeed, the terminology suggests a methodical and calculable way for man practically to measure and fulfill his contractual relationship with God – so much received, so much given, and the like.[199]

Bengel used this "commercial" terminology and made it very much a part of his theology of the divine economy. He talked, for example, about the Bible as a *Lagerbuch*, a ledger, in which were registered the debits and credits of man's account with God.[200] Given Bengel's discourse, one could argue, as many students of covenant theology in other contexts have, that the economization of the language of covenant theology reflected the "contractual" concerns of a world on the verge of secularization.[201] Thus, as McGiffert has observed,

Modern scholars have drawn distinctions between covenant and contract, describing the latter less as an extension or descendant of the former, newly applied to secular ends, than *as a radical departure from it*. The attributes and connotations of the two ideas tend to be seen as having been profoundly different, even antagonistic.[202]

As has already been suggested, however, this line of argument, while it certainly makes clear how eschatological modes might influence secular conceptions, misconstrues just how the "sociology" of covenant theology was meant to work among a godly people. As Walzer has perceptively noted, this mode of discourse, while certainly commercial and contractual, was seen more as "a way of activating men" in a religious sense than "of controlling God" in a secular sense.[203]

To understand why the economic mode of discourse points in the direction of religious reform and recollectivization rather than secularization and individualization, we need to remember that from the very beginning the intention of the contractual school of covenant theology had been, in Miller's words, "to incite men to preparedness, not in order that laws might be obeyed, but that souls might be saved."[204] The aim of the covenant was to redivinize man, not economize God; was to recollectivize *homo religiosus*, not turn Christianity into a mask for "utilitarian convenience."[205] In that sense, the contractual language of covenant theology, a mix of legal and economic terminology, had a religious and sociological dynamic in it, but it was a dynamic more concerned with collective redemption than with material acquisitiveness.

Michael Walzer, I think, has fully appreciated what is at issue here, for he has seen how the idea of covenant as contract mediated between the individual working in his calling and the recollectivization of a godly people.[206] In a society governed by this idea, Walzer has written, "the scheme of human relations would be effectively determined by the scheme of human employment."[207] In that context, he continued, a contract "was seen as an agreement between equals, . . . fully voluntary and unforced on both sides and a matter not of personal loyalty or fear, but of conscience."[208] According to Walzer, what made the voluntarism of contractual relations a matter of conscience was that the religious assurance one derived from fulfilling the covenant by working in a calling made

"long-term promises and agreements" as well as "the mutual recognition
of honest intention" possible.[209]

In this respect, the idea of the contract was less the correlate of "civil
society" in a modern secular sense than the objective expression and
collective result of a Christian's vocational commitment. In truth, the
consequences of the individual's attempt to exhibit religious personality
through vocational activity was collective assurance that "honest" labor
would be conducted in an atmosphere of trust, mutual recognition, and
reciprocity.[210] What held the collectivity together, then, was not the idea
of contract per se but the idea of contract as expressive of a covenanting
community of individual consciences. And since within that community
vocational activity was aimed at the sanctification of a godly people rather
than the acquisition of wealth by the individual,[211] contracts could be
envisaged as a means of collective discipline and work as part of the self-
realizing *telos* of a religious collectivity.[212]

Thus, the terminology Bengel employed to power his theology of the
divine economy enhanced vocational activity, gave added socioeconomic
impetus to Spener's ascetic notion of "dying into life," and made it
possible to explain the religious recollectivization of a godly people in
the down-to-earth terms of everyday commercial activity. Whatever else
it did, it is undeniable that the contractual form of covenant theology
encouraged *homo religiosus* to seek to realize himself in cooperation not only
with God but with his fellows as well.[213] And that meant that the covenant by which individuals were reborn in Christ carried with it a corporate
obligation, one to which Bengel clearly wished to rally Württemberg
Protestants in the early eighteenth century.

6. Covenant theology, religious recollectivization, and resistance theory

If the ideas of work, vocation, and contract received religious spins in
Bengel's thought, and if these spins provided the theology of the divine
economy with a kind of sociological justification, the sociology itself was
the axis upon which Bengel's soteriologically oriented theology of history
turned. And that was because as sociology and as soteriology the theology
of the divine economy had religious recollectivization as its end.[214]

That Bengel meant for us to appreciate this connection can be deduced
from his treatment of Abraham. As we have seen, Bengel had no qualms
about emphasizing the conditionalism of the covenant God had made
with Abraham.[215] It had certain obvious advantages for what he wished to
say about the biblical imperative of *praxis pietatis*. Just as important to
him, though, was the fact that this covenant was collective – it embraced
Abraham and "his seed."[216] That meant that the covenant with Abraham

had been between God and a religious people and that there was a religious precedent for saying that God would condescend to covenant with a godly people as well as with individuals. Viewed in that way, Bengel's interpretation of Abraham speaks to his collectivist as well as his activist religious concerns.

So how does a theology of history emerge from the interplay among conditionalism, activism, and collectivism in Bengel's rendering of covenant theology? To answer this question, we need to recall that the theology of the divine economy, whether in the form of Irenaeus' or Clement's covenants, Joachim's dispensations, or Coccejus' economies of grace, always discusses salvation as a process that unfolded in a discernible order, had clearly defined stages, and moved in a specific direction.[217] In Joachim, the process expressed itself in a law–grace–spirit sequence that was open to the future. Coccejus, we noted, presented a Calvinist re-working of this sequence. Its pattern was of a covenant of works followed by two economies of grace, with the possibility of a third economy that could be viewed in terms of a process of gradual sanctification. In both cases, however, the sequence culminated in a stage in which a Christian community with a truly associative religious life was realized on earth.

Bengel, I think, understood this dynamic very well, for his interpreta-tion of Abraham certainly aimed at putting the collectivist aspect of the first economy of grace at the service of his own collectivist commitments.[218] How else explain his statement that "Christianity has never *yet* attained the perfect form which it *is* to have by virtue of the Old Testament promises"?[219]

In saying this, Bengel implied that there were three rather than two economies within the covenant of grace. The argument was simple enough to make. God's covenant with Abraham had been conditional and collective; His covenant with Christians had been unconditional and personal; and now, after the Reformation had restored the integrity of the New Testament's covenant of faith, it was time for Christians to recollectivize themselves into a godly people who would be preparing for the arrival of the Kingdom of God on earth.[220]

For recollectivization to take place, of course, individuals, whose consciences in a religious sense were absolutely independent of those of their fellows, would have to come into covenant with each other in a social sense.[221] This, we have seen, was sociologically accomplished when man worked through his vocation, from inside out as it were, to form volun-tary and contractual networks of mutual subjection in which "trust" became the basis not only of Christian fellowship but of collective re-demption as well.[222] By living through one's vocation, and by denying one's self, the individual could collectivize his conscience and make it the basis for a conception of religious personality in which self-affirmation involved the inculcation of what Walzer has called "a new asceticism of duty" among a godly people.[223]

That this mode of exegesis served Bengel's reformist commitments well should be obvious: its combination of activism and collectivism neatly avoided the respective pitfalls of orthodoxy and separatism. That it fit in nicely with the thrust of the Second Reformation argument should be just as obvious, for social regeneration entailed collective discipline and co-operation. The theology of the divine economy, moreover, carried with it a number of other implications that Bengel was also eager to emphasize. For one thing it called attention to the presumptuousness of orthdoxy's claim to doctrinal infallibility. As the economy of salvation argument made clear, a distinction had to be drawn between the universal spiritual message and the particular historical forms of Christianity. Better, there-fore, to judge Christians by their conduct than by the lip service they paid to sterile doctrine.[224] From this premise followed related points that Bengel wished to make about toleration, *praxis pietatis*, and the impor-tance of the voluntarism of religious conscience in an age of spiritual maturity.

Equally as important, the economy of salvation argument made it possible for Bengel to reaffirm Spener's view that the basic appeal of Christianity lay in its capacity for spiritual growth. As Bengel envisaged it, Christianity was not time bound – it was constantly transcending the "local" forms it assumed in history. From this standpoint, it was no longer incumbent on the exegete to "explain away" historical changes within Christianity. Change now testified to the spiritual nature of the Christian religion – to its capacity to transcend itself perpetually by over-coming its own internal conflicts.[225]

Overall, then, the religious coherence of Bengel's theology of the divine economy was quite compelling. Indeed, in a fundamental way its con-ditionalism had the twin effects of reducing the hold original sin had on men's minds and of making salvation a collective process that one participated in through vocational activity.[226] Approached from either direction Bengel's conditionalist mode of biblical exegesis had the effect of greatly expanding the opportunities for Christian activism. The theology of the divine economy played a crucial role in turning pietists in general and Old-Württemberg Protestants in particular away from Augustinian and toward Pelagian religious conceptions.[227] Put slightly differently, the theology of the divine economy played to the process of gradual sanctifi-cation as evolutionary eschatology had to the assimilationism of self-realizing teleology.

For all its internal coherence, however, Bengel's theology would hardly have exercised the influence it did had its development not coincided with the emergence of a need among Württemberg Protestants to articulate a theory of resistance to their newly ascendant Catholic duke. What is striking here is that Bengel's theology transferred the locus of civil authority from the "godly prince" to a "godly people" coincidentally with the Württemberg Estates' call for political resistance to the absolutizing and catholicizing policies of the new duke of Württemberg. This, I think, was a remarkable convergence, for from then on it was possible for Württembergers to include the force of religious argument in their defense of the Estates' political right to resist the duke.[228]

That the ideas of the divine economy qua species of covenant theology and resistance theory qua species of constitutionalist political thought could become so aligned in Württemberg should not be surprising. As students of the history of political thought in Europe have shown, there had been ample precedent for such interplay in the thought of Protestants since the sixteenth century.[229]

On this score, Quentin Skinner has recently made the decisive arguments.[230] To summarize his very detailed account of the rise of Protestant resistance theory, he has shown that between Bucer and Zwingli in the 1520s and Hotman, Beza, and Mornay in the 1570s, Calvinists had developed a theory of resistance that combined aspects of feudal, scholastic, and covenant thinking;[231] that the idea of the Estates as a locus of "ephoral" resistance to princely power was first broached by Calvin in the *Institutes* and then made explicit by the monarchomachs in the 1570s;[232] that while many Calvinists may have been unclear as to whether their ephoral magistrates had been "ordained" by God, "elected" by a "godly people," or were just constitutional representatives in a legal sense,[233] the result of equating ephoral authority with the Estates system had the effect both of calling for "popular" resistance to arbitrary or ungodly rule and of vitiating the possibility of anarchist excesses;[234] that fundamental to almost all of Protestant resistance theory was the claim that resistance be restricted to those who had been endowed with the "vocation" to do so;[235] and that while use of the language of a "contract" theory of natural law very often gave resistance theory a "defensive" character, the framework within which that language was used was very often militantly activist and collectivist and informed by considerations of covenant theology.[236]

Within Protestant resistance theory, then, there were elements of political contractualism and covenant theology.[237] Perhaps the clearest expression of this can be found in Mornay's *Vindiciae* (1579).[238] As Barker appreciated long ago, the author of the *Vindiciae* availed himself of both elements in his argument for resistance.[239] On the one hand, Mornay exploited the contractualism of natural law to check excesses of the king.[240] On the other hand, he often justified this conception by making reference to the religious duties of a covenanting people.[241] In the first case, Barker had argued, Mornay presented us with "what we may call a natural people,...a political people with the political right of sovereignty."[242] In the second case, Mornay gave us a view of a godly people, of a "people *sub specie religionis*."[243] In the former, "*populus* and *Respublica*" are the same;[244], in the latter, *populus* and "*ecclesia*" merge into one "congregation of the faithful."[245]

It is certainly true that the argument of the *Vindiciae* is fraught with internal tensions. As Barker and Skinner have respectively noted, it expresses two different senses of what constitutes a "people" and offers "two distinct justifications of resistance," one "scholastic" and contractual, the other "providentialist" and covenantal.[246] Whether these tensions can be separated conceptually into a "purely political contract" and a purely "religious covenant" need not occupy us here;[247] what historically warrants attention is that there was a Protestant precedent for thinking that the two were compatible – were, in Barker's terms, "co-extensive and even identical."[248] How else explain the sustained and persistent effort to depict the civil piety of a Protestant people as "Israel and Rome redivinus"?[249] How else explain Beza's and Mornay's repeated linking of David and Brutus and their constant juxtaposing of the elders of Israel with the magistrates of Rome?[250] To use Julian Franklin's formulation of the matter, how else explain Protestants' efforts to interpret the covenant theology of the Old Testament "in a republican and constitutional spirit"?[251]

That this line of inquiry may be relevant to our discussion of Bengel's theology and Old-Württemberg's politics can be seen by probing Mornay's argument further. Like Bucer and Beza before him, Mornay regarded the premonarchical Hebrew people (the people of the so-called Mosaic covenant) as a model polity.[252] What was exemplary about this polity was the way power had been dispersed in it.[253] Since "it was dangerous," Mornay wrote, "to entrust the Church to a single, all-too-human individual," God "committed and entrusted it to the people as a whole."[254] Although Mornay quickly qualified this by explaining that by the "people" he meant the "assembly" of elders,[255] his overall intention was clearly to make "the people as a whole" responsible for fulfilling the Mosaic covenant.[256] Thus, like Bucer before and Harrington after him, Mornay cast the Mosaic polity in the mold of a classical republic that was held together by a religious covenant.[257]

To explain the emergence of kings in Israel, Mornay had to restructure his argument slightly.[258] The restructuring, I think, had momentous implications, for its success hinged first on bringing the king into Israel's covenant with God and then on making him a creation of the people.[259] To do this, Mornay argued for a *basic continuity* between the Mosaic and Davidic polities.[260] "When Kings were given to the people" he wrote, the covenant "did not lapse but was instead confirmed."[261] In saying this Mornay was claiming nothing unusual, for others had made the same argument about the continuity of development.[262] Yet, if Mornay is not original, he is at least clearer than others with regard to the argument he makes. He begins by citing examples from the monarchical period in which the coronation of kings involved an oath to preserve the convenant between God and the people of Israel.[263] In this covenant God is the "stipulating party; the King and the people as a whole – that is, Israel – are the promissory parties, both being obligated *of their own accord* for one and the same thing."[264] As such, Mornay reasons, the "King and Israel. . . are established as two co-signers equally obligated for the entire promise."[265] Mornay continues, using language that smacks of the vocabulary of the theology of the divine economy:

It seems, therefore, that God did what creditors so often do with borrowers of doubtful credit, which is to obligate several for the same account. . . each one of whom may be held responsible for the entire sum.[266]

If this is the case, Mornay concludes, God must have accorded the people "the authority, and the capacity. . . to be God's people *if they may*" – that is, they had "the right, not only of making a covenant, but also of *performing* it and of enforcing its performance on the King."[267]

Having assimilated the idea of kingship into the covenant – thus establishing the continuity of the monarchy with the Mosaic polity – Mornay proceeded to demonstrate that the kings, while chosen by God, had to be "established" by the people.[268] That is because "God willed that every bit of authority held by Kings should come from the people. . . ."[269] It was, Mornay insisted, their "votes" that made kings.[270] Therefore, people are "prior to the King" and thus "greater" than he is.[271] People make kings, he proclaims, "not the King the people."[272]

With this argument, Mornay realized, he had inserted a contractual and conditional covenantal element into the discussion of God's relationship with Israel.[273] It was necessary to do this, Mornay felt, because it was clear to him that when "the people of Israel" requested a king, and when they were granted one by God, the possibility of covenant corruption was greatly enhanced.[274] Hence, the need for a more explicit rendering of the relation between a king and his people. Hence, the need for *a contract* that was, in essence, an expression of the vigilance and watchfulness of a godly people.[275] The contract, in other words, was conditional and contingent upon the behavior of the king; the covenant was absolute and was the basis for the entire arrangement.[276]

What is at issue here may be illuminated in another way, a way that will bring us back to Bengel and his interpretation of Abraham. It has

been written of Beza and Mornay that they constantly drew on the idea of
God's covenant with Israel because it provided ample opportunities for
putting Old Testament images at the service of the contemporaneous
political ends of popular sovereignty and contractual government.[277] But
just as the figure of David could serve widely divergent political ends, so
could the covenant theology of the Old Testament.[278] Modern scholarship, for example, has identified covenants that focus on individuals
(e.g., Adam, Noah, Abraham, Moses, and David) and covenants that are
synonymous with experiences such as the Exodus, Sinai, Shechem, the
beginning of kingship, and the Exile.[279] Within these groupings, the
covenants with Moses and David are invariably singled out as of decisive
political importance, the reason being that the Mosaic covenant is associated with the *constitution* of Israel as a godly people and the Davidic
covenant with the *foundation* of empire and the divine right of kings.[280]
In the first case – in the theocracy, that is – the religio-political values
of voluntarism, activism, collectivism, and equality of status within a
decentralized polity are alleged to predominate.[281] In the second case,
centralization of authority and the organization of the people under the
monarchy for military purposes are depicted as the price of "Israel's"
survival against hostile Philistine forces.[282]

That there are clashes between the religio-political values of the two
systems of covenants should be obvious.[283] As scholars have been wont to
put it, there seems to be a "religious covenant" that derives its meaning
from Sinai and a "political covenant" that focuses on David, the
monarchy, and the divine right of Israel's kings.[284] In the Old Testament,
however, efforts were made to explain this tension. It is in these efforts, I
think, that we see most clearly why Abraham was a key figure for Bengel
and for Protestant resistance theory.[285]

According to Hillers and Voegelin, it is of the utmost importance that
the first of these efforts at explanation arose during the period of kingship
itself.[286] For that reason, both regard this effort to explain the relation
between Moses and David as "royalist" in nature – in Voegelin's terms, "a
piece of imperial propaganda" that aimed at showing how David's
kingship was the culmination of Israel's history.[287] What had begun with
Abraham's personal rebellion against the Amorites, so ran the argument,
had with time and collective discipline (i.e., the meaning of the Mosaic
covenant in this version) grown into, and consolidated itself in, the
Davidic monarchy.[288] Therefore, the rule of the kings and the foundation
of the monarchy could be presented as the center of meaning of Israel's
covenant with God.[289] Everything was meant to be related to this new
"nucleus" of Israelite experience.[290]

As Hillers has pointed out, all this was necessary because David had to
offer an account of how kingship fit into the Mosaic covenant tradition.[291]

David wished, of course, to use the covenant as a sanction for kingship; but he well knew that kingship played no part in the Sinai experience. So, to establish continuity of development between covenant and kingship he expanded the terms of God's covenant with Israel from a two-term to a three-term sequence. By doing this – by going back to Abraham and patriarchal history and by locating the beginning of covenant theology there – he bypassed the Mosaic covenant and made it a stage in the larger story of the emergence of Israel as a covenanted people whose very survival depended on the organization of the monarchy.[292] Instead of defining Israel in terms of the tension-filled covenant–kingdom sequence, David read the promise of a kingdom for Israel back into the story of Abraham and then brought the story forward in time so that the idea of the kingdom qua manifestation of Abraham's seed would take precedence over the Mosaic covenant, which was now relegated to an interim position in the unfolding of the covenant itself.[293] In terms of our earlier terminology, a "testament" had been made to Israel by God and it had both expressed and realized itself in the Abraham, Moses, and David experiences, experiences in which the people of Israel were by and large passive recipients of God's covenant with them.[294]

If this continuity in the development of God's covenant with Israel allowed David to posture as a leader who in some "democratic" sense represented the interests of the people,[295] that interest was totally determined by David's, not Israel's, covenant with God.[296] In Voegelin's terms, this arrangement made the idea of "a chosen king" rather than "a Chosen People" the center of God's covenant with Israel.[297] Therefore, David could present himself as sole interpreter of what that covenant was.

It was precisely at this point and over this issue that the "antiroyalist" version of Israel's covenant with God arose.[298] Vital to this undertaking was the claim that Israel under Moses and Israel under David were very different political entities. Government by judges in a theocracy was not the same as government by kings under a monarchy. Yet it was undeniable that David had not only saved Israel but had put the monarchy on a firm foundation as well. It was imperative, therefore, to the antiroyalist version of the history of Israel's covenant with God that the kingdom be assimilated to the idea of covenant rather than the covenant to the idea of kingdom. Continuity in this rendering obviously had a very different political meaning than in the royalist version, and to see that we need only note the way the antiroyalist argument used the idea of covenant to "bridle" the king.

At the center of this endeavor were the figures of Samuel and Jehoiada, both of whom would be cited repeatedly by monarchomach theorists of resistance in the sixteenth century.[299] What was asserted through the invocation of these figures was the priority of the covenant over kingship, of the rights of Israel as a Chosen People over those of David as a chosen king. The thrust of the antiroyalist argument is straightforward: there is a religious "covenant" between God and the people of Israel that takes precedence over the political "contract" between the people of Israel and their kings.[300] In this the story of Moses is paradigmatic, for his understanding of the covenant and law made clear what a proper arrangement of the two should look like. With this paradigm in mind, Samuel and Jehoiada, as manifestations of the conscience of a godly people, administer an oath to Saul and Joash, respectively. This oath, it turns out, is Mosaic in content, asserting the priority of the "words" of the covenant over the "ordinances" of the contract – that is, the latter are presented as elaborations, in more legalistic and institutional language, of the former.[301] One could say, in other words, that the oath that binds the people of Israel and their king to God is the antiroyalists' way of making a king truly a representative of a godly people rather than the people the passive recipients of the grace of a godly king.[302]

The connection between the antiroyalist version of Israel's covenant with God and the monarchomachs' use of the Old Testament should be clear.[303] What remains to be explained is how Bengel and Abraham fit into the larger picture. In considering this matter, we need to remember that "multiple meanings" invariably were attached to key figures in the Old Testament and that these meanings frequently were informed by political considerations.[304] Abraham, we have seen, was no exception, having been exploited by royalist forces for the purpose of legitimizing the Davidic covenant and its political correlate, the divine right of kings.[305]

For our purposes here, this mode of interpretation is decisive because it so obviously fits in with Paul's attempt to Christianize the Old Testament by way of his interpretation of the Abraham, Moses, David, and Christ sequence.[306] A testimony had been made by God to Abraham, and with time it had been affirmed by Moses and David before finally being realized in Jesus Christ. In Paul's scheme, moreover, the "initiative" remained wholly with God and the realization of the Testament had nothing at all to do with the "response" of the people.

This, however, is not the rendering of Abraham that we find in Bengel. His Abraham, to be sure, points toward Christianity, but the covenant Abraham had made with God was conditional and collective. For that reason, Bengel's Abraham is more easily assimilated to the Mosaic covenant than to the Davidic one. Once this is realized, any argument for a continuity in covenant theology from Abraham, through Moses and David, to Christ must also involve a redefinition of David's kingship, one that would depict it less in terms of the divine right of kings than in terms of an elective kingship argument.[307] This, of course, is precisely what we find monarchomach theorists doing during the sixteenth century –

turning David into a "humble monarch" who, in Mornay's words, "was established at Israel's initiative and for Israel's benefit" and who entered "into a covenant with all the elders of Israel, who represented the people as a whole."[308]

There is no reason whatsoever to doubt that Bengel meant to give his exegesis of Scripture this religio-political spin: everything points to a dual effort to put covenant theology at the service of religious collectivization and political resistance. The internal evidence – the stress on voluntarism, activism, collectivism, performance, conditionalism, covenants, and the religiocontractual language – speaks powerfully to this point. But there is external evidence for the affinity too, for covenant theology and resistance theory found a point of practical mediation in the constitutionalist posture assumed by the Estates of Old-Württemberg after 1733.

How this mediation worked is easy enough to explain, and we shall detail it in the next chapter. Suffice it to say here that while covenant theology pressed both for activism within a community of self-binding individuals and for progress in the spiritual life of a godly people,[309] the members of the Estates, Protestant almost to the man, were searching for a wider basis for constitutional resistance to the catholicizing and absolutizing policies of the new duke of Württemberg. Viewed in this way, it is easy to see how the Estates, as a cultural institution that had been formed by the interplay between religious, social, and antipolitical values, could assume the responsibility monarchomach theorists had previously assigned to "ephoral" authorities.[310] On the one hand, the Estates, in Mornay's words, "took the place of the people assembled as a whole" and acted as "ephors to Kings and associates to their rule."[311] On the other hand, it was guardian of the "laws" of the land.[312] In the first case, the Württemberg Estates provided a this-worldly institutional base for the ongoing reformation of a godly people; in the second case, it moderated the power of the duke by overseeing the legal aspects of the contractual political arrangement between the duke and the people.

Skepticism about the religio-political coherence and unity of the Württemberg people would be in order here were it not for the fact that for most of the century the Württemberg Estates constituted a fairly socially homogeneous group. Unlike the situation in sixteenth-century France, where the nobility led the resistance, the leaders of resistance in Old-Württemberg came from the cities and were "bourgeois" rather than aristocratic.[313] In fact, the Estates in Württemberg had been free of aristocratic influence for quite some time, so that the possibility that covenant theology was being used there to give old "feudal" interests a new constitutionalist face is not all that plausible.[314] In that respect, while the Estates can certainly be envisaged as the focus of an effort to institutionalize resistance and to limit resistance to those who had a "vocation" to do so, it can also be seen as the "epitome" of a single recollectivized religious conscience in which the people of Württemberg, like the people of ancient Israel, had political responsibilities that were largely defined by their religious duties.[315] What Walzer had said in another context about Mornay seems to hold for the people of Württemberg; namely, that the basis of their constitutionalism lay in a "trust" formed by an "identity of godly consciences."[316]

This arrangement, of course, was not without its tensions. For example, there was the problem of how constitutionally to mediate the contractual dualism between the Catholic duke and a Protestant people.[317] Then – and this became a glaring problem in Hegel's time – there was the problem of what to do when Protestants qua godly people and Protestants qua "bourgeois" individuals began to differ among themselves and within the Estates over the purpose and direction of collective life.[318] Finally, there was the problem of the character of a constitutional arrangement that required the Estates to pursue two different goals simultaneously: one was defensive and contractual and expressed itself in the traditionalism of the Good Old Law; the other tied the Estates to the godly people's quest for continuous reformation. The next chapter discusses these tensions with an eye toward how Hegel related to them.

3

◁══════════════════════════════════════▷

The political culture of
Old-Württemberg
The *Alte Recht* tradition

In the last chapter, it was suggested that down-to-earth Pietism, in the form of Bengel's theology of the divine economy, bore intimate relations to the satisfaction of several nonreligious needs in the culture of Old-Württemberg in the eighteenth century. As was noted, *praxis pietatis* and religious collectivization attracted Württembergers because they helped them mobilize for the purpose of social regeneration after the Thirty Years' War. In addition, we saw how these religious emphases could also serve the cause of political resistance. In those senses, Pietism provided Württembergers with incentives for developing new Protestant conceptions not only of *homo religiosus* but of his relation to the collective religious life as well.

In raising the question of the affinity between Pietism and the politics of Württembergers of the eighteenth century this study is in keeping with recent work that has identified pietists in general and Bengel and Moser in particular with reformist political impulses within the Württemberg Estates.[1] The argument of the last two chapters, I think, offers much support for this view; for it has shown how the Württembergers' preoccupation with the related religious ideas of *Lebens Reformation* and a Second Reformation enabled them to continue to use Christian values as a measure for contemporary political problems.

The purpose of what follows is to detail some of the ways in which these religious concerns found expression in the Estates' opposition to princely absolutism during the years 1733–1793.[2] During this period, the overriding concern among Württemberg Protestants was to check the power and authority of Karl Alexander and Karl Eugen, the two Catholic princes who reigned in Württemberg for most of the century, from 1733 to 1737 and from 1744 to 1793, respectively.[3] In this context, the interests of Protestant prelates and those of other members of the Estates converged – negatively in their antipathies to Catholicism and absolutism

113

and positively in their commitment to legitimizing the Estates as the guardian of the religious and civil liberties of all Württembergers.

Although a complete analysis of this convergence is impossible within the limits of this study, the dynamic of the interplay can be illuminated by examining a few select events in the political history of Old-Württemberg.[4] The sequence of events – which cluster around the dates 1514, 1551, 1607, 1733, 1743, 1755, and 1770 – may be envisaged as coterminous both with developments within the so-called *Alte Recht* (Old Law) political tradition and with the concerns of the men – the *Altrechtlern* – who used this tradition to justify the institutional resistance of the Estates to princely absolutism.[5] For most of the century these men politically served Protestant religious interests. By so doing, they gave the Estates of Württemberg a constitutional cast that tells us much about Württemberg as a Protestant culture around the time of Hegel's birth. In what follows, I shall try to explain the relation between the Estates as a focus of collective religio-political concern and the cultural values of Württembergers toward the end of the eighteenth century.

1. The making of a political tradition: 1514–1733

To understand how Pietism served the political purposes of Württembergers in the eighteenth century does not require a long digression in political history. As is well known, the constitutional ideal of the dualistic *Ständestaat* had survived the Reformation as a political arrangement in many German states.[6] By the seventeenth century, however, the efficacy of this constitutional arrangement had been undermined almost everywhere in Germany.[7] A crucial exception to this pattern of development was Württemberg, where the *Landschaft*, the political center of gravity in the territorial diet in which the Estates met when in plenary session, had managed to preserve some of its corporate rights well into the eighteenth century.[8] For that reason, the Estates of Württemberg were, in Walker's words, "the most famous" in all of Germany.[9]

The background to the prominence of the Estates in Württemberg's constitutional history is interesting. Since the 1550s, when representatives of the Lutheran church and the towns had agreed to remove the barriers between the different Estate orders (curiae), the Estates of Württemberg had consisted of a single house, the *Landschaft*, which was attended by fourteen prelates and some seventy representatives of the state's various administrative districts.[10] For better or worse, the Estates had carried out its political functions without the assistance or encumbrance of the nobility who, in 1514, had withdrawn from the *Landtag* (diet) in order to secure status as Free Imperial Knights.[11] Thus, without the nobility to contend with, the *Landschaft* was relatively free to pursue its own interest in the Estates when the *Landtag* was in session.[12]

In the long run, though, the uniqueness of the Württemberg Estates lay less in the simple fact of its survival than in the thoroughly urban character of its representatives.[13] Deputies to the *Landtag* (called *Landstände*) were appointed to their positions by local magistracies whose membership consisted of a mayor (*Bürgermeister*) and six to twelve members of a town "inner council" who themselves were selected from a larger body of citizens sitting on the town's "outer council." Citizens who were qualified to sit on these two governing councils constituted a group called the *Ehrbarkeit*.[14]

In theory, the *Ehrbarkeit* was supposed to be selected from an administrative area that encompassed rural as well as urban interests. In practice, however, selection of deputies to the *Landtag* was monopolized by the cities, with the result that the *Landschaft* became the exclusive preserve of a coherent urban interest group – the so-called "*bürgerlichen Ehrbarkeit*." Thus, as E. Hölzle has reminded us, to speak of "*Bürgerherrschaft*" in the context of one side of the constitutional arrangement in Old-Württemberg is not an exaggeration.[15]

In any event, prior to 1733 the political history of Old-Württemberg revolved around an abiding conflict between princes with absolutist ambitions and a *Landschaft* that sought to preserve a curious mix of corporate and urban interests.[16] Invariably, control of fiscal and taxation policy was the focus of this ongoing conflict.[17] The problem was that Württemberg's princes required financial resources to fund their projects, pay the salaries of an expanding bureaucracy, and finance a credible military force, and these resources were not readily available except through the agency of the Estates who, traditionally, had had the prerogative vis-à-vis the prince in matters of taxation and public finance. Not wanting to acquiesce in the support of policies that would eventually undermine the stability of the institutional arrangement that guaranteed its participation in the political life of the realm, the *Landschaft* understandably exercised great vigilance with regard to the prince's expenditures, especially when it came to the funding of military projects the prince might use to coerce the Estates into compliance with his wishes on any number of policy matters.

Precarious, no doubt, was the position of the *Landschaft*, but by 1733 it had posted a record of having vigorously and successfully resisted the efforts of Württemberg's princes to subvert a constitutional arrangement that had existed for more than two hundred years – since Duke Ulrich and the Estates had agreed in 1514 to the mutually binding terms of the so-called Tübingen Treaty of that year.[18] This treaty – which in the 1790s was still heralded as the "Magna Charta" of Old-Württemberg[19] – grew out of fiscal demands Duke Ulrich had made to the Estates in 1513.[20] With the aid and guarantees of Emperor Maximilian, the Estates persuaded Ulrich to consent to the provisions of a treaty that confirmed its right to oversee and regulate the expenditures of the duke and his court. Hence the institutional basis of *Landschaft* power for the next two hundred years.[21]

Obviously, this fiduciary function was an important political instrument in the hands of the *Landschaft*, for it enabled it to obstruct or blunt initiatives of the duke in almost every area of public life. In this, however, the *Landschaft* was not always successful: as F. L. Carsten has noted, an "energetic and determined prince" could, by hook or by crook, "rule without consulting the Estates."[22] Indeed, after 1514, there were long and intermittent periods in which the influence of the Estates was eclipsed.[23] Still, the Estates endured – partly because of "timely deaths" in the ducal house,[24] partly because of countervailing forces in the Holy Roman Empire,[25] and partly because of the sheer perseverance of the *Landschaft*, which never lost its sense of its own self-interest. And as fiscal pressure increased on Ulrich's successors, the fiscal prerogatives of the *Landschaft* became more important, a development that gradually brought it back to a position of relative political parity with the duke.

Still, even though the Estates had always been a political force to be reckoned with in Württemberg, it seldom engaged in more than "negative politics": as a corporate body it could respond to, but not initiate, policy.[26] There were two reasons for this.[27] First, although prelates and representatives of the towns had sat together in the *Landschaft* since the 1550s, they did not always share a common outlook. The church, after all, was beholden to the prince in matters pertaining to the administration of the income it derived from its property. For their part, prelates were dependent upon the prince for their appointments to any number of ecclesiastical positions, including those within the universities. Hence, prelates were generally reluctant to pursue religious interests in Württemberg that might provoke conflict with the prince.

If a lack of cooperation between religious and political leaders hurt the *Landschaft* in its struggle with the prince, so too was its unity impaired by the narrow sociopolitical base of the *Ehrbarkeit*.[28] As Hölzle has argued, much of the *Ehrbarkeit*'s prominence in the *Landschaft* had been won at the expense of the interests of the rural population. On two occasions – in 1514 and during the Peasants' War – the *Ehrbarkeit* chose to side with the court instead of the country.[29] As a result, the Estates lacked a popular political base in the countryside between 1514 and 1733.[30]

The negative character of the constitutional policies of the *Landschaft* changed, however, in 1733.[31] The events that culminated in the reign of Karl Alexander (1733–1737) did much to weld the prelates and the *Ehrbarkeit* into an "oppositional" force that for religious and political reasons made constitutional resistance to the prince an imperative for every Württemberger.[32]

The sequence of events leading up to this change is easy to sketch.[33] In 1733, Duke Eberhard Louis, a Protestant who had ruled for some forty years, died without having fathered an heir. Consequently, Karl Alexander, a cousin, and a man who had converted to Catholicism in 1712 and married a Catholic in 1727, assumed control of the government in Old-Württemberg. Needless to say, the presence of a Catholic on the throne of a state that for almost two centuries had been a Protestant enclave in southwest Germany alarmed Württemberg's thoroughly Protestant population.[34] What, they must have wondered, was to prevent Karl Alexander from exiling them as had happened to Protestants in Salzburg in 1731?[35]

And so, as the exiles from Salzburg began to wander through Württemberg in 1731, it was only natural that a religious dimension was added to the long-standing constitutional conflict between the ducal house and the *Landschaft*. Henceforth, the constitutional ideal of the dualistic *Ständestaat*, which had its roots in medieval corporatism, would merge with the kind of dualistic political outlook that had characterized monarchomach resistance theory in the sixteenth century.[36] The result was a much more complex constitutional arrangement than the idea of dualism might suggest.[37]

Indeed, when Württemberg Protestants realized how vulnerable they were, they set out to do something about it. As a result, significant changes took place in their political outlook. In the first place, the religious change in the ducal house considerably altered Württemberg's relation to the other states in the Holy Roman Empire.[38] Henceforth, Württemberg Protestants, whether politically motivated or not, would be unusually sensitive to the duke's foreign policy maneuvers, and especially to any overtures he might make to France or Austria (both Catholic) about military alliances. Conversely, Protestants would have to be more cognizant of efforts to undermine the power of Prussia within the Empire. Now, more than ever before, Württemberg Protestants would have to rely on Prussian influence within the Empire to preserve and guarantee their religious freedom (a fact that explains how Württemberg Protestants could herald eighteenth-century Prussian princes as preservers of freedom at a time when Lessing and Herder were voicing sharp criticism of them in other matters). Moreover, Württemberg's dependence on the mediative powers of other Protestant states within the Empire was all the more important because, with the change in the religion of the ducal house, Württemberg had lost influence in the *corpus evangelicorum*, an important administrative unit of the Empire that mediated disputes between Protestants and Catholics.

But in the late 1720s – in anticipation of Karl Alexander's accession and the consequent loss of their influence in the Empire – Württembergers had worked in the councils of the Empire to secure their future religious integrity. As a result, when Karl Alexander took power, something of an accord had been established (or so the *Landschaft* thought) between the Estates, the new duke, and the Empire, and that accord expressed itself in the form of the *Religionsreversalien* of 1733–1734.[39] According to this agreement, in return for pledging loyalty to the new prince, Württemberg Protestants were to receive assurances that the Empire would guarantee their religious freedom. More concretely, the *Reversalien* gave the *Landschaft* the right to administer the revenues from church property that the duke usually controlled through the privy council. Henceforth, these revenues, which were considerable, would be incorporated into the fiscal jurisdiction of the Estates.[40] There, obviously, they could be used to bridle the duke were the situation to require it.

Despite the precautions the *Landschaft* had taken, and despite the terms of the *Religionsreversalien*, Karl Alexander moved quickly between 1733 and 1737 to advance the causes of absolutism and Catholicism in Old-Württemberg.[41] A Catholic, General von Remchingen, soon headed the army; the duke's closest adviser, Frederick Charles, another Catholic, held the position of bishop of Würzberg and Bamberg, and was also a proponent of princely absolutism; and Süss Oppenheimer, who had been charged with circumventing the authority of the *Landschaft* in fiscal matters, was similarly inclined toward absolutism.

Through the combined efforts of these men, Karl Alexander found himself in 1737 in a position not only to catholicize Württemberg – that is, to give Catholics parity of legal status with Protestants – but also to break the political power of the Estates. But in 1737, as he was about to realize these political and religious ambitions, Karl Alexander died – through an act of divine Providence, eschatologically minded Protestants claimed.[42] And since the heir to the throne, Karl Eugen, was only nine years old at the time, a regency was declared – one that afforded Protestants an opportunity to consolidate their position and to clarify the religious and political traditions upon which their opposition to Karl Alexander had been based.[43] To do this, they recurred to history, to Württemberg's history since the Reformation, and to the role the "ancient constitution" had played in that history.[44] Since the days of Hotman the idea of the ancient constitution had been fundamental to the politics of European Protestants.[45] Thus, an appreciation of the case Württembergers made for their own "ancient constitution" should be politically and religiously illuminating.

2. Württemberg's "ancient constitution": A myth of politicoreligious concern[46]

What the foregoing means to suggest, of course, is that the impulse toward Protestant civil piety was very strong in Old-Württemberg after

1733.[47] Clearly, the boundaries between religious regeneration for the sake of the collective salvation of a godly people and political resistance for the sake of the Good Old Law were blurring. That convergence, in turn, posed something of a problem for the identity of pietist and *Altrechtler*. For the former, the issue was how to engage in practical politics without compromising religious values, how to become down to earth without succumbing to the temptations of this world. For the latter, conversely, the problem was how to define civil virtue and political duty in broad religious terms without actually allowing the values of the religious collectivity to dominate the political decision-making process.

Despite these problems, a commingling of religio-political interest took place, one that the close friendship between Bengel (the pietist) and Moser (the *Altrechtler*) testifies to in no uncertain terms.[48] Driven by the fear that Karl Alexander might take the kind of measures against Württemberg Protestants that Catholic authorities had taken against Protestants in Salzburg in 1731, pietist and *Altrechtler* found grounds for cooperation both in their mutual suspicions about the duke's intentions and in their dependence on the Estates as an institutional body that would preserve their interests against the duke were it ever to come to that.

Pulled together by the accession of 1733, Württemberg's religious and political leaders found some ideological justification for their alliance in the idea of the "ancient constitution," a key component of Protestant resistance theory since the sixteenth century.[49] As an ideal this idea simultaneously provided pietists with a religious reference for their conception of Protestant liberty and *Altrechtlern* with a legal basis for the Estates' resistance to the duke. Indeed, what came to be known as *Landschaft* patriotism in the eighteenth century had its roots (as we shall see) in this ideal,[50] an ideal that allowed Württembergers to combine aspects of covenant theology and legal traditionalism is one mode of constitutional thought.

To understand how this constitutional ideal functioned,[51] we need to recall the "origin time" of Württemberg's ancient constitution.[52] At the same time, we need to distinguish between appeals that were made to the constitution on traditional legal grounds and ones that were made to it on the basis of reformatory religious values. As will become apparent, the distinction is crucial in that it permits us to explain a political division that developed within the Estates itself after 1770; namely, one that turned on the issue of whether the constituent power of Württemberg Protestants rested in the hands of the collectivity qua a "godly people" or in the membership of the *Landschaft* qua a representative legal body.[53] Suffice it to say here that the distinction is quite important. In the first case the constitution remains religious in that it is assimilated to the idea of a covenanting community in which the people are alleged to have a single religious conscience that is quite distinct from the *Landschaft*. In the second case, the idea of a godly people is integrated into a constitutional structure in which judgments about the collective interests are matters internal to the *Landschaft* itself.

But before the political contours of that division can properly be drawn, we need to examine the argument for the ancient constitution itself. The place to begin our account is with the Tübingen Treaty of 1514. Looking back from the 1730s, it was easy to envisage that treaty as the beginning of a sequence of events that culminated in the 1550s in the agreement between the prelates and the *Ehrbarkeit* to sit together in one *curia*, the *Landschaft*.[54] Citing the developments of these years as normative for the present, the *Altrechtlern* insisted on holding the duke to the terms of the ancient constitutional tradition.[55] To that end, they elaborated a view of Württemberg's history in which the Estates, as a legally constituted corporate body, upheld the Good Old Laws of the land. Within that tradition, of course, there was room for princely prerogative. If, however, in the exercise of this prerogative the prince intruded on the jurisdiction of the Estates, tried to evade its authority, or violated the "fundamental" laws of the land, the Estates was legally justified to resist him, by force if necessary.[56]

Here the *Altrechtlern* had made a case for the legal rights of the Estates based on a custom of uninterrupted historical usage. Their brief was that the treaty of 1514, and its subsequent acceptance by members of Württemberg's ruling family, had guaranteed the Estates certain rights (e.g., with regard to finance) by which every duke had to abide. The *Altrechtlern*'s strategy, obviously, was to derive legitimacy for the Estates by making the ancient constitution normative for the present. In that way they hoped to remain coequal partners of the duke in the exercise of sovereignty – which meant that they envisaged a constitutional arrangement in which the *Landschaft* and the duke shared sovereignty by exercising it independently of one another in clearly delineated jurisdictional areas. Either way the constitutional result was the same: a dualistic polity in which the Good Old Law functioned in a very defensive and traditional way as a check on princely ambition.[57]

The thoroughly static character of this conception of Württemberg's ancient constitution might lead one to believe that this constitutional ideal had its legal roots in theories of late medieval corporatism. To draw this conclusion, though, would be to miss the importance of monarchomach resistance theory in Protestant constitutional thought from the 1560s on.[58] To appreciate the issue here we need only note the role the doctrine of double sovereignty played in the political history of Württemberg in the seventeenth century.[59] Christopher Besold, whom we have seen was Andreae's friend at Tübingen, was one of the first to articulate the doctrine and is, therefore, a crucial figure in its development.[60]

According to Besold, the duke and the Estates were coeval partners within a larger commonwealth within which "real majesty" or "sovereignty" resided. Real sovereignty, in turn, was linked by Besold with the "fundamental laws" of the land. Those laws, Besold argued, set limits to the duke's exercise of "personal sovereignty" and thus provided the commonwealth with protection against tyranny. Besold's point, of course, was that the Estates, as the guardian of the laws of the land, represented the real majesty of the commonwealth over and against the "personal majesty" of the duke. So, while on the surface the doctrine of double sovereignty seemed to be tailored to the needs of the dualistic *Ständestaat*, in substance it endowed the *Landschaft* with the kind of constituent power that proponents of the "mixed constitution" subsequently would allot to Estates and parliaments in several seventeenth-century Protestant countries.[61]

As an explanation of where sovereignty legally resided in a commonwealth the double sovereignty doctrine obviously worked best in situations where incidents of conflict between the duke and the Estates were minimal. But in crisis situations, when conflicts were likely to arise over the exercise of sovereignty, the doctrine provided little hope for mediated settlements. The exception to that rule, of course, was when the collectivity itself, as distinct from its established representatives, could be brought into the decision-making process by way of some galvanizing public issue. As a general rule recourse to the people was not an attractive option for either the duke or the Estates. But if points of dispute between the two parties could be defined in religious terms, appeal to the collectivity qua godly people was much more appealing. Hence, the political importance of religion in Württemberg after 1733.[62]

This point, I think, is rather important. It makes perfectly clear why the *Altrechtlern* found pietist arguments about activism, collectivism, and the need for a Second Reformation so congenial. How convenient for these *Landschaft* patriots that the case for "liberty" in Württemberg could be defined in opposition to "Roman" tyranny, in political and religious senses, and to the "foreigners" who had been appointed by Karl Alexander to key administrative positions in his government.[63] How convenient for these patriots that the matter of Protestant rights permitted them to broaden the basis of their support at a time when the *Landschaft* was being politically pressed by the duke. How convenient for them that reiteration of the argument for the Good Old Law as the "fundamental" law of the land could be presented in the form of an argument for preserving the Reformation as an ongoing force in Württemberg's history. How convenient, in short, that the legal appeal to "tradition," to Württemberg's ancient constitution, could be invested with "traditionalist" and reformist implications for Württemberg's religious future.[64]

It is in the context of considerations such as these that we need to take notice of just how Protestant religious conceptions worked their way into Württembergers' understanding of their ancient constitution. Again, the historical backdrop to this dimension of Württemberg's understanding of its own history has its origin in the early sixteenth century. Indeed, as we have seen, from that time on Württemberg Protestants conceived of themselves as a chosen people whose charge it was to preserve and expand the Reformation as a religious force in history.[65] We can appreciate their exaggerated sense of their own importance for the history of Protestantism when we recall the political and religious circumstances under which the Reformation was introduced into Württemberg.[66] The sequence of events is familiar enough: in May 1534, after almost fifteen years of exile, Duke Ulrich, with the military assistance of his cousin, Philip of Hesse, succeeded in driving "foreign" Hapsburg forces out of Württemberg. Within a matter of days, Ulrich made it clear to everyone that he intended to make Protestantism the official state religion.[67]

Now anyone reading the history of these years in the light of the events of 1733–1737 would be inclined to see the events of 1534–1535 – that is, the liberation of Württemberg from Roman tyranny and from foreign domination, the subsequent introduction of the Reformation into Württemberg, and Ulrich's confirmation of the inviolability of the Tübingen Treaty – as archetypal for what Protestants should be doing in the 1730s.[68] That, of course, is why the accession of 1733 was truly apocalyptic for Württemberg Protestants: once again they could see themselves as a godly people whose task it was to preserve and carry the standard of Christian liberty in a predominantly Catholic area of southwest Germany.

As we have seen, the *Altrechtlern* interpreted these events slightly differently. They approached the matter of Württemberg's ancient constitution from an historico-legal perspective that emphasized the way the formal aspects of the treaty of 1514 had restricted princely authority. Their views pointed in the direction of the sort of contractual theory of government that many Protestants had developed to cope with the increasing power of secular authorities in the sixteenth century. But there was more; for like the monarchomach theorists, many Württemberg Protestants insisted that the historical terms of this contract were binding only if they were consistent with the purposes and goals of a godly people, a people who had bound themselves together as a covenanting community. According to the terms of that covenant, prince and people were conjoined to uphold the ideal of godly rule, and the derogation of that duty on the part of either party constituted a breach of any contract that might otherwise obtain between them.[69] When that happened, as Württembergers thought it had in 1733, the people *sub specie religionis* were required not only to resist the agent of Antichrist, but also to organize themselves into a counterpolity within which preparatory work would then begin to reclaim the state from Antichrist in the name of a godly people and continuous reformation.[70]

On one level, this religiously informed conception of the ancient constitution and of the role a godly people played in its preservation had much in common with the political values of the legally minded *Altrechtlern*. Both sought constitutionally to limit the authority of the duke and both looked to the Estates as a rallying point for their cooperation and as the legitimate institutional base for their opposition to the duke. In one important respect, though, the legal and religious interpretations of Württemberg's ancient constitution were very different: where the one was traditional, defensive, and static, the other was traditionalist, reformist, and dynamic.[71] To put it another way, where the one would be content with preserving the status quo even if it meant permanent recognition of the duke, the other would be satisfied only after Württemberg had experienced a Second Reformation. Hence, the two faces of Protestant civil piety in Old-Württemberg;[72] hence, the conception of a constitutional arrangement that was backward looking in a socio-historico-legal sense and forward looking in a politico-eschatological-religious sense;[73] hence, finally, two different conceptions of liberty, one "law oriented" and quite "conservative" in a secular sense, the other participatory and "liberal" in a soteriological sense.[74]

3. The institutionalization of the tradition: 1733–1770[75]

For a time — say, from 1733 to 1770 — the two constitutional faces of Protestant civil piety in Old-Württemberg appeared as one, expressing the collective will of a single community whose representatives in the Estates legally safeguarded the religious rights of a Protestant people. The religio-political alliance that had organized itself in 1733 and had succeeded in securing the *Reversalien* of that year was confirmed repeatedly during this period:[76] in the early 1740s, when Charles VII, newly crowned head of the German Empire, vacillated on the matter of acquiescing in the settlement of 1733; in the 1750s, when Karl Eugen began to assert himself and exhibit absolutist tendencies, especially in the area of foreign policy; during the Seven Years' War, when prince and Estates split along confessional lines over the issue of whom to support in that conflict; and in the 1760s, when, once again, Karl Eugen contested the terms of the *Reversalien* of 1733. In each of these instances the interests of the people's representatives and those of the community itself proved to be equivalent, with the result that the unity of a Protestant people qua counterpolity was preserved.

To be more specific, pietists and *Altrechtlern* used these years, especially between 1737 and 1744, to reinforce their positions with Protestant forces within the Empire.[77] They did this by eliciting assurances from Protestant powers (e.g., England and Prussia) that they would continue to guarantee the 1733 agreement. Thus, in 1744, when Karl Eugen reached his majority, the *Landschaft* was in a position to hold him in check, at least for a while.

Within the framework of the existing constitution, then, it was difficult for a Catholic duke, especially one of sixteen years, to pursue absolutist or catholicizing policies. But pursue them Karl Eugen did, especially in the 1750s, when he began to show disdain for both the welfare of his subjects and the rights of the Estates.[78] Dissipation, self-indulgence, fiscal extravagance, and irresponsible behavior within the Empire soon became characteristic of his reign. Despite the fact that the regency had sent him to Berlin in 1741 for "schooling" in Prussian ways, little of the discipline, austerity, frugality, or dedication to the idea of state service that pervaded the Berlin court seems to have affected Karl Eugen's personality.[79] Like so many other German princes, he was always irresistibly drawn to French models and, as might be expected, he patterned his court after the Bourbons. But as was so often the case in the German principalities, the court at Stuttgart (later relocated to Ludwigsberg) was a caricature of Versailles; and its politics resembled those of Stendhal's Parma more than those of the great Sun King. The description Frederick the Great once offered of Karl Eugen might well be applied to all the "courtly cultures" in Germany: "Great only in small things and small in great ones."[80]

Although the issue between the duke and the Estates had been joined as early as 1752 – when Karl Eugen secured an independent income for himself by arranging a military treaty with Louis XV[81] – the tension between the two antagonists really culminated in the years 1763–1770.[82] At that time the fiscal burden of the Seven Years' War and the duke's repeated violations of the constitution weighed heavily on the land. Complacent as ever, Karl Eugen persisted in his "mania for building" and insisted on maintaining the "comic opera army" that had proved so inept during the recent war.[83] Needless to say, the *Landschaft* had resolved to hold the line against the duke, especially against his plan (proposed early in 1764) for the imposition of a "poll tax," the proceeds of which were to finance projects designated solely by him. So in June 1764 the *Landschaft* appealed to the Empire, specifically to the Aulic Council, to mediate the dispute with Karl Eugen.[84]

Through a series of rulings in 1764, 1765, and 1770, the Aulic Council, with strong Prussian promptings, arranged yet another constitutional settlement in Old-Württemberg.[85] The keystone of this arrangement was embodied in the *Erbvergleich* of 1770, the terms of which affirmed what some 250 years of history had already confirmed; namely, that constitutionally the Estates was an equal partner with the duke in managing the affairs of Old-Württemberg.

For all its success, however, the *Landschaft* after 1770 was becoming increasingly divided within itself. Granted, the *Erbvergleich* was a great victory for the *Landschaft*, but it was a "defensive" one that, while legally confirming the constitutional status quo, also testified to the primacy of the Small Council in determining *Landschaft* policy.[86] In that context, a split began to develop among Württembergers with regard to the purpose and direction of their collective life.[87] For its part the Small Council seemed content with constitutional dualism and with the negative politics that went along with it. And for this, the continuous and fixed opposition of an adversary prince was necessary. Other Württembergers, though, read the mandate of 1770 differently. Enforcing the contractual relations between a prince and the people was all very well, but there was more to *Landschaft* patriotism than that. For many Württembergers the victory of 1770 signaled an opportunity for Christian activism, for getting on with the business of the Second Reformation. For this, more positive political action was necessary, the kind of participatory action that Beza and Mornay had deemed appropriate for Calvinists in the late sixteenth century.[88]

Indeed, within the counterpolity formed by the *Landschaft*–godly people convergence, there was a group that sought to promote a more politically focused kind of Protestant activism. This group, which we shall examine shortly, drew a distinction between what might be called the "civil" and the "moral" character of a Protestant people.[89] The basis for this distinction was rooted in the belief that the legitimacy of the Small Council derived less from legal prescriptions than from a religious authority that came to it from God through the mediation of a godly people.[90] That meant that while the Council's "civil" authority – that which pertained to individuals – could be talked about in legal terms, its "moral" authority – that which derived from the collectivity understood as an entity distinct from the Estates – could only be discussed in terms of the religious goals of a covenanting people.[91]

After 1770, in other words, the political divisions in Old-Württemberg were no longer framed in terms of a simple constitutional dualism between prince and *Landschaft*. A third force had emerged on the scene – if not in reality, then at least as a conceptual possibility within the minds of those who regarded the interests of the Small Council and the ambitions of the duke as detrimental to the religious concerns of the community as a whole. For this group, the idea of citizenship among a truly Protestant people was meant to express the collective religious concerns of a covenanting people more than guarantee the civil and legal rights of particular groups or individuals. In keeping with this conviction, the politics of this group was more activist than passive; and that was because the imperative of a Protestant *Lebens-Reformation* sanctioned political activism as a necessary "moment" in the process of collective salvation.[92]

Here, obviously, the idea of constitutionalism had been assimilated to the Württembergers' conception of themselves as a godly people, as a people who had covenanted together to make the Reformation an expanding force in history. If that was their mission, they had argued, a *Lebens-Reformation* would have to take place, one that would be gradualist and would have religious recollectivization as its end. Viewed in this way, constitutionalism epitomized the collective will and eschatological hope of a Protestant people. On the one hand, it testified to Württemberg's involvement in sacred history, to its struggle against Antichrist and his agents. Hence, the negative political orientation of the counterpolity qua the *ecclesia* of a godly people. On the other hand, there was the more positive, reformist commitment to continuous reformation, to a process in which politics could be envisaged as an expression, extension, and revelation of the corporate covenant of a Protestant people. Hence, the activism that invested politics with the terms of collective religious significance and that made this worldly activity a crucial part in a people's attempt to assimilate to God.[93]

Several important consequences follow from this religiously inspired conception of the purpose and direction of collective life. First, insofar as *homo religiosus* is dedicated to *praxis pietatis* his concern with activism carries over into politics, first in the creation of a counterpolity and then in the gradual expansion of that polity into an all-encompassing godly one.[94] Expansion, of course, entailed the exercise of "will" as an "instrument" of activism.[95] In that sense, this particular conception of *homo religiosus* is quite Pelagian in that the object of will is not self-salvation so much as service to the collectivity for the sake of religious recollectivization.

There is, therefore, nothing "subjective" about this conception of will, for among these Protestants the expression of one's will was restricted to activity within a calling.[96] One's calling, in turn, was defined in terms that required the individual voluntarily to "die into life" and, thereby, to live for the collectivity. In other words, the idea of self-denial that was associated with *praxis pietatis* in a religious sense could easily be translated into asceticism in a political sense.[97] Either way, sacrifice of one's interests for the sake of service to the collectivity was imperative. That, too, is Pelagian, and testifies to the meaningful relatedness of religious and political values in Old-Württemberg in the eighteenth century.

To ensure this kind of commitment, moreover, people had to be allowed to participate in the processes that governed their lives.[98] Hence, the idea of Protestant civil piety as animated by an ethic of participatory virtue and as informed by a sense of trust and fellowship that made politics a vocation and "continuous labor" of a Protestant people.[99] Put another way, actualization of the eschatological hope of a covenanting people involved assimilation of individuals to a self-realizing teleological process that had collective religious salvation as its end.[100]

In keeping with their skepticism about individual perfectionism, however, Württembergers believed that the individual's capacity for virtue was limited. But even though individuals were forced to work through specific institutional structures, each individual could learn to subsume his identity in the collectivity, with the result that each would rise to a higher level of personal awareness by belonging to a collectivity of enhanced self-consciousness. The recollectivization of conscience, in other words, entailed more than asceticism and individual sacrifice: it involved self-realization as well.[101] In Peter Berger's terms, it involved a commitment to a religiopolitical ethic of "self-transcending participation."[102]

No doubt the idea of self-transcending participation smacks of mysticism but, as was noted earlier, this is a mysticism with a practical, this-worldly activist face.[103] And if this species of mysticism is not escapist, it is not characterized by automatism either. Rather, it is voluntarist and only operates in the context of a collective commitment to action. Thus, the affinity between a politics of participatory virtue and an eschatology that has religious recollectivism as its end. Thus, the possibility that the political concerns of Württemberg Protestants had less to do with the recovery of classical political thought than with the extension of the principles of covenant theology to political matters.

4. The "petrification" of a tradition: 1770–1793[104]

In discussing the importance of the culture of Old-Württemberg as a context for the development of Hegel's thought scholars often fail to take adequate note of the post-1770 ideological split within the ranks of the constitutionalist opposition to Karl Eugen.[105] Hence, they tend to attribute more homogeneity of outlook to the *Ehrbarkeit* than was present. Indeed, as we have seen, there were two modes of consciousness within the constitutionalist camp, and they existed simultaneously rather than successively in time.

Basically, the split in outlook can be explained in terms of some quite obvious constitutional considerations. First of all, it was neither practical nor customary for the *Landschaft* to meet as a diet, in plenary session, on a regular basis. In truth, between 1700 and 1770 the *Landschaft* was seldom in session – which meant that its policy and administrative functions were performed by the Small Council on a day-to-day basis.[106] This was especially true between 1739 asnd 1763, when the *Landschaft* did not meet as a diet at all.[107] What is more, there is evidence to suggest that the members of the Small Council (eight in all) thrived on that arrangement.[108] More to the point, they exploited the situation for their own advantage, with the result that from the 1750s on the Small Council could be said to have constituted itself as an oligarchy within the framework of the constitution.[109]

J. J. Moser, for one, saw the danger inherent in this situation.[110] As he saw it, and stated in his "Promemoria" of 1770, government *by* a Small Council, which was composed of lifetime members who were selected by surviving members, would invariably result in government *for* the Small Council and would lead to the monopolization of the Council by members of a few powerful families.[111] Moser, of course, knew these families well. As first counsel to the Small Council he had worked against their interests in the 1750s.[112] At the time, though, his only ally on the Council was Bengel,[113] and the latter's death in 1752 left Moser in a very isolated position vis-à-vis the other members of the Council and their main counselor, J. Stockmayer.[114]

In the face of the Council's oligarchic tendency, Moser warned the *Landschaft* in 1770 that it would lose its institutional credibility and compromise the values of the tradition for which it stood unless it delimited the authority of the Small Council.[115] Without such a delimitation, Moser argued, the *Landschaft* would become "an empty name" and merely a tool of the Small Council.[116] Despite Moser's pleadings, however, the *Landschaft* remained in the control of the Council, with the result that the oligarchy was able to rule behind a constitutional facade, a facade that after 1770 made the *Alte Recht* tradition less a tradition than an ideological fiction the Council very much wanted to perpetuate for the sake of self-justification.

With the ascendancy of the Small Council, the ideological dynamic of constitutionalist thought in Old-Württemberg arrived at a crucial historical juncture. The problem was that the identification of Württemberg's ancient constitution with the institution of the Small Council and with the authority of the few families in it had narrowed rather than enlarged the political focus of *Landschaft* patriotism.[117] In Weber's terms, the institutionalization of the idea of the ancient constitution had resulted in its becoming "frozen in traditionalism."[118] It had become an objective fact, fixed in its meaning, and required no further conceptualization to function as a cultural ideal.[119]

For Moser, this very institutional and legalistic reading of the ancient constitution represented what today's students of the idea of tradition would call an "abridgment" of tradition into an ideology of unreflective prescription.[120] That is, Moser regarded the Small Council's under-standing of its representative function as excessively narrow, *"dumm-patriotisch"* as he once put it.[121] There was more to tradition, he argued, than "just" hanging "onto received opinions."[122] If that were the only stuff of traditions, they would never change, and change they must in order to survive. That implied, of course, that traditions periodically had to be reconceptualized, had creatively to be restated in terms that would allow them to be adapted to the exigencies of new situations.[123] Such adaptations, Moser insisted, did not abridge traditions so much as enlarge them.[124] Thus, when Moser began to raise questions in the 1770s about the representativeness of the Small Council, he did so from a vantage point that stressed the ancient constitution's expansive rather than restrictive qualities.[125]

To correct this imbalance, this abridgment of tradition into an ideology of traditionalism, Moser began to remind Württembergers of the expansive, religious aspect of their ancient constitution.[126] He did this indirectly – by introducing to the *Landschaft*–Small Council dispute an external consideration; namely, the role that the *corpus evangelicorum*, an imperial institution that was created to assure Protestants of their legal rights in the Empire, could play in the internal affairs of Württemberg.[127] In the mid-1760s Moser had turned to this institution to defend Protestant rights against a usurping Catholic prince.[128] Now, in the 1770s, he appealed to the same institution to ensure that the Small Council would truly "represent" the interests of a Protestant people.[129] Imperial institutions, he argued, could guarantee these interests simply by insisting on the people's right to communicate to the Council continuously through their diet.[130] That assumed the diet would be in constant session, and that, obviously, is where Moser and the Council parted company.

What is vital to appreciate here is that Moser's appeal to the *corpus evangelicorum* was designed less to subordinate Württemberg to the authority of the imperial institutions than to reestablish the idea of the *moral* authority of the covenanting community as the ultimate source of *civil* authority in Württemberg.[131] As Moser saw it, a diet in session was like the "temple of God": *vox Populi, vox Dei,* he had written.[132] According to Moser, that simply meant that legal rights in "civil society" ultimately required religious sanction (i.e., "contracts" would only be honored among a trusting, covenanting people).[133] If that sanction were lacking, anarchy would be sure to undermine any constitutional arrangement, however secure its legal foundation.

Here, to be sure, the *corpus evangelicorum* figured prominently in Moser's thought.[134] Not only did it provide imperial guarantees for the defense of the *Landschaft* against the threat of Catholic encroachments, but it also proved useful in reminding Württembergers that confessional issues could still play a role in their constitutional considerations.[135] In that context, Moser meant to reintroduce religious considerations to the constitutional debate about just what it was that the *Landschaft* was supposed to represent when it acted as the agent of a Protestant people.[136] That is, he meant to recover the religious dimensions of Württemberg's ancient constitution and, by so doing, make the ideal of Protestant civil piety once again the measure of the Small Council's authority.[137] For that shift in priority to happen, though, Württembergers had once again to conceive of themselves as a covenanting, godly people, as a Protestant people with a reformatory religious mission. Promotion of that self-conception had been Bengel's principal concern when he served on the Small Council with Moser in the early 1750s,[138] and it certainly constituted the substance of Moser's criticism of the Small Council in the 1770s. To that end, Bengel and Moser had defined what was best for Württemberg (*das gemeine Beste*) in terms of a religious collectivism that was at once defensive vis-à-vis a Catholic prince and reformist with regard to the internal dynamic of its own constitutional position.[139] From what has been said in the last two chapters about Joachimism, evolutionary eschatology, covenant theology, and the sociopolitical dynamics of the theology of the divine economy, it should not be hard to see how and why the interests of Bengel and Moser converged.

After 1770, then, Württemberg Protestants had recourse to two different modes of constitutional awareness. In N. Frye's terms, one offered a "closed," the other an "open," conception of the "myth" of Württemberg's ancient constitution.[140] In the first case, the emphasis was placed on the rule of law and on the contract by which the people's representatives were given responsibility for safeguarding the collective interest against the prince. The stress, obviously, was on preserving the equilibrium between *Landschaft* and prince within the existing constitutional framework. Hence, the Small Council's reluctance to disturb the status quo went so far as to include acceptance of the duke as a permanent constitutional fixture. In the second case, recognition of the need to adapt the ancient constitution continually in order to preserve it yielded a more reformist conception of the meaning of Württemberg's constitutional tradition. More open to the future, it regarded the constitution in relative terms – as "immemorial custom in perpetual adaptation."[141] This, clearly, was Moser's view. Unwilling merely to reiterate the doctrine of a fixed and unchanging constitutional dualism, he gave the ancient constitution a reformist face by endowing it with the activism and collectivism of eschatological hope.

Looking backward and forward, to the ancient constitution of the past and to the eschatological hope of the future,[142] Moser offered Württembergers a program for constitutional reform that was informed by the same value complex that governed Bengel's understanding of the theology of the divine economy. To sum up the convergence in another way, the impulses toward constitutional reform and *praxis pietatis* were both powered by an eschatological hope in which the resacralization of politics was to be a consequence of the historicization of grace among a Protestant people. Thus, for *Altrechtler* and pietist there was an intimate connection between the idea of the political as an object of collective activism and the idea of the political as a moment in collective salvation. Therefore, ethical activism and political participation had redemptive religious value for reform-minded Protestants in Old-Württemberg at the end of the eighteenth century. When we realize that, it becomes easier to understand how Hegel in the 1790s could talk about man (i.e., *homo religiosus*) in terms of an eschatology that required active human participation (in a politico-teleological sense) to move it forward.

5. Enter Hegel

Given the importance of confessional issues in Württemberg politics in the eighteenth century, one might assume that Württembergers responded enthusiastically to Moser's constitutional promptings. Envisaging the constitution as a vehicle both of reformatory religious values and of collective salvation should have appealed to many Protestants. By the same token, the notion of the constitution as an instrument of participatory virtue should have attracted support from progressive political groups.[143] However, that was not the case, for two important reasons.

As we noted earlier, pietists and *Altrechtlern* – indeed, the entire *Ehrbarkeit* or *ehrbaren Bürgerstand* (the scribes, clerics, local officials, educators, and businessmen who peopled the *Landschaft* and constituted the "urban" group from which recruits for the court and councils of the Estates and ranks of the *Altrechtlern* were drawn) – shared a common ethos and practical "likemindedness" that included a consensus on many cultural ideals.[144] One of these ideals was education. For the *Ehrbarkeit*, the purpose of education was to make men better Christians – to make them ethically more active and to foster in them a sense of civil responsibility and belonging. Under the conditions of the day, this meant inculcating in the community a political commitment to the preservation and defense of the constitutional rights of the Estates against the prince and a religious commitment to *praxis pietatis* and to the pursuit of the Second Reformation.

Toward the end of the century, however, this cultural commitment, as it was reflected in the interests of the *Ehrbarkeit*, was showing some signs of strain.[145] In the 1750s, 1760s, and 1770s events had conspired to put great social and economic pressure on the unity of the *Ehrbarkeit*. A dramatic increase in population, a deteriorating economic situation, the fiscal extravagance of the prince, the economic pressure of the Seven Years' War, and the obstructionist economic policies of the Estates all mitigated upward socioeconomic mobility within the *Ehrbarkeit* and served to stifle "development" within Old-Württemberg as a whole.

One of the results of these changes was that social divisions began to appear in the once solid phalanx of the *Ehrbarkeit* – divisions that were also manifest in scrambled political loyalties within the *Landschaft* and among the *Altrechtlern*. Indeed, competition for fewer career opportunities created tensions between the upper and lower orders of the *Ehrbarkeit*, between the *Honoratorienstand* and everybody else – the *"niederen Bürgerstand,"* or, as it came to be called in the 1790s, the *"gemeinen Leuten."*[146] The problem was that the existing institutions of education – the Latin and cloister schools and the *Gymnasium* in Stuttgart – were designed to serve the needs of the *Honoratoren* first. For most of the eighteenth century, the education offered by these institutions provided students – generally the sons of the *Honoratoren* – with the requisite credentials for careers in the school system, the church, or the government bureaucracy.

In times of prosperity these same institutions also provided opportunities for sons of the lower clergy, teachers, minor functionaries, and retired military. But by the end of the century, the avenue to such careers was becoming increasingly restricted to members of the *Honoratorienstand*.[147] Even then, however, not everyone in that group could be accommodated. As contemporary accounts attest, there was avid interest within the *Honoratorienstand* itself over who would prevail in the fierce competition for positions in the "right" schools.[148] At any rate, by the 1790s the contracting socioeconomic situation threatened to divide the *Ehrbarkeit* internally. Unless an alternative to the declining fortunes of its lower orders could be found, the prospects for a continuation of the "united front" of the *Ehrbarkeit* against the prince seemed doubtful. And without that front Protestant civil commitments would have to change.

To complicate the situation still further, the *Erhbarkeit* had to contend with the political wheeling and dealing of the prince, Karl Eugen. Drawing on French and Prussian "models," Karl Eugen resolved in the 1760s to establish a school, ostensibly for the training of military officers, whose organization and curriculum manifested in its educational ideal all the characteristics of an Eastern European version of a "Western-style Enlightenment."[149] That is, the school sought to inculcate in its students and to pursue in its curriculum a utilitarian appreciation of the ethic of enlightened self-interest. With this the state established the basis for a convergence of interests between its own desire for trained state servants and the desire of those seeking opportunities for individual social mobility.[150]

Initially the school, the so-called *Karlsschule*, was designed to equip officer candidates with the most current forms of "hard," "scientific" knowledge.[151] To this end, the school's curriculum put an emphasis on aspects of military preparedness other than simple proficiency in drill. Mastery of such skills as fortification, use of artillery, strategies for the deployment of troops, and tactics were all stressed. In addition, students were expected to develop a firm grounding in mathematics, modern languages, and philosophy. And in keeping with the school's practical goals, the accent in the curriculum was on the teaching of subjects that had utility for the state.

As the school grew, however, it became clear that this institution, which was largely under the prince's control, could be used as a training ground not only for the military, but for the bureaucracy as well. With this in mind, the study of law and medicine, as well as of subjects associated with the "science" of cameralism, soon became commonplace in the school. A recruiting ground for civil servants who would be more indebted to the prince for their education and employment than to the *Ehrbarkeit* and Estates was in the process of formation. In effect, the founding of the *Karlsschule* coincided with the emergence of a social crisis within the *Ehrbarkeit*, with the result that the prince threatened to lure a portion of the *Ehrbarkeit* into state service in numbers far exceeding previous levels of recruitment.

But if the timing of the penetrations of the Enlightenment into Old-Württemberg was propitious in one sense, its association with the political force of absolutism made it difficult for Württembergers blithely to choose between the educational ideals of the German *Aufklärung* proper – with its traditional religio-political connection with the Estates – and those of the Enlightenment – with its "statist" and Western utilitarian overtones.[152] The problems were manifold: to side politically with the prince in this matter threatened the Estates, the guardian of Württemberg's constitutional liberties; and without those liberties there was little hope for the reconstitution of a godly polity in Old-Württemberg. To side with the Small Council, however, committed one to an educational ideal that in many respects lacked relevance for the modern world; and that was not acceptable because it did not square with the social aspirations of a large and increasingly vocal part of the *Ehrbarkeit*.

Thus, when the *Karlsschule* became an institutional reality in the 1770s it posed a challenge to the Estates – indeed, to the ethos of Protestant civil piety in Old-Württemberg. Church authorities felt threatened by the tenor of the program at the *Karlsschule*.[153] Besides a pseudoconfessional orientation that was in fact secular, too much philosophy was being taught, and by teachers who were responsible to the prince, not the church. For their part, the *Altrechtlern* had grave reservations about the school because, as a training ground for civil servants, it provided the prince with recruits who would be loyal to him instead of to the Estates.[154]

Given these circumstances, it is easy to see how the *Karlsschule* became a focal point for political discontent among the orders of the *Ehrbarkeit* and between the Estates and the prince. Aside from the obvious problem of political power, disagreements arose over the issue of what a "civil" education should consist in: was it to serve the collective interest in a religious sense or the interests of individuals and the state in a utilitarian sense?[155] Concurrently, the *Ehrbarkeit* were at odds over whether to offer piecemeal political support for the progressive aspects of state policy or to resist them totally for fear of promoting the interests of absolutism over those of the *Landschaft*.

Tensions such as these had important generational implications too. By the 1790s, the politicoreligious assumption around which the Protestant culture of Old-Württemberg had been organized was coming unglued and was in need of reconstitution. On the one hand, increasingly "enlightened" initiatives were coming from the state, from the prince in the case of the *Karlsschule*, and from the bureaucracy in much else. These initiatives, Hegel's generation must have felt, had to be considered on their intrinsic merits: they should not be dismissed en bloc because they originated in the ambitions of a prince with absolutist intentions.[156] Nor should the Estates command the unquestioning loyalties of the citizenry, for it was apparent, especially to the young, that the oligarchic families who controlled the Small Council were using the *Alte Recht* tradition as a rationale for not disturbing the status quo. As a result, respect for constitutional moderation and balance now meant giving sanction to a crude traditionalism – to the claim that what is, is right.

From that standpoint, Moser in the 1770s and others like him in the 1790s felt the need to articulate a view of contemporary affairs that would introduce an element of dynamic reformism into Old-Württemberg.[157] As they saw it, the *Alte Recht* tradition had to change in order to remain the same. For them, however, that did not mean assuming a posture of *Realpolitik* and acquiescing in the wishes of the prince. No reform movement could triumph in Württemberg that broke with the *Landschaft*, especially if the break involved a question of religious propriety. Nor was traditionalism, of the sort adhered to by the Small Council, much of an answer to the problems of the time. Indeed, rivalries for political power had taught some Württembergers that the state's politics was on the verge of degenerating into simple matters of private interest: those of the Estates versus those of the prince; of the Small Council versus the Estates; of Protestants against Catholics; of orthodox Protestants against reform Protestants; and, within the *Ehrbarkeit*, of the *Honoratoren* against the others.[158] The spectacle of groups competing for power and socioeconomic advantage, each claiming "patriotic" motives for programs that differed widely, convinced some that they had to put forward a new and powerful ideal of community that recalled man to public action and civil participation. Indeed, a new ideological consensus had to be established, a new basis for Protestant civil piety had to be found.

Putting the matter this way is to raise the question of how Protestant civil piety could have been reconstituted in Old-Württemberg as a cultural ideal in the 1780s and 1790s. Hegel, I think, confronted this question squarely in the early 1790s. The problem, of course, was that he had no institutional foundation upon which to develop his views. Neither the *Landschaft* nor the ducal government recommended itself as an appropriate tool for reform and reconstitution. This, it seems to me, is a crucial factor in understanding how Old-Württemberg, as a cultural context, relates to the development of Hegel's thought. Recognition of the *stasis* of existing institutions in Old-Württemberg ruled out the possibility of effecting reform through established channels. This, in turn, forced reform-minded Württembergers to take the position that the well-being of a society's religious and political institutions depends on the "spirit" of the people who stand behind them.[159]

There is nothing particularly mystical or German about this sort of appeal. As Pocock has observed, "the idea that peoples or their institutions possess a 'spirit,' or *historical character*, which may be understood by relating it to just such things as the 'manners, the religion and commerce of the people'" had been an eighteenth-century commonplace at least since Montesquieu.[160] However, when we notice different thinkers citing different factors or combinations of factors as decisive for the historical constitution of a people, it becomes possible to differentiate these thinkers according to the ways they proposed to *ground* "spirit" in reality.

Among Scottish thinkers, for example, it was understood that a focus that combined a concern with political economy with a concern with sociological realism would yield an accurate picture of how general social factors shaped the spirit of a people.[161] And since legitimation of that focus had to be historically grounded too, they developed an elaborate "four-stage" view of history to go along with it. Among the *Aufklärer* in general and Württemberg Protestants in particular, the idea of a people's spirit was handled differently. For them, the historical character of a Protestant people was invariably linked to the idea of history as a field of opportunity for the spread of reformatory religious values[162] – that is, they associated spirit with *homo religiosus*, with the impulse toward the continuous expansion of religious consciousness in history, and with the collective efforts of a godly people to assimilate to God through activism in this world.[163] And to justify their conception of spirit's role in history, they fleshed out an evolutionary eschatology that also had implications for the periodization of secular history.

From what we have learned about the internal dynamic of evolutionary eschatology, we might also expect to find "will" becoming the focus of pedagogic concern among Württemberg Protestants. And from Moser to Spittler that is what we do find as a principal preoccupation of reformers in Old-Württemberg.[164] Decisive for them was the fact that expansion of religious consciousness was only possible on a collective historical level when *homo religiosus* acted, through a sheer exercise of moral will, to move history forward. By that, however, they did not mean to cast *homo religiosus* in a subjectivist mold. On the contrary, Moser and Spittler inveighed against esoteric forms of mysticism and religious subjectivism as too self-indulgent and undisciplined to be efficacious in a civil context.[165] Both recognized, moreover, that history set limits to the expansion of religious consciousness during any particular moment of its development.[166] Yet both also believed that key groups could educate the collectivity properly to the existing possibilities for spiritual action in any given historical situation.[167] They could awaken the people's spirit and give it a realistic focus and point it in a concrete historical direction. By so doing, they *might* persuade the people to try to realize themselves as a *Volksidee* in which the collectivity constituted itself as a godly people.[168]

Clearly, this line of argument met the ideological needs of reform-minded Württemberg Protestants in the late eighteenth century. On the one hand, it could draw on religious tradition – on the related ideas of *praxis pietatis*, the collectivism of a covenanting people, the need for a Second Reformation, and so on. On the other hand, it could justify its short-term and nonpolitical focus in terms of the inertia of Württemberg's present institutional arrangement. And, as was the case with Bengel, what permitted this kind of religio-political convergence was the idea of Protestant civil piety as the eschatological imperative of a godly people who, while having organized itself into an *ecclesia* in a socioreligious sense, still needed time to expand in a political sense.

These were the concerns of reform-minded Protestants in Württemberg during Hegel's youth, and, as we shall see, Hegel identified both with the concerns and with the men who were exercised by them.[169] Therein, I think, lies the key to an historical understanding of Hegel's development in the 1790s – an appropriate point of contextual departure for what follows in Parts II and III of this study. Suffice it to say here that we shall see in Part II how Hegel initially conceived of the problem of political reform and how his reformist impulse, which combined Christian and classical conceptions of activism, had an ascetic cast to it.[170] Then, in Part III, we shall see why, in the face of his economic studies, he began to abandon asceticism as a context for reform and how, for an elongated moment between 1796 and 1804, he struggled to make the case for the religious ideal of Protestant civil piety from a point internal to a conceptual framework that had been suggested to him by his readings in late eighteenth-century Scottish thought.[171] During these crucial years Hegel came to realize that *homo religiosus* would survive as a collective ideal among Protestants only if it were first grounded in the context of *homo oeconomicus*. It is Hegel's attempt to explain the emergence of the former out of the concerns of the latter that constitutes the focus of what I would like to call the "dramatic action" of his development between 1796 and 1804.[172]

PART II

◁ ══ ▷

Württemberg's Hegel
Applied theology and social analysis

However incisive the social influences, economically and politically determined, may have upon a religious ethic in a particular case, it receives its stamp primarily from religious sources, and, first of all, from the content of its annunciation and its promise. Frequently the very next generation reinterprets these annunciations and promises in a fundamental fashion. Such reinterpretations adjust the revelations to the needs of the religious community. If this occurs, then it is at least usual that religious doctrines are adjusted to *religious needs*.

In view of the tremendous confusion of independent influences between the material base, the forms of social and political organization, and the ideas current in the time of the Reformation, we can only proceed by investigating whether and at what points certain correlations between forms of religious belief and practical ethics can be worked out. At the same time, we shall as far as possible clarify the manner and the general *direction* in which, by virtue of those relationships, the religious movements have influenced the development of material culture.

Max Weber

In the Preface it was stated that Part I of this study would provide a "thick description" of the Protestant culture of Old-Württemberg in the eighteenth century.[1] In setting this agenda I had a particular aim in mind: to establish *a* context within which *historical* sense could be made of what Hegel was "doing" when he began to engage in serious intellectual work in the 1790s.[2]

Our sense of Old-Württemberg as a cultural context, of course, was relatively inclusive: it had what Ricoeur would call ostensive and nonostensive referential dimensions.[3] It was ostensive when it addressed the unique religious and political concerns of Württembergers in the eighteenth century. It was nonostensive at points where Württembergers availed themselves of traditions of Christian and Protestant discourse that, they thought, were relevant to their immediate religiopolitical

139

situation.[4] Thus, for example, our conception of Württemberg as a culture allowed for covenant theology to enter Württemberg from *without*, because it operated as a mode of eschatological consciousness *within* Württemberg and among reformers for most of the eighteenth century.

Within this larger cultural setting, moreover, covenant theology, with its Pelagian and Joachimite tendencies, was assimilated to the Württemberg tradition of Protestant civil piety. At once a "motivational myth" and cultural ideal, Protestant civil piety was periodically invoked by groups of reform-minded Württembergers to justify their calls for religious or political activism. And because of its association with reform, civil piety was easily related to two other key ideas in the Württemberger conception of Protestant activism: *praxis pietatis* and the call for a Second Reformation. Hence, the clustering and coherence of a set of ideas that found a "creative circumference" in the concept of Protestant civil piety.[5]

As a schoolboy, I think, Hegel was very much an heir to this way of thinking. He was, as it were, a member of the "last generation" of Old-Württemberg Protestants – which is to say that his writings of the early 1790s may be approached, at least initially, from the vantage point suggested by the Württemberger preoccupation with civil piety as a Protestant ideal.[6] As the argument of Chapter 4 will try to show, Hegel's concepts of *Volksreligion* and *Sittlichkeit*, two of the key foci of his writings in the 1790s, are very much informed by the values of this cultural ideal. Could it really have been otherwise for the "old man"? As Locke would have reminded us,

Who is there almost that hath not opinions planted in him by education time out of mind, which by that means come to be as the municipal laws of the country which must not be questioned, but are there looked on with reverence as the standards of right and wrong truth and falsehood, when perhaps those so sacred opinions were but the oracles of the Nursery or the traditional grave talk of those who pretend to inform our childhood who receive them from hand to hand without ever examining them.[7]

In remarking upon Hegel's Württemberg origins, we do not mean to suggest that the writings of the 1790s merely "derive" from this cultural context. Certainly there is a relation between the two, just as there is between Parts I and II of this study. But the relationship, in both cases, is not one of cause and effect.[8] Rather, the relationship needs to be understood in terms of the flow of a narrative structure in which what comes first (Part I/the context) provides a "framework," or the "occasion" for what comes after (Part II/Hegel's writings in the 1790s).[9] To paraphrase Geertz, the purpose of Part I is to gain access to Hegel's conceptual world so that we can begin to think creatively and imaginatively with him as he himself tries to make sense of that world from a point *within* it.[10] To put it another way, Part I allows us not so much to know what "caused" Hegel to write what he did in the 1790s as to appreciate what choices were available to him for writing anything at all. Alasdair MacIntyre made the methodological point quite well when he wrote:

The explanation of a choice between alternatives is a matter of making clear what the agent's [Hegel's] criterion was and why he made use of this criterion [civil piety] rather than another and to explain why the use of this criterion appears rational to those who use it. . . . Explaining action is explaining choices; and explaining choices is exhibiting why certain criteria define rational behavior for a given society.[11]

Granted, the material presented in Part I was weighted toward highlighting the importance of Protestant civil piety as an impulse in, and conceptual resource of, the culture of Old-Württemberg.[12] In that sense, what took the form of a description of that culture was really an explanation of how one aspect of that culture functioned relative to its other dimensions.[13] There is, therefore, nothing determinist about this interpretative procedure.[14] Hegel could have chosen to pursue other alternatives. As we have seen, he could have identified very easily with the policies of the duke or the Small Council. Or he could simply have opted for compromise, for constitutional dualism as a way of preserving political peace between the duke and the Small Council. That Hegel chose *not* to associate himself with any of these alternatives and, instead, pursued the Protestant civil piety option (first under the rubric of *Volksreligion* and then under that of *Sittlichkeit*) tells us something historical about his thinking at this point in time. Again, to paraphrase Geertz, we may envisage Protestant civil piety as a " 'said' " of social discourse that was articulated by Hegel along a "curve of social discourse" that allowed for several other "inscriptions."[15]

In so doing, though, Hegel was not just unreflectingly repeating conventional wisdom about civil piety; from the very beginning, he sought à la Moser to adapt and extend that wisdom to the changed circumstances of the 1790s.[16] Indeed, as a resource in the culture of Old-Württemberg, the ideal of Protestant civil piety *enabled* Hegel to call for a certain kind of religiopolitical activism – that is, the cultural convention he chose to follow did less to constrain him than to encourage him to become a Protestant reformer.[17]

Once that is understood, the perspective that informs our approach to Hegel's writings in the 1790s comes into clearer focus. Instead of assuming, as so many have done, that the activism and reformism in these writings reflect the values of an anti-Christian radical, we can see very well how that activism and reformism manifest the concerns of a liberal Christian reformer who regarded the world as a field of Christian opportunity and who wished, therefore, to make political activism an integral part of his program of applied Christian theology.[18]

4

◁══════════════════════▷

The writings of the 1790s
The "old man" and the "young Hegel"

As a schoolboy, we have noted, Hegel exhibited personality traits that his biographers have characterized as excessively scholarly.[1] Indeed, when he was in his teens Hegel's personality was often likened to that of an "old man"; from the perspective of his peers, his academic work habits and aspirations were already those of a mature scholar.[2] And yet, like his Stuttgart neighbor Moser, who was also called the "old man," Hegel was regarded as more of a *"Collecteenmacher"* than a "thinker," the difference between the two being that while the collector excerpted from the texts of others the thinker created and worked with his own ideas.[3] Hence, the scholarly fuss we noted earlier about Hegel's originality as a schoolboy vis-à-vis his more precocious classmates Schelling and Hölderlin.

If the nickname "old man" hints at a Moser–Hegel personality parallel, Hegel's writings in the 1790s suggest a convergence of their religious and political interests as well.[4] As was noted in the last chapter, Moser's religiopolitical views found new spokesmen among, and a receptive audience within, the Württemberg reform group of the 1790s. During these years, when Moser's views were back in vogue,[5] Hegel was writing essays that set forth a reformist political position.[6] On the one hand, Hegel called, as Moser had, for greater participation on the part of "the people of Württemberg" in the political processes that governed their lives.[7] Through the exercise of collective will, Hegel argued, Württembergers would be "able to rise above" their "petty interests" and, by so doing, reveal both their "character" as a "people" and their commitment to the idea of the "general good."[8] For this, courage, sacrifice, and awareness of the need for reform were deemed necessary.[9] On the other hand, to ensure that this exercise of collective will would be truly selfless in an ethical sense rather than merely self-indulgent in a utilitarian sense, Hegel insisted that the reform aim at the cultivation of the people's "nobler wishes."[10] In setting that agenda, Hegel was appealing, obviously, to the idea Württembergers had of themselves as a people covenanting with God; and, as we have already seen, that idea – of the *Volksgeist* in Württemberg – was often tied by reformers to Protestantism and to the idea of the Reformation as an expanding force in history.[11]

In the writings of the 1790s – indeed, throughout his life – Hegel had much to say about the *Volksgeist* as an active and creative religiopolitical force in history.[12] And when he wished to talk about the force in specific historical terms, he often did so in the context of a discussion of what he called *Volksreligion*.[13] This conception, we have already observed, figured prominently in Hegel's thought in the early 1790s. It was through that concept that his conviction about the importance of civil piety for the *Volksgeist* of Old-Württemberg expressed itself.

For many scholars Hegel's interest in *Volksreligion* is a clear indication of the kind of "tyranny" Greek cultural conceptions exercised over "the German mind" at the end of the eighteenth century.[14] The argument is that Hegel's calls for courage, activism, self-sacrifice, and political reform were just so many ways of giving voice to the heroic ethic that (supposedly) governed public life in the Greek *polis*.[15] But Hegel did not have to read the Greeks to develop enthusiasm for *Volksreligion*. Württembergers had already admitted that kind of ethic to their conception of what public life should consist in among a Protestant people. And, as we saw, they ethicized piety and made it public as a prelude to sanctioning politics as a vehicle of religious recollectivization and collective salvation.[16]

There are good reasons, therefore, for arguing that important aspects of Hegel's writings of the 1790s follow as much from attempts to ethicize public life in the name of applied Christian theology as from an obsession with the classical model of public life. As any number of recent studies have shown, the ideas of "Christian redemption and the *vivere civile*," the "Christian notions of *martyr* and *caritas*" and "the classical notions of *heros* and *amor* (*patriae*)," and the figures of *homo religiosus* and *zōon politikon* were often linked in the intellectual history of early modern Europe.[17] And so they were in Hegel.

In what follows, I shall try to show that for most of the 1790s Hegel wrote within a framework suggested by the convergence of *homo religiosus* and *zōon politikon*.[18] I shall argue, moreover, that Hegel's basic aim in these writings was to cultivate what Heine would later refer to as "primordial *Sittlichkeit*." As Heine recalled:

I was young and proud, and it pleased my vanity when I learned from Hegel that it was not the dear God who lived in heaven that was God, as my grandmother supposed, but I myself here on earth. This foolish pride did not by any means have a corrupting influence on my feelings; rather it raised them to the level of heroism. At that time I put so much effort into generosity and self-sacrifice that

I certainly outshone the most brilliant feats of those good Philistines of virtue who merely acted from a sense of duty and obeyed the moral laws. After all, I myself was now the living moral law and the source of all right and sanctions. I was primordial *Sittlichkeit*, immune against sin, I was incarnate purity.[19]

In this statement we can see how easily the language of classicism can serve the purposes of Protestant activism and civil piety. The dynamic that Heine associates with the "heroic" conception of a life dedicated to public service and self-sacrifice could just as easily be associated with what was said earlier about the pietists' ideal of "dying into life."[20] After all, the idea of sacrifice *pro patria* had been a religio-political concern among eschatologically minded Württemberg Protestants long before the classical revival of the late eighteenth century. The influence of that revival, therefore, may very well be explained by the fact that Pietism, by tying "the coming of the Kingdom of God" to this-worldly activism and civil piety, had already made the idea of sacrifice *pro patria* a focus of ethical and political concern among Württembergers.[21]

To understand Hegel, then, it is important to realize that in the 1790s his conceptions of *Volksreligion* and *Sittlichkeit* were informed by reformatory religious values.[22] As we shall see, Hegel's understanding of the two conceptions reveals a commitment to *praxis pietatis*, to religious collectivization, and to the more general idea that by "stretching his soul" *homo religiosus* could prepare the world for the coming of the Kingdom of God.[23] As a spiritual exercise, stretching the soul involved both self-denial (i.e., "dying to the natural") and self-affirmation (i.e., "dying into life").[24] In the first instance, *homo religiosus* set himself against his natural self;[25] hence, the ascetic cast of much of Hegel's thought in the 1790s. In the second instance, *homo religiosus* aimed at developing himself as primordial *Sittlichkeit*, at developing himself as a "social I";[26] hence, the antisubjective, collectivist focus of so many of these early essays.

In the early 1790s, moreover, Hegel tended to identify *Volksreligion* and *Sittlichkeit* with a realm of experience *within* the objective world itself. The Kingdom of God was to be realized on earth, not in heaven. Thus, as *homo religiosus* died to the natural *within* himself, he was reborn in a collectivity that, objectively speaking, existed *outside* him.[27] This collectivity was religious in the original social sense of the word. It expressed the moral personality of a people who practiced piety together for the purpose of collective salvation. When, in other words, *homo religiosus* practiced piety he objectified himself in the world; that is, he gave something that was spiritual in him in a subjective sense (i.e., his *Geist* as *homo religiosus*) an objective, this-worldly, socioreligious form (i.e., *Sittlichkeit*).[28]

By setting himself against nature, then, *homo religiosus* ascetically freed himself as a subjective being from internal restraints on his Christian personality, on what Hegel regarded as the "idea" of man as *homo religiosus*.[29] So liberated, he was now (alleged to be) free not only to practice piety in the world but also to proclaim that world the proper object of applied Christian theology.[30] As Hegel once put it, "Secular life is the positive and definite embodiment of the Spiritual Kingdom – The Kingdom of the Will manifesting itself in outward existence."[31] Hence, Hegel's insistence that *homo religiosus* envisage the world as a "theater" for revealing what it meant to live a purposive Christian life.[32]

Most of the essays Hegel wrote in the 1790s present *Volksreligion* and *Sittlichkeit* in these terms: as "the divine of religion [realizing itself] as action" in the world.[33] Both conceptions, however, are also ideals, the objects of that action – that is, as ideals they are realized when the ideal of civil piety becomes the "ethical substance" of collective action itself.[34] Viewed in this way, Hegel's conceptions of *Volksreligion* and *Sittlichkeit* are linked to his sense of the world as a place of Christian opportunity for a Protestant people, as a place within which a Protestant teleology can realize itself. Hegel's conception of the *telos* of *homo religiosus* moves from "inside out," from "essence" to "existence," from subjectivity to objectivity, from *Geist* to *Sittlichkeit*, in the same way that earlier Protestants had conceived the relation between the First and Second Reformations.[35] And, in both cases, the movement from inside out is meant to recall men to public life so that the theoretical promise of Luther's *Lehrereformation* could be fulfilled in practice in a *Lebensreformation*.[36]

The point I am trying to make here about the relations between teleology, the concepts of *Volksreligion* and *Sittlichkeit*, and the sense of mission that some Protestants derived from the Reformation can be made another way. Mention of Hegel's conception of the *telos* of *homo religiosus* as involving a movement from inside out and as tying in with the Protestant notion of the Reformation as an ever-expanding force in history should recall to mind what was said earlier about how *homoiosis* (i.e., the ideology of assimilationism) had functioned as a teleological principle among groups of reform-minded Christians since the Alexandrians.[37] As we noted, the idea of assimilation to God had both ethical and eschatological dimensions to it. Often the two dimensions reinforced each other in ways that pedagogically helped Christian reformers persuade their fellows to take more responsibility for preparing the present for the future arrival of the Kingdom of God on earth.[38] Hence, the appeal of assimilationism to those *Aufklärer* who had Pelagian ethical leanings and to those eschatologically minded Württembergers who had Bengel's teachings on the economy of salvation before them.

As we saw, moreover, the doctrine of assimilationism had originally been used by ethically minded Christians to counter the Stoic claim of "divine immanence" and the "pantheistic materialism" that so often followed from it.[39] The argument was that this aspect of Stoicism discouraged men from taking ethical responsibility for their lives. In this connection, Clement of Alexandria had availed himself of the Platonic notion of *homoiosis* in developing a Christian conception of the *telos* of *homo religiosus*.[40] By stressing the implications for ethical activism that the doctrine of *homoiosis* held for man, Clement made transcendence of nature a condition of the *telos* of *homo religiosus*. In so doing, he made "assimilation to God" rather than "concord with nature" the measure of a purposive Christian life. That meant, in turn, that Clement's conception of teleology was ethical in a theological Platonic sense rather than naturalist in a pantheistic Stoical sense.[41] Thus, for him, and for many Christians after him, teleology was indistinguishable both from ethical self-realization and from the soteriological process whereby *homo religiosus* voluntarily and gradually separated himself from nature in order to realize the "idea" of himself as a Christian.[42]

The reason the teleological aspect of assimilationism is relevant to our study at this point is that many commentators have insisted that Hegel's teleology is thoroughly "classical" in inspiration.[43] Given this premise, it is but a short step to two further assertions: that Hegel's conceptions of *Volksreligion* and *Sittlichkeit* are also classically informed and that Aristotle is the main source of this inspiration. Three important implications follow from this series of related assumptions: *zōon politikon* is the subject of Hegel's work; the *polis* is the model for Hegel's conceptions of *Volksreligion* and *Sittlichkeit*; and Hegel's "Hellenic" ideal explains the focus of his writings in the 1790s.

There is no denying the many parallelisms between Aristotle's and Hegel's conceptions of teleology.[44] Both, for example, offered teleological accounts of why man was "impelled" to associate with his fellows and to cooperate with them in collective endeavors; both were convinced that the telic principle that drove man toward the collectivity was internally rather than externally generated; both agreed that "practice" and participation were crucial to realization of the ethical well-being of the collectivity; and, in the end, both defined virtue in terms of the *telos* of the collectivity. Conceptually, in other words, Aristotle and Hegel concurred in celebrating the idea of the associative life as the culmination of the human *telos*.

There is, however, an important difference between the two thinkers' views on teleology: mainly, that Aristotle wrote before and Hegel after Christianity had emerged as a system of belief in the West.[45] Consequently, the two offer quite different explanations of how the associated life comes into being and why it is "natural" to man.[46] In this context, it is well known that Aristotle's conceptions of teleology and of man as *zōon politikon* were modeled on his studies of nature. For that reason, "nature" in biological and material senses often figures prominently in discussions of Aristotle's teleology – which explains why *natural* necessity plays a key role in Aristotle's conceptions of *zōon politikon* and the *polis*.

Hegel, by contrast, had a more voluntarist and less naturalist conception of how the telos of *homo religiosus* worked itself out *in history*.[47] Within that conception, there was room at *certain points* for the activities of *zōon politikon*. But, according to Hegel, the conditions for those activities did not always exist. Thus, there was nothing "natural" for him about how *zōon politikon* came into being.[48] Hegel concluded, therefore, that "nature" provided no guide for a truly associative life. What the character of community should be, he realized, was something that man had to work out for himself, with others, and in and through history.[49] In that context, Hegel tells us, man will learn a simple lesson; namely, that what is "original and natural" about himself does not exist as "original and natural."[50] It must be "sought out and won"[51] – built up gradually in history, relative to time, place, and circumstance.[52] In the process, man will encounter many difficulties[53] – the theology of natural life (i.e., "man as he happens to be") will constantly collide with the theology of ethical life (i.e., "man as he could be if he realized his essential nature").[54] And yet, over time man gradually will overcome what is "merely natural" to him;[55] as Hegel put it, man will be able to transform his "first" into a "second" nature.[56] Hegel held, therefore, that at some moment in time man would become a self-defining subject who possessed a Pelagian-like "capacity for either direction." At that moment, willful and conscious preparation for the coming of the Kingdom could truly begin.[57]

With this argument, the importance of Protestantism for Hegel's conception of the *telos* of *homo religiosus* becomes evident. Much of what Hegel says about that *telos* is perfectly consistent with the Protestant conception of how history had been unfolding since the Reformation. In this connection, Hegel noted again and again that with the Reformation the "principle of Free Spirit" had been "made the banner of the World."[58] By that he meant that German Protestants, who were *now* the "bearers of the Christian principle," were in a position to effect a reconciliation between humanity and divinity *within history*.[59] Through Luther's efforts, Hegel declared, *homo religiosus* had "gained the consciousness of [his] freedom,"[60] with the result that men could now proceed to claim the "secular" both as a field of Christian opportunity and as the framework within which the Kingdom of God would be realized on earth.[61] Not surprisingly, though, Hegel qualified his endorsement of the Reformation as a pivotal event in Christian history for, like so many other Protestants before him, he regarded Luther's Reformation as one that had been fulfilled in theory but not in practice.[62]

At this point much of what was discussed earlier in this study becomes relevant to an explanation of what Hegel was "doing" in writing what he did in the 1790s. His position with regard to Luther can be explained not only in terms of the First and Second Reformation argument but also in terms of the ethical dynamic whereby eschatology as axiology becomes eschatology as teleology.[63] As Hegel's conception of the Protestant mission in history stood to the *telos* of *homo religiosus*, so the Christian conceptions of evolutionary eschatology and the theology of the divine economy stood to the doctrine of assimilationism. By putting the writings of the 1790s in this framework, many of Hegel's concerns – with the Old Testament (especially with the figure of Abraham); with Jesus' ethical teachings; with the "divine spark" in man; with education; with "drawing near to God" by way of "good works"; and with *Volksreligion, Sittlichkeit*, and the Kingdom of God – begin conceptually to "cluster" and form what Weber would call a "subjective-meaning complex of action."[64]

For all these reasons, I think it is misleading to explain what Hegel wrote in the 1790s by referring us, as Findlay does, to Aristotle or to the "objective" aspects of the Hellenic conceptions of subjectivity and teleology.[65] To be sure, there is, as Findlay perceptively notes, a self-realizing aspect to Hegel's teleology.[66] But the fact is that Hegel's understanding of teleology as a self-realizing process is *an historically specific conception*. Although Hegel would agree with Aristotle that man as a member of a species has a telos, Aristotle would not agree with Hegel that that telos was conditioned by history or that history itself had a telos. The difference is crucial. It means that a Christian theology of history rather than an Hellenic ideal constitutes the "motivational" situation within which the writings of the 1790s were written. As Hegel himself said in 1795, his interest was in employing the "legitimated idea of God" to clarify teleology, not the reverse.[67]

Much of what follows in this chapter aims at making this point clear. But the chapter has another purpose as well – which explains why in the section on Hegel at Tübingen and Berne I try to show how Hegel's conception of *Sittlichkeit* (i.e., civil piety) began to change toward the end of the 1790s. For Württemberg's Hegel, for the "old man," *Sittlichkeit* was an ideal – an inspiration for, and the *telos* of, religio-political activism.[68] In keeping with that ideal, Hegel tended to view the world as a field of Christian opportunity in which *Sittlichkeit* could be realized through acts of willed asceticism. Thus, when Hegel encountered obstacles to realizing *Sittlichkeit* as an ideal, he would envisage them as the inevitable consequences of translating theory into practice rather than as a shortcoming of ascetic theory itself. So conceived, these problems could always be "solved" simply by urging more discipline on the world.

Sometime between 1793 and 1799, while he was living outside Württemberg, Hegel began to abandon asceticism as a theoretical framework for the ideal of *Sittlichkeit*. In Part III I detail why Hegel did so at that time. Suffice it to say here that as Hegel's interest in economics developed, his conception of *Sittlichkeit* began to change. Instead of offering *Sittlichkeit* as a religious answer to the world's problems, the "young Hegel" started to search within the existing world for conceptual space within which *Sittlichkeit* could be preserved as an ideal.[69] Before that change was made, Württemberg's Hegel, the "old man," had been content idealistically to posit *Sittlichkeit* as an answer to the world's problems; after the discovery of economics the "young Hegel" pursued a mode of compromise with the world in which *Sittlichkeit* was realistically presented as requiring economic and social preconditions for its realization as an ideal.[70]

In this chapter, then, the concepts of the old man and the young Hegel have quite specific historical content. Their juxtaposition points to a "moment" when the line of development of Hegel's thought can no longer be "pulled out straight" from his Württemberg origins.[71] Much of the secondary literature on Hegel discusses this moment in terms of an "identity crisis" that the young Hegel experienced in the late 1790s.[72] For reasons that will soon be obvious, I have chosen to treat this crisis less as a psychological problem than as a theoretical one in which the values of the "old man" and the "young Hegel" struggled for control of his mind. Roughly, the struggle pitted the ideals of *homo religiosus* against the reality of *homo oeconomicus*. But to say that is only to refer to the surface of the conflict. At bottom, the struggle was much more involved than that. I explain what is at issue here in the remainder of this chapter.

1. Interpretations of Hegel in the 1790s

As was indicated above, there has been much scholarly debate over the "crisis" that allegedly consumed Hegel in the late 1790s, a crisis that Kroner says precipitated "an abrupt change in his intellectual and philosophic views, in his style and cast of mind, in his whole personality."[73] Scholars have offered widely divergent explanations of the origins of this crisis and of its importance for the development of Hegel's thought.[74] Whatever their explanations, though, scholars invariably cite evidence from Hegel's so-called "early theological writings" to add point to their arguments.[75] Since much of this chapter concerns those writings, it behooves us to be aware in advance of what Hegel scholars have said about them. Only then will it become clear how the argument of Part I of this study fits into recent interpretation of what the "young Hegel" is all about as a thinker.

Differences in scholarly opinion about the early theological writings begin with the debate over the appropriateness of the title Herman Nohl gave them in 1907. For our purposes, this debate is interesting less

because of what it tells us about Hegel than because of how it illumin-
ates the problems scholars have had interpreting Hegel's views on
Christianity.[76] Take, for example, what Lukács and Kaufmann have
said about these writings. To begin with, both have questioned Nohl's
designation of these writings as theological. If anything, both insist, these
essays are antitheological.[77] For Lukács, these essays exhibit a "sustained
hostility" to "theology";[78] Kaufmann agrees, claiming that they "consistently deprecate theology in any customary sense of the word."[79] Both
argue, moreover, that the "main thrust" of the early theological writings
"is directed against the Christian religion."[80]

The problem of whether these essays are as opposed to Christianity as
Lukács and Kaufmann claim is, I think, a crucial *conceptual* matter. It is
not just a semantic squabble among scholars. Nor is it a matter that can
be solved either by pointing out that Hegel used the term "theological" in
differing senses or by referring to him as an "ambiguous" Christian.[81]
What at bottom is at issue here is to what extent the young Hegel can be a
Christian and a political activist at one and the same time.

For Kaufmann and Lukács it is conceptually impossible to equate
Christianity with this-worldly political activism. The "positivity" and the
other-worldliness of Christianity, they argue, work against that proposition. To be specific, Kaufmann tells us that Hegel juxtaposed *Volksreligion*
and Christianity in order to contrast "glorious Greece" and "wretched
Christianity."[82] Obviously, Kaufmann continues, Hegel was protesting
"against the frozen dogmas and statutes of positive religion [i.e., Chris-
tianity]" and calling "for a living harmony" among men (i.e., a *Volksreligion*) based on the Greek model.[83] Kaufmann's thesis, then, is that
Hegel's initial conception of *Volksreligion*, as well as his later conception
of *Sittlichkeit*, was informed by classical, not Christian, references[84] –
which is to say, it was governed by religious values that Kaufmann
associates with classical "humanism."[85] According to Kaufmann, therefore, it is humanism, in a classical and not a liberal Protestant key, that
accounts for the reformist aspects of Hegel's political activism.[86]

Lukács, too, correlates Hegel's political activism with his interest in
classicism.[87] As he argued, Hegel's interest in the French Revolution and
its promised regeneration of the world "underlines his critique of Christianity and its positive content is the revival of the classical tradition."[88]
Despite some obvious differences, Lukács and Kaufmann agree on one key
issue: that Hegel's conception of political activism in the 1790s can only
be explained in terms of his campaign against Christianity. That Hegel's
political activism and his interest in classicism might have been part of a
program of applied Christian theology never seems to have crossed their
minds. And that is because both refuse to recognize civil piety as a basic
impulse within certain forms of Christian thought.[89] Had they been

willing to view things differently, they might well have seen that Hegel's aim in juxtaposing *Volksreligion* and Christianity was not so much to displace the latter with the former as to encourage Protestants to get on with the work of religious recollectivization.[90] That, after all, was what reform-minded Württemberg Protestants had been calling for for years, and that is what Hegel tells us he was calling for in the 1790s.[91]

Charles Taylor's recent study of Hegel offers an interesting perspective on some aspects of this problem. He also is critical of the way Kaufmann and Lukács have handled the problem of Christian modes of thought and value in Hegel's early theological writings.[92] What informs Taylor's criticism is his awareness that religion and politics cannot be separated in the thought of the young Hegel.[93] Unlike the "secular revolutionaries" in France, Taylor argues, Hegel had a "vision of regeneration" that involved "at its most fundamental level a renewal of religious life."[94] Instead of forcing himself to choose between a global opposition to Christianity or "traditional piety,"[95] Hegel pushed for what Taylor calls a "de-theologized Christianity," that is, a Christianity in which a voluntary commitment to "living piety" drew man outside himself and bound him to a collectivity that was social, religious, and political at once.[96] Through living piety, Taylor continues, Hegel expected the contemporary world to experience a "profound religious regeneration" that would carry over to the reform of political institutions as well.[97]

According to Taylor, this was Hegel's program for activism and reform as early as 1793.[98] At that time, while still at Tübingen, Hegel began to flesh out the conceptual dimensions of what he called *Volksreligion*, an ideal that at the time expressed his intention to weave religious and political values into one "civil" whole.[99] But here, in Taylor's statement of Hegel's conception of *Volksreligion*, a tension arises. On the one hand, Taylor identifies *Volksreligion* as the positive consequence of a detheologized Christianity, of the sort we have already seen down-to-earth pietists practice.[100] And, at several points in his discussion of *Volksreligion*, Taylor clearly links Hegel's interest in this ideal with an attempt to purify Christianity.[101] On the other hand, Taylor argues that this ideal was modeled "on the public religion of ancient Greece."[102] And like so many other scholars, Taylor suggests that Hegel's reading of Kant and Rousseau at Tübingen inclined him to move in this direction.[103]

Taylor's interpretation of Hegel's conception of *Volksreligion* presents us with several interesting conceptual and historical problems, ones that, I think, raise the issue of the relationship between the "old man" and the "young Hegel" very clearly. First of all, while Taylor's interpretation recognizes that *Volksreligion* grows out of an interplay between religious and political values, it tells us little about how to differentiate a conception of *Volksreligion* that aims at the reform of Christianity from one that is designed to replace it.[104] As a consequence, the possibility of construing the exact meaning of the early theological writings becomes difficult.

Second of all, Taylor's understanding of Hegel's commitment to *Volksreligion* entails a conception of the "young Hegel" that is almost indistinguishable from that of our "old man." In both cases religion, in the form of a commitment to living piety (*praxis pietatis*), is regarded as the principal source of the impulse toward civil well-being and pursuit of the public good (Protestant civil piety and *das gemeine Beste*).[105] And in both cases this impulse translates into a civil activism that has a political as well as a religious end.[106] As a result, the task of identifying the meaning of civil activism for Hegel becomes complicated, for by turns it can be part of a Christian or an anti-Christian program of reform.

An even more troubling problem emerges when we try to relate Taylor's interpretation of *Volksreligion* to the larger question of the meaning of the pattern of Hegel's development in the 1790s. Taylor argues, for example, that at Berne and Frankfurt (1793–1799) the young Hegel, who was still very much a Christian, had a "very man-centered" conception of religion.[107] As the centerpiece of his thought, Hegel allowed man to draw "his inspiration [for action] out of himself" rather than from "a larger order outside himself."[108] Hence, Taylor concludes that "the Hegel of the early theological manuscripts has a man-centered view of human regeneration."[109]

By 1800, though, Hegel's view of man had changed profoundly, and with that change, Taylor claims, Hegel arrived at his "mature" philosophical position.[110] At that time, Hegel abandoned religion for philosophy[111] and, by so doing, "displaced the center of gravity in his thought from man to *Geist*."[112] That displacement, in turn, made *Geist*, not man, "the subject of history."[113] And with this, Taylor tells us, Hegel became more concerned with getting men to *discern* the need for change than with getting them to see change as something that they had to initiate.[114]

In explaining this change, a change that carries us from the "young" to the "mature" Hegel, Taylor insists that the theoretical shift "from a man-centered theory to one centered on *Geist*" was "probably motivated by the political events of the time."[115] Indeed, Taylor's thesis is that the shift from man to *Geist* reflected Hegel's changed "conception of the role of willed action to political change."[116] As Taylor sees it, the young Hegel, the Hegel whose religious views informed his "man-centered conception of regeneration," was "quite radical politically."[117] By contrast, the mature Hegel was "not a political radical at all."[118] That was because

with the development of a notion of *Geist* as a subject greater than man, Hegel developed a notion of historical process which could not be explained in terms of conscious human purposes, but rather by the greater purposes of *Geist*. The transformations in political, social, religious institutions which must come about if man is to fulfill his destiny are no longer seen as tasks which men must consciously accomplish; on the contrary, although they are carried through by men, these do not fully understand the part they are playing until after they have come about.[119]

Thus, for Taylor the theoretical shift from man to *Geist* correlates very nicely with the shift from activist to passivist politics.[120]

Overall, Taylor's account of the pattern of Hegel's development in the 1790s may be understood, I think, in terms of a "thought–action–thought" explanatory structure. A failed attempt to translate *a theory* of religio-political regeneration into effective *action* is offered as an explanation for Hegel's shift *in theory* from man to *Geist*.[121] The implication, of course, is that Hegel's mature philosophy may be viewed as an expression of the frustrations of a generation of "young radical Germans" who had experienced profound political disappointments in the 1790s.[122] Faced with a world that lacked *the will* to initiate the kind of reformatory action for which he was calling, Hegel withdrew into a world in which the *vita contemplativa*, not the *vita activa*, received the highest-value priority.

This, of course, is an old saw of Hegelian scholarship.[123] As Taylor has correctly observed, it has been one of its axioms since the school of Hegel split into "old" and "young" Hegelians in the 1830s.[124] What is most interesting about this line of interpretation, though, is that it presents the "young Hegel" as an activist of the sort Taylor believes "the later young Hegelians" and the "young Marx" would have found most congenial.[125]

But there is an obvious problem here; for while Taylor's conception of the "young Hegel" is certainly a welcome corrective to that offered by Kaufmann and Lukács, it implies that Hegel's political radicalism follows (as action follows thought) from his concern with religious regeneration. Now *this* is a "young Hegel" with whom the "early Marx" would not have been comfortable.[126] Lukács, I think, understood this very well – which is precisely why he went to such lengths to dissociate *his* "young Hegel" from Christianity, from the religious conceptions of Württemberg's "old man."[127]

Lukács did this, of course, in the face of an historiographical tradition that, he claimed, had tried to depict Hegel during his crisis years as a romantic, as a philosopher of irrationalism, of mystical pantheism, of Christian mysticism, and so on.[128] Against this tradition, Lukács offered a rather different interpretation, one that conceptually located the "young Hegel" at a point of transition between an earlier and a later position.[129] This Hegel, Lukács admitted, had had his moment of crisis; and during that crisis Hegel had taken "a definite turn towards religious mysticism" and developed a "greater affinity with Christianity."[130] In this, Lukács concedes, Hegel went the way of many in his generation. But Lukács is quick to note that during these same years the young Hegel was pursuing "other studies" as well, studies that were socio-economic and historical in nature.[131] Through these studies, Lukács believes, Hegel thought he could find an explanation for why his program of religio-political regeneration had failed in practice.[132] In this, Lukács says, Hegel was most unique; and it is this Hegel, the thinker who was less concerned with philosophical escapism than with socioeconomic analysis, that Lukács wishes to identify as "the young Hegel."

At this juncture, four important points can be made about modern scholarship's different interpretations of Hegel in the 1790s. First, it is clearly a mistake to associate the young Hegel with an anti-Christian intellectual position. There is just too much evidence, including numerous statements from Hegel himself, that shows that although he was certainly not an orthodox Lutheran, he was also not about to abandon Christianity altogether.[133] Second, given what has been said in Part I of this study, it is imperative historiographically to separate the idea of the "young Hegel" from that of Württemberg's "old man." Taylor's conception of the young Hegel may be historically faulted here – which explains, I think, why his interpretation of the early theological writings as well as his assessment of the meaning Hegel assigned to his conceptions of *Volksreligion* and *Sittlichkeit* are difficult to follow. As was noted, that is because we are never exactly sure what the related ideas of "de-theologized Christianity" and "living piety" add up to in the context of Taylor's attempt to explain the differences between the Christian and the non-Christian (i.e., expressivist) impulses in Hegel's early thought.[134]

Third, it is obvious to me that Hegel's interest in economics, which Lukács emphasizes so much, has to be factored in as crucial to any conception of the *young* Hegel. Indeed, very little of what Hegel wrote after 1795 makes any sense without an appreciation of that factor.[135] Moreover, if there is any single issue that may be said to differentiate the old man from the young Hegel, it is the latter's interest in economics.

Finally, and this follows from the last point, a way must be found to reconcile the economic concerns of Lukács' young Hegel with the *Geist*-centered trajectory of Taylor's interpretation of the pattern of Hegel's development in the 1790s. The reason this reconciliation is necessary should be obvious: we cannot have Hegel around 1800 at one and the same time philosophically engaging the world through his economic studies (e.g., Lukács and Plant) and philosophically escaping from it through his conception of *Geist* (e.g., Taylor and Haym).

To meet the conceptual challenge posed by this last consideration requires only a slight adjustment in our perspective on the course of Hegel's development in the 1790s. What is decisive to realize, I think, is that from, say, 1796 to 1802, Hegel's philosophy operated on two theoretical levels at once.[136] On one level, Hegel was moving, as Taylor ably argues, from a man- to a *Geist*-centered theory of life. In this, Hegel's philosophy was indeed responding to what Taylor has described as "the external fact of [political] failure."[137] This failure, Taylor continues, cued Hegel that the sacrifices his program of regeneration asked of his fellows were too demanding.[138] Hence, the hard lesson Hegel learned about the efficacy of asceticism as a vehicle for translating a theory about Christian life into practice.

On another level, though, Hegel had come to realize through his economic and historical studies that if his program of religio-political regeneration were ever to be actualized, he would have to begin to take greater account of those social forces that militated against it. There were, as many of his contemporaries were saying, no "leaps" in nature or history[139] – everything unfolded in sequence, in a "chain" in which a certain order of development structured the opportunities for activism and reform in any given historical situation. Any call for regeneration, therefore, had to be fitted to the present before it could begin practically to project the possibility for reform into the future.[140]

In light of this new awareness – that "character and circumstance" were inextricably related in history – Hegel changed the theoretical context in which he had been thinking about regeneration.[141] Instead of appealing to the character and good will of *homo religiosus*, Hegel began to ask another question: in what respects would the circumstances of *homo oeconomicus* allow for the kind of religiopolitical regeneration he wished? The change, in other words, involved a shift in theoretical context: the problem of the *telos* of *homo religiosus*, which had been a problem of applied theology, was displaced by a theory in which socio-economic and historical analysis provided the framework out of which Hegel would try to draw the character of *homo religiosus*.[142] *Sittlichkeit*, to be sure, was the operative principle in each theory, but the spins on the concept as Hegel used it are, as we shall see, very different in the two cases.

In Part III I try to show how Hegel negotiates this shift in theoretical context. Suffice it to say here that he attempts to assimilate the first theoretical level of his thinking to the second. In that context, his conception of *Geist*, instead of drawing attention away from the pursuit of "conscious human purpose" in history, becomes the carrier of a telic principle of Christian activism *in history*.[143] Viewed in that way, *Geist* is still very much a man-centered conception. What is more, man's purpose is still defined in terms of a program of religious regeneration, of moving from inside out. The only difference is that *Geist* now operates as a metaphor for the consciousness of *homo religiosus* within a society that has reached *the* stage of commercial development in history.[144] In that sense, it is into a "civil society" that Hegel has assimilated *homo religiosus*; and it is to a dynamic peculiar and internal to that theoretical context that Hegel now looks for the hoped-for regeneration of the world.[145]

Hegel's conception of *Geist* expresses that hope, but it is a conditional hope – it exists only as a potential (i.e., as a subjective mode of consciousness) within a commercial society that is not yet truly *sittliche* in an objective sense.[146] The point of Hegel's analysis of that society, and of what at the time he began to call its "bourgeois" values, was to provide an explanation of how and under what circumstances that potential (i.e., *Geist* as the subjective consciousness of *homo religiosus*) could begin to express itself in objective terms.[147] Understood this way, it becomes clear that far from being a retreat from activism, Hegel's conception of *Geist* continued to carry his hopes for Protestant civil piety – that is, as a principle of Christian consciousness the telos of *Geist* is still to be realized in the recollectivized religious community of a Protestant people. Hence, the basic tension in Hegel's thought between Christianity in its conditional "liberal" mode and civil society in its presentist "bourgeois" mode.[148]

As we have tried to show, there is nothing particularly unusual about Hegel's having set this kind of agenda for himself. What is unique about Hegel, though, is the reasoning process he develops in order to arrive at a point where *Sittlichkeit* can be said to be a realistic option for ethico-political activism in the modern world. That reasoning process is examined in what follows.

2. Hegel at Tübingen and Berne: Christianity, *Volksreligion*, and Kantianism

After graduating from the *Gymnasium* in Stuttgart in 1788, Hegel enrolled at Tübingen as a candidate for a degree in theology.[149] For the next five years (1788–1793) he studied theology there [150] – which meant he was soon caught up in the conflict between the so-called "Old Tübingen School" of theology and a group of students whom Dieter Henrich has identified as "young Kantians."[151]

During the last twenty years, we have learned a good deal about the nature of this conflict.[152] In terms of two of the key personalities involved, the controversy was between G. C. Storr, a professor at the university and the "founder" of the Old Tübingen School of theology,[153] and K. I. Diez, a young tutor of theological students in the *Stift*.[154] For his part, Diez was a "radical" Kantian who is said to have exercised enormous influence on some of his charges between 1790 and 1792.[155] What Diez offered the *Stiftler* was an "enlightened" critique of religion based on the principles of Kantian philosophy.[156] Specifically, Diez provided a twofold indictment of the orthodox teachings of Storr and his colleagues. First of all, he identified Storr's school with what he called a theology of "transcendental illusion and empty chimeras."[157] Given this conviction, it was easy for Diez to push for what Henrich has said amounted to "a total rejection of Christianity."[158] Second of all, Diez wished to break the tie, conventionally drawn by orthodoxy, between morality and religion, so as to give impetus to the establishment of an ethical theory based on the autonomy of the human will.[159] According to Henrich, this made Diez a completely "practical" Kantian.[160]

In the face of this challenge, it was left to Storr to defend the orthodox teachings of the traditional Lutheran faith at Tübingen.[161] The substance of Storr's position has been well articulated by Pfleiderer. Of Storr and his colleagues he wrote:

They maintained their Biblical system against all the objections and doubts of the *Aufklärung* by an appeal to the Kantian philosophy; since, according to the critical philosophy, reason itself admits its inability to know anything of the supersensible, it has logically no right to protest against what has been made known to us concerning supersensible things by historical revelation; with regard to the practical reason, Kant himself allows that it demands a requiting Deity for the satisfaction of our desire for happiness, and is therefore in its own interest called upon to receive upon authority the historical revelation concerning God and his government of the world. Hence the truth of the Biblical doctrines stands higher than the critique of the speculative reason which confesses its own incompetence, and accords with the demands of the practical reason.[162]

With his strategy, Storr meant to exploit Kant for orthodox purposes. But by so doing, he drew attention to a fundamental tension in Kant's philosophy. On the one hand, as Henrich has observed, it would have been difficult to deny that Storr was well within his rights to use the skepticism of Kant's first *Critique* to buttress the case for "Biblical supernaturalism."[163] On the other hand, as Pfleiderer has noted, the young Kantians "perceived how little this appropriation of the Kantian philosophy to the service of theological dogmatism accorded with its real meaning and spirit."[164] In the first case, the "letter" of Kant's philosophy was put in the service of the "authority" of orthodoxy. In the second case, the "spirit" of Kant's philosophy was used to enlighten man as to his own "autonomy" and ethical responsibilities.[165]

In light of the uses being made of Kant's thought at Tübingen, is it any wonder that Kant's thought was at the center of the debates about theology there during these years?[166] But there is more. By all accounts, the debates were complicated still further by the fact that Diez's position was "too radical" for most of the *Stiftler*.[167] Few, it seems, were willing to go "all the way" with him with regard to the complete rejection of Christianity.[168] Schelling apparently was willing to do so;[169] Hegel was not – which means that "Hegel's Kantianism," if we can call it that, was of a special kind.[170] As Wacker noted, Hegel was "neither follower nor opponent of Kant" while at Tübingen.[171]

Yet Hegel's relation to Kant at this time was most important. We know, for example, that Hegel probably did not become involved in the Kant controversy at Tübingen until 1792–1793.[172] We also know that at the time Hegel's interest in Kant lay less in the philosophy of his three famous *Critiques* than in his recently published essay on religion.[173] What is more, one of Hegel's contemporaries insisted that "in Tübingen [Hegel] was not...really familiar with...Kant."[174]

To note these circumstances, however, is not to draw attention to anything new. We have known for years that Hegel's relation to Kant was complex.[175] W. H. Walsh has recently put it this way: "Hegel had an endless love/hate relationship with Kant. He admired him and at the same time he despised him."[176] Knowing that, however, has not led many scholars to probe deeper into their relationship, especially during the 1790s, when all agree that Hegel was in "a continuing *Auseinandersetzung* with Kant."[177]

Of this ongoing engagement, we know that Hegel had definitely "studied" Kant, without immersing himself in him, in 1789–1790;[178] that at Berne, he began a serious but limited study of Kant, reading only Kant's religious writings in the context of his own religious concerns;[179] and that at Frankfurt, he once again engaged Kant, this time in a more comprehensive philosophical fashion.[180]

It is obvious nonetheless that in 1792–1793, when the Old Tübingen School and the young Kantians (e.g., Diez and Schelling) began to square off over the meaning of Kant's philosophy, Hegel had to begin to think about his own position relative to that of the other Kantians in general and to their conflicting interpretations of Kant's *Religion* in particular.[181]

In this context, the position Hegel took is most illuminating. It is precisely what we would expect Württemberg's "old man" to have done. To appreciate this, we need to remember that Hegel had expressed himself on religion while still a schoolboy in Stuttgart. As Harris has reminded us, Hegel had been thinking as early as 1786 about what he as "a would-be *Volkserzieher*" would have to do in order to contribute to the establishment of the "Kingdom of God" on earth.[182] There were, of course, many reasons for his thinking this way at that time. For one thing, that mode of thought had been something like a *cultivated habitus* among down-to-earth pietists in Old-Württemberg for years. For another thing, Hegel had become a disciple of Lessing at an early age, and Lessing, we know, had had more than a passing interest in the relationship between eschatology, ethics, and the coming of the Kingdom of God.[183]

More specifically, we know that Hegel spent a good deal of time in 1786 excerpting from a book by Christian Wünsch in which ethical activism, religious recollectivization, and assimilationism were principal foci of concern.[184] A most revealing excerpted sentence runs: "The seed of goodness is planted in all our hearts by a benevolent Providence; but it is up to us to care for its development and growth."[185] This theological claim has anthropological implications of which we are most familiar.[186] And Hegel à la Lessing does not hesitate to talk about these implications in historical terms. In 1787 he wrote an essay in which cultivation of "the seed of Goodness" is discussed in terms of historical stages that, when viewed as a developmental sequence, reflect man's growing awareness of his responsibility for establishing the Kingdom of God on earth.[187] As Hegel saw it at the time, this process had reached a point *in the present* whereby the spread of religious enlightenment and the recollectivization of a Protestant people could lead to the constitution of Christianity as a *"Volksreligion."*[188]

Given this disposition, which clearly owes more to Lessing's *Education* than to Kant's first *Critique* (1781), it is easy to understand why at Tübingen Hegel was reluctant to side outright with either the Kantians of the letter or the Kantians of the spirit.[189] For him, the former espoused a supernaturalism that led to the kind of authoritarianism he associated with orthodox Lutheranism.[190] Conversely, he regarded the latter group as presumptuous in the autonomy and power it assigned to man's rational capacity.[191] Indeed, one could almost say that Hegel refused to go the way of either "theocentric" or "anthropocentric" religion.[192] To say this, of course, is to raise the question of which way Hegel did go.[193] The answer, I think, can be gleaned from documents Hegel left us from the years 1792–1793.

If one examines these documents closely, certain aspects of Hegel's thought about religion reveal themselves.[194] What they show, I think, is that Hegel's relationship to Kant in 1792–1793 is not what it is often said to have been.[195] To begin with, there is the matter of the substance of the sermons Hegel gave at Tübingen during his final two years there.[196] The first sermon we have (10 January 1792) is quite consistent with the religious themes Hegel chose to emphasize in 1786 and 1787. In it, Hegel stresses the importance of ethical activism, assimilationism, and religious recollectivization as parts of the providential plan for human redemption in history – that is, the sermon is "enlightened" in a Lessingian sense of the word.[197]

Several other sermons, delivered in May and June 1793, reiterated the same themes, only this time the main foci of concern are brought to bear on the question of what man can *do* in order to prepare for the establishment of the Kingdom of God on earth.[198] Hegel's message, one that informed his thought down to 1796, was simple: men should pay less attention to the doctrines of the visible church than to the way Jesus lived his life among men.[199] Were that life to become the focus of religious concern, *homo religiosus* would surely realize that his duty was both to imitate Jesus "within the limits of our human weakness" and to be "earnest to good works" that will "shine forth among men."[200] When that commitment is made, Hegel concludes, when religious truth "can let it be seen publicly and freely by anyone – then we are citizens of the Kingdom of God."[201]

Even more revealing of Hegel's religious thinking at the time is one of the essays that Nohl included in his collection of Hegel's early theological writings. This essay, the so-called "Tübingen Essay" of 1793, was written by Hegel shortly before taking his final examination at Tübingen in the fall of the same year.[202] According to Harris, it is in this essay that Hegel first began to "meditate on the Kingdom of God, and elaborate his conception of *Volksreligion* as his own contribution toward the coming of the Kingdom."[203] And it is clear from the essay that Hegel's intention was to offer a program of theological enlightenment that would stress what men needed *to do* in order to reform Christianity so that it would qualify as a *Volksreligion*.[204] To put it in the terms of our earlier discussion of the pietists' (e.g., Bengel's) distinction between *Lehre-* and *Lebensrevolutions*, Hegel wished to close the gap between *Lehre* and *Leben* by detheologizing orthodoxy in the name of the practice of piety.[205]

Since the substance of this essay has recently been detailed by Harris, I will not rehearse all its contents here. Suffice it to say that Hegel's dissatisfaction with the lack of focus orthodoxy gave to Christianity is clearly evident in the essay. Drawing selectively on various *Aufklärung* sources, Hegel uses the essay to advance the idea of *Volksreligion* as the organizing principle of a more broadly based effort to reform Christianity. Specifically, Hegel wishes to reinterpret Christianity so that its potentiality as a *Volksreligion* can be exploited by a *Volkserzieher* like himself for present religio-political purposes.[206] It is our thesis, therefore, that the essay in general and the concept of *Volksreligion* in particular aim at demonstrating what a would-be *Volkserzieher* would have to contend with if he were to promote Protestant civil piety as a religious ideal.

If the "Tübingen Essay" was designed to enunciate a program of Christian reform, we might expect Hegel to have built a call for ethical activism into his conception of *Volksreligion*. This, of course, is precisely what he does. Early in the essay he tells us that "the main thing in a *Volksreligion*" is the "degree to which [it] can influence how men act."[207] Its purpose, he stresses, is to promote "good action" among a people.[208] All too often, he continues, a people's sense of "its dignity" slumbers, with the result that periodically religion needs to aim at "the elevation" of the soul and the "ennobling of the spirit of a nation."[209] At this moment, religion needs to become *Volksreligion*, needs to become activist in a collectivist sense.[210]

As we might expect from someone who in 1787 had tried historically to correlate modes of religious consciousness with stages of civilization, Hegel conceded at the start of the "Tübingen Essay" that the form this ennobling appeal had taken in history varied, depending on "the spiritual culture and stage of morality that a people had reached."[211] And as we might also expect, Hegel argued this way because he believed a "seed" had been "buried" in man that gave him "a sense for what is moral, for ends that go beyond the range of mere sense."[212] This seed, Hegel insisted, was the source "from which religion springs,"[213] and as the seed is cultivated the religious conceptions of "sense-oriented people" gradually evolve into conceptions with decidedly more "moral" content.[214]

Given his view of how religious consciousness unfolded in history, it was only natural that Hegel would cast his conception of *Volksreligion* in terms of a theology of history that we by now must recognize as thoroughly reformist in an ethico-eschatological sense. *Volksreligion* functions in Hegel's thought as an ethico-political as well as an ethicohistorical or eschatological ideal. In the first case, *Volksreligion* expresses a people's desire for religiopolitical recollectivization (i.e., *Sittlichkeit*). In the second case, it expresses the focal point of a theology of history in which the Kingdom of God is expected to be realized on earth as *Sittlichkeit* becomes the collective ideal of a Protestant people.

Viewed in this way, it is very difficult to treat *Volksreligion* as an anti-Christian conception. Granted, Hegel has much to say in the "Tübingen Essay" about the historical circumstances that have prevented Christianity from developing into a *Volksreligion*. Indeed, it is in this context that he talks about "objective" religion, the transformation of "religion into theology," "positive" religion, "fetish faith," and, à la Rousseau, of a type of "enlightenment" that makes men "cleverer" without making them more "moral."[215] Of "objective" religion, Hegel had this to say:

[It] suffers itself to be arranged in one's mind [*im Kopfe*], organized into a system, set forth in a book, and expounded to others in discourse.[216]

Or again,

[It] is abstraction...[being composed of] frigid arguments and verbal exercises [instead of] the full and heartfelt experience of faith.[217]

And, in summing up why Christianity had not evolved into a *Volksreligion*, Hegel claims it had lost touch with people by allowing itself to become too "theological" and too "objective."[218]

By contrast, "subjective" religion was something Hegel identified with.[219] Moreover, it has a force he wished to associate with *Volksreligion*. He has this to say about it: "Subjective religion expresses itself in feeling and action."[220] It allows man to give "praise and thanks to [God] in his own deeds."[221] He continues: "Subjective religion is alive, it is effective in the inwardness of our being, *and active in our outward behavior*."[222] Everything, he tells us, "depends on subjective religion"[223] – which, for him, is to say that subjective religion "does not manifest its presence merely in putting the hands together, bending the knees, and abasing the heart before that which is holy; rather it spreads out into every budding branch of human impulse (without the soul being ever quite aware of it) and is everywhere active."[224]

In declaring that subjective religion entailed an activism that moved from inside out Hegel often talked as if the "heart" rather than "understanding" were the seed from which this impulse sprang.[225] But that is not really the case, for Hegel just as often used the term *Gemüt* to identify the source of this impulse in man.[226]

Gemüt is an interesting term.[227] In the late eighteenth century it was an anthropological–theological concept that entailed reference to the disposition in man to assimilate to God.[228] Kant often used the term in his work to identify this disposition.[229] Frequently, he used it interchangeably with the term *Herz*. In modern usage, though, *Herz* carries a sense of subjective feeling and emotion, where in the eighteenth century *Gemüt* generally connoted a practical and volitional rather than an affective drive.[230] In addition, eighteenth-century usage also ascribed an intellectual dimension to *Gemüt*. Hence, the translator of the "Tübingen Essay" has seen fit to render the German *Gemüt* with the English "mind" instead of "heart."[231]

But when *Gemüt* is translated as either heart or mind it loses a decisive aspect of its original meaning and lends itself to confusion. Not only does the translation permit what for us would be polar interpretations of Hegel's meaning (i.e., he is either a romantic or a rationalist), but it also makes *Gemüt* a completely anthropological concept. And it was not *just* an anthropological term in the eighteenth century.

This latter aspect of the translation problem becomes clear when we recall the importance *Gemüt* had in the tradition(s) of late medieval mystical theology.[232] As Ozment has observed, *Gemüt* was a crucial concept in "the Pelagian covenant theology" of late medieval theology.[233] In that context, it was used to signify an "active power" that embraced and penetrated the various faculties of the soul *and directed them toward God*.[234] On this reading, *Gemüt* operated through, but was distinct from, any particular faculty[235] – which means that *Gemüt*, like *Geist*, is best understood as a *spiritual energy* that orients man's faculties toward God and then leaves it to man himself to fulfill his destiny (i.e., his *Bestimmung*).[236]

There are good reasons, then, for detecting theological as well as anthropological intention in Hegel's use of this term, especially since it anticipates in so many ways the dynamic he later tries to articulate with his concept of *Geist*.

Be that as it may, it should be obvious that subjective religion, the appeal to *Gemüt*, and the call for activism in the service of *Volksreligion* are all part of a reform program that has its roots in a tradition of Christian thought that envisages assimilationism in an ethical sense as integral to the coming of the Kingdom of God in an eschatological sense. Hegel makes these kinds of connections himself. Explaining, for example, how a *Volksreligion* "whose doctrines are to be effective in life and work," is "to arouse and build up" a "sense of holiness," Hegel insisted that it define "service" to God as "that right action. . . that is most pleasing to him."[237]

It is crucial to understand that the "right action" the ideal of *Volksreligion* is designed to elicit from man is equivalent, in Hegel's words, to living a life of "virtue."[238] For a person to live that kind of life, though, the idea of "holiness" must be postulated as "the ultimate apex of ethical conduct [*Sittlichkeit*] and the ultimate limit of all striving."[239] In saying this, Hegel is well aware that he is establishing a convergence between the religious ideas of holiness and *Sittlichkeit* and the kind of "rational religion" (*Vernunftreligion*) that Kant had made central to moral philosophy.[240] What is more, Hegel also realized that many would object to his postulation of an ideal that "is not [in practice] attainable by man."[241] Hegel's response to this anticipated criticism, like Spener's and Lessing's, was that such an objection does "not so much go to show that man ought not to strive *to come ever closer* to that ideal. . . but only that in savagery and when there is a powerful propensity toward sensibility – we frequently have to be content to produce only a law-abiding habit in most men, and no purely ethical motives. . . are required to produce this."[242] Thus, "holiness," insofar as it is presented as the culmination or telos of *Volksreligion*, aims at inspiring "the whole soul with power and enthusiasm – with the spirit that is indispensable for greatness and sublimity in virtue."[243]

Presenting *Volksreligion* in these terms enabled Hegel to treat Christianity as a "subjective" religion that had the potential to become simultaneously a "virtue religion" and a *Volksreligion*. In the case of the last two terms, *Sittlichkeit* was to be their concrete historical expression.[244] But the realization of *Sittlichkeit* also required a political precondition, for as Hegel made clear throughout the "Tübingen Essay," *Volksreligion* could cultivate "noble dispositions" only if a people were politically free to take responsibility for its collective life.[245] If this condition were met, the *Volksgeist* of the people could be said to be both free and in concord with God's plan for the establishment of the Kingdom of God on earth.[246]

If the "Tübingen Essay" expresses a concern with *Volksreligion*, and if that concern reveals a commitment to *Sittlichkeit* and Protestant civil piety, we must ask what, precisely, is Kantian about it? It is not easy to answer that question, and for several reasons. First of all, we need to remember that while at Tübingen Hegel had not devoted anything like his full attention to the study of Kant. He was selective about what he read of Kant, preferring Kant's religious writings to his more "critical" ones.[247] Second of all, we should recall that Kant was being read in several different ways at Tübingen in the early 1790s. That Hegel could acquiesce in neither Storr's nor Diez's interpretative line means that we need to specify just what kind of Kantian Hegel was at the time he wrote the "Tübingen Essay."[248] Finally, and perhaps most important of all, recent Kantian scholarship had detected, especially in Kant's historical and religious writings from the 1784–1793 period, a number of arguments that are more "Hegelian" than "Kantian."[249] The claim, of course, is not meant to suggest that Hegel influenced Kant at this time, but it does hint at the possibility of Pietism as a common source for both thinkers' views about religion and its role in history.[250]

In light of these considerations, we must be careful about how we talk about the Hegel–Kant relationship in 1793. Take, for example, the way Harris describes the relationship for the period 1786–1793.[251] According to him, the excerpt that Hegel made from Wünsch in 1786 (quoted earlier) represents a "near-Kantian confluence of Enlightenment and Christianity."[252] Then, given what Hegel wrote in the "Tübingen Essay," Harris tells us that Hegel was using "Kant's moral philosophy" in general and his "postulates of practical reason" in particular as a "yardstick" for his own thought.[253]

Now it cannot be denied that there is a lot of Kant in the "Tübingen Essay."[254] But the Kantian source Hegel draws upon in this essay is the *Religion* of 1792–1793. All Hegel scholars acknowledge this.[255] But what Hegel scholars seldom comment upon is the very curious "Kantian" argument of that book. As Kant scholars have recently shown, the argument of the *Religion* is not easily reconcilable with the philosophical thrust of the *Critiques*, especially the first one.[256] If we look closely at the *Religion* – which in many ways is a typical down-to-earth pietistic statement about the relationship between ethics and eschatology in Christian thought – it is obvious that Kant's essay did not so much "influence" Hegel as confirm views he had held, and had been thinking about, since at least 1786.[257]

The *Religion* is a remarkable essay for a philosopher of Kant's stature to have written.[258] Indeed, if the essay is read in terms of the ethico-eschatological tradition discussed in Part I of this study, its main argument becomes strikingly Christian.[259] In Book One, which appeared as an independent essay in 1792, Kant makes a case for human perfectibility in history.[260] Rejecting the orthodox notion of original sin,[261] Kant insists that even after the Fall man is "capable of. . .improvement."[262] Kant is quick to qualify this, though; he writes:

When it is said, Man is created good, this can mean nothing more than: He is created *for good* and the original *predisposition* in man is good; not that, thereby, he is already actually good, but rather that he brings it about that he becomes good or evil, according to whether he adopts or does not adopt into his maxim the incentives which this predisposition carries with it ([an act] which must be left wholly to his own free choice).[263]

When man accepts these "incentives" for good action, Kant continues, he is "not yet holy by reason of this act (for there is a great gap between the maxim [i.e., as axiology] and the deed [i.e., as teleology])."[264] Yet, according to Kant, this acceptance puts man "upon the road of endless progress toward holiness" (i.e., *homoiosis*).[265] Once on this road man "passes from a tendency to vice, through gradual reformation of his conduct. . .to an opposite tendency."[266] At some point along this road that runs from "bad to better," Kant reasons, man will arrive at a moment of reversal when "by a single unchangeable decision" he will totally commit himself to "continuous labor" and "an ever-during struggle toward the better."[267] At this point, man's "predisposition" toward goodness will take the form of a moral "duty" that man pursues "for its own sake."[268]

Having stated this view, Kant next asks "what is it in us. . .whereby we, beings ever dependent upon nature through so many needs, are at the same time raised so far above these needs by the idea of an original predisposition. . .that we count them as nothing?"[269] His answer? The idea of "moral destiny" excites man and "acts perforce upon the spirit [das *Gemüt*] to the point of exaltation, and strengthens it for whatever sacrifices a man's respect for his duty may demand of him."[270] From this Kant concludes that the idea of holiness qua moral destiny enables man "to *hope* through his *own* efforts to reach the road which leads thither."[271]

For Kant a religion that demands of man that he "do as much as lies in his power to become a better man" is a "moral" religion, a religion of "good life-conduct."[272] Christianity, Kant declares, is the only "moral" religion that has ever existed.[273] He does not, however, claim that "salvation" can be secured through good life conduct alone, for in true synergist fashion he holds that "what is not within [man's] power will be supplied through cooperation from above."[274] Since, therefore, man cannot redeem himself without grace, Kant's view is that all religion must teach man is what he "*himself must do* in order to become worthy of this assistance [from above]."[275] And this is because Kant believed that although "some supernatural cooperation may be necessary to his becoming good, or to his becoming better, yet,...man must first make himself worthy to receive it."[276]

With the dynamics of this argument we are most familiar.[277] Following Pfleiderer, one could say that, à la Lessing, Kant viewed salvation as a process whereby "divine revelation" did not "descend upon man ready-made from without," but achieved "realization in man through the development of his religious capacity."[278] But in Book One of the *Religion* Kant inserted a new dimension into this theology of history. He did this by distinguishing two kinds of "virtue."[279] On the one hand, there was the "virtue of conformity to law." This type of virtue was "empirical" in that it arises when the "resolve to do one's duty has become habitual." On the other hand, there was a virtue that goes beyond mere legality. It was the kind of virtue that Kant associated with the truly "moral" man, the man who wished to be "pleasing to God."[280]

To give substance to this distinction Kant, à la Rousseau, differentiated between progress in "moral" goodness and the kind of progress that many eighteenth-century thinkers associated with "the process of civilization."[281] With regard to the former, Kant argued that "freedom," the "power of choice in respect of the moral law," must be "antecedent" to it.[282] With regard to the latter, Kant held that "civilization" is the framework within which man's capacity for freedom develops.[283] For Kant, though, the advance of civilization was no guarantee of progress in moral goodness.[284] And that was because Kant believed civilized man had historically reached a point of development where he valued "happiness" more than "virtue."[285] As Kant noted:

A man accounts himself virtuous if he feels that he is confirmed in maxims of obedience to his duty, though these do not spring from the highest ground of all maxims, namely, from duty itself. The immoderate person, for instance, turns to temperance for the sake of health, the liar to honesty for the sake of reputation, the unjust man to civic righteousness for the sake of peace or profit, and so on – all in conformity with the precious principle of happiness.[286]

Hence, Kant's need to distinguish between two types of virtue was based on a conception of history in which the matter of self-realizing teleology figured prominently.[287]

Having set the issue of moral progress in this "quasi-historical" framework,[288] Kant proceeded to link cultivation of the disposition toward moral goodness with different types of men.[289] First, there is man qua "living being," whose main disposition was toward "animality."[290] Then, there was man qua "living" *and* "rational being," whose disposition was toward "humanity."[291] Finally, there was man qua "rational" *and* "accountable being," whose disposition was toward "personality."[292] Of these dispositions Kant claimed that the first may be characterized as oriented toward the "physical";[293] the second, toward "acquiring worth in the opinion of others";[294] and, the third, toward "respect for the moral law as in itself a sufficient incentive of the will [to good life conduct]."[295]

According to Kant, the idea of virtue as conformity to law was a characteristic of the civilized man who had set his store in "happiness" rather than "virtue."[296] This man, though, while virtuous from a legal point of view, was not a morally good man from the point of view of God.[297] As Kant put it, the first man "obeys the law according to the letter," but the second man "obeys [it] according to the spirit."[298] What Kant meant to emphasize with this formulation, of course, was the difference between virtue that has happiness and legality as its ends and virtue that has the pursuit of holiness and morality as its ends.[299] As Kant claimed later in the essay, the "precepts of holiness" are "not mere laws of virtue" but maxims "we ought to pursue, and the very pursuit of them is called virtue."[300]

At this point in the argument, Kant concedes that promulgation of the law of virtue is socially necessary to prevent man from "falling back under [evil's] dominion" (i.e., to a condition of "animality").[301] Thus, his association of "humanity" with the stage of "civilization" in which the "juridical" sense is predominant.[302] At the same time, though, Kant regards "civilization" in its juridical mode as "a rallying point for all who love the good" for its own sake.[303] Kant's conceptions of humanity, law, and civilization, therefore, speak simultaneously to two different senses of virtue.[304] One is "juridico-civil" and is associated with "civilization" and "humanity." The other is "ethico-civil" and is linked with "noncoercive" laws of association that Kant regards as expressive of man's moral "personality."[305]

It is, I think, of the utmost importance that Kant is also drawing a distinction here between two conceptions of what constitutes a people: between people who are "merely" civilized and what he called "the concept of *a* people regarded as a commonwealth" (*eine Volkes als eines gemeinen Wesens*).[306] This commonwealth, Kant insists, emerges when it becomes the "special business" of men to make it their "ethical" duty voluntarily to unite themselves under "moral laws" for the purpose of establishing a "Kingdom of God" on earth.[307] This can only happen, he continues, "through religion"[308] – which is to say, "an ethical commonwealth can be thought of only as a people under divine commands, i.e., as a people of God, and indeed under laws of virtue."[309] This commonwealth, of course, begins as an idea among civilized people.[310] As Kant remarked,

a sign that the Kingdom of God is at hand appears, as soon as the basic principles of its constitution first become public, for (in the realm of the understanding) *that is already here* [i.e., the axiology problem] whose causes, which alone can bring it to pass [i.e., the idea of the commonwealth qua recollectivized religious community], have generally taken root, even though the complete development of its appearance in the sensuous world is still immeasurably distant [i.e., the teleological problem].[311]

But if the religious idea of an ethical commonwealth is properly cultivated, it will "like a grain of a seed in good soil...gradually, through its inner power, grow into a Kingdom of God."[312] And, for Kant, it was in his own day that "the seed of the true religious faith, as it is *now being publicly sown* in Christendom, though only by a few, [was being] allowed more and more to grow unhindered."[313] For Kant, the result was clear: "We may look for a continuous approximation to that church, eternally uniting all men, which constitutes the visible representation...of an invisible Kingdom of God on earth."[314]

In all this, we observe Kant presenting his readers with a picture of man at a moment of decision – at an historical crossroads, as it were.[315] The moment has been cast in ethico-historical terms, and in Books Two through Four of the *Religion* Kant offers various reasons man should choose "virtue" over "happiness," "morality" over mere "legality," and the pursuit of "holiness" over the "peace" and "profit" of civilization.[316]

Kant's understanding of this moment of decision, however, is informed by what he himself called "philosophical millenarianism." He makes this claim in 1784 in his famous essay "Idea for a Universal History from a Cosmopolitan Point of View."[317] What he says in that essay about philosophical millenarianism is most revealing. He writes, "Everyone can see that philosophy can have her belief in a millennium, but her millenarianism is not Utopian, since the idea can help, though only from afar, to bring the millennium to pass."[318] The millennium to which Kant is referring, the idea that will "help" realize the millennium from "afar," is the "ethical commonwealth," the recollectivized religious community (i.e., the Kingdom of God on earth) that allows for the full expression of man's moral personality.[319] This millennium, moreover, which beckons from afar and promises hope for a better future, is inextricably tied up in Kant's mind with the idea of holiness.[320] From that idea man borrows motives for the kind of ethical action in the present that will be necessary to overcome the obstacles "civilization" has placed in the way of the realization of his moral personality. Or, to put Kant's philosophical millenarianism in more familiar terms, the idea of holiness in the future stands to the pursuit of virtue in the present as eschatology as axiology stands to eschatology as teleology.[321] Whatever the terminology, the ethical dynamism of the *Religion* is that of an evolutionary eschatology shaped to the purposes of assimilationism and Christian reform.

That Kant meant for Christians to be ethical activists is clear from his criticism of those aspects of theology that "rob a man of his courage and reduce him to a state of sighing moral passivity in which nothing great or good is undertaken."[322] Indeed, Kant wants none of this "misconceived humility," none of this "slavish cast of mind."[323] For him, Christians must be *Gemüter*, men who have a sense of their "own moral worth" and who possess the "resolution" and "courage" to pursue virtue as a means of improving collective life.[324] These men, Kant continues in a telling Pelagian-like sentence, need not be "exiled into paganism" for their "self-conceit."[325] Rather, these men need to become the carriers of a new Christian standard of good life conduct, a standard whereby "godliness" is presented as "virtue's culmination."[326]

In associating virtue with the disposition of the man who has the courage to strive ceaselessly after moral improvement, Kant knew, as Lessing before him knew, he was introducing the idea of perfectibility into Christianity.[327] It is "our universal duty as men," Kant wrote, "to elevate ourselves to [the] ideal of moral perfection."[328] Kant specifically says that the possibility "of conforming our course of life to the holiness of the law is impossible of execution in any given time."[329] Yet, if man commits himself to this ideal (and he does this by accepting Jesus as a model for his behavior), his disposition will be such that, even though all his actions fall short of perfection, the "series of approximations [of action to ideal] carried on without end" may prove "well-pleasing to God."[330] In words that remind us of the Christian rendering of the Platonic notion of *homoiosis*, Kant writes that once man has "confidence in his moral disposition" he "has reasonable grounds for hope" that he will "approach ever nearer to, though he can never reach, the goal of perfection."[331] Assimilation to God, rather than self-deification, is what Kant is talking about here.[332] He is very clear on the matter: ". . . true religion is to consist not in salvation but in what we must do to become worthy of it."[333]

In the *Religion*, then, Kant offers us a philosophical millenarianism in which the eschatological notion of the coming of the Kingdom of God (i.e., as an "ethical commonwealth") acts as an incentive to this-worldly ethical activism (i.e., to the idea of virtue as the pursuit of holiness). That, Kant tells us, is how Jesus had employed the eschatological mode in his own teaching. As Kant noted of "Revelations,"

the account [which] closes with *the end of the world*. . .may be interpreted as a symbolical representation intended merely to enliven hope and courage and to increase our endeavors to that end. The Teacher of the Gospel revealed to his disciples the kingdom of God on earth only in its glorious, soul-elevating moral aspect, namely, in terms of the value of citizenship in a divine state, and to this end he informed them of what they had to do, not only to achieve it themselves but to unite with all others of the same mind and, so far as possible, with the entire human race.[334]

According to Kant, however, there is "nothing mystical" about this, for Jesus' use of eschatology "may be interpreted as a symbolic representation intended merely to enliven hope and courage and to increase our endeavors to [realize the Kingdom of God on earth]."[335] Once that is understood, Kant continues, Jesus' eschatological mode "can take on, before reason, [its] right symbolic meaning."[336]

For Kant, of course, that meaning expressed itself in philosophical millenarianism, in *Vernunftreligion*. But it was a *Vernunftreligion* that "freed [religion itself] from all empirical determining grounds and from all statutes which rest on history and which through the agency of ecclesiastical faith *provisionally* unite men for the requirements of the good."[337] So liberated, religion would "rule over all, so that God may be all in all."[338] That, we have seen, was precisely what Hegel was arguing for in his sermons and in the "Tübingen Essay" – which explains why he had no qualms about using Kant (i.e., the *Religion*) to advance the case for *Volksreligion* and the ideal of Protestant civil piety in his own work.[339]

Given the many points of contact between the *Religion* and the "Tübingen Essay" it seems appropriate to ask in what sense the latter is a "Kantian" tract. On one level, the essay is quite obviously Kantian, for its terminology and overall thrust show marked similarities with that of the *Religion*.[340] On another level, though, those similarities are precisely what make the "Tübingen Essay" so non-Kantian, and in two senses. On the one hand, the essay is contextually non-Kantian because it conforms neither to Storr's orthodox nor to Diez's strictly rationalist interpretation of Kant. On the other hand, the essay is historically non-Kantian because there is nothing particularly Kantian about its subject matter. In terms of the history of Protestant and Christian religious thought Hegel's essay and Kant's *Religion* are understandable as expressions of the ethico-eschatological tradition we discussed in Part I of this study. Hegel, we know, became heir to this tradition through the mediation of down-to-earth Pietism in Old-Württemberg, through its assimilation of covenant theology and the theology of the divine economy to the Württemberg context. And Kant had been moving toward that tradition since about 1784, when he realized that teleology in ethico-historical and religious senses was essential to the pursuit of holiness.[341]

Thus, when Hegel turned to the *Religion* in 1792–1793 and incorporated certain aspects of it into his thought, he was drawing upon arguments that were not Kantian in any conventional philosophical sense. If anything, they were the typical arguments of someone who wished synergistically to steer a course between orthodoxy and outright secularism. So, rather than talk about Kant's philosophical influence on Hegel at this time, it would be better to talk about Kant's and Hegel's attempts in 1793 to articulate a vision in which evolutionary eschatology and assimilationism served the purposes of ethico-political activism and Christian reform.[342]

Another sense of how Kant and Hegel were converging in their works of 1793 can be derived from the following considerations. In 1790, in *The Critique of Judgment*, Kant asked the following question: "Is [teleology] a branch of natural science . . . or of theology?"[343] From what he goes on to say, it is quite evident that he meant to regard teleology as a theological concept and to use it as an alternative to Pantheistic materialism.[344] Put in slightly different terms, Kant wished to distinguish "physico-theology" and "ethico-theology" and to apply the term "teleology" only to the latter.[345]

Earlier in this chapter and throughout Part I of this study we noted how teleology had been used in this ethico-theological sense by Christian reformers – that is, "assimilation to God" (i.e., ethico-theology) rather than "concord with nature" (physico-theology) was regarded as the telos of a purposeful Christian life. As Lovejoy has told us, early Christians had some difficulty with the Stoic notion of "conformity" to "Nature" as a norm of value and conduct.[346] Hence, their willingness to pursue the idea of progressive revelation as vital to the telos of the religious life.

Throughout his Berne period (1793–1796), Hegel continued to concern himself with the problem of "How far is the Christian religion qualified to serve as a *Volksreligion?*" He did so, I think, from the vantage point of teleology in the special sense we have been talking about. In a fragment from 1794, Hegel had asked this question;[347] in answering it he wrote: "Not all instincts of human nature have morality as their purpose – but the supreme purpose of man is to be moral, and among the tendencies that contribute to this end, his tendency toward religion is one of the most important."[348] As Hegel saw it, however, the present "public legal system" did "not have morality, but only legality as its immediate purpose."[349] A little later, in a letter of 1795 to Schelling, Hegel is even more specific. Remarking upon the condition of "humanity" (i.e., the juridico-civil state in man's religious development) in the present, Hegel contends that with "the spread of the ideas of how things ought to be [in a moral sense], the indolence of the law-abiding people to accept everything as it is will disappear."[350] At that moment, Hegel asserts to his friend, as he would later assert to Württembergers in the pamphlet of 1798 and in the long unpublished essay on the "German Constitution," *Gemüter* "will learn to sacrifice themselves" for the sake of a constitutional arrangement in which the "salvation of the human race" rather than "personal advantage" will be the end pursued.[351]

In another letter to Schelling, also from 1795, Hegel confided the following:

If I had time, I would try to determine more precisely how far – after the establishment of moral faith we may employ the legitimated idea of God backward, e.g., in the clarification of teleology, etc., how far we may take it back with us from ethical theology to physical theology and still exercise control with it there.[352]

What Hegel is saying here is quite interesting. He is posing, I think, Kant's question about teleology. Specifically, Hegel wants to determine at precisely what point, and under what circumstances, teleology in the form of ethical theology may be said to arise as a realistic alternative to physical theology. If that point can be identified, Hegel feels, then the religio-political issue of what a *Volkserzieher* needs to do in order to advance the case for *Volksreligion* and the "salvation of the human race" can be more precisely formulated.

Hegel recognized, of course, that his call to the *Gemüter* would be opposed by those "devoid" of "higher interests," by those whose concerns ran along the lines of "worldly advantage."[353] But their opposition, Hegel insisted, could be overcome if, as he put it in 1796, the *Volkserzieher* would "descend into the realms of physics" and set out *from there* to "give wings" to it.[354] That task, Hegel contended, was a collective endeavor – "the work of man"; and, as Hegel conceived it, the aim of that work, "the last and greatest of mankind," was to establish "eternal unity among us."[355] The question, then, of how to give "wings to physics" was Hegel's way of asking "how must a world [i.e., "civilization"] be constituted [in physical terms] for a moral being [both to exist in it and emerge *out of* it]?"[356] Or, as he put it in several letters of 1795, his concern during this period was to make clear to himself "what it may mean, 'to draw near to God'" given the situation of man in the present.[357]

In this context, it would seem that two of Hegel's most often discussed essays from the Berne period, the "Life of Jesus" and "The Positivity of the Christian Religion," were written to answer two questions:[358] first, there was the question of to what extent Jesus' teachings could be said to provide the basis for *Volksreligion*;[359] and second, there was the issue of what "drawing near to God" entailed for the life conduct of *homo religiosus*. As I see it, the two questions are related in that both culminate in arguments that make *Sittlichkeit*, the ethical striving of the collectivity for holiness, the ultimate aim of *homo religiosus*.[360] So conceived, *Sittlichkeit* becomes, for Hegel, the point of conceptual mediation between "virtue" qua the good life conduct of *homo religiosus* (i.e., *praxis pietatis*) and "holiness" qua the "highest good" (i.e., the arrival of the Kingdom of God on earth).

That this is Hegel's intention is evident from the opening paragraphs of the "Life of Jesus."[361] There, in words that remind us of how early Christians used the Fourth Gospel to make an ethicoeschatological case for Christian activism and reform, Hegel talks about "the divine spark" in man that John and Jesus alluded and appealed to in their effort to make "men conscious of... their dignity."[362] As *Volkserzieher* themselves, it was John's and Jesus' mission to acquaint men with their "true" selves as distinct from that side of them that inclined toward "happiness."[363] For Jesus, Hegel noted a few pages later, man was not entirely a "sensual being" whose "nature" could be fulfilled in "pleasure" alone.[364] Man was also a "spiritual" being who had a "spark" of "Godliness" about him.[365] To develop that "spark," Hegel tells us, was what Jesus' teaching was all about.[366] By the same token, it was man's "*Bestimmung*" to let that spark shine forth evermore into his life."[367]

Having presented Jesus thusly, Hegel proceeds to argue that the main thrust of Jesus' message was to remind a people of "the unique worth which *Sittlichkeit* confers on mankind."[368] Again and again, Hegel's point is that, vis-à-vis the statutory aspects of Judaism, Jesus called for cultivation of man's disposition toward *Sittlichkeit* (i.e., the covenant as fellowship) through the practice of piety.[369] And throughout the essay, Hegel presents ethical activism, *Sittlichkeit,* and the Kingdom of God as the core elements in Jesus' teachings. As Hegel had Jesus say, "Wait not on someone else... but take the responsibility for your improvement in your own hands.... For by so doing, you will bring the Kingdom of God about."[370] Hegel's Jesus, in short, is just what Haering said he was: an advocate of *Sittlichkeit.*[371] Therefore, the line Hegel followed in the essay was perfectly consistent with the needs of reform-minded Protestants in Old-Württemberg in the 1790s.

Besides Hegel's Württemberg origins, there is another very good, often neglected reason Hegel should have written the essay on Jesus the way he did. While Hegel was living in Berne he surely must have become aware of the uses to which Kant was being put by Swiss Protestants during the 1780s and 1790s. Granted, we know very little about Hegel's day-to-day existence in Berne between 1793 and 1796; even so, scholars generally agree that Hegel's detailed knowledge of Berne's political economy testifies to his deep interest in what was going on in the city during his stay there.[372]

Thanks to the work of Paul Wernle, though, we know quite a lot about what Protestants were thinking in Berne while Hegel was living there.[373] Among Swiss Protestants in general, Wernle tells us, there had been a strong tendency toward Pelagianism since early in the eighteenth century,[374] when Samuel Werenfels (1657–1740) began to remind Christians of the ethical aspect of Jesus' teachings.[375] By 1773, for example, a leading spokesman for orthodoxy in Berne was warning of the drift toward Pelagianism.[376] And with good cause, for J. J. Hess had just published a *Life of Jesus* that depicted the savior in very "down-to-earth," practical terms.[377]

More specifically, Wernle has given us information about the religious concerns of a group of Protestants in Berne who gathered around the theologian J. S. Ith.[378] According to Wernle, Ith and several of his followers, especially D. Müslin and P. Stapfer, worked hard in the 1790s to give Protestantism an activist and reformist face. In this, they availed themselves of Kant, whose writings, they thought, dovetailed nicely with their view of Jesus as the teacher of an ethical religion. As reformers, they sought to retrieve Jesus from the hands of orthodoxy and to put his teachings to purposes that would serve the interests of those who wished to continue the Reformation in the face of orthodox intransigence.

It is somewhat misleading, therefore, to treat Hegel's "Life of Jesus" as simply a Kantian philosophical tract.[379] Nor is it exactly helpful to claim that the *Problemstellung* of the essay "is Kantian."[380] From one perspective that is true, but it is a perspective that misses the point of what Hegel is trying to do in the essay. In the essay he is not trying so much to be a Kantian as to address a problem that reform-minded Protestants had been thinking about for some time. Thus, where Hegel has Jesus differentiate the "letter" and the "spirit" of the law, he is, to be sure, declaring himself a Kantian of the spirit.[381] But the spirit derives from the *Religion* and is, therefore, thoroughly Protestant in a reformist sense.[382] Small wonder, then, that Hegel's Jesus is a spokesman for *Vernunft-* and *Volksreligion* at one and the same time.

If scholarly doubt still exists about the reformist religious concerns that informed the "Life of Jesus," it can be dispelled further by examining the argument of "The Positivity of the Christian Religion," an essay Hegel also wrote while at Berne, toward the end of his stay there.[383] As in the "Life of Jesus," the essay on "Positivity" begins by focusing on Jesus and his relationship to Judaism. Once again Hegel's strategy is to juxtapose Jesus' teachings with the "burden of statutory commands" that "overwhelmed" the religious life of the Jews on a day-to-day level.[384] Because there was "a [religious] rule for every casual action of daily life," the Jewish religion had a "monastic" aspect about it.[385] According to Hegel, the result was that by Jesus' time "the service of God and [the call to] virtue, was ordered and compressed in dead formulas and nothing save pride in this slavish obedience to law. . .was left to the Jewish spirit."[386]

In this context, Hegel speculates, "there must have been Jews of a better heart and head" who refused "to become lifeless machines."[387] Among this group, Hegel continues, "there must have been aroused. . . the need for a nobler gratification than that of priding themselves on this mechanical slavery."[388] Jesus, Hegel tells us, was such a Jew. He "undertook to raise religion and virtue to morality and to restore to morality the freedom which is its essence."[389] Reminding his fellows that the laws of their sacred books were animated more by the spirit of *covenant* than by the letter of *contract*,[390] Hegel's Jesus urged Judaism to become once again "a virtue religion."[391] To do this, the "teacher of virtue" placed "all value in doing," in legislating for the self in terms of the collective interest (i.e., *Sittlichkeit*) of a religious people.[392]

As Hegel tells Jesus' story, though, Jesus found few listeners for his message. His fellows persisted in "the delusion that legality is the whole of morality."[393] In obeying the law a "pious Israelite had done what the divine commands required. . . and he simply could not believe that he had any further obligations."[394] Thus, Jesus' failure; thus, the initiatives of this "reformer" succumbed to the "immaturity" of a nation that preferred servility under a "yoke of law" to true freedom.[395]

Yet Hegel knew that on another level Jesus had not been a failure at all. Christianity, after all, did arise, survive, and prosper as a religion. But there, too, a problem arose for Hegel, a problem that he pursued over the course of the rest of the essay on "Positivity." That problem was to explain how a "virtue religion" that had failed to take hold among the Jews managed to survive with the Christians, but in a "positive" religious form of its own, i.e., in "a religion which is grounded in authority and puts man's worth not at all. . .in morals."[396]

In dealing with this problem Hegel offered two explanations. First, he conceded that Jesus' use of some of the categories of Jewish messianism[397] had "made it possible for the character of the Christian religion as a virtue religion to be misconceived in early times and turned at first into a sect and later into a positive faith."[398] By this Hegel meant to draw attention – as others had before him – to the tendency on the part of Jesus' disciples to make reverence for Jesus' moral teachings dependent on reverence for the authority of his "person."[399]

In this context, though, Hegel's historical sense obliged him to admit that the disciples' turn toward positivity "could not have been otherwise if the Christian religion was to be maintained, if it was to be established as a public religion and handed on as such to posterity."[400] In saying this, Hegel was not just offering the strategy of contextualization as an apology for the shortcomings of Jesus' disciples. No, for as the rewritten Preface to the "Positivity" essay clearly shows, Hegel intended to argue that it was precisely because positivity was *at the time* "necessary" to the survival of the "Christian religion" that its authoritarian teachings could be construed as of "accidental" rather than of "eternal validity" to "the religion of Jesus."[401] Hence, the possibility that in time the Christian religion would become the "virtue religion" (i.e., *Volksreligion*) that Jesus had spoken for against the positivity of Judaism and that Hegel was speaking for against the orthodoxy of Lutheranism. As Hegel clearly put it:

Jesus tried to draw his people's attention to the spirit and disposition which had to vitalize their observance of their laws if they were to please God, but under the government of the church this "fulfillment" of the laws was turned once again into rules and ordinances which in turn always need a similar "fulfillment."[402]

If Hegel cited Jesus' relationship to his disciples as one reason Christianity had become a positive religion, he also took careful note of how more general historical circumstances shaped that relationship. And with this shift of interest we begin to see the emergence of a new set of concerns that, ultimately, profoundly altered Hegel's thinking about Christianity and the role it could play in the modern world.

As has just been indicated, it was relatively easy for Hegel to demonstrate that the early Christians were as much in "bondage to the law" as the Jews had been.[403] Why, then, Hegel asks, were non-Christians drawn to this religion?[404] To answer that question Hegel looked to the political "spirit of the age" for some guidance.[405] What he discovered there were circumstances that made acceptance of the divinity of Jesus and the "authority" of his "person" easier to believe in.[406] Specifically, Hegel invoked the image of an imperial Rome in which "the despotism of the Roman emperors had chased the human spirit from the earth and spread a misery which compelled men to seek and expect happiness in heaven."[407] Slowly, "as depotism" poisoned more and more of the sources of life... the age revealed its hopeless triviality in the turn taken by its conception of God's divinity."[408] The result: a conception of a God whom we "no longer regarded as like ourselves...to which we contributed nothing by our activity, but into which...we could beg or conjure our way."[409]

In light of this religio-political convergence, men lost the "will" to moral activism.[410] Instead, they began "to wish" for "the realization" of religious ideals that were "beyond the boundaries of human powers" and that were expected to be acquired "without our co-operation."[411] Given this self-conception, Hegel argued, men must have "despised themselves from the moral point of view,"[412] with the consequence that they "were bound to create the doctrine of the corruption of human nature and adopt it gladly."[413] Small wonder, Hegel concluded, that "belief in human potentialities" soon was viewed as "a sin."[414] Like Kant, Hegel regarded this as misconceived "piety";[415] and by setting himself in opposition to this conception of the divine–human relationship he served notice on orthodoxy that he, too, was a religious reformer and that, like Kant, he would not acquiesce in exiling the call for virtue to paganism.[416]

That this religio-political argument was perfectly consistent with the basic thrust of the "Tübingen Essay" should be obvious. In both cases, Württemberg's Hegel, the "old man," posited close relationships between religious and political activism and reform. And that, we know, was a "cultural given" for many Württemberg Protestants in the eighteenth century. But toward the end of the "Positivity" essay Hegel touched upon another subject that, as we shall see in Part III, was to have enormous importance for his thought for the next few years, until at least 1804. That subject was economics.

The topic arises in the context of Hegel's discussion of Roman imperialism, for, Hegel tells us, one of the consequences of Roman expansion was an "increase of wealth" as well as an "acquaintance with luxury."[417] Using their newfound wealth to great effect, the aristocracy "acquired a dominion and an influence over the masses,"[418] with the result that the idea of "the state as a product of [man's] own energies disappeared from the citizen's soul."[419] Citing Montesquieu in support of his view, Hegel held that with this development "virtue" vanished from the political scene and from among the Roman people.[420] From that time on "the end [the Roman people] set before themselves in their political life was gain, self-maintenance, and perhaps vanity."[421] Citizenship came to be defined in economic terms, as "a right to the security of that property which now filled his entire world."[422] For Hegel, in other words, there were positive politicoeconomic as well as negative politico-religious reasons for the turn of Christianity toward positivity.[423]

In light of that awareness, Hegel began to realize that an effective program of religious reform in the present would have to do more than provide a high-minded ethico-religious alternative to men who had for so long been taught to despise themselves "from the moral point of view." The appeal to human dignity, to the spark of divinity in man, was, of course, still necessary. But it had to be made in a more "roundabout" way[424] – the appeal had to be framed so as to persuade men that the satisfaction they derived from the economic advantages of citizenship qua "security of property" were not sustainable on any long-term basis.[425] Hence, Hegel's new interest in economics was "dialectically" related to his continuing interest in religious reform.[426] That is, as was noted before, his thought from about 1796 on was moving around two figures at once: that of *homo religiosus* and that of *homo oeconomicus*.

In Part III I shall try to show how the key to the development of Hegel's thought between 1796 and 1804 lies in appreciating this religio-economic interplay. Moreover, I shall try to demonstrate how this interplay reveals itself in terms of what might be understood as a linguistic exercise in the synonymizing and desynonymizing of two key concepts – nature and *Sittlichkeit*.[427] Indeed, what Hegel does in several of the writings of this period is use a socioeconomic mode of presentist discourse to synonymize nature and *Sittlichkeit* and then a politico-religious mode of conditional discourse to desynonymize them. It is, I think, in that linguistic context that *Sittlichkeit* becomes a resource of ambiguity in Hegel's thought.[428] It is the purpose of Part III of this study to show how this ambiguity manifested itself in Hegel's social and political theory.

PART III

Toward the *Phenomenology*

Sittlichkeit becomes a problem in social
and political theory

Works of nature and art one does not get to know as they are finished; one has to
catch them in their genesis to comprehend them.

Goethe

I am persuaded that one can be clear, even in the poverty of our language, not by
always giving the same meanings to the same words, but by arranging it so that
as often as each word is used, the meaning given it be sufficiently determined by
the ideas related to it.

Rousseau

In the past, it was the work of the intellectuals to sublimate the possession of
sacred values into a belief in "redemption." The conception of the idea of redemption, as such, is very old, if one understands by it a liberation from distress,
hunger, drought, sickness, and ultimately from suffering and death. Yet redemption attained a specific significance only where it expressed a systematic and
rationalized "image of the world" and represented a stand in the face of the world.
For the meaning as well as the intended and actual psychological quality of
redemption had depended upon such a world image and such a stand. Not ideas,
but material and ideal interests, directly govern men's conduct. Yet very frequently the "world images" that have been created by "ideas" have, like switch-
men, determined the tracks along which action has been pushed by the dynamic
of interest. "From what" and "for what" one wished to be redeemed and, let us
not forget, "could be" redeemed, depended upon one's image of the world.

Weber

To say, as I do in Chapter 5, that Hegel "discovered" economics while at
Berne is slightly misleading. There are hints in the "Tübingen Essay" that
Hegel already understood how economics qua the force of habit, interest
and material circumstance conditioned the ethical choices men made
about the conduct of their lives in concrete historical situations. He
noted, for example, that because "sensibility is the principal factor in all

181

the action and striving of men," it was difficult "to decide whether mere prudence or actual morality is the determining ground of the will."[1] Having admitted this – that "in dealing with human nature and human life...we must take particular account of man's sensibility, his dependence on external and internal nature, upon his surroundings and the environment in which he lives, and upon sense impulses and blind instinct"[2] – Hegel proceeded to argue that "when there is a powerful propensity toward sensibility we frequently have to be content to produce only a law abiding habit in most men, and no purely ethical motives... are required to produce this."[3] From the context in which this remark is made, it is clear that Hegel regarded this "law abiding habit" as "a gain" insofar as it involved the refinement of a "grosser sensibility" he associated with man's "strictly animal drives."[4] In that sense, Hegel's "law abiding man" mirrors the qualities Kant had ascribed to man in his "human" condition.[5]

Further light is thrown on what Hegel is driving at here from two comments he made early in his Berne period. In the "Berne Plan" of 1794 Hegel wrote that "Not all the instincts of human nature...have morality as their purpose – but the supreme purpose of man is to be moral."[6] Continuing, he claimed, though, that the "civil legal system" existing in his era did "not have morality, but only legality as its immediate purpose."[7] Shortly thereafter, in a letter to Schelling, he made the same point in a more illuminating way. After noting that "at present the spirit of the constitution has made a pact with personal advantage and has based its rule upon that," he expressed the hope that the prevailing "apathetic" attitude of law-abiding interest groups, who "accept everything always just as it is," would soon give rise to a disposition to see "how things *ought* to be" in a moral sense.[8] Clearly, then, Hegel regarded the kind of prudence he associated with civility in a legal sense as an advance for men;[9] but he did not accept that advance as sufficient in itself to warrant moral praise.[10]

In this, we have seen, Hegel's position was not unique. In Württemberg, reform-minded Protestants had been criticizing the oligarchic tendencies within the Small Council for years.[11] Concurrently, thinkers such as Lessing and Kant were raising hard questions about the relationship between civil and moral values in the thought of the German bourgeoisie as a whole.[12] But as we saw in the "Positivity" essay, there was something relatively new about Hegel's position on all this. Although much of the argument of that essay confirmed Hegel's view that the orthodox Christian notion of original sin had marked affinities with despotic political rule,[13] another part of the argument hinted at the possibility that both forms of oppression had an economic underpinning. That is, Hegel sensed a certain dovetailing of interest between the economic and legal concerns citizens exhibited about the security of their property and the apathy they manifested toward the "hidden game" orthodox religious and despotic political leaders played with regard to their conspiracy perpetually to dishonor the human race.[14]

Therefore, we do not need to wait for Marx and Engels to tell us about the Luther–Adam Smith convergence.[15] Hegel was aware of it very early on – that is, for him it was not just a question of disabusing men of a negative religiopolitical self-conception but also of persuading them voluntarily to enlarge their self-conception so that they could pursue moral values that lay above and beyond those that clustered around the security of property issue in a civil sense.[16] To do this, Hegel had to begin to study economics, and it is in that context that his reading of the Scots becomes important.

I believe that the religious concerns of Württemberg's "old man" and the economic ones of the "young Hegel" come into juxtaposition at precisely this point and provide Hegel with what Kenneth Burke would call a "perspective by incongruity."[17] That, according to Burke, is a "moment" in time when ideas "that had been considered mutually exclusive" merge in the mind of a thinker to form a new complex of symbolic action.[18] On the one hand, as a reform-minded Protestant, Hegel remained committed both to *Sittlichkeit* as a religious ideal and to the recollectivization of public life in Württemberg. On the other hand, as a student of the Scots (especially of Ferguson, Steuart, and Smith), he had come to understand how emergent, irreversible, and centrifugal socioeconomic forces in Europe as a whole would soon conspire against the realization of his religious ideal.[19] In that context, the question was: could *Sittlichkeit* be translated into the language of social and political theory without having its religious sense lost in the stuff of economics?

The answer to this question, Hegel thought, was yes; and therein lies the key to the ambiguities Hegel purposefully builds into his concept of *Sittlichkeit* during these years. As we shall see, from about 1796 to 1804 *Sittlichkeit* became a conceptual axis and point of mediation between his religious values and what he was learning from the Scots about socioeconomic processes and patterns of development in history.[20] To put it in Schiller's terms – and he was reading Schiller carefully at this time – Hegel accepted the Scottish claim that "physical man does in fact exist" in a civil context, but unlike the Scots and like Schiller he believed "the existence of moral man [*der Sittliche*] is as yet problematic."[21] Hegel's problem, then, was to solve the latter problem in terms of the former while at the same time allowing *Sittlichkeit* to retain its collectivist religious dynamic.[22]

Once Hegel's conception of *Sittlichkeit* is placed in this religioeconomic context, it is easy to see why it has lent itself to such divergent interpretations. Working backward from the notion of modernity as a value complex with a strongly individualist cultural bias, Hegel's reformist and collectivist religio-political interests will appear as reactionary or conservative; but working forward from the eighteenth-century German religious context these same concerns will appear progressive, even liberal, vis-à-vis the political culture that had formed around orthodox Lutheranism. Aside from guarding against the anachronistic aspects of the former interpretation, what is important to realize here is that what makes *Sittlichkeit* progressive in a religious context makes it reactionary in a socioeconomic one.[23] That is, *Sittlichkeit* in its liberal religious mode may be envisaged not only as a progressive religious alternative to orthodoxy, but also as a response to, and criticism of, the relatively progressive socioeconomic views of the Scottish thinkers, at least as we have come to think of them as proponents of a laissez-faire world view.[24] In other words, as a *liberal* Protestant reformer, Hegel's commitment to *Sittlichkeit* entailed both acceptance of and an *after the fact* criticism of bourgeois socioeconomic interests and values.[25] As Hegel saw it, the increasing organization of collective life along the socioeconomic lines of a commercial society made the need for *Sittlichkeit* all the more necessary.[26] Without *Sittlichkeit*, there was nothing to prevent society from slipping back from a condition of humanity, where the possibility for moral improvement existed, to one of animality, where it did not.[27]

Here, moreover, it is important to remember that prior to his Scottish exposure Hegel had meant for *Sittlichkeit* to encompass objective experience as a whole. In this form, *Sittlichkeit* had been a principle of collective unity as much as a religious value. Now, it seemed that in order to preserve *Sittlichkeit* as an ideal Hegel would have to scale down his expectations for its objective scope. The more his Scottish-inspired realism forced him to expand his understanding of the dynamics of objective experience, the more his religiously inspired idealism had to confine itself to smaller and smaller strategic enclaves within it. Put another way, the more Hegel learned about the socioeconomic aspects of "civil society" from the Scots, the more conditional his own thought became with regard both to the problem of *Sittlichkeit* and to the prospects for the recollectivization of public life in the modern world.[28]

This interplay between realism and idealism, this overlay between progressive European socioeconomic thought and progressive German religious thought, I think, governs the development of Hegel's thought between 1796 and 1804.[29] During those years this interplay and overlay prompted Hegel to begin to differentiate socioeconomic aspects of objective experience from political ones. As we shall see, the upshot of this is that Hegel's concern with *Sittlichkeit* evolved after 1796 into an elaboration of the differences between the political and the socioeconomic "moments" of objective experience. This elaboration, in turn, led Hegel toward the state–civil society conceptual split that became all-important to his thought in later years.[30]

In the four chapters that follow, I try to identify the thought processes that lay behind the state–civil society conceptual split as it appeared in the early Jena period. Hegel, we shall see, came to the distinction while trying to find conceptual space and positive institutional correlates within objective experience for the religious ideal of *Sittlichkeit*. To this end, Part III of this study envisages Hegel's development between 1796 and 1804 as an exercise in applied religion, as part of an attempt to use secular arguments to advance the case for religious reformism. This exercise, I think, informs much of Hegel's social and political theory. Indeed, if we are ever to make historical sense of his writings, we need to grasp this aspect of his thought. This is especially true of our understanding of the *Phenomenology*. So, if the focus of Part III is on the implications the reconsideration of *Sittlichkeit* had for Hegel's social and political theory, it also offers insights into the prehistory of the *Phenomenology*.

5

Hegel discovers the economy

While discussing the respective Christian and classical components of Savonarola's and Guicciardini's thought, Pocock has claimed that the two thinkers, despite some sharp differences, agreed on one thing: that "luxury" corrupted men.[1] According to Pocock, while "Savonarola had seen luxuries and vanities as distracting the soul from the pursuit of salvation, Guicciardini [saw] them as distracting the citizen from the pursuit of the public good."[2] Given this parallel, Pocock concluded that "what should be stressed here is less the secular divergence between the Christian and civic traditions than the extent to which they found common ground in an ideal of austerity and self-denial [vis-à-vis luxury]."[3]

That there was a good deal of this kind of asceticism in Pietism in general and in Hegel's thought in the early 1790s in particular has been a recurring theme in Parts I and II of this study. As has been shown, *homo religiosus'* concern with collective salvation and *zōon politikon's* concern with civic virtue were closely connected. Indeed, for many pietists the notion of "dying into life" by way of one's vocation made self-sacrifice in the name of the collectivity at once a religious and a political duty. So construed, "dying into life" could be regarded both as a means of political participation and as a step toward the fulfillment of one's religious "personality."

Still, as was becoming increasingly evident in the eighteenth century, the call for ascetic self-denial vis-à-vis the passions and the impulse toward luxury that was so often associated with them was gradually being undermined by concrete historical developments[4] and by the arguments of countless "apologists" for luxury, who were stressing its "utility" not only for economic development but also for the advance of "civilization" itself.[5] Instead of depraving morals, as conventional wisdom had had it, luxury was being celebrated or tolerated as a vital spur to "ingenuity," "industry," "employment," and the promotion of the "mechanical arts."[6] In Hume's words, luxury was "innocent" so long as it was not "pursued at the expense of some virtue, as liberality or charity."[7]

Apologists for luxury went still further when they began to herald it as crucial to the cultivation of the "liberal" arts, the arts that, according to Hume, aimed at the cultivation of "the pleasures of the mind" in a moral sense rather than those of the body in a physical sense.[8] Indeed, in the eighteenth century a concerted effort was being made by some "progressive" thinkers in England and France to link the ideas of luxury and civilization together so that the prosperity they associated with the former term and the high-minded moralism they wished to associate with the latter term could be construed as different yet positively related aspects of one and the same "enlightened" age.[9] As Hume put it, "industry, knowledge and humanity, are linked together by an indissoluble chain, and are found, to be peculiar to the more polished, . . . the more luxurious ages."[10] The principle that informed Hume's claim was simple: civilized men knew how to use the leisure that their wealth gave them wisely.[11] Thus, the more refined they became, the less inclined they were, in his words, to "indulge in excesses of any kind."[12]

Against the moderates and outright "libertines" who defended luxury on the grounds of utility, men such as John Brown and T. Smollett had little to offer their fellows in the way of new disincentives to its pursuit.[13] They tended to reiterate the conventional wisdom about luxury – that its causes could be eradicated by more vigilance, more asceticism, more fear of God's damnation, and greater "repression" of the body by the mind.[14] These were men whom Hume would have called "severe moralists"[15] – men whom, he charged, "blame even the most innocent luxury, and represent it as the source of all the corruptions, disorders and factions, incident to civil government."[16]

To a man of Hume's moderate persuasion, the views of both the "libertines" and the "severe moralists" were extreme.[17] Ever alert to the "many ills" of what he called "vicious luxury,"[18] he nevertheless recognized that luxury was an ill generally "preferable to sloth and idleness"[19] and that given human nature, it was not likely to be cured by repression or prohibition. For Hume as well as for Saint-Lambert luxury was beneficial to society until it became vicious.[20] And it only became vicious, so they argued, when it ceased to promote "industry" in a "solid" *economic* sense and became associated with status seeking in a "vain" *social* sense.[21] If, however, luxury were to become vicious, appropriate "police" actions would have to be initiated to curb the danger of real and potential *social* excesses.[22] For these moderates, in other words, luxury needed to be "contained" for social, not economic, reasons. Its causes were not to be "repressed" in an "ascetic" sense so much as its effects were to be "harnessed" in a "civil" sense.[23] This quite clearly was Hume's position in the early 1750s. And in a very general sense this was the way the Scots viewed the relationship between commerce, luxury, and civilization at the time the Germans began reading them in the late eighteenth century.[24]

But the Germans did not just read the Scots: they adapted them to their own purposes. A good indication of how this was done can be seen in how the Germans received the work of Adam Ferguson in the 1760s, 1770s, and 1780s.[25] His two early works – *An Essay on the History of Civil Society* and *Institutes of Moral Philosophy* – were quickly translated into German.[26] It is not hard to see what the Germans found attractive about them, particularly about the *Institutes*, which C. Garve translated in 1772. Ferguson's text makes the argument that, although man is by nature a social animal, the character of man's social experience will vary depending upon whether the pursuit of "preservation" in a material sense or the pursuit of "excellence" (*Vollkommenheit*) in a moral sense governs his collective life.[27] In the former condition, man lives a social existence in a rational manner but does so with an eye toward ever increasing his "comfort" in a material sense.[28] In the latter condition, man exhibits "a greatness of mind" that entails a commitment to moral excellence and the pursuit of spiritual values.[29] Thus, Ferguson's work made two telling points about social life: it recognized the economic origins of society but, at the same time, it refused to accept the related premises that society was *merely* an economic organization and could be justified to men solely in terms of its satisfaction of their physical needs.

In light of what was said in Chapter 4 about Lessing's "honest man," Kant's concept of "civilization," and Hegel's attitude toward the property –legality–morality problem,[30] it is not hard to see why Ferguson appealed to the Germans. The Germans found a "sociological realism" in his work, presented in the form of a philosophy of history, that could be used to underline the call for ethical activism so essential to the emergent Protestant theology of history. It is surely no accident that this is precisely what Garve stressed in the commentary he included in his translation of the *Institutes* in 1772.[31] According to Garve, what distinguished men from animals was not social existence per se but the opportunity social existence qua material foundation gave man to realize himself as a moral being.[32] As Garve saw it, the material dimension of social existence afforded man an opportunity to realize his true telos in the sense that it provided him with a "reflective" moment, a moment of "leisure" and freedom, when he could choose just what kind of person he wished to become in a moral sense.[33]

To make the right choice, Garve argued, man's "imagination" had to be liberated somewhat from material restraints.[34] Once in that condition, however, imagination had to be directed properly – in Kant's terms, it had to be "disciplined" properly by culture[35] – that is, without that discipline man's imaginative faculty might very well incline in the direction of "fantasy," "fashion," and "recreation" (in a word, toward luxury in a pejorative sense) rather than in the direction of the pursuit of a redemptive *telos* in a spiritual and moral sense.[36] If that were to be the case, there would be every justification for civilized men to begin to take issue with the values of "civilization" from the vantage point of "culture."[37]

This, of course, is what many Germans did, Garve among them. Following Ferguson, he conceded that historically man had always been under enormous physical and social pressure to secure his survival and the perpetuation of the species. In those circumstances, Garve thought, it was foolish to talk about discipline as a way of life.[38] Garve noted, though, that Ferguson's account of how man would realize his true moral telos did not require this kind of presumptuousness, for Ferguson's work showed historically rather than abstractly how the possibility of mind disciplining body, of culture disciplining society, could be presented in evolutionary terms, in terms of a "chain" in which the links of physical necessity were gradually loosened so as to permit man to pursue moral ends of his own choosing.[39] Ferguson's work, in other words, enabled Garve to provide a socio-historical explanation of that moment of reflection when man qua *animal rationabile* could voluntarily and consciously begin to put his imagination to the service of collective redemption in a theo-teleological sense.[40] And when Garve did that he was providing an easy point of entry for sociological realism and historical evolutionism to move into German thought and establish contact with the tradition of Protestant thought that had developed around the theology of the divine economy argument.

On the level of ideas, the connection between these two modes of thought is not that hard to establish. Nor is the fact of the connection unusually German. As Viner, Tuveson, and Crane have convincingly shown, a similar convergence of ideas and interests can be detected in much English Protestant thought in the seventeenth and eighteenth centuries.[41] Crane, I think, is most instructive here. He has demonstrated that many English thinkers (i.e., Anglican apologists) who had previously been committed to the notion of progressive revelation in history found it easy to assimilate the principles of socioeconomic realism to their own religious purposes.[42] What enabled them to do this, Crane argues, was their willingness to regard commercial activity and the material prosperity that went with it as part of a "great providential design" for human redemption in history.[43] Given their understanding of that design, commercial prosperity was envisaged as a divine dispensation given to men by God at *that* point in history so as to provide them with leisure time that, when used properly, would lead, in John Taylor's words, to both greater "cultural" and greater "religious Attainments."[44]

According to Edmund Law, one of the key figures in Crane's study,[45] there was a close connection between a society's form of economic organi-

zation and the sophistication of its religious conceptions.[46] Indeed, as Law
saw it, there was a clear link between advances in "natural and civil life"
and a fully mature Christianity.[47] "Improvements" in the "Sciences" and
"Arts," he asserted, were essential if one were to experience Christianity
in its "fulness."[48] Clearly, the assumption was that as "civilization"
advanced, so did the *telos* of *homo religiosus*; that is, from the point of view
of the theology of the divine economy civil society could be construed – in
an accommodationist sense – as an instrument of salvation.[49] Hence, the
ease with which "progressive" Scottish thought in a socioeconomic sense
was assimilated into "progressive" German Protestant thought in a
religious sense.

In addition to Garve, other Germans were reading Ferguson this way,
And one of them was Hegel's hero, Lessing.[50] According to several
scholars, Ferguson's work persuaded Lessing that the Christian notion
of "progress toward perfection" could be "retrieved" and brought up to
date by means of some of the principles of mainline "enlightenment"
thought.[51] As Flajole put it, with Ferguson's "assistance" Lessing could
"now see history as the concrete record of human progress, a progress that
is the development of the divine immanent cause of nature."[52] As such,
Flajole continued, Lessing "can now speak of *men as responsible beings* who
are progressing with the basic purposefulness of the divinity toward a
lofty moral and intellectual perfection and a happiness that is always in
harmony with human nature *and its state of development*."[53]

This last statement, I think, captures reasonably well what was at issue
when Lessing remarked that "we are all sufficiently like God to be able to
do something else than just sin. We can weaken that power [of sensual
desire] and use it [if properly directed] for good as well as for evil
actions."[54] The decision as to which way to direct that power, however,
was now in man's hands. As William Worthington, one of Crane's apologists, observed, "free Agents may suffer their Liberty to Evil, to Gain
such a Head as to destroy Grace and Liberty to Good."[55] Yet, Worthington continued:

...there is a Possibility, that they may all improve their Liberty to Good, and
the Grace given them in Aid of it, to that Degree, as to destroy their Liberty to
Evil; and there is the highest Degree of Probability, that the Bulk of them at
length will. Because it is most reasonable to suppose, that reasonable Creatures,
after the continued Experience of the Benefits of Good, and Inconveniencies of
Evil, will at last perceive their true Interest, and act accordingly – that after
Vibrating for a Time from one Extreme to the other, the Centre of moral
Oscillation will at length be fix'd.[56]

And so it was with Lessing, who used a theology of history to challenge
"honest" men to move beyond mere prudence and legalism and become
religious in a high-minded moral sense.[57]

Schiller, too, seems to have read Ferguson this way.[58] As we shall see in Chapter 8, a good many of Ferguson's and Garve's points are reiterated in the *Aesthetic Education of Man*. Suffice it to say here that in the twenty-third letter Schiller drew attention to what he called "the indifferent sphere of physical life."[59] It was here, Schiller argued, that "man must make a start upon his moral life."[60] In saying this, Schiller recognized that for "human dignity" to survive in the modern world, for man to "be able *to wing* his way toward autonomy and freedom," the "war against matter" must be carried "into the very territory of matter itself, so that [man] may be spared having to fight this dread foe on the sacred soil of freedom."[61] Given this conviction, Schiller insisted that calls for moral activism be developed from a point *within* the physical world of sensuous man himself.[62] This was a conviction that Hegel shared, having developed it just about the time he was reading Schiller and the Scots. Whether the one or the other was more of an influence on Hegel at this time need not detain us here. Either way the result was the same: Hegel was persuaded to "lay hold on life" so as all the better to "lay hold on salvation."[63] Hence, his movement away from asceticism in the middle 1790s.

What this endeavor consisted in for Hegel will be discussed in detail in the remainder of this chapter, as well as as in subsequent ones. Suffice it to say here that Hegel's concern with economics was always governed by the principle of what Clement had called "learned leisure"[64] – that is, by the principle that wealth, riches, and even luxury were not, in Clement's words, "intrinsically" either "good" or "bad."[65] What mattered to Clement was "not to accuse what of itself has neither good nor evil qualities, but rather the mind of man, which has power to use [wealth] well or ill, being free to decide and responsible for its employment of the gifts of God."[66] Clement recognized, moreover, that "it was difficult to keep the luxuries of unusual wealth from dazzling [man's] soul."[67] He aimed, as Ferguson, Schiller, and Hegel later would, at persuading men who had some wealth and leisure to put both in the service of a higher moral life.[68] As he put it in his "Sermon on Riches,"

Wealth, for the Christians who understand, is their given material, their instrument, their tool. . . . It may serve for good or evil purposes, and its proper nature is to serve, not to rule.[69]

That statement, I think, expressed well the principle that guided Hegel in his economic studies. It was a principle that fit in nicely with the accommodationist teachings of the theology of the divine economy and with key aspects of Scottish thought, especially those associated with the work of Ferguson. That this is true will be evident from what follows.

1. Hegel and the Scots: The problem of economic containment[70]

According to Paul Chamley, Hegel's interest in economics began at Tübingen, with the study of Locke.[71] This is something of a conjecture, for while Rosenkranz has told us that Hegel had read Locke as a young man,[72] it is not at all clear that Hegel had read Locke the way Chamley implies he did; that is, as a natural "rights" theorist in whom one can observe the emergence of a new understanding of the relationship between labor, property, and human personality.[73] An argument, no doubt, can be made for this view, but without evidence to support Chamley's position it is more prudent, I think, to argue that Hegel began his serious economic studies at Berne. It was at Berne that he developed his interest in the fiscal policy of the Berne oligarchy, in the English debates on the Poor Law, in Steuart's work on "political oeconomy," and, if Harris is correct, in Adam Smith.[74]

Whatever the impetus for these studies, one thing is clear: from the Berne years on Hegel was acutely aware of the close tie that many eighteenth-century social and political theorists had been drawing between economic and civil (i.e., legal and cultural) developments in history. In this, the Scots occupied a prominent position. As is well known, many of them had found their way to political economy by way of the study of moral philosophy or law.[75]

What we know conclusively about Hegel's reading of the Scots is that it occurred sometime during his residences at Berne, Frankfurt, and Jena, roughly over the ten-year period of 1794–1804. Hegel definitely had read James Steuart by 1799, for we know – again from Rosenkranz – that by May of that year Hegel had written a long (now unfortunately lost) commentary on one of the two German translations of Steuart's *Principles of Political Oeconomy* (1767).[76] We also know that by 1803–1804 Hegel had read Adam Smith's *Wealth of Nations* (1776), for several references to it appear in the Jena manuscripts of those years.[77] Scholars also have inferred from some of the excerpts in Hegel's *Tagebuch* that he had read Ferguson while a schoolboy at Stuttgart,[78] probably as an outgrowth of his interest in *"Popularphilosophie"* in general and in C. Garve's work in particular.[79] Moreover, it is highly probable that Hegel's interest in Ferguson was stimulated again in the mid-1790s by Schiller, whose *Aesthetic Education* was deeply influenced by Ferguson's work.[80]

Among Hegel scholars, there has been much speculation about the collective impact these readings had on Hegel. Rosenkranz, who for his own reasons wanted to depict Hegel as a thinker of liberal persuasion, contended that the (now lost) manuscript he once had had in his possession showed Hegel to be against "what was dead" in the "mercantile system" that Steuart (allegedly) supported.[81] This, Rosenkranz claimed, was proof that in the late 1790s Hegel was already moving away from mercantilism and toward Smith's more liberal economic views. Lukács and Hyppolite, each for different reasons, likewise regarded Hegel as "the disciple of Adam Smith (and his teacher Ferguson)" and held that Hegel's exposure to Smith was "a turning point" in his development not only because it taught him much about economics but also because it provided him with a concrete example of how the economic, social, political, and cultural aspects of objective experience might be differentiated and yet related.[82] Ritter, Plant, and Avineri have traced Hegel's interest in economics to his reading of Steuart.[83] Chamley and Plant have carried Hegel's interest in Steuart one step further, claiming that much of the Hegelian conception of history stems from Steuart.[84] Häring and Vogel, while conceding Smith's importance, have argued correctly, I think, that Hegel's interest in economic liberalism was immediately *aufgehoben* in a more socially and religiously responsible framework.[85] Pascal, Plant, and Lukács, moreover, have stressed the influence Ferguson's criticism of the sociopsychological implications of the division of labor had on the development of Hegel's "critical humanism."[86] And Hoffmeister regarded Ferguson as the source of much of Hegel's interest in the dynamics of "public spiritedness."[87]

Today, no serious Hegel scholar can ignore the Scottish influence on Hegel's thought.[88] But given the diverse views scholars have expressed on this subject, the exact nature of that influence remains something of a puzzle. The traditional view, held by liberals and Marxists alike, that Hegel's encounter with the Scots made him a liberal or bourgeois thinker, simply will no longer do, if only because twenty years of recent scholarship on Scottish thought has considerably altered our current understanding of what it was all about. Whereas earlier generations of scholars could (naively) view the Scots as articulating an internally consistent and liberally progressive "party line" on economic matters, Hegel scholars today must contend with a more nuanced and complicated picture of what the Scottish Enlightenment was all about.[89]

Albion Small notwithstanding, it used to be enough to associate the Scots with the emergence of classical political economy.[90] That no longer is the case. As recent scholarship has persuasively shown, there was a classical sociological as well as a classical economic ideological current within late eighteenth-century Scottish thought.[91] In fact, it is fast becoming an historiographical commonplace to see the former developing as a criticism of the latter.[92] Even Adam Smith is no longer regarded as fitting, simply, into the classical economic framework.[93] The same, of course, is true of Steuart, who, along with many other eighteenth-century "mercantilists," has recently been "rehabilitated" to the point where he now appears to have been what we might call a *"conditional* economic liberal."[94]

In light of these recent revisions, Hegel's relationship to the Scots needs to be examined more closely, even if it must still remain on the speculative level for want of any new concrete information about how he read them. As we shall see, Hegel read the Scots quite selectively, borrowing as he saw fit to suit his own needs. In what follows I shall attempt to reconstruct the "ideological context" in which Germans in general read the Scots in the late eighteenth century. This will be done less to identify causal influences than to establish the kinds of problems and themes Germans found interesting in Scottish thought. Then, on the basis of what we know about Hegel's interests in the late 1790s, I shall offer some conjectures as to how Hegel probably read his Scottish sources.

German thinkers had been highly interested in the Scots at least since the 1750s, when Lessing decided to translate Hutcheson's *System of Moral Philosophy* into German.[95] As was noted earlier, Ferguson's *Essay* was translated in 1768 by Jünger and his *Institutes* in 1772 by Garve.[96] The 1770s also witnessed translations of Smith's *Wealth of Nations* (by Schiller's cousin), Steuart's *Principles*, John Millar's *The Origin of the Distinction of Ranks*, and Henry Home's (Lord Kames') *Elements of Criticism*.[97] In 1794, moreover, Garve came out with a new translation of the *Wealth of Nations* that would go through three editions by 1810.[98]

In that general context, German interest in the Scots followed two different but, as we shall see, ultimately related lines of development.[99] One, which focused on the so-called "Scottish School of Primitivists," concerned itself with aesthetic theory, much of which was prominently displayed in Ferguson's *Essay*.[100] Lessing, Herder, Hamann, Garve, and Schiller often cited Ferguson to the effect that "art" was "natural to man"; that man was, therefore, "the artificer of his own nature"; and that each culture had an inner aesthetic principle that, given the proper occasion, would emerge to give objective expression to "the genius of that people" at a particular moment in history.[101] The other line of interest in the Scots fastened on their periodization of history and emphasized the role socioeconomic processes played in shaping the civil institutions and cultural values of different peoples at different moments in history. Here all the Scots were important, but pride of place certainly goes to Ferguson, Steuart, and Smith.[102]

Initially, Hegel's interest in the Scots coincided with the late eighteenth-century German interest in the relationship between socioeconomic processes in history and the development of civil institutions. By and large, this German interest was centered in two universities, Göttingen and Königsberg. Since both universities were noted for training civil servants for service in the respective bureaucracies of the states of Hanover and Prussia, their concerns with this aspect of Scottish thought is not surprising. What is somewhat surprising, though, is that in both states there was a growing late eighteenth-century interest in the doctrine of free trade, as it was proposed first by the physiocrats and then by Adam Smith.[103] Hence, the convergence of economic and institutional interests within German thought during this period.

As German interest in Scottish views on economics developed, it tended to focus on whether the emergent school of "political economy" was a form of *economic theory* or a guide for *economic policy*. More specifically, the debate turned on the question of whether liberal economic theory was correct in assuming that the economy was governed by natural laws that would provide, if left to run their course, not only economic growth but socioeconomic stability as well, or whether it was a theory that needed to be adapted to circumstances of time and place before it could be implemented as policy.

In the first case, the liberal economic theory could pass itself off as *science*; in the second case, as *art*.[104] In turn, if the liberal theory were judged to be a science – as classical economists would later have it – it followed that the economy must be granted absolute autonomy relative to the state; conversely, if liberal theory were judged to be policy oriented in an artistic sense – as thinkers from Aristotle, through Petty, to Steuart and the German cameralists would have it – it needed to be envisaged as a sphere that was separate from, but not independent of, some sort of collective political control and judgment.[105] In the first case, to use Polanyi's terms, the "economy" is "disembedded" from society; in the second case, it is "embedded" in it.[106] To use terms more relevant to the Hegel–Scot connection, in the first case we tend to get a typical textbook version of Smith as an economic liberal, and in the second case, a rehabilitated Steuart as a neomercantilist or conditional economic liberal.[107]

Between the mid-1770s and mid-1790s, something of a consensus had been established among German thinkers on this question. During these years – in journal reviews and in classroom lectures – Germans expressed two basic reservations about liberal economic theory in general and about Smith's work in particular.[108] First, they feared the social (and, ultimately, the political) consequences of unlimited competition, both within a nation and between nations.[109] Second, they were not sure that a theory that derived from English circumstances could be taken over *en bloc* and applied to the continent without major adjustments.[110] As one reviewer pointed out, it was not so much a question of the theory being right or wrong as of what it presupposed in the way of preconditions; mainly, "a certain stage of industry, wealth, and enlightenment" within a nation.[111]

From the very beginning, then, the Germans were inclined to approach economics less from the vantage point of theory than from within a larger

sociological and historical framework. That did not mean they were
indifferent to the significance of Smith's work. At least since Petty,
cameralists had regarded economics as the "art" of producing wealth for
the social whole.[112] Insofar as Smith's work could be envisaged as a
contribution to how to stimulate industry and the production of wealth in
society, the German cameralists were eager to put his teachings in the
service of what is often called "social" mercantilism.[113] But the Germans
insisted that those teachings had to "fit" into a larger framework of effective police administration.[114] Thus, as among the French officials whom
Steven Kaplan has studied, the Germans who were reading Smith in the
late eighteenth century saw no inherent tension between their views and
his on the matter of policing the economy.[115] As one German student of
Smith was to put it later, "Cooperation on the part of the government
in advancing the national wealth . . . is . . . to be recommended, provided it
remains within proper bounds. These bounds in part vary according to
condition and circumstances, but can in part be determined by general
principles."[116] In other words, it was not a question of either mercantilism or laissez-faire, of Steuart or Smith, but rather of a new compact for
civil society in which police policy was to steer a *via media* between too
much regulation and too much liberty.[117]

Even Smith's strongest supporter in Germany, C. J. Kraus, thought
the principles of liberal economic theory had to be adapted to the German
situation.[118] According to Kraus, Smith had provided an "economic
model" against which contemporary policy could be measured. But for
Kraus the policy decisions of skillful bureaucratic statesmen, not the
genius of Smith's theory itself, would determine whether the gap between
the economic model and the German reality would ultimately be bridged.
In that sense, even those who were most enthusiastic about Smith tended
to absorb him into the conventional framework of late eighteenth-century
cameralist police administration. That this was the case in Germany
should not be surprising; after all, was it not Dugald Steward who
"recommended his students to begin their studies [of economics] with the
[*Wealth of Nations*] and then to consult Steuart's [*Principles*] as one which
contains 'a great mass of accurate details . . . ascertained by his own
personal observations during his long residence on the Continent' "?[119]

Once we realize how Smith was being read in Germany, it is easier to
see why James Steuart's views on political economy found such a receptive
audience there.[120] From the German vantage point, Steuart's doctrine contained many of the advantages of Smith and few of the disadvantages.[121]
That is, Steuart made it possible to ascribe to the essentials of economic
liberalism without having to give up the idea of politics as a means of
economic containment.[122] Like Smith (and the other Scots) Steuart held
an evolutionary view of socioeconomic developments in history;[123] and

like Smith he identified labor, the division of labor, trade, and industry as the key forces of change in the evolutionary process.[124] Steuart also accepted self-interest as the "ruling principle" for economic, though not for all, human action.[125] Similarly, Steuart acknowledged that economic exchange often created bonds of solidarity in a society. Yet he also perceived, as Ferguson had and Millar would, how an uneven distribution of economic wealth between employer and employee could give rise first to *social* tensions between rich and poor and then to the kind of *political* tensions that invariably resulted from the subordination of the latter to the former.[126]

Steuart, however, was quite modest in the claims he advanced for his views,[127] for several reasons. First of all, he had traveled widely and had lived on the continent for many years.[128] His work, therefore, had a built-in comparative dimension.[129] Questions of time and place mattered for Steuart and, as we have already seen, his lack of British "conceit" appealed enormously to the Germans.[130] Second, Steuart always questioned the capacity of the market to regulate itself.[131] In a most revealing passage Steuart used a mechanical analogy to make a case not only for the complexity of modern economics but also for the need for political controls. Comparing the economy of modern states to watches, "which are continuously going wrong," he wrote:

sometimes the spring is found too weak, at other times too strong for the machine: and when the wheels are not made according to a determinate proportion, by the able hands of a Graham, or a Julien le Roy, they do not tally well with one another; then the machine stops, and if it be forced, some part gives way; and the workman's hand becomes necessary to set it right.[132]

Clearly, then, Steuart doubted whether the market, if it were to become unbalanced, could reestablish its own equilibrium without some form of political intervention. On this score, too, Steuart's "artistic" sense appealed to the Germans;[133] among the cameralists economics had always been more a matter of art than of science.[134]

Finally, and perhaps most important of all, the large role Steuart assigned the "statesman" in controlling economic processes fit in nicely with the reigning German orthodoxy of cameralism. The cameralists, as Small told us long ago, regarded economics as a subdivision of politics and, therefore, subordinated it to the police function of government.[135] For them, civil society was like a tabula rasa upon which the statesman etched a rational design for collective well-being. Here, as G. Parry has well understood, Steuart's appeal to the Germans lay in his forward-looking rationalism rather than in his backward-looking traditionalism.[136] Had the Germans been simple traditionalists in this matter they would certainly have preferred Smith to Steuart.[137]

Here it behooves us to examine more closely just what kind of authority and responsibility Steuart assigned to the "statesman" or, as he later was to put it, to "the legislative and supreme power, according to the form of government."[138] In England, A. Skinner has noted, Steuart was widely criticized for this aspect of his work.[139] But Steuart, as Skinner has also observed, was not an "unenlightened" seventeenth-century mercantilist; nor was he a supporter of the kind of "enlightened despotism" that was so congenial to the physiocrats.[140] Although he granted the "statesman" wide administrative powers, he made it perfectly clear, as our earlier quotes have illustrated, that his statesman performed the function of a "watchmaker" rather than a "wedge."[141] His statesman was a technician, a manager, a planner, not a reckless despot.[142] In fact, Steuart went so far as to claim that the statesman's economic responsibilities would prove to be "the most effectual *bridle* ever...invented against the folly of despotism."[143] By this Steuart meant that as industry developed, and as the mechanisms for the policing of industry became more complex, the sovereign power, whatever its form, would become "so bound up by the laws of...political economy, that every transgression of them would run into new difficulties."[144]

Steuart's use of the term "bridle" here is most interesting. It speaks, I think, to several dovetailing lines of argument in eighteenth-century thought. Before Steuart, Nicole and Mandeville had used the term in contexts where economic excesses (i.e., "unbridled appetites") needed to be managed artfully by effective police administration.[145] But, as Keohane and Skinner have shown, the "bridle metaphor" had also been used since Seyssel as a check on "absolutism."[146] In that sense, the term had "constitutionalist" tendencies built into it. Still more revealing is the fact that Calvin had used the bridle metaphor to express the right of the "people" to defend against "the excessive cupidity and licence of Kings."[147] And it is surely no accident that Beza and Mornay put the term to use in service of the cause of the monarchomachs.[148]

In light of these connotations and Steuart's use of the term, it seems safe to say both that Steuart wished to harness rather than repress the passions of individuals with regard to their pursuit of economic interest and that he wished to do so without going as far as, say, the physiocrats in granting unlimited police powers to the sovereign.[149] Thus, his conception of the "statesman" is carefully crafted and balanced. On the one hand, Steuart's statesman is ever watchful for social dislocations that stem from what we today would call economic cycles.[150] When new technological advances threw men out of work, Steuart expected the statesman to act to stabilize the situation. As he put it:

In treating every question of political oeconomy, I constantly suppose a statesman at the head of government, systematically conducting every part of it, so as to

prevent the vicissitudes of manners, and innovations, by their natural and immediate effects or consequences, from hurting any interest within the commonwealth. When a house within a city becomes crazy, it is taken down; this I call
systematical ruin: were it allowed to fall, the consequences might be fatal in
many respects. In like manner, if a number of machines are all at once introduced
into the manufactures of an industrious nation (*in consequence of that freedom which
must necessarily be indulged to all sorts of improvement*, and without which a state
cannot thrive), it becomes the business of the statesman to interest himself so far
in the consequences, as to provide a remedy for the inconveniences resulting from
the sudden alteration.[151]

On the other hand, Steuart was not opposed to "freedom," innovation,
and "improvement" in the economic realm. For this reason, it is perfectly
possible and even probable that Hegel read Smith and Steuart as complements to each other rather than – as the conventional view would have it –
as spokesmen for two antithetical interpretations of the purposes of
"political economy."

2. Steuart's "statesman" and the conception of the *Polizeistaat* in Old-Württemberg

In Old-Württemberg there was an additional, very important reason for
receptivity to Steuart's view of political economy. It was not just that
Steuart had lived in Tübingen in the late 1750s or that during his stay
there he had dedicated a tract on the "velocity" of money to the duke of
Württemberg.[152] The very fact of the dedication – with its "statist"
implications – might have given the ever-wary Estates occasion to ignore
the economic views he was later to express in his *Principles*. But Steuart, as
we have seen, was not a "statist" of that sort. This becomes obvious when
we realize that his statesman was charged with another all-important
responsibility; namely, that of influencing "the spirit of those whom he
governs."[153] As Steuart saw it, one of the statesman's principal duties was
to manipulate "the spirit of the people" – that is, its "morals, government
and manners" – so as to allow him and his subjects to take full advantage
of new and emergent economic forces in history.[154]

   This, Steuart felt, was the major task of eighteenth-century statesmanship. What the statesman had to do was oversee the "great alteration in
the affairs of Europe" that was at present taking place as Europe changed
from a "feudal and military" society to a "free and commercial" one.[155]
For that alteration, Steuart argued, a people had to be properly
prepared.[156] If the "right plan of political oeconomy" were to be followed,
a people's habits and expectations would certainly have to change.[157] On
the one hand, "idleness" would have to give way to "industry."[158] On the
other hand, however, a sense of "frugality," which would militate against

the "infinite allurements" of "luxury," would have to be cultivated.[159]

For Steuart, luxury was both an inducement to industry and a result of it.[160] And within limits Steuart was perfectly willing to live, as so many others were, with "moderate" luxury.[161] What he objected to, though, was having to live with the consequences of "excessive" luxury, with what he called its "seducing influence."[162] Hence, Steuart urged statesmen to contain luxury by promoting a sense of "frugality" among a people through an educational program in which traditional religious values were accented.[163] In this respect, Steuart's statesman had to offer religious as well as economic guidance to his people. And that was an expectation that squared nicely with the cameralist conception of the German *Polizeistaat* in the eighteenth century.

What Marc Raeff has told us about the German conception of the *Polizeistaat* during the early modern period of European history explains, I think, how this dovetailing of interests may have been effected.[164] At least since the sixteenth century, Raeff argues, and certainly since the Thirty Years' War, the Protestant states of Germany had been obliged (for reasons of *Innen- und Aussenpolitik*) to assign significant "police" powers to their respective princes.[165] The problem was that these police powers embraced two seemingly contradictory aims. On the one hand, the prince was expected to be an activist, an interventionist, in regulating the economic affairs of society.[166] On the other hand, however, the rationale offered for this intervention was very often religious, not economic, in nature.[167] That is, Raeff notes, the intervention was generally sanctioned as a means of providing a proper foundation for a Christian life of active piety.[168]

In the first case, police policy expressed itself in "the tyrannical control and supervision of every facet of public and economic life."[169] In the second case, though, police policy was supposed to maximize the opportunities for a voluntarist program of *praxis pietatis*. Instead of imposing demands on society, the thrust of police policy here was to develop and draw out – in a pedagogic sense – the religious personality of a people. Thus, the German conception of *Polizeistaat* was informed by a double directive: it was to stimulate and manage the economy as well as to prepare the way for *praxis pietatis*, continued moral reformation and collective salvation.[170]

Obviously, this dual responsibility made for tensions, ambiguities, and outright contradictions in the German conception of the *Polizeistaat*. The prince was expected to command a knowledge of man's religious, as well as his economic, needs.[171] And yet, as Raeff observes, this was a satisfactory arrangement as long as Protestants believed in "the notion of the prince's calling and Christian obligation to the welfare of his subjects."[172] That is, as long as this notion persisted there would be, as Manfred Riedel has acutely observed, no manifest tension between a statist conception of "police" and the socioeconomic and socioreligious unity of "civil society" (in the pre-Hegelian sense of the term).[173]

In Old-Württemberg, where at least since 1733 it had not been in the interest of Protestants to assign to a Catholic duke such extensive police powers, the traditional idea of the *Polizeistaat* had much less to recommend it.[174] This, I think, has recently been illustrated by Mack Walker's study of J. J. Moser, a man with whose importance in the history of Old-Württemberg we are already somewhat familiar.[175]

What Walker has taught us about the way this religious–economic interplay worked itself out in Moser between the 1750s and the 1780s is most illuminating.[176] In the 1750s, before the duke of Württemberg's absolutizing and catholicizing tendencies emerged full blown, Moser had regarded the duke as a potential instrument of economic reform. In this, he was vehemently opposed by the members of the Small Council who, as we have seen, had economic interests of their own to protect. Thus, Moser in the 1750s was viewed by many as a "projector," a pejorative term for one who would take the duke's side versus the Small Council's on economic matters, especially if the matter revolved around the question of how to stimulate trade in Württemberg.[177] Moser, in turn, regarded the Small Council as an obstructionist institution with regard to economic policy and, at just about the time Steuart was writing his tract for the duke on the importance of the "velocity" of money for trade, he was recommending increasing the circulation of money to stimulate trade as a police policy for the duke.

As the Seven Years' War unfolded, though, Moser realized how dangerous his work on behalf of the duke could be relative to Protestant religious interests. Hence, by 1764 Moser had withdrawn his support from the proposals the duke was offering in the way of police administration.[178] And by the 1770s Moser would see clearly that the police policies of the physiocrats, which the duke found increasingly congenial, were as inimical to Protestant interests as those he himself had been pushing in the 1750s.[179] In both cases, it had naïvely been assumed that "plenty" for the people rather that "power" for the prince would be the ultimate justification of effective police administration.[180] Moser conceded, of course, that a truly "wise ruler" would pursue that end.[181] But who was to say that Karl Eugen, a Catholic and an absolutist, would be wise?

Faced with the problem of who should assume responsibility for the public police function, Moser began to perceive the merits of a system in which the principle of the division of labor dictated the diffusion of police power throughout the administration of "government."[182] Thus, in a series of publications in the 1760s and 1770s Moser stressed the pivotal role the professional civil servant could play in ameliorating the constitutional tensions being generated by the diverging economic and religious interests of the duke and the Estates, respectively.[183] As Merk has noted, in these writings Moser aimed at augmenting the police function of "government" without either encroaching upon the traditional religious rights of the Protestant collectivity (i.e., the Estates) or contributing to the duke's personal power and glory (i.e., the state).[184]

As Moser argued it, "enlightened government," working through the agency of a professional bureaucracy, could bridge the gap between the duke and the Estates by aggressively promoting a wide range of economic reforms. Moser insisted, though, that these reforms had to be defined in terms of the *gemeine Beste*, in terms of "plenty" for the people rather than "power" for the duke.[185] At the same time, Moser assigned to another group of bureaucrats – within the same institutional structure – responsibility for promoting public morals. This group's task was to use the schools in general and a religious education in particular to instill senses of altruism and a commitment to public service in the people.[186]

Like J. J. Reinhard, one of the "bureaucratic statesmen" in late eighteenth-century Baden whom Helen Liebel has written about, Moser was trying here to strike a balance between innovation and tradition in police policy.[187] There are two ways to look at this. First, one can regard Moser's position as that of a moderate, as a compromise that appealed on the one hand to the Estates in language that guaranteed the traditional religious rights of Württemberg Protestants and on the other hand to the new statesmen in language that recognized the importance of economic planning and that implied support for the rational organization of government around the principles of the division of labor and the figure of the disinterested civil servant.

But Moser had done more than that, I think, for in striking the balance the way he did, he proposed to institutionalize within the bureaucracy the conflict that existed in Old-Württemberg not only between the duke and the Estates but also between new economic and old religious values. As a consequence of this he had to posit professional civil servants as a kind of "universal class" who, because of their keen sense of duty and dedication to service, were *Unparteilichkeit*.[188] This, Moser claimed (à la Steuart's statesman), permitted the civil servant to gain an objective and disinterested perspective on the interplay between the religious and the economic values of civil society and, from that vantage point, to develop a plan of police administration that preserved a healthy balance between the spiritual and the physical needs of the people.[189]

Given Moser's views, it is not hard to see why other Württembergers might have found Steuart congenial. This is especially true of the group of reformers whose political views in the 1790s we have discussed at various points in this study.[190] For this group – which was eager to seize the occasion of the calling of the Estates in the mid-1790s to implement constitutional reforms – the Moser–Steuart combination must have been most compelling. As was noted earlier, much of the thrust of the reform program hinged on a conception of statesmanship that made the civil servant the disinterested representative of the public interest. In economic matters, Moser and Steuart recommended "economic planning" without endorsing either the "statist" implications of the physiocrats or the "anarchism" of wholesale laissez-faire.[191] In political matters, both regarded "power and plenty" as inextricably tied to each other – which meant they approached the health of "civil society" in terms of a balance between political and socioeconomic interests. And, in the matter of religion, they both recognized how instrumental a proper religious education could be when it came down to checking social impulses toward "vicious luxury," whether in the court or among a people. In short, Moser and Steuart presented a balanced view of life in the modern world, a view that balanced innovation in economics with traditional political and religious programs of police. And this was what many educated Württembergers were trying constitutionally to establish in their homeland in the mid-1790s.

In a very general sense, this was the ideological context in which Hegel read the Scots. The context, I think, explains why he may have been inclined to read Steuart and why he may have been disposed to approach the issue of political economy (i.e., Smith's theory of the free market economy) from the vantage point of neomercantilism (i.e., Steuart's conditional or qualified economic liberalism).

Be that as it may, two additional aspects of Steuart's relation to Hegel need to be clarified before we proceed to the next three chapters, in which Hegel's own views on economics, politics, and religion will be discussed.

First, and most obviously, there is the matter of the Württembergers' very high-minded conception of the professional civil servant. This conception, I think, brings us back to Raeff's notion of the *Polizeistaat*. The fact is that Moser and Steuart offered Württembergers an updated bureaucratic version of the older German conception of the well-ordered *Polizeistaat*. Indeed, Moser and Steuart asked bureaucratic statesmen to perform the same double political function that Raeff contends the Christian prince had been expected to perform; namely, to improve the economy while preserving the traditional religious integrity of the people.[192]

In Old-Württemberg, as well as in much of Europe, this proved to be a most difficult undertaking. Raeff, for example, has hinted that the bureaucratic version of *Polizeistaat* had about the same order of probability for success in managing this interplay as the Christian prince had had: none.[193] If this is true, Moser might be depicted as having wished away rather than as having solved the contradiction Raeff has argued proved fatal to the *Polizeistaat*.

Here a problem of Moser's and Steuart's bureaucratic rendering of the German conception of the *Polizeistaat* emerges full blown. The more successful police policy was in promoting economic growth, the more aggressive and vigilant it had to be with regard to its religiopedagogic function.[194] And, as our discussion of Moser and Steuart has made clear, there was little hope of "containing" economic expansion without that kind of vigilance. Hence Steuart's concern that unchecked economic expansion would usher in the kind of moral, social, and political problems he associated with a society that could not resist the temptation to "excessive" luxury.[195]

Viewed in this way, it is quite probable that the way Hegel handled the problem of luxury in the writings that date from the Frankfurt and Jena periods (1797–1807) will tell us a great deal about how he proposed to bring his religious values into line with his new economic awarenesses. How he conceived that alignment, in turn, will explain how and why he came to envisage *Sittlichkeit* less as a religious problem than as one in social and political theory.

6

Sittlichkeit reconsidered

I. The essay on *Natural Law*

Against the general ideological background set in the last chapter, it is not hard to see why Hegel felt compelled to rethink his conception of *Sittlichkeit*.[1] The cumulative impact of his study of the fiscal policy of the Bernese oligarchy and his reading of various Scottish writings on political economy as well as his awareness of the foreclosure of opportunities for political reform in Württemberg after 1798 convinced him that his initial understanding of *Sittlichkeit* had been rather naively formulated.[2] He realized that his early conception of *Sittlichkeit* had ignored the economic interest factor as a powerful determinant not only of men's actions but also of their perceptions of the possibility of action in any given social situation.[3]

Before Hegel, Ferguson had understood this very well. Hence, the importance of the distinction Ferguson drew in the *Essay* between "wisdom" and "interest," a distinction he believed his commercially minded contemporaries had badly confused.[4] According to Ferguson, this confusion reduced wisdom to a matter of utility and material calculation,[5] with the result that man's sense of wisdom was now being measured less in terms of his "human" (i.e., moral) than in terms of his "animal" (i.e., economic) nature.[6] As Ferguson saw it, this was a dangerous way of thinking, for it made "preservation of our animal nature" not just a "constant" and necessary everyday concern of man but the "principal constituent of human felicity" as well.[7]

This economic factor – this way of thinking by which man in commercial society gave increasing priority to the importance of material interests in the organization of collective life – is precisely what Hegel tried to address in his work between 1796 and 1804. But during this period Hegel never wavered in his resolve to do this in a way that did not compromise the religious aspect of his conception of *Sittlichkeit*. Thus, during these years *Sittlichkeit* was not so much a matter of applied theology for

Hegel as the center of a problem that grew out of his new understanding of how economics could militate against the realization of *Sittlichkeit* in the public realm of experience. In that respect, if *Sittlichkeit* were to remain, for Hegel, a historically relevant and progressive ethicopolitico-religious ideal, it had to be presented in a new way, in a form that aimed at "laying hold on life" for the sake of carrying "the war against material-ism" into the "territory of matter itself."[8]

Still, if Hegel's reconsideration of *Sittlichkeit* can be explained in terms of this religious–economic overlay, his reflections on the overlay need to be approached carefully. With regard to economic matters Hegel was not a "libertine," a *doux-commerce* "evolutionist," a "severe" moralist, or a straightforward advocate of "modernizing mercantilism."[9] He was not drawn toward the libertine position because he accepted neither the providentialism of the laissez-faire market nor the libertine view of human nature; he was not an evolutionist because he refused to de-emphasize the political realm of objective experience as a forum of importance for the collective ontological fulfillment of *homo religiosus*; he rejected – as we shall see in this chapter – severe moralism because it assumed an overly ascetic (i.e., "formalist") political posture toward the socio-economic aspects of collective life; and he never quite came around to subscribing to modern-izing mercantilism because he balked at "economizing" politics, at reducing questions of political value to the managerial perspective of effective regulation of the economy in both productive and distributive senses. Rather, Hegel was committed to developing a conception of politics that while promoting ethical activism and religious recollectivi-zation did so in a manner that was empirically grounded in a curious, some would say "dialectical," way. In this chapter I shall begin to explain what that means.

That Hegel chose to pursue the strategy that he did testifies at once to his idealism and to his realism. It testifies to his idealism because he refused to abandon his belief that *Sittlichkeit* could vie with what I shall call the economic ethic for control of men's minds.[10] At the same time, it manifests his realism in that it obliged him to develop a more nuanced understanding of the socioeconomic and sociopolitical aspects of the objective context in which *Sittlichkeit* was to be actualized as a religious ideal in the modern world. And the combination of the two, and the weighting Hegel gave to them, suggests that while Hegel's realism made him a great social theorist, it was the embattled idealism of a very reli-gious and political man that explains the "spins" on the concepts he used in what he wrote between 1796 and 1804. In the mode of realist, as an observer of broader European socioeconomic and sociocultural processes, Hegel was a spectator: he described and analyzed what was happening around him. In the mode of idealist, as a liberal Württemberg Protestant, he was an actor: he evaluated what was happening around him and posited alternative structures for action when existing structures threatened to inhibit or actually arrested realization of his values.

In what follows, our task will be to specify how Hegel concretely tried to reconcile his idealism with his realism. A careful reading of two texts from this period is illuminating. In the remainder of this chapter and in the next one I propose specifically to examine two texts Hegel wrote in the early 1800s. In these – the texts on *Natural Law* and on *Ethical Life* – Hegel tries to translate *Sittlichkeit* into the language of social and political theory.[11] At the same time, he boldly confronts the economic interest problem, in its socioeconomic and sociocultural (i.e., ideological) forms, and tries to devise an authentically political solution for it. From these works it becomes perfectly clear not only what prompted Hegel to make the civil society–state conceptual split but also what the "illocutionary force" behind it was.

1. The problem of philosophy: "Empiricism" and "moral formalism"

After his father died in 1799, Hegel received a small inheritance from the estate. The financial cushion that this bequest provided made it possible for him to give up his tutorial position in Frankfurt and to move early in 1801 to Jena. There, with a minor teaching position in the philosophy department of the declining but still relatively vigorous University of Jena, Hegel was able to pursue his intellectual interests in more formal philosophical fashion. Indeed, from 1801 through the completion of the *Phenomenology* in the fall of 1806, Hegel versed himself and was caught up in most of the major philosophical disputes of the day.

Before discussing the *Natural Law* text, in which Hegel demonstrates a working knowledge of the intricacies of these philosophical disputes, we need to remember several important things about Hegel's "early" Jena period. First, in the early Jena years – say, from 1801 to 1804 – Hegel was closely tied to Schelling. He was personally indebted to Schelling for helping him secure the position at Jena. At the same time, he was philosophically involved with Schelling through their joint editorship of the *Critical Journal of Philosophy*.[12] From this collaboration emerged a line of criticism that sought to move German philosophy beyond the positions and principles of Kant and Fichte.

Second, the criticism Hegel offered of Kant and Fichte – in 1801 in the *Difference* essay and in 1802 in *Faith and Knowledge* – is just that: criticism.[13] That is, Hegel does not move very far in the development of his own position relative to Kant and Fichte on the one hand and to

Schelling on the other. His thought is still evaluative and diagnostic rather than evaluative and prescriptive.[14]

Finally, it is important to remember that between 1802 and 1804, Hegel wrote *Natural Law* and *System of Ethical Life*, in both of which he made an effort to be philosophically constructive. For Hegel, however, being constructive philosophically meant being concrete. For this reason, both essays begin very abstractly and philosophically and then gradually work toward more concrete formulations of the problems Hegel wanted German philosophy to confront. As we shall see, this procedure – which henceforth will be a characteristically Hegelian procedure – proved most effective, for it allowed Hegel to do several things at once. Professionally he could show an academic world that had never heard of him that he was conversant with the subject matter of philosophy; intellectually he could establish an identity of his own by staking out a philosophical position vis-à-vis those established by Kant, Fichte, and Schelling; and personally he could present his criticism in a way that, while appearing to be philosophical, actually compelled the reader to confront the substantive political problem that lay at the center of the religious–economic overlay in his thought.

These two texts are pivotal, then, because they allow us to see Hegel fleshing out a conceptual framework and developing a vocabulary for translating the problem of *Sittlichkeit* into the language of social and political theory. To be sure, there is much talk in these essays about "philosophical method"; but the structure of the essays themselves suggests the development of an argument that involves a reconsideration of *Sittlichkeit* beyond anything else.

Given these concerns, I think the *Natural Law* text is designed to make three main philosophical points. The first point, which Hegel develops over the first half of the essay, is methodological.[15] It indicates to the reader his reservations about the methodological principles that seem to govern much of modern European and German philosophy. This argument, which is wholly negative (in that it tries to draw positive conclusions from a series of negative philosophical deductions), is then followed by two other arguments that are meant to be more positive and constructive.

At this point, however, Hegel has some organizational problems that take some of the edge off the arguments advanced in the second half of the text. His organizational problem is threefold. First, he wants to derive a positive set of methodological guidelines from the line of philosophical criticism developed in the first half of the essay. Second, he wants to translate his own positive methodological convictions into a language that will allow him to discuss philosophical method substantively rather than abstractly – that is, in the context of concrete problems of socioeconomic, religious, and political experience. Finally, he wants to offer substantive solutions to these problems. This is clear enough; but in his eagerness both to translate methodological questions into matters of substance and to solve the substantive problems that arise once the translation process has been completed, Hegel often runs the two arguments together, and the result is that there is much confusion in the second half of his essay.

Hegel, though, must have been aware of this, because in the text on *Ethical Life*, which was written shortly thereafter, he tries to sort out some of the confusions that arose in the second half of the *Natural Law* text. Hence, the justification for my treating the two texts together – as constituting two different but related phases of the reconsideration of *Sittlichkeit*.[16]

In the first half of the *Natural Law* text Hegel expressed deep dissatisfaction with the "scientific" method of philosophers who had written on natural law in the late eighteenth century.[17] Hegel divided these philosophers into two groups.[18] On the one side were those who approached natural law from the perspective of an "empiricism" whose "governing principle" was the a priori of the a posteriori;[19] on the other side – and this is the group Hegel truly wants to engage – were the "formalists," those who opposed empiricism with an "a priorism" of their own.[20] Here Hegel meant to take issue with Kant and Fichte, the "moral formalists,"[21] who claimed that for philosophy to be philosophy (i.e., truly universal) it had to "regard as contingent and dead what it can subsume" under the concept of particularity (i.e., under all that is mutable).[22]

For Hegel, the consequence of the methodological debate between these two competing schools of philosophy was a "no win" situation for philosophy both as a science and as a vehicle for *Sittlichkeit*. As he saw it, the contemporary approaches to natural law asked philosophy to choose between "empiricism" and "theory" (i.e., formalism).[23] In the first case, Hegel argued that philosophy would be swallowed up in "experience"; in the second case, it would be divorced from it.[24] In both cases, however, the result was the same: each philosophy falsely posited a true absolute in what Hegel regarded as only a one-sided "negative absolute."[25]

Schelling, of course, had been saying something like this for years. Moreover, in his conception of the absolute he had tried to show that the true absolute must be philosophically explained in terms of a "principle of opposition."[26] As he conceived it, the absolute concept must embrace unity and multiplicity, particularity and universality, the finite and the infinite, empiricism and formalism, and so on. On this point Hegel found Schelling's methodology most congenial. But Schelling, Hegel thought, like Kant and Fichte before him, had posed the problem of the absolute too abstractly. Hegel conceded that Schelling's conception of the absolute marked a methodological advance beyond Kant and Fichte (i.e., it marked the advance from "subjective" to "objective" idealism). But what really drew Hegel to Schelling was not method per se but the practical uses to which that method could be put. Hegel realized that Schelling's conception of the absolute held out the possibility of a concrete reconciliation of the tension in his own thought between his old religious values (i.e., the elevation of man to the infinite) and his new awareness of the role economics played in men's lives. In short, Schelling represented not only a methodological corrective to Kant and Fichte, but also a point of departure for Hegel's development of his own conception of philosophy's relation to the problem of *Sittlichkeit*.[27]

There is nothing particularly new or profound about the philosophical criticisms Hegel presents in the first half of the *Natural Law* text. His discussion of empiricism is most conventional.[28] While acknowledging the legitimacy of empiricism's complaints about formalism – that is, about "a universality which is totally empty"[29] – Hegel condemns empiricism for its own "unscientific character,"[30] for its willingness to pass off as "healthy common sense" and as "the culture of the day" the reality of an "animal life" that "does not even rise to formal ideality."[31] Just as conventional is his criticism of formalism, which he critiques more or less from the point of view of empiricism.[32]

Again, all this is quite unoriginal. But as we have already noted, Hegel's principal concern in this essay is to translate matters of philosophical method into matters that relate substantively to *Sittlichkeit*. As he takes up this challenge, the essay becomes both more original and more concerned with concrete problems of socioeconomic and political theory.

Hegel reaches this point about a third of the way through the essay, when he begins to focus on the practical legislative problem that arises from moral formalism in general and from Fichte's philosophy in particular.[33] Hegel knew quite well that his own philosophy was very likely to be confused with the views of those whom he had identified as moral formalists (e.g., Kant and Fichte). Specifically, what bothered Hegel about moral formalism was the political implication that seemed to follow from its methodological principles. As Hegel saw it, moral formalism insisted on a legislative (i.e., political) doctrine that was bent on the "annihilation of the specific."[34] The legislative thrust of formalism aimed at achieving universality simply by canceling that which was not universal.[35] As such, it refused to "lay hold on life."

In philosophical terms, moral formalism was a position with which Hegel was quite familiar. After all, there was an "ascetic" dimension to this kind of formalism, and Hegel was certainly no stranger to the attractions of asceticism.[36] In Kant, this ascetic dimension expressed itself in the self-coercion of the autonomous man; in Fichte, it assumed the more objective and overt political form of legal "compulsion." Insofar as

Hegel's early conception of *Sittlichkeit* had had an ascetic dimension, he too had once been inclined toward moral formalism. But, as we have seen, some time in the late 1790s he abandoned asceticism as a possible solution to social and political problems. From the Scots, if not from Montesquieu, he had learned that asceticism, especially in the form of the "compulsion and supervision" of Fichte's political philosophy, was inadequate and unacceptable as a political solution to modern socioeconomic problems.[37] As Hegel noted, the "content" of *Sittlichkeit* is bound up as much with the "living body" as with *Geist*.[38] That meant that *Sittlichkeit* could be divorced from neither the one nor the other without succumbing either to "libertinism" or to "severe moralism."

Much of what Hegel has to say in the *Natural Law* text about the ascetic dimension of moral formalism focuses on Fichte.[39] In Fichte's philosophy, Hegel thought, the political implications of asceticism were most obvious and the connection between political preferences and methodological convictions was most apparent. These two aspects of Fichte's thought, I believe, explain why Hegel devotes so much space to him in *Natural Law*.

The criticism Hegel makes of Fichte's philosophy of compulsion comes at a crucial point in the text. It is by way of his criticism of Fichte – in whom he thought the connection between moral formalism and political despotism was clearest – that Hegel himself begins to move the focus of the argument from a discussion of philosophical method to one of political substance. It was not enough just to establish a tie between Fichte's method, his idea of compulsion, and political despotism, however. That, Hegel thought, was easy enough to do. It would be more challenging to develop a criticism of Fichte that while endorsing the idealism of moral formalism made the case for it empirically and in terms of a hardheaded realism – a realism that while rooted in the dynamic of everyday life put the case for corrective action in a conditional ethical mode.[40]

Hegel begins his criticism of Fichte with this agenda in mind. He claims that Fichte's notion of compulsion was faulty because it involved a "leap from the real to the ideal."[41] Implicit in this leap, Hegel argued, was a dualistic view of human experience that, at bottom, tried to achieve a "union of universal and individual freedom" by "compelling the activity of every individual" to be "regulated by the universal and the abstraction that are set up in opposition to him [as particularity]."[42] From this Hegel concluded that Fichte's leap involved positing "a negative absolute" in which "there is nothing absolute... except just pure abstraction, the utterly vacuous thought of unity."[43]

Hegel thought, moreover, that Fichte's formalism had disastrous political implications, for it seemed to "destroy civic freedom" and to sanction "the harshest despotism."[44] Fichte's "empty abstraction of the concept of the universal freedom of all [which is really] separate from the freedom of individuals" ultimately annihilates individuality for the sake of conceptions of freedom and unity that lack real "substance."[45] The thought of moral formalism, Hegel argues, is governed by "a principle of coercion" that, when allowed to run its course, leaves us with conceptions of free men and unified communities that are just "creatures of imagination, without reality."[46] As he noted, in Fichte's philosophy:

... a system is built whereby both the concept and the individual subject of ethical life are supposed to be united despite their separation, though the unity is on this account only formal and external, and this relation between them is called "compulsion." In this way the external character of oneness is utterly fixed and posited as something absolute and inherently necessary; and thereby . . . the union of universal and individual freedom, and ethical life itself, are made impossible.[47]

In view of the lack of voluntarism in Fichte's philosophy, Hegel concluded that "we must completely reject that view of freedom whereby freedom is supposedly a choice between opposed entities,"[48] one real and bound up with particularity, the other ideal and part of a timeless universal continuum. Indeed, for Hegel philosophy should not be presented (i.e., burdened) with this kind of either/or choice. Rather, philosophy had to devise a way to reconcile the two; and this, Hegel maintained, had to be "exhibited" on the level of *Sittlichkeit*, in the daily life of "a people," and not just on the level of abstraction.[49]

Abstractly put, what Hegel was striving for was a reciprocal relation between the ideal and the real within "absolute ethical life" itself.[50] By this, Hegel meant to designate the real and the ideal as "necessary moments" in the life of the "absolute" (i.e., still to be equated with objective experience itself).[51] But if "both are linked together" it is also "absolutely necessary" for both "to be separate and to be kept distinct, so that . . . they both are equally positive for that reason."[52] He continues by noting that "the one is negative for the other; but so they both are. It is not that one is absolutely positive, the other absolutely negative; each is both in their relation to one another . . . and since each of them is just as positive as the other, both are absolutely necessary."[53] Neither the ideal nor the real, in other words, "is absolutely positive or genuinely ethical."[54] Hence, the clear link in the essay between methodological and political conceptions.

2. Economics and the "bourgeois" conception of ethical life

At this point Hegel's "discovery of the economy" becomes central to the argument of the *Natural Law* text. To see this one need only realize that basic to Hegel's criticism of moral formalism was the claim that it tried to avoid making any concessions to, or compromises with, what it regarded as "negative" or "contingent" or "inorganic" or "accidental" or "particular" or "finite" or what have you.[55] At various points in this text Hegel is quite specific about what he thinks is the major consequence of the moral formalists' attitude toward "reality": it is that they are unable to come to terms with the economic aspects of modern social and political life. This, Hegel argues, is their fatal flaw, and he means to correct them while retaining some of their high-minded moral idealism.

That Hegel wishes philosophy to confront "reality" (i.e., economics in general and political economy in particular) is obvious throughout the remainder of the essay. "Reality," Hegel writes, "in the context [of the science of political economy]...and of which some different aspects are physical necessity, enjoyment, possession, and the objects of possession and enjoyment, is pure reality."[56] By this Hegel means that there is "a system of reality" *within* objective experience itself of which philosophy, especially a philosophy of *Sittlichkeit*, must take full account.[57] Hegel goes on to equate this "system" with "the real practical realm" of objective experience – the realm, that is, of "feeling or physical necessity and enjoyment" and of "work and possession."[58] Through what he calls "knowledge of necessity," philosophy must come to appreciate both man's physical needs and the ways in which these needs shape social existence.[59]

More specifically, Hegel identifies this practical realm of physical necessity with what he calls the "inorganic," as distinct from the "organic," dimension of *Sittlichkeit* (i.e., still to be understood as synonymous with objective experience as a whole).[60] The presumption here is twofold: that the inorganic relates to man's physical needs and the organic to his spiritual needs and that the philosophy of absolute *Sittlichkeit* must, somehow, encompass both.[61] As Montesquieu (whom Hegel mentions several times in the essay) and the Scots understood, man experienced both kinds of needs simultaneously.[62] Hegel offers an adequate, albeit highly abstract, summary of what he has done here when he writes:

This reconciliation lies precisely in the knowledge of necessity, and in the right which ethical life concedes to its inorganic nature, and to the subterranean powers by making over and sacrificing to them one part of itself. For the force of the sacrifice lies in facing and objectifying the involvement with the inorganic. This involvement is dissolved by being faced; the inorganic is separated and, recognized for what it is, itself taken up into indifference while the living, by placing into the inorganic what it knows to be a part of itself and surrendering it to death, has all at once recognized the right of the inorganic and cleansed itself of it.[63]

In less abstract terms Hegel has partitioned or segregated his conception of absolute ethical life into two different but related "moments" of experience.[64] But if this differentiation of, say, the "organic" and "inorganic" seems to mirror the dualism of the moral formalists, Hegel offered very different reasons for drawing the distinction. He claimed that by confronting "the negative [i.e., the inorganic] as objective...and by consciously conceding to the negative a power and a realm, at the sacrifice of a part of itself, it maintains its own [organic] life purified of the negative."[65] Put another way, Hegel posits the distinction between organic and inorganic not so much to eliminate or escape from the latter as to bring it under the conscious control of the former. This, of course, is not what the moral formalists had in mind when they developed their split vision of objective experience – the illocutionary force of the split is quite different in the two cases.

This becomes quite clear as Hegel proceeds to equate the "inorganic nature of the ethical" with economics. And yet, when Hegel concedes economics its "right" to exist,[66] he means to grant it, to borrow a phrase from Schumpeter, "definite but not separate existence."[67] That is, he means to "contain" it. For example, while discussing "the system of reality" (i.e., the realm of physical needs) that, "as a science, is the system of so-called political economy," Hegel argues that it "must remain subject to the domination" of "the positive totality."[68] Or again: "in order to prevent this system of reality from becoming a self-constituting and independent power...the ethical whole must...impede both its burgeoning in point of quality, and the development of ever greater difference and inequality for which its nature strives."[69] Again: the "positive [organic] ethical life of the state" is endangered if it permits "the purely real system [i.e., the inorganic] to become independent and the negative and restrictive attitude [toward human self-realization that goes along with it] to be upheld."[70] Finally, Hegel insists, "Ethical organization can remain pure in the real world, only if the negative [i.e., the economic] is prevented from spreading all through it."[71]

Viewed in this way, it becomes clear that Hegel has succeeded in working the subject matter of *Natural Law* to a point where it now dovetailed with the concern about *Sittlichkeit* that had been developing in his thought since he had read the Scottish thinkers. He began this essay by using Schelling's conception of the absolute to criticize the moral formalists. Then, by way of a series of specific criticisms of Fichte, Hegel managed to translate problems of philosophical method into ones of political substance. Finally – and here Hegel offered an implicit criticism of Schelling – he drew attention to German philosophy's neglect of the economic interest factor in human behavior. Moreover, in making this latter point Hegel developed a conception of *Sittlichkeit* that involved assigning different conceptual space to different kinds of behavior. On the one hand, there was behavior geared toward satisfaction of physical needs; on the other, behavior aimed at spiritual fulfillment. Citing Montesquieu, Hegel made it clear that these two kinds of needs are interdependent and constitute the two causal chains out of which the "general spirit" of a particular people develops.[72]

At this point in the essay, Hegel's task will be to spell out in concrete detail and in the language of social and political theory what he thinks is the nature of the reciprocal relationship between these two types of behavior. His problem is that over the course of the essay he has eliminated a number of possible ways of conceptualizing the relationship. For example, he has ruled out various forms of what might be called the equilibrium model of reciprocal relationships.[73] He has also dismissed the possibility of allowing these two types of needs to develop on their own without really touching each other.[74] Rather, Hegel insists that each be depicted as having "a living bearing on the other."[75] In light of what he objected to in the thought of others, Hegel had no choice but to begin to argue that spiritual fulfillment grew naturally out of physical needs and that man's spiritual growth must be understood more in terms of the positive attraction he feels for spiritual self-realization than in terms of the revulsion he feels for "the empirical."[76] In the last part of the essay, in other words, Hegel's agenda is very much like the one Schiller had set for himself in *Aesthetic Education*.[77]

Much of what Hegel says on this matter in *Natural Law* is more precisely formulated in *Ethical Life*. Even so, Hegel makes some remarkably important statements about the economy and its relation to man in *Natural Law*. So, at the risk of some overlap in the discussion of the two texts, we shall take up Hegel's discussion of the economy here as well as in *Ethical Life*.

Having divided absolute *Sittlichkeit* into organic and inorganic moments, Hegel proceeds to argue that as a real historical force "political economy" has created a "system of universal mutual dependence in relation to physical needs and work and the amassing [of wealth] for these needs."[78] In this sentence, the phrase a "system of universal mutual dependence" is crucial, because it implies that through the dynamic of economic production and consumption men form patterns of interaction that may make for social solidarity.[79]

Hegel's appreciation of the *social* benefits of economic growth was by no means unique. Since Mandeville, many of the most influential thinkers of the eighteenth century had been arguing the point.[80] Steuart, for example, had said something quite similar when he wrote:

Hence I conclude, that the best way of binding a free society together is by multiplying reciprocal obligations, and creating a general dependence between all its members. This cannot be better effected, than by appropriating a certain number of inhabitants, for the production of the quantity of food required for all, and by distributing the remainder into proper classes for supplying every other want. I say farther, that this distribution is not only the most rational, but that mankind fall naturally into it.[81]

Ferguson had expressed himself on the subject this way: "As a bond of society, . . . pursuit [of] the objects of sense [i.e., of economic gain] make an important part of the system of human life."[82] Still others, approaching the subject from the point of view of religious providentialism, argued that "God intended commerce to operate as a unifying factor for all mankind."[83] And it was but a short step from here to the claim that commerce held the key to "perpetual peace" among the nations of the world.[84]

While conceding that increased *social* unity may be one of the benefits of economic expansion, Hegel goes still further, hinting that this "cohesive system" even possesses a kind of "justice" and "universality."[85] Hegel understood, that is, that this system required more than a people's common participation in commercial life to sustain itself. If work and commerce encouraged men to cooperate in a *socioeconomic* endeavor that was "common to all," the endeavor itself only constituted the foundation upon which a more complex system of *sociocultural* values had been erected.[86] Drawing upon Montesquieu and Ferguson, Hegel noted how systems of political and civil law had historically grown up around the idea of property, with the result that patterns of socioeconomic relations were finding sanction in noneconomic (e.g., sociocultural and political) areas of objective experience. Things "particular" and "finite" often came to be thought of as "inherent, absolute and unconditioned."[87] That is, a "system of property and law," which was animated by a "fixation of individuality," could easily come to be regarded as something "absolute and eternal" rather than "wholly finite."[88]

Hegel was quite specific in formulating his objections to this system of interlocking socioeconomic and sociocultural values, and the language he used to present them is most revealing. As might be expected, he dismissed any conception of ethical life that was "preoccupied with fixed reality, with possession and property and not with courage."[89] According to him, however, "the ethical life of the bourgeois or private individual" was governed by just this kind of "fixation."[90] As Hegel depicted it, the bourgeoisie's conception of ethical life was characterized by a desire for "peace and gain and perfect security in their enjoyment" of the "fruits" of political economy.[91] In this ethical conception, the idea of "possession is taken up into formal unity [i.e., into law]" where it "fixes, and posits absolutely, individual separate existence."[92] Every individual, therefore, is related to every other in terms of common participation in "a universal private life" that is organized around the principle of man's material comfort, around his "interests."[93]

Throughout this discussion Hegel was obviously trying to establish grounds for a criticism of this bourgeois ethical conception. Just as obviously he was trying to present this conception as "something negative" because "it expresses itself in the individual [i.e., in the inorganic] as such" and not in a truly collective [i.e., an organic] form.[94] We need to be careful here, though, for Hegel does not mean to deny men the opportunity to pursue their economic interests. Hegel, after all, had already conceded that "right" to them. Like Ferguson and Steuart he recognized "that the care of subsistence is the principal spring of human actions."[95] But construing this spring as the most "constant" and "uniform" feature of human nature was not equivalent to saying that it was the only or even the most powerful spring of human action.[96] Yet that is how bourgeois theorists were presenting it, with the consequence that "interest" and the pursuit of wealth were, to quote Ferguson, becoming "the principal idol of [the contemporary] mind."[97]

What Hegel has done here is most interesting. In addition to differentiating between the organic and the inorganic, he seems to be suggesting that the "inorganic" itself (i.e., the interlocking system of socioeconomic and sociocultural values) can be divided into something like substructural and superstructural components. In terms of basic principles of eighteenth-century social and political thought Hegel is implying that the bourgeois conception of ethical life is both a composite and a consequence of dovetailing "physical" (i.e., socioeconomic) and "moral" (i.e., sociocultural) influences.[98] Indeed, Hegel has conceptualized the bourgeois ethic in a way that suggests the influence of Montesquieu's, Steuart's, and Ferguson's understandings of the basic "causes" from which the "general spirit" of a people is derived (in this case, the "people" being a specific "class" of people with a specific orientation toward ethical life). But by dividing the realm of the bourgeoisie into socioeconomic and sociocultural components Hegel makes it easier for himself to be more specific and selective both about what he objects to in the bourgeois system and about how he will derive *Sittlichkeit* from it without having to ask others to join him in making – à la Fichte – a metaphysical "leap" from the real to the ideal. To appreciate how Hegel does this, we need to pay close attention to the conceptual role he begins to assign to politics in *Natural Law*.

As the text makes clear, there is a basic political concern at the core of Hegel's criticism of the bourgeoisie's overly economic conception of ethical life. This concern, in turn, is inextricably tied to his conception of *Sittlichkeit* as the key to religious recollectivization, collective salvation, and the ontological fulfillment of *homo religiosus*. Specifically, what disturbed Hegel about the bourgeois conception of ethical life was its willingness to accept economic "security" as "compensation" for acquiescence in its own "political nullity."[99] The problem, as Hegel presented it, was that the bourgeois ethic had allowed the fact of economic mutualism to dominate man's conception of himself as a social being. Like Ferguson, he realized that an economic orientation toward life had gained ascendancy in men's minds "at the expense of other pursuits [i.e., values]."[100] As the orientation established its hegemony, as it "forgot" its conditioned character, it began "to encroach on [other areas of human endeavor] and subjugate them."[101] This, Hegel argued, had led to the economization of *Sittlichkeit* and to the bolstering of the individualist tendency in modern thought.

However, Hegel was not objecting to the economic component of the bourgeois system here. Like many late eighteenth-century thinkers who had reflected on economics, commerce, and luxury, he differentiated between the moderate and the immoderate pursuit of these things.[102] As Ferguson had put it, man's involvement in "commerce is a blessing or a curse, according to *the direction his mind* has received."[103] Nor was Hegel inclined to find fault with this economic orientation toward life because it had been emancipated from moral sanctions. On the contrary, Hegel's concern with the bourgeois conception of ethical life suggested that he clearly perceived the higher moral and rational sanctions to which the economic orientation could appeal in order to justify itself.[104] Schiller had seen this clearly. In his truly remarkable twenty-fourth letter he had likened this orientation to the condition of "animality striving toward the Absolute."[105] In this condition, Schiller continued:

. . . the moral is still at the service of the physical: in either case the sole principle prevailing within him is a material one, and man is, at least in his ultimate tendency, a creature of sense – with this sole difference, that in the first case he is an animal void of reason, in the second *an animal endowed with reason*.[106]

It is important to realize, therefore, that Hegel's criticism of the bourgeois system was designed to change its sociocultural more than its socioeconomic orientation toward life.[107] That is, it was concerned less with exhorting men to reverse a socioeconomic pattern of historical development than with providing them with a new sociocultural perspective within which economic development, commercial expansion, and the pursuit of luxury might be pursued in both a civil and an ethical way. In terms that would have been familiar to Rousseau and Ferguson, Hegel had defined his philosophical task as one that entailed giving a new "direction" to man's conception of his ethical life.[108] Needless to say, the new direction pointed away from the bourgeois "system of reality" (i.e., away from the "inorganic" with its socioeconomic and sociocultural layers) and toward a system (i.e., an organic one) in which man could add a political dimension to a "personality" that was being stifled in a socioeconomic and sociocultural framework of his own making.[109]

Viewed in this way, the argument of *Natural Law* has arrived at a point where *Sittlichkeit* as an ethicopoliticoreligious ideal can be proposed as an alternative to the centrifugal socioeconomic and sociocultural forces of the period. On the one hand, it was obvious to Hegel that despite its *social* benefits commercial expansion was fostering *political* apathy in society as a whole.[110] On the other hand – and here Hegel takes leave of the managerial perspective of modernizing mercantilism – this apathy was being encouraged by those "statesmen" who sought to define political responsibility almost wholly in terms of management of the economy.[111] Either way, Hegel thought, the idea of the political as a vehicle of ethico-religious self-actualization was being made economic. It was in this context that Hegel decided to offer *Sittlichkeit* as a vehicle for a "new direction" in politics.

Before Hegel, Ferguson had made many such observations. In his *Essay* he had noted how laws that "secure the person and property of the subject, without any regard to his political character," invariably permit men "to immerse" themselves "in their separate pursuits of pleasure [and]. . . gain, which they may preserve without any attention to the commonwealth."[112] With only bonds of commerce uniting them,[113] and with the principle of the division of labor dictating their employment in different "callings" (i.e., vocations), men "ceased to be citizens" and "society" came to "consist of parts, of which none [was] animated with the spirit of society itself."[114] What has happened in Europe, Ferguson claimed, was that the "provision of wealth" had become "the idol of a covetous. . . mind."[115] "Interest," he claimed, was triumphing everywhere and at the expense of some of the "higher engagements of life."[116] Instead of "cultivating their own nature," men now seemed satisfied to accumulate "wealth and external conveniences."[117]

For Ferguson and Hegel, therefore, the commercial advance was rapidly laying "the political spirit" of peoples to "rest."[118] Men were losing that "elevation of mind" and that "sense of honor which gave rules to. . . personal courage."[119] Nobility of character was now defined, as Montesquieu and Rousseau had also noted, in terms of "the sumptuous retinue which money alone may procure."[120] Ferguson, commenting on how eager men seemed to be to "yield up their dignity as citizens,"[121] put his finger on what he thought, and what Hegel later would think, was the problem when he wrote:

If those principles of honour which save the individual from servility in his own person, or from becoming an engine of oppression in the hands of another, should fail; if they should give way to the maxims of commerce, to the refinements of *a supposed philosophy*, . . . if they are betrayed by the cowardice of princes; what must become of the nations of Europe?[122]

Here we arrive at a crucial "moment" in *Natural Law*, in Hegel's development, and in European intellectual history on the whole. To appreciate this fully, we need only recall that at several points in the text Hegel had argued that the bourgeois conception of ethical life was singularly devoid of one essential quality – "courage."[123] Like Gibbon, whom he quoted at length on this point,[124] Hegel believed that the bourgeoisie's lack of "courage" was both cause and effect of their "political nullity."[125] But Hegel thought that the contemporary political problem was best explained in terms of what Ferguson had called mankind's "voluntary neglects and corruptions."[126] By this Ferguson had meant that some of the "active virtues" – "magnanimity, courage, and the love of mankind" – were being "sacrificed to avarice and vanity."[127] Reflecting on how to remedy this situation Ferguson made a remarkable point. He wrote:

. . . if the individual, not called to unite with his country, be left to pursue his private advantage; we may find him become effeminate, mercenary, and sensual; not because pleasures and profits are become more alluring, but because he has *fewer calls to attend to other objects*; and because he has more encouragement to study his personal advantages and pursue his separate interests.[128]

What is remarkable in this statement is the implication that the threat commerce posed for the political identity and integrity of a people could be offset by "calls" that challenged the privileged position many men were giving to the economic ethic in their lives.[129]

These calls, of course, were understood by Ferguson to be "political" in nature and were meant, therefore, to contest in an ideological sense the positions taken by cultural spokesmen who wittingly or unwittingly lent support to the drift toward luxury and avarice.[130] The calls, moreover, were to come from those "higher orders of men" who, unlike "men of business," had not lost "that courage and elevation of mind" that is so central to the preservation of a peoples' political identity.[131] It is precisely the *political* problem of how to promote that "courage and elevation of mind" that Hegel is conjuring up toward the end of *National Law*. And, as we shall see, it is through the idea of courage (i.e., *Tapferkeit*) that *homo religiosus* emerges from the life of *homo oeconomicus*.

3. The idea of *Tapferkeit*: The conversion of *Geist* to *Sittlichkeit*[132]

The fact that in *Natural Law* Hegel repeatedly juxtaposes *Tapferkeit* with the bourgeoisie's preoccupations with "fixed reality," with "possession and property," and with "peace and gain and perfect security" is quite revealing.[133] It allows him to discuss economic factors in terms of the negative condition of political apathy and the positive, albeit conditional, condition of political activism. Indeed, like Ferguson, Hegel used the idea of "courage" to impugn those who formed their identities around "the indulgences of animal appetite."[134]

Other influential eighteenth-century thinkers, many of whom Hegel had read, had employed the idea of courage to make the same point. In the *Persian Letters* Montesquieu characterized as "cowards" those whose sole "ambition" was to "languish amidst the pleasures" of acquired "riches."[135] Adam Smith, in his *Lectures* of 1762–1763, and then again in the *Wealth of Nations*, had remarked that "Another bad effect of commerce is that it sinks the courage of mankind, and tends to extinguish martial spirit. . . . By having their minds constantly employed on the arts of luxury, they grow effeminate and dastardly."[136] Smith continued: "These are the disadvantages of a commercial spirit. The minds of men are contracted, and rendered incapable of elevation."[137] The same problem, it seems, exercised the author of the article on "Luxury" in the *Encyclopedia*. Discussing the question of whether "luxury weakens courage,"[138] Saint-Lambert conceded that it would (i.e., it would become a "vice") unless it were "subordinated" to "civic spirit and patriotism."[139] Though Saint-Lambert wavered over whether the "government" or the "poets"[140] should be assigned the task of rekindling "waning patriotism," he was quite sure that somebody must take responsibility for the "elevation of spirit" that turns "minds. . .to patriotic feelings and true virtue."[141]

Finally, there was Rousseau, who quite unabashedly took up the subject of "courage" in his "Discourse on Political Economy" as well as in his two *Discourses*.[142] In assessing the deleterious effects of luxury on human virtue, Rousseau offered patriotism, "the most heroic of all the passions,"[143] as a check on "egoism," the ethic of acquisitiveness, and the ascendancy of "private interest" at the expense of "public interest" in the affairs of men.[144] For patriotism to take hold of men's minds, citizens had to be trained, their souls had to be elevated, so that "that contemptible activity [i.e., the pursuit of economic self-interest] that absorbs all virtue and constitutes the life of petty souls" could not become "entrenched" as a "habit" (i.e., as the defining characteristic) of collective life.[145] To contain this centrifugal movement, Rousseau wanted a group of "illustrious warriors" constantly to "preach courage" to men so that the "virtue" of citizenship would not perish as an ideal among them.[146] Rousseau was even more explicit about this in the *First Discourse*. There he had complained that modern science, instead of arousing "courage" in men, was enervating it in them.[147] He noted that as "luxury spreads" it gives rise to the kind of specialization in the arts that deprives the collectivity of its binding ethos. Insofar as science was complicit in all of this, it could be implicated in the enervation of "true courage."[148]

Rousseau often discussed courage in a militaristic textual context.[149] And like Machiavelli before him and Ferguson after him, he often used examples from the history of Roman antiquity to point up the role courage might play in the life of a truly political people.[150] Whether the focus was on antiquity or on the eighteenth century, though, the refrain was always the same: the advance of commerce and luxury enervated courage and undermined the military prowess of a people. But there was more to Rousseau's concern with courage than that. It was not just "brute" courage of a militaristic kind that he wanted to promote.[151] No, Rousseau like Monboddo was interested in "true courage"; and for him, true courage only expressed itself in the political life of a people.[152] As he wrote in the *First Discourse*, if luxury "is harmful to warlike qualities, it is even more so to moral [i.e., political] qualities."[153] It made men forget "what the words magnanimity, equity, temperance, humanity, courage are."[154]

Seen in this light Rousseau's understanding of courage seems to have a "portable quality" about it: it can serve a political as well as a military end.[155] In this, Rousseau's view of courage is not unlike that of Plato.[156] Indeed, there were many antecedents within the classical tradition of political philosophy for what Rousseau was saying about courage.[157] In the *Republic*, for example, Plato posited courage (*thymos*) as the distinguishing quality of the guardian class.[158] Moreover, it is clear throughout the *Republic* that courage was essential to the process whereby a people became politicized, whereby men came to define their collective living arrangement in terms of the benefits of a truly political *association* rather than in terms of the benefits of mere social *aggregation*.[159]

Like Rousseau, though, Plato never meant to make the "natural passion" that expressed itself as courage the basis for political association. Animals as well as men could exhibit that quality in their behavior. And since Plato meant to differentiate men from animals by reference to the political aspects of their behavior, he had to develop a perspective on courage that was uniquely political as well as peculiar to man. As Allan Bloom has noted, this concern lies behind Plato's criticism of Achilles and behind his attempt to distinguish *thymos* (i.e., courage as a natural passion common to men and animals) from *Andreia* (courage as informed by an appreciation of the virtue of an associative political life).[160] Thus, in Plato, too, courage has a portable quality.[161] And just as in Rousseau, this portable quality allows Plato to regard courage as a "mode of conduct" in which the heroic figures of the warrior and the citizen merge and become one.[162]

When, therefore, Rousseau makes a point of calling on "illustrious warriors" to "preach courage" to men, he is really asking them to preach a doctrine with a very specific political content. For Rousseau, of course, that content could be summed up in the word "patriotism."[163] But there was more. The patriotic call was also a way of reminding men of what it meant to be free "human," as distinct from enslaved "animal," beings.[164] Insofar as men who indulged in "animal" pleasures could be said to be slaves to their appetites, they were not human beings (i.e., truly free) at all.[165] Conversely, men of courage were human precisely because they were free from that kind of dependency. They were free, that is, in the classical political sense of the term.

From these examples, some of which certainly must have caught Hegel's attention, it should be clear that in the late eighteenth century many influential political theorists were using the idea of courage as a vehicle for political arguments – arguments advanced in the name of man's *human* as distinct from his *animal* nature.[166] Hegel, I think, had these references clearly in mind when he posited *Sittlichkeit* as an alternative to the bourgeois conception of ethical life.

In *Social Contract* Rousseau used the terms *citoyen* and bourgeois to express this distinction.[167] In *Natural Law*, Hegel employed the same distinction with one important qualification: he was careful never to present the opposition between *Bürger* as citizen and *Bürger* as bourgeois in the kind of exclusive terms that were so congenial to the moral formalists. In this Hegel may very well have been following Garve, who had insisted that the double meaning of the German word *Bürger* aptly expressed the modern political problem, whereas the French words *citoyen* and *bourgeois* enabled one to avoid it.[168] On the contrary, Hegel had been committed from the mid-1790s to showing how the idea of *Bürger* as citizen develops from the idea of *Bürger* as *bourgeois* (i.e., to showing how the organic–political develops from the inorganic–economic). In *Natural Law* the idea of "courage" is offered as the key to the "conversion" process.[169] But the explanation Hegel offers of the conversion process itself is empirically grounded and for that reason is very different from other late eighteenth-century political versions of the courage–conversion argument.

That Hegel meant to be rigorously empirical in explaining how courage figured in the transformation of the bourgeois into the citizen becomes clearer if we remember how Schiller had handled the same problem in *Aesthetic Education*. There, in the twenty-third letter, Schiller had remarked that "the sign of a noble soul" was the capacity to transform the "most limited matter and the pettiest object into something infinite" (note that earlier Hegel had defined religion in similar terms).[170] Schiller called someone who possessed this "gift of transforming" *ein Gemüt*.[171]

Gemüt is an untranslatable term.[172] Yet, as we have already noted, it was a key word in German cultural life at the end of the eighteenth century.[173] Indeed, it was central to emergent religious, philosophical, and aesthetic arguments, and had even been used by Hegel in the mid-1790s in overtly political contexts.[174] All that notwithstanding, *Gemüt* is still derived from the German word *Mut* (courage) which, in Greek, would be rendered *thymos*. The word *Gemüt*, in other words, is etymologically connected with the idea of courage and generally is meant to convey something about the nobility of one's soul.[175] For Schiller, this nobility expressed itself aesthetically, in the "transforming" power one may exhibit in dealing with "everyday actuality."[176] And this aesthetic meaning lies behind the scholarly claim that *Gemüt* is best understood as an "indeterminent [*sic*] striving for general satisfaction, *not directed at any particular aim*, but rather concerned with the entire condition of the soul."[177]

Hegel, we observed earlier, used *Gemüt* in a rather different way in his early theological writings. There the transforming power was construed in quite specific religious and political rather than general aesthetic terms.[178] As we argued, Hegel was using *Gemüt* as an anthropological–theological concept that had its roots in the "Pelagian covenant theology" of late medieval German thought.[179]

Given his previous usage of the term, we might expect Hegel to have continued to use *Gemüt* in contexts where "courage" was being employed as part of a broader argument for man's elevation and conversion to the higher things in life. But in *Natural Law* Hegel employed another word for courage.[180] The word is *Tapferkeit*. That substitution, I think, is extremely revealing, for it tells us worlds about the very specific political connotation Hegel wanted to assign to *Sittlichkeit* in *Natural Law*.[181]

Why, then, the substitution? The answer, I think, lies in the continuing influence of Garve on Hegel's political thinking.[182] Between 1798 and 1801 Garve's translation of Aristotle's *Ethics* had been published.[183] The translation appeared in two volumes. In the first volume Garve presented an essay on the history of *Sittlichkeit* from Aristotle through the Scottish thinkers Hutcheson, Ferguson, and Smith. In addition, the first volume contained Garve's commentary on each of the chapters of the first two books of the *Ethics*. In this commentary, Garve stressed how essential *thymos* had been to Greek political conceptions.[184] But he also drew attention to the fact that *thymos* was a characteristic of animals as well as of men. Therefore, Garve proposed using the word *Tapferkeit* to express the reflective sense of courage that was a unique characteristic of human political association. Garve granted, in other words, that while *thymos* might be the empirical source of *Tapferkeit*, it was not identical with it. That was because *thymos* lacked not only the specific political quality of *Tapferkeit* but also the general reflective quality of the "magnanimous" man whose *Bestimmung* (i.e., *telos*) was realized in political action.

A corollary of the work Garve did for the Aristotle translation was the publication in 1798 of a long essay on *Sittlichkeit*. In one of the sections of this essay Garve offered his own reflections on the meaning of

Tapferkeit.[185] According to Garve, *Tapferkeit* was the specific form that virtue assumed when it was directed toward a political end.[186] Here Garve was careful to differentiate *Tapferkeit* from mere physical bravado, the difference being that he regarded the former as a quality that only "civilized men" exhibited and only in their political behavior.[187] In that sense, Garve's understanding of *Tapferkeit* is to be seen more as a consequence of the conscious and voluntary development of man's political (i.e., collective moral) personality than as a mere transfer of *thymos* to the political realm of behavior. As Garve put it, *Tapferkeit* was *Geist* that had been given a political focus, a focus that Garve and Hegel talked about in terms of *Sittlichkeit*.[188]

For Garve, then, *Tapferkeit* is an "energy" that finds expression in politically oriented action. This action was political for Garve for several reasons.[189] First of all, it was political because it had its roots in man's longing to be part of a collective moral agency (i.e., the state). Second of all, it was political because it was an "active" expression of human fellowship. Finally, it was political because it had – à la Rousseau – a patriotic edge to it.

In making this latter point, though, Garve did not mean to equate patriotism with nationalism. What made the patriotic impulse "noble" was that in the final analysis it had "justice" as its highest end.[190] And justice, as any student of Aristotle's *Politics* would know, has a relative political aspect about it. But, as Garve saw it, it was only through the agency of politics that justice could be pursued at all. Garve believed that politics was the arena in which man learned to order and establish his value priorities. This made an active political life imperative if man wished to be a truly human being. Through political participation and the setting of value priorities man announced to the world what kind of person he wished to be – if not in the immediate present, then in the immediate future. In this sense, politics could be regarded as an expression of man's confidence in his own future, in his own ability to live a virtuous life. As Garve remarked, "Keine bürgerlich Gesellschaft bestehen kann, wenn sie nicht muthvolle und tapfere Bürger hat,"; that is, for Garve what made society "civil" was its political, not its socioeconomic, "moment."[191]

In *Natural Law* Hegel used *Tapferkeit* in just this way; and in juxtaposing it with the bourgeois conception of ethical life it is obvious that he meant to challenge the view that collective solidarity could be measured solely in terms of reciprocal socioeconomic relations. Truly human cohesiveness, Hegel felt, had to have an explicit political dimension. That is, it had to arise from what the Greeks called *praxis*, from behavior that was "free" and purposefully designed to express that aspect of human personality that lay beyond the realm of physical necessity. *Praxis*, in other words, was the realm of the "organic," the realm of true *association*. What remained was the "inorganic sphere," the sphere of physical necessity, the sphere of mere *aggregation*, in which cohesiveness, were it momentarily to exist, had an accidental quality about it.[192]

Several interesting points emerge from viewing the "*Tapferkeit–bourgeois*" juxtaposition in the *Natural Law* text this way. First of all, it is clear that Hegel used the word *Tapferkeit*, rather than *Gemüt*, to express a specific political rather than a very general aesthetic commitment. In that context, of course, both words could be construed as part of a philosophy of "expressionism"; [193] but to see the two that way, I think, is to confuse idealism with romanticism (in the same way that we earlier showed that Pelagianism had often been confused with pantheism). *Tapferkeit* is not, therefore, to be equated with *Gemüt*. It was, indeed, related to it, but the conceptual "subscript" is very different in the two cases.

Second, *Tapferkeit*, at least in Garve's and Hegel's hands, was not a quality that was prominent in the political thought of the moral formalists. They, after all, had tried to divorce things political (i.e., the organic) from things nonpolitical (i.e., the inorganic). Granted, *Sittlichkeit* was an ideal shared by Garve and Hegel on the one hand and by the moral formalists on the other. But in Garve's and Hegel's work *Tapferkeit* had its roots in the inorganic and developed from a dynamic internal to the inorganic itself.[194] It did not, as the moral formalists would have had it, emerge as a force or entity that was independent of the inorganic from its inception.

Third, although Garve and Hegel presented *Tapferkeit* as an empirically rooted spiritual energy, they never celebrated it, as the "empiricists" would have, as a "natural" phenomenon. On the contrary – for Garve and Hegel *Tapferkeit* comes into play precisely at the point at which men were obliged for ethico-politico-religious reasons to move beyond the realm of nature. So, even though *Tapferkeit* had a "natural" origin, it was not "naturally necessary" to men except insofar as they came to see politics as a way of developing their personalities beyond what was given to them "by nature."[195] In this sense, the end of *Tapferkeit* is an "artificial" creation that, somehow, grows out of "nature." Explaining how this happens will be Hegel's task in *Ethical Life*.

Finally, it would be wrong, I think, to treat *Tapferkeit* simply as a category of classical political philosophy. To be sure, in Garve and Hegel *Tapferkeit* seems to stand to *Gemüt* as *Andreia* did to *thymos*. Moreover, *Tapferkeit* and *Andreia* have *Sittlichkeit* as their end. Therefore, both might be rendered in terms of the classical trope of "civic virtue." But if *Tapferkeit* has *Sittlichkeit* as an end, it also has its source in *Gemüt* or *Geist*. That means, of course, that *Tapferkeit* is what might be called a "conversion principle," part of the process whereby *Geist* or *Gemüt* becomes transformed into *Sittlichkeit*. We know that this was Hegel's main concern during these years and we know that we regarded the conversion process itself as an exercise in applied theology. On those terms, *Tapferkeit* might very well be envisaged as part of the ontology of *homo religiosus* in general and of religious recollectivization in particular. If that was the case, we need to be especially careful about how we measure the classical and the Christian components of *Natural Law*. Had not Hegel cued us to his true intention when in that text he wrote that "the movement of the absolute contradiction between [the organic and inorganic] presents itself in the Divine nature as courage"?[196]

4. Hegel and the problem of Aristotelianized Protestantism

Having said this we should try to conclude our discussion of *Natural Law* by trying to explain how classical and Christian political motifs may have figured in it. An answer to this question, I think, can be fashioned by adapting some of the arguments of J. G. A. Pocock's *Machiavellian Moment* to the German context in which *Natural Law* was written.[197]

In *The Machiavellian Moment* Pocock has argued that a good part of the intellectual history of early modern Europe, especially in the Anglo-American world, can be explained in terms of continuity and change in the ideological tradition of what has come to be known as "civic humanism."[198] At its simplest level Pocock's thesis is that some time between the Renaissance and the later Enlightenment the humanists' perennial concern with the relation between "virtue" and "corruption" gave way to a more specific concern with the relationship between "virtue" and "commerce." Confronted with what they perceived to be the centrifugal economic tendencies of the period, many humanists felt compelled to develop political strategies for preserving the integrity of man's "civic personality." For this, ways had to be devised for insulating politics against the "corruption" of "commerce" and the lure of "luxury." This, Pocock argues, forced thinkers in the civic humanist tradition into assuming a conservative posture with regard to much of the dynamic of "early modern capitalism."

According to Pocock, however, the humanists were conceptually ill equipped for this task because they lacked a theory of historical change that went beyond ascribing the adverse effects of commerce to "fortune."[199] When, during the eighteenth century, "fortune" was seen as an inadequate explanation of historical change, humanists were forced to develop another view of man's relation to history. Thus, Pocock writes, what began "with Florentine humanists" culminated in the eighteenth-century European context in "the beginnings of a dialectical perception of history" that stressed the interplay between economics and human alienation in history.[200]

This thesis, I think, has a subtle relevance to the situation in Germany during Hegel's life. The Germans, of course, were strangers neither to the classical tradition nor to the civic humanist form it assumed in much of the early modern period. However, as has been pointed out earlier, some Germans, especially in Old-Württemberg, viewed this tradition from a very specific Christian vantage point. That is, they tended to place the language of civic humanism in the service of a futurist program of religious recollectivization rather than a presentist defense of the status quo. In that context, neoclassical conceptions of politics were placed in the service of what has variously been described as "messianic nationalism," "apocalyptic republicanism," "quasi-millennial republicanism," "philosophical millenarianism," and, more aptly, "civil millenarianism."[201] In other words, a Christian eschatological hope for the future rather than a classical fear of decline relative to the past governed much of the discussion about politics in Old-Württemberg in the eighteenth century. The result: Württemberg Protestants could discuss the problem of religious recollectivization (i.e., the need for a Second Reformation) with the teleologically informed language of Aristotle's political thought. In this way religious recollectivization could be presented in terms of a vital "political" moment in a broader process that Pocock has explained in terms of "Christian redemption" in history.[202] Hence, Pocock's claim that among liberal Protestants Aristotle was instrumental in "the reunion of political history with eschatology."[203]

More than most, Pocock has seen what has been lost from our understanding of the political thought of the seventeenth and eighteenth centuries by frequent and uncritical use of the by now coventional distinction between the classical and the Christian. Though he has not pursued his thesis into the German context (as Felix Gilbert has suggested he should),[204] he has appreciated how certain forms of eschatological thought made it possible, especially for Protestants, to incorporate the classical (i.e., Aristotelian) notion of man as *zōon politikon* into a Christian soteriological framework.[205] This meant, of course, that much of Aristotle is compatible with a view of man as *homo religiosus*; that is, with the ontological framework within which Hegel was working as a young man.

Central to Pocock's thesis is the view that under certain conditions the motivation of "citizen and saint" could have, and did become one in the intellectual history of early modern Europe. Still, there are deep and important differences between the citizen's and the saint's political conceptions. For one thing, as we have already noted, citizen and saint have different conceptions of political time. This point is crucial to Hegel scholarship, because his thought is clearly more indebted to the latter's than to the former's sense of time.[206] For Garve and Hegel, for example, *Tapferkeit* expressed a political hope for the future far more than a fear of the possibility of decline in the present. It expressed, in other words, a liberal Christian hope for the future more than a conservative political hope for the present.

For another thing, citizen and saint may have different attitudes toward the economic interest factor in the collective life. In the civic humanist tradition *economics* was generally viewed as a disruptive *social* force, so much so that by the eighteenth century the major *political* imperative of this tradition was to guard against socioeconomic inequality.[207] As a result, there was a moral formalist tendency in civic humanism that often expressed itself politically in terms of a mind–body dualism and asceticism. Among certain groups of Protestants, however, there was a tendency to view economics "indifferently." Indeed, from Calvin to Rousseau and Ferguson economics was measured less in terms of man's physical involvements per se than in terms of the spiritual attitude he had toward them.[208]

This, I think, is crucial, especially for the line of argument we shall see Hegel develop in *Ethical Life*, discussed in the next chapter. Suffice it to say here that liberal Protestants held that wealth only became a social problem when the collectivity began to sanction the pursuit of wealth and interest as the *telos* of a civil existence. According to this view, when "luxury" rather than "wisdom," when the value of bourgeois security and comfort rather than *Bürgerliche Vollkommenheit* (excellence), defined the collective living arrangement, man, however rational and law-abiding he might otherwise be, remained, like an animal, a slave to his desires.[209] These desires, though, were not rooted in man's physical needs; they were creations of his imagination, of the "civilization" in which he lived at a specific moment in time.[210]

Here our previous discussions of the theology of the divine economy, of the three-stage view of history, of the voluntarist aspects of self-realizing teleology, and of the relation between commerce and luxury in eighteenth-century thought begin to converge. In terms of the Christian attitude toward wealth that we have been discussing, the impulse toward luxury was, as Rousseau clearly saw, rooted more in "our affections" than "our needs," more in the misdirected spiritual desires of our souls than in the material needs of our physical constitutions.[211] At the same time, the liberal Protestant view recognized that the scale of the contemporary contagion of luxury was unprecedented in the history of Western civilization – that is, it was not enough for individuals to struggle heroically against luxury; the collectivity had to do so as well. That meant that someone had to begin to articulate the call for a collective commitment that required civilization to submit to the discipline of culture, civil society to that of *Sittlichkeit*, and the spirit of a people to that of its true telos. In *Ethical Life*, written shortly after *Natural Law*, Hegel developed the infrastructure for this argument. We shall now turn to *Ethical Life* to see why Hegel chose to cast his argument in a socio-economic form.

7

Sittlichkeit reconsidered
II. The essay on *Ethical Life*

Hegel's *System der Sittlichkeit* (*System of Ethical Life*) was written as a companion piece to the essay on *Natural Law*.[1] Though not published during his lifetime, the essay is best regarded as a position paper in which Hegel fleshes out in more detail the practical political problem he had encountered and perfunctorily discussed in the *Natural Law* text, namely, how *Tapferkeit* could be set up as a conceptual axis that would allow for the conversion of the "inorganic" moment of *Sittlichkeit* into the "organic" one.[2] Since it is clear from the *Natural Law* text that Hegel associated the organic with the political moment of objective experience, the essay on *Ethical Life* must surely on that account be considered one of Hegel's most pointedly political tracts.

Still, the political intentions of the essay are not immediately obvious. Even though the text addresses many of the same political problems as the essay on *Natural Law*, the political dimension of the text has been obscured by the language Hegel used to talk about it. We know, of course, that politics was very much on Hegel's mind when he wrote *Ethical Life*. There is an obvious political overlap between that text on the one hand and the essays on *Natural Law* and the *German Constitution* on the other.[3] Yet, even though the essay on *Ethical Life* offers a detailed explanation of the "political moment" in human experience, it does so in a philosophical language that not only complicates an already complicated subject matter but also makes it impossible for the text to speak for itself. Thus, if we are to appreciate the decidedly political thrust of this text — how it provides an insight into Hegel's understanding of the origin and purpose of the political moment of objective experience — we need to bear in mind that the philosophical language Hegel uses in the text has a concrete reference in the religious–economic overlay problem that we previously argued propelled Hegel toward the political in the first place. Indeed, without an understanding of this overlay and of Hegel's political

231

commitment, it would be very difficult to make philosophical sense of the essay.

As if this were not enough, there are other reasons the essay on *Ethical Life* is a notoriously difficult text to decipher. First, it is hard to follow because, as Plant has noted, "it is clearly a work in progress and was not meant for publication."[4] And even if we grant, as Plant and Harris do, that the text was meant to be supplemented by lectures, it is still repetitive and tentative in the argument it advances.

Second, Hegel wrote this text when he was still Schelling's collaborator on the *Critical Journal*. In this context, much of the language in the essay shows Schelling's influence. The problem, however, was that Hegel was using this language in a conceptual framework that was not conducive to Schelling's terminology. That is, he was using Schelling's language (e.g., the concept *Potenz*) to discuss a relation within objective experience itself (i.e., between *Sittlichkeit* in its relative "inorganic" and absolute "organic" moments) that Schelling had all but ignored in his own work.[5] Consequently, Hegel encountered great difficulty and fell into many confusions when he tried to adapt Schelling's language to his own purposes. And even though he abandoned Schelling's terminology shortly after *Ethical Life* was written, it had to carry the burden of that terminological problem.

Third, the essay is one of Hegel's first properly philosophical texts. If the move from Frankfurt to Jena was made with the hope of gaining an opportunity to teach philosophy at the university level, the realization of that hope carried with it an obligation to speak the language of philosophy in the lecture hall. And at this date that was the language of Schelling. For Hegel, who was already committed to discussing philosophy against the backdrop of contemporary problems of socio-economic and political experience, this was no easy matter. Granted, it had been relatively easy for him to slide from the language of religion (i.e., *praxis pietatis*) to the language of philosophy (i.e., *Sittlichkeit*) and then again from there to a critique of the political asceticism implicit in moral formalism. But it was quite another thing, as Hegel soon discovered, to translate *Sittlichkeit* into the language of social and political theory and at the same time into the language of Schelling. This double linguistic burden, needless to say, made for a certain lack of clarity in the argument. And, ultimately, it forced Hegel to develop his own philosophical conceptions and terminology.

Finally, in *Ethical Life* Hegel is still not clear in his own mind about what kind of conceptual framework would adequately encompass the socioeconomic and political dynamic he had detected in the world of objective experience. Hegel knew where he wanted to go: he knew what values he held dear and what his priorities were among them. This was evident in the *Natural Law* text, when he tried to draw a clear distinction between socio-economic (i.e., inorganic) and ethicopoliticoreligious (i.e., organic) kinds of behavior. As we have seen, he made this distinction in order to develop a political conception of *Sittlichkeit* that would take account of economics without impeding religious collectivization and the collective quest for salvation.

In *Natural Law* this distinction was given concrete form in the differentiation between the citizen and the bourgeois. Yet, as was noted earlier, it is clear from this text that Hegel, like Garve, meant verbally to exploit the double meaning of *bürgerlich Gesellschaft*.[6] That Hegel did this is, I think, fraught with significance for understanding his conception of politics during these years. On the one hand, *bürgerlich Gesellschaft* could stand for the old values and priorities of the Protestant conception of the *Bürger* qua citizen. Here, as Manfred Riedel has reminded us, the idea of the *Bürger* expressed a very old European conception of community (i.e., "civil society" in its pre-Hegelian usage).[7] On the other hand, *bürgerlich Gesellschaft* hinted at the meaning-complex of the *Bürger* qua bourgeois. Here the idea of *Bürger* was pervaded by a new socioeconomic conception of community.[8]

Taken together, then, the potential double meaning of *bürgerlich Gesellschaft* allowed Hegel philosophically to pose a politico-historical problem for his readers, a problem that, like his philosophy at this time, turned upon the conception of *Sittlichkeit*. Indeed, as Hegel saw it, the question of the day in the Germanies (if not in all of Europe) was with which set of meanings Germans would choose to identify. Both meanings, Hegel thought, were real historical possibilities. If his reading of the Scots had told him that elsewhere in Europe the balance had been tilting toward the conception of *Bürger* as bourgeois, the argument of the essay on the *German Constitution* made it clear that Hegel thought Germans had a chance to pursue the other alternative. Because of what we today would call "economic backwardness," and because of the political possibilities that the collapse of the Holy Roman Empire had opened up, Germans might still be receptive to "calls" for action that would differ markedly from those that wittingly or unwittingly provided sanctions for the bourgeois conception of ethical life.

Hegel, in this respect, has built "dramatic action" into the text and into his conception of *Sittlichkeit*.[9] What he has done here is what H. White has claimed Tocqueville tried to do in his own work; namely, to put "living men in a situation of choice, to enliven them to the possibilities of choosing, and to inform them of the difficulties attending any choice they might make."[10] Put another way, Hegel was asking men to choose a *political* future for themselves, a future that Hegel understood full well was conditional in that it depended upon the active and voluntary consent of his readers.[11] Seen in this light the essay on *Ethical Life* had a twofold purpose: to alert Germans to what was at stake in the meaning they assigned to *bürgerlich Gesellschaft* and to persuade them to make the "right choice" (i.e., one that was consistent with Hegel's own preferences in the matter).

For Hegel, therefore, the dramatic action of *Ethical Life* consists, above all, in a call for historical action.[12] What is more, the action for which the text is calling is specifically political – it asks the audience to engage in collective action that has *Sittlichkeit* as its end. Moreover, as we have seen, Hegel's conception of *Sittlichkeit* had been designed to address a specific historical problem; namely, how to prevent the "bourgeois" conception of ethical life from encroaching upon all other areas of collective life. There is, in short, nothing "existential" about what Hegel is writing about here. True, what he says is presented in the form of symbolic political action – but that action emerges from a constellation of forces that is historically grounded in basic eighteenth-century concerns.

Thus, in the essay on *Ethical Life* Hegel's problem was this: while describing as realistically as possible the dynamic of the current socio-economic and political situation, he had to permit his own preferences to emerge as an alternative to what he regarded as a drift toward a thoroughly "bourgeois" conception of ethical life. To use the conceptual language of Kenneth Burke, Hegel's conception of the socioeconomic and political dimensions of objective experience was at once "regulative" and "constitutive": regulative in that it posited what may be realized politically "on condition that its offer is accepted" and constitutive in that its conditional political mode was grounded in present-day socio-economic reality.[13] It is Hegel's attempt to do this – to attach his own values to the analysis without seeming arbitrary and without ignoring real historical forces – that, I think, compelled him at this time to develop a unique understanding of objective experience, an understanding that soon was to express itself in the famous state–civil society conceptual split.

1. Natural *Sittlichkeit* and the origin of societies problem

Hegel begins the essay on *Ethical Life* more or less where the *Natural Law* text ended – by dividing objective experience into two "moments," each of which is governed by a different principle of action. But where *Natural Law* discussed the division in terms of the inorganic and organic, *Ethical Life* expresses the differentiation in terms of the relation between natural *Sittlichkeit* and absolute *Sittlichkeit*. Hegel, however, meant for these new terms to embrace several of the antitheses of the *Natural Law* text: for example, between man's physical and spiritual drives; between socioeconomic and political conditions of objective experience; and between the values of the bourgeois and those of the citizen. There is, in this respect, a marked continuity of development between the two essays.

Still, the very fact that Hegel felt compelled to write this essay indicates some dissatisfaction with the way he had handled these antitheses in the earlier essay. It must have been quite obvious to him that the argument of *Natural Law* was, at bottom, slightly formalist in character. That meant, of course, that it was vulnerable to the same kinds of criticisms Hegel himself had made of the work of Kant and Fichte. Thus, to avoid repeating the mistakes of the formalists Hegel had to show how the political moment of experience grew naturally and purposefully (i.e., endogenously, to use what we shall see is an apt economic term) out of the bourgeois pursuit of economic self-interest itself. That is, the desire for politics (i.e., for the organic) had to be internally "pushed" out of, rather than externally "pulled" from, the socioeconomic (i.e., inorganic) sphere of action.[14]

Without this kind of argument – one implicit in positing *Tapferkeit* as a conversion principle – Hegel's attempt to distinguish his position from that of the formalists and empiricists would fail, for without that argument his differentiation of objective experience into two different realms of action could be construed in either of two ways: à la the formalists as an argument for liberating the state from civil society (in order to insulate things political from corrupting socioeconomic "interests") or à la the empiricists, as an argument for liberating civil society from the state (in order to free the productive forces of the former from the regulatory encumbrances of the latter). In the following discussion we shall show how Hegel tried to steer clear of the horns of this formalist–empiricist dilemma. And since little of his argument can be understood apart from his conception of *natürliche Sittlichkeit* (what Hegel discussed in the *Natural Law* text in terms of the inorganic), we shall start our exegesis of the essay on *Ethical Life* with an analysis of that concept.

Hegel begins his discussion of natural *Sittlichkeit* with what appears to be a straightforward account of what Durkheim, writing about Rousseau, termed "the origin of societies" problem.[15] It is obvious from the text that this problem provides the *textual* context in which Hegel means initially to set the concept. As we shall see, the meaning Hegel assigns to natural *Sittlichkeit* can only be appreciated against the backdrop of positions he takes on the kinds of problems of continuity and change that invariably arise in discussions of man's movement from a presocial to a social condition.

On the surface, the text on *Ethical Life* seems to be making three conventional eighteenth-century points about this movement.[16] First, Hegel indicates that man's entry into social relations with others was a consequence of fears and needs that could only be satisfied by a collective living arrangement.[17] Second, he claims that to sustain this collective living arrangement man must labor;[18] and for the collectivity to meet the continuing challenge of demographic pressure man must, to speak with Steuart, learn to "labor ingeniously" and with "industry."[19] That is, to ensure his preservation man had to learn to organize his labor and the pursuit of subsistence in a systematic (i.e., social) way. As a result, man enters into cooperative relations with others and gradually becomes accustomed to what the Scots were wont to call "the habit of society."[20]

Finally, Hegel suggests that the effort to organize society along economic lines entailed an expansion of man's consciousness.[21] The more physical and psychical contact man had with others, the more opportunity he had to exercise his faculties – which meant that he began to develop his intelligence, but in a very practical, down-to-earth, need-oriented sort of way.[22] For Hegel, however, this development could not be understood in terms of increasing self-consciousness (self consciousness, we shall see, is only expressed for Hegel in the political moment of objective experience). As he saw it, the object of social intelligence continued to be bound up with man's conception of himself as a physical (i.e., animal) rather than spiritual (i.e., human) being.[23] Though Hegel is not exactly clear on this, I take it that when he remarked that natural *Sittlichkeit* was characterized by "formlessness. . .and the absence of wisdom"[24] and that a people is not a people without that wisdom,[25] he was echoing Schiller, who had made the general point quite clearly:

In the very midst of his animality the drive towards the Absolute catches him unawares – and since in this state of apathy all his endeavour is directed merely towards the material and the temporal, and limited exclusively to himself as individual, he will merely be induced by that demand to give his own individuality unlimited extension rather than to abstract from it altogether: will be led to strive, *not after form, but after an unfailing supply of matter*; not after changelessness, but after perpetually enduring change; and after the absolute assurance of his temporal existence.[26]

Hegel granted, of course, that the development of tools and organizational skills entailed exercise of intelligence.[27] But since the purpose of this intelligence was to satisfy physical needs, social man's consciousness did not differ significantly from that of presocial man. Thus, for Hegel, as for others before him, what distinguished social from presocial man had less to do with consciousness than with specific aspects of social organization. These aspects (e.g., the division of labor) may have made man a *social* animal, but, according to Hegel, they did not make him a *human* being. For that, man had to become political – which meant that for Hegel the presocial and social were similar because both were prepolitical in character.

This is an extremely important point. It means that for Hegel the difference between man's presocial and social conditions is one of degree, not kind. To be sure, Hegel acknowledged that the movement from one condition to the other involved many changes: restraints invariably were imposed on what Rousseau had called man's "natural liberty"; man's labor was organized differently, principally along lines dictated by the idea of the division of labor; new patterns of social dependency and subordination developed from the way labor was organized; and problems of possession became matters of law (i.e., they became questions of the civil "recognition" of property).[28] Despite the changes, though, Hegel refused to explain this transition in terms of radical antitheses. Rather Hegel insisted on a fundamental continuity of development between the presocial and social conditions.[29] This is obvious from the elastic quality he has given to the concept of natural *Sittlichkeit*: it can be stretched to cover man's actions in both realms of experience and can be used, therefore, to collapse the two into one "prepolitical moment" of experience.

In this, Hegel's conception of natural *Sittlichkeit* as an institutional value complex is very similar to the conceptions of the *Notstaat* and the *Naturstaat* that Schiller developed in *Aesthetic Education*.[30] There, Schiller claimed that "need" and "compulsion" initially dictated to man that he live, collectively, in the *Notstaat* – a mode of organization governed by "purely natural laws," not those of "Reason."[31] According to Schiller, the *Notstaat* became a *Naturstaat* when civil and political institutions were developed that sanctioned pursuit of this kind of need.[32] In both the *Notstaat* and the *Naturstaat*, then, man's orientation toward life is governed by "appetite alone"[33] – he lives as a "taught animal" in the *Naturstaat* and an "untaught one" in the *Notstaat*.[34] The problem for Schiller, of course, was that in both conditions "morality [was] at the service of the physical."[35] For Schiller, this simply meant that man was not yet a truly moral being. In Kant's terms, man had "civilization" but not "culture." Thus, Schiller's insistence that man's moral task was to make himself a "person," to "transform" his "Natural State" (*Naturstaat*) into an "Ethical one" (*sittlichen*).[36] Hegel, I think, was making exactly the same point.

Here, though, we need to be careful. While Hegel appears to be endorsing the evolutionists' equation of the necessary and the natural,[37] it is precisely this equation that he exploits in his criticism of societies that are organized around and celebrate the existence of natural *Sittlichkeit*. As Hegel sees it, man had been forced out of his presocial condition by need.[38] Though Hegel does not indicate whether this need arose solely from demographic pressure (e.g., Steuart's "principle of generation")[39] Hegel's points are that man is forced to leave his presocial condition because of "physical need"; that he is obliged to "labor" to alleviate this need; and that through labor and industry man develops social habits and a type of consciousness (reflective of his material interests) that binds him to others in a network of reciprocal socio-economic relations.

Much of this had been common fare of the Scottish thinkers whom Hegel had been reading in the 1790s. From them he had learned that "the habit of society" among man was both variable and historical. That is, from them he had learned about the four-stage theory of history.[40] Specifically, he had learned that the way men met their subsistence needs (i.e., first as hunters, then as shepherds, next as husbandmen, and finally as artificers and manufacturers) shaped the social as well as the economic structures in which they lived. As the Scots conjectured, man laboring alone or in small family units quickly exhausted the productive capacity inherent in labor-intensive methods of subsistence provision.[41] This, in turn, led to the expansion of the family living group so that it could take advantage of the geographic distribution of nature's spoils.[42] Implicit in this arrangement, of course, was a nascent exchange of goods between different units of the same family and then between different family units. Gradually, so runs the conjecture, men became aware of the advantages of this living arrangement – of trade and of production specialization – with the result that *societies* were formed around the principle of the division of labor, the key to successful trade and the exploitation of production specialization.[43]

The upshot of all this was that man moved *naturally,* albeit through a series of stages, from a presocial to a social condition. For the Scots, moreover, the movement culminated in the "modern" mode of socio-economic organization, one that allowed "civilized" man to reap the benefits of his industry and commerce. And so it was that by becoming industrious, by engaging in trade, and by using the principle of the division of labor to organize that trade, man began to provide for his own physical needs as well as for those of his fellows. What is more, man became, in Mandeville's phrase, "fond of Society" for the "Ease and Security" it offered him.[44]

All this, of course, struck the Scots as quite "natural" – they contended that man's entry into society was the result of adaptive responses to the exigencies of physical necessity. For this reason, the Scots discussed society in natural, historical, and evolutionary terms. Implicit in their outlook was the twofold claim that in its origins the "habit of society" was economically conditioned and that men fell "naturally into it" even as their societies became more rationally organized.[45] As Steuart put it, society could be explained as the result of a "natural chain" that began with demographic pressure and ended with the rational organization of agriculture and commerce.[46]

Hegel, it seems to me, adapted many of these arguments to his own purpose of establishing a continuity of development between man's presocial and social conditions of existence. To be sure, for him society was both necessary and natural to man.[47] Society, at least in its nascent form, was a natural extension and expression of man's physical nature – that is, in society man remained a natural being albeit in a very social way. What man did in his presocial condition – which was to act under the increasing pressure of immediate physical necessity – he continued to do in society but in a more systematic fashion. Hence, as was noted earlier, the difference for Hegel between man in his two conditions was not one of kind but of degree. Thus, however different social man was from presocial man, he was not yet human for Hegel. He was, that is, still "natural" in the sense that he remained a prepolitical being.[48]

Hegel, then, is saying that insofar as social organization is governed by what Schiller had called the "force of his [physical] needs," its purposes are not very different from those that shaped life in the presocial setting.[49] Certainly there is nothing as yet "artificial" about society for Hegel (as there was, say, for Rousseau).[50] Nor is there anything inherently alienating about man's having to acquiesce in the division of labor to alleviate his physical needs (as there was for Marx in some of his writings). Society and the division of labor, in fact, were natural to man.[51] Their institutionalization, therefore, did not entail "denaturing" him. By the same token, however, society as such did not do much to advance man beyond his natural condition. And that, according to Hegel, was the essence of the problem of *Sittlichkeit*.[52]

That Hegel argued for continuity between the presocial and the social conditions of life is fraught with meaning for understanding the basic political thrust of *Ethical Life*. Granted, on the surface his account of the origin of societies appears innocent enough – it expresses the kind of "sociological realism," so prominent in Montesquieu and among the Scots, which held that social life is material, necessary, and natural to man.[53] The issue, however, is not whether Hegel uses the language of sociological realism in his attempt to run presocial and social man together – unquestionably he does that, and in several important ways – but whether the idea of natural *Sittlichkeit*, which he uses to express the fact of this continuity, is being employed descriptively, prescriptively, or in some other way.

As is so often the case with Hegel this question cannot easily be answered. Still, some sense can be made of his use of the concept if we bear the following considerations in mind. To begin with, it is undeniable that at the most elementary level Hegel wanted to explain the emergence of society and man's *social* consciousness in the way the Scots had: in terms of material considerations in general and in terms of the dynamic of the division of labor in particular. He wanted, as it were, to "lay hold on life" before trying to guide men beyond what was natural and necessary to them. To use this argument, however, seemed to require acknowledgment of a basic *change* between presocial and social man. Hegel did not want to do this. On the contrary, it was his intention to establish a *continuity* of development between the two. Establishment of this continuity enabled Hegel to go on to stress the need for development of the kind of *political* consciousness he thought *homo religiosus*, the quintessential human being, needed to have in order to survive as the carrier of *Sittlichkeit* in the modern world.

To make both of these arguments at once Hegel had to give a particular conceptual spin to the meaning of natural *Sittlichkeit*. He did this by emphasizing on the one hand the *continuity* of development *in consciousness* between presocial and social man. Because both were primarily concerned with physical necessity, they were both prepolitical in character. On the other hand, however, he argued for a *discontinuity* between the two on the level of socioeconomic organization (i.e., labor was governed by the principle of the division of labor in the social situation). Hegel, in other words, was arguing for a *continuity* of consciousness within an otherwise *discontinuous* socioeconomic mode of argumentation.

By giving the conception of natural *Sittlichkeit* this spin, Hegel was able to be both realistic and idealistic at once: he could use the matter-of-fact principles of sociological realism to place man in society without having to endorse as a norm the natural mode of social consciousness that went along with it. One could say, then, that as a concept *natürliche Sittlichkeit* was both descriptive (Hegel in the mode of realist) and (potentially) negatively normative (Hegel in the mode of idealist). Although at this point in the essay Hegel is neutral about natural *Sittlichkeit* as social consciousness, the direction of the essay itself suggests an intention eventually to subordinate social consciousness qua *natürliche Sittlichkeit* to political consciousness qua *absolute Sittlichkeit*.

This latter point warrants more consideration, for within the general context of the essay on *Ethical Life* it occupies a prominent place. The points that need to be made are these. First, like Montesquieu, Steuart, Ferguson, and Schiller, Hegel appears inclined to argue that insofar as men are "united by sensation" (Montesquieu),[54] by the "physical-necessary" (Steuart),[55] by "interest" (Ferguson),[56] or by "blind necessity" (Schiller),[57] the basis for their collective interaction is neither "knowledge" (Montesquieu and Steuart) nor morality (Ferguson and Schiller), but their simple and common involvement in an "animal economy."[58] This kind of social solidarity, these thinkers argued, was the result of an *accidental*, albeit natural, convergence of interests that could never provide man with more than what Ferguson had termed "mere existence."[59] For these thinkers, in short, there was something asocial about a social solidarity that was exclusively based on economic mutualism.[60] In keeping with this conviction, they argued that for man to become truly human and truly "social" he had to develop a *substantive* (i.e., self-conscious) sense of *Sittlichkeit* – had to develop a sense of himself as a political being.

From the *Natural Law* essay we know that Hegel equated the human, the self-conscious, the absolute, the organic, and the substantive with the "political." What is more, we know that he identified the political as the "species-specific" quality that distinguished man as a human being from man as an animal being (i.e., man in his narrow socioeconomic mode). In the essay on *Ethical Life* he makes the same point,[61] only this time he ventures an explanation of just how this kind of consciousness develops.

Viewed in this way, natural *Sittlichkeit* would seem to constitute for Hegel a necessary *social moment* in man's evolution. It reflects Hegel's belief that society is necessary for the exercise and development of human consciousness.[62] Yet Hegel also insists that man's consciousness in its social moment is not human consciousness (i.e., political consciousness). There is an architectonic vision implicit in Hegel's discussion of natural *Sittlichkeit*; that is, the discussion must be said to have been programmed from the start for *natürliche Sittlichkeit* (i.e., socioeconomic consciousness) to be superseded by *absolute Sittlichkeit* (i.e., political consciousness).

However, knowing that this was Hegel's "project" really does not allow us to distinguish his vision from that of many others who had built a political component into their architectonic speculations. Where Hegel differs from all others, I think, lies in the way he explains the emergence of political consciousness among a people. Where others had tried to awaken the political impulse in men by appealing to divine intervention or to some great legislator, Hegel did so by way of an analysis of the socio-economic dynamic of collective existence itself.[63] In the next two sections of this chapter we shall see how he employs the tools of political economy and sociological realism to advance his aggressively ontological vision of man both as *zōon politikon* and as *homo religiosus*.

2. Natural *Sittlichkeit* as an institutional and value complex

If in his discussion of natural *Sittlichkeit* Hegel had tried to show that society came into being for natural, necessary, and primarily economic reasons, his analysis of that society itself (i.e., natural *Sittlichkeit* conceived of as an institution, as a habit of society, that had taken hold among men) was critical in that he stressed what "needs" a society organized along those lines could not fulfill. It is easy to miss this shift in the argument, for Hegel's terminology conceals it. Indeed, if in the context of the origin of societies problem the term "natural *Sittlichkeit*" often blurred the distinction between presocial and social man, in the context of the social moment of objective experience it obscured the difference between what we today would call socioeconomic *base* and sociocultural *superstructure*.[64]

The point of departure for this all-important aspect of Hegel's argument is an idea he had formulated in the essay on *Natural Law*. There, we saw, Hegel had divided the "inorganic" moment of objective experience into something like substructural and superstructural elements. In *Ethical Life* he begins to flesh out this distinction. He starts by reiterating the view, repeatedly stressed throughout the essay, that socioeconomic organization shapes consciousness.[65] Because men initially banded together for the sake of their physical well-being, and because this arrangement afforded them a great deal of material "comfort," they decided to define their social interaction in economic terms, in terms of what Ferguson called their "interests" and Hegel their "system of need."[66]

In this essay, however, Hegel adds another dimension to the discussion. As he saw it, the "system of need" generated a "system of recognition" such that the latter came to reflect the materialist priorities of the former.[67] That the two systems could be distinguished was obvious to Hegel; that he chose to treat them as mutually reinforcing entities indicates that he regarded them as different expressions of one and the same "general spirit" (i.e., natural *Sittlichkeit* as a "social whole," as a meaning complex that, in *Natural Law*, had been discussed in terms of the "life style" and value priorities of the bourgeoisie).[68]

Given this layered view of natural *Sittlichkeit* as an institutional and a value complex, it is not surprising to find Hegel groping for a way to explain how man is to break out of it, how he is *voluntarily* to advance beyond the *social* moment of objective experience. Hegel had reached a similar point in the essay on *Natural Law*; there, however, he had gotten no further than positing *Tapferkeit* as the answer to the problem.[69] But Hegel, ever the realist, knew that identifying *Tapferkeit* as the source of man's political impulse was not the same as explaining how and why it should develop as an impulse in the first place. Hegel knew, in other words, that it was time to provide an *endogenous* explanation of *Tapferkeit*.[70] That, I think, is what the essay on *Ethical Life* is all about.

Initially, of course, Hegel wanted to express all this in the language of philosophy – with the categories of universality and particularity and so on. There, however, a problem arose. On the one hand, he wanted to say that man's movement from a presocial to a social condition constituted a movement from universality (i.e., man as an abstraction, as pure potentiality) to particularity (i.e., man as a concrete socioeconomic being). On the other hand, though, he recognized that from the point of view of the agent (i.e., the consciousness of social man) the social moment of existence not only encompassed the whole of his *experience* (i.e., for him it was a "totality"), but constituted the horizon of his *expectations* as well.[71] There was, in short, something like universality within what Hegel regarded as the particular social moment of experience itself.[72] As he put it, the system of natural *Sittlichkeit* "transferred" the "universal" to the "particular," thus making an "ideal," a "totality," of the particular itself.[73]

This idea, Hegel discovered, could not be expressed in the current language of philosophy. So, to solve the problem of how to concede universality to particularity (i.e., to the social moment of objective experience) he qualified this conception of universality by arguing that it was only "relative," only a "moment."[74] Hence, the meaning both of the phrase "totality of relative ethical life" and of the claim that "relative identity has the form of universality."[75]

With this qualification we arrive at a crucial juncture in Hegel's development as a thinker. It seems to me that his conception of "relative ethical life" relates not just to his conception of natural *Sittlichkeit* but also to the eighteenth-century debate on the relation between commerce, luxury, the economic containment.[76]

This becomes clear when we remember that Hegel was not the first to use the idea of relativity to characterize the social situation of civilized man. In *Émile*, for example, Rousseau had written the following: "Remember that as soon as amour-propre has developed, the *relative I* is constantly in play."[77] And before that Rousseau had written that "amour propre is only a relative sentiment, artificial and born in society, which inclines each individual to have greater esteem for himself than for anyone else."[78]

It is well known that amour propre was, for Rousseau, an "instrument" of "unhappiness" for civilized man.[79] As he presented it, the ascendancy of amour propre among civilized men had led to a confusion of "our vain desires with our physical needs,"[80] with the result that man had extended his desire for superfluous things (i.e., for luxurious living) to a point where he had become a "slave" to "all the attachments" he had created for himself.[81]

According to Rousseau, though, the more man "increases his attachments [to these kinds of things], the more he multiplies his pains";[82] "the more [he] gains an *enjoyment* [from consuming them], the further happiness gets from [him]."[83] Man's great mistake, however, was to seek in the "false wisdom" of an already overly fanciful imagination the terms for his future happiness.[84] As Rousseau saw it, so long as amour propre governed one's orientation toward life, man would invariably search for a "physical" rather than a "moral" solution to his unhappiness.[85] And that, for Rousseau, simply was to perpetuate the unhappiness that civilized man had experienced in the first place.

Hegel's interlocking conceptions of natural *Sittlichkeit* and of "relative ethical life" are understandable in terms of Rousseau's argument. There are, I think, three ways to make this point. First there is Hegel's claim that "intelligence" in the system of natural *Sittlichkeit* is both "subjective and an accident of it."[86] By that Hegel means – and he stresses the point throughout the text[87] – that what passes for intelligence within the system of natural *Sittlichkeit* is not really rational, not really "true intelligence."[88] And it is not truly rational because it lacks what Hegel called "wisdom" or "spiritual shape."[89] As he succinctly put it, in this system the universal dimension of intelligence is measured in terms of "the crude, the purely quantitative, and [is, therefore, a] wisdomless universal."[90] Put another way, the system "lacked wisdom" because it was governed by only a "practical intelligence" whose sole concern was with "enjoyment" and with the *legal* sanction of "enjoyment and possession."[91]

The point Hegel is making here about the material concerns of intelligence within the system of natural *Sittlichkeit* becomes more obvious when we remember that Schiller and Ferguson had talked about the social –civil moment of existence in similar terms. Schiller had put it this way:

Because in his experience the sense-drive precedes the moral, [civilized man] assigns to the law of necessity a beginning in time too, a positive origin, and through this most unfortunate of all errors makes the unchangeable and eternal in himself [i.e., his true *telos*] into an accidental product of the transient.[92]

Ferguson, too, had argued that what was "accidental" to human nature, what was habitual rather than essential to it, had often become an "idol" of the mind.[93] True, as such it served to unite men; but according to Ferguson it did so on the basis of "interest" rather than "truth."[94] For Hegel, Schiller, and Ferguson, in other words, there was a close correlation on the one hand between man's material concerns and the shape of his intelligence and on the other hand between the "accidental" aspect of natural *Sittlichkeit* and the idea of "relative identity."

Hegel is more specific later in the text. There he makes it quite clear that he associates natural *Sittlichkeit* with the bourgeois conception of ethical life as well as with relative identity.[95] Earlier in the text he had argued for a close connection between need, labor, enjoyment, possession, relative identity, and the process by which these things and activities received legal sanction (i.e., "recognition").[96] In doing this he used the language of political economy, especially the language of property, to show how in the system of natural *Sittlichkeit* the idea of relative identity assumed "the form of universality"[97] and presented itself to man (i.e., to the consciousness of the individual) as a "totality" in which "individuality" constituted "an absolutely entire system [of need and recognition]."[98]

In this context, and in a section of the text entitled "relative ethical life," Hegel begins to discuss what the idea of "honesty" means in a system in which the "totality of relative ethical life" is measured in terms of "the empirical existence of the single individual."[99] Without question, Hegel means to relate this discussion to the thoughts on the bourgeois conception of ethical life that he had previously developed in *Natural Law*. He proceeds to *sociologize the idea of honesty* so that it becomes the distinguishing characteristic of the bourgeoisie.[100] He then tells us that the interest of the "class of honesty lies in work for needs, in possessions, gain, and property."[101] This class, he continues, is law-abiding (almost to a fault),[102] conceives of "justice in connection with property in things,"[103] and is incapable of "courage."[104] Still, despite its "honesty," Hegel felt the group lacked "wisdom," because its material interests refused to allow it to move beyond the present "empirical situation."[105] In Rousseau's telling phrase, Hegel's view was that this group's conception of law was "occupied with property" far more than with "persons."[106]

Hegel is even blunter about the shortcomings of the relative conception of ethical life toward the end of the *Ethical Life* essay.[107] Referring to the bourgeois conception of ethical life as one organized around a "system of need" that is itself held together by "a system of universal physical dependence" of each on everyone else,[108] Hegel claims that in this system "what rules appears as the unconscious and blind entirety of needs and modes of their satisfaction."[109] Then Hegel makes the point that within this system "enjoyment" is "limitless," "endless," "infinite."[110] In this situation the "business class"[111] – those "needy intelligences...who are concerned with both a surplus and an unsatisfied need at the same time"[112] – begin to exhibit "the bestiality of contempt for all higher things."[113] As a result, the "absolute bond of the people, namely [true] ethical principle, has vanished, and the people is dissolved."[114]

Given Hegel's language and the substance of his concerns, it should be obvious that economics had come to figure prominently in the "young Hegel's" conception of *Sittlichkeit*. Nonetheless, there is still a good deal of the "old man," of Württemberg's Hegel, in *Ethical Life*. At a decisive point in the text – the point at which Hegel's argument obliges him to offer an alternative to natural *Sittlichkeit* – he informs us that "true intelligence" (i.e., wisdom) arises with and issues forth from "the divinity of the people."[115] To this end, Hegel insists that a people is "not a disconnected mass, nor a mere plurality."[116] Rather, a people exists at the moment when "the God of the people"[117] reveals itself through a collective action that Hegel discusses in terms of a "transition from subjective [*Sittlichkeit*] to objective [*Sittlichkeit*]."[118] In keeping with the basic thrust of Hegel's thinking between 1796 and 1803, it is no accident that this transition from subjectivity to objectivity, which takes place *within* objective experience itself, and which arises from and is related to the collectivity's conception of itself as a godly people, is both powered and pulled forward by the promise and principles of true *Sittlichkeit*. That is, Hegel's argument for transition here seems conceptually to culminate in a politico-religious moment of recollectivization.

3. Hegel's conception of "bad infinity"

If this were all Hegel had to say about society, he could be said to have done little more than offer a verbal solution to how political consciousness (i.e., true universality, absolute *Sittlichkeit*) superseded social conscious-ness (i.e., relative universality, natural *Sittlichkeit*). But Hegel has more to tell us about the social moment of experience than that. In *Ethical Life* Hegel also offers an endogenous explanation of how political consciousness emerges from the social moment of objective experience. The remainder of this chapter will be concerned with how he begins to explain the conversion of social into political consciousness by way of his conception of "bad infinity."[119]

Again, Rousseau's work proves helpful for framing Hegel's problem. In a key section of *Émile*, Rousseau tells us that "work is. . .an indispensable duty for social man."[120] By that Rousseau means something quite specific. He does not mean work in the sense of "practice of the natural arts, for which a single man suffices," but work in the sense of practice of "the arts of industry, which need the conjunction of many hands."[121] Having made this point, Rousseau proceeds to argue that "introduction of the superfluous [i.e., luxury] makes division. . .of labor indispensable [to society]."[122] As a result, Rousseau says, man finds himself living in an exchange society, in a "society of the arts" that "consists in exchange of skills, that of commerce in exchange of things, that of banks in exchange of. . .money."[123] Gradually, Rousseau continues, "money" becomes "the true bond" of this society.[124] And while Rousseau concludes this section with the claim that he will "not enter into an explanation of the moral effects" of money on social man, he does tease us with the suggestion that "all the chimeras of opinion are born from money."[125] As we shall see, that is the point Hegel wishes to establish with his idea of "bad infinity."

From what has been said so far about *Ethical Life* it should be obvious that Hegel's conception of labor had much in common with Rousseau's. Suffice it to say that Hegel made labor basic to man in two ways. First, labor was central to the constitution of the "system of need" in a physical sense. To preserve himself man had to cooperate with others, with the consequence that labor became a crucial tie between the satisfaction of individual need and the goal of social action. Second, Hegel claimed that labor was social in yet another sense – one that he related to his conception of the social moment as a "system of recognition." Here the argument was that validation of one's objective social being depended on receiving recognition (i.e., legal sanction) from others for what one earned from one's labor (i.e., property).

In this argument Hegel was, of course, accenting the positive aspects of labor in its various forms as socioeconomic *praxis*. Like Rousseau, he wished that the uses of labor in this system "be well presented before the abuses are shown."[126] What did alarm Hegel, though, was the prospect that men would be content to make socioeconomic *praxis* the sole measure of their existence. However "natural" such *praxis* might be to man it hardly required him to be more than *homo oeconomicus*. Thus, Hegel's problem was quite similar to the one that exercised Schiller in *Aesthetic Education*. There Schiller had noted how the "practical spirit" of business was so "enclosed within a monotonous sphere of material objects" that it had rendered man "incapable of extending [his imagination] to appreciate other ways of seeing and knowing."[127] To use Rousseau's splendid phrase, Schiller thought social man had become "stupidly ingenious."[128]

After having established man in society and *after* having shown that the "habit of society" brings the interplay between labor, the division of labor, exchange, and contract together in one coherent whole in which the market mechanism is established as universal, Hegel begins to criticize natural *Sittlichkeit* as an institutional and value complex. The problem, as Hegel perceived it, was that as a "total institution" the market did not permit man truly to constitute himself as an objective being. To be sure, it allowed him to produce himself in the world and to become instrumental to the material well-being of others. But it could not provide him with the recognition that was essential to substantiation of his objective being in a *moral* sense. That was because insofar as man consumed the production of others he negated the objective being of those from whom he expected to derive social recognition. For Hegel, therefore, the market consisted in a network of self-creative and self-canceling mechanisms. As it was constituted, it involved a trade-off: in exchange for the objective satisfaction of physical needs it asked man to forsake the objective recognition that was required for him to become a moral being. The market, in short, allowed man instrumentally to labor for others, but it did not permit him expressively to labor for himself.

According to Hegel, then, the market system operated effectively as a system of need but not as a system of recognition. The questions Hegel wished to raise, therefore, were these: could a society organized around exchange become human? And how could a society be persuaded to redirect its thinking toward the pursuit of more high-minded objects?

Hegel's conception of bad infinity emerges in the context of his attempt to answer these two questions in general and to discredit the bourgeois conception of life in particular.[129] And the key, I think, to understanding his conception of bad infinity lies in his conception of money and its relation to luxury.[130]

Like Aristotle, Locke, and Steuart before him, Hegel saw an intimate connection between money and the unleashing in society of an unlimited desire for the acquisition of wealth. As Steuart had written, when "imaginary wealth [money] becomes well introduced into a country, luxury will very *naturally* follow; and when money becomes the object of our wants, mankind becomes industrious."[131] Soon, Steuart continued, "trade comes to be extended among men" and "manufacturers, more ornamental than useful, come to be established."[132] The result: "Every person becomes fond of money."[133]

For Hegel, the relationship between industry, money, trade, and luxury expressed itself most clearly in the activities and values of the "commercial class."[134] As was noted previously, Hegel's conception of this class was, from a moral perspective, negative – it had lapsed into "barbarism" by its single-minded pursuit of enjoyment.[135] And, by refusing to set limits to enjoyment, it had turned the "ideality of enjoyment" into an "empirically endless" pursuit.[136] As Hegel put it, "The urge to increase wealth [i.e., enjoyment] is nothing but the necessity for carrying to *infinity* the specific individual thing [i.e., enjoyment] which possession is."[137]

Here, of course, our previous discussion of eighteenth-century conceptions of luxury becomes important to understanding what Hegel is "doing" in the *Ethical Life* essay with the concept of infinity.[138] On one level the conception of infinity is clearly related to the *political* argument Hegel had made in the *Natural Law* essay; namely, luxury was distracting the commercial class from its political duties. On another level, though, Hegel's conception of infinity speaks the language of the religious tradition we have been discussing in Part III of this study; namely, the language that regards riches, luxury, and wealth only as problems when they penetrate the soul and proceed to corrupt the imagination of *homo religiosus*.[139] When this happens, when man loses his *telos*, when he succumbs to the lure of vanity and gives into amour propre, wealth is neither used "indifferently" nor put in the service of "life."[140] As a result, in Schiller's words, man, "through a misunderstanding (almost unavoidable in this early epoch of prevailing materiality)," directs his energy "towards physical life, and instead of making [himself] independent [i.e., "truly human"] plunge[s] him[self] into the most terrifying servitude."[141]

Hegel's conception of infinity, I think, is governed more by the religious than by the political implications of the eighteenth-century debate on luxury. On the one hand, Hegel seemed willing to accept the pursuit of luxury as important to economic prosperity. There is no indication either in *Ethical Life* or in *Natural Law* of a desire on Hegel's part to suppress or eliminate the impulse toward luxury. As so many of Hegel's sources had argued, it was not the existence of luxury but the value priority it received in men's minds relative to "higher" pursuits that determined whether it was excessive or not.[142]

On the other hand, Hegel certainly recognized that modern society and its market economy presented – indeed, encouraged and thrived upon – the temptation to vicious luxury. To translate Hume's terms into those Hegel used in *Ethical Life*, the pursuit of luxury was likely to cease being "innocent" and socially "beneficial" when luxury qua "system of need" found sanction in a "system of recognition" that set no limit to that pursuit.[143] Thus, Hegel's contention that because "the ideality of enjoyment" knows no limits and because "civilized enjoyment volatilizes the crudity of need," enjoyment itself had to be contained by, be made subservient to, a more noble disposition.[144]

What Hegel objected to, in other words, was the "transubstantiation" of commerce, money, and luxury from mere agencies of economic action into a coherent set of pursuits that defined money-making as the overall *purpose* of civilized man.[145] For Hegel, of course, that purpose expressed itself in the system of natural *Sittlichkeit* that, in turn, encompassed the activities and value orientation of the bourgeoisie. In Kenneth Burke's terms, Hegel objected to natural *Sittlichkeit* because it enabled the bourgeoisie to substitute "the monetary motive" for "the religious motive," to make it the " 'symbolic' or 'spiritual' ground" of collective identity.[146]

We have already seen how Rousseau, Ferguson, and Schiller faced this problem: they urged men to redirect their imagination to objects more worthy of truly *human* endeavor.[147] As Rousseau had observed:

> ...it must...be agreed that although men cannot be taught to love nothing, it is not impossible to teach them to love one thing rather than another, and what is truly beautiful rather than what is deformed.... Not only does philosophy demonstrate the possibility of these new directions, but history provides a thousand stunning examples. If they are so rare among us, it is because no one cares whether there are any citizens.[148]

The same concern, I think, permeates the work Hegel did at Jena. While leaving more or less intact what he had identified as the bourgeois "system of need," he wished to replace the bourgeois "system of recognition" with one that had more ethical content in both political and religious senses. For that a conversion, or "turning," had to take place in men's minds – in men's value orientation toward life. And it could only take place if it could be shown that the prestige value the bourgeois associated with consumerism was not likely to bring much satisfaction (i.e., it was a world of "bad infinity") and that there were resources *within* the bourgeois system of need that would provide the occasion for the cultivation of a more satisfying ethical definition of collective well-being. Hegel, that is to say, believed one could be "bourgeois" with regard to the organization of society's "system of need" and "Christian" with regard to society's "system of recognition."[149]

In the final chapter of this study, we shall see how Hegel dealt with the problem of giving "spiritual shape" to the collective identity of a people. Suffice it to say here that he identifies the division of labor principle as the resource within civil society, within the bourgeois system of need, that permits the conversion of natural *Sittlichkeit* qua system of recognition into absolute *Sittlichkeit* qua the collective religio-political identity of a people. I wish, however, to conclude this chapter with a few further remarks on how Hegel's conception of bad infinity relates to the problem of religious–economic overlay in his thought.

As I understand the bad infinity argument, it has much in common with the "conspicuous consumption" thesis that was advanced in the work of the twentieth-century economist Thorstein Veblen.[150] In *The Theory of the Leisure Class* Veblen argued that consumerism was driven by man's need for distinction in a world in which prestige value was measured in terms of the accumulation and consumption of wealth. Writing about the craving modern man exhibited for wealth, Veblen contended that

However widely, or equally, or "fairly," it may be distributed, no general increase in a community's wealth can make any approach to satiating this need, the ground of which is the desire of everyone to excel everyone else in the accumulation of goods....Since the struggle is substantially a race for reputability [i.e., status] on the basis of [the equation of "wealth" and "honor"], no approach to a definitive attainment is possible [on those terms].[151]

Speaking to the same point, Lovejoy and Hirschman have both observed that Veblen was "merely repeating and elaborating propositions which may be described as commonplaces of the late seventeenth and eighteenth centuries."[152] According to Lovejoy, many writers of this period realized that since the desire for economic goods was "essentially limitless,"[153] it had what we would call a relative disappointment factor built into it. Three passages, two from Ferguson's *Essay* and one from Diderot, make the point:

No ultimate remedy is applied to this evil, by merely accumulating wealth; for rare and costly materials, whatever these are, continue to be sought; and if silks and pearl are made common, men will begin to covet some new decorations, which the wealthy alone can procure. If they are indulged in their humor, their demands are repeated. For it is the continual increase of riches, not any measure attained, that keeps the craving imagination at ease.[154]

We live in societies, where man must be rich, in order to be great; where pleasure itself is often pursued from vanity; where the desire of a supposed happiness serves to inflame the worst of passions, and is itself the foundation of misery.[155]

Diderot had noted the same thing:

Society makes it easier for men to possess those things for which they feel a natural need, and it renders such possession secure. At the same time, however, society gives men a notion of an infinite number of imaginary needs. These urge them on a thousand times more keenly than real needs, and they make men perhaps even more unhappy when they are gathered together, than they would have been in an isolated existence.[156]

It had been a primary concern among many religiously minded men in the seventeenth and eighteenth centuries to *relativize* the satisfaction one could derive from material well-being. Here the Calvinist doctrine of indifference (discussed earlier) was very helpful;[157] theoretically it allowed these thinkers to deal with men's passions and interests without practically forcing them to deny desire as a primary source of human motivation.[158] All that was required was to show that luxury was a "Divine blessing" so long as it was "indifferently used"; so long as it did not involve immersion in "sensual delights," inebriation of the "heart and mind with present pleasures," and the perpetual pursuit of new sources of abundance.[159]

How did one know where to draw the line between man as a naturally "restless" being whose desires sometimes carried him beyond physical need and man as a "fallen" being, a sinner?[160] In the *Critique of Judgement*, Kant gives us an answer, one that anticipated Hegel's position on the problem. Writing with reference to contemporary civilization qua a "culture of skill," Kant claimed that

...with the advance of this culture — the culminating point of which, where devotion to what is superfluous begins to be prejudicial to what is indispensable, is called luxury — misfortunes increase.... Yet this *splendid misery* is connected with the development of natural tendencies in the human race, and the end pursued by nature itself, *though it be not our end*, is thereby attained.[161]

Here, as was noted earlier, Kant is reading a double meaning into the concept of civilization.[162] On the one hand, there is civilization qua a culture of skill. This culture Kant associates with a "natural" tendency in man that leads to "luxury" and "splendid misery" (i.e., bad infinity).[163] On the other hand, there is civilization qua a culture of discipline. This culture "consists in the liberation of the will from the despotism of desires whereby, in our attachment to certain natural things, we are rendered incapable of exercising a choice of our own."[164]

What is striking about this is that Kant's "culture of discipline" requires man to exercise his will not in order to come into "accord" with nature but in order to free himself from it.[165] What this culture asks man to do is define his *telos* less in terms of the ends of nature than in terms of the end of creation.[166] Both ends, of course, are in some sense teleological; but in the latter case teleology is self-realizing and shaped by theological considerations.[167] Kant is very clear about this. He dismisses, for example, enjoyment and happiness – ends of nature – as appropriate ends for man: to wit, "For his own nature is not so constituted as to rest or be satisfied in any possession or enjoyment whatever."[168]

For Kant, though, there is no denying that the unleashing of "a crowd of insatiable inclinations," which are linked to the "idealization" of luxury, have led to a "preponderance of evil" in the modern world.[169] Some of this evil has been "visited upon us" by nature, some by "the truculent egoism of man" himself.[170] Whatever the source of the problem, Kant says, we must "overcome the tyrannical propensities of sense" because they render man "incapable of positing a final end for his own real existence."[171] That existence, Kant continues, can only be realized if the "energies of the soul" are evoked so that they "give [us] strength and courage to submit to no such force, and at the same time quicken in us a sense that in the depths of our nature there is an aptitude for higher ends."[172] Kant, in short, was asking man to realize his *telos* as *homo religiosus* by *institutionalizing the doctrine of indifference* in the form of a culture of discipline.[173]

Hegel, I think, was trying to make the same point in *Ethical Life* when he began to separate systems of need and recognition and to replace the bourgeois conception of the latter with one more consistent with his own conception of the *Sittlichkeit*. Suffice it to say here that it is precisely at the moment of substitution – at the point at which Hegel's understanding of the principle of the division of labor permits him to substitute the idea of Christian pride for that of bourgeois avarice[174] – that his commitment to the ideal of Protestant civil piety begins to reassert itself as a governing principle of his thought. In the final analysis Hegel's appeal to man to aspire to more than comfort, security, and the never-ending pursuit of wealth was an appeal to the *telos* of *homo religiosus*, to a Christian pride that required man through an act of will to separate himself from nature in a way that the mere fact of his social existence had not. How Hegel made this appeal is the subject of the next chapter.

8

Hegel's conception of the division of labor

Thus far the basic thrust of Part III of this study has been to emphasize the importance of the religious–economic overlay in the development of Hegel's thought after 1796. This overlay, after all, prompted him to try to translate *Sittlichkeit* into the language of objective experience in general and into the principles of eighteenth-century social and political theory in particular. In this endeavor, moreover, Hegel's reading of the Scots was of vital importance. From them he learned not only about political economy and sociological realism, but also about how to use these conceptual tools to ground *Sittlichkeit* in the world of "objective experience."

Initially, Hegel's effort to develop a more up-to-date philosophy of *Sittlichkeit* involved identifying the division of labor principle as essential to the constitution of the *social* moment of objective experience. As we saw in Chapter 7, the idea of the division of labor played a prominent role in Hegel's essay on *Ethical Life*: it was one of the driving forces behind man's movement from a presocial to a social condition of existence, and it was the key to the establishment of a network of interconnected institutional and value relationships that governed man's life within what Hegel called the system of "natural *Sittlichkeit*." Indeed, in some respects it could be said that the division of labor constituted the core of Hegel's conception of the *social moment* of objective experience itself.

What follows pursues this conception a bit farther. It does so because I believe the division of labor concept provides the key to Hegel's endogenous explanation of how the *political moment* of objective experience emerges from the *social moment* in general and from its system of recognition in particular. What Hegel ultimately does with the conception of the division of labor is to "work it" to a point *in the text* where he can begin to build a case for a new political awareness around it.[1] To do this, he has to introduce several other important conceptions to the *Ethical Life* text. Thus, Hegel's discussion of "intuitions and concepts,"

253

"indifference," "*Bildung*," and the "first class." All these ideas, I think, cluster conceptually around the division of labor principle. Understanding how these ideas relate to each other will enable us to see how Hegel proposed to move from the social to the political moment of objective experience. And in the process, we shall see him reintroduce religious values into his philosophy of *Sittlichkeit*.

1. Schiller: The "wisdom" of "indirection"

Scottish thought, again, offers a convenient point of departure for understanding Hegel's conception of the division of labor. Today it is generally recognized that the Scots, especially Smith and Ferguson, were aware of, and disturbed about, some of the noneconomic consequences of the division of labor.[2] On the one hand, they lauded it as the motor force of progress: it increased economic production, helped expand the market, promoted trade, enhanced the quality of goods produced for the market as well as the "dexterity" of workers, and provided the economic underpinning for those leisure-time pursuits that were synonymous with advanced "civilization." On the other hand, however, they saw how, in Smith's words, it contributed to the "corruption and degeneracy of the great body of the people."[3] Routinized work, Ferguson claimed, tended "to contract and to limit the views of the mind."[4] By making men "parts" of an "engine,"[5] Ferguson argued, the division of labor withdrew "individuals from the common sense of occupation" and, by so doing, deprived society of "the spirit of society itself."[6] Smith, in a passage worth quoting at length, put it this way:

In the progress of the division of labor, the employment of the far greater part of those who live by labor, that is, of the great body of the people, comes to be confined to a few very simple operations; frequently to one or two. But the understandings of the greater part of men are necessarily formed by their ordinary employments. The man whose whole life is spent in performing a few simple operations, of which the effects too are, perhaps, always the same, has no occasion to exert his understanding, or to exercise his invention in finding out expedients for removing difficulties which never occur. He naturally loses, therefore, the habit of such exertion and generally becomes as stupid and ignorant as it is possible for a human creature to become.[7]

Scottish ambivalence toward the division of labor was not lost on the Germans.[8] This was especially true of Schiller, whose insights into the dynamics of the division of labor principle anticipate much of what Hegel said on the subject. For example, in the sixth letter of *Aesthetic Education* Schiller rehearsed for his readers the pros and cons of the division of labor argument. While "readily" conceding that specialization and the division of labor were necessary to the progress of "the species," and while recognizing that if men "wished to proceed to a higher state of development" they would have "to surrender their wholeness of being and pursue truth along separate paths," Schiller could not see how "individuals might benefit from this fragmentation of their being."[9]

On another level, moreover, he argued that the division of labor posed a threat not just to the individual but to the values of true community as well. As he noted,

Once the increase of empirical knowledge, and more exact modes of thought, made sharper divisions between the sciences inevitable, and once the increasingly complex machinery of State necessitated a more rigorous separation of ranks and occupations, then the inner unity of human nature was severed too, and a disastrous conflict set its harmonious powers at variance.[10]

Pursuing this thought further, Schiller wrote:

Everlastingly chained to a single little fragment of the Whole, man himself develops into nothing but a fragment; everlastingly in his ear the monotonous sound of the wheel that he turns, he never develops the harmony of his being, and instead of putting the stamp of humanity upon his own nature, he becomes nothing more than the imprint of his occupation or of his specialized knowledge.[11]

This alarmed Schiller. He thought the idea of "function" was rapidly becoming society's "measure of a man."[12] À la Ferguson, this meant for Schiller that collective life was degenerating "into a crude and clumsy mechanism."[13] For society, Schiller noted, was now "an ingenious clockwork, in which out of the piecing together of innumerable but lifeless parts, a mechanical kind of collective life ensued."[14] Instead of "hastening upward into the realm of organic life," society was "elapsing into its original elements,"[15] into a "state of primitive morality" where "selfishness" (*der Egoism*) and a "materialistic moral philosophy" reigned supreme (i.e., reigned as that society's system of recognition).[16] Summing up the lesson of the sixth letter, Schiller reiterated the Scottish ambivalence toward the division of labor when he concluded that "however much the world as a whole may benefit through this fragmented specialization of human powers, it cannot be denied that the individuals affected by it suffer under the curse of this cosmic purpose [*Weltzwecke*]."[17]

Schiller's views on this matter, then, resemble those expressed by Rousseau and Ferguson.[18] And, as had already been shown, they anticipate those later expressed by Hegel. Faced with what has come to be known as the problem of *Gemeinschaft* and *Gesellschaft*, these thinkers responded to it in the following way. First of all, they tended to reduce the larger problem to a smaller one: that is, the problem of *Gemeinschaft* and *Gesellschaft* was approached by way of the concept of the division of labor. Second, neither Ferguson, Schiller, nor Hegel was inclined to regard socioeconomic inequality, class conflict, or a class-dominated state as the inevitable consequence of the division of labor. It was not so much that they did not perceive these things as that they approached the problem of the division of labor from another angle, one that located the problem of modern society more in shortcomings in its "system of recognition" than in inequalities within its "system of need." Finally, and this is related to the last point, they believed that the "class" based approach to the division of labor carried with it political solutions (i.e., either the redistribution of wealth by political means or a social revolution against property) that, in one way or another, made politics an instrument of man's economic rather than ethical advance.

In this context, Schiller's *Aesthetic Education* is representative of a line of argument that runs, I think, from Ferguson through Schiller to Hegel. According to Schiller, the most deleterious consequence of the division of labor lay in the way it contributed to and sanctioned the perpetual oscillation of society between "two extremes of human depravity."[19] On the one hand, there were the "crude" and "lawless instincts" of "the lower and more numerous classes."[20] On the other hand, there were the "enervation and perversity" of the "civilized classes."[21]

In the first case, Schiller claimed, the division of labor brutalized the intelligence and dulled the imagination of "the majority of men."[22] Too exhausted "by the struggle for existence to gird themselves for a new and harder struggle against error," they gladly assigned "to others the guardianship of their thoughts."[23] Schiller continued: "And if it should happen that higher promptings stir within them, they embrace with avid faith the formulas which State and Priesthood hold in readiness for such an event."[24]

In the second case, the division of labor was the cause of the "repugnant spectacle" of the "civilized classes."[25] For this group, which he associated with those who had been "freed [by civilization] from the yoke of physical needs but who *by their own choice* continued to bow beneath it," Schiller had nothing but contempt.[26] These so-called carriers of "Enlightenment," Schiller pointed out, were passing off the "sham propriety" of civility and refinement as "culture" when, in fact, their civility was but a mask for "materialistic ethics."[27] Instead of using its liberty to exercise "an ennobling influence" on the collectivity, this group preferred to pursue "fashion" rather than "improvement."[28] For this, Schiller scored the civilized classes, for as he saw it, they remained "barbarous" in the midst of an advanced civilization[29] precisely because they had mistakenly tied "the law of society" to "self-interest" rather than to the wisdom of "true enlightenment."[30]

Much of what Schiller is talking about here should be familiar from what has been discussed in Chapters 5, 6, and 7. As was noted there, the confusion of "wisdom" with "interest" was a main concern of Rousseau, Ferguson, Kant, and Hegel.[31] And like these thinkers Schiller made a point of noting that it would take "courage" to reorient man's priorities such that wisdom could then be used for "the ennobling of character."[32]

It is decisive to realize that Schiller meant for the ennobling of character to serve the purposes of politico-moral reform.[33] More important to realize, though, is that Schiller did not expect "the State" to serve as the agent of ennoblement.[34] On the contrary, he implicated the State as well as the civilized classes in the process that had led to the "deep degrada-tion" of the present age.[35] To set things right, to establish true enlightenment among men, another "instrument" of reform had to be found[36] – that is, Schiller proposed to pursue the ends of true *Sittlichkeit* (i.e., politico-moral ends) by nonpolitical means.[37] Hence, his tendency to identify this instrument with the "art of the ideal"; the "Fine Arts"; "aesthetic culture"; "the rational concept of Beauty"; and "culture."[38]

Given Schiller's argument, it should be obvious that he meant to posit a connection between the basic need to "ennoble" character and the overall purpose of "aesthetic culture." In an age when "material needs reign supreme and bend a degraded community beneath their tyrannical yoke,"[39] he wrote, it is art's task to rescue "humanity" and restore its lost "dignity" to it.[40] To do this, art must introduce man to "the shape of things to come"[41] – that is, it "must abandon actuality and soar with becoming boldness above our wants and needs, for Art is a daughter of freedom, and takes her orders from the necessity inherent in minds [*Geister*], not from the exigencies of matter."[42]

In designating art as the instrument that would ennoble man's character, liberate him from his materialistic obsessions, and provide him with the principles of "true enlightenment," Schiller knew he was approaching the problem of politicomoral reform "indirectly" – by nonpolitical means.[43] Anticipating being misunderstood on this point, Schiller denied that his aesthetic concerns were irrelevant to politics.[44] Rather, he said, "if man is ever to solve [the] problem of [contemporary] politics in practice he will have to approach it though the problem of the aesthetic."[45] What Schiller meant by this becomes clear in the seventh, eighth, and ninth letters of *Education*.[46] There he remarks that "all improvement in the political sphere is to proceed from the ennobling of character."[47] Having already identified the State as hostile to this kind of politicomoral initiative,[48] Schiller proceeded to argue that art "will not join battle directly with this savage force which resists her weapons."[49] What art will do, though, is appeal to "man's inner being";[50] and it will do this during man's "leisure hours."[51] At that time, art can lay its "shaping hand" on men's minds: it can begin to "Banish from their pleasures caprice, frivolity and coarseness and imperceptively . . . banish these from their actions and, eventually, from their inclinations too. Surround them . . . with symbols of perfections . . . and Art [will] triumph over Nature."[52]

In making the case for the wisdom of indirection, Schiller was assuming several things about aesthetic culture. First, he was equating the purposes of art with the cultivation of truth – that is, he made art serve the pedagogic purposes of moral didacticism. Hence his designation of art as the "champion [of Truth] in the realm of phenomena."[53] Second, Schiller assumed that artists would possess "the steadfast courage" to disdain the "enlightened" opinions of the age – to live out of season, as it were.[54] To this group, Schiller exhorted:

Live with your century; but do not be its creature; render to your contemporaries what they need, not what they praise . . . think of them as they ought to be, when called upon to influence them; think of them as they are, when tempted to act on their behalf.[55]

Finally, Schiller held optimistically to the belief that if artists "appeal to what is best" in mankind, mankind will respond with a display of its inherent "nobility."[56]

In all this, of course, Schiller was assuming something about man's receptivity to, and potential for, moral development.[57] And he was explicit about what political consequences would follow were artists successful in their endeavor to cultivate this potential. As he wrote:

Every individual human being, one may say, carries within him, potentially and prescriptively, an ideal man, the archetype of a human being, and it is his life's task to be, through all his changing manifestations, in harmony with the unchanging unity of this ideal. This archetype, which is to be discerned more or less clearly in every individual, is represented by the State, the objective and, as it were, canonical form in which all the diversity of individual subjects strive to unite. One can, however, imagine two different ways in which man existing in time can coincide with man as Idea, and, in consequence, just as many ways in which the State can assert itself in individuals: either by the ideal man suppressing empirical man, and the State annulling individuals; or else by the individual himself becoming the State, and man in time being ennobled to the stature of man as Idea.[58]

From what Schiller goes on to say, it is clear that he preferred the latter of the two alternatives, for he speaks favorably of the ennobling of "subjective humanity" in the direction of the "ideal and objective humanity" represented by the State.[59] More to the point, Schiller insisted that art's task in all this was preparatory: it did not so much wish to guarantee "any particular result" as restore to man "the freedom to be what he ought to be."[60] By establishing a counterweight to "the one-sided constraint of nature in the field of sensation,"[61] art provided man with "the gift of humanity itself" – "the power of becoming human" voluntarily, by his "own free will and decision."[62]

2. Schiller: Enthusiasm, indifferences, and reflection

All this has obvious relevance to what Hegel thought he was doing in the essays on *Natural Law* and *Ethical Life*. Schiller's challenge to the narrow, materialistic values of the "civilized classes" is governed by the same concerns that informed Hegel's criticism of the "bourgeois" conception of ethical life. Indeed, in both cases a concerted effort has been made to recall men to public life by holding out to them the imperative of, and possibilities for, politico-moral reform. But we can draw more insight into Hegel from Schiller if we look even more closely at the latter's conception of "indirection," for it helps to illuminate just how Schiller and Hegel used the idea of "indifference" to advance the purpose of politico-moral reform (i.e., true *Sittlichkeit*). And since indifference is the key to Hegel's conception of the first class, it is important to our understanding of that idea, too.

As has previously been noted, Schiller posited a direct connection between the advance of the division of labor and civilization's increasing neglect of "the aptitudes of the psyche" (*Anlagen des Gemüts*).[63] To arrest this development, Schiller urged artists to cultivate these neglected "aptitudes." He asked them to uncover ways to liberate man's "imagination" (*Einbildungskraft*) from the narrow confines set for it by civilization.[64] Having said this, however, Schiller goes to great lengths to avoid any hint of the kind of "intuitionism" that soon would become associated with romantic subjectivism.[65] Surely it is no accident that in the process of qualifying his position, he found another use for the idea of indirection, one that Christian reformers had used for centuries to separate themselves from "enthusiasts."[66]

Schiller's qualification of his position begins with the argument that not every artist has been endowed with "the spirit of long patience" that is required to cultivate man's imagination.[67] All too often, Schiller remarks, "the impatient spirit of enthusiasm" drives "vigorous souls...toward action," toward the insistence that "the Absolute" be realized immediately.[68] Blinded by the "misfortunes of the human race," these men "of feeling" hurl themselves "*directly* upon present-day reality," seeking "specific and prompt results."[69] Then, in a most revealing statement, Schiller claims that for enthusiasts "time does not exist, and the future turns into the present from the moment that it is seen to develop...out of the present."[70] They wish, as it were, to "leap" directly to the Absolute without having to tolerate any of the inconveniences and frustrations of "in-betweenness."[71]

As an alternative to this, Schiller counseled patience and a willingness to proceed toward the realization of politico-moral reform in a "round-about" way – "indirectly," as he put it.[72] In language that smacks of Lessing and of the theology of the divine economy,[73] Schiller says art's task is to build a "third joyous kingdom" to which man can come in order to be "released from all that might be called constraint, alike in the physical and in the moral sphere."[74] From this "aesthetic State" the artist will reach out to man;[75] but to do this "the mightiest genius must divest itself of its majesty, and stoop in all humility to the mind of a little child."[76] And instead of forcing free citizens "beneath the yoke" of his purposes, as the enthusiast would do, the truly patient artist will ask them to "assent" both to joining him in this Kingdom and to trying to expand its scope.[77] And should the artist despair of having to proceed so "indirectly," Schiller is quick, à la Lessing, to remind him that "as in much else, a kindly *dispensation*" has seen to it that the quickest way to fulfill the "ideal of equality" in the world is to force art to work for an "ideal" world through "the real" one.[78] Thus, the connection in Schiller's mind between "indirection," "popularization," "assent," and the commitment to carry "the war against matter into the very territory of Matter itself."[79]

On these terms, then, the "aesthetic state" emerges as a "dispensation" given by God–Providence–Nature to man for the sake of deliverance from the twin perils of materialism and enthusiasm. That art had certain redemptive powers is, of course, a very old trope; Curtius and Kantorowicz have shown us that.[80] That trope, however, is often misunderstood. Most often it is associated with the romantic conception of the artist. But on this issue there is a major difference between Schiller (and Hegel) on the one hand and the romantics on the other: the former insist on submitting to, and gaining assent from, the collectivity for "art's" values whereas the latter do not.[81] For Schiller, therefore, the redemptive power of art is linked to the doctrine of indirection, which in turn, is linked to a conception of history as a kind of *Bildungsroman*, in which characters gradually came to self-consciousness by way of a series of progressive revelations about themselves.[82] And because aesthetic values must receive collective assent in the real world before they can become truly realized, the artist must be patient – must be a good "husbandman," willing to use the "blessing of time" to his advantage. He must, as Schiller puts it, be willing to live in a condition of "indifference" between the eternal and the temporal, to fulfill his pedagogic purpose.[83]

What Schiller tells us about this condition of indifference is very revealing – in its own writ and for the insights it offers us to Hegel's own rendering of the conception in the essay on *Ethical Life*. In the eighteenth and twenty-third letters of *Education* Schiller speaks of art's need to establish a "middle state" between the "sensuous" and "spiritual" dimensions of human experience.[84] This "middle state of aesthetic freedom,"[85] Schiller continues, is a place to which "sensuous man" must be "transported" if his "nature" (i.e., his "animal" nature) is ever to be "altered."[86]

By this, Schiller means to be quite historical. This becomes clear when we recall that in the third letter Schiller had juxtaposed "physical" with "moral" man and then wondered how, given the configuration of contemporary civilization, the latter could be coaxed to emerge from the former.[87] This, he insisted, was the problem of the age in which he lived. Now in letters nineteen through twenty-four he offers the "middle state" as an axis and point of mediation between the two; between the physical and the moral, between the temporal and the eternal.[88] What he argues is that since "sensation precedes consciousness," since the physical idea of the "individual" exists before the moral idea of "a Person," there must be a point, a moment of transition between the two.[89] That point, according to Schiller, is the "middle-state" – the state where man "emancipates himself" from "the dominion of nature"[90] without, however, immediately attaining the status of a moral being for himself.[91] Here man gains relative "autonomy" vis-à-vis his sensuous nature and acquires the capacity to make decisions about what kind of "person" he should be[92] – that is, Schiller conceives of the middle state as a "precondition" of freedom,[93] a precondition that must be realized before "spiritual" man can emerge from "the physical according to the laws of freedom."[94] This three-step sequence, I think, is what Schiller had in mind when he wrote "Man in his physical state merely suffers the dominion of nature; he emancipates himself from this dominion in the aesthetic state; and he acquires mastery over it in the moral."[95]

In the middle state, then, man achieves something like a condition of equilibrium between his sensuous and moral natures.[96] Instead of equilibrium, though, Schiller speaks of a condition of "indifference": to wit, "It is here . . . in the indifferent sphere of *physical life* that man must make a start upon his moral life."[97] It is here that he "must learn to desire more nobly"; that he receives "the gift of humanity itself"; and so on.[98] Schiller is quite clear about his meaning, for he equates indifference with a "state of reflection" in which the power of sensation loses its hold on physical man as the power of morality begins to assert itself on spiritual man.[99] In this condition of indifference qua state of reflection man is "momentarily free of all determination."[100] What we have at this moment, Schiller says, is "a happy medium" in which man qua *Gemüt* is as "removed from the constraint" of the physical as from that of the moral.[101] Man in this condition is "a Nought" (*Null*)[102] – not so much an "empty" being as a being with a differentiated consciousness who is "neither exclusively matter nor exclusively *Geist*."[103] For that very reason, however, he is free – free actively and voluntarily to define "what he ought to be."[104]

Man does not *automatically* become "what he ought to be" by arriving at the point of indifference. That he does was the view of the enthusiasts – of those who wished to leap directly to the Absolute from the physical without having to engage the physical itself.[105] To them, Schiller offered the following counsel: "take one step backward" and by doing so open up "within the domain of sense" an "indifferent sphere of physical life" where man can begin to "make a start upon his moral life."[106] By calling "spiritual man...back to matter," Schiller believed, the possibility of drawing "sensuous man" toward the aesthetic state of indifference was greatly enhanced; [107] by requiring art to ground its speculations about man's nature in experience, he believed, a counterweight to materialism could be established within "the territory of Matter itself";[108] and by learning how to instruct by indirection, Schiller believed, art could establish a "negative condition," a state of indifference among man, that was a precondition for man to display his moral personality.[109]

Throughout *Aesthetic Education*, then, Schiller meant to be a "realist" without having to sacrifice his credentials as an "idealist."[110] As we have seen, in this, as well as in many other things, he anticipated Hegel. But there is one aspect of Schiller's thought that Hegel must have found a little disconcerting. On the one hand, Schiller made recognition of the "priority of the sensuous drive" in man the key to understanding "the whole history of human freedom."[111] Hegel, we have seen, would have agreed. On the other hand, Schiller left the force that "awakens our Personality" (in a self-conscious, moral sense) shrouded in mystery.[112] He failed to explain what precipitates the development of man's moral nature. As he observed:

Ineluctable, incorruptible, incomprehensible, the concepts of Truth and Right make their appearance at an age when we are still little more than a bundle of sensations; and without being able to say whence or how it arose, we acquire an awareness of the Eternal in Time, and of Necessity in the sequence of Chance. Thus sensation and self-consciousness both arise entirely without any effort on our part, and the origin of both lies as much beyond the reach of our will as it is beyond the orbit of our understanding.[113]

Surely Hegel would not have concurred in this judgment. Schiller's argument, that it is "by the grace of Nature" that man arrives at "indifference" qua "state of reflection," must have struck the hardheaded

Hegel as "tender-minded."[114] To avoid succumbing to this kind of mysticism himself, Hegel had to find a way, a "realistic" way, to bring man to the point of indifference. As we shall see, he chose to exploit the division of labor principle to do so and, by so doing, made sociological and economic Schiller's notion of the "grace of Nature."

3. Conversion by inversion: Intuitions and concepts in Hegel

In *Ethical Life* it is not easy to see Hegel making these changes to Schiller's argument. Nevertheless, it is exactly what he is doing toward the end of the essay.

To be fair to Schiller, it should be noted that there are hints within *Education* that point in the direction Hegel will follow – in the direction Hegel will move with the aid of his conception of how the division of labor works in modern society. In the fifth and eighth letters, for example, Schiller had suggested that because "civilization" had "freed man from the yoke of physical need," he should have begun to move beyond the "materialistic" ethic of the present.[115] Ferguson had been even more explicit. Writing about the impact of the division of labor on modern life, he noted that while it tended "to contract and to limit the views of the mind," it led in some areas "to general reflections, and to the enlargement of thought."[116] Indeed, for Ferguson, "thinking itself" was becoming "a peculiar craft" in "this age of separations."[117] Thinkers, Ferguson continued, belong "to that station" in which men are "bound to no task," where "they are left to follow the disposition of the mind and to take that part in society, to which they are led by the sentiments of the heart, or by the calls of the public."[118] In words that Schiller and Hegel could hardly have missed, Ferguson urged men to "look for the elevation of sentiment, and *liberality* of mind, among those orders of citizens, who, by their condition, and their fortunes are relieved from sordid cares and attentions."[119] In truth, Schiller did not miss what Ferguson had said. According to him, certain artists have achieved this condition. And like Ferguson, he referred to that condition of "indifference" and "reflection" in terms of man's "first liberal relation" with the world.[120]

It is extremely helpful to approach certain arguments in *Ethical Life* with the Ferguson–Schiller convergence in mind. What the convergence suggests is that the conceptual tools of political economy and sociological realism, both of which revolved largely around the division of labor principle, have become resources for those who would question for ethicopoliticoreligious reasons the values of what Hegel had called the "bourgeois" conception of ethical life. We are, in short, at that point in time when some of the principal conceptions of the "Enlightenment" merge into the patterns of either "anti-Enlightenment" or "true Enlightenment" thought; when the ideas of "liberality" and of the "bourgeoisie" begin to go their separate ways in history, at least for a while.[121]

Hegel, I think, was very much aware of how the convergence of the one informed the divergence of the other. What makes this difficult to see is the language Hegel uses to pose the problem. To that end he initially sets the problem in philosophical terms — in terms of the interplay between "intuitions" and "concepts" — and, only after doing that, in terms of the "indifference" and division of labor arguments.

First things first, then. The argument Hegel makes about intuitions and concepts is, I think, rather easily put. Earlier we noted that in the essays on *Natural Law* and on *Ethical Life* Hegel had divided the inorganic, the social moment of objective experience, into something like substructural (i.e., the system of need) and superstructural (i.e., the system of recognition) elements. We noted, in addition, that Hegel had posited *Tapferkeit* as a key impulse *within* social man that, when activated, would impel him toward politics, the organic, substantive *Sittlichkeit*, and so on. In this Hegel was very much like Schiller, for both were committed to avoiding "leaps" and to deriving the organic from "the indifferent sphere of physical life" (i.e., from a psychological point internal to man whose self-conception was still very much rooted in *social* experience).

Although we did not pursue the idea at the time, it should have been obvious that Hegel's conception of natural *Sittlichkeit* had three, not two, dimensions. In addition to the manifest need and recognition systems there was (so Hegel posited) a latent disposition for true unity within this otherwise disconnected mass. Seen in this light, Hegel's task was to explain how this latent impulse toward unity might become manifest and, following from that, how the bourgeois conception of recognition would first be contested and then superseded by that which had just become manifest. To put it as simply as possible, Hegel's problem was to effect a *conversion* of the social into the political by way of an *inversion* of the value priorities in the consciousness of social man.

It is toward this point that Hegel wishes to work his discussion of intuitions and concepts in *Ethical Life*. He begins with what he calls the subsumption of intuition under the concept.[122] By this he means to identify a condition (i.e., man in his social moment) in which "the absolute ethical order appears as nature, because nature itself is but the subsumption of intuition under the concept."[123] When we ask what this subsumed intuition is, Hegel tells us: it is "the unity" that "remains the inner" when the "concept" (i.e., nature), in all its "multiplicity," has become outer (i.e., established itself institutionally as natural *Sittlichkeit*).[124]

The "unity" that "remains the inner" is the latent impulse to which Hegel will have to appeal in order to effect conversion by inversion. Since what "remains inner" is an impulse, man's intuition of this unity is real – it is rooted in his real-life experience as sensuous (i.e., socio-physical) man. As such the impulse "belongs to nature" (i.e., to the socioeconomic realm for Hegel) and is experienced by man involuntarily (i.e., it is part of social experience itself).[125] Still, if this intuition exists in man as need, it does so only as "feeling" – that is, it has yet to be realized in consciousness or to become the object of reflection or deliberate action.[126]

For Hegel, then, although intuitions exist in man they are generally "concealed" from him.[127] This is an extremely important point and goes far to explain why Schiller rather than Schelling is so decisive for Hegel's development during these years. Both Schelling and Schiller had much to say about "the point of indifference." But what they said about it was really quite different and led in very different directions: Schelling's toward the cult of romantic genius and the philosophy of nature; Schiller's toward the idea of the reflective self and the philosophy of *Sittlichkeit*. Thus, it is worthwhile to take careful note of the differences between the two thinkers' conceptions of the point of indifference.

Schelling, we know, wished to establish intuition as a nonrational faculty of the human mind.[128] As Schelling understood it, this faculty was the key to human transcendence because through it flowed those influences he deemed capable of ennobling character and of giving true meaning to life. These influences, he argued, came to man from nature, and it was the task of artistic or philosophic genius to use imagination to intuit these influences and to make them available to all mankind in the form of art.

More specifically, Schelling posited a "psycho-natural parallelism" between man and nature.[129] Genius, Schelling insisted, is "a free gift of nature" that allows certain men to bridge the gap between themselves and nature.[130] With this gift, these men situate themselves at a "point of indifference" that, according to Schelling, allows genius to appreciate both the profusion of nature and its inner coherence. That is, from the point of indifference genius becomes aware of how unity and diversity are one and the same thing in the creative processes of nature.[131]

This is the insight genius and art must reveal to mankind. But there is more to Schelling's conception of genius than the label of pantheism would suggest. If genius comes to know the Absolute in nature it also comes to know it in itself.[132] And if it succeeds first in giving artistic expression to that knowledge and then in communicating it to others, all of mankind will be so illuminated – that is, the Absolute will become immanent among men if the offerings of the artistic imagination are internalized as social norms.

From here, of course, it is but a short step to romanticism, to an aesthetic vision that prides itself on "the intrusion of personal traits" into art, on introspection, and on the artists' gradual withdrawal from the world into one of their own making.[133] As M. H. Abrams has noted, when a work of art "is concerned to imitate something inside the artist himself; and when its criterion is thus made both intuitive and introspective, art readily slips its mooring in the public world of sense and begins to rely instead on a vision which is personal and subjective."[134]

This twist, which begins with man looking for the Absolute, the point of indifference, in nature and ends with the internalization of the Absolute in the mind of the artist – that is, which begins with emanationism and pantheism and ends with the colossal egoism of romanticism – has important implications for Schelling's conception of the relations between intuitions, concepts, and the point of indifference.[135] These implications, in turn, are precisely why Hegel chose to follow Schiller on the point of indifference rather than Schelling.

Three of these implications are especially important. First, there is very little in Schelling's thought that allows him to separate "sensations" from "intuitions." Indeed, the parallelism that Schelling posits between man and nature is designed more to accent complementariness than conflict. If that is the case, genius becomes a receptable, a *tabula rasa* upon which nature registers its design.[136] Genius could be said to "display" nature's aggregate of elements but not to "master" them. And mastery of nature's profusion was something to which Schiller and Hegel were both committed.[137]

Second, Schelling implied – and Hegel specifically disputed him on this – that intuitions were the same as concepts.[138] That is, Schelling believed in "automatism," in the direct translation of aesthetic intuitions into artistic conceptions that would give concrete expression to the presence of the Absolute in the artist's life itself.[139] The effect of this, of course, was to assimilate nature qua sensation and intuition to the dynamic of artistic production. That assimilation, in turn, made the Absolute a much more subjective anthropological conception even while it was making it a much more objective aesthetic one.

Third, by running sensations, intuitions, and conceptions together Schelling opened the way for the entry of religious mysticism into his thought. By proposing to use art to reconcile man and nature in the Absolute Schelling had to grant the artist insight into the creative processes of nature itself; and that, for a pantheist, entailed developing first-hand knowledge of nature's designer. Insight into nature, then, enabled the artist to use his imagination to redeem his fellows in the same way that religious mystics had used prophecy to regenerate fallen man. On that reading the artist is not just producing works of aesthetic inspiration, he is offering them to mankind as a means of religious grace as well. But because there was no longer any need to verify these works empirically, there was little to prevent mere aesthetic "fancy" from trying to pass itself off as redemptive religious grace, little to prevent the artist from claiming a prophetic privilege for himself based on personal knowledge of the Absolute.[140]

What all this adds up to in Schelling is a conception of the point of indifference that envisages it as an explicit expression of the identity between man and nature, the artist and the Absolute. Culminating in artistic creation, the point of indifference becomes shorthand for the consciousness of redivinized man. Instead of representing – as it did for Schiller and would for Hegel – a point where reflective self-evaluation *was possible*, a point where the condition of *Bestimmbarkeit* allowed man to choose freely between a higher human or lower animal mode of existence, Schelling's point of indifference stood as testimony to an already redeemed self. For the artist, redemption took the form of artistic creation; for his audience, it took the form of communion with the Absolute through individual acts of aesthetic appreciation. In both cases, however, redemption was highly subjective;[141] indeed, it was almost always the consequence of some solitary mystical experience made possible by the transcendental imagination. That made the Absolute qua point of indifference accessible only to private intuition and left it closed to "intersubjective activity," to collective discussion of what standards art had to meet for it to qualify as redemptive and worthy of human emulation.[142]

Like Schiller, Hegel had no intention of endorsing this kind of naive philosophic aesthetic. So, in the essay on *Ethical Life* he carefully avoids formulations that even hint at leaving human redemption in the hands of Schelling's man of genius. As Plant has well understood, for Hegel to have done otherwise would have been to leave the problem of substantive *Sittlichkeit* (i.e., of the establishment of a truly political community based on intersubjective communication) "at the mercy of the private intuition of a transcendent, even mystical entity."[143] Hegel saw, that is, that Schelling's point of indifference, his whole conception of the Absolute, had an indefinable and esoteric quality about it. This quality, in turn, tended to diminish audience participation in the determination of the values that were to govern the collectivity.

Rather than commit himself to the prophetic pretensions of Schelling's conception of genius, rather than read an overly optimistic automatism into the conception of the point of indifference, Hegel, like Schiller, chose to present the point of indifference as central to the gradual "roundabout" way in which men come to determinations about their collective identity and destiny as a people. Granted, there is a hierarchical aspect implicit in

Schiller's and Hegel's conception of the point of indifference, too; but as Schiller and Hegel present it the emphasis is less on offering sanction for the prophetic gifts of certain social groups, less on justifying their right to political power, than on getting the collectivity qua people to think about the value priorities in their lives.[144] To use M. H. Abrams' terminology, Schiller and Hegel have a "pragmatic" rather than an "expressive" conception of the point of indifference; or, rather, they are more concerned with stimulating discussion about the ends for which men should exist than with imposing values on them in the name of genius.[145]

What is crucial here is that Schiller and Hegel both recognized the need to keep imagination qua mere intuition in check.[146] This did not mean, however, that they wished to dispense with it as a mode of experience in, and source of knowledge about, the world. On the contrary, they both accepted intuition, feeling, and imagination (in the narrow sense) as essential to the process of reflective self-evaluation. But they did insist on treating intuition as only the start of this process – they regarded intuition as the initial phase of a long and drawn-out *Bildung* process that, at bottom, involved giving conceptual form to intuition itself.[147]

According to Schiller and Hegel, then, for this to happen intuition and understanding, feeling and thinking, had to be coordinated. For Schiller this was the task of aesthetic imagination (in the broad sense); for Hegel it was the task of philosophy in general and of a philosophy of *Sittlichkeit* in particular. In Hegel's case, however, this process of coordination and self-evaluation had very definite correlates in the objective world of experience. That is because he regarded self-evaluation as a collective process to which a people must subject itself if it were to become a truly political and truly human entity. Thus, if Schelling had moved the point of indifference from external nature to internal man, Hegel was committed to moving it from a point internal to man to a point that would be external to him in the sense that it would be located in the world of a shared socio-economic and political experience. There, it was to become a subject of collective debate; and out of that debate, in which intuitions could become concepts and concepts intuitions, was to emerge, for better or worse, the political character of a people. In that context, Hegel's conception of the point of indifference is a point of departure for, rather than the culmination of, thinking about the Absolute.

Viewed in this way it should be clear why Hegel's discussion of intuition (i.e., the sense of "unity" that "remains inner") has a very specific political edge to it. Indeed, in the essay on *Ethical Life* intuition will become surrogate for what Hegel discussed in the *Natural Law* essay under the rubric of *Tapferkeit* – that is, each has a teleological aspect built into it. As such, his discussion of the process by which intuitions are converted into concepts should tell us much about how the political moment of objective experience is to emerge from the social one. A main question in *Ethical Life* is how the intuition of unity that remains concealed in man arises and becomes a subject for and of collective and reflective self-evaluation. According to Hegel there are three steps in the process. First of all, Hegel à la Schiller allows social man to intuit through "feeling" that natural *Sittlichkeit* is an inadequate expression of true community.[148] Man knows this because feeling itself is a legitimate source of information that, while not speaking directly to the mind, conveys to the individual the kind of moral truths around which the spirit of community must be formed. When these truths are lacking man becomes aware of a "contradiction" between his "inner light" (i.e., his innate sense of substantive *Sittlichkeit*) and the "universal light hovering over him" (i.e., natural *Sittlichkeit* institutionalized as system of recognition).[149]

Hegel likens the resultant "feeling of separation" to the conditions of animals.[150] "An animal's voice," he writes, "comes from its inmost part, or from its conceptual being, but, like the whole animal, it belongs to feeling."[151] He continues: "Most animals scream at the danger of death but this is purely and simply an outlet of subjectivity, something formal" (i.e., undirected in the way *Tapferkeit* is before it becomes *Andreia*)[152] As such, Hegel goes on to tell us, the animal's "voice is empty, formal, void of totality."[153] That, of course, is because it is neither "the product of intelligence" nor the product of some intersubjective communication (i.e., it has not yet been elevated from *Gemeinsinn* – common feeling – to *Gemeingut* – a common possession of a self-reflective collectivity).[154] In this animals and social man (i.e., bourgeois man) have much in common: both share a condition of existence in which a "feeling of separation" generates a need for true unity.[155]

Presenting the problem of intuition this way enabled Hegel to focus more easily on the next step in the process, the step whereby intuitions are converted into concepts and, thereby, become socialized, become subjects of public discussion and collective self-evaluation. Having claimed that this "feeling of separation" gives rise to a latent sense of "need" for "unity," for substantive *Sittlichkeit*, Hegel now wants to show how "this feeling" is to "display *itself* as a totality," as an alternative form of *Sittlichkeit* in which "the separation of subject and object" (i.e., social man's sense of separation from his fellows) will be "superseded."[156] For this to happen feeling qua intuition must begin to express itself conceptually – in the form of a new system of recognition that offers an alternative value system to the one that governs life in the condition of natural *Sittlichkeit*.[157] Someone, that is, must begin to give *voice* to this latent feeling and need;[158] and this must be done from a point internal to the social moment of objective experience itself (i.e., as with Schiller it cannot, therefore, come from the State). In short, it must come from a *social* group whose condition of existence allows it to think politically about collective, human needs without being political itself. That group is Hegel's "first class."

4. The first class and the division of labor: Hegel sociologizes indifference

Mention of the first class brings us to Hegel's conception of the point of indifference. It also brings us to the point where we see him exploiting to great advantage the Ferguson–Schiller convergence. What he proceeds to do is offer a socio-economic explanation for the ideas of indifference and reflective self-evaluation.

Early in *Ethical Life* Hegel poses the issue of the "feeling of separation" in terms of a tension between inner and outer man.[159] He notes how outer man, while initially enjoying sensuous pleasures, soon becomes "satiated" with them and, thus, begins to develop a sense of indifference toward them.[160] In terms that articulate the essence of the "bad infinity" of excessive consumerism, Hegel contends that "satiation" testifies to "the indifference and emptiness of the individual."[161] Moreover, the experience of satiation reminds the individual that very little of the "specific character" of his social existence "arises" from true interaction with his fellows.[162] He begins to long for "the possibility of being ethical," for true *Sittlichkeit*.[163]

As outer man becomes disillusioned with *a merely social existence*, inner man becomes more resolute about establishing himself as the measure of reality. That is, inner man begins to assign "universal" significance to himself and to the "need" he feels for a unity that will supersede his sense of social indifference.[164] Hegel uses the image of a seesaw to convey what he is driving at here: namely, a social condition in which the inner and outer aspects of man's existence are at war with each other with regard to the problem of which is universal and which is particular.[165] Many, of course, would characterize this condition as one of simple "alienation"; for Schiller and Hegel, however, it was the point of indifference, the negative condition of creativity, the point of "nullity" where the two aspects of social man's existence neutralize each other and, by so doing, create the state of "complete indeterminacy" that is necessary for reflective self-evaluation.[166]

For Hegel, then, the point of indifference refers, psychologically, to the condition in which a feeling about the need for unity (i.e., an intuition) becomes transformed into a conscious public ideal (i.e., a concept). With this transformation – which Hegel equates with the process of education itself – "intelligence" is produced among men (i.e., what was previously

Gemeinsinn is now *Gemeingut*).[167] That is to say, the need for unity is no longer "concealed" from social man, and, in fact, may now become the possession of collective wisdom. When this happens "speech" becomes possible and a mass finds itself in a position to constitute itself as a people (i.e., as a prepolitical entity that has formed itself into a collectivity that is committed to the discussion of what it means to be human).[168]

Hegel's discussion of intuitions and concepts leads directly to the idea of nullity, indeterminacy, and indifference. We must ask, however, whether that discussion is an improvement on Schiller – on his claim that "indifference" arises "by the grace of nature." Obviously it is not; and Hegel knew that – which is precisely why he turns at this moment to the division of labor principle to ground indifference in socioeconomic reality.

To see this, we ourselves need to step back, need to realize that by explaining the transformation of intuitions into concepts in terms of a process of gradual public enlightenment Hegel was implying that *Bildung* had a social function.

To that end, Hegel was inclined to explain the interplay between intuitions and concepts in terms of the process by which a teacher brings out what is best in a student. Furthermore, as Hegel presents it, the transformation of intuitions into concepts also involves the movement of consciousness from an inner psychological to an outer sociological point. In that context the process of public enlightenment must be understood in terms of intersubjective communication – that is, *Bildung* is a collective social as well as individual psychological process. For that reason, Hegel's discussion of the process whereby man's inner intuition of unity comes to express itself in an outer conceptual form reveals much about his understanding of the dynamic of education and of its relation to social experience itself. And since what is being given conceptual form is the impulse toward unity (i.e., the organic, true *Sittlichkeit*, the distinctively human), Hegel's discussion of this dynamic should tell us just how the political moment of objective experience emerges from the social one.

If we think about intuitions and concepts in terms of a *Bildung* process involving a student–teacher relationship, the following interplay reveals itself. The student becomes the carrier of the intuition of unity. As such, he is disposed toward collective action that has a political focus in that the action aims at realizing the "concealed unity" that lies within him.[169] By the same token, the teacher becomes the embodiment of the concept. He is the outward expression of the student's intuition.[170] Or, as Hegel puts it in a slightly different context elsewhere in the essay, the teacher stands to the student as the objectivity of "corporeal sign" stands to the subjectivity of "gesture."[171] In this sense, the student is able to see in the teacher his own intuition in objective form (i.e., the student's intuition is now "distinguishable" from itself).[172] Conversely, the teacher, who is inclined toward the political for reasons that we shall see relate to the division of labor, finds in the student a receptive audience whom he will *try to persuade* to translate his "need" for "unity" into something objective in an organic–political rather than inorganic – socioeconomic sense.[173]

Given this framework, Hegel's pedagogic conception of how intuitions evolve into concepts seems to depend on two things. First, it depends on the existence of a group of "students" (i.e., Germany's middling groups) who, having experienced "bad infinity" and the disappointment of "relative identity," are psychologically disposed toward hearing *calls* for organic forms of integration and identity formation. Second, it depends on the existence of a group of "teachers" (i.e., Hegel's first class) who are in a position to offer a vision of what organic unity might consist in. According to Hegel, when these conditions are met, the possibility for formation of a "social counterwill" among a people becomes very real indeed. This counterwill, in turn, becomes a vehicle of political educa-tion, if not of political action itself – that is, Hegel's entire discussion of intuitions and concepts, indifference and *Bildung*, is an evocation of politics. Put another way, *Bildung* stands to *Sittlichkeit* in *Ethical Life* as *Tapferkeit* had stood to *Andreia* in *Natural Law*. Indeed, in both cases something that had been potentially political has acquired a specific conceptual focus. And although that focus is political and lies beyond the social it has arisen from a point *within* the social moment of objective experience itself.[174]

What Hegel has done here is quite revealing: he has used the idea of *Bildung* to sociologize the psychological dynamic by which intuitions are converted into concepts. When *Bildung* "takes" among a people it raises inner intuition to the stature of outer conception and, by so doing, neutralizes the difference between inner and outer man. In a word, it places man in a condition of "indifference," sociologically considered. And since what was once inner has become outer, there are now two competing systems of recognition within the social moment of objective experience: one points toward liberality, the organic, the political, the human; the other seeks to preserve the inorganic, the socioorganic, the bourgeois.[175]

In this situation, Hegel tells us, "all [social man's] specific determinacy is annulled"[176] – that is, man has become "truly infinite" in the sense that he is now aware of his own "nullity."[177] And since man is now conscious of this nullity, he is in a position to engage in reflective self-evaluation in a collective social rather than individual psychological sense. In short, Hegel has sociologized the point of indifference and, thereby, made socio-economic processes essential to collective self-evaluation. As such, indifference denotes for him that "moment" in time when a collectivi-ty has the opportunity to decide whether it wishes to become a political "people" or remain a "disconnected mass" or "mere plurality."[178]

That Hegel meant for this to be the case is confirmed by the way he works his concept of "a people" into the essay on *Ethical Life*.[179] For Hegel, *Bildung* brings the collectivity to a social point of indifference. It is the point where all things – body and spirit, the one and the many, intuitions and concepts, universals and particulars, subjectivity and objectivity, the organic and the inorganic, the infinite and the finite – converge in one very pregnant textual and historical moment of "dramatic action." In a simple phrase, it is what Hegel called the moment of "living indifference," the point where "all natural difference is nullified" such that "the individual intuits himself as himself in every other individual."[180] This moment, Hegel suggests, is when the idea of "a people" becomes a practicable political possibility. A people, he tells us, is neither a "mass" nor a "plurality."[181] Rather, it is a "living indifference" with the potential for "organic totality" within itself.[182] By that Hegel means the people have the possibility of becoming "self-constituting," of becoming a "cause" for itself.[183] And should it act to realize that possibility it will be drawing nearer to "the Absolute," to true *Sittlichkeit*, "rising" toward the organic "from below," as he put it.[184] In other words, "the people" are now the objective, social carrier of the "intuition" that had longed for unity, true *Sittlichkeit*. And were a people to try to realize itself as such, Hegel thought, it would open itself to the future and begin the kind of "pilgrimage" that leads ultimately to religious recollectivization.[185]

The politico-religious edge Hegel has given to *Bildung*, to the sociologized point of indifference, and to the idea of a people should be clear. It should be just as clear that Hegel, like Schiller, left it to the people to decide whether or not to act on this political imperative.[186] Indeed, for Hegel, the very idea of a people entailed collective and voluntary decision-making as to what kind of system of recognition would govern life. Hegel, obviously, had his own preferences here – he was hardly indifferent to the choice a people made. In terms of the dramatic action of the text and of the historical moment, he most assuredly identified with a people who had opted for substantive rather than natural *Sittlichkeit*.

If this were all Hegel had said about the origins of political consciousness (i.e., the impulse toward true *Sittlichkeit*), we could, with some adjustments, find a place for him in the history of idealism qua moral formalism. But Hegel knew – as his criticisms of Fichte and Schelling have revealed – that the conventional fare of this kind of idealism contained not a little bit of wishful thinking. For this reason, I think, he chose to link the general problem of *Sittlichkeit* and the particular problem of sociological indifference to the concept of the division of labor. It was Hegel's way of grounding his version of idealism in the contemporary dynamic of social and political experience.

How, then, does Hegel use the division of labor concept to pull all this together? As has already been noted, the concept figured prominently in the *Ethical Life* text – in the discussion of man's movement from a presocial to a social existence. Similarly, it played an important role in fostering conditions that led to vicious luxury and the experience of bad infinity. In this, of course, there was nothing new. The Scots and Schiller, after all, had arrived at a similar position: one that held that the division of labor had progressive and retrogressive edges to it. If it did much to advance man's material *interest*, it also detracted from his *wisdom*. If it propelled "civilization" forward, it pulled "culture" backward.

All that notwithstanding, Hegel's treatment of the division of labor became original when he linked it to the ideas of *Bildung* and sociologized indifference. Hegel made this connection after having first discussed the role of the division of labor in two other prior contexts: in nature and in the social moment of objective experience itself.[187] Early in the essay he had discussed the division of labor in *natural* terms – as manifest in the sexual division within the family.[188] This division, he proceeded to argue, was overcome by "love," itself a natural, rather than ethical, form of action. One of the consequences of this response to division was the propagation of children who, as the motor force of demographic pressure, became instrumental in the emergence of the *social* moment of objective experience.[189] This moment, in turn, had its own form of division, a division that revolved around the principle of the division of labor as we know it today – as a principle of socioeconomic organization.[190] Here, as was noted earlier, the basis of division is built into the labor experience itself: in the form of a whole series of "mechanical" (i.e., inorganic) relationships that develop among men who, despite their varied interactions, are "dead" to each other, "tools" for each other.[191]

With this argument, we arrive at the point where our previous discussions of intuitions and concepts, *Bildung*, and the point of social indifference become relevant to Hegel's conception of the division of labor. In that discussion, it was suggested that Hegel's concern was to show how students qua intuitions came to identify with teachers qua concepts; how the inner becomes the outer such that a point of indifference is socially established; and how the convergence of intuition and concept provided not only an opportunity for self-evaluation, but also a possibility for politicoreligious recollectivization. Hegel, I think, invokes the division of labor principle both to explain these changes and to give socioeconomic substance to his argument. He does this in the following way.

Just after noting the "mechanical" consequences the division of labor has had in the socio-economic context, Hegel begins to discuss what he calls the emergence of rational "intelligence."[192] This intelligence, as we have seen, constitutes a challenge to what passes for "intelligence" among the bourgeoisie. By "intelligence" Hegel here means something that is intersubjective and is designed to help overcome social difference as well as social indifference.[193] Without question Hegel wishes to link this form of intelligence both to wisdom and to the principle of true *Sittlichkeit*.[194] As Hegel puts it, it must be "real [i.e., social] but in such a way that this reality is itself ideal [i.e., political, oriented toward true *Sittlichkeit*]."[195] As such, the intelligence will be "in intelligent individuals, but objectively universal in its corporeality" (i.e., "its subjectivity" will "immediately [be] objectivity").[196]

What is Hegel talking about here? And how does it relate to the division of labor? As simply as possible, he is referring, à la Ferguson, to the emergence of a social group whose specific function is to think intelligently and with wisdom about man's social condition.[197] Specifically the group's function is twofold: to create a vision of true *Sittlichkeit* and thereby challenge the orthodoxy of the inorganic mode of social organization qua system of recognition and to persuade others to make that vision their own. In Ferguson's terms the group's task was to use its freedom to "produce" its "mind in public" in order to turn men to "human affairs" and away from "inanimate nature."[198] In Hegel's terms, this group embodies "the freedom of intelligence" and expresses that intelligence when it raises what is finite (e.g., intuition) to what is infinite (e.g., the concept) without abolishing what was finite about it.[199] As such, this group represents "the ethical organic...in contrast to the inorganic."[200]

When we ask Hegel what permits this exercise of intelligence he tells us: it begins to appear when economic development and specialization, both integral to the division of labor concept, free intelligence qua social group from "need and labor."[201] In this condition of "negative" freedom this group is free from determinacy and, therefore, can make itself into an "essence," into a self-creating entity capable of positing and pursuing ends of its own choosing.[202] The group's "calling," in other words, is to persuade men to begin thinking and talking about creating themselves as human beings. Thus, if Hegel associated the division of labor with modern forms of social division and specialization of function, he also tied it to a development that made it possible for a group to emerge whose "calling" was very similar to that which Hegel identified with the impulse toward substantive *Sittlichkeit*. Thus, Hegel used the division of labor principle not only to "lay hold on life" but also to work through society for the purpose of realizing a spiritual end, an end that expressed the *telos* of *homo religiosus*.

In the essay on *Ethical Life*, Hegel refers to this group as the "first class"

and as "the absolute class."[203] This group, he argues, "has absolute and
pure" *Sittlichkeit* "as its principle."[204] Freed from the obligation to
provide itself with its "purely practical" (i.e., physical) "needs," this
group's only concern is the "universal."[205] Or, as he also put it, this
group's immediate activity in the people is not work but something
organic in itself [i.e., *Sittlichkeit*] and absolute."[206] Hegel warns,
however, that it would be a mistake for those whose "surplus" supports
this group to feel that the group's activity has no relation to their own
needs. On the contrary, insofar as a people wishes to become truly "a
people," it must look to this group as the "model" of self-constituting
activity.[207] Rooted in the everyday, the "classes" who support the "first
class" can never by themselves "get beyond" the "intuition" of true
Sittlichkeit.[208] For this, they require the nurture and service of the "first
class," whose function consists in giving conceptual form to this
intuition.[209]

Thus, according to Hegel, this group fills a very important nonmaterial
social "need."[210] It is a need that social man "intuits" (i.e., "feels"); it
arises at the historical moment when the division of labor is fairly well
advanced in both its positive and negative aspects; and it is inextricably
connected with the ideas of the organic, the political, and the
distinctively human. As Hegel summed it up, "the first class is clear,
mirror-bright identity, the spirit [*Geist*] of the other classes."[211] That
spirit, of course, is inseparable from the ideal of *Sittlichkeit* and, hence,
from Hegel's philosophy of these years.

In all this Hegel's philosophy of *Sittlichkeit* was the expression of
conclusions he had worked out by bringing his religious values and
economic studies into juxtaposition. Like all his thinking during these
years, it was designed to offer an alternative to what he understood to be
the "relativity" of "bourgeois" identity – which, for Hegel, was not truly
an identity at all. But the philosophy of *Sittlichkeit* was also informed by
what Hegel had learned from Schiller about *Bildung* and the point of
indifference. One might say, therefore, that Hegel's philosophy of
Sittlichkeit voiced prepolitical concerns.[212] Without question Hegel
understands the first class more as a "social" group that has been freed
from "need" by the advance of the division of labor than as a "political"
group endowed with political authority. Hegel's first class, in short,
influences politics, but only indirectly. While it is allowed conceptually
to point the way toward what politics should consist in, it is bound by the
meaning of *Bildung als Beruf* to leave to the people the decision as to just
how politics will be constituted in fact.[213]

In this, Hegel means for the first class to exercise its influence in a
roundabout way – in a way that is perfectly consistent with Schiller's

conception of the "doctrine of indirection." What political implications flow from Hegel's effort to locate the first class at the point of social indifference and to explain *Bildung* in terms of a philosophy of indirection is a fitting subject for the Epilogue of this study.

Epilogue
Bildung and politics: The "first class," Christian pride, and "absolute spirit"

A neat summary statement of the issues this study has tried to raise, confront, and resolve is not easy, for my contextualist commitment to "thick description" makes such an exercise somewhat gratuitous. So, rather than be redundant, I shall conclude this study with a brief description of "Protestant *Bildung*," a conception that, I think, brings Hegel's ideas on the theology of history; on *praxis pietatis*, civil piety, and the Second Reformation; on *Sittlichkeit* and its relation to social and political theory; and on the eschatological dimension of self-realizing teleology into coherent focus.

A convenient point of departure for this undertaking can be found in the main thesis of Part III of this study: in the argument that in the 1790s and early 1800s Hegel was a critic of what he called the "bourgeois" conception of ethical life. In that context, we need only remember that Hegel had argued for a separation of the bourgeois system of need from the bourgeois system of recognition and that he had tried to replace the latter with one with more "substantive" ethical content. In his terms, he proposed to substitute a system of absolute *Sittlichkeit* for a system of natural *Sittlichkeit*.

In light of what we know he had said during these years about *Sittlichkeit* in general and about the relationship between *Tapferkeit* and "bad infinity" in particular, it would not be a distortion to say that in the early 1800s Hegel was working with a conceptual framework within which the ideas of "pride" and "avarice" figured prominently.[1] To that end, a key sentence in the *Ethical Life* text runs as follows:

... the first class has in its consciousness the difference of the second class and the crudity of the third, and so it separates itself from them and maintains a sense of its lofty individuality or the *pride* which, as *inner consciousness of nobility*, abjures the consciousness of the non-noble and what is precisely the same as that consciousness, namely, the action of the non-noble.[2]

278

In this passage, Hegel uses the idea of "nobility" in the sense that Schiller had used it in the twenty-third letter of *Aesthetic Education*.[3] There, Schiller had equated the idea of nobility with the point of indifference, with the "war against matter," with the transformative power that enabled man to transcend himself as a merely physical being; and with the pursuit of "human dignity."

In the essay on *Ethical Life* Hegel takes that idea, reformulates it in terms of human pride, and assigns the first class the duty of cultivating it publicly. From here, of course, it is but a short step to declaring *Sittlichkeit* both the object of collective pride and the alternative to the materialistic excesses of natural *Sittlichkeit*. Put another way, pride is for Hegel a latent resource within the collectivity, and the first class's task is to bring that resource to public consciousness. Hegel's reference to pride, therefore, has an obvious political connotation that fits in nicely with his overall strategy of converting social into political consciousness. And since it had also been customary to attach a political spin to the idea of pride in the ancient world – in the Hellenic debate over the proper uses of leisure (*scholē*) and in the Hellenistic discussion of the relationship between *otium* and *negotium*[4] – modern scholarship has concluded that Hegel's concern here is best explained in terms of a recovery of the teachings of classical political philosophy.

But there is also a Christian aspect to what Hegel was doing when he tried to separate pride and avarice. To understand this, we need to recall what Christianity under Augustine's auspices had done to the idea of pride. Before Augustine, early Christians had wavered as to whether pride or avarice was the foremost religious vice.[5] When Augustine arrived on the scene, he insisted on collapsing the latter into the former, with the result that after Augustine "pride" was equated with "sin" itself.[6] As Herbert Deane has noted, pride for Augustine was shorthand for an all-pervasive "egoism": from it "the sins of cupidity, the unlimited desire for material and sensual gratifications, [and] the lust to dominate all other men" followed.[7] And, as Deane also noted, "if pride is the root of sin [for Augustine], sin can be overcome only by complete humility and by attributing to God any good that man does."[8]

We know from Part II of this study that Hegel and Kant objected to making this kind of humility the defining characteristic of *homo religiosus*.[9] For them, and for many other *Aufklärer*, Augustine's conception of humility had permeated orthodox Lutheranism and, in that form, had imposed a darkly pessimistic vision on the Protestant conception of religious man.[10] As we have seen, Kant and Hegel wished to contest this view, proposing the eschatological doctrine of assimilationism as an alternative. They were careful, of course, to distinguish their reformist commitment to assimilationism from the more mystical commitment to deification.[11] Yet both were quite convinced that through the exercise of will men, *in certain situations*, could aspire to, and strive for, something more than a "creaturely" existence. For that, however, men had to be encouraged à la Pelagius to have an ethical will and to be allowed à la Joachim to participate in the soteriological process.

That did not mean that Hegel thought man could become "God"; nor did it mean that he thought man possessed the power of self-salvation. As was noted earlier, there is a big difference between the mystical idea of divinization and the more modest ideal of *homoiosis*, a big difference between the idea of *attaining* identification with God and *striving* to become like him. In any event, Kant and Hegel, like many of their Calvinist and pietist predecessors, preached a doctrine of "relative perfection";[12] and for that reason they tried to cultivate Christian "pride" among their readers. Thus, in separating pride and avarice Hegel was contesting not only the overly economized bourgeois conception of ethical life but also the orthodox Lutheran conception of *homo religiosus*.[13] From that perspective, Hegel's concern with pride – nobility – courage – dignity could be said to aim as much at Christian reform as at recovery of classical political philosophy.

For our purpose, of course, what is especially attractive about viewing the separation of pride and avarice in this way is that it speaks directly to the problem of religious–economic overlay in Hegel's thought. In addition, awareness of the religious issues that lie behind the separation permit us to see more clearly just what Hegel was trying to do with his conception of the first class. If we insert the first class into this conceptual framework, it becomes clear that Hegel meant for this class to be the carrier of, and the force behind, a Protestant conception of *Bildung*, a conception that simultaneously addressed the economic and the religious aspects of the overlay problem.

To see this, we need only note the symmetry Hegel builds into his overall argument at this point in his development. First of all, there is symmetry between Hegel's theology of history and his conception of *Sittlichkeit* as a problem in social and political theory. The moment of symmetry arises when indifference is sociologized – when a group of men (i.e., the first class), for reasons that are historically specific to a commercial society, find themselves in a position reflectively and voluntarily to initiate the kind of action that Hegel associated with self-realizing teleology.[14]

Second of all, there is symmetry between Hegel's conception of "dying into life" and his notion of the division of labor. Here the moment of symmetry emerges when the social division of labor reaches a point that allows a specific social group, the first class, to exist independently of physical need.[15] Instead of having to practice a rigorous, ascetic program of self-denial to ensure that they are "dead" or "indifferent" to the material seductions of the world, the members of the first class are excused from the wrenching experience of the "self-emptying" process by writ of the division of labor principle.[16] Put another way, Hegel conceives of this aspect of the division of labor in terms of a dispensation from God that offers *homo religiosus* the opportunity to realize his telos on a collective basis.[17] God, as it were, has condescended once again to deal with man on the latter's terms, choosing to move indirectly through the division of labor to place man in a position to participate once again in his own salvation.

Given these points of symmetry, it should not be hard to see how the juxtaposition of pride and avarice, the conception of the first class, and the idea of Protestant *Bildung* become "meaningfully related" at this point in Hegel's work.[18] All "cluster" around the question of how to convert natural *Sittlichkeit* into absolute *Sittlichkeit*. That question, in turn, hinged on another, equally important consideration – how to convince *homo religiosus* that political activity could be envisaged as a legitimate extension of, rather than an illegitimate substitute for, Christian piety.[19] The answer to both questions, Hegel discovered, lay first in equating the first class's cultivation of pride with the political education of a godly people and then in explaining the resultant political activity in terms of a theology of history in which political activity was defined as a moment in a pilgrimage that, in the end, would lead *homo religiosus* beyond the political itself.[20] Let us say, then, that Hegel's conception of the interplay between the first class, pride, and politics was "architectonic" in that it sought to define political activity in terms of a religious vision of the telos of man that was itself informed by a very specific theology of history – that of the divine economy.[21]

Having said all of this, we need now to ask a decisive question: what political implications follow from Hegel's placement of the first class in this conceptual framework? Though the question has drawn the attention of many fine scholars, it has, to my mind, never been answered properly, and that is because scholars all too often fail to see that Hegel's political thought – at least during this period of his life – is not, strictly speaking, *political* at all.[22] It is socioeconomic on the one hand and socioreligious on the other – that is, Hegel's conception of the political arises from, and is basically governed by, the interplay between the religious and economic aspects of his thought. And since the first class is presented as the living objective expression of that interplay it is to the first class – in its prepolitical setting – that we must look if we are to make sense of Hegel's conception of politics.

The proper place to begin that inquiry is with the realization that Hegel's conception of the first class is designed to solve the problem of religious–economic overlay in his thought. On the one hand, its origins are explained in terms of the dynamic of the division of labor principle. In addition, its function is explained in terms of Hegel's perception of its relation to other social groups. On the other hand, however, Hegel's first class is also made to be religiously aware of society's overall need for a new binding social ethos. On this score, Hegel conceived of the first class as "in the *arche*," as a group whose task was to initiate public discussion about what the *telos* of politically oriented action should be.[23] We know, however, that the concerns of Hegel's first class were not those of its bourgeois rivals – its concerns were those of a militant minority group that was struggling against the overall bourgeois value orientation of the system of natural *Sittlichkeit*. In that sense, Hegel charged the first class with a double task: first of creating a new socioreligious "counterwill" to that of the bourgeoisie;[24] and then of giving that counterwill a political focus that was consistent with his religious conception of true *Sittlichkeit*.[25]

Still if Hegel presents the first class as the initiator of political discussion, he does not designate the first class as the sanctioning agent of what has been initiated.[26] This, I think, is of the utmost importance. Clearly Hegel meant for the initiatives of the first class to receive "confirmation" from the collectivity qua deliberative socio-religious body before they could be sanctioned as appropriate vehicles for realizing the *telos* of the social whole.[27]

Again, the overall symmetry of Hegel's argument is striking. In Hegel's thought the first class stands to the collectivity in the same way that God stands to man in the synergist's conception of the theology of the divine economy.[28] Both have pedagogic purposes; both are dealing with men whose horizons of expectations are historically circumscribed; both insist on a gradualist and voluntarist approach to conversion; both proceed toward the goal of collective salvation indirectly – God by way of a series of dispensations in history, one of which is linked to the division of labor principle; the first class by accepting the sovereignty of the people and by recognizing that any attempt to bypass the collectivity would violate the principle of self-realizing teleology; both are committed to assimilationism and are, for that reason, critical of "enthusiasts" who believe man can "become God" by way of some mystical and direct identification with Him; and, finally, both are committed to reformist rather than vitalistic programs of religious renewal. On those terms the first class has a pedagogic as well as a redemptive purpose: it is the carrier and symbol of the *telos* of *homo religiosus* in history.

In this context, it is most important to realize just how Hegel expected the first class to accomplish its mission. Clearly, he meant for his audience to construe the first class as a "new order of men" – independent of established political and religious groups and institutions.[29] Freed from "need," this group was to symbolize what was possible in the way of collective ethico-religious self-realization if "indifference" toward material well-being were to become institutionalized as the dominant social ethos. Along those lines, Hegel casts the first class in the image of a spiritual aristocracy; but from what he has told us about enthusiasts in religion and romantics in philosophy,[30] it is clear he meant for the first class to pursue its ends according to the moderate pedagogical principles of *spiritum intelligentiae* rather than according to the mystical principles of *spiritum prophetiae*.[31]

In this, he assumed a position we have seen was common to Joachim, Coccejus, and Bengel.[32] And because he aligned himself with this pedagogical tradition of eschatological thinking, it would be a mistake to equate him with the kind of esoteric mysticism one so often encounters among his romantic contemporaries. Granted, Hegel's conception of the first class parallels the romantic conception of the artist in that both are "out of season" with their times and both are in some sense "free floaters." But there is a major difference here; whereas Hegel presents the first class as an agent through whom the Word of God passes, the romantic presents the artist as a privileged soul whose task it is, in M. H. Abrams' terms, to offer the world an "index" of his own "personality."[33] In the first case, the first class serves as the agent of the truth of the Word, of a truth it does not invent, but reveals for the consideration of others. In the second case, the artist creates a truth he wishes others to accept. Hegel's first class, in other words, wished to lead, to be in the *arche*, not to rule in any personal way.[34] It wished to instruct man in the essentials of Christian pride and collective piety and it did so by reminding him, in a public fashion, that he had been created in the image and likeness of God.

Ever troubled by "cults of personality," Hegel cast his conception of the first class in impersonal terms – that is, he conceived of the activity of the first class in terms of a religious vocation. It was called to office to point the collectivity away from the bad infinity of natural *Sittlichkeit* and toward the religious promise of true *Sittlichkeit* and self-realizing teleology.[35] As such, the class was a guide to, an "instrument" for, and a symbol of, the collective *telos* of a godly people.[36]

It is, therefore, of the utmost importance to differentiate Hegel's conception of the first class's cultivation of pride from the romantic conception of the artist's creative ability. Quite simply, they are not the same thing; one is Pelagian, the other pantheistic.[37] To put the difference in M. H. Abrams' terms, Hegel's concern with pride is more "pragmatic" than "expressive."[38] He is more concerned with directing and turning his *audience's* attention to politics than with offering the world an "index" to his *own* personality. Hegel, in short, is much more a collectivist in a socioreligious sense than an individualist in an aesthetic sense.

Understood in these terms, the position Hegel assigns the first class seems to be informed by the kind of religiopedagogical considerations that are so prominent in the theology of the divine economy. As a class it is to represent to the collectivity the potential the collectivity itself has for becoming a godly people – for becoming an "instrument" of God.[39] Lessing, Hegel's hero, understood this very well. In *Education* he was able to equate revelation and education by endowing à la Hegel's first class a select group of teachers with the patience and wisdom that would be necessary if a proper foundation were to be prepared for the collectivity gradually and collectively to enter the "third age" of religious history.[40] This group, Lessing insisted, must offer "guiding" clues to the collectivity on the destiny of the human race;[41] and it must do so, he continued, without succumbing to either enthusiasm or despair.[42] In soteriological matters, Lessing noted, men could not be rushed – could not be made "at one stroke. . .worthy of their third age."[43] God understood this – hence the economy of his revelations, his patience, and his willingness to deal with men indirectly. Lessing and Hegel, I think, meant for mankind's educators to internalize that divine model of education and redemption and to make it the basis of their vocation – which is to say *Bildung* and true *Sittlichkeit* were united by the idea of the divine economy qua theology of history.

In this respect, it is crucial to Hegel's argument that the *nobility* of the first class, its dignity and moral courage, be *recognized* by the collectivity.[44] When that happens, when a reciprocal relation of service and recognition arises, respectively, between the first class and the collectivity, then a "people" is founded and a consensus formed as to what overall meaning and purpose the collective will should have. Rousseau's conception of a "people" is similarly informed;[45] and Ferguson's effort to differentiate "the rule by which [a people's] will is collected" from the mere movement of a people as a "crowd" exhibits the same concern.[46] Like Hegel, then, Rousseau and Ferguson were concerned more with constituting a godly people in a socioreligious (i.e., prepolitical) sense than with making a case for a specific set of political institutions in a utopian sense. Put slightly differently, the three were more concerned pedagogically with turning men toward the pursuit of godly goals than politically with identifying a specific set of political institutions as divine.

The first class, then, has a twofold function in Hegel's thought: pedagogically, and in the original sense of the Latin word *classicus*, the first was to be socially "imitated" because it represented excellence (*Vollkommenheit*) in an ethico-religious sense;[47] and politically, in the sense of the moral authority of the proverbial wise man, it was to "guide" the discussion about the political agenda so that the sovereignty of the people could assert itself in an informed way.[48] Either way, however, the commitment of the first class was to an educational process in which communication about moral values passed between the first class and the collectivity.[49]

To say this, of course, is not to deny that there is a tension here between the moral authority of the first class, its endeavor "to moralize" the collectivity, and the supposed independence of the collectivity as the sanctioning agent of the moral initiatives of the first class.[50] A danger clearly exists that the promotion of *Bildung* in a theological sense will turn into a system of indoctrination in an ideological sense.[51] But the way Hegel has presented the first class suggests another reading. Insofar as the first class is successful in propagating the values it wishes to institutionalize among a people, it renders its own function relative to the collectivity more and more superfluous.[52] As the moral character of the collectivity develops, the authority of the first class recedes from view as the idea of "all in all" becomes reality. One could say, therefore, that the religious "calling" of the first class involves three things: gaining a public hearing for principles of Protestant *Bildung*; winning through debate public recognition for these principles such that they become the motor force of a self-sustaining civil piety; and monitoring the progress of the collectivity as it seeks to translate the theology of the divine economy into principles of collective action.

Here again a double perspective is needed to understand Hegel's argument. If many scholars have treated the first class as part of Hegel's love of antiquity, we can also explain the role the first class plays in terms of a Protestant conception of how *gnosis* is translated into *pistis*. To see this, we need to remind ourselves briefly about the history of the idea of statesmanship in Western thought. First, we need to remember that for Plato and Cicero the political wisdom of the "statesman" was often associated with "godlike" men who, while not holding political office themselves, exercised enormous influence on politics because they were regarded as instruments of "divine intervention" in history.[53]

Second, it is worth recalling what Rousseau did with the idea of statesmanship in his work. Take, for example, Rousseau's discussion of the Great Legislator in *Social Contract*.[54] As Rousseau tells us there, his concern with the Great Legislator stemmed from his interest in "the act by which a people becomes a people."[55] And, as he saw it, this "act of association" was "necessarily" prepolitical in character: it constituted "the true basis of society" upon which specifically political sets of obligations were then to be erected.[56] The Great Legislator for Rousseau, then, was one who dared "to undertake the founding of a people" from a point within the collectivity itself.[57] In that context, Rousseau carefully points out, the Legislator represents neither the "magistracy" nor the principle of "sovereignty," but a principle of "wisdom" independent of both.[58] Hence, Rousseau's statement that the Great Legislator must accomplish his task with "an authority that amounts to nothing."[59] In a word, all the Great Legislator has to recommend him to others is his "moral" authority.

To give substance to what he is talking about, Rousseau links the idea of the Great Legislator to the "images of authority" that have grown up around the figures of Moses, Muhammad, and Calvin.[60] Great Legislators all, the three were for Rousseau "fathers of nations."[61] But, as Rousseau notes, all three were also founders of a godly people in a religious sense.[62] They were "chiefs," not "masters,"[63] men who not only could "make the Gods speak," but also make them "be believed,"[64] They were not "lucky imposters" so much as geniuses whose "wisdom" made it possible for a people both to be founded and to endure.[65] And by enduring a people proves both that it has internalized the wisdom of the legislator and that it has made that wisdom the basis of "public morality."[66] The internalization and socialization of wisdom, in turn, offers proof (i.e., *pistis*) of the legitimacy of the legislator's mission.[67] The conscience (i.e., *gnosis*) of the legislator, as it were, has been collectivized in the form of a people whose voice is now that of God.[68]

What Rousseau says here about the Great Legislator tells us a good deal about the function and purpose of Hegel's first class. In both cases, the function of each is to found a people; and in both cases the wisdom of each is presented as a dispensation "given by God" to mankind at a specific moment in history. What is interesting about this line of argument is that it fits in nicely with a main ethico-religious concern of certain groups of Protestants in the history of Europe.[69] From Zwinglianism, through Calvinism and Puritanism, to Pietism, there had been a tendency among Protestant pastors, in Troeltsch's words, to compare "themselves with the Prophets of the Old Testament and their mission to the people."[70] According to Troeltsch, these pastors wished to control "public life" after "the manner of the Prophets."[71] Claiming to be the "instruments" God was using to disseminate His Word,[72] these pastors regarded the *Cri au Peuple* as their special calling and as the appropriate basis of collective religious life.[73]

What brought the preacher and the people together, of course, was the conviction that the *proof* of the preacher's election lay less in the self-proclaimed power of his personal *faith* than in the public's *belief* that what he was preaching was true.[74] *Listening* to a preacher did not necessarily mean *believing* what he said; but if one believed what one heard then *obedience* to his *office*, legitimation of his function, was supposed to follow. Put another way, the *gnosis* of the word became the *pistis* of the collectivity when the public trumpeting of the pastor was consented to and acted upon by those who had gathered together in God's name and on a voluntary basis to form a godly people. Obligation to the Word, in short, presupposed legitimacy of office; it did not entail, however, acceptance of the divinity of the preacher. And that was because the people had itself become a socioreligious "office" with a single "voice" informing it.

To speak once again in terms of inversion and conversion, one could say that in Hegel's thought the *gnosis* of the first class stood to the *pistis* of the collectivity as the *status* of the first class qua the potentiality of the collectivity for becoming a godly people stood to the *actus* of the collectivity qua its actualization of the *gnosis* of the first class.[75] More simply put, *gnosis* and *pistis* could be said to constitute two different moments in a realm of socioreligious discourse in which the object of intersubjective communication, of *Bildung*, was the establishment of a godly people who would possess a single conscience and will.[76]

In this realm of *conditional* or regulative discourse, the identity of *bürger* and Christian was meant to be one[77] – that is, the action of both was meant to be governed by the principles of *Bildung* and "civil piety." Those principles, we know, were informed by a theology of history – and it is Hegel's commitment to that theology, especially to its voluntarist aspects, that required him to bring the *gnosis* of the first class and the *pistis* of the collectivity into a reciprocal relationship. If piety and learning, *pistis* and *gnosis*, were to coexist among a Protestant people, then this, he thought, was an adequate socio-religious way of expressing the whole of the relationship.

Overall, then, Hegel's conception of the first class resonates with the pedagogic and socioreligious overtones of the religious tradition we have been discussing throughout this study. To that end, both are concerned with ethical life on a practical, collective level. They are "pragmatically" oriented in a Pelagian sense, not "expressively" oriented in a pantheistic sense.[78] The task of both, moreover, is to remind the collectivity of the heroic effort that is required when a godly people voluntarily commits itself to the "progressive sanctification" of the world.[79] And if that task entails turning the attention of Protestants to their political responsibilities, that was just another way of announcing that it was time for them to reclaim the state in the name of a godly people.[80] Finally, both take frequent recourse in a theology of history that provided in the economy of salvation argument incentives for just this kind of Christian activism.[81] And both tie this activism to a "new order of men" that is to persuade man that "active holiness" is a legitimate way of realizing his telos as *homo religiosus*.[82]

Understood this way, Hegel's political conceptions – really, his millenarian hopes for the growth and increasing maturity of a Protestant people – derive more from the tradition of covenant theology in a religious sense that from natural law in a contractual, secular sense. There is, of course, nothing unusual about this – Calvinists of one sort or another had for years been interpreting contractual relations within society in the religious light of covenant theology.[83] They wished, as it were, to organize politico-legal obligations around the idea of the covenanting people rather than to have a covenanting people absorbed into a secular, pluralistic, constitutional structure.[84]

The difference is not unimportant, and for several reasons. First, it means Hegel is more concerned with the founding of a people, with the "enactment" of a constitution, than with constitutional specifics per se.[85] As Rousseau has noted, there is a difference between the "sacred" bonds on which a "people" (i.e., society) is founded and the laws that govern the collectivity once a "founding" has taken place.[86] Hence, the point of envisaging the first class's mission in prepolitical, socioreligious terms.

Second, it is precisely because Hegel's politics is rooted in covenant theology that he requires the first class to submit its initiatives to the people.[87] According to covenant tradition, the third dispensation from God to man was meant to be collective and voluntartist. Indeed, if the idea of a self-realizing teleology were to have historically specific content, the sovereignty of the people had to be recognized in a "procedural" sense. Thus, the prepolitical pedagogic purpose of the first class's attempt patiently to cultivate *Bildung* and the disposition to civil piety among a Protestant people.[88]

A further corollary of this last point is that Hegel, at least during these years, was reluctant to talk about politics in a specific institutional sense. Because he refused to indulge in utopian speculation about politics, Hegel had to leave political arrangements as such to the play of circumstances.[89] His procedural commitment, that is, obliged him to allow for gaps to exist between "initiative" and "debate" on the one hand and between "debate" and "result" on the other.[90] Putting the matter this way, in turn, required Hegel to define public discussion of society's political agenda in what Lovejoy would call "adjectival" terms.[91] Hegel had to acknowledge that the value of political debate lay less in what was attained by a people as a result of political discussion than in the qualities it attached to itself for having taken the time to debate political issues at all. Adjectival politics, in other words, is supposed to enhance a people's self-esteem – pride, in Hegel's terms.[92] The argument is that from the act of political discussion itself agents are supposed to become more self-conscious about their own purposes and direction. They become aware of their freedom and take political responsibility for it. They have arrived, in short, at the "moment" when self-realizing teleology is a real historico-religious possibility for them.[93] Hegel's conception of the politics of pride speaks to that "moment of voluntarism" in the life course of "*homo religiosus*."[94]

If covenant theology explains Hegel's procedural commitment to the idea of the sovereignty of the people, it also explains how and why he proposed to "protect" the "people" against itself.[95] Like Rousseau before him, Hegel wished to win collective consent for the initiatives of the first class (Great Legislator), but he did not wish to oblige the first class to be implicated in whatever the people consented to. This, of course, was no problem for a thinker who had already contested bourgeois hegemony in an ideological sense and who had always operated with a highly idealized conception of what a people substantially was supposed to be. All that was necessary was to distinguish between the idea of "a people" and that of a "mass."[96] Indeed, one could say that Hegel conceived of a people, religiously characterized, as the carrier of Christian *gnosis* in the world.[97] In that sense, the idea of a people was associated for him with standards of collective excellence.[98] At this point in the argument, though, that excellence was meant to express itself more in action than in thought — that is, Hegel's notion of a people was an "as if" conception.[99] It was conditional, regulative, and meant to express a "supersensible purposiveness" that was hypothetical in a teleological sense precisely because of the voluntarist theological convictions that informed it.[100]

All the same, there is an obvious problem here. Even if we allow Hegel to distinguish his substantive from his procedural commitment to the people, he must confront the possibility that on some occasion the two might coincide. The "legitimate" state in a procedural sense could be the "good" state in a substantive sense.[101] If the first class were successful in its pedagogic attempt to moralize society in the name of theology, it would seem to follow that regenerated society would then seek to translate the theological values upon which it was founded into political terms. And if that were the case, the state might very well be seen, as Perry Miller has put it, as "a kind of second incarnation, a Messiah fathered by God and born of the people."[102] In that context, God could be said to have created the state indirectly — through the agency of a godly people exercising its freedom.[103] Still, it would be God's state — the political analogue of a regenerated people who, while striving collectively to assimilate to God, would very likely be intolerant of any diversity within its ranks.

We must ask, then, whether this kind of politico-religious oppressiveness is the inevitable consequence (or price) of assigning first the people, then the state, to an active role in realizing the kingdom of God on earth.[104] Is an authoritarian theocracy the result of translating the religious values of covenant theology first into socio-religious and then into political terms? The answer to these questions, I think, is yes and no. Yes, in the obvious sense that in Hegel's "lexical series" the activity of the state was meant to be seen as a corporate registration of the collective will of a Protestant people[105] No, for two different reasons. First, because in

Hegel's scheme hierarchy existed without arbitrariness and subordination. The state was not a substitute for socio-religious community so much as an extension of it. It dotted the "I," as it were. And second, what permitted Hegel to envisage "state and society" in terms of congruency was his belief that each by itself was but an objective "moment" in a larger theology of history that unfolded according to the logic of the divine economy.

Thus the state was assimilated to the economy of salvation argument. It, too, had a special role to play in the soteriological process – that is, the possibilities for activism on the part of the state were limited by "substantive" (i.e., teleological or supersensible purposive) considerations After implicating the state as well as society in the soteriological process, Hegel had to expand his theology of history, expand it beyond the two moments of objective experience itself. That was the only way to safeguard against the state proclaiming itself to be the Kingdom of God on earth. Hence, Hegel's need to transcend the state, to have recourse to a "teleological architectonic" whose informing vision of man's *telos* was still that of the theology of the divine economy. Only this time, fulfillment of that economy was presented in postpolitical terms – in terms of what Hegel called "absolute Spirit."

It is well known that Hegel developed the conception of absolute Spirit in *Phenomenology* and that he began to work with that idea shortly after writing the essays on *Natural Law* and *Ethical Life*.[106] In these essays, we have been, Hegel had been dealing with the state–society conceptual problem in the textual context of an argument about *Sittlichkeit* and its relation to the dynamics of objective experience. Moreover, there was no mention in those essays of absolute Spirit. Why, then, the change? Because development of the idea of absolute Spirit enabled Hegel to finesse several problems that confronted him at this stage in his development.[107]

First of all, the idea gave him an opportunity to avoid having to vouchsafe the state as a religious end in itself. Absolute Spirit, in that sense, was a final court of appeal for the "conscience" of any Christian who felt oppressed by the godly people in its socio-religious or politico-religious incarnations.[108] At the same time, though, as a disembodied set of "terminal values" that transcended the state but not the world, absolute Spirit constituted a religious (some would say a cultural) resource from which the first class could draw to make the religious case against "bourgeois" values.[109]

Here, of course, a great deal of confusion arises. The implication is that absolute Spirit can be at one and the same time a postpolitical religio-cultural defense against theocracy and, when retrieved by the first class, the basis for a prepolitical, socioreligious assault on bourgeois materialism.[110] Can Hegel have it both ways? I think so, primarily because in both cases Hegel used the idea of absolute Spirit to check a perceived threat to religious voluntarism, first in a collective, then in an individual, sense. Just as bourgeois materialism inhibited the recollectivization of a godly people, so religious collectivism, at least when institutionalized, undermined the theological voluntarism upon which the idea of self-realizing teleology was based. Man qua individual could not, on Hegel's terms, be forced to be free. The meaning of absolute Spirit, in other words, depends upon the context in which it is used. It can offer either consolidation for the religious "heretic" or cultural "outsider" in a postpolitical context or incentive for socioreligious reformers in a prepolitical context. On those terms, the idea of absolute Spirit, religiously characterized, insists on the one hand on the integrity of the conscience of the individual believer and on the other hand on the need for religious collectivism organized along the lines of Christian gnosis.[111] In both instances the watchwords are voluntarism, patience, toleration, persuasion, and consent – the core values of the Protestant conception of *Bildung*.

What is crucial to realize here, I think, is that Hegel never meant for the two functions of absolute Spirit to be collapsed into one another, because the result would be an all-too-subjectivist rendering of the relationship between the conscience of the individual believer and the gnosis of the collectivity. Believing and knowing, intuitions and concepts, were not the same for Hegel.[112] That is precisely why his conception of *Bildung*, religiously considered, is simultaneously the means and the end of his Protestant activism. It also accounts for the so-called circular quality of his thought.[113]

Despite all the qualifications Hegel introduced to protect against extremism in either individualist or collectivist senses, interpreters of his political thought continue to insist on rendering it in "either–or" terms. Along these lines, two basic criticisms have emerged. Eric Voegelin, for example, regards Hegel as the main theorist of Gnostic intellectualism.[114] According to him, Hegel's designation of the first class as a spiritual, elite group is an invitation to authoritarianism and to the ideological politics of the intelligentsia. The argument is that Hegel meant to place the collectivity in the perpetual tutelage of the first class – Voegelin sees Hegel's first class less as a selfless instrument of collective education in an open-minded religious sense than as an agent of ideological indoctrination in a closed-minded political sense.[115]

Related to this view, but internally at odds with it, is the argument that Hegel's conception of the first class is an invitation to totalitarianism, to the politics of mass movements.[116] The claim here is that the first class's attempt to moralize and mobilize the collectivity blurred the line between theology and ideology – led, that is, to a dangerous confusion of religious revivalism and popular political activism. The result: the institutionalization from "below" rather than from "above" of "civil religion" among a people.[117]

Clearly, if we isolate aspects of Hegel's thought there is something to be said for these criticisms. Each singles out a "moment" in Hegel's thought and offers it as the key to understanding his political values. But in order to present Hegel this way critics have had first to freeze, and then to generalize from, individual moments in his thought. As we have seen, however, this is a procedure Hegel did not countenance and would not have countenanced. He was much too moderate for that kind of extremism.

A good way to see this is to compare his "typically German" way of thinking with some of the startlingly similar things Tocqueville said in *Democracy in America* about the relation between religion and politics in the modern world. "In 'Ages of Faith,'" Tocqueville writes, religion instills a "general habit of behaving with the future in view."[118] In "skeptical ages," by contrast, when "the light of faith grows dim, man's range of vision grows more circumscribed," with the result that he falls back "into a complete and brutish indifference about the future."[119] In this context, Tocqueville continues, man becomes impatient and impulsive, prone to indulgence of his "ephemeral and casual desires."[120]

Having said this, Tocqueville then offers a "long-term" strategy to "philosophers and men in power" who might wish to regenerate society in a moral sense.[121] To this end, he advises them to "strive to set a distant aim as the object of human efforts."[122] If they are successful in giving "men back that interest in the future," men will again "become accustomed to foresee from afar" – that is, "they will *gradually* be led without noticing it themselves toward religious belief."[123] This, he says, in a telling phrase, would result in "bringing mankind back, by a long and roundabout path, to a state of faith."[124]

Somewhat later in *Democracy*, Tocqueville is more specific. Again, in typically German fashion, he complains about how "the constant trivial preoccupations of private life" were impeding "the progress of the body social" toward "greatness."[125] He concludes this line of argument with a statement that could easily have been penned by Kant or Hegel:

Thus far from thinking that we should counsel humility to our contemporaries, I wish men would try to give them a higher idea of themselves and of humanity; humility is far from healthy for them; what they lack most, in my view, is pride. I would gradually surrender several of our petty virtues for that one vice.[126]

This, of course, is what Hegel asked the first class to do – to begin to educate modern man to his collective moral responsibilities. For this,

Tocqueville thought a "new political science" would be necessary.[127] Hegel, whose views on these matters were similar to Tocqueville's, was not so sure, for his conception of the first class's political responsibilities was cast in "nonpolitical" terms that had been prevalent among Protestants since the Puritans.[128] He did this, though, less to escape from politics in a Lutheran sense than to prepare people for participatory political responsibilities in a Calvinist sense.[129] Rousseau had done this with Émile; Hegel meant for the first class to do it with the German *Bürger* who, at odds with himself, was undecided whether to seize the opportunity to indulge his bourgeois appetites or to heed the liberal Christian call to "civil piety."

It is in this sense – and only in this sense – that Hegel may be designated the philosopher of the "bourgeois Christian world."[130] That he was that world's "last" philosopher should not be held against him; for since Hegel wrote what he did, history has gone another way. But only because history has gone the way that it has is Hegel still very much with us today, both in the East and in the West. The idea of absolute Spirit continues to furnish both camps with ideological resources with which to engage the other. Whether that should be taken as a testimony to, or a criticism of, Hegel need not detain us here: it is not a question a historically oriented study of Hegel can answer.

Abbreviations

AE	F. Schiller, *On the Aesthetic Education of Man*, E. Wilkinson and L. Willoughby, eds. (Oxford, 1967)
AHR	*American Historical Review*
ANCL	*Ante-Nicene Christian Library*
Anmk.	"Anmerkenung" to Adam Ferguson's *Grundsätze der Moralphilosophie*, C. Garve trans. (Leipzig, 1772)
BP	G. W. F. Hegel, "The Berne Plan of 1794," in H. S. Harris, *Hegel's Development* (Oxford, 1972), pp. 508–510.
Brf.	J. Hoffmeister, ed., *Briefe von und an Hegel*, v. 1 (Hamburg, 1952)
BWKG	*Blätter für Württembergische Kirchengeschichte*
CH	*Church History*
CJ	Immanuel Kant, *Critique of Judgement*, J. Meredith, trans. (Oxford, 1952)
CP	J. V. Andreae, *Christianopolis*, F. Held, ed. and trans. (New York, 1916)
CR	J. Franklin, ed., *Constitutionalism and Resistance in the Sixteenth Century* (New York, 1965)
CTJ	*Calvin Theological Journal*
Cultures	C. Geertz, *The Interpretation of Cultures* (New York, 1973)
DHE	J. Hoffmeister, ed., *Dokumente zu Hegels Entwicklung* (Stuttgart, 1936)
DP	O. Ritschl, *Dogmengeschichte des Protestantismus*, 4 v. (Leipzig, 1908–1927)
DVLG	*Deutsche Vierteljahrsschrift für Literaturwissenschaft und Geistesgeschichte*
ES	N. Hoyt and T. Cassirer, eds., *Encyclopedia Selections* (Indianapolis, 1965)
Essays	A. O. Lovejoy, *Essays in the History of Ideas* (New York, 1948)
Ethical	G. W. F. Hegel, "System of Ethical Life," in *Hegel's "System of Ethical Life" and "First Philosophy of Spirit,"* H. Harris and T. Knox, trans. (Albany, 1979)

ETW	G. W. F. Hegel, *On Christianity. Early Theological Writings*, T. Knox, trans. (New York, 1961)
Exo.	M. Walzer, *Exodus and Revolution* (New York, 1985)
Founda.	Q. Skinner, *The Foundations of Modern Political Thought*, v. 2 (Cambridge, England, 1978)
GA	K. Holl, *Gesammelte Aufsätze zur Kirchengeschichte*, v. 3 (Darmstadt, 1965)
GGR	*Geist und Geschichte der Reformation*, Festgabe für H. Ruckert (Berlin, 1966)
GNET	E. Hirsch, *Geschichte der neuern evangelischen Theologie*, 5 v. (Güterslohe 1949–1954)
HD	H. S. Harris, *Hegel's Development* (Oxford, 1972)
HPR	D. Christensen, ed., *Hegel and the Philosophy of Religion* (The Hague, 1970)
HPW	G. W. F. Hegel, *Hegel's Political Writings*, T. Knox, trans. (Oxford, 1964)
HS	*Hegel-Studien*
HT	*History and Theory*
HTR	*Harvard Theological Review*
Instr.	"Instruction," in M. Leube, *Geschichte des Tübingen Stifts*, v. 2 (Stuttgart, 1930), pp. 218–232
Insts.	J. Calvin, *Institutes of the Christian Religion*, 2 v., J. Allen, trans. (Philadelphia, 1945)
JBS	*Journal of British Studies*
JEH	*Journal of Ecclesiastical History*
JHI	*The Journal of the History of Ideas*
JMH	*The Journal of Modern History*
JTS	*Journal of Theological Studies*
Kirche	H. Hermelink, *Geschichte der evangelischen Kirche in Württemberg von der Reformation bis zur Gegenwart* (Stuttgart, 1949)
KOH	Immanuel Kant, *Kant: On History*, L. Beck, ed. (New York, 1963)
KS	*Kant-Studien*
Law	G. W. F. Hegel, *The Scientific Ways of Treating Natural Law, Its Place in Moral Philosophy, and its Relation to the Positive Science of Law*, T. Knox, trans. (Philadelphia, 1975)
Lessing	H. E. Allison, *Lessing and the Enlightenment* (Ann Arbor, 1966)
LTW	G. Lessing, *Lessing's Theological Writings*, H. Chadwick, trans. (Stanford, 1956)
Mind	P. Miller, *The New England Mind. The Seventeenth Century* (New York, 1939)
MP	*Modern Philology*
OH	E. Voegelin, *Order and History*, v. 1 (London, 1956)
Order	D. Little, *Religion, Order and Law* (Chicago, 1969)
PD	P. J. Spener, *Pia Desideria*, T. Tappert, ed. and trans. (Philadelphia, 1964)

PH	G. W. F. Hegel, *The Philosophy of History*, J. Sibree, trans. (New York, 1956)
PMLA	*Publications of the Modern Language Association*
Politics	J. G. A. Pocock, *Politics, Language and Time* (New York, 1973)
PP	*Past and Present*
Protestant	K. Barth, *Protestant Theology in the Nineteenth Century* (Valley Forge, 1973)
PTM	C. Montesquieu, *The Political Theory of Montesquieu*, M. Richter, trans. (Cambridge, England, 1977)
RWL	Immanuel Kant, *Religion Within the Limits of Reason Alone*, T. Greene and H. Hudson, trans. (New York, 1960)
Saints	M. Walzer, *The Revolution of the Saints* (New York, 1973)
SCJ	*Sixteenth Century Journal*
SE	R. Sher, *Church and University in the Scottish Enlightenment* (Princeton, 1985)
SHR	M. Reidel, *Studien zu Hegels Rechtsphilosophie* (Frankfurt, 1969)
Soc.	F. E. Cranz, "The Development of Augustine's Ideas on Society Before the Donatist Controversy," *Harvard Theological Review*, v. 47 (1954)
SR	*Social Research*
ST	E. Troeltsch, *The Social Teaching of the Christian Churches*, v. 2, O. Wyon, trans. (New York, 1931)
TC	J. Arndt, *True Christianity*, 6 v., A. Boehm, trans. (Boston, 1809)
TE	G. W. F. Hegel, "The Tübingen Essay of 1793," in H. S. Harris, *Hegel's Development* (Oxford, 1972), pp. 481–507
TMM	J. G. A. Pocock, *The Machiavellian Moment* (Princeton, 1975)
WVL	*Württembergische Vierteljahrschrift für Landesgeschicht*
ZKG	*Zeitschrift für Kirchengeschichte*

Notes

Preface

1. Max Weber, *The Theory of Social and Economic Organization*, T. Parsons and A. Henderson, trans. (New York, 1947), pp. 94–96. Note especially Parsons' note, p. 94.
2. In the first case one gets the conventional Kant–Fichte–Schelling–Hegel sequence; in the second case, what George Kelly has called "an intelligent defense" against this tendency. See his *Idealism, Politics and History* (Cambridge, England, 1969), p. 303. I have more to say about the inadequacies of the conventional sequence in the Introduction.
3. W. Wallace, *The Logic of Hegel*, W. Wallace, trans. (Oxford, 1874), p. xiii. For surveys of the diversity see W. Beyer, *Hegel Bilder*, 3rd ed. (Berlin, 1970), and H. Ottman, *Individuum und Gemeinschaft bei Hegel*, v. 1 (New York, 1977). Old, though still useful, is H. Rosenberg's youthful essay, "Zur Geschichte der Hegelauffassung," in R. Haym, *Hegel und seine Zeit*, 2nd ed., H. Rosenberg, ed. (Leipzig, 1927).
4. The return to the "innocence" of the text has recently been championed by A. Bloom, "The Study of Texts," in *Political Theory and Political Education*, M. Richter, ed. (Princeton, 1980), esp. p. 127.
5. I have found these assumptions stated in the following "textualist" literature: P. Riceour, "The Model of the Text: Meaningful Action Considered as a Text," in *SR*, 38, 3 (1971); H. White, "The Historical Text as Literary Artifact," in *Clio*, v. 3, 3 (1974); A. Bloom, "Study"; and M. White, "Why Annalists of Ideas Should Be Analysts of Ideas," in *Georgia Review*, v. 29, 4 (1975).
6. On the general issue of scholarship and interpretation, Bloom, "Study," pp. 127 and 131, seems to be quite willing to accept the "denigration of. . . historical scholarship" that is implicit in his position. For intelligent responses to this presumption, see J. G. A. Pocock, "Political Ideas as Historical Events: Political Philosophies as Historical Actions," in *Political Thought and Political Education*, M. Richter, ed. (Princeton, 1980); Q. Skinner, "Some Problems in the Analysis of Political Thought and Action,"

297

in *Political Theory*, v. 2, 3 (1974), esp. p. 282; and R. A. Jones, "On Understanding a Sociological Classic," in *American Journal of Sociology*, v. 83, 2 (1977).

7. Ricoeur, "Text," p. 548.

8. C. Geertz, *Cultures*, Chapter 1. Geertz's work, I think, is invaluable for intellectual history. See, e.g., n. 10 below.

9. In their haste to explain Hegel's thought in terms of his Prussian connections, scholars too often forget this. For the necessary corrections, see the essays by T. M. Knox, S. Avineri, and W. Kaufmann in *Hegel's Poitical Philosophy*, W. Kaufmann, ed. (New York, 1970). Above all, see E. Weil, *Hegel et L'État* (Paris, 1974). For those who have not made this mistake, see n. 29 to the Introduction.

10. Here an awareness of the cultural diversity of the Germanys in the eighteenth century is crucial. Indeed, how to handle the problem of "German particularism" requires some thought. To this end, I have found Geertz, *Cultures*, very useful because "thick description" is best used in "confined contexts" (p. 23) in which "small facts speak to large issues" – that is, in contexts that allow us to "generalize" within a case study rather than "across cases" (p. 26).

11. As I shall point out shortly (n. 15 below), a *setting* is not the whole of the context. I borrowed the concept from A. MacIntyre, *After Virtue* (Notre Dame, 1981), p. 192.

12. On the open-endedness of *histoire total*, see J. Hexter's review of Braudel in *JMH*, v. 44, 4 (1972), esp. pp. 510–511 and 530–531.

13. The emphasis on "a" in this sentence is meant to capture the spirit of Geertz's remarks about cultural analysis as "guessing at meanings" (*Cultures*, p. 20). Peter Berger's notion of "plausibility" structures is, perhaps, a more apt way of putting it. See his "A Sociological View of the Secularization of Theology," in *The Journal for the Scientific Study of Religion*, v. 1, 1 (1967), p. 10. I will be offering, therefore, a description of the culture from a certain point of view, not a description of the culture itself.

14. See K. Burke, *A Grammar of Motives* (Berkeley, 1969), pp. 29 and 75–88. As Burke notes, the word "circumference" reminds us that we can place the object of our study (i.e., Hegel) "in contexts of varying scope" (p. 77). In Geertz's terms, it allows us to cut the concept of culture "down to size" (p. 4).

15. To summarize, my conception of Hegel's cultural context has three dimensions. First, there is the "setting" – Old-Württemberg; next, there is what Burke (*Motives*, pp. 26ff) would call the "ancestral" references to down-to-earth Pietism and the Good Old Law; and, finally, there is the "circumference" of the context – the concept of Protestant civil piety that is formed by the interplay between the two ancestral references and that makes the Old-Württemberg setting unique. In saying this I am well aware that I am allowing "traditions" to become part of the larger context. On this, see A. Lockyer, "Traditions as Context in the History of Political Thought," in *Political Studies*, v. 2, 2 (1979); and, above all, R. D. Cumming's extremely useful and erudite *Human Nature and History*, 2 v. (Chicago, 1969), esp. v. 2: n. 118, p. 445.

16. On the "spins" of concepts, see J. Pocock's *Politics, Language and Time* (New York, 1973), Chapter 1, esp. pp. 17–32, and pp. 281–282.

17. Burke, *Motives*, p. 107, is very clear on this: namely, "whereby a part can be taken as consistent with the whole." The idea of "derivation" is another way Burke talks about the problem (pp. 16 and 28).

18. Ibid., p. 26, puts it this way: "the more thorough one is in carrying out [the contextual] enterprise, the more surely [it] opens [itself] to the charge of failing to discuss man 'in himself.'" More recently, C. Tarlton, "Historicity, Meaning, and Revisionism in the Study of Political Thought," *HT*, v. 12, 3 (1973), esp. p. 320, has warned of this danger. I am fully aware of the pitfalls of doing contextual intellectual history. Many of these pitfalls, however, are creations of critics who insist on regarding contextualism as a form of "functional" analysis (e.g., H. White's remarks, *Metahistory* [Baltimore, 1983], pp. 17–19). No doubt there has been a functional–contextual tendency in the "radical" tradition of the sociology of knowledge that goes back to Mannheim's ideologically oriented work. But there is a "moderate" current in the sociology of knowledge that is contextual without being functional. It is, as T. Parsons would have it, only "halfheartedly" functional – which means for me that it sees ideas as relevant to society but reserves judgment as to whether or not ideas in any specific context are functions of societal development. This current has its origins in the work of Max Scheler and Max Weber. It is concerned less with knowledge as socially distorted thought (ideology as a cause or source of intellectual error) than with the way knowledge is used in what Berger and Luckmann have called the "social construction of reality." Weber, it seems to me, was very clear on this point. While recognizing the functionalist tendencies in contextual analysis, he always tried to use contextualism to assess the "motivational situation" of historical actors and to illuminate what he called "the subjective-meaning complex of action" (see his *Theory*, pp. 97–101). "Meaningful," not "causal," relationships were what Weber was trying to establish in much of his work. Recently, E. D. Hirsch, *Validity in Interpretation* (New York, 1967), pp. 86–88; A. I. Melden, *Free Action* (London, 1961), pp. 100–104; and S. Marcus, *Engels, Manchester and the Working Class* (New York, 1974), p. 30, have all argued for a contextualism that is not functionalist. Two influential and intelligent defenses of contextualism may be found in R. Jones, "Classic," and Q. Skinner, "Hermeneutics and the Role of History," in *New Literary History*, v. 7, 1 (1975), esp. pp. 215–216. Exemplary in this regard is J. Dunn's Weberian-inspired study of *The Political Thought of John Locke* (Cambridge, England, 1969). It is exemplary and Weberian because of the relative autonomy it permits Locke's religious ideas to have vis-à-vis his socioeconomic interests.

19. Remarks in J. Shklar's *Men and Citizens* (Cambridge, 1969), pp. 216–218, point in this direction.

20. L. W. Beck, *Early German Philosophy* (Cambridge, 1969), p. 4, has made the same general point: though "genius" may escape the "uniformity" of culture, "the path of . . . escape at least begins from a common . . . stock of ideas and challenges."

21. It should be noted that I am not using "representative" in the sense of

'average type," for what might be taken as the sum total of common traits in the culture of Old-Württemberg. Rather, I am using it in the Weberian sense of a "typical" characteristic of a certain reference group. Used in this way, the concept of a "representative" thinker implies something about the "social distribution" of a culture's public stock of knowledge. That is, as Berger and Luckmann, *The Social Construction of Reality* (New York, 1967), pp. 15, 23, 46, and 77–79, have pointed out, certain forms of public knowledge are "role-specific." In addition, communication theory has shown how in the history of early modern Europe the public stock of knowledge had very definite geographical boundaries – which for our purposes would mean that as a resident of Stuttgart Hegel lived in, and had access to, a communications network very different from the one someone living in the country, just thirty miles away, would have had access to. Thus, it is possible to talk about Hegel as a representative thinker without depriving him either of his uniqueness or of his stature as a thinker. And if we take Hegel as representative in this sense, there seems to be no need to argue the case against those who would have us believe that the study of second-level thinkers somehow brings us closer to the "real" intellectual tendencies of any given cultural epoch. Prominence and typicality need not work at cross-purposes. Put another way, it is not necessarily true that it is better to learn some things about a large group of second-level intellectuals (or about the "intellectual history" of "nonintellectual" classes) than to learn a lot about one strategically placed genius. Weber discusses typicality in *Theory*, pp. 99 and 111, and in "Objectivity in Social Science and Social Policy," in *Methodology of the Social Sciences*, E. Shils and H. Finch, trans. (Glencoe, IL, 1949), pp. 83–84. In this, moreover, I believe I am following Geertz, *Cultures*, p. 14, who writes, "Understanding a people's culture exposes their normalness without reducing their particularity."

22. Cumming, *Human*, passim. I repeat, this is a remarkable, important, and neglected book. What Cumming means by "other studies" are intellectual exposures that create what Burke (*Motives*, p. xix) would regard as "resources of ambiguity" in a thinker's thought. That is, the exposure creates problems for the "derivation" of thought, and, thereby, forces shifts in "contexts" and the "transformation" of thought. Geertz, *Cultures*, p. 27, makes the same point: to wit – "ideas are not created wholly anew in each study; . . . they are adopted from other, related studies, and, refined in the process, applied to new interpretive problems."

23. Though I had worked out my own theory of Hegel's pattern of adjustment before reading Cumming's book, I found Cumming's discussions of Cicero's and Mill's development very helpful in framing this preface. See, esp., v. 2: n. 66, pp. 439–440, and n. 141, p. 447.

24. I have more to say about this in the Introduction.

25. I borrow here from L. Althusser, *Montesquieu, Rousseau, Marx*, B. Brewster, trans. (London, 1972), p. 137. He develops the idea of "modality" in the context of explaining Rousseau's relation to Hobbes.

26. K. Burke, *Motives*, pp. xviii–xix and 192, is apposite here. To wit: "what we want is not terms that avoid ambiguity, but terms that clearly reveal the strategic spots at which ambiguities necessarily arise" (p. xviii); or, again:

"the great departures in human thought can be eventually reduced to a moment where the thinker treats as opposite, key terms formerly considered apposite, or v. v." (p. 192). I realize, of course, that this ambiguity could be considered to be unintentional (see, e.g., A. O. Lovejoy, *Reflections on Human Nature* [Baltimore, 1961], pp. 67–68). I doubt, however, that in Hegel's case it was, because it is the tension created by the ambiguity that he hopes to use to compel his reader to accept the premises of his philosophical argument. I make the case for this in Part III.

27. For more on Hegel's use of the "conditional mode" of discourse, see Part III.

28. I stress this because it is precisely Hegel's refusal to "leap" beyond objective experience that makes him a great *social*, though not necessarily a great *political*, theorist. More on the problem of "leaping" below, Parts II and III.

Introduction

1. See, e.g., G. Santayana, *The German Mind: A Philosophical Diagnosis* (New York, 1968), Chapter II, esp. p. 25, where Hegel is termed a "superior Lutheran"; G. Mure, "Hegel, Luther, and the Owl of Minerva," in *Philosophy*, v. 41, 156 (1966). Much of this goes back to Rosenkranz, *Hegels Leben* (Berlin, 1844), who celebrated Hegel as a Protestant philosopher (p. xxvii). Also of interest: those who note the "Christian" character of Hegel's thought. On this, see K. Löwith, *From Hegel to Nietzsche*, D. Greene, trans. (New York, 1964), esp. p. 47 (Hegel as "the last Christian philosopher"); and J. Findlay, *Hegel: A Re-examination* (New York, 1958), esp. p. 359 (Hegel as "the most Christian of thinkers").

2. A notable exception: L. Beck, *Early German Philosophy*, esp. pp. 88 and 99, who realizes how Calvinistic much Lutheran thought was in the eighteenth century.

3. Not untypical in this regard is H. Marcuse, *Reason and Revolution*, 2nd ed. (Boston, 1954), pp. 14–15. In *Re-examination*, p. 359, Findlay calls Hegel "the philosopher of Reformation 'inwardness,'" a claim that is repeated by W. Walsh, *Hegelian Ethics* (New York, 1969), p. 19.

4. Throughout this study, I shall try to show that in Old-Württemberg Protestants "went public" for religious reasons as well as practical political ones.

5. In the Preface (n. 10), I mentioned the problem of German particularism. This fact has been appreciated by P. Reill, *The German Enlightenment and the Rise of Historicism* (Los Angeles, 1975), p. 4, and by L. Beck, *Early*, p. 5. The point seems to have been lost on B. Cullen. *Hegel's Social and Political Thought: An Introduction* (New York, 1979), p. 1, who hints at the unity of German culture during "the *Goethezeit*."

6. Indispensable for this period of Hegel's life are J. Klaiber, *Hölderlin, Hegel Und Schelling in Ihren schwäbischen Jugendjahren* (Stuttgart, 1877); F. Nicolin, ed., *Der Junge Hegel in Stuttgart* (Marbach, 1970); H. Harris, *HD*; D. Henrich, *Hegel in Kontext* (Frankfurt, 1967), and his "Leutwein über Hegel," in *HS*, v. 2 (1965); and W. Betzendorfer, *Hölderlins Studienjahre im Tübinger Stift* (Heilbronn, 1922).

7. Henrich, "Leutwein," is excellent on the problem of contemporary assessments of Hegel.

8. The source for Christiane's views is a letter she wrote to Hegel's widow in 1832. Part of the text appears in W. Kaufmann, *Hegel: A Reinterpretation* (New York, 1965), pp. 299–301. Nicolin, *Stuttgart*, pp. 83–84, discusses the letter.

9. See *DHE*.

10. Nicolin, *Stuttgart*, p. 9, suggests the diary is "untypical" in that it is so formal and devoid of youthful fantasies. Klaiber, *Hegel*, sees this as evidence of Hegel's early "realism." R. Haym, *Hegel und seine Zeit*, 2nd ed., H. Rosenberg, ed. (Berlin, 1927), suggests it is a measure of Hegel's dry personality. E. Caird, *Hegel* (London, 1883), p. 5, has called the period "the age of diaries." Indeed it was, and precisely because Francke had made the keeping of a diary an imperative for measuring the pietists' academic as well as spiritual "progress."

11. Excerpting was a quite common procedure among eighteenth-century thinkers. Note, e.g., Rousseau's comment about his own work habits in C. Hendel, *Jean-Jacques Rousseau*, 2 v. (New York, 1934), v. 1: pp. 6–7.

12. Klaiber, *Hegel*, p. 101, and T. Haering, *Hegel, sein Wollen und sein Werk*, 2 v. (Leipzig, 1929), v. 1: p. 32, offer apologies for their speculations about Hegel's youth.

13. Haym, *Hegel*, p. 16, cautions against reading future developments into the past.

14. See, for example, K. Rosenkranz, *Leben*, p. 12; W. Dilthey, "Die Jugendgeschichte Hegels," in *Gesammelte Schriften*, v. 4 (Stuttgart, 1959), p. 6; Haym, *Hegel*, p. 20; Klaiber, *Hegel*, pp. 90–91; and H. Glockner, *Hegel*, 2 v. (Stuttgart, 1929), v. 1: pp. 279–280.

15. Again, Rosenkranz's *Hegel*, p. 4, set the direction for Hegelian scholarship. Also see Haym, *Hegel*, p. 20; Dilthey, "Hegels," p. 6; Klaiber, *Hegel*, pp. 67 and 91; Harris, *HD*, has tried to make Hegel's vocation for scholarship an interpretive device for the whole of his thought; Nicolin, *Stuttgart*, p. 6, argues that Hegel's mother inclined him in this direction; but Glockner, *Hegel*, v. 1: pp. 269 and 354, notes a "schoolmaster mentality" in both branches of Hegel's family.

16. Nicolin, *Stuttgart*, p. 5; Haym, *Hegel*; Klaiber, *Hegel*, p. 64; J. Loewenberg, *Hegel Selections* (New York, 1929), p. x; J. Royce, *The Spirit of Modern Philosophy* (Boston, 1892), p. 195; and F. Rosenzweig, *Hegel und der Staat* (Berlin, 1920), v. 1: p. 11.

17. See her letter in Kaufmann, *Hegel*, pp. 299–300.

18. Besides the prestige of high ranking, one's *Lokation* in the promotion, the equivalent to our class ranking, was important for future career opportunities. The first three places were traditionally offered teaching positions at the university upon completion of the degree requirements. These rankings, however, seldom changed. Nevertheless, as Leutwein tells us, Hegel was demoted to fourth place soon after his arrival at Tübingen, with the result that upon graduation he had to seek employment elsewhere as a *Hofmeister*. Harris, *HD*, pp. 65ff and 155, offers some insight into the different dimensions of this matter.

19. W. Bohm, *Hölderlin*, 2 v. (Halle, 1928), v 2: p. 35, makes the point about Hegel. R. Rürup, *Johann Jacob Moser* (Wiesbaden, 1965), p. 6, makes the point about Moser. Rürup also has noted (p. 32) how Moser combined religious and political interests within the framework of "Christian philosophy." Not an insignificant point for a study of his namesake.

20. Haering, *Hegel*, v. 1: p. 13.

21. See Klaiber, *Hegel*, pp. 63, 105, and 138–139. Also see Glockner, *Hegel*, v. 1: p. 372.

22. Glockner, *Hegel*, v. 1: pp. 274–275; E. Caird, *Hegel*, p. 5.

23. Rosenkranz, *Hegel*, p. 6; Hoffmeister, *DHE*, p. 15.

24. The source for this is Leutwein, quoted in Kaufmann, *Hegel*, p. 7. But Harris, *HD*, p. 69, quite rightly notes the lack of "manuscript authority" for the phrase.

25. Harris, *HD*, p. 22; Haering, *Hegel*, v. 1: pp. 13–18; both perhaps are relying on Leutwein's statement that Hegel was an "eclectic" while at *Tübingen*. What Rousseau says about his own work habits (n. 11, above) is also relevant here. Also see n. 30 below.

26. R. Kroner, *Von Kant zu Hegel*, 2 v. (Tübingen, 1921–1924), is the major work here.

27. Haering, *Hegel*, v. 1: pp. vii–xv.

28. I borrow the phrase qua concept from Cumming, *Human Nature and History*, v. 1: p. 284.

29. Nicolin, *Stuttgart*, p. 5, discusses Hegelian scholarship's neglect of Hegel's Württemberg origins. F. Rosenzweig, *Hegel*, pp. 8–17, has understood the importance of the generational aspect of Hegel's cultural origins in Old-Württemberg. And R. Schneider, *Schellings und Hegels schwäbische Geistesahnen* (Wurzburg, 1938), has offered an appreciation of what it meant to come from Schwabia in the eighteenth century. But Schneider's study fails to discuss the relationship of religion to politics. That omission has been rectified by G. Rohrmoser, "Zur Vorgeschichte der Jugend-schriften Hegels," in *Zeitschrift für Philosophische Forschung*, v. 14, 2 (1960). Others who have noted the Württemberg connection are K. Barth, *Protestant Theology in the Nineteenth Century* (Valley Forge, 1973), esp. p. 395; E. Benz, "Johann Albrecht Bengel und die Philosophie des deutsche Idealismus," in *DVLG*, v. 27, 4 (1953); N. Lobkowicz, *Theory and Practice* (Notre Dame, 1967), pp. 166–176; and M. Brecht and J. Sandberger, "Hegels Begegnung mit der Theologie in Tübinger Stift," in *HS*, v. 5 (1969). Vital to all these studies is the tie between Hegel and the eschatological orientations of Württemberg pietists in the eighteenth century.

30. Eclecticism was something of an intellectual style in Stuttgart and Tübingen during these years. See the remarks of Klaiber, *Hegel*, pp. 77 and 80. For eclecticism in the *Aufklärung* as a whole: Reill, *Rise*, passim. Also n. 25 above.

31. See L. Febvre, *A New Kind of History*, K. Folca, trans. (New York, 1973), p. 9.

32. Brecht and Sandberger, "Hegels," are very helpful here, as are Harris, *HD*, and Henrich, *Kontext*, pp. 41–72. Old but still useful: O. Pfleiderer, *The*

Development of Theology in Germany Since Kant, J. Smith, trans. (London, 1890). I discuss the philosophical currents at Tübingen in 1790s below, Chapter 4.

33. Rosenzweig, *Hegel,* v. 1: pp. 8–17, on the generational aspect.
34. Rürup, *Moser,* p. 12, makes the point well.
35. For the particularism of Old-Württemberg, see M. Walker, *German Home Towns* (Ithaca, 1971); F. L. Carsten, *Princes and Parliaments* (Oxford, 1959); and E. Hölzle, *Das Alte Recht und die Revolution* (Munich, 1931). Very helpful for intellectual currents: B. von Wiese, *Friedrich Schiller* (Stuttgart, 1959).
36. The phrases are borrowed from Geertz, *Cultures,* p. 9, and K. Mannheim, *From Karl Mannheim,* K. Wolff, ed. (New York, 1971), p. 39.
37. For the role-specific dimension of this, see n. 21 to the Preface.
38. I develop the importance of the tie between "ethics and eschatology" in Chapter 1. The phrase "down-to-earth Pietism" comes from K. Barth, *Protestant,* p. 122.
39. Here Q. Skinner's recent discussion of the presence of Protestant "resistance theory" among sixteenth-century German Lutherans is important. See *Founda.,* esp. v. 2.
40. Berger and Luckmann, *Social Construction of Reality,* pp. 53ff. The idea of a "tacit" dimension of cultural knowledge has been developed by M. Polanyi, *Personal Knowledge* (Chicago, 1958), esp. Part Two.
41. Berger and Luckmann, *Social,* pp. 15, 23, 53ff, and 65. L. Dumont, *From Mandeville to Marx* (Chicago, 1977), makes similar points while discussing "ideology" as a non–class-bound concept (see, e.g., pp. 19–20).
42. The importance of pretheoretical knowledge for the sociology of knowledge has been appreciated by Berger and Luckmann, *Social,* pp. 8, 15, and 64–65. Mannheim, *From,* pp. 38ff, also discusses the notion. It would be unwise to regard this kind of knowledge as "unconscious." Better, as Dumont (*Marx,* p. 20) understands, to regard it as "unstated."
43. See N. Frye's essay in *Daedalus* (Spring 1970), pp. 276–277. Also see Chapter 3, pp. 130–131.
44. As I noted in n. 18 to the Preface, the idea of meaningful relatedness is Weberian.
45. G. Kelly, *Idealism, Politics and History,* p. 352. Obviously, he is playing on the original Greek meaning of the term.
46. On Bengel, I follow G. Mälzer, *Johanne Albrecht Bengel* (Stuttgart, 1970); on Moser, Rürup, *Moser,* and Rohrmoser, "Hegels." I discuss both at length in Part I.
47. The basic conceptual point has been made by L. Dumont, *Marx;* by R. Bellah, "Civil Religion in America," in *Daedalus* (Winter 1967); idem, "American Civil Religion in the 1970's," in *American Civil Religion,* R. Richey and D. Jones, eds. (New York, 1974); and by N. Hatch, *The Sacred Cause of Liberty* (New Haven, 1977), pp. 3–6.
48. Bellah, "Civil," pp. 3 and 19, and "1970's," pp. 257ff. Also see T. Luckmann, *The Invisible Religion* (London, 1967), pp. 17–19. Examples of this argument: F. Raab, *The English Face of Machiavelli* (London, 1964);

and H. Arendt, *Between Past and Future* (New York, 1961), esp. p. 69.

49. Bellah, "1970's," p. 257.
50. Luckmann, *Invisible*, passim.
51. Skinner, *Founda.*, makes the general point about Lutheran resistance theory. In Part I, I examine this closely.
52. See Richey's and Jones' introductory remarks to the essay in *American*.
53. Especially important here: the increasing interest in the tie between eschatology and political activism in Europe and America in the seventeenth and eighteenth centuries. I cite the literature in Chapter 1.
54. Bellah, "1970's," pp. 257 and 271. I am well aware – as S. Wolin has noted – that civil religion has most often been discussed in situations where it has been shaped by the *state* and imposed on *society*. In certain contexts, however, the dynamic works the other way. Old-Württemberg, I think, is such a case. For more on this important point see Wolin, "America's Civil Religion," in *Democracy*, v. 2, 2 (1982), and Skinner, *Founda.*, p. 81. I develop the point about Württemberg in Part I.
55. As Bellah ("1970's," p. 256) notes: the concept's "reality depends less on the existence of certain things out there than on a consensus that it is a useful way of talking about things that indubitably are out there."
56. See, e.g., n. 3 above.
57. For example, K. Pinson, *Pietism as a Factor in the Rise of German Nationalism* (New York, 1934); H. Brunschwig, *Enlightenment and Romanticism in Eighteenth-Century Prussia*, F. Jellinck, trans. (Chicago, 1974), esp. pp. 13, 93, 190, and 245; and P. Hazard, *The European Mind 1680–1715*, J. May, trans. (New York, 1963), pp. xix and 418ff.
58. I list the literature in Chapter 1.
59. Here I am using "reform" and "revival" as distinct forms of religious "renewal." On this, I follow G. Ladner, *The Idea of Reform* (Cambridge, England 1959), pp. 9–34.
60. I stress the relative quality because there were Catholic as well as Calvinist precedents for this conception.
61. V. Weise, *Schiller*, p. 59, makes the point, as does H. Burger, *Schwabentum in der Geistesgeschichte* (Stuttgart, 1933), pp. 10–11.
62. On these points much that T. Parsons says is relevant. See his "Christianity and Modern Industrial Society," in *Secularization and the Protestant Prospect*, J. Childress and D. Harned, eds. (Philadelphia, 1970).
63. Weber, "Objectivity," pp. 112–115, develops the conceptual idea of "historical" clusters of "meaningful action."
64. Reill, *Rise*, p. 108, makes the point about the "new religiosity" of the *Aufklärung*. Also of interest: L. Beck, *Early*, pp. 10, 159, 245, and 288–289.
65. I have borrowed the idea of a "tradition of discourse" from S. Wolin, *Politics and Vision* (Boston, 1960), pp. 22ff and 357ff.
66. Here, obviously, I am allowing a tradition to be part of a context. See n. 15 to the Preface.
67. For accommodationism in the *Aufklärung* see P. Reill, *Rise*, esp. pp. 162–171. M. H. Abrams, *Natural*, p. 394, and, esp., n. 5, p. 507,

discusses accommodationism among German pietists and in Lessing. Following the brilliant article of R. S. Crane (cited below in Chapter 5), Abrams ties accommodationism in Germany to that which developed in England. He also cites Tertullian as a resource for much of this. On the tie between Tertullian and Lessing see Lovejoy's *Essays*, Essay XVI. Clement and Irenaeus are also central to the accommodationist doctrine. Most often Joachimism is identified as the source for this among the Germans. See, e.g., J. Moltmann, *Theology of Hope*, J. Leitch, trans. (New York, 1967), esp. pp. 261–264. For him, Lessing and Kant are Joachim's heirs. Also see H. J. Mähl, *Die Idee des Goldenen Zeitalters* (Heidelberg, 1965), where Lessing, Kant, and Hegel are linked to Joachimism. Though I do not question this connection, I now believe that Joachimism's influence among the Germans was a consequence of their "crypto-Calvinist" tendencies. In sum, I would say that accommodationism is common to covenant theology in a variety of forms: in Clement; Joachim; Calvin and Coccejus; and the "philosophical millenarians" among the Germans (Lessing, Kant, and Hegel). I discuss all this below in much more detail.

68. For more on the activism inherent in this idea see n. 70 below.

69. Though I follow Ladner, *Reform*, I do not endorse all his findings or understand some of his emphases. For example (p. 2), he claims that Christian reform "has no true equivalent in pre-Christian times." Yet, throughout the study (e.g., pp. 9, 54–55, 61–62, and 83), he concedes how important "non-Christian renewal ideology" is to Christian reform. This is especially true of two ideas that, by his own admission, are crucial to his whole undertaking: *paideia* and *homoiosis* (see esp. n. 61, p. 47; n. 30, p. 90; n. 43, pp. 94–95; and n. 56, p. 60). Nor do I understand quite how he runs the Greek Fathers, who do use these ideas to explain salvation, into Augustine, who clearly does not. I discuss all this below. Suffice it to say here that I am following Ladner primarily in what he has to say about the Church Fathers *before* Augustine.

70. Here a problem arises. Ladner (*Reform*, pp. 166 and 330–331) contends that the "activism" of the Alexandrian Fathers was not "directed toward the world outside the soul." *Theoria*, not praxis, he argues, governed the theology of the Alexandrian reformers. In saying this, however, Ladner ignores a crucial element; namely, that among the Alexandrians *logos* and *bios*, theory and practice, were complements to each other. That is, the true Christian will make "the word" relevant to "his life" through action that is directed outward. Several students of the Alexandrians' Platonic exegeses of Genesis 1.26 have made the point. S. Lilla, *Clement of Alexandria* (Oxford, 1971), esp. pp. 66 and 108, insists that the practice of virtue is essential to Clement's understanding of the passage. Here Lilla follows H. Merki, "Ὁμοίωσις Θεῶ" *Von der Platonische Angleichung an Gott zur Gottähnlichkeit bei Gregor von Nyssa* (Freiburg, 1952), who discusses Clement in terms of the specific character traits of the man who wishes to assimilate to God. Decisive here, though, is the context in which the Alexandrians were thinking. Vis-à-vis "Stoic pantheistic materialism" (Lilla, p. 48) and the

ethical indifferentism of Gnostic mystery cults (see E. DeFaye, *Origen and His Work*, F. Rothwell, trans. [London, 1926], pp. 79ff and 95; J. Daniélou, *Origen*, W. Mitchell, trans. [London, 1955], pp. 87ff, 98, 103, 123, and 168; and A. Nygren, *Agape and Eros*, P. Watson, trans. [New York, 1953], pp. 290ff), the Alexandrians stressed the need for moral activism. Hence, their relatively optimistic theological anthropology and their reformism. Perhaps the most compelling argument for activism among the Alexandrians is R. B. Tollinton, *Clement of Alexandria*, 2 v. (London, 1914), esp. v. 1: pp. 240–242, and v. 2: pp. 94 and 235–237.

71. Two points are crucial here. First, as Ladner (*Reform*, p. 31) notes, the Alexandrians had a sense of "progress" qua man's gradual "assimilation to God." It is this idea that prompted H. Chadwick to argue for a close connection between the Alexandrians and Lessing (see the Introduction to *LTW*, esp. pp. 40–48). Second, it is clear that while the Alexandrians believed in "progress" they did not equate assimilation to God with "deification" or "self-salvation." As E. R. Dodds has observed (*Pagan and Christian in an Age of Anxiety* [Cambridge, England, 1968], pp. 74–76), there is a difference between assimilation and deification. Suffice it to say that assimilation to God is a "moral" doctrine and deification a "mystical" one. In the first one strives for "relative perfectibility"; in the second for "absolute perfection." (The terms are Ladner's, p. 31.) G. Butterworth is very clear on this. See his "The Deification of Man in Clement of Alexandria," *JTS*, v. 17 (1916) esp. p. 169. Also see n. 81 below.

72. W. Jaeger, *Early Christianity and Greek Paideia* (Cambridge, MA, 1961), esp. pp. 15–16 and 60–62, is a fine introduction to the problem. Much can also be learned from S. Lilla, *Clement*, esp. pp. 9–11, 55, and 190, and from H. Chadwick, *Early Christian Thought and the Classical Tradition* (Oxford, 1966), esp. pp. 40–50.

73. On the importance of all this see A. Nygren, *Agape*, pp. 290ff and 349ff; C. Bigg, *The Christian Platonists of Alexandria* (Oxford, 1886), pp. 1–50; J. Dillon, *The Middle Platonists* (London, 1977), pp. 114ff; and Lilla, *Clement*, passim. On Philo, see A. Wolfson's *The Philosophy of the Church Fathers*, v. 1, 3rd ed. (Cambridge, 1970), and idem, *Religious Philosophy* (Cambridge, MA, 1961).

74. Dillon, *Middle*, pp. 122–123, 139–145, 157ff, and 166ff, discusses Philo's and Eudorus' perceptions of the connection, as does Lilla, *Clement*, pp. 17–21 and 107ff. Lilla also has much to say about Clement's Platonic exegesis of the Genesis passage, pp. 30, 58, and 106–117. J. Danielou, *Origen*, pp. 294–295, focuses on Origen's rendering of the connection. For a more general treatment of the subject, see R. Wilson, "The Early History of the Exegesis of Genesis 1:26," in *Studia Patristica*, v. 1 (Berlin, 1957). Very useful also is Jaeger, *Early*, p. 99 and n. 30 pp. 144, who stresses the importance of the tie for Gregory of Nyssa: "For Gregory, Genesis 1.26 is the link between Christianity and the philosophical tradition of the Greeks."

75. In addition to the literature cited in n. 74 above, see H. Merki's (*Gott*)

study of the history of the idea of *homoiosis* from Plato to Gregory of Nyssa. Ladner, *Reform*, pp. 54–55, 83, and n. 43, p. 94, discusses the point. For Clement, see Tollinton, *Clement*, v. 1: pp. 168 and 319, and v. 2: pp. 90–91, 209, 290–291, and 304–305. Above all, see R. Markus, "'Imago' and 'Similitudo' in Augustine," in *Revue des études augustiniennes*, v. 10, 1 (1964), for a fine account of Augustine's "innovations" here.

76. Ladner, *Reform*, p. 83, calls the translation a "fateful event in the history of ideas." It is so because if assimilation is understood in soteriological terms, then human effort may enter into salvation – in which case we get "synergism." On synergism, see n. 82 below.

77. Here we begin to see the idea of the "fortunate fall" emerge as crucial to Alexandrian thought. Ladner, *Reform*, pp. 146ff, has seen this clearly. The idea involves minimizing the Fall and maximizing man's capacity for moral progress. Nygren, *Agape*, pp. 382ff, and Daniélou, *Origen*, spell out the implication for Origen.

78. Ladner, *Reform*, p. 35, and Lilla, *Clement*, pp. 106ff, are clear on the point. So, too is Jaeger, *Two Rediscovered Works of Ancient Christian Literature* (Leiden, 1954), esp. p. 93 and Tollinton, *Clement*, v. 1: pp. 310–314, and v. 2 pp. 243–244.

79. I realize that the idea of a plastic nature is a verbal creation of the Cambridge Platonists. I do not think, though, that my usage here is anachronistic. After all, Cudworth, who used the phrase, openly celebrated the Alexandrians' achievement. On this see C. Patrides' introduction to *The Cambridge Platonists*, C. Patrides, ed. (Cambridge, England, 1970), esp. pp. 26–27 and 41, where he links Cudworth and Clement and Origen. J. Passmore, "The Malleability of Man in Eighteenth-Century Thought," in *Aspects of the Eighteenth Century*, E. Wasserman, ed. (Baltimore, 1965), has noted the Pelagian connection. Not insignificant is the fact that "plastic power" was a conception designed to combat the kind of materialism mentioned in n. 70 above. On this see W. Hunter, "The Seventeenth-Century Doctrine of Plastic Nature," in *HTR*, v. 43, 3 (1950). Basil Willey puts it this way: The Cambridge Platonists "were the modern counterparts of... Clement and Origen...." See his *English Moralists* (London, 1964), p. 172.

80. This gradualism has been fully appreciated by Tollinton, *Clement*, v. 1: p. 343.

81. The qualification "as far as" is important. Ladner, *Reform*, pp. 80 (n. 70), 89, 94–96, and 106, seems to disregard this (and much of the literature in n. 71 above) when he equates "assimilation ideology" with "deification ideology." Augustine (n. 228 below) will do the same thing. What is at issue may be illuminated in the following way. First, the Greek words *hagios* and *hieros*, although they both mean "sacred," have different connotations. *Hieros* has a positive one, implying dedication to the divine; *hagios* is more negative, suggesting the presumptuousness of such dedication. T. Pangle, *The Laws of Plato*, T. Pangle, trans. (New York, 1980), p. 526 (n. 2), makes the point.

82. As with the idea of a plastic nature, I do not regard my usage of synergism

here as anachronistic. Although the "synergists" were a sixteenth-century group of Protestants who took many of their cues from Melanchthon, those cues had been framed (as Melanchthon knew) by the Alexandrian Fathers. As a group, these Protestants objected to the extremism of Luther's conception of the tie between grace and salvation, a conception that they felt deprived man of moral dignity and militated against *praxis pietatis*. The alternative they offered allowed for human participation in the salvation process in much the same way as the Alexandrians had. That the synergists lost the struggle with "orthodoxy" only means synergy was later available to the *Aufklärer* as a resource for their criticism of orthodoxy. The synergism of the Alexandrians has been noted by Lilla, *Clement*, p. 66, and above all by Jaeger, *Two*, pp. 87–96. Significantly, Jaeger [pp. 72–73, 97–98 (n. 2) and 102–106] uses the ideas of *homoiosis* and *paideia* to group the Alexandrians, Gregory of Nyssa, and the Pelagians (in their moderate form) into one synergistic whole. These ideas, in turn, are decisive for the *Aufklärer*. Perhaps the best evidence for the presence of synergism in the ancient world comes from J. J. Mosheim, a key figure in the *Aufklärung*. In his influential *Ecclesiastical History*, 6 v., A. MacLaine, trans. (London, 1811–1819), v. 4: pp. 329–330, he links the Protestant synergists with Semi-Pelagianism (which was Pelagius' position in the first place – see n. 196 below).

83. That the idea of striving is central to Lessing's theological purposes has been appreciated by H. Chadwick, *LTW*, pp. 40–48. It is important for this study that Chadwick also ties Lessing to Joachim; this supports my argument about the connection between the ethical activism of the Alexandrians and Pelagius and the eschatological concerns of Joachim. Also important is J. T. McNeill's claim in *The History and Character of Calvinism* (London, 1954), p. 213, that Lessing's eschatology was influenced heavily by Calvin's covenant theology.

84. Lilla, *Clement*, pp. 108ff.

85. What Jaeger, *Two*, pp. 87–106, says about synergy is relevant here. Tollinton, *Clement*, v. 2: p. 52, says this about Clement.

86. Origen, quoted in Ladner, *Reform*, pp. 87–88. My emphasis. Compare with Gregory of Nyssa (in Jaeger, *Two*, p. 93): "the further we extend the efforts of our works the more the soul grows through our efforts." Jaeger (p. 73) notes the tie between the two. Tollinton, *Clement*, v. 2: p. 14, says Clement ascribed to the belief that "the world of God became man's, that [man] may learn from a man [Christ] how man becomes God."

87. Ladner, *Reform*, pp. 86 (n. 12), 87 (n. 19), and 187, discusses the idea of potential in Clement and Origen; he refers to *homoiosis* as a "process" on pp. 33 and 86. The idea of *homoiosis* as telos has been noted by Lilla, *Clement*, pp. 42–44 and 105ff, and Dillon, *Middle*, esp. pp. 121-122. With regard to the last point it must be remembered that this telos is not stoical because (as Dillon argues, pp. 9, 114–122, 192, and 229) it refuses to define itself in terms of a "concord with nature." Rather, it is Platonic and theological and involves *separation* from nature for ethical purposes. Willey, *English*, p. 186, applies the distinction to the Cambridge

Platonists. This distinction is also fundamental for separating Hegel from his romantic contemporaries. I discuss the problem below, Part III.

88. Ladner, *Reform*, p. 86.

89. One of the principal themes of Jaeger, *Early*, and Ladner, *Reform*, pp. 136 (n. 17), 60 (n. 56), and 90 (n. 30), is that the Alexandrians were the heirs of "the ideology of *paideia*."

90. J. Daniélou, *Gospel Message and Hellenistic Culture*, J. Baker, trans. (Philadelphia, 1973), pp. 254–255. W. Jaeger, *Early*, pp. 61–62.

91. See n. 67 above.

92. See Clement's "The Miscellanies" in *ANCL*, v. 12 (Edinburgh, 1869), pp. 326–328. Tollinton, *Clement*, v. 1: pp. 350–355, and v. 2: pp. 10–14, 199–205, 253, and 291–305, has much to say about accommodationism in Clement. H. Koch, *Pronoia und Paideusis* (Berlin, 1932), esp. pp. 60–61 and 70–71, does the same for Origen. J. Taubes, "Äbendlandische Eschatologie," in *Beiträge zur Soziologie und Sozialphilosophie*, v. 3, R. König, ed. (Bern, 1947), esp. pp. 133–134, ties the Alexandrians directly to the late eighteenth-century German idealists.

93. Tollinton, *Clement*, v. 2: pp. 57ff, identifies Maricon as Clement's main concern here.

94. Clement, *ANCL*, v. 12, p. 327.

95. Ibid., p. 56. As Koch notes, *Pronoia*, p. 44, Origen used the same image. In both instances the image is linked to the economy of salvation argument. In Chapter 2 I show (esp. nn. 89, 121, and 197) how prevalent this image is among Calvinists.

96. Very helpful for understanding how the idea of economy was used among the Alexandrians is G. L. Prestige, *God in Patristic Thought* (London, 1936), pp. 57–75.

97. Clement, *ANCL*, v. 12, pp. 74–75, makes the connection between Christian theology and Platonic teleology very clear.

98. The *pistis* to gnosis argument is a main theme in all the literature on Clement.

99. For Clement's activism see Tollinton, *Clement*, pages cited n. 70 above.

100. Ibid., v. 1: p. 310, and v. 2: pp. 244 and 301, stresses the cooperation theme.

101. S. Ozment, *Homo Spiritualis* (Leiden, 1969), uses the phrase "Pelagian Covenant theology" to express this convergence.

102. Ladner, *Reform*, pp. 35, 43, and 70–71. He writes, "In Alexandrian theology, spiritual reform on earth is bound up with eschatology."

103. Ibid., pp. 107–109, 115, and 118.

104. Ibid., p. 118, discusses the relationship between eschatology and preparation in Origen. S. Bercovitch, *The American Jeremiad* (Madison, 1978), pp. 47–49, has explained how this relationship worked in an eighteenth-century American context. Essential also: P. Miller's brilliant "Preparation for Salvation," in *JHI*, v. 4, 3 (1943). More to the point are the following scholarly parallels. Passmore, "Malleability," esp. p. 26, uses Miller's "preparation" argument to illuminate English patterns of ethical thought in the seventeenth century. Conversely, Tuveson, who had

previously discussed preparationism in seventeenth-century England, pursued the argument among American millennialists in *Redeemer Nation* (Chicago, 1968). Miller argues for a dovetailing of the two currents in his classic *The New England Mind. The Seventeenth Century* (New York, 1939), esp. p. 366, where the covenant tradition, in the form of "federal theology," constitutes the point of convergence.

105. Surely it is not an accident that for many scholars – E. Benz, *Evolution and Christian Hope* (New York, 1966), pp. 21–34; E. Tuveson, *Millennium and Utopia* (Berkeley, 1949), pp. 15–19; and Taubes, "Eschatology," pp. 77–82 – Augustine "de-eschatologized" Christianity. Conversely, other scholars – e.g., E. Voegelin, *The New Science of Politics* (Chicago, 1952) – regard attempts to provide eschatological alternatives to Augustine as fraught with political danger.

106. P. Gay, *The Enlightenment: An Interpretation*, 2 v. (New York, 1966–1969).

107. Ibid., v. 1: pp. 31ff and 256–321.

108. Hazard, *European*, pp. xviii and 44–50.

109. Gay, *Enlightenment*, v. 1: p. 3.

110. Ibid., pp. 31–38.

111. Ibid., p. 33.

112. Here I follow C. Becker, *The Heavenly City of the Eighteenth-Century Philosophers* (New Haven, 1932), pp. 105–106 and 111. Gay makes the point about Condorcet in *Enlightenment*, v. 2: pp. 113–114.

113. Gay, *Enlightenment*, v. 1: pp. 3–8.

114. Ibid., v. 2: p. 144.

115. Ibid., v. 1: pp. 17–19 and 318.

116. Hazard, *European*, pp. 3–110; Gay, *Enlightenment*, v. 1: p. 351; Becker, *Heavenly*, p. 73.

117. Cassirer, *Enlightenment*, pp. 134–136, and H. Dieckmann, "Themes and Structure of the Enlightenment," in *Essays in Comparative Literature*, Levin and Motekat, eds. (St. Louis, 1961), pp. 67–70, discuss the problems of the antireligious interpretation of the Enlightenment.

118. See, for example, A. Kors, *D'Holbach's Coterie: An Enlightenment in Paris* (Princeton, 1976). A. MacIntyre, *After*, p. 36, makes the point well.

119. Gay makes the point in *Enlightenment*, v. 1: p. 203, by referring to Voltaire's representation of Leibniz in *Candide*.

120. The shortcomings of Gay vis-à-vis the *Aufklärung* have been discussed by Reill, *Rise*, pp. 49ff, 174ff, and p. 233 (n.'s 6 and 9); and by Beck, *Early*, p. 525, who is well aware of the uniqueness of the German situation (e.g., pp. 245 and 288–289).

121. Hazard, *European*, pp. 65ff, and E. Hirsch, *GNET*, v. 2: p. 342, elaborate.

122. Gay, *Enlightenment*, v. 1: p. 203.

123. I discuss this below.

124. D. P. Walker, *The Ancient Theology* (London, 1972), pp. 3–10, cites several instances.

125. Hirsch, *GNET*, v. 2: p. 124, contrasts Voltaire and Lessing on the issue. K. Aner, *Die Theologie der Lessingszeit* (Halle, 1929), says as much about the *Aufklärung* in general and Lessing in particular.

126. I found much that was useful in H. Baron, "Secularization of Wisdom," in *JHI*, v. 21, 1 (1960). Beck, *Early*, p. 322; Hirsch, *GNET*, esp. v. 2; and Aner, *Theologie*, esp. pp. 28−31, 80−81, and 151−152, stress the *Aufklärers'* moral and civil activism.

127. See, e.g., O. Chadwick, *The Secularization of the European Mind in the Nineteenth Century* (Cambridge, England, 1975), pp. 7−15.

128. These terms are my own but the distinction Bouwsma makes between "biblical" and "Hellenistic" understandings of Christianity comes very close to my own. See his "Two Faces of Humanism" in *Itinerarium Italicum*, H. Oberman, ed. (Leiden, 1975), pp. 8−9. I have found similar support for the distinction in O. Ritschl, *DP*, where the distinction takes the form of a contrast between "determinant" and "indeterminant" conceptions of man's relation to God. Whatever the terminology, both make a case for a contrast between "biblical Augustinian" and "classical Pelagian" strains of Christian thought. (I prefer the term "classical" to "Hellenistic" because it allows me to pick up Plato and Aristotle.) See also n. 142 below.

129. I borrow these useful terms from Nygren, *Agape*, pp. 205−207 and 315. Especially important here is Nygren's distinction (p. 51) between "vulgar" and "heavenly" eros. Only the latter is truly Platonic and egocentric in a religious sense. So regarded, egocentric religion fits in nicely with *homoiosis* as telos discussed in n. 87 above. There is, moreover, a source within the *Aufklärung* itself for the distinction. See the important note in Aner, *Theologie*, pp. 158−159, where "subtle" and "crude" Pelagians are discussed. What I say in n. 81 is relevant here.

130. Very helpful here: E. TeSelle, *Augustine the Theologian* (New York, 1970), pp. 347ff. The phrase comes from Cochrane, *Classical*, p. 379.

131. Vital here are the many points Hirsch, *GNET*, v. 4: pp. 27−47 and 75−76, and Aner, *Theologie*, esp. p. 162, make about the *Aufklärers'* antipathy for Augustine. Also see H. Allison, *Lessing and the Enlightenment* (Ann Arbor, 1966), pp. 38−41.

132. A. Harnack, *Outlines of the History of Dogma*, J. Millar, trans. (London, 1985), v. 5: p. 203, makes the charge.

133. See, respectively, J. Morris, "Pelagian Literature," *JTS*, v. 16, 1 (1965), p. 55; and P. Brown's magnificent *Augustine of Hippo* (Berkeley, 1967), p. 367.

134. Harnack, *Dogma*, v. 5: pp. 188−189.

135. J. Ferguson, *Pelagius* (Cambridge, England, 1956), p. 68, says even Augustine attested to this.

136. Ibid., pp. 48ff and 70; above all, see T. Bohlin's *Die Theologie des Pelagius and ihre Genesis* (Wiesbaden, 1957), p. 9. Also very useful: G. Bonner, "How Pelagian was Pelagius?" in *Studia Patristica*, v. 9 (1966).

137. Brown, *Augustine*, pp. 381ff; and Bonner, "How," p. 350.

138. G. Bonner, "Rufinus of Syria and African Pelagianism," in *Augustinian Studies*, v. 1 (1970). Ferguson, *Pelagius*, p. 131, stresses the importance of Rufinus as a conduit between Origen's and Pelagius' commitments to "moral progress."

139. B. Warfield, *Studies in Tertullian and Augustine* (New York, 1930), p. 301.

140. A Souter, *Pelagius' Expositions of Thirteen Epistles of St. Paul* (Cambridge, England, 1931).

141. Two points here. Ladner, *Reform*, pp. 409–410, argues that the Semi-Pelagians believed Augustine, not Pelagius, had deviated from tradition in the matter of grace. Jaeger, *Two*, pp. 86–106, argues persuasively that synergy lay at the core of that tradition of grace.

142. This is an extremely important point of revisionism. First, as Brown (*Augustine*, p. 355) notes, this makes the contest between Augustine and Pelagius an internal dispute within Christianity. This means, in turn, that Souter and Bohlin have been right to stress Pelagius' continuity with the thought of the Alexandian Fathers. And since Pelagius' views on grace and moral progress (i.e., *homoiosis* as telos) are quite consistent with those of the Fathers, many scholars have begun to see Augustine, not Pelagius, as a theological innovator. See, e.g., Jaeger, *Two*, p. 98; and P. Brown, "Pelagius and His Supporters," in *JTS*, v. 19, 1 (1968), esp. p. 107. Ladner, *Reform*, pp. 162–167, is clear on this, but takes Augustine's side in the matter. It is, obviously, this effort to establish Pelagius as a religious reformer rather than a secular heretic that informs my distinction between biblical and classical tendencies within Christianity (n. 128 above).

143. D. P. Walker, *Ancient*, pp. 9–10, has appreciated this. Essential, though, are Brown, *Augustine*, passim, and TeSelle, *Augustine*, p. 310.

144. Brown, *Augustine*, pp. 381ff.

145. Ibid., pp. 279 and 369.

146. Ibid., pp. 385–389.

147. Souter, *Pelagius*, p. 185; Bohlin, *Pelagius*, pp. 46–54.

148. G. Bonner, *St. Augustine of Hippo* (London, 1963), pp. 323–324.

149. A. Smith, "Pelagius and Augustine," in *JTS*, v. 31 (1929), p. 27.

150. E. Gilson, in *St. Augustine*, M. D'Arcy et al., eds. (New York, 1957), p. 292.

151. Passmore, "Malleability," has shown that very well, as has Aner, *Theologie*, passim.

152. Nygren, *Agape*, pp. 220 and 240–242, has been helpful here.

153. Cassirer, *Enlightenment*, Chapter IV, makes many of these points, as does Aner, *Theologie*, esp. pp. 28–31, 43, 80–81, 104, 151–152, 298, and 329.

154. Brown, *Augustine*, pp. 347, 349, and 371, makes these points about Pelagius. For him, "The good Pelagian was a 'good citizen' [p. 371]." Brown has elaborated the collective–civil–political implications of Pelagianism in "Supporters," esp. pp. 98–103. J. Passmore, *The Perfectibility of Man* (London, 1970), esp. p. 204, has concurred with him about Pelagius' environmentalism. Ferguson, *Pelagius*, p. 121, discusses Pelagius' "service" ethic.

155. The phrase "humanized" comes from Barth, *Protestant*, pp. 84ff. With it, he means to draw attention to what I would call the Pelagianizing tendency of eighteenth-century thought. Aner, *Theologie*, esp. p. 172, refers to the "humanization" of Christ during the *Aufklärung*, especially in the 1770s. By this he means to draw attention to Pelagius' conception of the

incarnation as liberating because the incarnation made men responsible for living a Christian life (as best they could).

156. Beck, *Early*, p. 289, addresses the issue.

157. Stephen, quoted in Dieckmann, "Themes," p. 70.

158. Hazard, *European*, p. 46.

159. See, e.g., n. 154 above, for how this leads to civil activism.

160. Hirsch, *GNET*, v. 4: p. 111; Aner, *Theologie*, pp. 61ff.

161. Here is where the recovery of synergy (n. 82 above) in the service of Christian reform is important.

162. L. Beck, *Early*, focuses specifically on this theme. Essential to his argument (esp. pp. 99–114) is the tie between Melanchthon and Aristotle. Hence, the idea of Aristotelianized Protestantism discussed below, in Chapter 6. As Beck notes, the tie is really a "Pelagian" one (p. 99). Just as important: H. Liebing, "Das Äusgange des europaischen Humanismus," in *GGR*.

163. Beck, *Early*, pp. 99ff, for a quick overview. I discuss the Protestant view of Aristotle below, in Chapter 6.

164. Liebing, "Humanismus," p. 373.

165. O. Ritschl, *DP*, v. 1: pp. 40ff, and v. 2: p. 437, is a basic source for this. A useful introduction to the conflict can be found in Beck, *Early*, pp. 101–114.

166. A problem would seem to arise here as to how synergism can be related to Calvinism. Beck, *Early*, pp. 107–113, has not flinched before the problem of how Calvin's "theocentric" views could possibly reinforce Melanchthon's synergism and worldly reformism.

167. Liebing, "Humanismus," and L. Spitz, "Humanism in the Reformation," in *Renaissance Studies in Honor of Hans Baron*, A. Molho et al., eds (Dekalb, Ill., 1971).

168. Beck, *Early*, p. 8, refers to this development as the key to the "great dialectic of German Philosophy."

169. C. McClelland, *State, Society and University in Germany, 1700–1914* (Cambridge, England, 1980), has all the details of this and of what follows.

170. My reason for locating the *Aufklärung* within this chronological framework is that several of the leading spokesmen for neologism – which for most commentators is synonymous with the theology of the *Aufklärung* – delineated their opposition to orthodox Lutheranism during this period. Spalding, Sach, and Jerusalem all articulated telling (i.e., Pelagian-like) arguments against orthodox (i.e., Augustinian) anthropology between 1747 and 1748. On this see Aner, *Theologie*, esp. pp. 28–31, 43, 61–82 and 158–162; Cassirer, *Enlightenment*, pp. 139–141 and 159–160; and Hirsch, *GNET*, v. 4: pp. 45ff. These arguments, in turn, culminate in the early 1770s with the publication of several books deploring the idea of original sin (Aner, p. 298). I prefer this periodization to that of others (e.g., Beck), which focuses too much on Prussian developments.

171. Reill, *Rise*, p. 8, puts it this way: "The Aufklärers' religious convictions led them to espouse an idea of history that postulated an interaction between spirit and nature." (cf. pp. 161–162). One further point here. Aner, *Theologie*, pp. 184–193 and 206–227, shows how this conviction led the

Aufklärer back to the Alexandrians' theology of history, which, as we have shown, is proto-Pelagian.

172. Aner, *Theologie*, pp. 61–82, is quite good on the neologians, as is Hazard, *European*, pp. 65ff. Reill (*Rise*, passim) is also instructive. Barth, *Protestant*, pp. 165ff, divides the neologians into practical–political and academic groups.

173. Consult Aner, *Theologie*, for all the details, esp. pp. 158–162, where he discusses Jerusalem's famous letter to Gottsched (1747) on Augustine's inadequacies and his unfair treatment of Pelagius. Hirsch, *GNET*, v. 2: pp. 266–272, and v. 4: pp. 75–76, offers Arnold and Semler as other examples.

174. Aner, *Theologie*, pp. 104, 158–162, and 329.

175. Hirsch, *GNET* v. 4: p. 187.

176. Aner, *Theologie*, p. 304, and Barth, *Protestant*, pp. 137ff and 165ff, stress the directional aspect of *Aufklärung* theology.

177. Barth, *Protestant*, p. 165, follows Aner in proclaiming the *Aufklärer* as action oriented. Also see n. 126 above.

178. That this was their concern is clear from Aner, *Theologie*, pp. 28–31 and 80–81. Also see n. 154 above for Pelagius' civil activism.

179. Ibid., pp. 158–162.

180. Hirsch, *GNET*, v. 4, esp. p. 27; Aner, *Theologie*, p. 43; and Reill, *Rise*, p. 142.

181. These qualities, I think, give the *Aufklärung* its particular coherence. The coherence, however, needs to be understood in terms of the potentialities within *homo religiosus*. They must be developed, therefore, as Lessing well knew; and for that time is necessary. (See, e.g., Aner, *Theologie*, pp. 351–353.)

182. Harnack, *Dogma*, v. 5: p. 169; Brown, *Augustine*, p. 368; and Bonner, "How," p. 350.

183. See n. 181 above.

184. Bohlin and Ferguson are informative on what follows. Also see R. Evans, *Pelagius. Inquiries and Reappraisals* (New York, 1968), esp. pp. 90–121.

185. See n. 142 above.

186. Ferguson, *Pelagius*, p. 175; and Bohlin, *Pelagius*, pp. 16–22.

187. Bonner, "How," pp. 353ff.

188. Evans, *Pelagius*, pp. 95ff, elaborates.

189. Brown, "Supporters," pp. 105ff.

190. Ferguson, *Pelagius*, pp. 67 and 166, notes how this possibility did not entail "deification" for Pelagius. See n.'s 71 and 81 above for the deification argument.

191. Brown, *Augustine*, p. 342.

192. Ibid., p. 372, uses this quote to characterize Pelagius' position.

193. See n. 190 above.

194. Cochrane, *Classical*, p. 453, says Augustine specifically denounced this "pagan" conviction.

195. This, of course, is part of the fortunate fall argument (see n. 77 above).

196. All modern commentators agree that Pelagius' theological views were

contingent upon grace. He was, as it were, always a Semi-Pelagian.
197. Bohlin's language here is unfortunate. It is quite clear that he is talking about religious synergy. What is at issue in the choice of terms? Whether Pelagius should be understand as a pagan Neoplatonist or as a Christian synergist.
198. This is crucial. Clement, we have seen, made the covenant theology argument. And Pelagius – as Evans, *Pelagius*, pp. 95ff, shows – is using a modified version of it. After Pelagius, this theology of history is modified again – by Joachim [see Ladner, *Reform*, p. 29 (n. 13)]. The Joachimite tradition then develops, but it always has its roots in Alexandrian and Pelagian religious thought. Henceforth, the Joachimite tradition and what Ozment calls "Pelagian covenant theology" are connected in a single ethico-eschatological framework of moderate synergism. On covenant theology in Protestantism, see Chapter 2 below.
199. Clement's *Christ the Educator* is an important source here for Pelagius.
200. Pelagius, quoted in Brown, *Augustine*, p. 352.
201. Ibid., has clearly understood Pelagius' use of this "brilliant image." Yet to appreciate the image fully we need to remember what Tillich, *A History of Christian Thought*, 2nd ed., P. John, ed. (Providence, 1956), pp. 46ff and 237–238, has told us: that the Christian *persona* was less one of concealment than one of constant revelation; and that its "autonomy" did not imply "personal" independence from God.
202. Brown, *Augustine*, pp. 371–375.
203. Ibid., p. 343.
204. Ferguson, *Pelagius*, p. 175. Here, obviously, synergy and covenant theology intersect. The point has been elaborated on brilliantly by P. Miller, *Mind*, esp. p. 385, in the context of his discussion of Coccejus' federal theology. For more on Coccejus, who writes in the Joachimite tradition, see Chapter 2.
205. Bohlin, *Pelagius*, p. 24; Brown, *Augustine*, p. 371.
206. Brown, "Supporters," is clear on the point. Ferguson, *Pelagius*, p. 124, insists that Pelagius' sense of *conscientia* was collective. Clearly, then, Pelagius' synergy was not just "penitential."
207. See n. 154 above.
208. See n. 54 above. Miller, *Mind*, p. 414, implies this while discussing covenant theology. Passmore, *Perfectibility*, p. 115, makes the same connection while discussing Pelagianism.
209. Augustine, quoted in Brown, *Augustine*, p. 373.
210. Augustine, quoted in TeSelle, *Augustine*, p. 258.
211. Augustine, *The Anti-Pelagian Works*, v. 2, P. Holmes, trans. (Edinburgh, 1874), p. 13.
212. Augustine, *The Confessions of St. Augustine*, R. Warner, trans. (New York, 1963), pp. 93, 149, and 249.
213. Ibid., p. 248.
214. Ibid., pp. 168–169.
215. Ibid.
216. Ibid., p. 180.

217. Brown, *Augustine*, p. 371. Also see H. Deane, *The Political and Social Ideas of St. Augustine* (New York, 1963), p. 57.
218. Deane, *Ideas*, p. 71, is clear on Augustine's disbelief in "historical progress." Above all, F. E. Cranz's very fine "The Development of Augustine's Ideas on Society Before the Donatist Controversy," in *HTR*, v. 47, 4 (1954), esp. pp. 278ff: to wit, the idea of "gradual progress" in history is "dropped" by Augustine after 393 (p. 279).
219. Brown, *Augustine*, pp. 264–269; and Cochrane, *Classical*, pp. 392ff and 451ff. Cranz, "Society," p. 290, would put it this way: education is a process of "dis-tension" of the religious personality rather than one of "extension"; that is, of progressive confusion rather than of revelation and self-clarification.
220. Brown, *Augustine*, p. 265.
221. The implication, of course, is that "assimilation to God" qua "approximation" is the same as "deification."
222. Augustine, quoted in Ladner, *Reform*, p. 194.
223. Deane, *Ideas*, pp. 16 and 49.
224. Ferguson, *Pelagius*, p. 46, tells us that Pelagius distinguished false from true pride, perhaps just as Plato distinguished vulgar from heavenly eros (n. 129 above). On the presence of the same distinction in Kant and Hegel see Part III.
225. I have discussed the idea of preparation for salvation above, n. 104. Among the *Aufklärer* preparation is more a matter of "patience" than of "enthusiasm," of gradual reform than of revolution. Miller, "Preparation," pp. 279–280, is clear on the point. I develop the argument in Parts II and III.
226. Lessing, *LTW*, p. 83. In paragraphs 80–86 Lessing makes it clear that the "goal" of "education" should have a spiritual "purpose."
227. What I say in n. 71 above is relevant here.
228. What I say in n. 89 above is relevant here.
229. Three points here. First, K. Bolle's remark that often "full scale religious renewal is not possible except through secularization" seems apposite here. (See his "Secularization as a Problem for the History of Religions," *Contemporary Studies in Society and History*, v. 12, 3 [1970], p. 251.) Second, the issue of what has been called "physico-theology" (Tuveson, *Millennium*, p. 104; Beck, *Early*, p. 525; and Reill, *Rise*, n. 10, p. 227) arises here. And third, the problem of "redivinization" (Voegelin, *New*, p. 107) needs to be confronted.

Part I

1. Again, I have learned much from Geertz, *Cultures*, on how to approach the problem of religion when it is viewed as "a cultural system."
2. See M. Reeves, *The Influence of Prophecy in the Later Middle Ages* (Oxford, 1969), for the basic dimensions of this tradition. Reeves justifies her use of Joachimism as a label for what she concedes (p. 75) is a "very miscellaneous collection of prophecies," first by equating Joachimism with the "belief in

the coming Age of the Spirit" (p. 242) and then by identifying "the dynamic quality" of this belief with the eschatological expectations of the entire period (p. 135). Reeves has since advised me that she has altered her views on this. As n. 67 to the Introduction indicates, I think Joachimism is a species of covenant theology and its influence among the Germans needs to be understood in that theological context.

3. I explain below, Chapter 1.

4. One can make the point historically by looking at Mosheim's attitude toward Servetus. Reill, *The German Enlightenment and The Rise of Historicism*, pp. 164–165, notes how Mosheim was impressed with the activism inherent in Servetus' call for "a total reformation of contemporary religion." Approaching Servetus by way of Joachimism, Reeves (Prophecy, pp. 484–486) explains his activism in terms of the trinitarian view of history. Much of what she says about Servetus is substantiated by R. Bainton *Hunted Heretic* (Glouchester, 1973), especially pp. 46–52 and 195–196), who sees much of the theology of the divine economy (i.e., Joachimism in the service of the "deification of men") in Servetus.

5. I discuss the Joachim–Augustine conflict below, Chapter 1.

6. Passmore, *The Perfectability of Man*, p. 214. The same argument is often made in discussion of Coccejus and "federal theology." It comes up in that form in Old-Württemberg (see below, Chapter 2) and, according to Miller, in seventeenth-century America. S. Ozment, *Homo Spiritualis*, p. 25 (n.1), hints at the tie when he invokes Coccejus in the midst of a discussion of late medieval Pelagian covenant theology.

7. J. Vann, *The Making of a State: Württemberg, 1593–1793* (Ithaca, New York: 1984), n. p. 124, provides a percentage breakdown.

8. My conceptualization of this owes much to W. Haller, *Foxe's Book of Martyrs and the Elect Nation* (London, 1963), and to W. Lamont's *Godly Rule* (London, 1969), especially pp. 23–24 and Chapter 2.

9. It is instructive here that Foxe (see Haller, *Book*, pp. 124 and 130), saw himself as writing in the Eusebius tradition that is often characterized as "Caesaropapism." Yet, as R. Markus has shown, "The Roman Empire in Early Christian Historiography," *Downside Review*, v. 81 (1963), especially p. 344, the notion of political rulers fulfilling "the divine purpose in history" is "derived" from a very old "Hellenistic tradition." The idea of a "godly polity" is Eusebius', as Cranz, "Kingdom and Polity in Eusebius of Caesarea," *HTR*, v. 45, 1 (1952), p. 62, has noted. Obviously, I understand much of this – the tie between "godly polity," Caesaropapism, and Foxe – in terms of the civil religion argument discussed in the Introduction, n. 54.

10. Reeves, *Prophecy*, p. 309.

11. Ibid., p. 311.

12. Ibid.

13. Ibid., pp. 299ff and esp. 311.

14. Note comment in ibid., p. 311: "Joachim's vision of a spiritual revolution has made significant difference to the image of the great World Emperor in that he was now seen as the just chastiser and renewer of a depraved Church." Clearly, this is important to the "godly prince" argument that so

dominates Protestant thought in the sixteenth century. The literature on Foxe, while weighted toward the minimalist position, does acknowledge a maximalist tendency in Foxe also.

15. I have found Lamont's discussion of the English peoples' conception of itself as a "godly people" useful here. See Lamont, *Godly*, Chapter 4, and especially pp. 50–51 and 94–95. Also see Tuveson, *Redeemer Nation*, Chapter V.

16. The phrases come from Hatch, *The Sacred Cause of Liberty*, p. 153, and Reeves, *Prophecy*, p. 312, respectively. Hatch (pp. 17–24 and 152–154) is especially good on drawing out the political implications this eschatological approach to kingship had for Protestants in America. It is from him that I have borrowed the phrase "civil millenarianism."

17. Hatch, *Sacred*, p. 83, hints at a similar shift in America.

18. Ibid., esp. pp. 73–76, is important. Tuveson, *Redeemer*, p. 24, labels this self-conception "apocalyptic Whiggism." Hatch (pp. 3 and 148) prefers the idea of "republican eschatology."

19. On the counterpolity concept, see M. Walter, *Saints*, p. 51.

20. The phrase is Tuveson's, *Redeemer*, p. 25. It is clearly tied to the idea of a "godly people" (n. 15, above) and not to the idea of a "godly prince."

21. Throughout Part I I make much of the shift in the focus of Protestant eschatological imagination away from things political to things social. The "directional cast" (Geertz, *Cultures*, p. 97) of the argument is important, I think, for showing why Protestant "motivations" that appear to be "secular" are, in fact, religiously inspired. One could say that an overriding concern with the preservation of Protestant religious liberties led Württembergers to recast the eschatology that had previously focused on the prince so that it would suit a collective Protestant (i.e., socioreligious) interest. Pocock, *Politics Language and Time*, pp. 177–178, discusses the shift in terms of the difference between "the magisterial and the Radical Reformations." More relevant, though, is the extensive body of literature that deals with the relationship between "Calvinism and democracy." See, e.g., H. Baron cited in Chapter 2 below.

22. A basic theme of Hatch's, *Sacred*, passim.

23. In addition to n. 15 above, see Hatch, *Sacred*; Haller, *Book*, especially Chapter VII; and Bercovitch, *The American Jeremiad*, for discussions of the "election," "persecution," and "chosen" people argument.

24. Among others, Miller, *The New England Mind*, pp. 469–470, has appreciated the importance to Protestants of the Reformation as an "expanding force" in history. This, of course, is precisely why covenant theology and Joachimism appealed to so many Protestants in the early modern period of European history: it opened the future to them. Troeltsch, *ST*, pp. 592 and 599–604, explains this "force" in terms of the Calvinist commitment to the "progressive sanctification" of the world.

25. Tuveson, *Redeemer*, p. 33, is clear on this point.

26. I develop the Second Reformation argument below. Troeltsch, *ST*, p. 678, uses the idea to point up Protestant awareness of the need for "reform in life" even after the Reformation.

27. As a "millennial people" the Protestants had a collective sense of election. Hatch makes the point, *Sacred*, pp. 39 and 57. Bercovitch, *American*, p. 44, comes close to this argument when he writes that among Puritans "the way of salvation was made into a mode of socialization." Note that "socialization" here, while certainly "ideological," is not an imposition of a reigning political power. Troeltsch's chapter on Calvinsim, *ST*, is the classic statement.

28. What makes that responsibility prepolitical rather than antipolitical is that the Protestant conception of a millennial people is tied on the one hand to the Reformation as an expanding force in history and on the other to the millennium as the end of that expansion. In both cases, the goal of religious life is what I would call "recollectivization." That, I think, is a fair description of what Protestant politics consists in *once it has* abandoned the godly prince argument (i.e., once it has displayed its antipolitical convictions). On recollectivization also see n. 175, Chapter 1.

29. The counterpolity argument (n. 19 above) is decisive here.

30. Burke, *A Grammar of Motives*, pp. 235–236. For our purposes here this is a remarkably important argument. It allows us to show quite clearly how what appears to be a Protestant *withdrawal* from politics is actually a precondition for the *reform* of politics. M. McGiffert, "Covenant, Crown and Commons," in *JBS*, v. 20, 1 (1980), is excellent on this point.

31. The concept is Hatch's (see *Sacred*, especially Chapter 1) and is useful because it permits us to appreciate how certain modes of eschatology permit the fruitful interplay between religious and political sets of values that we generally consider to be antithetical.

32. Reeves, *Prophecy*, pp. 501–502, is right to trace this mode back to Joachim. And Tuveson, *Millennium and Utopia*, pp. 19–20, is just as correct to regard Joachim as an anticipation of "later Protestant attitudes" on this point.

33. I have more to say about the Joachimite eschatological "mood" below. Suffice it to say here that Reeves, *Prophecy*, pp. 55, 135, 175, 178, 384, 431, 481, 502, and 506, very often talks about Joachimism more as "mood" than a "tradition" or "motivation." For the difference between "mood" and "motivation" see Geertz, *Cultures*, p. 97.

34. Benz, "Bengel," and Rohrmoser, "Hegels," cited in n. 29 of the introduction, are the key sources on this tradition.

35. Geertz, *Cultures*, p. 113.

36. P. Berger, *The Social Reality of Religion* (London, 1967), p. 154.

37. The epigraphs to Part I come, respectively, from Tocqueville's *Democracy in America*, Mayer, ed., pp. 287, 287, 293, and 530. Anyone familiar with the work of Weber will appreciate the parallel with Tocqueville on the matter of "affinity." See, for example, *From Max Weber*, Gerth and Mills, eds. (New York, 1958), pp. 284–285.

38. The phrase is from Weber's famous statement on "elective affinities" as quoted in R. Bendix, *Max Weber* (New York, 1960), p. 63.

39. Parsons, quoted in ibid., p. 261.

40. The phrase is Bendix's, in ibid., p. 259.

Chapter 1

1. I cite the most relevant literature below, n. 35. Suffice it to say here that W. J. Bouwsma, *Concordia Mundi: The Career and Thought of Guillaume Postel (1510–1581)* (Cambridge, MA, 1957), was one of the first to exploit eschatology as such a resource. More recently, Pocock (*Politics Language and Time*, p. 162) remarked, "Prophecy and eschatology. . . were not merely a system of dogmas for believers, but a highly important component of the conceptual equipment possessed by Christian Europe." In another context, Abrams, *Natural Supernaturalism*, has brilliantly shown what can be done by developing this kind of focus. Very useful as a general introduction to the topic: Y. Talmon, "Millenarian Movements," in *Archives Européenes de Sociologie*, v. 7, 2 (1966).

2. E. von Dobschütz, *The Eschatology of the Gospels* (London, 1910), p. 60. Although this book is quite old, it is a useful introduction to the problem of eschatology in Christian thought.

3. At least one commentator has suggested that this approach to eschatology is "neo-Weberian." See W. Lamont, "Debate: Puritanism as History and Historiography," *PP*, no. 44 (1969), pp. 133. In *The New England Mind*, especially Chapters XIII and XIV, Miller provides a classic example of this approach.

4. As H. Guy, *The New Testament Doctrine of the "Last Things"* (Oxford, 1948), p. 179, has observed: there is no such thing as "orthodox eschatology."

5. Benz, *Evolution and Christian Hope*, pp. 11ff, notes how different were early Christian attitudes toward the appropriate means of salvation – e.g., "prayer," "prophetic vision," "asceticism," and "progressive development in salvation history." Also of interest here: B. Wilson, *Magic and the Millennium* (New York, 1973), pp. 21ff, where he offers a typology of different means of salvation that help us understand different modes of religious activism.

6. See, respectively: A. Schweitzer, *The Quest of the Historical Jesus*, W. Montgomery, trans., 3rd ed. (London, 1954); and C. Dodd, *The Interpretation of the Fourth Gospel* (Cambridge, England, 1953), pp. 7 and 447 (n. 1), who credits G. Florovsky with the idea of "inaugurated eschatology;" von Dobschütz, *Gospels*, p. 56, makes much of "consequent eschatology"; Dodd, "Eschatology and History," in *The Apostolic Preaching and Its Development* (London, 1936), develops the idea of "realized eschatology"; A. Funkenstein, *Heilsplan und natürliche Entwicklung* (Munich, 1965), differentiates revolutionary and evolutionary eschatology; J. F. C. Harrison, *The Second Coming: Popular Millenarianism, 1780–1850* (London, 1979), p. 228, alludes to "apocalyptic and existential eschatologies"; and von Dobschütz, *Gospels*, pp. 150, 156 and 179–180, and Guy, *New,* p. 170, refer respectively to "transmuted" and "sublimated" eschatology.

7. Lamont, "Debate," pp. 143–146, discusses these three political types of the eschatological imagination. Also consult J. Gebhardt, *Politik und Eschatologie* (Munich, 1963), where a similar distinction is drawn.

8. Talmon, "Movements," esp. p. 188, argues the point from several different perspectives.
9. Dodd, *Fourth*, p. 7, gives a concise summary.
10. One student of eschatology has depicted thoroughgoing eschatology in the following terms: by it "[Schweitzer] meant that the entire ministry of Jesus was based on his conviction that he himself was destined to bring history to a close in the immediate future." See G. Buchanan's Introduction to R. H. Charles' *Eschatology* (New York, 1963), p. ix. Dodd, *Apostolic*, pp. 80–81, traces "futurist" eschatology back to the Hebrew conception of the "Day of the Lord."
11. Wilson, *Magic*, pp. 21–22, refers to this as a "conversionist" means of salvation.
12. Ibid.
13. This kind of "logic" has prompted one scholar to refer to thoroughgoing eschatology as "consistent" eschatology with a "futurist" dimension. See W. Kümmel, *The New Testament*, S. Gilman and H. Kec, trans. (New York, 1972), esp. pp. 226–244.
14. Much can be learned about "futurist" eschatology from R. Bultmann, *History and Eschatology* (New York, 1957), Chapters III and IV; and from Benz, *Evolution* pp. 25–34.
15. Bultmann, *History*, p. 51.
16. I follow K. Löwith, *Meaning in History* (Chicago, 1949), pp. 155–157.
17. Useful, especially with regard to the relation between Augustine's eschatology and ecclesiology, are: Bultmann, *History*, pp. 53–55 (to wit: "In the sacramental Church eschatology . . . is neutralized."); Benz, *Evolution*, pp. 25ff, refers to Augustine's "ecclesiastical positivism" and his "'de-eschatologization'" of Christianity; and Löwith, *Meaning*, pp. 155–157, demonstrates how the exclusion of "the temporal relevance of the last things" by postponing "indefinitely the expectation of their actual occurrence" effectively "neutralized" the "radical eschatology of the early Christians."
18. Bultmann, "History and Eschatology in the New Testament," in *New Testament Studies*, v. 1, 1 (1954–1955), p. 15. Also see Benz, *Evolution*, p. 21.
19. This is what Bultmann means to address with his "The Problem of Eschatology" chapter heading in *History*, pp. 38ff.
20. Bultmann, "Eschatology," p. 14, and Löwith, *Meaning*, pp. 155ff and 184f, discuss the problem of the "interim." For Augustine's view, see T. Mommsen, "St. Augustine and the Christian Idea of Progress," in *JHI* v. 12, 3 (1951), p. 371.
21. Dodd develops the idea of "realized" eschatology in *Apostolic*, esp. pp. 85ff. Later, in the face of criticism, he modified his position, admitting that his conception of realized eschatology had an "unrealized" dimension to it also. For the criticism, see Buchanan, "Introduction," p. xiii; for Dodd's modification see his *Fourth*, p. 447, and accompanying note.
22. Dodd, *Apostolic*, p. 87.
23. Ibid., p. 93.

24. Ibid., pp. 82–83 and 87.

25. Ibid., p. 87.

26. Ibid., pp. 83–84. It is important to realize that this claim is often used in descriptions of Augustine's eschatology. See, e.g., H. Grundmann, *Studien über Joachim von Floris* (Leipzig, 1927), pp. 73–78 and 89, and J. Ratzinger, *The Theology of History in St. Bonaventura*, Z. Hayes, trans. (Chicago, 1971), Chapters 1 and 2.

27. Dodd, *Apostolic*, p. 85.

28. Ibid.

29. Dodd, *Fourth*, p. 447 (n. 1).

30. This is an extremely important point in the history of ideas. It makes clear what Voegelin, *The New*, p. 121, means to evoke with his ideas of "active mysticism" and "intramundane mysticism." Dodd has understood this well (*Fourth*, p. 7): to wit, the Fourth Evangelist has not "turned eschatology into mysticism" because this mysticism "is based upon a fulfillment of history, within history." Later (pp. 197–199), Dodd shows how John's mysticism aims at activism, not ecstasy. This, in turn, explains the "programmatic" aspect of this kind of mysticism, a point appreciated by Tuveson, *Redeemer Nation*, p. 5, and by Ozment, *Homo Spiritualis*, Part One, in his discussion of Tauler. In addition, Tuveson (p. 7) argues that the programmatic aspect of this kind of mysticism "is in its way progressive." Hence, the importance of the idea (see Ladner, *Reform*, n. 34, p. 24) of "self-perfecting mysticism" that, for Dodd (p. 447, n. 1) would be equivalent to "self-realizing eschatology" (i.e., synergism). Vital to our purposes here is the fact that it is this kind of "mysticism" that we wish to associate with Joachim's eschatology. M. Bloomfield, "Joachim of Flora," in *Traditio*, v. 13 (1957), p. 261–262, sees this clearly. The distinction is all the more important because it has been tied to Hegel by Findlay, *Hegel*, p. 65.

31. With this shift of emphasis we move, for some, from eschatology to teleology. For example, Bultmann: "Eschatology has wholly lost its sense as goal of history and is in fact understood as the goal of the individual." See his "Eschatology," p. 13. Von Dobschütz, *Gospels*, p. 56, prefers "consequent eschatology" to teleology. As we shall see, this is what is at issue in Joachim: did he put eschatology at the service of *homoiosis* as a teleological concept or not? See n. 34 below.

32. This distinction grows naturally out of the discussion of n.'s 30 and 31 above. One can find useful explanations of the distinction in Taubes "Eschatologie," pp. 12–13; and in H. Balthasar, *Prometheus* (Heidelberg, 1947), pp. 12–14 and 29–35. G. Buchanan, "Introduction," p. xxiv, says of axiology: "Expectations of ends that were nonteleological so far as time and history are concerned but emphasized ends in terms of meaning should be called 'axiology.'"

33. Taubes, "Eschatologie," pp. 12–13, regards the interplay as basic to what he calls "apocalyptic ontology." Balthasar, *Prometheus*, argues that the interplay becomes an historical reality in the eighteenth century.

34. Funkenstein, *Heilsplan*, uses the term. As nn. 30–33 above indicate,

however, many crucial distinctions are implicit in the innocent label. Dodd, *Apostolic*, p. 95, regards this kind of eschatology as a disguise for "evolutionary teleology" and a doctrine of "progress." Nygren, *Agape and Eros*, pp. 102–103, makes the same point: to wit, "The Kingdom of God. . .is not built up, it comes."

35. In addition to the literature cited in n. 1 above, see the following: Tuveson, *Millennium*; idem., *Redeemer*; Bercovitch, *American*; Hatch, *Sacred*; Lamont, *Godly*; Harrison, *Second*; Haller, *Book*; Reeves, *Prophecy*; idem., "History and Eschatology," in *Medievalia et Humanistica*, n. 4., N.S. (1973); N. Cohn, *The Pursuit of the Millennium*, rev. ed. (New York, 1970); C. Garrett, *Respectable Folly: Millenarians and the French Revolution* (Baltimore, 1975); C. Hill, *Antichrist in Seventeenth-Century England* (London, 1971); W. Peuckert, *Die Rosenkreusser* (Jena, 1928); G. Schrenk, *Gottesreich und Bund* (Gütersloh, 1923); and F. Yates, *The Rosicrucian Enlightenment* (London, 1972).

36. See, especially, Tuveson, *Redeemer*, pp. 17 and 31–32; and Lamont, *Godly*, pp. 31–33. The latter singles out J. Foxe as the man who "made the pursuit of the Millennium respectable. . .who domesticated the Apocalypse. . . ." For tendentious reasons, Talmon, "Movements," pp. 167, 176–177, and 194–195, refuses to accept reform-oriented millennialism.

37. Above all, Lamont, *Godly*, and Tuveson, *Millennium*. Wilson, *Magic*, has a "reformist" classification in his typology of millenarianism. It is very close to Ladner's more historically oriented concept.

38. Talmon, "Movements," p. 194, is clear on the matter.

39. Obviously, this relates to the "intramundane mysticism" comment in n. 30 above.

40. Berkovitch, *American*, p. 23, puts it concisely: "Its function was to create a climate of anxiety that helped release the restless 'progressivist' energies required for eschatological fulfillment."

41. See Grundmann, *Studien*, p. 70; Bouwsma, *Postel*, pp. 264–265; Reeves, *Prophecy*, p. 506; and Bloomfield, "Joachim," pp. 266–267.

42. As we shall see, there is a scholarly dimension to Joachimism that is important to its reception among "establishment" scholars.

43. Geertz's (*Cultures*, pp. 96–98) discussion of the relation between "moods" and "motivations" helps us appreciate the "directional" aspect of the reformers' use of eschatology as a vehicle of change.

44. Reeves, *Prophecy*, passim, notes many Catholic uses of Joachim, too.

45. Tuveson, *Redeemer*, p. 26. For a fuller appreciation, see D. Kelley, *Foundations of Modern Historical Scholarship* (New York, 1970), pp. 152–163, and idem, *The Beginning of Ideology* (Cambridge, England 1981), pp. 157–158 and 247–248, where martyrology is explained as the basis of Protestant propaganda and as a philosophy of history.

46. Haller, *Book*, pp. 130–134, and esp, p. 130: Foxe "set before the Elizabethan public the current Protestant version of the traditional Christian conception of the meaning of history." Also see Tuveson, *Redeemer*, p. 140, where Foxe is presented as the formulator of the "Protestant myth" of Christian history.

47. I follow Haller, *Book*, pp. 162–169. The "war of the elect" phrase is Haller's (p. 68), made with reference to Bale, from whom Foxe drew much inspiration. Bale, like Knox, made Joachim a key figure in all of this. See Reeves, "History," pp. 103–107.
48. Haller, *Book*, p. 165. For an elaboration of the sequence see Skinner, *Founda.*, pp. 34–50, where the martyrs, who become precursors, are discussed.
49. Tuveson, *Millennium*, pp. 22–23.
50. Reeves, *Prophecy*, p. 83; and M. Bloomfield, *Piers Plowman* (New Brunswick, 1961), esp. Appendix I and p. 226 (n. 2).
51. Reeves, *Prophecy*, p. 107.
52. The reference to Renan may be found in Löwith, *Meaning*, p. 246 (n. 19). It is not a new observation; as we shall see Andreae noted as much in the seventeenth century and Lessing in the eighteenth century. Tuveson, *Millennium*, pp. 19–20, remarks upon Joachimism's anticipation of Protestantism here.
53. Grundmann, *Studien*, pp. 73ff, argues the point, as does Ratzinger, *Bonaventura*, Chapters 1 and 2.
54. Consult the Introduction, section 4, for the argument. Mommsen, "Progress," pp. 356 and 363–365, confirms the point made by many others.
55. With reference to this, Pocock (*Politics*, p. 177) writes: "The medieval Church thus rested largely upon the minimization of the eschatological perspective and the diversion of attention from the historical to the institutional. . . ." On Augustine and "de-eschatologization" see n. 17 above and n. 105, Introduction.
56. Ibid., p. 177.
57. Markus, "Empire," p. 342; Mommsen, "Progress," pp. 347–348.
58. Markus, "Empire," p. 342.
59. On Eusebius, I have consulted Ladner, *Reform*, pp. 115–121; Cranz, "Kingdom;" Markus, "Empire;" Mommsen, "Progress;" Funkenstein, *Heilsplan*, pp. 31–34; and Cochrane, *Classical*, p. 183ff.
60. Markus, "Empire," p. 343; Voegelin, *New*, p. 104, regards Eusebius as a "political" eschatologist.
61. Eusebius, quoted in Mommsen, "Progress," p. 361. Mommsen draws attention to Eusebius' penchant for "synchronizing" the "birth of Christ and the reign of Augustus." See, e.g., the long quote from Eusebius, pp. 361–362.
62. Cranz, "Kingdom," p. 55, writes: Eusebius "establishes an essential parallelism between the Empire and Christianity."
63. Ibid., pp. 53–55.
64. Ibid., pp. 54–55.
65. Ibid., p. 55.
66. Ibid., pp. 51–55. Cf. Voegelin, *New*, p. 104; and Ladner, *Reform*, p. 121.
67. Ibid., pp. 55; Markus, "Empire," p. 343. From this, Mommsen ("Progress," pp. 362–363) argues, we get the "Christian idea of progress."
68. Mommsen, "Progress," p. 363.

69. Given what has been said previously about the relationship between eschatology as axiology and as teleology this is an important change. See n.'s 30 and 31 for reference to the "self-realizing" eschatology argument.

70. See Ladner, *Reform*, pp. 109, 115–121, and 151 (n. 83), on the convergence between Origen and Eusebius. The connection is also noted by Mommsen, "Progress," p. 361, and by Cranz, "Kingdom," p. 55.

71. Earlier (n. 31) I noted how Bultmann envisaged this shift. In *History*, p. 59, he elaborates, suggesting that the shift involves "the secularizing of the concept of providence." Much is at stake here, for it is not clear whether the shift is made to "humanize" God or to "deify" man. Bultmann opts for the former, arguing that teleology here is based on an "analogy with the process of nature." That, Dillon (*Middle*, pp. 9 and 114–122) shows, is true of the stoics' "concord with nature" argument but not of those who used the *homoiosis* argument. If Dillon is right (see n. 87 to the Introduction), then the shift is made to "redivinize" man, and that is not what we mean by "secularization."

72. Cranz, "Soc., " pp. 279ff, is very clear on this. Also very helpful: R. Markus, *Saeculum: History and Society in the Theology of St. Augustine* (Cambridge, England, 1970), pp. 33–42.

73. Cranz and Markus agree about this but offer slightly different datings as to when the change occurred.

74. Mommsen, "Progress," p. 364, argues that Origen and Eusebius were those whom Augustine had in mind. Markus, *Saeculum*, pp. 51–55, is explicit.

75. This was Augustine's concern from the Donatist controversy on.

76. Another concern drawn from the Donatist conflict.

77. This is Cranz's dating of the change. Markus, *Saeculum*, p. 33, insists on a later dating.

78. Markus, "Empire," p. 347, puts it clearly: "In Augustine's hands the Roman Empire. . . is no longer God's chosen instrument for the salvation of men, no longer is it indispensable for the unfolding of his plan in history."

79. By this, of course, I mean to identify Augustine with "realized" eschatology.

80. Markus, *Saeculum*, pp. 64–71.

81. Cranz, "Kingdom," p. 47.

82. Cranz, "Soc.," pp. 313ff, makes the "neutrality" argument; Markus, *Saeculum*, the "agnostic" argument.

83. Cranz, "Soc.," pp. 284ff and 310ff; Markus. *Saeculum*, Chapter 4.

84. Cranz, "Soc.," pp. 284ff and 310ff.

85. Though I cannot develop the argument here, this question of "value" lies at the core of the Augustine – secularization argument. That is, what makes him appear to be a realistic and secular thinker is the contempt he has for worldly values.

86. Markus, *Saeculum*, Chapter 4; also consult Cochrane, *Classical*, pp. 82–84.

87. Markus, *Saeculum*, Chapter 4.

88. This is important because it makes "creative politics" part of the salvation process. Cochrane, *Classical*, pp. 82–84, pejoratively ties the idea to

"environmentalism" and thus establishes Augustine as a liberator.

89. Deane, *Ideas*, is excellent on Augustine's antiperfectionism.

90. Cranz, "Soc.," esp. 279ff.

91. Besides ibid., see Markus, *Saeculum*, Chapter 2, and Mommsen, "Progress," pp. 372–374.

92. Cranz, "Soc.," and Markus, *Saeculum*, pp. 17–23.

93. To wit, Mommsen ("Progress," pp. 373–374): "Whereas according to Eusebius...the history of man had taken a fresh start [with the Incarnation] and had 'progressed' [thereafter]... Augustine stopped his historical account precisely with the appearance of Christ."

94. Ibid., p. 374; Markus, *Saeculum*, pp. 17–23.

95. Cranz, "Soc.," pp. 290ff, develops the argument.

96. Mommsen, "Progress," p. 371, explains why *excursus* should not be equated with "progress."

97. Bultmann, *History*, p. 53, is illuminating, as is Taubes, "Eschatologie," pp. 77–80. This shift from Rome to the church keys the depoliticization and de-eschatologization arguments.

98. As R. Bainton has noted (*Studies in the Reformation*), eschatology "slumbered" between Augustine and Joachim (p. 125).

99. I am reminded of C. Dawson's remark (*Religion and Culture*, p. 59) that "it is only by religion that a religious culture can be changed."

100. Here eschatological renewal must be understood in terms of attempt to "redivinize" man *vs.* Augustine.

101. That Joachim fits into this more general pattern has been shown by Funkenstein, *Heilsplan*; Grundmann, *Studies*; and Ratzinger, *Bonaventura*. Others have tended to overemphasize Joachim's uniqueness.

102. There are several very useful review essays of the literature on Joachim and Joachimism. See M. Bloomfield, "Joachim;" idem, "Recent Scholarship on Joachim," in *Prophecy and Millenarianism*, A. Williams ed. (Essex, England, 1980); and G. La Piana, "Joachim of Flora," in *Speculum*, v. 7 (1932). On Joachim's biography, H. Bett, *Joachim of Flora* (London, 1931) is still useful. Most of the key literature has already been cited: to wit, Reeves, *Prophecy*; idem, *The 'Figurae' of Joachim of Fiore* (Oxford, 1972); Löwith, *Meaning*, Chapter XIII and Appendix I; Voegelin, *New*; Passmore, *Perfectibility*, Chapter II; Ratzinger, *Bonaventura*; Funkenstein, *Heilsplan*; Grundmann, *Studien*; Benz, *Evolution*, Chapters III and IV; Cohn, *Pursuit*; Mähl, *Idee*, Chapter 2; and Taubes, "Eschatologie," Chapters II and III.

103. Reeves, *Prophecy*, p. 90, refers to these anthologies. I discuss below, n. 122, her sense of "later" Joachimism. On her use of Joachimism, see n. 2 to the Introduction to Part I.

104. Benz, *Evolution*, p. 36; Reeves, *Prophecy*, p. 21; and Löwith, *Meaning*, p. 147, discuss Joachim's moments of illumination. There were several, each with slightly different contents. I thank M. Reeves for making this clear to me.

105. Löwith, *Meaning*. p. 147. A similar formulation in Piana, "Joachim," p. 265.

106. Reeves, *Joachim of Fiore and the Prophetic Future* (New York, 1976),

pp. 6–8, carefully separates Joachim's argument about a "third status" from his followers' argument about a "third age." It is the latter that concerns us here.

107. Löwith, *Meaning,* pp. 147–148. My emphasis for reasons that will soon be apparent. For a useful introduction to the idea of "divine economy" see G. L. Prestige, *God,* esp. pp. 55–75. I develop the theme in Chapter 2.

108. Two points. The three-age scheme is, of course, very old, as is the idea of successive revelation in time. Where Joachim is different is in his location of the third age *in history* and at a point in the future in a *soon-to-arrive* age.

109. La Piana, "Joachim," p. 276, argues that history shapes theology here, not vice versa.

110. I thank M. Reeves, again, for telling me that Joachim never worked out the date 1260 himself.

111. La Piana, "Joachim," p. 266, has appreciated this along with many others (e.g., Grundmann and Benz).

112. Löwith, *Meaning,* p. 151, writes: "the real significance of the sacraments is not, as with Augustine, the signification of transcendent reality, but the indication of a potentiality which becomes realized within the framework of history." With regard to the matter of continuity and change here, see G. Leff, *Heresy in the Later Middle Ages,* 2 v (New York, 1967), v. 1: p. 71, who argues for a mode of continuity within a discontinuous sequence. Benz, *Evolution,* p. 47, makes the same point.

113. Reeves, *Figurae,* passim, makes much of the "tree" metaphor.

114. As Lovejoy makes clear with regard to Tertullian, *Essays,* this is a constant of covenant theology. It is, moreover, quite relevant among Calvinists and the German idealists.

115. The phrase is Joachim's, quoted in Bloomfield, "Joachim," p. 262 (n. 59). Also in Reeves, *Figurae,* p. 2.

116. Löwith, *Meaning,* p. 149, has appreciated this and (pp. 244–245, n. 8) he links the view to Kant.

117. Very clearly stated in Bloomfield, "Joachim," p. 281: "One might say that Joachim historicized the Greek...idea of 'deification' and increase in perfection." By deification he means assimilation (see n. 135, p. 281).

118. Very clear in Grundmann, *Studien,* pp. 3–7, 71, 73–78, and 89.

119. Bloomfield, "Joachim," p. 261: Joachim "was a lyrical, not a systematic, thinker." But compare with idem, "Recent," p. 24: Joachim "carried systematization to an extreme."

120. Benz, *Evolution,* p. 44, is especially good on explaining this: "the history of salvation becomes a history of the education of humanity in which the Spirit is the creative, pedagogical principle."

121. The phrase is Voegelin's, *New,* p. 111.

122. This is when "later" Joachimism begins for Reeves. See *Prophecy,* pp. 14, 41, 44, 48, 55, 59–60, 65, and 156–157.

123. La Piana, "Joachim," pp. 266 and 280.

124. The logic of the argument, which culminates in the Eternal Gospel, was worked out by Joachim's followers, not by Joachim himself.

125. Benz. *Evolution,* p. 46.

126. Löwith, *Meaning*, p. 151.
127. Here is where Protestants (e.g., Bale, Foxe, and Knox) found Joachim most helpful. See Reeves, "Eschatology," pp. 99–107.
128. For some the line here runs from Montanism, through Joachim, to Münzer. See, e.g., Benz, *Evolution*, pp. 16–19, 35, 45, and 56. Bloomfield, "Joachim," pp. 274–275, specifically refutes the Montanism connection.
129. Reeves, *Prophecy*, pp. 135ff, discusses this, as does Benz, *Evolution*, pp. 39–41.
130. See Reeves, *Prophecy*, pp. 10, 16–17, and 21, for the particulars.
131. Very solid here, Bloomfield, "Joachim," pp. 261–262.
132. Ibid., p. 262 (n. 59) – an excellent note about the relation between learning, humility, and exegesis.
133. Reeves, *Prophecy*, p. 140; Bloomfield, "Recent," p. 31, where the distinction between *spiritum prophetiae* and *spiritum intelligentiae* is developed, and La Piana, "Joachim," p. 265.
134. This becomes vital for eighteenth-century Protestant thought in Württemberg.
135. Reeves, *Prophecy*, p. 10; Bloomfield, "Joachim," p. 262.
136. Reeves, *Prophecy*, pp. 139 and 170. Crucial here is her description (p. 96) of a picture of Joachim (from 1516) in a very scholarly guise.
137. As noted by Löwith, quoted above, n. 107.
138. Much that P. Worsely says, *The Trumpet Shall Sound*, 2nd ed. (New York, 1968), pp. ix–xix, is useful here. What he shows is how some prophetic movements have little to do with the personality and charisma of individual leaders.
139. Reeves, *Prophecy*, p. 140, stresses the collective aspect of Joachimism. Above all, though, see La Piana's ("Joachim," pp. 274ff) discussion of E. Buonainti's work on Joachim.
140. Consult the Epilogue for the Lessing–Hegel parallel.
141. Compare this with what Benz, *Evolution*, p. 17, says of Montanism: "Montanus and his community...believed that the promise of the Paraclete's coming...had been fulfilled in them, that the age of the Paraclete had already begun."
142. Reeves, *Prophecy*, pp. 140ff, emphasizes the teaching–preaching aspect of Joachimism. It is crucial also to German Idealism. Consult the Epilogue.
143. Bengel uses Joachim's strategy when he gives 1809 as the date for the beginning of the millennium.
144. Lessing's "Education," in *LTW* makes much of the patience aspect of all this.
145. Löwith, *Meaning*, p. 156, writes of Joachim: "religious perfection is possible...only in a definite period at a definite juncture." Reeves, *Prophecy*, p. 473, agrees.
146. I make much of this in the Epilogue – in the context of Hegel's conception of the "first class."
147. The phrase is Reeves, *Prophecy*, p. 140.
148. I have in mind here Voegelin's argument about Gnostic intellectualism. Also see n. 325 below.

149. I base this statement about the ongoing character of the Reformation on Reeves' rendering of Brightman's view of how what started in Germany in 1521 would be finished in England in the early seventeenth century. See Reeves, "Eschatology," pp. 110–111. Also see McGiffert, "Crown," where Perkins' work is the focus.

150. Reeves, *Prophecy*, p. 107.

151. Reeves, "Eschatology," pp. 103–104, pays particular attention to Bale, Knox, and Foxe. Skinner, *Founda.*, pp. 103–107, is perceptive on Bale's "apocalyptic nationalism" (p. 107).

152. On Osiander and Joachim, see Reeves, *Prophecy*, pp. 453–454, and Bainton, *Studies*, pp. 62–66. On Flacius, see Reeves, *Prophecy*, p. 487, and idem, "Eschatology," p. 103.

153. Reeves, "Eschatology," p. 105.

154. Reeves, *Prophecy*, pp. 487–490.

155. Ibid.; also see Kelley, *Ideology*, p. 158.

156. Reeves, *Prophecy*, pp. 487ff, is explicit about the "conservative" political implications of Joachimism. Lamont, *Godly*, makes much of the conservatism of Foxe's "godly prince" arguments and then proceeds to link Foxe with Erastianism. In addition, Skinner (*Founda.*, p. 74) detects a "deeply conservative" strain in the godly prince literature of early Protestantism.

157. Pocock, *Politics*, pp. 177–179, has seen this very well, remarking upon the conservative and radical faces of Joachimism as a form of political eschatology among sixteenth-century Protestants.

158. Reeves' argument [*Prophecy*, pp. 5–6, 14, 19, 41 (n. 1), 48, 55–65, and 151] about patterns of "twos and threes" in Joachimism helps illuminate the political dynamic we are addressing here. Also see n. 122 above.

159. I rely heavily on Reeves, *Prophecy*, for what follows.

160. On the commentary, see ibid., pp. 56, 149–152, and 156–158 (n. 2).

161. Developed in ibid., pp. 307–309: to wit, "The future in the third status belongs chiefly to a rejuvenated Roman Catholic Church."

162. Ibid.; also see Cohn, *Pursuit*, p. 111.

163. Reeves uses these phrases, *Prophecy*, p. 309.

164. The leader in question is one "Brother Arnold," a Dominican. He has been discussed in ibid., pp. 170 and 310–311; by Cohn, *Pursuit*, pp. 112–113; and by E. Kantorwicz, *Frederick the Second*, E. Lorimer, trans. (New York, 1931), p. 618. Here, Reeves writes (p. 311), "We meet what is really Joachim's third status recast in political terms." Kantorowicz, though, speaks only of a desire for "the reformation of the church."

165. Kantorowicz. *Second*, pp. 506–507.

166. Ibid., pp. 506 and 617: "The Emperor pointed to the sacred and exalted mission of his own Empire and the sanctity of his own Caesar-majesty."

167. Reeves, *Prophecy*, esp. Part Three.

168. Ibid., pp. 372–373 and 490. Luther, apparently, was responsible for some of this.

169. Tyndale, quoted in Skinner, *Founda.*, p. 73.

170. In what follows, I have benefited enormously from ibid., pp. 65–81, especially pp. 73–78.

171. Most stimulating here is Lamont, *Godly*, pp. 25, 52, 67, and 95, who tries to explain the political dynamic of the magisterial and radical Reformation in terms of "centripetal" and "centrifugal" millenarianism. Specifically, he uses these distinctions to set Foxe off against Brightman. Though there are problems with this formulation (see n. 175 below), Lamont has ably shown how certain forms of eschatology may serve conservative interests (i.e., Foxe's, for example). When coupled with Walzer (*Saints*) and McGiffert ("Crown"), Lamont gives us a rich view of the various eschatological currents in Puritan England.

172. The archetypal character of Knox's development has been noted by J. Gray, "The Political Theory of John Knox," in *CH*, v. 8 (1939).

173. The idea of "Reformation without tarrying" has been stressed by Skinner, *Founda.*, pp. 75–78; Gray, "Knox," pp. 137ff; and W. Haller, *The Rise of Puritanism* (Philadelphia, 1938), Chapter V.

174. The importance of this shift was appreciated long ago by J. Figgis in his classic essay "Erastus and Erastianism," in *The Divine Right of Kings* (New York, 1965). There, Figgis argues that Erastus was concerned less with making religion "the creature of the state" (p. 293) than with preventing "ruling elders" from establishing themselves as overseers of public morality "independent of the civil power" (p. 273). What is radical about this shift, obviously, is the notion that *nonpolitical* agents or agencies could become responsible for policing public morality. The point has been ably made by Walzer, *Saints*, p. 57, and by McGiffert, "Crown," pp. 33 and 44–48. It is crucial to the Calvinism–democracy argument.

175. This, I think, is where Lamont's notion of "centrifugalism" breaks down as a political metaphor for the radical Reformation. Certainly it captures the sense of moving away from the prince as the center of Protestant political gravity. And in the case of the Anabaptists it expresses the sense of anarchism that was associated with that movement (see, e.g., Skinner, *Founda.*, pp. 77–78). But as a metaphor it fails to capture what I shall call the imperative of "recollectivization" that is central to other groups of activists within the radical Reformation. Among these groups the movement away from the prince was simply a prelude to a more godly form of socioreligious and sociopolitical collectivism. Centrifugalism does not account for that movement back toward collectivism and political engagement. To take account of it, one must realize that covenant theology always had a collectivist aspect to it when used by Protestants. It was, therefore, an alternative to the despotism–anarchy modes of discourse.

176. Reeves, *Prophecy*, pp. 59–65. Also see her discussion of Gerard (pp. 187–188), whom she singles out as the one "who first explicitly appropriated the Joachimist future for the Franciscan Order" and who fully exploited "Joachim's Trinitarian conception of history."

177. Reeves, "Eschatology," p. 103, notes how Joachimism served this purpose. In idem, *Prophetic Future*, p. 165, she lists the groups that tried to claim election for themselves.

178. N. Cohn, *Pursuit*, hints at this when he distinguishes "social" from "political" Joachimism.

179. Skinner, *Founda.*, is very clear on the constitutionalist aspect of certain

groups within the radical camp. Walzer, *Saints*, pp. 112–113, carefully differentiates the radicalism of saints "in and out" of office.

180. Both Skinner and Walzer imply this about Mornay.

181. One could almost say that the differences among radical groups turned on the question of "who" would be responsible for guiding the process of continuous reformation. For the constitutionalists the task was reserved for those with a "vocation" to do so. For the revolutionaries (e.g., Müntzer) and the anarchists the agents of reformation were, as might be expected, much more vaguely defined.

182. Milton, quoted in Ladner, *Reform*, p. 34. The concept of a "Second Reformation" has only been hinted at in the secondary literature. The phrase can be found in Troeltsch, *ST*, p. 678, and in Hill, *Antichrist*, p. 101. It is connected, I think, with the ideas of a "real reformation" (Lamont, *Godly*, pp. 97–98) and a "general reformation" (Yates, *Rosicrucians*, p. 139). Crucial, though, is the fact that students of J. V. Andreae (see below, section 3), a key figure in Württemberg's history, have tied him to the idea of a Second Reformation. See, e.g., J. Montgomery, *Cross and Crucible*, 2 v (The Hague, 1973), v. 1: p. 232; and F. Held, "Introduction," to Andreae's *Christianopolis*, F. Held, trans. (New York, 1916), p. 10 (n. 2). Also see n.'s 14 and 28, Chapter 2, below.

183. Tuveson, *Redeemer*, p. 20, stresses the importance of the radicals' need to break the "unholy alliance" between the Church and State that had developed under orthodox influence. Also see Lamont, *Godly*, p. 36, where Bancroft's speech of 1588 is seen as pivotal; and Hill, *Antichrist*, pp. 54–55. I should note here that there is precedence for this separation in Joachim. (See Bloomfield, "Joachim," pp. 268–269.) The point certainly was not lost upon the Puritans as they viewed the Anglican arrangement.

184. Some of the Young Hegelians, one should note, go back to the idea of a Second Reformation in the 1830s.

185. On Studion consult Yates, *Rosicrucians*; Peuckert, *Rosenkreusser*; and, above all, Montgomery, *Cross*, who offers more detail than the others. Much more is available on Andreae. Yates, Peuckert, and Montgomery all have extensive discussions of Andreae. For specific contextualizations of Andreae's life and work in terms of Old-Württemberg see the following: F. Fritz's essays in *BWKG*, v.'s 29, 31, 32–34, 39; H. Hermelink, *Geschichte der evangelischen Kirche in Württemberg von der Reformation bis zur Gegewart* (Stuttgart, 1949); Karl Holl, *GA*, pp. 302–384; and E. Schmid, *Geschichte des Volksshulwesens in Altwürttemberg* (Stuttgart, 1927), esp. pp. 81–87.

186. Montgomery, *Cross*, p. ix.

187. F. E. Stoeffler's *The Rise of Evangelical Pietism* (Leiden, 1965), Chapter IV, is filled with useful information on this.

188. The date 1580 is to be associated with the Formula of Concord and with the ascendancy of orthodox Lutheranism.

189. See, e.g., Stoeffler, *Rise*, pp. 182ff.

190. As I show below, this is a common theme among pietists from Arndt, through Andreae, to Spener et al.

191. On Arndt see Stoeffler, *Rise*, pp. 202ff; A. Boehm's preface to the translation of Arndt's *TC*, pp. ix–xxiv; and F. J. Winter, "Johann Arndt," in *Schriften des Vereins für Reformationsgeschichte* (Leipzig, 1911). Stoeffler is unequivocal: "The father of Lutheran Pietism is not Spener but John Arndt" (p. 202). Or, as Winter (p. 91) notes, "Spener could be called a new Arndt."

192. R. Friedman, quoted in Stoeffler, *Rise*, pp. 202–203. Here it is crucial to realize that this is a theological formulation of moderate Calvinism. See, e.g., D. Little's discussion of Calvin and Perkins in *Order*, pp. 54 and 109. The key here, of course, is the shift from "justification" to "sanctification." Troeltsch, *ST*, p. 601, is excellent on Calvinism and the "ethic of sanctification."

193. Arndt, *TC*, p. 73. Also see pp. 94, 99, and 185.

194. Ibid., p. 87.

195. Ibid., p. xxvii.

196. Ibid., p. xxviii.

197. Ibid., p. xxv.

198. Boehm stresses this in his preface to *TC*. On the general problem of the relation between justification and sanctification in Protestantism, see P. Miller, "Preparation," and *Mind*, esp. Book IV; and Troeltsch, n. 192 above. Troeltsch, *ST*, p. 604, brilliantly ties the ideas of "externalization" and "progress" together in Calvinism.

199. Many scholars, I think, miss the importance of this shift because they invariably regard Arndt as a "mystic." Granted, he took some important cues from Tauler (Winter, "Arndt," p. 79), but as Ozment has shown (*Homo*) Tauler was a curious mystic indeed. According to Ozment, Tauler is very much an activist of the Pelagian sort. In fact, most of the points Ozment makes about Tauler (e.g., his activism, his "assimilationism") can be made about Arndt too. Essential to both Tauler and Arndt is the idea of the "spark" of divinity that continues to exist in man after the Fall. Arndt, *TC*, p. 335, uses the image, as does Tauler (Ozment, pp. 21ff). Put another way, Ozment's argument (p. 46) about "grace" and "preparation" in Tauler is true of Arndt's understanding of "justification" and "sanctification." All this is further illuminated by n. 30 above.

200. Important here is the reference to "the whole economy of God" in the subtitle of the English translation of *TC*. It suggests the relevancy of this line of interpretation for Arndt. Critics of Arndt at the time accused him of synergism (Winter, "Arndt," p. 34).

201. See Introduction, pp. 12–17.

202. The relationship between the "spark" argument (n. 199 above), "assimilationism," and the "image of God" idea is crucial here. It is most clear in Arndt, *TC*, p. 317. One should note, though, that Arndt was often viewed as a crypto-Calvinist. That would be because there is much of the "spark – assimilationism" argument in Calvin's *Institutes* (see Chapter 2, below, for this).

203. Arndt, *TC*, pp. 335 and 317.

204. Ibid., pp. 152 and 317. Another major theme in Calvin's *Institutes*.

205. We should remember here that the "Plato" we are talking about is the one

334 Notes to pp. 62–64

who regarded the telos of religious life (i.e., *homoiosis*) in theological rather than stoical (i.e., pantheistic) terms. There is, therefore, no contradiction between Platonic theology (of this sort) and sanctification. Consult n. 71 above, too, for how this fits into the redivinization argument. In addition, Little, *Order*, pp. 35–36, makes the fine point that Calvinism's theological concerns put it in opposition to Stoicism.

206. Arndt, *TC*, p. 317.
207. Ibid., p. 344.
208. Ibid., p. 350.
209. Ibid., p. 317. My emphasis to call attention to the "approximationism" of the argument.
210. Ibid., p. 322.
211. Ozment, *Homo*, pp. 35ff, makes the point about Tauler; Stoeffler, *Rise*, p. 209, about Arndt.
212. Technically, Arndt's *TC* consists of six books that came out in 1–3–2 groupings over the years 1605–1621. See Stoeffler, *Rise*, pp. 202 (n. 2) and 205, for particulars.
213. See Winter, "Arndt," pp. 34 and 90; and Stoeffler, *German Pietism During the Eighteenth Century* (Leiden, 1973), p. 2.
214. Arndt, *TC*, p. xxvii, refers to continuing the "work of reformation."
215. The idea of a "general reformation" seems to be tied to the emergence of Rosicrucianism. See below, n. 218, for the specifics.
216. I remind the reader of Brother Arnold, n. 164 above, a Württemberger.
217. Yates, *Rosicrucians*, p. 35.
218. On the connection between Rosicrucianism and Protestantism see Montgomery, *Cross*, Section Four; and Yates, *Rosicrucians*, esp. p. 99, where the link between "Rosicrucian writers" and the "refreshing of contemporary Lutheran piety" is explicitly stated. The phrase "general reformation" is used in the Rosicrucian manifesto, *Fama*, reprinted in Yates, esp. pp. 239 and 249.
219. There is a possibility that Studion's name was once Studian [Montgomery, *Cross*, p. 202 (n. 148)]. Is there a connection between the name change and "the Studion" monastery that had such great influence in Calabria during Joachim's time?
220. Most of the possible source can be found in Reeves, *Prophecy*; Bouwsma, *Postel*; and Peuckert, *Rosenkreusser*.
221. Peuckert, *Rosenkreusser*, p. 40.
222. Yates, *Rosicrucians*, p. 35.
223. Peuckert, *Rosenkreusser*, pp. 51–52, refers to this mood, as does Fritz, *BWKG*, v. 49: pp. 116–134.
224. Peuckert, *Rosenkreusser*, pp. 38–40, regards the formation as an esoteric group of gnostic-type intellectuals. Yates, *Rosicrucians*, pp. 36ff, treats it as an actual alliance among Protestant princes. Montgomery, *Cross*, p. 202 (n. 145), reviews the literature. D. Kelley, *Francois Hotman* (Princeton, 1973), pp. 266ff and 293–298, doubts a Protestant one ever existed.
225. The significance of the date, 1604, has been appreciated by Montgomery, *Cross*, pp. 169 (n. 31), 202–203, and 232–233; Yates, *Rosicrucians*,

p. 256 (n. 1), offers an astrological view of the date.

226. Yates, *Rosicrucians*, pp. 33–35.

227. Here, of course, is where "political Joachimism" as a tradition is important.

228. Montgomery, *Cross*, pp. 202–203 (esp. n. 148); and Yates, *Rosicrucians*, p. 31.

229. Montgomery, *Cross*, pp. 232–233.

230. Peuckert, *Rosenkreusser*, pp. 77–80, explains how Joachimism gives coherence to this mood of simultaneous crisis and expectation. Reeves, *Prophecy*, p. 384, says as much of the psychology of Postel's use of Joachim. That this mood had a political correlate in Württemberg has been noted by J. Salmon, *The French Religious Wars in English Political Thought* (Oxford, 1959), pp. 52–54. There, C. Besold, Andreae's friend, is cited as a proponent of the "double sovereignity" doctrine. For more on Besold, see Chapter 3, pp. 120–121. The point is that Besold used the double sovereignty argument as a means of widening the participation of "society" in "political" affairs.

231. The tie between the two is made obvious by Yates and Montgomery in addition to Peuckert.

232. Yates, *Rosicrucians*, p. 35; and Montgomery, *Cross*, pp. 174 and 204 (n. 157). Both the *Fama* and the *Confessio* are printed in the appendix to Yates.

233. In the *Fama*, the opening of the vault, which could be calculated to have taken place in 1604, was "the signal for the general reformation." See Yates, *Rosicrucians*, p. 44.

234. Here the Gnostic–election current within Joachimism begins to surface in a *socioreligious* rather than *political* context. As Little (*Order*, Chapter 4) notes, this is a Calvinist tendency as well.

235. See n. 218 above.

236. Montgomery, *Cross*, pp. 204ff; Peuckert, *Rosenkreusser*, pp. 96–99.

237. The opening paragraph of the *Fama* (Yates, *Rosicrucians*, p. 238) speaks of the "perfection" of knowledge by this group.

238. Ibid., pp. 232–233.

239. Ibid., pp. 145–155, is very good on the mixture of science and religion in Rosicrucianism. She speaks (p. 148) of it as promoting "a kind of divinized science."

240. Ibid., p. 232.

241. Here we have again the two basic currents in Joachimism: political Joachimism of the "godly prince" sort and the Joachimism of election that itself has "reform" and "vitalistic" faces. What distinguishes the former from the latter is its patient pedagogical thrust. The parallel with the Puritan situation in England, mentioned by Lamont and McGiffert, should be noted.

242. Andreae's use of Joachim is detailed by Montgomery, *Cross*, p. 57, 173, and 198–199. Compare with Lessing, *LTW*, p. 97. Bloomfield, "Joachim," pp. 289–290, notes the seventeenth-century "pro-Joachim boom."

243. Montgomery, *Cross*, pp. 55–56 and 69 (n. 191).

244. The "circle" is discussed in depth by Montgomery, *Cross*, pp. 160ff, 171ff, and 178ff. Andreae's desire to form these societies, Yates tells us (*Rosicrucians*, p. 151), was spurred by his devotion "to Christian and intellectual renewal." The desire became manifest in 1618–1619, when Andreae established his "Societas Christiana." Montgomery, esp. 211ff, discusses Andreae's involvements with these kinds of associations in the 1620s and 1630s. Clearly, the associations are socioreligious, not political, in nature.

245. Held's introduction to *Christianopolis* stresses the pedagogical thrust of Andreae's work. Yates makes the comment, *Rosicrucians*, p. 147. She also emphasizes the educational aspects of Andreae's thought, as does Hermelink, *Kirche*.

246. For the experience, see Montgomery, *Cross*, pp. 43ff and 105. As Montgomery has appreciated (p. 105), the "social merits of Calvinism" were crucial to Andreae's (and Arndt's) attempt "to make Christianity [i.e., Lutheranism] a matter not merely of theory, but also of practice." As I note in n.'s 248, 250, and 254 below, Calvinism becomes crucial to Württemberg Protestantism at this point.

247. For Andreae's social activist commitments, see Montgomery, *Cross*, p. 141, and Yates, *Rosicrucians*, pp. 145–154. "Civil" here refers to a "socioreligious" argument.

248. On Andreae and the war, see Hermelink, *Kirche*, pp. 136ff; Fritz, *BWKG*, v.'s 32–34; Montgomery, *Cross*, pp. 66ff; and Schmid, *Geschichte*, pp. 81–87. Also important: Karl Holl, *GA*, p. 309, where he argues that the war forced Lutherans to begin to talk like Calvinists.

249. Montgomery, *Cross*, pp. 84ff. Hermelink downplays the influence.

250. Hence the idea that Andreae was trying to "Calvinize Lutheranism." The phrase is O. Ritschl's, *DP*, v. 1, p. 403.

251. There is a hint of this relationship in Holl, *GA*, p. 331.

252. One could say, I think, that on the level of ideas Arndt, Andreae, and Spener represent three different "moments" in the unfolding of a theology of the divine economy. One deals with the sanctification of the individual, one with the regeneration of society, and one with the apotheosis of history itself. All come together in Bengel and in Old-Württemberg.

253. Montgomery, *Cross*, pp. 55, 74, and 105, cites a variety of these influences.

254. Andreae, quoted in ibid., p. 44.

255. See, e.g., *CP*, pp. 205–206.

256. In ibid., p. 174, a key phrase runs: "So there would seem to be a need of cooperation which only Christianity can give – Christianity which conciliates God with men and unites men together, so that they . . . do good deeds . . . and finally die happily to live eternally."

257. I think the sixteenth-century origins of much of the Second Reformation argument undercuts the Thirty Years' War focus as an explanation for the call for activism among seventeenth-century Lutherans.

258. Montgomery, *Cross*, pp. 74–75, makes much of Vives' influence.

259. E. Troeltsch, *ST*, p. 717, has understood this well.
260. Holl, *GA*, pp. 331–345, is very helpful on Andreae's fears of Caesaropapism, another way of talking about Erastianism and political Joachimism. Fritz, *BWKG* v. 32, esp. p. 88, puts it in a 1630s framework. Also see Montgomery, *Cross*, pp. 75–76.
261. Montgomery, *Cross*, pp. 75–76; I should note here that with this shift the center of gravity of authority begins to move toward "the people" qua religious collectivity. In M. Walzer's terms (*Saints*, p. 57), "Christian discipline" was being "substituted for secular repression." The political is giving way, in some sense, to the "social."
262. Andreae, *CP*, p. 134.
263. Ibid., p. 135.
264. Ibid., p. 196.
265. Holl, *GA*, pp. 313–314, notes how the war helped put eschatology at the service of renewal, especially in education. Fritz, *BWKG*, v. 29, reiterates.
266. Fritz, *BWKG*, v. 32: p. 88.
267. Andreae, *CP*, p. 206. Here, I think, the two faces of Protestant civil piety begin to emerge.
268. In the Introduction, n. 54, I made the point about civil religion working from the state to society and vice versa. The argument is relevant here.
269. What Andreae says (n. 256 above) expresses this dynamic and comes close to the passage quoted in R. Flew, *The Idea of Perfection in Christian Theology* (Oxford, 1968), p. 92: "Then Love's circuit is complete, from God to us, from us to our brother, and through our brother back to God."
270. Troeltsch, *ST*, pp. 715–716.
271. The dates for Pietism as a movement generally run from 1675, when Spener's *Pia Desideria* (*Pious Desires*) was published, to 1740, when Frederick the Great took control of the Prussian state.
272. Both are celebrated in *PD*, T. Tappert, ed. and trans. (Philadelphia, 1964). The book itself was written as an introduction to a new edition of Arndt's sermons.
273. Spener, quoted in Stoeffler, *Rise*, p. 235.
274. The point, of course, of writing *PD*.
275. Arndt, quoted in T. Tappert's "Introduction to Spener," *PD*, p. 9. See also Spener, pp. 54–55.
276. Spener, *PD*, pp. 43–44.
277. Ibid., p. 32.
278. The phrases appear in ibid., pp. 69, 73, 75, and 32.
279. Ibid., p. 95.
280. Stoeffler, *Rise*, pp. 200 and 203, insists on the "Arndt–Spener type of piety within Lutheranism." Both, I think, are also involved in the call for a Second Reformation.
281. This is a crucial theme in the study of Pietism. As early as the 1680s, Spener was alarmed by the separatist movement. See Tappert, *PD*, pp. 19–20. I elaborate on the theme in Chapter 2. Moser, a key figure for us, insisted on the distinction in 1734 (see Chapter 3).
282. Hermelink, *Kirche*, p. 153.

283. C. Kolb, *Die Anfänge des Pietismus und Separatismus in Württemberg* (Stuttgart, 1902), pp. 28−29. For more on this development in Old-Württemberg, see Chapter 2, pp. 82−87 and 87−96.

284. Troeltsch, *ST*, pp. 714−717, speaks of Pietism as "the sect ideal within the Church." Also see n. 43, Chapter 2, for more on this distinction.

285. A complication arises here, for while Troeltsch (*ST*, p. 715) notes that pietists always eventually broke with the church, they did not do so in Württemberg. Troeltsch has conceded this elsewhere. Compare R. Knox, *Ethusiasm* (Oxford, 1950), p. 109: "The enthusiast always begins by trying to form a church within the Church, always ends by finding himself committed to sectarian opposition." Thus, in Old-Württemberg, the pietists, technically speaking, were neither pietists nor enthusiasts.

286. Very clearly stated by Lessing, quoted in Beck, *Early*, p. 350: "The true Lutheran does not wish to be defended by Luther's writings but by Luther's spirit."

287. Stoeffler, *Pietism*, p. 52; Weber, *The Protestant Ethic and the Spirit of Capitalism*, T. Parsons, trans. (New York, 1958), p. 129, has the right argument. Indeed, the latter makes the connection between Pietism and *praxis pietatis* most explicit. In Chapter 2, I link the idea to the notion of the Second Reformation as a *"Lebens-Reformation."*

288. With this shift, German Protestantism begins to operate according to the theoteleological "logic" of assimilationism. At the same time, Lutheran eschatology is cast in "evolutionary" rather than "realized" terms.

289. Spener, *PD*, p. 104. Compare with Kant, Chapter 4 below.

290. Barth, *Protestant*, p. 132, speaks of Pietism pushing the doctrine of justification "into the background in favor of the doctrine of conversion and sanctification." Compare with Weber, *Protestant*, p. 129: "The emphasis was placed so strongly on the *praxis pietatis* that doctrinal orthodoxy was pushed into the background." Cf. the notes on "sanctification" above, n.'s 192 and 198.

291. Tappert, *PD*, pp. 24−25.

292. Following Gerhard, Arndt, and Andreae, Spener, *PD*, p. 54, attacks this kind of "scholastic" orthodoxy.

293. As we shall see, this emphasis on "will" does not make the pietists subjectivists. On the shift itself, see Spener, *PD*, p. 50: ". . .the study of theology should be carried on not by the strife of disputation but rather by the practice of piety."

294. E. Rice, *The Renaissance Idea of Wisdom* (Westport, Conn., 1958), p. 141.

295. Ibid., pp. 183−186, argues that this liberation of the will tends toward Pelagianism. I agree, but disagree with Rice's association of "Pelagianism" with secularism.

296. What M. Schmidt (quoted in Tappert, *PD*, pp. 27−28) says about the mix of mysticism and activism, eschatology and ethics, in Spener fits in very well with my argument here. Compare with n. 199 above.

297. Much of what Troeltsch, *ST*, says about Calvinist activism applies here as well.

298. Stoeffler, *Pietism*, pp. 23ff, is solid on the connection.
299. Consult the Epilogue for the persistence of this theme among the German idealists.
300. Spener, *PD*, p. 44.
301. Ibid., p. 45.
302. Francke, quoted in Stoeffler, *Pietism*, p. 27.
303. Spener, *PD*, p. 103.
304. Ibid., his emphasis.
305. Ibid., pp. 103 and 107–108.
306. Ibid., p. 104; my emphasis – to remind the reader that Arndt (*TC*, v. 1, p. 106) and Andreae (n. 248 above) both used the "die to life" metaphor.
307. Spener, *PD*, p. 107, writes: students of theology "during their early years of study [must] realize that they must *die unto the world* and live as individuals who are to become examples to the flock." My emphasis.
308. Hermelink, *Kirche*, pp. 178ff, makes the point with specific reference to Pietism's penetration into Old-Württemberg. For more on this, see Chapter 2.
309. Andreae, *CP*, pp. 166–167, 250–251, and 205–206, respectively.
310. Ibid., pp. 173, 196, and 207, runs the three areas of interest together.
311. Ibid., p. 206.
312. Spener, *PD*, p. 78; compare Troeltsch, *ST*, p. 716: "Spener also held that the greatest impulse towards reform lay in the idea of the coming Kingdom of God." The connection between eschatology and ethics in Spener has been ably discussed by J. Wallmann, "Pietismus and Orthodoxie," in *GGR*, pp. 437ff. For him, Spener's eschatologically inspired idea of a "hope for better times" signaled a shift toward activism among Lutherans.
313. Spener, *PD*, p. 45. Francke often speaks of "self-effacement" as the beginning of "true cultivation of character." Arndt also said this in *TC*, v. 1, pp. 125–135.
314. Here is a crucial point in the argument, the point where the German conception of "vocation" begins to play a crucial role in pedagogy. As I point out in Chapter 8 and the Epilogue below, the concept is essential to Hegel's thought, but to appreciate his use of it, we need to realize the religious "spin" the concept originally had. Suffice it to say here that the idea of vocation initially involved an "abnegation of self" and a commitment to live through the collectivity by way of service to it. On this, see R. Douglas, "Talent and Vocation in Humanist and Protestant Thought," in *Action and Conviction*, J. Seigel et al., eds. (Princeton, 1969), esp. p. 295. I spell much of this out in Chapter 2, section 5.
315. Basic here is the sense of vocation as an expression of humility rather than hubris. In fact, Spener (*PD*, p. 80) is clearest on this: "in spiritual matters ... there is more cause to be concerned about beginners [i.e., enthusiasts]...than about those who have already taken some steps towards perfection." Why? Because "patience" must take precedence over "enthusiasm." See n. 322 below.
316. One should consult studies of the pietists (e.g., Francke) at Halle to fill in

the picture. I discuss Pietism at Tübingen in Chapter 2.

317. In the Epilogue, I argue that this idea informs Hegel's conception of the "first class."

318. Lessing, *LTW*, p. 83. For more on this theme, consult the Epilogue.

319. Spener, *PD*, p. 80

320. Ibid.

321. I have detailed the importance of the distinction throughout this study. There is, for him, no such thing as "quantitative" perfection (Flew, *Idea*, p. 276).

322. Spener, *PD*, pp. 37–38. My emphasis, to stress the tie between patience and humility.

323. No accident, I think, that Spener's "model" for much of this is the success achieved by pre-Augustine Christians in the "work of sanctification." Spener, *PD*, pp. 81–85. Schiller, Chapter 8 below, reiterates this theme.

324. Ibid., p. 81; Spener makes this point before going on (pp. 92ff) to argue for a specifically Protestant view of the "spiritual priesthood" of all believers.

325. Here the parallel with Joachim (n. 139 above) is strong as both point toward a theory of the "equality of salvation." McGiffert, "Crown," pp. 45–50, offers a similar argument for Perkins. In Chapter 8, I show how the "equity" argument appears in Schiller and Hegel.

326. I try to prove this in Chapter 2 by focusing on Bengel.

327. Spener, *PD*, pp. 78 and 85. We can, Spener writes, "hinder" God's "work of sanctification in us."

328. See Wallman, "Pietismus," pp. 437ff.

Chapter 2

1. For Bengel's life, I have relied heavily on Mälzer, *Bengel*, and K. Hermann, *Johann Albrecht Bengel* (Stuttgart, 1973). The latter is especially informative about Bengel's life before 1713. Bengel has also received recent attention from scholars who have appreciated his influence on the culture of Old-Württemberg in the eighteenth century. See, e.g., Benz, "Bengel," and G. Rohrmoser, "Hegels," cited in n. 29 to Introduction; R. Heinze, *Bengel und Oetinger als Vorläufer des deutschen Idealismus* (Münster, 1969); and H. Bauch, *Die Lehre vom Wirken des heiligen Geistes im Frühpietismus* (Hamburg, 1974). Each of these studies discusses the Bengel–Hegel connection. Much can also be found on Bengel in Stoeffler, *German Pietism*; Hirsch, *GNET*, v. 2: pp. 177ff; and Hermelink, *Kirche*, esp. pp. 208ff.

2. As far as I can determine, no one has explored this relationship. Benz, "Hegel," p. 551, hints at it, though, without mentioning Bengel specifically.

3. On the *Instruction* see M. Brecht, "Philipp Jakob Spener und die Württembergische Kirche," in *GGR*; idem, "Die Entwicklung der Alten Bibliothek des Tübinger Stifts," in *BWKG*, v. 63 (1963); and M. Leube, *Geschichte des Tübinger Stifts*, 2 v. (Stuttgart, 1921 and 1930), v. 1: pp. 80ff. The *Instruction* is reprinted in v. 2: pp. 218–232.

4. For the particulars consult Mälzer, *Bengel*, p. 11.

5. Ibid.
6. Discussed in detail by Hermann, *Bengel*, pp. 33ff. Needless to say, these wars have figured prominently as a backdrop for discussion of religious changes in Württemberg during these years. See, e.g., Stoeffler, *German Pietism*, pp. 88ff. Above all, see Barth, *Protestant*, pp. 92–93, where he cites the wars of the seventeenth century as precipitants of the shift from theology as "perverted theological understanding" to theology as "the practical use of the Christian creed."
7. Hazard, *The European Mind 1680–1715*, p. 83.
8. The general point has been made by Holl, *GA*, esp. p. 314, and Fritz, *BWKG*, v. 29, esp. p. 138.
9. J. A. Bengel, *Gnomon of the New Testament*, 5 v., A. Fausset, ed. (Philadelphia, 1860), v. 1: pp. 3 and 8 (n. 1).
10. Spener, *PD*, p. 40.
11. This, of course, is consistent with what was said in Chapter 1 about the importance of the persecution–election connection in sixteenth-century Protestant thought. On the election of Württemberg Protestants, see Fritz, *BWKG*, v. 29, pp. 150–151. Bengel himself drew the parallel between Württemberg and Israel. See J. Burk, *Johann Albrecht Bengel* (Stuttgart, 1831), p. 168. The parallel was quite commonly drawn by Württemberg pietists (see H. Lehmann, n. 81 below, pp. 61 and 78–79).
12. The point has been well made by Hermann, *Bengel*, p. 411; and Benz, "Bengel," pp. 532, 539, and 549.
13. Reference here is made to the argument about "eschatological mood" in Chapter 1, esp. n. 43.
14. In this, of course, Bengel fits into the Second Reformation argument of the last chapter. See Stoeffler, *German*, p. 90. For specific mention of the connection, see n. 28 below.
15. See n. 3 above for the *Instruction*.
16. The convergence of Andreae's and Spener's interest in reform has been noted by many scholars. See Brecht, "Spener," pp. 447ff, and Kolb, *Anfänge*, p. 2.
17. According to Brecht, "Spener," p. 443, and Mälzer, *Bengel*, p. 351, Tübingen had never been a stronghold of orthodoxy. Stoeffler, *German*, p. 92, cites Andreae's work as the reason for the easy penetration.
18. On the tension, see Kolb, *Anfänge*, pp. 34–37, and Brecht, "Entwicklung," p. 49.
19. Appreciated by Brecht, "Entwicklung," pp. 48–54.
20. Ibid., pp. 51–54. See the *Instruction*, in Leube, *Stifts*, v. 2: pp. 227–228.
21. Brecht, "Entwicklung," pp. 32ff. See the *Instruction* itself, pp. 221 and 229–230.
22. On the development of this method in European thought see D. Kelley, *Foundations*, esp. pp. 100–101, where the philology–Calvinism connection is clearly elucidated. G. Schrenk, *Bund*, pp. 25ff, notes the importance of philology in reformed exegesis. He points out, moreover (pp. 300–316), that this method was most prominent in Coccejus and his student Vitringa, both of whom had enormous influence on Spener and

Bengel. Brecht, "Entwicklung," pp. 34 and 59, and Bauch, *Lehre*, discuss the specifics of the influence on the *Instruction* and on Spener and Bengel, respectively. Just as important is the tie Brecht (p. 60) and Hermelink, *Kirche*, p. 170, make with regard to reformed exegesis and Tübingen from 1720 on. It tells us much, they argue, about the historical-mindedness of Württemberg Protestants later in the century.

23. Holl, *GA*, p. 309, has noted how during the late seventeenth century many Lutherans began to talk like Calvinists. I would also suggest that in Old-Württemberg they began to think like Calvinists (i.e., the philological connections) and to act like Calvinists in politics (i.e., the resistance theory connection discussed below, section 6). Holl's point has recently been reasserted by Beck, *Early German Philosophy*, pp. 88 and 99. Also see n.'s 248–250, Chapter 1.

24. See the *Instru.*, pp. 227 and 230–231.

25. On the key figures involved see Brecht, "Spener"; Leube, *Stifts*, v. 2, pp. 45 and 259ff; Hermelink, *Kirche*, pp. 153ff; Stoeffler, *German*, pp. 91ff; Kolb, *Anfänge*; Fritz, *BWKG*, v.'s 55–57; and idem, *Altwürttembergische Pietisten* (Stuttgart, 1950).

26. By this I mean to equate down-to-earth Pietism with the activism and practical-mindedness that is so clearly articulated in the *Instru.*, esp. pp. 223–224. In 1712, Bengel put it this way: "To arrive at the proper point of mediation between activism and quietism is the main obligation of a Christian." See Bengel, quoted by Hermann, *Bengel*, p. 128.

27. See *Instru.*, pp. 223–224. Noted by Schmid, *Geschichte*, pp. 85 and 126; and Brecht, "Spener," p. 455. For reflections of this in Bengel, see Mälzer, *Bengel*, pp. 205–206 and 292, and Hermann, *Bengel*, pp. 246ff. It is not insignificant that Calvin expressed the same conviction. See J. Calvin, *Insts.*, v. 2: p. 327. According to D. Kelley, *Ideology*, pp. 150ff, this combination of piety and learning is "Erasmian."

28. As Heinze, *Bengel*, pp. 35–36, and Mälzer, *Bengel*, pp. 344 and 354–355, have noted, the "Reformation der Lehre" was to be followed by what Bengel called a "Lebens-Reformation." The latter, it should be noted, was championed by the "three angels" of Lutheranism: Arndt, Spener, and Bengel himself. Bengel mentions these angels in *Gnomon*, v. 5: p. 332.

29. Hermann, *Bengel*, pp. 12ff, offers a full discussion of the family background. I follow him closely.

30. Fritz, *BWKG*, v. 49, pp. 116ff, discusses Hafenreffer who, Fritz tells us, baptized Andreae and introduced him to eschatology.

31. I discuss the political importance of the *Ehrbarkeit* in Chapter 3. For the religiopolitical views of the people in the 1690s, see J. Vann, *Making*, pp. 159–166.

32. Again, I rely on Hermann, *Bengel*, pp. 17ff, for what follows.

33. Ibid., p. 20, makes the point about the diary and the apocalyptic images in it.

34. Ibid., pp. 23–30, for what follows.

35. Ibid., p. 32, details Bengel's retrospective account.

36. This is the thrust of ibid.'s (pp. 33–37) discussion of the Bengel family history in the 1690s. The argument fits in nicely with more broadly based

accounts (e.g., Fritz and Holl) of the eschatological "mood/motivation" connection within Württemberg culture during these years.

37. Noted in Hermann, *Bengel*, p. 35.

38. Bengel's decision to live with the contradiction might well be summarized with the words of G. K. Chesterton, to wit: "Christianity got over the difficulty of combining furious opposites, by keeping them both, and keeping them both furious." See Chesterton, quoted in A. Hoekema, "The Covenant of Grace in Calvin's Teaching," in *CTJ*, v. 2 (1967), p. 135.

39. Hermann, *Bengel*, pp. 38ff and 78ff, provides an overview of Spindler as a force in Bengel's life.

40. In addition to ibid., I have drawn on the following for accounts of Spindler: Mälzer, *Bengel*, pp. 27ff, and C. Kolb's series of essays on pietists and separatists in Old-Württemberg. See *WVL*, v.'s 9–11 (1900–1902), esp. v. 10, pp. 202ff. There Spindler is identified as *the* key figure among the separatists.

41. Hermann, *Bengel*, p. 62.

42. Bengel's total silence on Spindler has been noted in ibid., p. 82.

43. At this point, I should reiterate what was said in Chapter 1 (n.'s 281–285) about the pietist–separatist terminological problem. M. Brecht, "Die Anfänge der historischen Darstellung des Württembergische Pietismus," in *BWKG*, v.66 (1966), has made it perfectly clear that while pietists and separatists were not clearly differentiated until the 1740s the distinction was implicit much earlier. According to Brecht ("Entwicklung," p. 57), from the 1690s on Lutherans distinguished pietists from separatists by using a "church–sect" distinction. In this context, the Arndt–Spener line of piety was, with some qualifications, acceptable to church officials (e.g., Jaeger and Hedinger). In truth, several key officials invoked Spener as a model for dissent (see Kolb, *Anfänge*, pp. 28–29, 40–42, and 46–47); that is, Troeltsch's point (n. 284, Chapter 1) about the "sect-ideal within the Church" is most relevant here. By the 1740s someone like Mosheim, *History* v. 3: pp. 377–384, could deplore the confusion of pietists with "fanatical" separatists.

44. See Kolb, "Anfänge," v. 10, esp. pp. 202ff, on what follows.

45. Hermann, *Bengel*, pp. 78–82; and Kolb, "Anfänge," v. 10: pp. 364ff.

46. See Hermelink, *Kirche*, p. 185.

47. I have in mind, of course, the Arndt–Spener line – the two "angels" of Lutheran piety, as Bengel would later call them (see n. 28 above).

48. In the Introduction to this study, I made the point about Ladner's differentiation of reformism and revivalism as different modes of regeneration. In Chapter 1, I noted how eschatology very often served purposes of Protestant reform. Given the thrust of these two arguments, it seems appropriate to concur with Brecht ("Spener," p. 459) and Bauch (*Lehre*, pp. 37–39 and 53), who regard Bengel as having domesticated (i.e, institutionalized) eschatology and put it in the service of reform. We need, therefore, to distinguish eschatology within the church from eschatology outside of it carefully. Otherwise, we shall confuse two quite different modes of eschatological thought.

49. For discussions of Spener's associations in Old-Württemberg see the

literature, n. 25 above. I follow it closely with regard to the dynamics of the penetration.

50. See, esp., Kolb's discussion of Hedinger's essay on Pietism, in *Anfänge*, pp. 46–47. For Hochstetter's similar views, see Hermann, *Bengel*, p. 138.

51. The association of separatism with "enthusiasm" has been remarked upon by Brecht, "Spener," p. 455; and by Kolb, "Anfänge," v. 10: pp. 364ff. Also see n. 285, Chapter 1.

52. On the Edict see Brecht, "Spener," pp. 456–457; Kolb, *Anfänge*, pp. 22ff, 28ff, and 34ff; and Fritz, *BWKG*, v. 50: pp. 119ff. Jaeger's reference (Kolb, p. 29) to "our Spener" takes on significance in this context.

53. The increasing tolerance of Pietism among orthodox Lutherans in Old-Württemberg after 1694 has been the focus of Kolb's and Fritz's essays. Consult them for details.

54. Kolb, *Anfänge*, passim.

55. Essich, Hermann tells us (*Bengel*, pp. 65–67), was representative of the new attitude in Old-Württemberg about the need to combine piety and learning (n. 27 above) so that activism and civil regeneration could be promoted. Crucial to the whole endeavor, though, was the attempt to make teaching part of the religious vocation. As we have already seen, this focus was vital to Spener. It was carried on by Francke, who in 1713 influenced Bengel precisely along these lines (see Hermann, pp. 217–218 and 244ff). E. Schmid, *Geschichte*, pp. 141ff, focuses the same theme on the figure of Hedinger.

56. Mälzer, *Bengel*, pp. 292ff, makes the point about Bengel's inaugural address at Denkendorf in 1713, as does Hermelink, *Kirche*, p. 218. In the address, piety and *Bildung* are the keys to a Christian "character."

57. For details of the university insofar as it relates to Bengel's years there, see Hermann, *Bengel*, passim. Brecht, "Entwicklung," esp. pp. 58ff, and H. Liebing, *Zwischen Orthodoxie und Aufklärung* (Tübingen, 1961) provide more broadly based overviews of the university. All three sources stress the importance of the Pietism–Coccejanism interplay for the theological trajectory of Protestant thought at Tübingen during these years. That trajectory has been variously characterized as *"Übergangstheologie"* (Brecht and Hirsch); *"Universitatstheologie seiner Zeit"* (Liebing); and *"föderaltheologischen Orthodoxie"* (Liebing).

58. Consult Hermann, *Bengel*, for discussions of the particular personalities.

59. Jaeger is a crucial figure in the history of German Protestantism in the eighteenth century. There is, however, very little in English that relates to him. The German literature, though, is quite aware of his importance; see esp. the relevant sections of Hermann, Hirsch, Brecht, Hermelink, Liebing, Schrenk, and Bauch.

60. In section 4, I explain the meaning of this terminology. Suffice it to say here that federal theology may be divided into two currents within the reformed tradition of biblical exegesis; that Coccejus was a key figure in one of these currents, the "contractual school"; that Coccejanism may itself be divided into early academic and later speculative phases (see Bauch, *Lehre*, p. 23, and Stoeffler, *German*, pp. 226–227); that the Coccejanism that was

taught at Tübingen by Jaeger was a balanced version of the two phases
(Fritz, *Pietism*, p. 60); and that it was balanced precisely because it had to
contend with orthodox and separatist critics at once.

61. One should consult Wallmann, "Pietismus," esp. p. 430, on the problem
of differentiating "reform orthodoxy" and "late orthodoxy" from Pietism à
la Spener during this period. For what follows on Jaeger, see the literature
cited in n. 59 above.

62. This convergence of eschatology and ethical activism, of reformed exegesis
and the Arndt–Spener line of practical piety, is the focus of most of the
scholarship on Jaeger. It points up very well the links between orthodoxy,
Pietism, and federal theology on the one hand and their united opposition
to separatism on the other. See, e.g., Brecht, "Entwicklung," pp. 49–61;
Liebing, *Zwischen*, pp. 7ff; Mälzer, *Bengel* pp. 354–355.

63. The point has been developed by Hermann, *Bengel*, pp. 123ff.

64. On the importance of his conception of the purpose of disputations among
sixteenth-century Protestants see D. Kelley, *Ideology*, pp. 101ff, and Little,
Order, p. 92. On the specifics for Bengel, see ibid., pp. 145–170.

65. The similarity between Spener's conception of the "educational" function of
conventicles (see *PD*, pp. 37, 49, 75, 85, 91, and 97) and Jaeger's sense of
the disputation is striking.

66. The phrase is Spener's, *PD*, p. 49.

67. Spinoza was a key figure in several of these disputations. Too much should
not be made of that exposure, however, because Spinoza's mode of
historical exegesis was quite common among federal theologians of a
Coccejan persuasion.

68. See Liebing, *Zwischen*, pp. 4, 7, and 128ff.

69. Hirsch, *GNET* v. 2: pp. 109, 121, 148–154, 318ff, 367, and 390ff.

70. Two points need to be addressed here. First, Brecht, "Entwicklung,"
pp. 58ff, makes it clear that although Pietism and federal theology are not
identical they reinforced each other in positive ways in the eighteenth
century and are, therefore, historically important for the way Protestants
thought in Old-Württemberg. Second, the reformist aspect of evolutionary
eschatology, which is a major theme of this study, permits us to link
Joachim, Coccejus, and Bengel in a tradition of ethico-eschatological
discourse. Many scholars have noted the Coccejus–Bengel connection.
Only Mälzer, *Bengel* pp. 241–243, and Heinze, *Bengel*, pp. 17–20, have
discussed the Joachim–Bengel affiliation.

71. There is a clear line of academic concern here: it runs from Coccejus,
through Jaeger, to Bengel. For Bengel's attitude see *Gnomon*, v. 1: p. 8,
and v. 5: p. 186. For Coccejus' opposition to subjectivist interpretations of
the Bible, see C. McCoy, *The Covenant Theology of Johannes Cocceius*,
unpublished dissertation, Department of Philosophy, Yale University
(1956), esp. p. 144.

72. Kolb, *Anfänge*, pp. 19–27, discusses the growing dissatisfaction from
1688 on. I follow him here.

73. Brecht, "Spener," p. 457, offers an overview of the contents of the
Kompendium. Kolb provides a detailed account in "Die Kompendium der

Dogmatik in Altwürttemberg," in *BWKG*, v. 51 (1951).

74. Hermann, *Bengel*, pp. 157–158, discusses Jaeger's church history – published, with Bengel's help, in 1709 and 1717.

75. Ibid., pp. 123–124. Again, the Calvinization of Lutheranism argument is relevant here.

76. Kolb, "Kompendium," pp. 46ff, makes the point, as does Hermelink, *Kirche*, p. 172.

77. As to Coccejus' representativeness, see Schrenk, *Bund*, p. x.

78. It is important, though, not to exaggerate Coccejus' uniqueness. Mosheim, *History*, v. 3: p. 429, regarded Coccejus as an "innovator," but that is simply wrong, as Mälzer, *Bengel*, pp. 223 and 243, and McCoy, *Cocceius*, pp. 71ff and 84ff, have made clear.

79. For the Pietism, reform orthodoxy, and federal theology convergence see n. 62 above. For the clustering of Pietism and Coccejanism among Protestants in general and in Bengel in particular see, respectively, Schrenk, *Bund*, pp. 300ff, and A. Ritschl, *Geschichte des Pietismus*, 3 v. (Bonn, 1880–1886), v. 1: pp. 505–506.

80. Kolb, "Kompendium," pp. 42ff, notes the responses.

81. Hence the scholarly characterizations of Württemberg reformers as "three-quarters" orthodox and Jaeger as "half-Coccejan." For the characterizations see, respectively, H. Lehmann, *Pietismus und Weltliche Ordnung in Württemberg* (Stuttgart, 1969), p. 64, and G. Möller, "Föderalismus und Geschichtsbetrachtung im xvii. und xviii. Jhr.," in *ZKG*, v. 30 (1931), p. 432.

82. Hermann, *Bengel*, passim.

83. See n. 74 above.

84. The "school" of Bengel has been discussed in detail by Hermann, *Bengel*, pp. 320–339; by A. Ritschl, *Pietismus*, v. 3: pp. 84ff; and by Mälzer, *Bengel*, pp. 370ff. The latter is quite right to point out that the "school" divides into reformist and revivalist groups after 1750.

85. That this was the case can be seen by the opposition provoked by Bengel's and other pietists' work. Discussed by Hermelink, *Kirche*, pp. 166ff.

86. I have made this point about Joachim already (n.'s 134–136, Chapter 1). McCoy, *Cocceius*, and Schrenk, *Bund*, stress the scholarly and objective quality of Coccejus' work. For Bengel, see Stoeffler, *German*, pp., 99–102; Hermann, *Bengel*, p. 374; and Heinze, *Bengel*, pp. 14 and 151 (n. 96), where the Joachim–Bengel exegetical tie is noted.

87. Without employing this terminology, Möller, "Föderalismus," passim, makes this conceptual point about Coccejus. But instead of Joachim she uses Irenaeus as the source of the economy of salvation argument. No problem there, for both are covenant theologians.

88. On Coccejanism as an exegetical strategy see ibid.; Schrenk, *Bund*, is broader and, hence, less focused. McCoy, *Cocceius*, is quite descriptive and sticks very close to Coccejus' texts. J. Moltmann, "Jacob Brocado als Vorläufer Coccejus," in *ZKG*, v. 71 (1960), plays down Coccejus' activism but acknowledges a Joachimist transmission to the early German pietists from Brocado, who influenced Coccejus.

89. McCoy, *Cocceius*, esp. pp. 168–170, brings out the "dia-logical" aspect of Coccejus' thought. As we have already seen, discussion of covenants had long been a device for making synergist arguments. This is clear in Clement, Origen, Pelagius, and Joachim. G. Möller, "Föderalismus," cites Irenaeus as *the* key source for much of this. Similarly, the idea of divine condescension is generally part of this idea complex. E. Emerson, "Calvin and Covenant Theology," *CH*, v. 25 (1956), p. 137, and J. Møller, "The Beginnings of Puritan Covenant Theology," *JEH*, v. 14 (1963), pp. 48–49, discuss the early Protestant sources for this idea. In the latter, Calvin is quoted, to wit: "See how kindly [God] indulge thee: for [he does] not require integrity from thee simply on account of [his] authority...; but whereas [he owes] thee nothing, [he] condescends graciously to engage in a mutual covenant." There is much also in the *Insts.* to this effect. See v. 1: pp. 374, 405, 469, and 503–504, where "accommodationism" is the topic. Also see Calvin, quoted in Hoekema, "Covenant," p. 142, and n. 121 below.

90. For details, consult McCoy, *Cocceius*, pp. 195ff, and Schrenk, *Bund*, pp. 85ff. On the origin of the covenant of works idea see L. Trinterud, "The Origins of Puritanism," in *CH*, v. 20 (1951), esp. pp. 48–49.

91. By "natural" Coccejus understands the coordinated activity of reason and will in the human personality.

92. The point is well made by Schrenk, *Bund*, p. 86.

93. McCoy, *Cocceius*, pp. 71ff, 195ff, and 204ff.

94. For the origins of this idea, see Schrenk, *Bund*, p. 75. On how it works in Coccejus, ibid., pp. 75ff, 149ff, 175ff, and 206ff.

95. See Calvin, quoted in Hoekema, "Covenant." p. 153.

96. The passiveness associated with the idea of "receptive faith" is well brought out by J. v. Rohr, "Covenant and Assurance in Early English Puritanism," in *CH*, v. 34 (1965), pp. 199–201, and by R. Greaves, "John Bunyan and Covenant Theology in the Seventeenth Century," in *CH*, v. 36 (1967), pp. 157–161.

97. Trinterud, "Origins," pp. 48–49, discusses the main line of development in terms of the "double covenant" thesis, one of "works," the other of "grace." More balanced is L. Bierma's helpful overview of the literature on covenant theology among sixteenth-century Protestants. See his "Federal Theology in the 16th century: Two Traditions?" in *The Westminster Theological Journal*, v. 45 (1983), p. 2.

98. This, of course, is a crucial point, and has been touched upon by most of the literature cited in this chapter on covenant theology. Several points about the literature are in order. First of all, there is a terminological problem, for very often (e.g., in P. Miller) covenant theology is read out of Calvinism when it tends toward contractualism–bilateralism–conditionalism and so on. Others (e.g., v. Rohr) insist that the idea of a "covenant" is by definition bilateral, etc., and, therefore, they use the term "testament" to express the idea of a "unilateral" promise. To avoid this kind of confusion, it might be best to divide covenant theology into one-way testament and two-way contractual schools of thought. This

distinction raises another problem, for it is often used (e.g., among students of Puritanism – Trinterud and Møller) to divide covenant theology into passivist and activist schools. The former, so goes the argument, is Calvinist and Genevan, the latter an essential feature of the "Rhineland Reformation" (Trinterud, p. 40). In the first school, gratuitous grace is emphasized; in the second, ethical activism (Møller, p. 66), Finally , there are those (e.g., Emerson and Hoekema) who claim that the moderate Calvinists (e.g., Coccejus), who stressed the contractualism of covenant theology, were truly Calvinists in that vis-à-vis strict determinists they sought to return to the kind of "balance" of determinism and free will that is the core of Calvin's own teaching on the covenant.

99. On the Genevan school see Trinterud, "Origins," and Møller, "Covenant."

100. Greaves, "Covenant," p. 157, is clear on the ethical implications of the point, for Bunyan said, "The Covenant itself was Christ, as given of God unto us." For this reason, Greaves classifies Bunyan as a "strict" Calvinist and distinguishes him from the "moderate" contractualists.

101. A good example of this is quoted in v. Rohr, "Covenant," pp. 199–200. An excellent discussion of the conceptual point as to whether faith is inherent in the covenant itself or is part of man's response to God's offer of a covenant can be found in K. Hagen, "From Testament to Covenant in the Early Sixteenth Century," in *SCJ*, v. 3, 1 (1972), pp. 11–12 and 22. There he shows how the Zürich line of covenant theology in particular and the "Rhineland Reformation" in general separated from Luther.

102. See the well-made point of J. Møller's "Covenant," p. 66.

103. That Coccejus opted for the "two-way" covenant thesis has been appreciated by McCoy, *Cocceius*, pp. 168–170 and 279ff, and esp. p. 312, where Coccejus is quoted to this effect. Also see Schrenk, *Bund*, p. 84.

104. That Zwingli, Bollinger, and Calvin used covenant theology against the Anabaptists is well known (see, e.g., Schrenk, *Bund*, pp. 36ff). Hagen, "Covenant," pp. 18–20, is especially clear on Zwingli. He argues persuasively that contractualism was the result of Zwingli's rescue of the Old Testament from the Anabaptists, who regarded that book solely as a covenant of works and law. M. McGiffert, "The Problem of the Covenant in Puritan Thought," in *New England Historical and Geneological Register*, v. 130 (1976), is lucid on how this development also occurred in Peter Buckeley's thought. Calvin, *Insts.*, v. 1: pp. 390–391, 394, 462ff, 474, and 503–505, expresses a similar concern with those who wished totally to exorcise law and works from Christianity. Greaves, "Covenant," is good on Bunyan and the Antinomian problem.

105. Clearly stated by Calvin, *Insts.* v.1: pp. 466 and 489. From this Calvin draws the all-important distinction between the "letter" and the "spirit" of Scripture. I should point out here also that the relationship between economy, modes of administration, covenants, progressive revelation, accommodationism, and condescension is a very old one and has decided pedagogic and developmental edges. The point is clearly made by Möller, "Föderalismus," in her discussion of Irenaeus' relation to Coccejus. Also of

particular interest on the idea of economy in patristic thought: G. L. Prestige, *God*, pp. 57ff. Also see n. 121 below.

106. I take up the matter of why the covenant starts with Abraham rather than Moses below.

107. McGiffert, "Covenant," pp. 115–116; Schrenk, *Bund*, pp. 130–131, makes the point specifically about Coccejus.

108. McGiffert, "Covenant," p. 116.

109. Møller, "Covenant," pp. 49–50, has appreciated the point.

110. Calvin, *Insts.*, v. 1: pp. 388–390.

111. Møller, "Covenant," p. 64, and McCoy, *Cocceius*, pp. 226–231 and 293–294, speak of the latter understanding of law in terms of the "will" to a "new life." It is significant, I think, that Calvin, *Insts.*, v. 1: p. 657, links "newness of life" to "restoration of the Divine image within us."

112. McGiffert, "Covenant," p. 115.

113. McCoy, *Cocceius*, p. 40, and Emerson, "Covenant," pp. 138–139, regard Coccejus as a critic of overly "scholastic" Calvinism.

114. I develop this argument, section five.

115. See Møller, "Covenant," pp. 66–67.

116. The terminological point (n. 98 above) is important here, because while for some scholars the word "covenant" connotes a "two-way" proposition, for others that arrangement is best described as a "contract." Coccejus clearly advocated the two-way argument, but did so with both sets of terms.

117. Calvin, quoted in Hoekema, "Covenant," p. 141, insists on God's initiation. Coccejus, according to McCoy (*Cocceius*, pp. 168–170 and 279ff), follows Calvin on this, but still is able to bend the vocabulary in the direction of "contract" terminology.

118. See McCoy, *Cocceius*. Here "keeping" the faith must be understood in contractual and activist terms. As Calvin said (quoted in Hoekema, "Covenant," p. 144), "We must show by our deeds that we are the people of God."

119. Miller, *Mind*, p. 376, has put it clearly: "The covenant between God and man is an agreement of unequals upon just and equal terms."

120. I borrow this helpful formulation of the dynamics of grace from R. Greaves, "The Origins and Early Development of English Covenant Thought," in *The Historian*, v. 31, 1 (1968), p. 22.

121. The idea of "indirection" is crucial to the argument of Part III of this study. In n. 89 above I spoke of divine condescension and accommodationism. In the *Insts.*, v. 1: p. 405, and v. 2: pp. 316–317, Calvin links these ideas to God's pedagogic purposes. There are good patristic precedents for such linkages and many of them cluster around the idea of "economy" (see Prestige, *God*, esp. p. 61). Crucial here – and for the argument of this study – is the parallel between Calvin and Clement on this point. In *The Miscellanies* (Book VI, Chapter 5) Clement discusses God's "indirect" method of dealing with men, and does so within the framework of "covenant" theology (see Clement, *ANCL*, v. 12, pp. 326–328). Just as decisive is the fact that Clement (pp. 74–75) developed the idea of "indirection" in the context of having earlier cited Plato's "image and

likeness" of God argument as the basis for it. There is also much "indirection" in the Old Testament itself. See, e.g., Walzer, *Exo.*, pp. 53–54, who ties it to the politics of covenant theology.

122. Møller, "Covenant," p. 51, traces much of this activism to Tyndale, a key figure in the Zürich school of covenant theology. As Hoekema, "Covenant," p. 143, and Bierma, "Two," note, though, there is much of this in Calvin, too.

123. That there is much "assimilationism" in Calvin, Calvinism, and covenant theology has been pointed out by R. W. Battenhouse, "The Doctrine of Man in Calvin and in Renaissance Platonism," in *JHI*, v. 9, 4 (1948), esp. pp. 453–454, 457–458, and 462. Throughout Battenhouse's essay, the *Insts.* are cited as a source of Platonic–Pelagian assimilationist arguments. Many of the same points are made by W. Niesel, *The Theology of Calvin*, H. Knight, trans. (London, 1965), Chapters 4 and 6–9.

124. The argument for expansion has been detailed by Schrenk, *Bund*, pp. 135ff, and hinted at by McCoy, *Cocceius*, p. 177. The implication of this argument, of course, is that Christ becomes the "*Middelpunkt*" of an ongoing process of regeneration. He fulfills what came before while inaugurating what will be. For the idea of *Middelpunkt* in covenant theology see Möller, "Föderalismus," esp. pp. 406–407 and 409–410. Obviously, the idea of *Middelpunkt* allows us to treat the Incarnation as part of evolutionary eschatology in the teleological rather than axiological sense. For this also see n.'s 31–32 to Chapter 1.

125. McGiffert, "Covenant," p. 116.

126. Ibid.; and McCoy, *Cocceius*, p. 231. Here an important change of dynamic takes place. Hindsight entails looking backward, but the idea of Christ as a "mirror," a frequent image used by Calvin, implies a reflection forward. That is why the idea of the "imitation of Christ" (see Kelley, *Ideology*, p. 21) is so crucial to Reformation activism in the sixteenth century.

127. In light of the discussion of n.'s 124 and 126 above this argument should be easier to understand. Whether Christ is depicted as the axis of human redemption in history or as a mirror for imitation, he is in both cases the center of an economy of salvation that is assimilationist in both teleological and eschatological senses. Christ, as it were, becomes a manifestation of a dispensation in which economy takes the form of an educational ideal (see Schrenk, *Bund*, pp. 132–133). This idea is discussed further in the Epilogue.

128. If the latter, Coccejus' position parallels that of many Joachites.

129. For some, this call to "glory," so prevalent in the language of Calvinists, is equivalent to an anthropological activism of a Pelagian kind.

130. Coccejus, quoted in McCoy, "Johannes Cocceius: Federal Theologian," in *Scottish Journal of Theology*, v. 16, 4 (1963), p. 359.

131. For this reason, Schrenk, *Bund*, p. vii, has characterized Coccejus as a "momentous event" in the history of Protestantism. Möller, "Föderalismus," p. 429, argues that the turn to Coccejus signaled the end of orthodox Lutheranism in the Germanies.

132. Chapter Five of Hermann, *Bengel*, discusses the issues surrounding the text

and its composition. Much of the impetus for this undertaking, Hermann (pp. 133–135) tells us, came from Hedinger's attempt in 1704 to meet the same challenge. Also discussed well by Stoeffler, *German*, pp. 97ff. The word *Gnomon* means "index or pointer."

133. See *Gnomon*, v. 1, esp. p. 67. A key passage there makes it clear that Scripture gradually increased in "clearness and explicitness" as exegetes came to understand their vocation better. Crucial in all of this (see v. 5, p. xi) is Bengel's concern to use scholarship to keep the church intact against the separatists. Elsewhere (v. 5, pp. xiii and xvii) he dissociates exegesis both from "scholastic" pedantry (i.e., orthodoxy) and from "forced" and "mystical" biblical interpretation (i.e., the separatists).

134. W. Haller, *Puritanism*, p. 181. For what follows, see esp. pp. 169–170, 175–176, 179–181, and 188.

135. One of the great confusions in eighteenth-century German intellectual history arises here. As G. Kaiser, *Pietismus und Patriotismus im literarische Deutschland* (Wiesbaden, 1961), p. 7, has noted, while the trajectory of "Pietism" in the century runs in the direction of increasing subjectivism, withdrawal, and inwardness, the early "pietists" (e.g., the main line in Württemberg) were clearly not so inclined. Thus, the distinction Beck (*Early*, pp. 158–159) makes between early "hard" and later "soft" pietists is important. It shows that the line from Luther, through Pietism, to idealism is not direct. On this see C. Hinrichs' classic essay in *Preussen als historisches Problem* (Berlin, 1964), pp. 171ff. Also of importance, Weber, *Protestant*, pp. 137–138, where the "emotionalism" of Pietism is properly handled. Lehmann, *Pietismus*, p. 18, reverses Weber's emphasis, preferring to regard emotionalism rather than *praxis pietatis* as the key characteristic of "historic" Pietism.

136. Hermann, *Bengel*, p. 32, relates this "calling" to Bengel's rationalization of his father's death. Later (pp. 369–374) he roots it squarely in exegesis as a scholarly vocation. Also see Stoeffler, *German*, p. 102.

137. *Gnomon*, v. 1: pp. 5–6.

138. Ibid., pp. 22ff.

139. Hermann, *Bengel*, pp. 371ff, discusses this within the framework of biblical traditions.

140. Bengel, *Gnomon*, v. 1: p. 18.

141. Ibid., p. 8

142. In ibid., p. 54, Bengel speaks of chronology as the mainspring of biblical interpretation. Elsewhere (v. 5: xvii) he writes: "The expositor who nullifies the historical ground work of Scripture for the sake of finding only spiritual truths everywhere, brings death on all correct interpretation." Kelley, *Foundations*, and idem, *Ideology*, explains how and why philology found its way into Protestant exegesis.

143. See Bengel, *Gnomon*, v. 1: pp. 9 and 43–45; Bengel (pp. 41ff) associates this concern with the problem of "style" in Scripture and goes on to make philological and historical points about it.

144. Schrenk, *Bund*, pp. 27ff, discusses the distinction. As Kelley, *Foundations*, p. 38, has observed, this mode of exegesis goes back at least to Valla, who

stressed "the priority of grammar to theology." On this also see McCoy, *Cocceius*, pp. 109ff and 120ff.

145. Bengel, *Gnomon*, v. 1: pp. 9 and 44.

146. What is at issue here is nicely explained by Kelley, *Ideology*, pp. 59–63 and 96ff. There he shows how "conscience" in Protestant thought changed radically over the course of the sixteenth century from an "antisocial" to a collectivist concept.

147. On this I have found Miller, *Mind*, Chapters XIII and XIV, most stimulating. There, he has much to say about "corporate registrations of the Covenant" (p. 415). One should note, though, that Miller equates this process with the "constitution" of a people more in a political than a social sense. More in line with my argument is the thrust of Walzer's (*Saints*, p. 170) claim that there was a "constant tendency" in Calvinism "to turn the theology of salvation into a sociology." It is, of course, in the idea of the corporate covenant that contractualism plays such an important part. Walzer and Miller both emphasize this, and do so in the context – all-important for us (see section 6) – of a Protestant recovery of the Old Testament.

148. Walzer, *Saints*, p. 168, has summed up the collective aspect of this well: "Covenant theology had its source in the solemn promises made by God to the Israelites and it was in the form of a national covenant that the contractual idea first entered Protestant minds." That Bengel had Israel in mind as a model is clear from Burk, *Bengel*, p. 168, where Bengel is quoted to that effect. Troeltsch, *ST*, pp. 583, 586, 600–601, and 618, offers more insight into the Calvinism–Old Testament connections.

149. Bengel, *Gnomon*, v. 1: pp. 5–6. His emphasis.

150. Ibid., p. 6; also see pp. 42 and 46 for the accommodation–condescension arguments, both crucial to the theology of the divine economy position. See n. 89 above for parallels in Calvin.

151. Ibid., v. 1: p. 42; also see v. 2: pp. 453–454.

152. Ibid., v. 2: p. 277.

153. Ibid., v. 1: p. 6.

154. Ibid., p. 67; also see v. 2: pp. 297–298, where Bengel notes the wisdom of the "succession" that "has been instituted in the Divine economy. . . . The Divine economy has its delays exactly answering the end contemplated." Later (pp. 453–454) Bengel turns this into an argument for pedagogical "gradualism." Two other points. First, one should remember Joachim's notion of salvation moving from "clarity to clarity" (n. 115, Chapter I) and, second, one should compare Bengel here with Calvin, *Insts*. v. 1: pp. 393, 397–398, 403, 459–463, 485, and 500. Hagan, "Covenant," pp. 14–20, discusses the clarity to clarity argument in Melanchthon and Zwingli, respectively. For gradualism and covenant theology in the Old Testament, see Walzer, *Exo.*, pp. 54–66.

155. See Chapter 1 as well as Prestige, *God*, pp. 57ff. Also see n. 121 above. There I tie Clement and Calvin together. Möller, "Föderalismus," makes the same argument with the figures of Irenaeus, Calvin, and Coccejus.

156. Bengel, *Gnomon*, v. 2: p. 537, writes: "The Christianity of all and each

individually, is to be estimated, not merely from Divine worship, but also from the daily mode of life." Compare with Spener (n. 293, Chapter 1) and Coccejus (n. 130 above).

157. This is a crucial point appreciated by Schrenk, *Bund*, pp. 146–147, when he argues that the emphasis in covenant theology had less to do with what "God could do for us" than with what "we could do for God." According to Schrenk, moreover, the latter was understood to involve a collective endeavor. So, when Bengel speaks (*Gnomon*, v. 3; p. 154) of a "time" when "the fulness of the Gentiles, who have been long since called, may entirely come in," he is making a three economies of salvation argument. Kelley, *Ideology*, p. 26, refers to the "mythical" component of "formation, deformation, reformation" in the thought of Protestant reformers. Walzer, *Saints*, p. 56, discusses the same rhythm in terms of a "social, personal, and social again" sequence. Both, I think, are making what I have called a "recollectivization" argument.

158. Discussed in *Gnomon*, v.5: pp. 1–22.

159. Ibid., p. 17.

160. Very clearly stated with regard to Paul, in ibid., v. 3: p. 2.

161. Ibid., v. 5: pp. 1ff.

162. Ibid., pp. 16ff.

163. Ibid., p. 368.

164. Ibid., v. 4: pp. 10–11.

165. See, e.g., *Insts.*, v. 2: pp. 50ff.

166. Bengel, *Gnomon*, v. 2: p. 537.

167. See my explanation in n. 157 above.

168. Bengel, *Gnomon*, v. 5: pp. 22 and 16, respectively.

169. Ibid., pp. 16 and 22, respectively. Here Bengel follows Calvin closely.

170. A delicate but important point arises here. Whereas Calvin's exegesis of Paul and James was designed to save Paul from the Antinomians, Bengel's was to rehabilitate James. This maneuver, I am sure, is typical of liberal Protestants in the eighteenth century. Compare Bengel, e.g., with the famous Scottish preacher and High Church official, Hugh Blair. Specifically, note what Blair says about Paul and James in *Sermons*, 3 v. (New York, 1802), v. 2: p. 302. For Blair's liberalism, consult R. Sher, *SE*, passim.

171. Bengel, *Gnomon*, v. 5: p. 17.

172. Ibid., pp. 17–18. Yet (p. 21) Bengel is careful to say that "Works do not give life to faith; but faith produces works, and works make perfect faith." All this is part of what Bengel regards as "attaining...Divine friendship"; and friendship, as Bengel following Coccejus well knew, was the key to understanding the idea of "covenant" in the Old Testament.

173. Ibid., p. 17.

174. Ibid., pp. 19 and 20, respectively.

175. Ibid., p. 20, my emphasis. There is, as it were, a gap, an interim, between justification and salvation, and that is the realm of sanctification qua preparationism in this world through *praxis pietatis*. See Miller, *Mind*, p. 383.

176. Abraham is a key figure in all of this for political as well as religious reasons. I connect the two in section 6. This background, I think, is vital to a full appreciation of Hegel in the 1790s.
177. Bengel, *Gnomon*, v. 5: p. 20. On Paul's Christianization of Abraham see McGiffert, "Covenant," pp. 115–116. For the reverse process, the Judaizing of Christianity, see n. 277 below.
178. Bengel, *Gnomon*, v. 5: p. 20; the temporal interim here is crucial for Bengel. Why? Because it allows for a "test of faith" within the terms of God's covenant with Abraham. The test, then, constitutes the condition of the two-way covenant in that it can be equated with man's *response*.
179. Ibid., p. 21.
180. Ibid.
181. Ibid., pp. 21–22.
182. Abraham, then, is an archetype of the conditional covenant for Bengel.
183. Bengel, *Gnomon*, v. 5: p. 21: "...at what part of Abraham's time," Bengel asks, was God's covenant with him "fulfilled?" The temporal dimension is important to the justification–sanctification question (see n. 175 above).
184. The sequence is hinted at in ibid., v. 2: p. 466, where belief, solid knowledge, and full faith are used to chart "progress" in faith.
185. Ibid., v. 3: p. 172.
186. Ibid.; also nicely summarized by Miller, *Mind*, p. 385, where he notes how faith is supposed to guarantee *walking* in faith.
187. Bengel, *Gnomon*, v. 3: p. 172.
188. Ibid.; my emphasis to point out the anticipation here.
189. Ibid.; one could say here that while Paul used Abraham to Christianize the Old Testament, Bengel used Abraham qua archetype to conditionalize the New Testament. The general point has been appreciated by Möller, "Föderalismus," pp. 419–423, in her discussion of Coccejus' relation to the Old Testament.
190. Bengel, *Gnomon*, v. 2: p. 121.
191. Ibid.; and v. 5: pp. 3–5.
192. Ibid., v. 5: pp. 3–5, and v. 3: p. 154, bring out nicely the patience–perfectionism aspect of Bengel's sense of "trial." Much of what Bengel says here corresponds to what W. Bouwsma ["Christian Adulthood," in *Daedalu*, v. 105, 2 (1976), p. 77] would call a uniquely Christian conception of "adulthood."
193. Bengel, *Gnomon*, v. 3: pp. 60ff.
194. Like Joachim, Bengel believed that as exegetes became wiser (i.e., better scholars), so, eventually, would the collectivity. See n. 154 above also.
195. On this point see n.'s 147 and 157 above. Little, *Order*, p. 71, makes several fine points on the relationship between covenants and socioreligious compacts.
196. As Prestige, *God*, makes clear, the economy of salvation argument is a very old Christian religious conception. Among Protestants, though, it acquired a more specific focus. Calvin (quoted in Hoekema, "Covenant," p. 161) remarked, e.g., that God promises man "recompense...to stir us up to take courage better to serve him, seeing that our labors are not lost

before him, but are credited to our account, and the profit of them returns to us." Zwingli, Hagen ("Covenant," pp. 16–18) tells us, used fiscal and legal language to discuss the idea of the covenant in the mid-1520s. Ozment (*Homo*, pp. 32–34) claims Tauler (much earlier) has likened God's covenant with man to "a good business deal" in which "a fair bargain" was struck between the two contracting parties. Very useful for the merging of religious and economic language in Calvinism is Little, *Order*, pp. 58–67 and 96. Also consult Walzer, *Exo.*, pp. 24–25, for the Hebrew precedent.

197. The relation between economy and pedagogy is very clear in Calvin. While discussing God's accommodationism (*Insts.* v. 1: pp. 503–504), Calvin likens Him to a "husbandman" who knows how to cultivate with the seasons. Möller, "Föderalismus," p. 420, cites passages from Coccejus and Vitringa to the same effect. Clement (*ANCL*, v. 12: p. 56) cites husbandry as an appropriate metaphor for religious instruction. Origen (*ANCL*, v. 23; p. 161) offers a similar formulation. Again, as in n.'s 89 and 121 above, economy and accommodationism are inextricably connected here.

198. The entry of legal terminology into covenant theology has been discussed by McCoy, *Cocceius*, pp. 72ff, 89ff, and 164ff, and by Hagen, "Covenant," pp. 18–20. Two key points must be made here. First, the language was vital in the 1520s to the Protestant cause against the Anabaptists. Later, in the 1560s, it was central to Protestant resistance theory, especially among the Huguenots. D. Kelley ties much of this together, including the philology–legal–Calvinist mode of exegesis, in *Ideology*, esp. pp. 141–142, 176ff, 191ff and 256ff, and 309–310.

199. Miller, *Mind*, pp. 375, 389, and 485, speaks of this in terms of a "business" arrangement and as "spiritual commercialism." Also see McGiffert's "Covenant," p. 122; Miller's "Preparation," pp. 283–284; and Walzer's *Saints*, p. 168.

200. See Bengel, quoted in Hermann, *Bengel*, p. 369; Mälzer, *Bengel*, pp. 283–284 and 356; Hermelink, *Kirche*, p. 172; Benz, "Bengel," pp. 533 and 553–554; Heinze, *Bengel*, pp. 22 and 26–27; and Burk, *Bengel*, p. 403. Very useful, moreover, is Bauch, *Lehre*, esp. pp. 67–68 (n.'s 100 and 105), who points out the contractual connotation the term *Lagerbuch* had in Schwabia at the time. From Weber, *Protestant*, p. 246 (n. 124), we learn that Francke, certainly one of Bengel's models, had a very developed and methodical conception of "religious account books" that were to measure progress in salvation. It is possible, as n. 196 above reveals, that there were earlier sources for the idea.

201. Kelley's argument, *Ideology*, passim, about the role of lawyers in the "secularization" of Protestant thought is important here. The best argument for secularization is still Miller, "Preparation," pp. 283–286. But we must be careful. As we shall see (section 6) with regard to Mornay and Bengel, religious covenants could express themselves in the language of secular contracts. The point is well made by J. Eusden, "Natural Law and Covenant Theology in New England, 1620–1670," in *Natural Law Forum*, v. 5 (1960), esp. pp. 10 and 17.

202. McGiffert, "Covenant," p. 125; my emphasis.

203. Walzer, *Saints* p. 167; cf Little, *Order*, pp. 59ff.
204. Miller, "Preparation," p. 284.
205. The phrase is from ibid., p. 283. Note, e.g., Walzer's argument, *Saints*, p. 211, where "industry" and "work" are construed as marks of "saintliness."
206. Walzer makes the argument, *Saints*, pp. 54–57, 82–85, 167–171, and 212–215. Also very helpful: Miller, *Mind*, pp. 382–385, where it is remarked that entering into the covenant meant voluntarily accepting the conditions of a contract that obliged one "to external behavior."
207. Walzer, *Saints*, p. 213.
208. Ibid., p. 214; Miller, *Mind*, pp.. 382–383, is clear on the voluntarism of all this also. Walzer, *Exo.*, pp. 80 and 88, elaborates in terms of *"Exodus politics."*
209. Walzer, *Saints*, pp. 213 and 214, respectively.
210. Ibid.
211. Ibid., p. 215.
212. In effect, conscience had been collectivized and would henceforth be construed as a "social force." On this see ibid., p. 57, and Kelley, *Ideology*, p. 96. For the latter, the shift entailed the transformation of "religious ideas" into "a form of ideology" (also see pp. 59–61).
213. As Miller, *Mind*, p. 414, has noted, covenant theology involved a blurring of the distinction of the "religious and the social" in cultural self-conceptions. He argues (p. 415) that this gave covenant theology a "corporate" character. Crucial for our purposes, though, is that in Old-Württemberg the registration of this corporate covenant takes place in opposition to the prince. It is, therefore, different from Miller's New England, where "rulers" were included in it.
214. I have made the point in nn. 147 and 157 above. Troeltsch, *ST*, pp. 586, 604 (n.), and 610 makes this a consequence of Calvinist activism.
215. As we shall see in a moment this was a radical step in itself.
216. See n. 148 above and Miller, *Mind*, pp. 377–378 and 414–415. As Miller well understood (p. 415), reading collectivism as well as conditionalism into the covenant with Abraham was fraught with political implications. Walzer, *Exo.*, pp. 77, 107, 119, and 123, draws out the political implications.
217. The "order" of salvation argument, of course, is crucial. Miller, "Preparation," is most helpful here. Besides Irenaeus and Clement, Calvin (*Insts.*, esp. v. 1: p. 480) articulated an "order" of salvation argument. In all three the argument is part of the larger "clarity to clarity" thesis of the theology of the divine economy.
218. As Bengel, *Gnomon*, v. 5: p. 193, observed: "the end depends upon the origin." Hence, the rhythm of the three economies of grace argument is confirmed.
219. Ibid., p. xii; reiterated, v. 3: pp. 153–154.
220. Clearly, then, recollectivization is critical to Bengel's "Lebens Reformation" argument (n.'s 14 and 28 above). See Chapter 4 for Hegel's view of this.

221. Kelley, *Ideology*, esp. pp. 59–63, is most penetrating here. Also see n. 147 above.

222. Earlier (n. 172 above) we mentioned the relation in Bengel's mind between friendship and covenant. In Coccejus (see McCoy, *Cocceius*, pp. 165ff), a covenant was an "act of trusting." From his knowledge of Hebrew, Coccejus also knew that this act had a "public" dimension to it. As such, he associated it with the "self-binding" of a people among themselves. Walzer, *Saints*, p. 85, is very sharp on the "politics" of this kind of "trust." So, too, is Troeltsch, *ST*, p. 618. Walzer, *Exo.*, pp. 75, 77, and 90, elaborates further.

223. Walzer, *Saints*, p. 85.

224. See Bengel, quoted in n. 156 above.

225. Tension, in short, was vital to the expansion of religious consciousness in history. Hence, Bengel's interest in heretics and his toleration of separatists.

226. Miller, *Mind*, pp. 401–402, 411, and 415, is clear on the relation betwen original sin and the contractualism of covenant theology.

227. For Bengel, Pelagius represented a balanced view of the "grace–nature" argument. See Bengel, quoted in Burk, *Bengel*, p. 238, where Pelagius is dissociated from the extremism of modern Pelagianism.

228. By "political" right I mean the Estates' capacity to exist as an independent entity within a constitutional framework that was at once political, social, and religious.

229. In formulating my position on this interplay I have found the following studies most helpful: E. Barker, "A Huguenot Theory of Politics," in *Church, State and Education* (Ann Arbor, 1957), esp. pp. 86–88; H. Baron, "Calvinist Republicanism and Its Historical Roots," in *CH*, v. 8 (1939), esp. pp. 36 and 40–41; J. Figgis, "The Monarchomachi," in *Political Thought from Gerson to Grotius* (New York, 1960); J. Franklin, "Constitutionalism in the Sixteenth Century: The Protestant Monarchomachs," in *Political Theory and Social Change*, D. Spitz, ed. (New York, 1967); R. Giesey, "The Monarchomach Triumvirs: Hotman, Beza and Mornay," in *Bibliotècque d'Humanisme et Renaissance*, v. 32 (1970); Kelley, *Ideology*, esp. Chapters VI–VIII; G. Pinette, "Freedom in Huguenot Doctrine," in *Archiv für Reformationsgeschichte*, v. 50 (1959), esp. pp. 215–222; J. Salmon, "Bodin and the Monarchomachs," in *Jean Bodin*, H. Denzer, ed. (Munich, 1973); and, above all, Q. Skinner, *Founda.*, esp. pp. 235–236, where the connection between resistance theory and covenant theology is quite specifically addressed.

230. Skinner, *Founda.*, pp. 235–236.

231. Ibid., passim.

232. The "ephoral" argument is decisive for ibid., pp. 229–236 and 314–316, where the idea in Calvin and Hotman is discussed. Melanchthon (in 1530) and Zwingli (1523) had used the idea earlier [see C. Shoenberger, "The Development of the Lutheran Theory of Resistance: 1523–1530," in *SCJ*, v. 8, 1 (1977), p. 70, and J. McNeill, "The Democratic Element in Calvin's Thought," *CH*, v. 18, 3 (1949), n. 28, p. 163]. Giesey,

"Mornay," n. 14, p. 48, roots the idea in the "Aragonese tradition" of political thought.

233. Skinner, *Founda.*, pp. 229–233 and 306–316, is very careful here to distinguish the "inferior magistrate" theory of resistance, which depended on "ordination" from God for its justification, from the "popular magistrate" theory, which hinged on election and representativeness.

234. Crucial here is the development of a theory of resistance that is at once "democratic," in that it implies popular control of certain political processes, and "aristocratic," in that it leaves much of the initiative for politics in the hands of duly authorized institutional authorities. Barker, *Church*, p. 92, stresses the latter; McNeill, "Calvin's," the former; and Pinette, "Freedom," p. 203, emphasizes a balance.

235. See Skinner, *Founda.*, pp. 306–307.

236. Ibid. is aware of this (pp. 235–236) but goes to great lengths (pp. 325–332 to argue for the divergence rather than convergence of the covenant–contract argument. Others, though, have pursued, or alluded to, the latter alternative. See, e.g., Barker, *Church*, pp. 86–88; Figgis, *Gerson*, p. 175; Eusden, "Law," p. 17; Pinette, "Freedom," pp. 221–222; Troeltsch, *ST*, p. 632; and, above all, Baron, "Calvinist," pp. 40–41, who subordinates contract to covenant. Decisive for the latter group of scholars is the persistent recourse among Protestants to the Old Testament to make the "contractual" argument; that, for them, is proof of covenant priority. The relationship between covenants, Old Testament citations, and nonsecular political arguments has been noticed by H. Trevor-Roper, "George Buchanan and the Ancient Scottish Constitution," *English Historical Review*, Supp. 3 (1966), pp. 9 and 15 (n. 2) and, above all, by Troeltsch, *ST*, pp. 586, 600–601, 618, 623, and n.'s pp. 887–890.

237. Kelley, *Ideology*, pp. 293 and 309–310, suggests a convergence of covenant and contract in the language of resistance in the 1570s. According to Kelley, Beza, and Mornay on the one hand and Hotman on the other represent the dovetailing of interests. For J. Salmon, *Religious Wars*, pp. 6–7, there is development here from an historically based constitutionalism to elective kingship. Also extremely helpful: H. Höpfl and M. Thompson, "The History of Contract as a Motif in Political Thought," in *AHR*, v. 84 (1979), esp. pp. 929–933.

238. A convenient translation of key portions of the *Vindiciae* can be found in *CR*, 138–199. Giesey, "Mornay," p. 42, regards the *Vindiciae* as the most popular monarchomach tract.

239. Barker, *Church*, pp. 85–88. Skinner, *Founda.*, pp. 325–326, notes this too; but, in a key passage (p. 326), he argues that it was "unusual" to place such emphasis on the idea of covenant. Hence, his "divergence view" of covenant and contract noted in n. 236 above.

240. Skinner, *Founda.*, p. 325, refers to this as a "typically scholastic" resistance argument.

241. The point is made by Kelley, *Ideology*, p. 310; Franklin, *CR*, p. 42; and Pinette, "Freedom," p. 222. Here the Old Testament figures begin to become important *political* actors.

242. Barker, *Church*, p. 86.
243. Ibid.
244. Ibid.
245. Ibid.; the association of *ecclesia* with people is not unimportant, as Troeltsch, *ST*, p. 593, has observed. Note Skinner's comments, *Founda.*, pp. 10–11, 71 and 98. Crucial here is the way in which *ecclesia* becomes tied up with the "godly people" argument, a point appreciated by Pocock, *TMM*, pp. 397–399. There, Harrington's politics and his interest in the Old Testament are explained with reference to the godly people qua theocracy argument. Also see n. 309 below.
246. Barker, *Church*, pp. 86–87, and Skinner, *Founda.*, pp. 325–326.
247. This, of course, is Skinner's concern (*Founda.*, p. 331), given his divergence focus.
248. Barker, *Church*, n. 1, pp. 86–87; when this compatibility is stressed, it explains much about the sixteenth-century fascination among Protestants with the Israelite polity – at once a republic and a theocracy. Not enough has been written on this subject. Hans Baron, *Calvins Staatsanschuung und des confessionnelle Zeitalter* (Berlin, 1924), esp. pp. 24, 35, 53–54, 60–62, and 71–72 (n. 3), has offered an argument for the importance of the theme, as has one of his sources, G. Beyerhaus, *Studien zur Staatsanschauung Calvins* (Bern, 1910), esp. Chapter IV.
249. The phrase is Pocock's, *TMM*, p. 399.
250. For the references, see Franklin, ed., *CR*, pp. 110–113, 116–118, 149, and 159.
251. Franklin, "Monarchomachs," p. 122. For Beza's and Mornay's high appraisals of the Israelite constitution, see *CR*, pp. 116 and 163, respectively. For Bucer's similarly inspired views, see Baron, "Calvinist," pp. 36–37 and n. 23, p. 40.
252. Mornay, *CR*, p. 163. Baron, "Calvinist," p. 41, sums up the situation well: "...Calvinist writers and politicians...regarded the pre-monarchic Jewish state as a divine example" of why monarchy was not "agreeable to God" unless it was limited by law.
253. Skinner, *Founda.*, p. 205, Shoenberger, "Theory," p. 68, and Baron, "Calvinist," pp. 35–37, make the point about Bucer. Franklin, *CR*, pp. 37–38, argues the point with regard to Beza.
254. Mornay, *CR*, p. 147.
255. Ibid., pp. 149–150. Here Mornay likens Israel's elders to the Estates system and provides them with "ephoral" authority.
256. Ibid., p. 146. It is decisive, I think, to realize that Mornay inserts the elder-king contractual relationship into a larger framework in which God and the people figure prominently. His claim is that only a people who had covenanted with God and among themselves were in a position to authorize representatives. This, then, is a "godly people" argument in which power flows from God, through the people, to the king by way of their representatives.
257. One could also make the argument about covenants and contracts in terms of the conceptual differences between *universitas* and *societas*. The issues

involved are nicely discussed by Salmon, *French*, pp. 41–42.

258. Mornay, *CR*, pp. 146ff.

259. On the "establishment" of the king by the people, see ibid., pp. 158–161, 169, and 180–181. With this, Mornay transforms the question of constitutional resistance to one of elective kingship by, and sovereignty of, the people.

260. There is much at political issue in the continuity argument. Calvin, we know (McNeil, "Calvin's," pp. 159–162), regarded the prerogative of elective kingship in Israel as a divine gift given by God to a godly people who were vigilant about their liberty. To make the continuity argument, therefore, election had to carry over from the judges to the period of Kings. To this end, Beza (*CR*, p. 110) had argued that the Mosaic polity "was not abolished with the change from aristocracy to monarchy, but was retained, and organized with more precision." To do this, though, Calvinists had to draw heavily on the picture of David, the "humble monarch." who had been willing both to submit himself to the people for "ratification" and to take an "oath" of allegiance to them. (On these points, see Skinner, *Founda.*, 228, and Salmon, "Bodin," pp. 367–368.) The problem, of course, was that there were other ways to interpret the figure of David in the Bible. As J. Mazzeo, "Cromwell as Davidic King," in *Renaissance and Seventeenth-Century Studies* (New York, 1964), has noted, there is also a "divine right" of kings line of interpretation associated with David. In that respect, the continuity–discontinuity argument about developments within the Old Testament has contemporary relevance for sixteenth-century resistance theorists. Only Beyerhaus, *Studien*, pp. 133–145, has appreciated the political significance of this, concluding first that Calvinists distinguished "legitimate" (i.e., David) and "illegitimate" (i.e., Saul) monarchs and, second, that for them monarchy in any form was obsolete, given the modern religious sensibility.

261. Mornay, *CR*, p. 146.

262. See n. 260 above.

263. Mornay, *CR* p. 143. Mornay cites the Jehoiada–Joash exchange. Note Miller's (*Mind*, p. 415) comment on the use of the same citation by federal theologians in America. Also see n. 273 below.

264. Mornay, *CR*, p. 147; note the language parallel with Zwingli (Hagen, "Covenant," pp. 18–21), and with the covenant theologians we have examined. Were the covenant not bilateral, Mornay tells us, it would be "an empty covenant."

265. Mornay, *CR*, p. 147. For the language parallel, see n. 196 above.

266. Ibid.

267. Ibid., p. 148; the idea of "performance," obviously, is at once conditional and collective. It is the idea of a people enforcing the covenant that makes Mornay so radical and militantly religious. Proof of this can be found in a revealing statement made by H. Ferne, quoted in J. Franklin, *John Locke* (Cambridge, England, 1978), p. 36, (n. 32). There the politics of Mornay's contract within the covenant argument is clearly delineated.

268. Mornay, *CR*, pp. 149–150, 158–161, 169, and 180–181; cf. Beza, pp. 104 and 117–118. In the latter (p. 150), Mornay writes that "Israel,

which chose and established its king as a kind of public representative, was superior to Saul."

269. Mornay, *CR*, p. 158. Also see n. 256 above.
270. Ibid., p. 159.
271. Ibid., pp. 160–161.
272. Ibid., pp. 180–181.
273. Note Beza's formulation of the problem, *CR*, p. 118: "There was first an oath by which King and people obligated themselves to God...and then a mutual oath between the king and the people." A clear case, I think, of a political contract *within* a religious covenant.
274. Mornay, *CR*, pp. 179–180; cf. Beza, *CR* p. 116.
275. Beza (n. 260 above) hints at this with his "precision" remark. Calvin, *Insts.*, v. 1: pp. 389–390, speaks revealingly about the "Law" as "a day to day" guide to the Divine will and as a "perpetual spur" to, and "goal" of, day-to-day activity itself.
276. For this reason, students of the Old Testament often speak of covenants and contracts in terms of the relationship between "policy" and "technique" (see, e.g., D. Hillers, *Covenant: The History of a Biblical Idea* [Baltimore, 1969], pp. 94–95). More extensively discussed by E. Voegelin, *OH*, pp. 328–332 (see n. 300 below). The precondition for political liberty, in other words, is the cohesiveness of a covenanting people.
277. See, e.g., Pinette, "Freedom," esp. pp. 215–222. For a hostile view of this development in the Reformed church see P. Wernle, quoted in Niesel, *Theology*, p. 104. There, Wernle implies that "Christianization of the Old Testament" really involved Judaizing the New Testament in a way that allowed Calvinists to use "Law" as a device for political oppression. Troeltsch, *ST*, p. 601, corrects Wernle on this.
278. I rely on Hillers, *Idea*, and Voegelin, *OH*, for much of the argument that follows.
279. The Mosaic (Sinai) and Davidic (Kingship) covenants are thoroughly discussed by Voegelin, *OH*; Hillers, *Idea*, has much to say about Schecham and David.
280. The formulation is Voegelin's *OH*, pp. 176–178. Hillers, *Idea*, pp. 104–112, links the Davidic covenant specifically to the divine right of kings tradition. Cf. n. 260 above.
281. Hillers, *Idea*, pp. 78–81 and 118–119, puts it this way.
282. On the military exigencies that occasioned David's rise to power see Voegelin, *OH*, p. 142 and Chapter 8 and 9, esp. pp. 249–282.
283. Very clearly stated throughout by Voegelin, ibid., esp. pp. 295–298, and Hillers, *Idea*, pp. 112–113.
284. Voegelin, *OH*, p. 186.
285. While Hillers, *Idea*, pp. 102ff, focuses on how Abraham figures in the struggle between supporters of the Mosaic and of the Davidic covenant, Voegelin, *OH*, addresses the question of the substance of the political differences between the two groups.
286. Hillers, *Idea*, pp. 98ff and 111ff; Voegelin, *OH*, pp. 138–139, 185, and 223.
287. Voegelin, *OH*, p. 276. Also see pp. 189, 194, 256, and 269–277. Hillers,

Idea, pp. 100–106.

288. Voegelin, *OH*, pp. 178, 194, and 268–276, explains how David's supporters did this.

289. Ibid., p. 137, refers to the Mosaic and Davidic covenants as "rival centers of meaning" around which the religious history of Israel was written.

290. Ibid., p. 138. The nucleus is "new" relative to the Mosaic precedent.

291. Hillers, *Idea*, p. 100.

292. See n. 288 above.

293. See the very precise formulation of the issue in Voegelin, *OH*, p. 179.

294. If there is a strength in Hillers, *Idea*, it lies in his appreciation of this point (pp. 100–103 and 112).

295. Both Hillers, ibid., p. 110, and Voegelin, *OH*, pp. 229–230, refer to this as pseudo-democratization.

296. Hillers, *Idea*, pp. 102–112, notes the movement here from a two-way to a one-way covenant.

297. Voegelin, *OH* p. 272.

298. Ibid., discusses the two versions in Chapter 8, pp. 226ff.

299. Ibid., pp. 243–248.

300. Ibid., p. 171, differentiates a "Great Berith" from "berith as a legal institution."

301. I follow ibid, pp. 325–332.

302. In Voegelin's terms, ibid., pp. 272 and 334, the struggle between royalists and antiroyalists is over the power of "mediation." For the latter, the "carriers" of God's spirit are the historians, not the king.

303. Ibid., p. 245, alludes to the connection without pursuing it. The connection is also most obvious in Locke's "First Treatise."

304. Ibid., p. 276 (n. 17), notes some of the different conceptions of Abraham in the Old Testament. J. Mazzeo, "Davidic," discusses different lines in the exegesis of David.

305. Hillers, *Idea*, pp. 106–112, and Voegelin, *OH*, pp. 189 and 276–277, both make the connection.

306. Specifically noted by Hillers. *Idea*, pp. 104 and 184.

307. Mazzeo, "Davidic," is very helpful on the switch from the one to the other.

308. See e.g., Mornay, *CR*, pp. 150 and 180, respectively. For Beza's David, see *CR*, pp. 104 and 117–118, where David's oath is construed as evidence of elective kingship.

309. A crucial point emerges here: namely, that the millennialist conception of Württemberg Protestants as a godly people translated into a *social* ideal in which civil and religious liberty were part of the same equation of Christian progress. The unity of the *ecclesia* – the people as a congregation of the faithful – was sustained by the collectivism of a voluntary association that had the cohesiveness of a religious sect.

310. The tie between ephoral authority and the Estates system is specifically made by Calvin, *Insts.*, v. 2: p. 804, and by the monarchomach theorists. Also see n. 232, above.

311. Mornay, *CR*, p. 149.

312. Ibid., pp. 170 and 180; there the "lex regia" is cited as "the condition of

[a king's] rule."

313. A parallel between Württemberg and the Scottish situation in the late sixteenth century suggests itself here. Much of what Skinner, *Founda.*, pp. 189–190 and 339–340, says about the religio-political dynamic in Scotland would seem to be relevant to Württemberg after 1733.

314. Walzer, *Saints*, pp. 73 and 83, links Huguenot resistance theory and constitutionalism directly to feudalism. The absence of the nobility from the Estates in Württemberg is, therefore, of some importance. This was appreciated by A. Ritschl. *Pietismus*, v. 3: pp. 6–8, and confirmed recently by M. Walker, *German*, passim.

315. Mornay, *CR*, p. 147, refers to the people as a "corporate body" that acts "as a single individual." Mornay offers this idea while discussing Israel as the embodiment of a godly people, and the elders qua Estates as the "epitome" (p. 149) of the Kingdom.

316. Walzer, *Saints*, p. 85. Because of this, Walzer questions whether this kind of constitutionalism is political in any meaningful "representative" sense.

317. It has been claimed that this kind of dualism is "characteristic of monarchomach theory" (see J. Franklin, *John Locke*, p. 65). At the same time, we know that the idea of the "dualistic" *Ständestaat* is a very old Geman conception that predates monarchomach theory (see R. Benert, "Lutheran Resistance Theory," in *Il Pensiero Politico*, v. 6, 1 [1973], esp. pp. 20–21). The two, I think, must be distinguished; and to do so, we must allow the religious factor to enter the political situation.

318. Franklin, *Locke*, pp. 42 and 67, is relevant to the conceptual point here for two reasons. First, he distinguishes *moral* and *civil* aspects of the constitution of a people. And second, he correlates the distinction with the idea of a people as an abstract group and as a group with established representatives. In Old-Württemberg, the former is informed by decidedly religious conceptions; the latter, by much narrower, political ones. The split is all-important to an appreciation of Hegel's political orientation in the 1790s.

Chapter 3

1. See, e.g., R. Rürup, *Moser*, where the connection between Pietism and political reform is presented through a study of the life and works of J. J. Moser. Rurup's views have recently been challenged by M. Walker, *Johann Jakob Moser and the Holy Roman Empire of the German Nation* (Chapel Hill, 1981), exp. p. 190 (n. 2). The difference between Rürup and Walker, I think, is one of emphasis.

2. Catholic dukes reigned in Württemberg until 1797. I focus on the 1793–1797 period in Part II below.

3. Between 1737 and 1744 a regency was established in Württemberg. I discuss the importance of the period throughout the chapter.

4. F. L. Carsten, *Princes and Parliaments*, offers a useful introduction to the subject. For more detail, especially about the late eighteenth-century situation, see E. Hölzle, *Das Alte Recht*. Much can be learned from Rürup

and Walker, n. 1, above, and from Vann, *The Making of a State.*

5. Hölzle, *Alte*, makes the *Alte Recht* tradition the focus of his study. For this he has been criticized. See M. Hasselhorn, *Der altwürttemberische Pfarrstand im 18. Jahrhundert* (Stuttgart, 1958), pp. 73–74. The basis of the criticism is that Hölzle has overemphasized the legalistic aspect of Württemberg's cultural history and missed the importance of its religious concerns. Walker, *Moser*, offers a nice balance between the two.

6. The general point has been made by Hölzle, *Alte*, p. 4. L. Krieger, *The German Idea of Freedom* (Chicago, 1957), pp. 14ff, draws out the political implications for "German" political thought. As I point out (n. 36) below, I think the "dualistic" argument misses the dynamic of religious opposition in Old-Württemberg. Also see n.'s 317 and 318, Chapter 2.

7. Carsten, *Princes*, p. 436. Also see K. Epstein, *The Genesis of German Conservatism* (Princeton, 1966), p. 261.

8. Württemberg's uniqueness in this regard has been noted by Carsten, *Princes* p. 5, and by Epstein, *German*, p. 264.

9. Walker, *Moser*, p. 269.

10. Carsten, *Princes*, pp. 24ff. Epstein, *German*, p. 261, offers slightly different figures.

11. Carsten, *Princes*, pp. 3, 11, 23, 26, 423, and 425 on the nobility. A problem arises in Carsten's analysis, however, when (p. 23) he contends that the absence of the nobility hurt the Estates and then (p. 26) claims just the opposite. Walker, *Moser*, p. 272 (n. 188), discusses others who have vacillated on the issue. Given the situation, it is difficult to know just what J. Toews, *Hegelianism* (Cambridge, England, 1980), pp. 13–15, has in mind when he proposes to root Hegel in the *social* structure of the "ancien regime."

12. Two points. First, the nobility was absent from the Estates in many places in southwest Germany (Carsten, *Princes*, p. 425). Second, what was unique about Württemberg was the unicameral system in which burgher and prelate sat together. Hence, the importance of the confessional issue that is lost if the "dualistic" argument (n. 6 above) is overstressed.

13. The urban character of the Estates in Württemberg has been appreciated by Hölzle, *Alte*, pp. 9ff, and by Carsten, *Princes*, pp. 4, 11, 52, and 432. M. Walker, *Home Towns*, regards this as particularly important for Württemberg's political culture.

14. Much has been written on the *Ehrbarkeit* in Württemberg. Besides Hölzle, Carsten, and Walker (n. 13 above) consult Hasselhorn, Keck, and Uhland (noted in section 5). The issue is whether this group can be regarded as a "progressive" political force. Carsten, *Princes*, esp. pp. 432–434, argues that it can. K. Epstein, *German*, p. 260, claims Carsten is "romanticizing" this reactionary group. Vann, *Making*, pp. 38–43, is useful here, for he claims that the *Ehrbarkeit* is more a *political* than a *social* group.

15. Hölzle, *Alte*, p. 11.

16. Here, obviously, is where the "medieval" reactionary versus "modern" progressive argument (n. 14 above) comes into clear focus.

17. The fiscal problem figures prominently in H. Trevor-Roper's "The General

Crisis of the Seventeenth Century," in *Crisis in Europe, 1560–1660*, T. Aston, ed. (New York, 1967). Epstein, *German*, p. 261, applies Trevor-Roper's thesis to Old-Württemberg, claiming that the Estates' fiscal obstructionism was a drag on "modernization." In this, Epstein quite clearly presents the politics of the Württemberg Estates in terms that would have been familiar to F. Hartung, who made the same argument (see, e.g., Carsten, *Princes*, pp. 433–434).

18. On the treaty, see Carsten, *Princes*, pp. 6–13.

19. Ibid., p. 12 (n. 2). The oft-cited quote comes from L. Spittler, a key figure in the 1790s. I discuss him below, section 5.

20. Ibid., p. 12.

21. Ibid., pp. 429–432.

22. Ibid., pp. 23 and 430.

23. Ibid., cites Duke Ulrich's rule (1534–1550) and that of Duke Frederick (1593–1608) as two examples.

24. The "timely deaths" argument is repeatedly cited in literature. It fits in well, I think, with Württembergers' conception of themselves as a chosen people. See, e.g., ibid., pp. 50, 128, 147, and 439. Also see Hölzle, *Alte*, p. 5; Rürup, *Moser*, pp. 13–14; and Lehmann, *Pietismus*, p. 85. Karl Alexander's death (1737) was so construed.

25. A principal theme in Walker, *Moser*.

26. I think Rürup, *Moser*, pp. 14–15, has this right in that he regards the period after 1733 as less "negative" and more reformist.

27. I follow Walker, *Moser*, pp. 72–76, on what follows.

28. Carsten, *Princes*, pp. 23–24.

29. Hölzle, *Alte*, pp. 4–11.

30. Carsten, *Princes*, twists and turns in order to present the Estates as a "representative" body despite its narrow social base.

31. Appreciated by Rürup, *Moser*, pp. 14ff. Walker, *Moser*, p. 120, sees the 1733–1739 period as a crucial political moment for Württemberg Protestants, because during those years the religious issue gave the Estates popular appeal. Also see ibid., p. 124.

32. I've learned much about "oppositional men" of this sort from Walzer, *Saints*, esp. p. 3. A. Ritschl, *Pietismus*, v. 3: p. 19, terms the convergence "oppositional patriotism."

33. Consult any of the histories mentioned above for particulars.

34. Walker, *Moser*, Chapter 7, details the alarm in Moser. For the figures, see Vann, *Making*, p. 124 (n.)

35. Walker, *Moser*, pp. 69–71, details the impact of the Salzburg episode on Moser.

36. The dualisms, I shall argue, are very different. In the first, the dualism translates into a doctrine of permanent consitutional negativism. In the second, the dualism is conditional and, very often, a prelude to political activism.

37. Toews, *Hegelianism*, pp. 15–17, while discussing this neglects to bring in the "resistance theory" aspect of the problem.

38. Walker, *Moser*, provides much useful information on this insofar as it

concerned Moser. For the larger picture: K. von Aretin, *Heiliges Römanisches Reich 1776–1806*, 2 v. (Wiesbaden, 1967).

39. Ably discussed by Walker, *Moser*, pp. 120ff.

40. Since roughly one-third of the public revenue fell under this rubric, the shift in control was politically significant. I follow ibid., pp. 72–76, here.

41. See, e.g., Carsten, *Princes*, p. 124, and Lehmann, *Pietismus*, pp. 84–85.

42. Lehmann, *Pietismus*, p. 85; Walker, *Moser*, p. 120; and Vann, *Making*, n. 12, p. 222.

43. The consolidation is perceptively discussed by Lehmann, *Pietismus*, pp. 88ff.

44. Carsten, *Princes*, p. 147: to wit, after Karl Alexander's death "a marked pride in the ancient consitution" manifested itself among Württembergers. By that Carsten means pride in the "Good Old Law." Crucial, moreover, is the connection between these two thematic foci and the idea of "*des gemeinen Besten*", a watchword of Württembergers (e.g., Bengel and Moser) that had clear religious implications. For the tie between the latter two themes see W. Merk, "Der Gedanke des Gemeinen Besten." in *Festschrift Alfred Schultze*, W. Merk, ed. (Weimar, 1934), p. 483. For use of the phrase in Bengel and Moser see Lehmann, *Pietismus*, p. 97, and Rürup, *Moser*, p. 99, respectively.

45. D. Kelley, *Hotman*, is very helpful in showing how the sixteenth-century French search for an ancient constitution could play such an important role in Huguenot resistance theory.

46. In this section my conception of the ancient constitution comes very close to the one J. Pocock hints at in *TMM*, pp. 340–347. There, Pocock quite deliberately assimilates the ideas of "the Elect Nation" and "a national apocalyptic" to the "ideology of the Ancient Constitution." In his appreciative review of Pocock, J. H. Hexter (*HT*, v. 16, 4 [1977], esp. p. 328) has drawn attention to the conceptual possibilities of treating the ancient constitution as a "sacred–secular" idea complex. I try to exploit that here.

47. Here, of course, the impulse is toward establishing a counterpolity. Over the course of the century the impulse becomes more politically focused in a positive sense.

48. Mälzer, *Bengel*; Lehrmann, *Pietismus*, pp. 97–104; and Hermann, *Bengel*, esp. p. 456, discuss the Bengel–Moser association.

49. See n.'s 44–46 above for this.

50. Hölzle, *Alte*, p. 79, uses this phrase.

51. To borrow Pocock's terminology, it functions "as a mode of civil consciousness."

52. A. List, *Der Kampf ums gute alte Recht* (Tübingen, 1913), p. 8, points out how the idea of origins here is constitutionally, not chronologically, focused. It has, as it were, a mythical component.

53. Krieger, *German*, pp. 54–55, has some quite interesting things to say about this in the context of a discussion of Pufendorf's distinction between "physical and moral persons." J. Franklin, *Locke*, pp. 2 and 42, also reflects on the difference. See n. 318, Chapter 2, also.

54. Carsten, *Princes*, pp. 24–28, is most helpful on the 1514 to 1550s aspects of the consolidation.

55. In ibid., pp. 42–48, the importance of the duke's oaths to the treaty are examined.

56. Ibid., p. 47, cites the crisis of 1607, when the duke established his own interpretation of the treaty, as a key moment in the struggle for sovereignty in Old-Württemberg.

57. Here, obviously, the idea of constitutional dualism presents itself as a static force in political life. As I noted below, though, that interpretation of dualism changes in the seventeenth century – from 1607 on, that is.

58. I have discussed the difference in the dualisms in n. 317, Chapter 2, and in n. 36 above.

59. The doctrine has been discussed most ably by Franklin, *Locke*, pp. 64–68; and Salmon, *French*, pp. 52–53. Both follow O. Gierke, *Natural Law and the Theory of Society*, E. Barker, trans. (Boston, 1957), pp. 50–61. It is not insignificant that this doctrine was developed in Württemberg around the time of the 1607 crisis. Nor is it insignificant that Besold, Andreae's friend, was involved in the doctrine's development or that the doctrine emerged at a time when Württembergers were moving away from the godly prince argument (discussed in Chapter 1).

60. On Besold, see the literature cited above, n. 59. In addition, see Gierke, *Law*, pp. 37, 67, and 155. I follow these scholars in the remainder of this paragraph.

61. Gierke, *Law*, p. 155, makes the "mixed constitution" argument. In this, he is followed by Franklin, *Locke*, pp. 65–67. The implication is that the idea of mixed constitution and that of monarchomach resistance theory are closely connected in that both allow for greater popular participation in government. That was not a concern of the medieval *Ständestaat*.

62. My conclusion here coincides with the claims of Pocock and Hexter (n. 46 above) that increased participation in politics was very often a consequence of the eschatological considerations of a godly people. Also see n. 74 below.

63. For a parallel see Kelley's discussion of Hotman's reaction to Catholic foreigners in the French government (see *Hotman*, p. 242).

64. Two conceptual points here. First, Pocock (*TMM*, p. 341, and idem, *Politics*, Chapters 6 and 7) is very stimulating on the "tradition–traditionalist" argument. Second, Kelley, *Hotman*, p. ix, talks about this in terms of "fundamentalism" and "Utopianism." More on these points below, nn. 104 and 142.

65. A theme of Chapter 2 of this study.

66. Carsten, *Princes*, pp. 19ff.

67. As ibid. notes, p. 14, Württemberg was sold to the Hapsburgs in 1520.

68. That is not to say that Ulrich kept his word; he did not, as ibid., p. 21, has observed.

69. The focus of Chapter 2, is relevant here.

70. Lehmann, *Pietismus*, pp. 75–79, makes the point. The idea of continuous reformation, of course, entails a shift away from merely "negative" politics.

71. Ibid., p. 100, refers to the latter position as "conservative" and the former position as "sterile" conservative.

72. With this argument I come back to the theme of the introductory section to Part I of this study.

73. Note how there is little room for individual liberty ("civil rights" in T. H. Marshall's sense) in either of these constitutional modes of consciousness.

74. Hexter, "Review," pp. 330–334, makes some fine conceptual points about the "language of liberty" issue here. To be precise, he detects one language that is "law" oriented and another that focuses on "participation." Furthermore, he notes, as I do here, that very often the two languages inhabited the same conceptual space.

75. On the institutionalization of tradition I have found Berger and Luckmann, *The Social Construction of Reality*, pp. 53–67, most useful.

76. Carsten, *Princes*, pp. 123–148, for the general situation after 1733. Consult Walker, *Moser*, pp. 120ff, for the *Reversalien*, and pp. 208–216 and 248ff for the points that follow.

77. As Walker (*Moser*, p. 120) has observed, the result of the 1733–1744 series of events was the introduction of "a religious component to a more general constitutional contest between [the prince] and the Protestant diet."

78. A sense of Karl Eugen's idiosyncratic personality comes through very clearly in A. Fauchier-Magnan's *The Small German Courts*, M. Savill, trans. (London, 1958).

79. R. Uhland, *Geschichte der hohen Karlsschule in Stuttgart* (Stuttgart, 1953), p. 4.

80. Frederick, quoted in Fauchier-Magnan, *Small*, p. 171.

81. Carsten, *Princes*, pp. 136ff; Walker, *Moser*, pp. 198ff.

82. For details, see Walker, *Moser*, Chapters 25 and 26.

83. Fauchier-Magnan, *Small*, pp. 180ff; Uhland, *Geshichte*, pp. 6–7.

84. For details of the petition to the Aulic Council, see Epstein, *German*, p. 263.

85. Carsten, *Princes*, pp. 140–144, offers an overview.

86. Epstein, *German*, p. 264, refers to 1770 as a great "defensive victory." Walker, *Moser*, pp. 277–278, notes Moser's concern with the Small Council predominance.

87. Lehmann, *Pietismus*, pp. 112–117, regards the defensive character of the Small Council's interpretation of the victory as a missed opportunity for activism. Walker, *Moser*, p. 215, depicts Moser as trying to seize that opportunity in the name of Protestant liberty. Moser, as it were, presented himself as a spokesman for the conscience of a godly people.

88. Walzer, *Saints*, p. 90, has captured the religious essence of the activism well. Writing of Mornay and Beza he notes how for them "it was [a people's] duty not merely to resist heretical kings but to transform the secular state into...'the temple of God.'"

89. See n. 53 above and n. 318, Chapter 2, for other references to the political implications involved in the distinction. Franklin, *Locke*, esp. pp. 34, 42, and 67, implies that the "moral" integrity of a godly people is clearly exhibited in the monarchomach theory that (p. 34) "the kings's authority

derives from God by mediation of the people." By people Franklin understands (p. 67) a "right of the community" as distinct from the rights of its "established" representatives.

90. Walker, *Moser*, esp. 269ff, points out how Moser made this distinction in terms of a "private right"/"public capacity" differentiation.
91. Ibid., pp. 326–327, hints at the problem here.
92. Pocock's claim (*TMM*, p. 463) about Puritanism is relevant here: to wit, "it became increasingly necessary [for it] to affirm that civic was one with religious liberty, and virtue...one with salvation."
93. Merk, "Besten," pp. 486–490, insists that salvationism had been integral to the Good Old Law tradition at least since the Reformation. I concur with this.
94. Formation of a counterpolity becomes a precondition for a self-realizing teleology in an eschatological sense.
95. Significantly, Moser becomes a "will" oriented activist around 1770. See Walker, *Moser*, pp. 284–285, 308–309, and 326–327. As Barker (*Church*, p. 114–117) has noted, one of the paradoxes of Protestantism is that "the resolute practice of individual will" was meant "to issue in a stringent form of theocracy." The paradox, I think, may be explained in terms of Protestant civil piety.
96. See n. 73 above. J. N. Findlay, "Hegel's Conception of Subjectivity," in *HS*, Beiheft 19 (1979), has brilliantly exploited this notion in illuminating Hegel. More on this below, Part III and n. 164 below.
97. Hexter, "Review," p. 321, has understood this very well indeed. Also see n. 99 below.
98. I've made the point about participation above, n.'s 46 and 62.
99. When Walzer (*Saints*, p. 85) speaks of Calvinism as the carrier of a "new asceticism" he is elaborating the point he made (p. 2) about politics as "a continuous labor." It applies here.
100. See n. 94 above, a summary of Chapter 1.
101. Hexter, "Review," p. 321, and Walzer, *Saints*, p. 212, both have appreciated this.
102. P. Berger, *Social Reality of Religion*, p. 63.
103. See n.'s 30 and 199, Chapter 1, on the mysticism argument.
104. The phrase "petrifaction of tradition" comes from J. Levenson, *Confucian China and Its Modern Fate: A Trilogy*, 3 v. (Berkeley, 1958–1965), v. 1: p. xxx. Levenson has many wise things to say about how intellectual historians might go about approaching the problem of intellectual traditions (esp. v. 1: pp. xxvii–xxxiii). I have detected, though, some confusion in this terminology (compare v. 1: pp. xxx and 59); I do not, therefore, follow his usage, especially for the term "traditionalist."
105. Toews, *Hegelianism*, pp. 19–23, has the right focus here, but blurs the dynamic of the situation by not appreciating the presence of the *ideological* tension within the constitutionalist camp. In important ways, it cuts across the *social* tensions on which Toews ably comments.
106. Consult Walker, *Moser*, pp. 192–193.
107. Ibid., p. 247; Carsten, *Princes*, pp. 140ff.

108. Walker, *Moser*, p. 207, indicates that this had been the Committee's position since the 1730s; Carsten, *Princes*, p. 146, that this had been its position from 1770 on.
109. Walker, *Moser*, pp. 273–278; Carsten, *Princes*, p. 145–146.
110. Walker, *Moser*, p. 277; and Rürup, *Moser*, pp. 192ff.
111. Moser had one particular family in mind: the Stockmayers. On the family, which Walker (*Moser*, n. 21, p. 199) calls a "dynasty," see Walker, pp. 193, 199, 206, 214, and , esp., 231.
112. As Walker impressively details (ibid., pp. 194–207 and 217–228) economic policy figured in the conflict. I pick up this theme in Part III as a backdrop to Hegel's "discovery of economics."
113. Hermann, *Bengel*, p. 456; Lehrmann, *Pietismus*, pp. 97–101.
114. J. Stockmayer was Moser's principal adversary, and although he relinquished his counsel position in the late 1750s, he continued to exercise enormous influence. See Walker, *Moser*, pp. 231 and 247.
115. Rürup, *Moser*, pp. 192–196; ibid., p. 277.
116. Walker, *Moser*, p. 277; Carsten *Princes*, p. 145.
117. Pocock, (*Politics*, p. 241) is useful here: to wit, "Institutionalization, the necessary cause of traditionalism. . . ."
118. Weber, *From Max Weber*, p. 284.
119. On the need for traditions to reconceptualize themselves, see Pocock, *Politics*, Chapter 7.
120. I follow ibid. here, pp. 245 and 252–253.
121. Walker, *Moser*, p. 272.
122. Ibid.
123. Note the parallel here with Bengel's positive view of the role of change within the history of Christianity. For the conceptual point, consult Pocock, *Politics*, pp. 220ff and 236–245.
124. Walker, *Moser*, p. 272; Rürup, *Moser*, p. 177.
125. In Levenson's terms (*China*, v. 1: p. 59), Moser did so because he had "a traditionalistic bias" against identifying tradition with a single institutional arrangement.
126. Walker, *Moser*, pp. 264–267 and 317–328, is very solid here. Merk, "Besten," p. 517 (n. 55), suggests that this entailed changes in Moser's economic policy, a point I pursue in Part III.
127. See Walker, *Moser*, pp. 264–267 and 317–328.
128. Ibid., pp. 266–267.
129. Ibid., pp. 267–269 and 322.
130. Ibid., pp. 269–271, is helpful on the participation theme.
131. To ibid., p. 326, I would simply add the "moral–civil" distinction discussed elsewhere in the chapter (e.g., n. 90 above). That done, the idea of the "civil" becomes a key term in the struggle for linguistic hegemony. Also see n.'s 137 and 155 below.
132. Walker, *Moser*, p. 271. This formulation is repeated by Hegel. See Part III below.
133. Ibid., p. 303, brings this out clearly.
134. Ibid., pp. 321–323.

135. Ibid., p. 326.

136. Ibid., pp. 328–342.

137. What we have here, of course, is a struggle for linguistic hegemony – whether "private right" or "public capacity" will define the purpose *"des gemeinen Besten."* Also see n. 155 below.

138. Lehrmann, *Pietismus*, pp. 97–98.

139. See n.'s 44 and 137 above.

140. Frye, "Path," *Daedelus* (1970). pp. 308–309.

141. The phrase is Pocock's, *Politics*, p. 220. Later (p. 227) Pocock refers to this position as a "theory of conservative traditionalism."

142. What Kelley (n. 64 above) says about Hotman would seem to be relevant to Moser here.

143. This should not be confused with a call for participation based on "democratic" rights. Even in the mid-1790s few Württembergers were inclined in that direction. See, e.g., Epstein, *German*, p. 500.

144. In addition to Uhland, Hölzle, Carsten, and Walker also consult R. Keck, *Geschichte der Mittleneren Schule in Württemberg* (Stuttgart, 1968).

145. Toews, *Hegelianism*, pp. 23–24, is clear on the split, but fails to appreciate the full range of its ideological implications.

146. Keck, *Schule*, pp. 28–32. Hasselhorn, *Pfarrstand*, p. 33, offers a figure of 4,000 (out of a population of 600,000) as a rough approximation of *Ehrbarkeit* numbers around 1790.

147. Keck, *Schule*, pp. 40–52.

148. Klaiber, *Hegel*, p. 119; Keck, *Schule*, p. 40–49; Hasselhorn, *Pfarrstand*, pp. 40–41.

149. Uhland, *Geschichte*, has thoroughly studied the school. He (p. 26) as well as others (Keck, *Schule*, p. 56; Hölzle, *Alte*, p. 55; and Leube, *Stift*, p. 75) have concurred with Spittler's contemporaneous claim that Karl Eugen's school was an institution of "enlightened" persuasion.

150. With this convergence, the idea of the professional civil servant who would mediate between prince and Landschaft often crops up in the literature on Württemberg. Above all, see Hölzle, *Alte*, pp. 130ff.

151. Keck, *Schule*, pp. 52–58 and 78ff; Uhland, *Geschichte*, pp. 4 and 53–57.

152. Moser, I think, is archetypal here. In the late 1750s he was inclined to support Karl Eugen in matters of economic policy, but he drew back from that position when he realized how that strategy enhanced the power of the duke. Hence his criticism of the physiocrats in the 1770s. More on this in Part III below.

153. Hasselhorn, *Pfarrstand*, pp. 93 and 103; Uhland, *Geschichte*, pp. 65 and 79–80.

154. In this context, the fact the Hegel's younger brother was sent to the *Karlsschule* is interesting. Consult Leube, *Stift*, for what the institution symbolized for Württembergers in the 1780s.

155. Ibid., p. 36, notes how Karl Eugen meant to offer an alternative education. Hasselhorn, *Pfarrstand*, pp. 36 and 46–47, comments specifically. The choice has been discussed in more general terms by R. Vierhaus, "Politisches Bewusstsein in Deutschland vor 1789," in *Der Staat*, v. 6

(1967), esp. pp. 179–184. And though he employs a different terminology, he is clear on the linguistic hegemony argument (n. 137 above).

156. Hegel's essay on the Württemberg constitutional situation in the mid-1790s made these points. More on this below, in Part II.

157. There is a clear line that runs from Moser to the reformers of the 1790s. Two of them, Spittler and Georgii, have been discussed by Hölzle, *Alte*. Hölzle (pp. 92ff and 180ff) links Hegel's politics in the 1790s to this group of reformers. Harris, *HD*, pp. 416–434, also places Hegel in this context.

158. The tensions listed here explain, I hope, why the "dualistic" model needs to be rethought.

159. Walker, *Moser*, p. 326: to wit, ". . . Moser had growing doubts about the efficacy of institutions, and growing conviction that the wills of persons inhabiting them mattered more." Walker proceeds to argue that Moser looked to "religion" to focus individual and collective will. Hegel, I argue below, will try to do the same.

160. Pocock, *Politics*, p. 225. Pocock is quoting Burke; my emphasis.

161. I discuss the Scottish thinkers below, in Part III.

162. Very helpful here is P. Reill, *Rise of Historicism*, pp. 163–174.

163. While ibid. is useful on what the *Aufklärer* understood by "spirit," he tends to decollectivize the point of their activism by pitting (p. 167) "accumulated historical tradition" against "individual moral reinterpretation" of tradition. From here it is but a short step to pitting (p. 167) "community values" against "individual spirit," and that formulation of the problem does not work for Württemberg at all. Reill (p. 169) is quite right to stress that activism here "entailed a wrenching denial of past history," but the focus of that denial is consistent in Württemberg with a long tradition of collective faith in the dynamic of sacred history. In that sense, the activism is a fulfillment of history as much as a reaction against it.

164. In addition to n. 159 above note what ibid., pp. 175ff, says about Spittler's attitude toward the "will."

165. Ibid., p. 178. Also see n.'s 73 and 96 above.

166. Ibid., pp. 179–180.

167. Ibid., pp. 176–180, on Spittler. On Moser: Rürup, *Moser*, pp. 31 and 179–180. On Hegel: see Part III and the Epilogue below.

168. What Reill, *Rise*, pp. 179–180, says about Heeren's notion of *Volksidee* may be assimilated, I think, to the idea of a covenanting community constituting itself as a Protestant people. In both instances, "moral–political" change was the goal of collective action. As to who would be responsible for initiating that action, see below, Part III.

169. See n. 157 above.

170. Hexter, "Review," p. 321: "Republican virtue, like Christian virtue, insists that the way to self-fulfillment lies through self-denial."

171. See the Preface to this study for a fuller statement of the shift in Hegel's interest.

172. I discuss the idea of "dramatic action" below, in Part III.

Part II

The epigraphs come from Weber, *From Max Weber*, p. 270, and *Protestant Ethic*, pp. 91–92.

1. See the Preface and notes 11 and 13–15 to the Preface.
2. A good discussion of how the focus on "doing" adds up to a methodical prescription for the study of thinkers–texts–ideas in terms of their contexts can be found in A. MacIntyre, *After Virtue*, pp. 192–196.
3. Ricoeur, "The Model of the Text," *SR* (1971), esp. pp. 535–536 and 557–558.
4. To put the matter this way is, of course, to raise a question about Ricoeur's distinction (ibid., pp. 543ff) between the "importance" of the action of a text and its situational "relevance."
5. On the idea of "creative circumference," see Burke, *A Grammar of Motives*, p. 77.
6. I say "initially" in light of Beck's statement, n. 20 to the Preface. Indeed, one could say that for many Württembergers civil piety was a "cultivated habitus." I would agree, though, that in Hegel's case the preoccupation with civil piety was not "unconscious" – that is, civil piety was more a "mental tool" for him than an unconscious "habit." On this distinction see R. Chartier's essay in *Modern European Intellectual History: Reappraisals and New Prespectives*, D. La Capra and S. Kaplan, eds. (Ithaca, 1982). Also see nn. 40–42 to the Introduction and nn. 16 and 17 below.
7. Locke, quoted in Dunn, *The Political Thought of John Locke*, n. 3, p. 257.
8. As MacIntyre has reminded us, "to look for the antecedents of an action is not to search for an invariant causal connection, but to look for the available alternatives and to ask why the agent [Hegel] actualized one rather than another." See "A Mistake About Causality in Social Science," in *Philosophy, Politics and Society*, 2nd Series, P. Laslett et al., eds. (Oxford, 1962), p. 61. I have defended this position, so crucial to the contextual strategy of intellectual history elsewhere. See my "Context Construction in Intellectual History," a paper given at the National Humanities Center, May 2, 1984. Suffice it to say here that in the paper I argue that the methodological idea of context construction, as originally formulated by "moderate" sociologists of knowledge (e.g., Weber and Scheler), was designed, in Weber's words (*Economy and Society*, v. 1: p. 15), "for provisional orientation" in the service of "interpretative understanding" rather than for "merely demonstrating functional relationships."
9. MacIntyre (*After*, pp. 194 and 197) points out how "narrative history" is "the basic and essential genre" for the kind of methodological orientation that is concerned with noncausal explanations of social action.
10. Geertz, *Cultures*, pp. 23–24.
11. MacIntyre, "Mistake," p. 61.
12. K. Burke, *Permanence and Change*, 2nd ed. (New York, 1954). and P. Boudieu, "Intellectual Field and Creative Project," in *Social Science Information*, v. 8, 2 (1969), discuss the idea of "weightedness" within a cultural context.

13. Geertz, *Cultures*, p. 27, notes how "description" and "explanation" often converge in the "interpretive" sciences.

14. Burke, I think, would regard this use of context as a way of "directing the attention" to some things rather than to others. It reveals, therefore, more about one's principles of selectivity than one's causal commitments. See Burke's *Motives*, pp. 18–19, and especially his essay "Terministic Screens," in *Language as Symbolic Action* (Berkeley, 1966), p. 45. Also of interest here is J. Searle's *Intentionality* (Cambridge, England, 1983), esp. Chapter 5: "The Background." There [p. 158] he says "Background" (i.e., context) "functions causally, but the causation...is not determining."

15. Geertz, *Cultures*, pp. 19–20, and esp p. 27, where the "'said' of discourse" is related to "the conceptual structures that inform" the actions of the subject(s) under investigation.

16. This is why I do not believe the term "unconscious" (n. 6 above) applies to Hegel's preoccupation with civil piety. In Pocock's terms (*Politics*, Chapter 7), Hegel was reconceputalizing civil piety as a tradition, not just paying mindless lip service to it. He was, at this point in his life, something of a "maintenance" specialist, in Hexter's sense of the term.

17. And it is precisely because this ideal was a cultural resource available to Hegel that it needs to be understood as a "mental tool" rather than an "unconscious habit." In Searle's terms (*Intentionality*, pp. 157–158), the context qua background provided "a set of enabling conditions that made it possible" for Hegel's particular form of "Intentionality to function."

18. I have learned much from Dunn, *Locke*, pp. xi–xii, and from idem, "From Applied Theology to Social Analysis," in *Wealth and Virtue: Political Economy in the Scottish Enlightenment*, I. Hont and M. Ignatieff, eds. (Cambridge, England 1983), on how to conceptualize the chapter that follows.

Chapter 4

1. A clear recent example: Harris, *HD*, p. 5.

2. Ibid., pp. 68, 71 n. 1, p. 72, and 258.

3. Compare, for example, Walker, *Moser*, pp. 334–335, and Harris, *HD*, p. 5.

4. For the convergence theme, consult the literature in n. 157, Chapter 3. At some point in this chapter the reader will certainly ask: why not cite Bengel here? The answer is that Hegel does not acknowledge him as a source during these years. What are we to make of this? According to some (Lobkowicz, *Theory and Practice*, pp. 169–170), appreciation of Bengel's ideas was "common knowledge in Swabia" and, therefore, it can be taken for granted that Hegel knew about them. Others (e.g., Rohrmoser, "Hegels," and Brecht and Sandberger, *HS*, v. 5) are not so sure. For the former, Hegel's exposure to Pietism cannot be questioned; but whether that exposure focused specifically on Bengel is debatable. For the latter, Hegel was not informed by Pietism at all. They point out that Hegel did not associate with pietists in the *Stift*. We know, though, that by the 1790s Pietism had evolved in Württemberg into a form of mystical sub-jectivism that Hegel could not countenance. So his lack of interest in the

pietist circle is really not surprising. Hegel's silence about the "down-to-earth" pietists is more troubling. I can only note that he seldom cited his sources during these years – which explains why Storr, Sartorius, and even Kant are hardly ever mentioned in his written work.

5. Walker, *Moser*, pp. 278–279, cites the restoration of Moser's official portrait to the dining hall of the estates in 1797 as evidence of his new standing among the reformers of the 1790s.

6. That Hegel was a political reformer during these years has never been doubted. See J. Hyppolite, *Studies on Marx and Hegel*, J. O'Neill, trans. (New York, 1969), p. 39; Kaufmann, *Hegel*, p. 34; R. Plant, *Hegel* (London, 1973), p. 53. Plant's claim, that Hegel was a radical democrat, has been seconded by Harris, *HD*, pp. 223 (n. 1), 429 (n. 2), and 430. S. Peczynski (n. 7 below, p. 73), though, urges us not to exaggerate "the democratic character" of Hegel's writing in the 1790s.

7. The most oft-cited example is Hegel's (now lost) essay on "Recent Domestic Affairs of Württemberg," a fragment of which appears in *HPW*, T. Knox, trans. (Oxford, 1964), pp. 243–245. Harris, *HD*, pp. 418–419 and n. 3, 427–428, and Z. Pelczynski, "An Introductory Essay," in *HPW*, pp. 73–74, discuss some of the issues, including the matter of the essay's dedication "To the People of Württemberg." Three points about this essay. First, though the essay has a political focus, its language is very much that of an essay Hegel wrote in 1793 [I discuss the essay, the "Tübingen Essay," in section (2) below], in which the relationship between religion and politics is most obvious. Second, in *PH*, J. Sibree, trans. (New York, 1956), pp. 50 and 74, Hegel makes it very clear that, for him, the idea of "a people" has a religious as well as a political connotation. Finally, the source of the fragment translated by Knox is Haym, *Hegel*, pp. 65–68. Not translated by Knox was another section (also in Haym, pp. 483–485) in which Hegel echoes Moser's indictment of the Small Council. It is decisive here that in Hegel's so-called "Berne Plan" (*BP*) of 1794 the Moser legality–morality distinction (discussed in Chapter 3) is quite prominent.

8. Hegel, *HPW*, pp. 243–245. Compare the language with which these concerns are expressed with that of a letter from the year 1795 – in *Brf.*, v. 1, p. 24 – and with the "Fragment" of 1800 – in *ETW*, T. Knox, trans. (Chicago, 1948), pp. 311 and 317. The idea of "rising above" material interests has been discussed in terms of Hegel's religiously inspired conception of "overreaching" by E. Fackenheim, *The Religious Dimension of Hegel's Thought* (Bloomington, 1967), pp. 20, 98, and n. 35, 256. In Royce's terms the idea carries with it the notion of "active self-enlargement." Hence, its importance for the telos of *homo religiosus* argument.

9. As we shall see, it is not unimportant that Hegel, both in 1798 (*HPW*, p. 243) and the letter of 1795 (n. 8, above), uses the term *Gemüter* to characterize the kind of man who possesses these qualities. For more on *Gemüter*, see section 2, n.'s 229, 230, and 324 below, and Chapter 6.

10. As was noted in Chapter 3, Hegel was not inclined to equate "a mass of individuals" with "a people." See Hegel, *DHE*, p. 269. This distinction, I

think, underpins his conception of the difference between "legality" and "morality" in 1794 (n. 7, above). See Hegel's *BP*, pp. 508–510. Also note his distinction (*PH*, p. 76) between the "real" and the "ideal" existence of a people. I also discuss Hegel's idea of "people" in the Epilogue.

11. And so it was with Hegel as G. Kelly, *Hegel's Retreat from Eleusis* (Princeton, 1978), pp. 124–127, C. Taylor, *Hegel* (Cambridge, England 1975), p. 505, and Harris, *HD*, pp. 166–169, have noted but not elaborated. For a clear statement of Hegel's later position, see *PH*, pp. 416–424 and 441–442.

12. This is what I take Kelly, *Retreat*, p. 15, to mean by the following: "Hegel's notion of Volksgeist is much closer to Montesquieu's *esprit général d'un peuple* than it is to any Romantic supercorporate spirit, though it is *more teleological* and less positivistic and 'structural–functional' than Montesquieu's concept." What informs the teleology, of course, is the Second Reformation argument, as Kelly later appreciates (pp. 124–127).

13. See Harris, *HD*, pp. 121–131, for a helpful discussion of the relationship between the two terms. Hegel refers to the relationship in *TE*, p. 506.

14. Kaufmann, *Hegel*, pp. 82–84; and E. Fackenheim, *Dimension*, p. 260 (n. 17).

15. G. Lukács, *The Young Hegel*, R. Livingstone, trans. (Cambridge, MA, 1975), pp. 53–54, develops the theme.

16. When Plant, *Hegel*, p. 32 (n. 3), argues that civil piety is a "recognizable theological genre" and then in the text (pp. 32–40) invokes Rousseau as its source, I wonder about the weighing of the influence here. The genre certainly dates to sources earlier than Rousseau. And many of them, especially in Rousseau's case, were Calvinist.

17. In order, the quotations come from Pocock, *TMM*, p. 85 (also see pp. 7 and 135–137); E. Kantorowicz, *The King's Two Bodies* (Princeton, 1957), p. 248 (also see pp. 234–235 and n. 146, 240–241); and Pocock, *TMM*, p. 462. Cf. Hexter, n. 170, Chapter III.

18. That the two are linked in Hegel's mind is clear in 1793, in *TE*. Appreciated by Harris, *HD*, pp. 125, 134, and 149.

19. Heine, quoted in Kaufmann, *Hegel*, p. 367.

20. I made the point about "dying into life" in Chapter 2. Relevant here is Kantorowicz's remark (*Two*, pp. 234–235) that "The Christian martyr... who had offered himself up for the invisible polity...was to remain – actually until the twentieth century – the genuine model of civic self-sacrifice." See n. 24, below, for Hegel. And note M. Greene, *Hegel on the Soul* (The Hague, 1972), pp. 44–45, on Hegel's philosophical rendering of the "dying to life" theme.

21. In section 2, I make the case for Hegel's inclusion in this tradition. See n. 30, below also.

22. Well made by T. Knox, "Hegel's Attitude to Kant's Ethics," in *KS*, v. 49, 1 (1957–1958), pp. 79–80, where *Sittlichkeit* and the establishment of "the Kingdom of God on earth" are linked. Also see Löwith, *From Hegel to Nietzsche*, pp. 45–46, where the same point is made.

23. Hegel uses the phrase in *Hegel's Theologische Jugendschriften*, H. Nohl, ed.

(Tübingen, 1907), p. 66. It functions, I think, in the same way as "overreaching" does (n. 8 above).

24. Clearly stated by Hegel in *PH*, pp. 73 and 78, to wit: Spirit "perishes in fulfilling its own destiny and proper function." Hegel likens this (p. 78) to the experience of the "life of a people." In Greene, *Soul*, pp. 44–45, Hegel is quoted to the effect that "from the 'dead husk' of nature 'proceeds a more beautiful nature, Spirit.' " See n. 55 below for a key issue here.

25. Hegel, PH, pp. 40, 55–56, 377, and 424.

26. For the phrase, see Hegel, *Encyclopedia of Philosophy*, G. Mueller, trans. (New York, 1959), p. 215.

27. When Hölderlin credits Hegel with being the "conductor of my thoughts into the external world" this is what he is talking about. See Harris, *HD*, p. 101 (n. 1).

28. A key theme in *PH*, pp. 22, 25, 57, 417. As we shall see on section 2, Hegel was talking about "sparks" and "seeds" of potential in man from the 1780s on. One of the few to appreciate this: G. Adams, "The Mystical Element in Hegel's Early Theological Writings," in *University of California Publications in Philosophy*, v. 2 (1910), esp. p. 80, where he notes that Hegel viewed the Reformation as having failed "in its social task of building up a joyful social *Geist*."

29. In *PH*, pp. 417–424 and 441–442, Hegel makes it clear that the Reformation constituted this moment of freedom.

30. Ibid., pp. 422–424. To wit (p. 424): the spirit of *homo religiosus* "does not assume [its] complete form immediately after the Reformation. . . it was not yet expanded into a system [i.e., of *Sittlichkeit*] by which the moral world could be regulated."

31. Ibid., p. 442.

32. Hegel uses the phrase in *TE*, p. 502.

33. Hegel, quoted in Kaufmann, *Hegel*, p. 272.

34. Hegel uses the phrase in *Hegel's Philosophy of Right*, T. Knox, trans. (Oxford, 1952), p. 105. The remark Hegel makes there about the "circle" of ethical necessity constitutes what Kelly (*Retreat*, p. 25) regards as the "psychological motor" of Hegel's concept of *Sittlichkeit*.

35. In n. 27, above, Hölderline hinted at this "inside out" movement. Hegel is very clear on the movement himself. See *Right*, p. 284, and n. 31, above. For the movement's roots in German Protestantism see Chapters 1 and 2. For a parallel in Schiller, see *AE*, pp. 73–77.

36. Kelly, *Retreat*, p. 125, speaks here of Hegel's Protestantism and its relation to his call for "the recovery" both of " 'ethicality' (*Sittlichkeit*)" and of "politics." In Chapter 2 we saw how the *Lehre*- and *Lebensreformation* arguments fit together in Bengel. Hegel uses the formulation in *TE*, p. 504. Also note Harris' apt comment, *HD*, pp. 323–324. Lessing, too, used the distinction. See Allison, *Lessing*, p. 53.

37. Discussed in the Introduction and Chapter 1.

38. When Lessing (*LTW*, p. 96) claimed that soon man will "not need to borrow motives for his actions from this future," he was referring to this

kind of interplay. Clearly, what Lessing is doing is moving the emphasis in eschatology from "anticipation" to "participation." Kelly (*Idealism*, p. 170) links Lessing and Kant to Joachim on this score. Kant seems to have borrowed this formulation from Lessing. See n.'s 317 and 318 below.

39. See, e.g., Lilla, *Clement of Alexandria* (Oxford, 1971), pp. 42–51; Cochrane, *Christianity and Classical Culture*, pp. 167–168; and Tollinton, *Clement of Alexandria*, v. 1, pp. 170, 216, and 234. Throughout, Tollinton makes clear that Plato was Clement's ally in all of this.

40. Lilla, *Clement*, pp. 45–56. Lilla (p. 49) specifically links Clement's "polemic against Stoic materialism" to "Middle Platonism." On this he has received much support from Dillon, *The Middle Platonists*, especially Chapter Three.

41. In terms of the argument of Part I, Clement may be said to offer an "egocentric" rather than "anthropocentric" conception of religion. It is, therefore, proto-Pelagian rather than proto-Pantheist.

42. Clearly Hegel's position in *PH*, especially pp. 39–40 and 55. Note Findlay's claim ("Subjectivity," p. 16) that in Hegel subjectivity "becomes Mind . . . in proportion as it liberates itself from . . . immersion in the natural."

43. I cite the literature, section 1.

44. Useful here is MacIntyre's discussion (*After Virtue*, p. 172) of the "parallelism" between Aristotle and Christianity on the matter of virtue. As we shall see, though, there is an important difference between Aristotle's teleology, which, according to MacIntyre (pp. 139, 152, and 183) "presupposes his metaphysical biology," and Hegel's teleology, which, I think, presupposes a Protestant theology of history. As Löwith, *From*, p. 13, has observed, "the 'idea' as understood by Hegel was not intended to describe a process of nature but a process of spirit. By it Hegel did not mean the reason of nature . . . but the reason of [Christian] history." Also see n. 11 above.

45. Taylor, *Hegel*, pp. 14–17 and 81, is very good on showing how Hegel and Aristotle differ here. With this argument about the "self-realizing" aspect of Hegel's teleology (especially p. 81), Taylor offers a correction to M. B. Foster, *The Political Philosophies of Plato and Hegel* (Oxford, 1935), pp. 136–137, who faulted Hegel for not recognizing the Judeo-Christian notion of voluntary will "as the subjective spring of activity." That the self-realizing aspect of Hegel's teleology informs his conception of subjectivity has been appreciated by Findlay, "Subjectivity." But Findlay regards "self-realizing teleology" as Hellenic rather than Germanic" in inspiration. By Germanic Findlay (p. 23) means a "modern" conception of subjectivity – a point that brings him, in the end, into conflict with Taylor, who treats self-realizing teleology as a modern creation.

46. Appreciated by Kelly, *Retreat*, p. 90.

47. I stress "in history" here because Hegel's historical sense clearly differentiates him from Aristotle. On the lack of this sense in Aristotle, see MacIntryre, *After*, p. 149. On its importance in Hegel see Löwith, quoted in n. 44 above. In Aristotle, in other words, there is "meaning in history."

but not a "meaning of history."

48. Made in numerous passages in *PH*, pp. 40–41, 54–57 and 73–77.
49. Ibid., p. 24.
50. Ibid., pp. 40–41.
51. Ibid.
52. Hence, the historical orientation of Hegel's conception of *Volksgeist*, expressed in ibid., pp. 73–78.
53. Ibid., pp. 24, 55, 73, and 78.
54. As I show, section 2, this distinction is crucial for Hegel – in 1795 and 1796 as well as in *PH* later (especially pp. 39 and 55). Useful here: MacIntyre, *After*, pp. 50–51.
55. Hegel, *PH*, pp. 55. So when Hegel claims there that "Spirit is at war with itself; it has to overcome itself as its most formidable obstacle," he is exploiting an ambiguity that has been associated with the word "nature" since antiquity. On this ambiguity see A. O. Lovejoy and G. Boas, *Primitivism and Related Ideas in Antiquity* (Baltimore, 1935). For K. Burke, *Language as Symbolic Action*, p. 46, such exploitation is "tender minded" in that the term " 'nature' exists to provide us with terms for the physical realm that are transferable to the moral realm." For Burke, this kind of exploitation is a form of "coy theology." It applies to Hegel, I think.
56. Hegel uses the phrase in *PH*, p. 40. In 1796 Hegel characterized this transformation as one that involved giving "wings" to physics. See Hegel, in Harris, *HD*, p. 510. Löwith, *From*, p. 8, discusses Hegel's usage of this very old Ciceronian phrase.
57. Hegel's conception of the Kingdom of God is discussed in section 2.
58. Hegel, *PH*, p. 344. It is instructive here that Hegel's conception of the Reformation (pp. 344–345) is presented in terms of a three-stage theology of history that culminates in an age of "spirit" and collective redemption. This is the age, moreover, in which God becomes "all in all." That is a main-line Protestant conception. See, e.g., Littler, *Order*, pp. 75 and 115.
59. Hegel, *PH*, p. 341. Also see pp. 422 and 447.
60. Ibid., p. 422.
61. See the quotation in n. 30 above.
62. Hegel's view of this is clear in *PH*, pp. 424 and 441–442. He held this view as early as 1794. See the fragment in *Jugendschriften*, p. 42.
63. In an otherwise fine study of Kant, Y. Yovel, *Kant and the Philosophy of History* (Princeton, 1980), contends (pp. 116–121) that teleology and theology are at loggerheads in Kant. Yovel is forced, therefore, to claim throughout that the theological language Kant uses to talk about teleology is only "metaphorical." I disagree (see n. 342 below) and would make the same point about Hegel's language relative to other Hegel scholars who wish to discount the religious dynamic within it (e.g., Findlay, *Hegel*, p. 16). For the correct formulation of the teleology – theology language issue see Plant, *Hegel*, pp. 131–135, and n. 127 below. On Kant's "reconceived teleology" see P. Riley, *Kant's Political Philosophy* (Totowa, 1983).
64. I discuss all these themes, section 2.

65. Findlay, "Subjectivity," and idem, "Hegel's Use of Teleology," in *New Studies in Hegel's Philosophy*, W. Steinkraus, ed. (New York, 1971). By making this claim, Findlay is forced to insist ("Teleology," p. 102) that Hegel used religious language to mask his non-Christian intentions. E. Voegelin, *OH*, v. 4, p. 263, says Hegel retained religious language "as a cover" for his non-Christian endeavor. The same claim has been made by many scholars with regard to Lessing's "exoteric" use of religious language. See, e.g., Allison, *Lessing*, n. 12, pp. 194–195.

66. See n. 45 above.

67. Hegel, *Brf.*, v. 1, p. 17. Also see n. 38 above for Lessing's and Kant's variations on this theme.

68. I show, section (2),that this was Hegel's position in 1793–1794.

69. I stress "within" here to draw attention to the crucial "shift of context" in Hegel's thinking. Lukács, *Young*, p. 122, has put it well: "His philosophical formula was to lead to a revitalization of society from within and not to importing any extraneous principle into society [from without]." I have learned much from Cumming, *Human Nature and History*, v. 1, pp. 21–33, as to how to conceptualize his "shift of context." Also see Harris, *HD*, p. 407; and Plant, *Hegel*, pp. 44–45.

70. This is what I meant earlier by saying that Hegel's conception of self-realizing teleology was an "historically specific" notion. Several points are relevant here. First, in Part III I detail what is at issue here. Second, as I try to show in section 2 there is a good deal of this in the essays Kant wrote on history in the 1780s. Third, many scholars have treated the covergence of religion and economics in Hegel as a simple matter of "secularization" when, in fact, Hegel's intention was to "redivinize" the world. As Kaufmann (*Hegel*, pp. 77–78) has noted, while the phrase "God is dead" appears in Hegel, it does so in contexts in which Hegel wishes to proceed "beyond [His] death to [His] resurrection."

71. Again, Cumming, *Human*, v. 1, pp. 52–53, has been helpful conceptually.

72. Consult Harris, *HD*, pp. 258–265, for specific aspects of the literature. And see section 1.

73. R. Kroner, "Hegel's Philosophical Development," in *ETW*, p. 8.

74. For example, Kaufmann, *Hegel*, pp. 8, 15–19, and 81–85, stresses Hegel's Greek exposure. Kroner, ibid., p. 10; Dilthey, *Jugendgeschichte*, pp. 41–43, 53–54, and 138; and D. Henrich, "Some Historical Presuppositions of Hegel's System," in *HPR*, pp. 39ff, credit Hölderlin with the key influence. Others (e.g., Lukács) make much of Hegel's economic studies. Schmidt, "Recent Hegel Literature," in *Telos*, no. 46 (1980–1981), offers a broad and intelligent commentary on much of the recent literature in this area. For earlier scholarship, see W. Walsh, "A Survey of Work on Hegel 1945–1952," in *Philosophical Quarterly*, v. 3 (1953).

75. Many of these writings can be found in *ETW*.

76. Fackenheim, *Dimension*, pp. 6–11, summarizes some of the larger issues (e.g., the problem of "secularized Christianity") that arise in the interpretation of Hegel's religious thought. For Löwith (*From*, p. 47), Hegel is "the last Christian philosopher"; for Hyppolite, *Studies*, p. 39, and Lukács,

Young, p. 123, Hegel was "ambivalent" about Christianity; and for many authors (e.g., Heine) Hegel was an "atheist" pretending to be a Christian.

77. Lukács, *Young*, p. 64; and Kaufmann, "Hegel's Early Antitheological Phase," in *Philosophical Review*, v. 63 (1954), p. 3. For contrary views, see J. Gray, *Hegel and Greek Thought* (New York, 1941), pp. 22–23; S. Avineri, *Hegel's Theory of the Modern State* (Cambridge, England, 1972), pp. 13 and 25 (n.); and Löwith, *From*, p. 324, who regards Hegel as "discriminating" in his criticism of Christianity.

78. Lukács, *Young*, pp. 8 and 23.

79. Kaufmann, "Early," p. 5. Also see pp. 6 and 13. Kaufmann (p. 13 n.) ties himself to Lukács by complimenting him on his exposure of "Hegel's early theological phase" as a "fiction." Though I disagree with both about the religious dimension of Hegel's thought, I think both are correct in stressing (versus Kroner) that Hegel was not a Romanticist.

80. Lukács, *Young*, p. 9; Kaufmann, "Early," p. 13, and idem, *Hegel*, pp. 32–3, 41–43, and 271–273. In a telling paragraph Kaufmann ("Early," p. 7) runs without pause Hegel's criticism of orthodox Lutheranism into a rejection of Christianity per se. Obviously, the one does not imply the other.

81. A careful reading of how Hegel uses the term "theological" in *TE* reveals this. Croce, *What Is Living and What Is Dead of the Philosophy of Hegel*, D. Ainslie, trans. (London, 1915), pp. 70–72, discusses the "ambiguous" Christian point.

82. Kaufmann, *Hegel*, pp. 31–32.

83. Ibid., p. 37.

84. Ibid., pp. 82–84, ties *Sittlichkeit* and *Volksreligion* together and proceeds à la R. Haym to treat both as classically inspired.

85. Ibid., p. 273.

86. In ibid., Kaufmann tries to separate "humanism" from liberal Protestant theology. Much is at stake in the distinction. Hyppolite, for example, argues that the difference between the ideas of an "individual I" and a "human I" should be explained in terms of the difference between "Christianity" and "religious humanism." If, however, I am right about liberal Protestant theology's concern with religious recollectivization, then Hyppolite's religious humanism and my liberal Protestant theology arguments begin to converge, with the result that the distinction Kaufmann wishes to draw becomes problematic.

87. Lukács, *Young*, pp. 16 and 35.

88. Ibid., p. 35. For Lukács, "One of the greatest failures of the historiography of ideology is that the relationship between the classical revival and the struggles of the bourgeoisie for emancipation has never been adequately explored." In this context, Lukács claims (p. 104) that Hegel's religious views were those of bourgeois humanism and (pp. 52–54) that that humanism was "heroic" in a classical sense. And (pp. 9–16) Lukács insists that the latter is a "religion of freedom" relative to Christianity that, for him, is a "religion of despotism." For these reasons, Lukács' Hegel is a main-line "Enlightenment" thinker.

89. Plant, *Hegel*, Chapter I, especially n. 3, p. 32, has the correct position. But also see n. 16 above.

90. Although Plant (ibid.) has seen this clearly, his own presentation is confusing. With regard to the juxtaposition, he says (p. 36) *Volksreligion* will "replace" Christianity. Then (p. 42) he mentions Hegel's intention of developing "a Volksreligion *out of* Christianity." My emphasis. The difference is important.

91. I cite the evidence in section 2.

92. Tayor, *Hegel*, n. 1, p. 55.

93. See the key passages in ibid., pp. 51–56 and 65–66.

94. Ibid., p. 53. As we shall see, it is decisive here that Taylor says this view of renewal manifests "a religion of *Aufklärer* in terms defined by Kant."

95. Ibid. Taylor's detheologization argument is most perceptive. Where we disagree is with what he proceeds to do – or not do – with it.

96. Taylor uses the phrase, ibid., p. 495. Taylor ties this to "liberal Protestantism" (p. 495) and to "living piety" (pp. 53–55 and n. 1, p. 483). In this, he seems to follow Knox, "Attitude," p. 73, where Hegel is said to wish "to substitute for orthodoxy...a living religious faith."

97. Taylor, *Hegel*, p. 54, and n. 1, p. 55.

98. His source here is *TE*.

99. Consult the argument of *TE*, pp. 499–507. The term "civil" here retains its collective, moral aspect. It is, therefore, "pre-Hegelian."

100. See n. 96 above, and Taylor's statement (*Hegel*, p. 65) that this was to take place "in the context of a purified Christianity."

101. Hence Taylor's claim (ibid., p. 52) that Hegel really "never broke away" from Christianity.

102. Ibid., p. 54.

103. Ibid., pp. 53–54.

104. In this, Taylor succumbs to the confusion noted in Plant, n. 90 above.

105. Taylor, *Hegel* p. 53–55.

106. Ibid., p. 54.

107. Ibid., p. 71

108. Ibid., p. 71.

109. Ibid., p. 72.

110. Ibid., pp. 72–73.

111. Ibid., p. 74. Taylor (pp. 67 and 69) explains part of this shift in terms of Hegel's career prospects as a professional philosopher.

112. Ibid., p. 71.

113. Ibid., p. 74.

114. Ibid., pp. 73.

115. Ibid., pp. 74–75.

116. Ibid., p. 73.

117. Ibid., pp. 74 and 73. Plant, *Hegel*, p. 53, and Hyppolite, *Studies*, p. 39, also advance the radicalism thesis. Also see n. 6, above.

118. Taylor, *Hegel*, p. 73.

119. Ibid., p. 74.

120. A problem arises here if one views, as I do, Hegel's political writings of the

late 1790s as still reformist in nature. Avineri (in *Hegel's Political Philosophy*, Kaufmann, ed.); Kelly, *Retreat*, p. 24; and Harris, *HD*, pp. 434ff, all argue for this view. Many others (e.g., Hyppolite, *Studies*, pp. 40–42) see Hegel as acquiescing in the status quo. Taylor holds to the latter position, and I do not agree with it. Also see n. 123, below, for more on the philosophical implications of this argument.

121. Taylor, *Hegel*, pp. 53 and 75.

122. Ibid., p. 75.

123. R. Haym, *Hegel*, pp. 160–162, was one of the first to articulate the view fully. For Lukács, *Young*, p. xxv, this maneuver constitutes the "idealist abstraction from real human activity." For Hyppolite, *Studies*, p. 42, the move "is marked by a shift from a reformist attitude to an attitude of contemplation, from the 'sollen' to 'the comprehension of what is.' "

124. Taylor, *Hegel*, n. 1, p. 72, and p. 74.

125. Ibid., a similar argument in Löwith, *From*, p. 324.

126. There is no problem, of course, if the Christian aspects of Hegel's thoughts are defined as "humanist." But that is simply a terminological solution to the more involved problem of Hegel's relation to Christianity and of the relation of both to Marx.

127. A most revealing passage in Lukács (*Young*, p. 363) runs: Hegel failed to notice "that the consistent application of his own *teleological* principle leads him back into the old *theological* conception of teleology." My emphasis. I doubt that this blind spot is true of Hegel. But the statement is most pertinent to Lukács and his desire to solve the Hegel–Marx problem. A. Funkenstein, in *Medievalia et Humanistica*, n. s., v. 5 (1974), p. 22 (n. 50), has noted the connection between Hegel's teleological terminology and the religious "accommodationism" argument. It is a crucial point.

128. Lukács, *Young*, pp. xviiiff.

129. A key section in ibid., pp. 99–123.

130. Ibid., pp. 100 and 122.

131. Ibid., p. 99.

132. Ibid., pp. 98, 119, and 122, where Lukács moves the focus of Hegel's concerns to a point *within* civil society itself.

133. As was pointed out in the Introduction, few *Aufklärer* were willing to abandon Christianity.

134. In Hegel, p. 495, for example, Taylor associates "detheologized" Christianity with "liberal Protestantism" and " 'death of God' theologies." For the correct view, see Kaufmann, *Hegel*, pp. 77–78, where the claim is made that the "resurrection" of God, not his "death," was Hegel's aim. Also see nn. 70 and 96 above.

135. I pursue the theme in Part III of this study.

136. In n. 26 to the Preface I referred to the strategic role the ambiguity of words can play in assessing a thinker's thought at certain pivotal "moments" of its development. Between 1796 and 1802 such ambiguity surrounds Hegel's conception of nature. And in n. 55 above, I noted how Hegel exploited the ambiguity for "tender-minded" purposes. Mention of these two points is relevant here because the "two theoretical levels"

referred to in the text are religious and economic in nature and find their point of mediation in Hegel's conception of "nature." Hegel, in other words, is using language here as a "symbolic" mode of action.

137. Taylor, *Hegel*, p. 53.

138. Ibid., pp. 66 and 54.

139. As we shall see in Part III, esp. Chapter 8, Schiller used the idea in *AE*; Hegel used the phrase "overleaping of nature" in *ETW*, p. 278. In this, though, both were objecting to those who believed the idea of "what ought to be" was a simple matter of postulation. It is, for both, a key argument against romantic enthusiasm.

140. Hence my argument (n. 120 above) about the reformist character of Hegel's essay on the "German Constitution."

141. This, of course, is why Hegel's conception of teleology, alluded to above, is an historically specific conception. What makes it so is the priority Hegel assigns to his theology of history.

142. In their own ways, this is what Lukács, *Young*, pp. 98, 119, and 122, and Harris, *HD*, p. 407, are driving at, albeit in very general terms.

143. In the Preface, n. 27, I referred to the "conditional mode" of Hegel's discourse. It applies here. In Part III I show how Hegel relates this telic principle to "middling" social groups in civil society.

144. What Löwith, *From*, p. 323, says about the concept of "human being" is relevant here. To wit, when Hegel talks about *Geist* he is talking about a human being whose self-conception "is basically determined by the idea which the Christian has of himself *as the image and likeness of God*." (My emphasis). It is what Kant and Schiller mean to express with the term "personality."

145. Thus Löwith's concern (*From*, Part Two) with the tensions and dynamics of what he calls "the bourgeois-Christian world."

146. See n. 143 above. I should note here that the "hope" that *Geist* expresses is at once teleological and eschatological, participatory and anticipatory.

147. A major theme pursued in Part III below.

148. Löwith's theme, nicely summarized by Fackenheim, *Dimension*, pp. 232–235.

149. Consult Harris, *HD*, pp. 58–64, for Hegel's reasons for pursuing a degree in theology despite his reservations about it.

150. Ibid., n. 3, pp. 59–60, speculates on Hegel's frustrated wish to be a lawyer.

151. Three sources are vital for what follows: Pfleiderer, *The Development of Theology in Germany Since Kant*, pp. 85ff; Harris, *HD*, especially Chapter II; and Henrich, "Presuppositions," especially pp. 31–39.

152. In addition to n. 151, above, see Brecht and Sandberger, "Hegels," and M. Leube, *Das Tübinger Stift*.

153. Harris, *HD*, p. 90; Pfleiderer, *Theology*, p. 86.

154. On Diez, see Henrich, "Presuppositions." In Pfleiderer's older study (*Theology*, p. 87) Schelling is placed at the antipode of Storr. Brecht and Sandberger, "Hegels," have much to say about the views of the tutors at Tübingen during these years, as does Leube, *Stift*.

155. Henrich, "Presuppositions," pp. 35–36. Also see Harris, *HD*, n. 2, p. 81, and n. 3, pp. 98–99.
156. Henrich, "Presuppositions," pp. 33–34. There is a problem here, for Henrich does not really tell us what the difference is between this "radical critique" and that of (p. 34) "a religious Enlightenment which makes use of Kantianism as the most progressive system of insight." To lump both groups under the rubric of "young Kantians" (p. 31) is to miss an important nuance that differentiates Kantians of the spirit from each other. Also see n. 248 below.
157. Diez, quoted in ibid., p. 35.
158. Ibid., p. 36.
159. Ibid., p. 31; Pfleiderer, *Theology*, p. 88.
160. Henrich, "Presuppositions," p. 36.
161. On Storr, see ibid., pp. 32–37, and Harris, *HD*, pp. 90–92.
162. Pfleiderer, *Theology*, p. 86.
163. Henrich, "Presuppositions," pp. 31 and 37. Also see Harris, *HD*, p. 94. The "supernaturalism" phrase is Pfleiderer's, *Theology*, p. 86.
164. Pfleiderer, *Theology*, p. 87. Pfleiderer has Schelling in mind here. Henrich, "Presuppositions," p. 37, refers to the orthodox use of Kant as "an inversion" of Kant's meaning.
165. The distinction between the letter and the spirit gained prominence in the 1770s when Lessing began to publish Reimarus' fragments. For specifics, see Allison, *Lessing*, pp. 95, 108, 112–113, and 115. Crucial, I think, is that Lessing used the distinction versus orthodoxy to argue for progressive revelation in history. Kant used the distinction in *RWL*, pp. 25–26; Schiller used it in *AE*, p. 87; Schelling in a letter to Hegel, *Brf.*, v. 1, p. 14; and Hegel in *TE*, *BP*, and *ETW*.
166. Harris, *HD*, p. xxiii, argues that Kant's philosophy and the interpretation of Jesus' character and teaching were at the core of the debate.
167. Henrich, "Presuppositions," p. 36, and Harris, *HD*, n. 3, p. 98.
168. According to Harris (*HD*, p. xxiii), Diez denied Jesus was the "true Messiah."
169. See Schelling, quoted in Harris, "The Young Hegel and the Postulates of Practical Reason," *HPR*, p. 67. For Hegel's reservation, idem, *HD*, pp. 210–211.
170. Appreciated by Henrich, "Presuppositions," p. 38.
171. H. Wacker, *Das Verhältnis des jungen Hegel zu Kant*, (Berlin, 1932), p. 71. Harris, *HD*, p. xxxiii, seems to make the same point when he claims Hegel meant to defend Jesus as well as Kant against both sets of their detractors. Yet Harris (n. 2, pp. 495–496) becomes confusing when he terms this a "narrowly Kantian" position.
172. Harris, *HD*, p. xxiii, and n. 3, pp. 98–99.
173. Kant's *RWL* appeared in two parts, in 1792 and 1793. Book One was published as a separate essay in 1792 and then was included with Books Two through Four in 1793. The impact this essay had on Hegel has been testified to by all scholars. See, e.g., Knox, "Attitude," p. 71; Kaufmann, *Hegel*, pp. xii, 8, and 13; Gray, *Hegel*, p. 22; Harris, *HD*, p. 108.

174. Leutwein, quoted in Kaufmann, *Hegel*, p. 8. Also see Wacker, *Hegel*, p. 66.
175. At least since Pfleiderer, *Theology*, made an issue of it.
176. W. Walsh, "Kant as Seen by Hegel," in *Idealism Past and Present*, G. Vesey, ed. (Cambridge, England, 1982), p. 109.
177. Ibid., p. 94; Also see Harris, "Postulates," p. 61, for roots of the thesis in Dilthey et al.
178. Wacker, *Hegel*, pp. 65–66; Harris, *HD*, p. 83; and Kaufmann, *Hegel*, p. 8.
179. Wacker, *Hegel*, p. 75; Knox, "Attitude," p. 71.
180. Lukács, *Young*, Chapter Four.
181. This is what I take Harris, *HD*, p. xx, to mean by his reference to Hegel's desire to "formulate the right interpretation of Kant" while at Tübingen.
182. Harris, following Haering, develops the *Volkserzieher* theme in ibid., esp. pp. 59 and 157. He discusses the Kingdom of God theme, and its importance for Hegel, pp. 101, 104–105, 116, n. 2, p. 128. For the relation of the latter theme to Hegel's view of Christianity see n.'s 188 and 204 below.
183. Ibid., pp. 99,101, and n. 3, pp. 186–187, makes it clear that Lessing had been Hegel's hero for years. H. Allison, *Lessing*, pp, 53, 78, and 115, and n.'s 1, 3, and 11, pp. 193–194, offers specific details.
184. Ibid., pp. 23–26. The excerpt itself appears in *DHE*, pp. 87–100. See, especially, pp. 86, 89, and 93–95.
185. Translated by Harris, *HD*, p. 25.
186. See, e.g., the quotations from Spener, Chapter 1, above, n.'s 319, 320 and 322.
187. *DHE*, pp. 43–48, especially p. 46.
188. A key theme in light of the argument of section 1 of this chapter. I make the argument below with regard to Hegel's relationship with Kant's *RWL*. I think Harris (*HD*, pp. 26, 34, and xxiii) has understood this well, for at several points he claims that *Volksreligion, Vernunftreligion*, and Hegel's attempts to reform Christianity are of a piece with each other. See also n. 204 below.
189. Noted by Harris, *HD*, n. 2, pp. 212–213.
190. In *TE* this becomes expecially clear.
191. See n. 169 above.
192. Pfleiderer, *Theology*, p. 19, offers this kind of formulation for Kant. I think it applies to Hegel as well.
193. Obviously I think the notion of "egocentric" religion as developed earlier (Introduction, especially n. 129) is relevant here. It becomes apposite in the context of the distinction Hegel draws in *TE* between loving God and loving oneself. Also see Kant, *RWL*, p. 41, for the same distinction.
194. I am referring here to the sermons collected in *DHE*, pp. 175–192, and to *TE*.
195. I take issue here with some of Harris' claims. See, e.g., n. 251, below.
196. Discussed by Harris, *HD*, pp. 108–119.
197. See *DHE*, pp. 176–179.

198. As Allison, *Lessing*, has noted, this was a main theme of Lessing. It is also a very old pietistic precept, as we saw in Part I.

199. Harris, *HD*, Chapter II, and, especially, n. 2, p. 105, relates the theme to Lessing.

200. *DHE*, p. 181.

201. Ibid.

202. I agree with Harris, *HD*, p. 153, that the essay is not "a fragment." As Harris notes (p. 119), it is the key to "a fairly large-scale project" that was to occupy Hegel for years. That project, Harris suggests (p. 107), was one of "theological enlightenment."

203. Ibid., p. 116.

204. Of all recent Hegel scholars, Harris has understood this the best. In addition to the references cited in n. 188 above, consult his intelligent handling of the Christianity–*Volksreligion* problem in *HD*, pp. 231–233 and 252–253. Suffice it to say that Harris makes it clear that in 1793–1794 Hegel was concerned with the "rehabilitation of Christianity as a *Volksreligion*." Hence, the importance of the question Hegel asks himself in *TE*, pp. 495–499, and in *BP*, p. 509, as to "How far is Christianity qualified to serve as a *Volksreligion?*"

205. See n.'s 95–96 above.

206. Noted by Harris, *HD*, n. 1, p. 233.

207. Hegel, *TE*, p. 483.

208. Ibid.

209. Ibid.; this *religious* theme correlates very nicely with the *political* theme pursued in the 1798 essay on the constitutional situation in Old-Württemberg.

210. The collectivist aspect of the argument emerges clearly in *TE*, pp. 499–507

211. Ibid., p. 500. Clearly, this theme is decisive for our argument about religious "accommodationism." Other statements in *TE*, pp. 482–483 and 485–487, support this thesis.

212. Ibid., p. 485; the "seed" metaphor also is used in essays Hegel wrote in 1795 and 1796.

213. Ibid., p. 487.

214. Ibid.; again, the religious accommodationism and teleological assimilationism convergence is important.

215. Ibid., pp. 484, 488, 492, 499ff, and 490–494, respectively.

216. Ibid., p. 484; here Hegel has in mind "the *Buchstabenmensch*," a figure discussed by Harris, *HD*, p. 140, and used by Hegel, *TE*, p. 494. Clearly, Hegel is juxtaposing this man, whom he associates with "enlightenment," and the man of "wisdom" who, he holds, recognizes the need for "elevation of the soul." As Lovejoy (*Primitivism*, p. 270) has recorded, setting the "cunning" and "clever" man against the "wise" man is a very old theological strategy. Kant uses a very similar formulation in *RWL*, p. 149, and in *CJ*, pp. 94ff, in his discussion of cultures of skill and cultures of discipline. In that context, he associates the former with "happiness," the latter with "virtue." In part III, I shall show how Hegel gives this idea an economic

twist by linking it to the idea of "luxury."

217. Hegel, *TE*, p. 488.

218. Ibid., p. 486.

219. Ibid., pp. 484ff.

220. Ibid., p. 484.

221. Ibid.

222. Ibid.; my emphasis to bring out the "ethical" aspect of Hegel's conception of subjective religion. This aspect, I think, allows Hegel to tie subjective religion and *Volksreligion* together. It confirms, moreover, the "inside–outside" thrust of Protestant reformism, noted in n. 35 above.

223. Ibid., p. 485.

224. Ibid., p. 486.

225. Ibid., pp. 486–488.

226. Ibid., pp. 485–486 and 500. Hegel uses the term throughout the 1790s in political as well as religious contexts. It appears frequently in his correspondence too.

227. H. Dreyer's essay on the concept of *Geist* in late eighteenth-century German thought, in *KS*, Ergangshefte, no. 7 (1908), also discusses usage of the term *Gemüt*. Also consult the Glossary in *AE*, pp. 313ff.

228. Dreyer, "Geist," pp. 28ff.

229. See, e.g., Kant, *RWL*, pp. 43–45, 73, and 77–78, where *Gemüt* (p. 45) is "the spirit" in man upon which the memory of his "divine origin" acts to inspire virtuous behavior. Also see n. 324, below.

230. For a fine statement of the point see M. Foster, *Plato and Hegel*, p. 127. There, Foster relates *Gemüt* to "will" and perceptively notes that, as such, it is "a potentially practical principle" rather than just "a theoretical" one. The etymological link Foster posits (n. 2, p. 127) between *Gemüt* and the idea of "courage" becomes important for us in Part III. See also n. 324, below.

231. Harris, *HD*, pp. 485–488. Elsewhere (p. 184) he translates the term as "heart." The editors of *AE* prefer "psyche" as a translation.

232. See Ozment, *Homo Spiritualis*, especially pp. 1–46. The subject of Ozment's work on *Gemüt* is J. Tauler, whom, Harris tells us (*HD*, pp. 230–231), Hegel studied and excerpted from in the early 1790s. Much of what Ozment says about Tauler's conception of *Gemüt* applies to Hegel. For example, Ozment (pp. 16–19) indicates that while in Tauler *Gemüt* often correlates with the latin *mens*, it embraced "the disposition of the heart" as well. Its "illumination," moreover, was directional rather than a possession of man's. As such, it expressed an awareness about man's *Bestimmung*, about man's *adult* conception of his true telos. For a Tauler – Kant parallel, see n. 289 below.

233. Ozment, *Homo*, p. 3.

234. Ibid., pp. 15–16, 22, and 46.

235. Ibid., pp. 16 and 19. Also see *AE*, pp. 313ff.

236. The idea of man's *Bestimmung* is important here. Since Spalding (see Allison, *Lessing*, n. 155, p. 175), the term had been vital to the "humanistic tendency" in eighteenth-century German religious thought. According to

the editors of *AE*, pp. 305–306, the term was often linked with the idea of the telos of man's "'true' nature." Kant, Schiller, and Hegel, I think, used the term in this religioteleological rather than natural–teleological sense.

237. Hegel, *TE*, p. 492.

238. Ibid., p. 495. It would be easy to credit Kant (*RWL*) with the decisive influence here. But note what Clement said much earlier (quoted in Tollinton, *Clement*, v. 2, p. 298): "Above all, they should bear in mind the fact that by nature we are born for virtue, not so as to possess it from our birth, but with an aptitude for its acquisition. By this consideration we can solve the dilemma of the Heretics, whether Adam was formed perfect or imperfect. If imperfect, say they, how could the work of God, who is perfect, be imperfect, especially such a work as man? But if perfect, how comes his transgression of the commandments? We, too, will make reply that man was not created constitutionally perfect, but only with an aptitude for the reception of virtue. Certainly, for the pursuit of virtue, it makes all the difference to be born with an aptitude for its acquisition. And it is God's will that we should originate our own salvation."

239. Hegel, *TE*, p. 495. Another version of this statement may be found in Hegel's *Jugendschriften*, p. 362.

240. In *TE*, Hegel uses the phrase *Vernunftreligion*. On p. 486 he ties it specifically to the demands "practical reason" makes on men for ethical activism.

241. Compare ibid., p. 495, with Spener, quoted in Chapter 1, n.'s 319, 320, and 322. For Lessing's famous formulation, see Allison, *Lessing*, p. 135. Chadwick, *LTW*, pp. 42–43, takes it all back to Clement. Tollington, *Clement*, v. 1, p. 193, discusses Clement's usage. Generally speaking, the idea of "striving" enables Christian reformers to bridge the gap between axiology and teleology without having to equate striving for perfection with its actual attainment. There is much of this kind of "striving" in Schiller, *AE*, pp. 77 and 95.

242. Hegel, in *TE*, p. 495. With this statement a decisive argument emerges. Throughout this essay one of Hegel's concerns has been to ask how to differentiate acts of "mere prudence" form acts of "actual morality" (p. 482). From what he says (p. 484), it is clear that he wishes to associate the latter with acts that are "'pleasing to God.'" Given what Hegel says about the "law-abiding habit," it is just as clear that "prudence" stands to "legality" as "actions pleasing to God" stand to acts of "actual morality" in Kant's sense and to truly "ethical" acts in Hegel's sense. In this context, prudence, legality, and the "propensity toward sensibility" (i.e., toward acquisitiveness) are linked in Hegel's mind with the refinements of civilization. Against that value complex he wishes (p. 496) to awaken men to higher-minded pursuits. In this Kant (n. 280 below) and Lessing are decisive: to wit the latter: "Religion has far higher purposes than to mold the honest man. It presupposes him; and its chief aim is to raise the honest man to higher insights." See Lessing, quoted in Allison, *Lessing*, p. 66. Later, we shall see how this value complex becomes associated with "bourgeois" interests and with the frustration of Hegel's attempt to constitute

Sittlichkeit as a collective ideal. In terms of the argument of Part One, Hegel wished men to adhere to the spirit of the *covenant* of a godly people rather than to the letter of the *contract* they had consented to among themselves.

243. Hegel, *TE*, p. 497.

244. Thus, the importance of *Sittlichkeit* as a conceptual axis in Hegel's thought.

245. Throughout *TE*, pp. 483 and 505–506, Hegel makes it clear that *Sittlichkeit* as a religious ideal cannot exist among a politically "oppressed" people.

246. Ibid., p. 506.

247. The point was made earlier, n. 173 above.

248. As was noted previously, there were differences not only between Kantians of the letter and those of the spirit but also among Kantians of the spirit themselves. See n. 156 above.

249. See, e.g., Yovel, *Kant*, especially pp. 9, 11, 23ff, 279–283, and 300ff. Put another way, it is when Kant tries to reconcile the dualism of the first *Critique* that he begins to prefigure Hegel.

250. It is well known that Kant's background had much Pietism in it. T. Greene, "The Historical Context and Religious Significance of Kant's *Religion*," in Kant's *RWL*, especially pp. xxvii–xxx, brings this out. Most instructive, though, is M. Despland, *Kant on History and Religion* (Montreal, 1973), pp. 101ff, for he shows how the aspects of Pietism to which Kant adhered were down-to-earth. There is, he insists (p. 103), a good deal of Calvinism in Kant's religious views.

251. Though I am most indebted to Harris, I do have "intimate" disagreements with him with regard to how he handles the Hegel – Kant issue between 1786 and 1796. For Harris, *HD*, p. 234, the issue turns on the dovetailing of Kantian and Greek modes of thought and value. For me, the issue of dovetailing involves an appreciation of how after 1784 Kant became drawn more and more toward covenant theology, a movement that, I think, brings him closer to Württemberg's Hegel.

252. Ibid., p. 24. On p. 26 Kant is identified as the carrier of the "ideal of rational enlightenment." A sentence later he is associated with "the rationalist humanism of the Enlightenment." For most *Aufklärer*, the latter would have been compatible with Christianity; the former would not.

253. Ibid., p. 234.

254. I will bring out some of the many parallels in the notes below.

255. See, e.g., n. 173 above.

256. On this see Walsh, "Seen," pp. 99–100; Henrich, "Presuppositions," p. 29; E. Fackenheim, "Kant's Concept of History," in *KS*, v. 48, 3 (1956–1957), pp. 381 and 389ff; Despland, *Kant*, especially pp. 48 and 67; and Yovel, *Kant*, especially pp. x and 127.

257. That there was an eschatological aspect to Kant's thinking, especially between 1784 and 1793, is well known. See, e.g., the literature cited in the Introduction (n. 67) and Despland's remarks and citations, *Kant*, pp. 277 and 317 (n. 19). Despland (p. 196 and n. 57, p. 339) links Kant's thinking to federal theology in general and to covenant theology in parti-

cular. Just as helpful, P. Cornehl, *Die Zukunft der Versöhnung* (Göttingen, 1977), pp. 59–81. Much that Yovel, *Kant*, says about Kant's teleology has an eschatological dimension to it; but Yovel insists that the dimension is "exoteric." Despland (pp. 104–105 and 111) disagrees with the "exoteric" thesis. I agree with him.

258. I say this because of the lengths Kant scholars have gone to to explain away the "Messianic prophecies" of *RWL*. Note Fackenheim's discussion, "Kant's," pp. 381–384.

259. Most fully elaborated by Despland, *Kant*.

260. Kant, *RWL*, p. 39. Compare this and much of what follows with Clement, quoted in n. 238 above.

261. Ibid., pp. 39, 46–47, and 172–173.

262. Ibid., p. 39. On p. 40 Kant writes "For despite the fall, the injunction that we ought to become better men resounds unabatedly in our souls."

263. Ibid., p. 40. Note the voluntarism and activism in the statement.

264. Ibid., p. 42. Also see p. 139.

265. Ibid., p. 42 As Despland has recorded (*Kant*, p. 199), Kant used the assimilationism argument to explain the dynamic of elevation of the soul.

266. Kant, *RWL*, p. 42. Also see pp. 43 and 46.

267. Ibid., p. 43.

268. Ibid., p. 44. Here the truly moral man is expected to emerge as a being whose interests are not merely prudential.

269. Ibid.

270. Ibid.; also n.'s 229 and 236 above, for more on the interaction between *Gemüt* and *Bestimmung* that is expressed in this sentence. One could say that the interaction constitutes the dynamic of what Kant called "philosophical millenarianism." On this see n. 317 below.

271. Ibid., p. 46; compare with Clement, quoted in n. 238 above.

272. Ibid., p. 47. W. H. Walsh, "Kant's Moral Theology," in *Proceedings of the British Academy*, v. 49 (1963), is most illuminating on Kant's turn to activism.

273. Kant, *RWL*, p. 47.

274. Ibid.; compare with Hegel (in *TE*, p. 486) where "special arrangements of God for the benefit of man are not excluded."

275. Kant, *RWL*, p. 47. In the sentence immediately preceding this one, Kant contends that the relation between God's "cooperation from above" and man's *doing* will vary according to time and place. In this, he is very much an accommodationist. Also see n. 318 below.

276. Ibid., p. 40. Clearly, the "preparationist" argument, discussed in Part I. Also see Kant, quoted in n. 332 below.

277. See Part I of this study.

278. Pfleiderer, quoted by Greene, "Context," in *RWL*, p. xx. This is a fine formulation of the axiology–teleology thesis.

279. See Kant, *RWL*, pp. 42–43, for what follows.

280. See n. 242 above.

281. Kant, *RWL*, p. 15. Also see Kant, *KOH*, pp. 21–22. Despland, *Kant*, pp. 32ff, and Kelly, *Idealism, Politics and History*, pp. 89ff, relate Kant to

Rousseau in this context.

282. Kant, *RWL*, pp. 16–17.
283. Ibid., p. 86. Earlier in the essay (pp. 16–18) Kant had hinted that "civilization" was the "middle ground" between optimistic and pessimistic conceptions of human nature. This is what Kelly means (*Idealism*, p. 89) when he refers to civilization as a "mediating term" for Kant. For Despland (*Kant*, pp. 32, 38, and 57) Kant is being deliberately ambiguous here in order to impress upon his readers the need to *make* a moral choice. Hegel, *TE*, pp. 495–496, follows Kant closely on this.
284. Clearly indicated by Kant, *RWL*, n. p. 21, where a gap is posited between civilization qua rationally organized system of legal rights and obligation and civilization qua pursuit of the truly moral law.
285. Ibid., p. 42. According to Kelly (*Idealism*, n. 2, p. 109) and Yovel (*Kant*, p. 71 and n. 18, p. 101), Kant became more conscious of this split after 1788. Also see n. 363 below, where Hegel's understanding of the split is discussed.
286. Kant, *RWL*, p. 42.
287. This, I think, is the "practical" concern alluded to in Beck, *Early German Philosophy*, n. 157, p. 487 – that is, the ethical consideration of a religiously informed philosophy of history had much influence on the direction of Kant's thought in the 1784–1793 period.
288. The phrase is Fackenheim's, "Kant's," pp. 387–388. By it he means to bring out the self-realizing and conditional aspects of Kant's very moral and religious conception of freedom.
289. Kant, *RWL*, pp. 21–23. Later (pp. 86–87), the types of men are located in different types of societies. The societies, in turn, represent different stages of religious fulfillment. For a revealing parallel see Ozment's quotations from Tauler, *Homo*, pp. 15 and 30, where the stage sequence, respectively, is as follows: "Man exists as if he were three men. The first is the outward, animal, sensing man; the second, the rational man . . . ; and the third is the *Gemüter*." Or again, "First a formless material . . . attains an animal form. But this form awaits and thirsts after a human form [then] it thirsts after an . . . in-the-image-of-God constructed form." Compare n. 232 above, where *Gemüt* is discussed.
290. Kant, *RWL*, p. 21. On the level of religious ideas the "animality" reference is obviously revealing. For a stimulating account of how the idea of "animal economy" fits into the divine economy argument, see Irenaeus, *ANCL*, v. 5: pp. 25–31.
291. Kant, *RWL*, p. 21.
292. Ibid.
293. Ibid., p. 22.
294. Ibid.; a clear reference to a Mandeville–Rousseau–Smith line of eighteenth-century intellectual development.
295. Ibid., pp. 22–23.
296. Ibid., pp. 42–43. Compare with Lessing, quoted in n. 242, above, where honesty and religion are subtly contrasted. Hegel will later talk about the "security" conscious bourgeoisie.

297. Ibid., pp. 25–26 and 42. Note Yovel's fine discussion (*Kant*, pp. 188–189) of the point about citizenship and morality. Cf. Walsh, "Moral," p. 269.
298. Kant, *RWL*, pp. 25–26. Also see n. 165 above, and n. 337 below.
299. Ibid., p. 43.
300. Ibid., p. 148.
301. Ibid., p. 86.
302. Ibid., pp. 86–87.
303. Ibid., p. 86.
304. Well appreciated by Kelly, *Idealism*, pp. 89ff. It is vital to realize, therefore, that these three terms exist, in both their modes, simultaneously rather than successively in time for Kant. The ambiguity created by Kant's usage is, I think, purposeful. It adds what Burke would call "dramatic action" to Kant's argument.
305. Kant, *RWL*, pp. 86ff.
306. Ibid., p. 131.
307. Ibid., p. 139. Also see pp. 89 and 130. That Kant was moving here toward what I have called "recollectivization" has been noted by Despland, *Kant*, pp. 181–182 and 202–208, and Yovel, *Kant*, pp. 40–41, 51–54, 66, 77, 98, 138, 171, and 202. For the latter, Kant's *RWL* represents an attempt at (p. 202) "the historical totalization of morality, i.e., the actual creation and propagation of . . . an ethical community." Also see n.'s 319 and 334, below.
308. Kant, *RWL*, p. 139.
309. Ibid., p. 91.
310. Ibid., p. 139.
311. Ibid. Another clear rendering of the axiology–teleology distinction. See n. 279 above also.
312. Ibid., p. 148.
313. Ibid., p. 122. My emphasis to bring out how Kant meant to frame the "dramatic action" (n. 304 above) of his argument in *historical* as well as *human* terms.
314. Ibid.; as Harris has observed (*HD*, pp. 96ff), the idea of the "invisible church" was a watchword among the *Stiftler* at Tübingen. Hegel uses the phrase in *Brf.*, v. 1, p. 18, and in some of his sermons of 1792–1793. It is an old Protestant conception.
315. Kant, *RWL*, pp. 77–79, 112, and 122, provides and overview of his scheme of progressive revelation in history. The point has been noted by Yovel, *Kant*, pp. 206–209. In the Epilogue, I discuss this as a moment of religious "voluntarism."
316. Ibid., p. 42.
317. Kant uses the phrase in this essay. See *KOH*, pp. 21–22. The idea has been discussed in the literature cited in n. 67 to the Introduction, above. Kant's point about "philosophical millenarianism" is aptly summarized in his statement (*RWL*, p. 21) that "The most rational mortal being in the world might still stand in need of certain incentives . . . to determine his choice [to pursue holiness]." Also see n. 270 above.
318. Kant, *KOH*, pp. 21–22. Compare this with *RWL*, p. 79, and with Lessing,

n. 38 above. In each case, the informing principle is accommodationism shaped to the *teleological* needs of a theory of progressive revelation in history. Also see n. 275 above.

319. Kant, *RWL*, p. 89, where, while discussing the coming of the ethical commonwealth, Kant claims: " Now here we have a duty which is *sui generis*, not of men toward men, but of the human race toward itself. For the species of rational beings is objectively, in the idea of reason, destined for a social goal, namely, the promotion of the highest as a social good. But because the highest moral good cannot be achieved merely by the exertions of the single individual toward his own moral perfection, but requires rather a union of such individuals into a whole toward the same goal – into a system of well-disposed men, in which and through whose unity alone the highest moral good can come to pass – the idea of such a whole, as a universal republic based on laws of virtue, is an idea completely distinguished from all moral laws (which concern what we know to lie in our own power); since it involves working toward a whole regarding which we do not know whether, as such, it lies in our power or not. Hence this duty is distinguished from all others both in kind and in principle. We can already foresee that this duty will require the presupposition of another idea, namely, that of a higher moral Being through whose universal dispensation the forces of separate individuals, insufficient in themselves, are united for a common end."

320. Ibid., p. 171.

321. Ibid., pp. 60ff, 98–114 (especially 104–109), and 150.

322. Ibid., p. 172.

323. Ibid., the notes pp. 172–173. I make much of this statement about "misconceived humility" in Part III and in the Epilogue, where I discuss Hegel's notion of Christian "pride."

324. Kant, *RWL*, p. 173, uses the term *Gemüter* here and in connection with the "courage–activism" argument. On p. 50, he had spoken of courage and virtue in the classical context; he here is assimilating that argument (as Foster, n. 230, hints above) to Christianity. Two points. First, Kant is indeed critical of "Pietism" here; what he has in mind, though, is not the down-to-earth variety of the early eighteenth century but the inner-directed, emotional variety of his own day. Second, the attempt to assimilate virtue into Christianity through the "practice of piety" constitutes the "heroic" aspect of Kant's (and Hegel's) religious faith. Hence, their refusal to allow virtue qua *praxis pietatis* to be exiled to paganism.

325. Ibid., 172 n.

326. Ibid., p. 173. Also see p. 189, where piety and virtue are juxtaposed.

327. In addition to the next few n.'s below, see ibid., pp. 69–70. Kant, as Despland (*Kant*, pp. 163 and 236) has observed, seems to follow Lessing here in that he makes striving for holiness rather than perfection itself the measure of a conscientious Christian life. For Lessing on striving, see Lessing quoted in Allison, *Lessing*, p. 135. That Kant was using striving in this sense is evident from *CJ*, p. 114. Also see n. 241. above.

328. Kant, *RWL*, p. 54.

329. Ibid., p. 60. Also see p. 69.
330. Ibid., p. 61. For Jesus as a model of liberation see, e.g., pp. 77 and 110.
331. Ibid., p. 62.
332. That Kant has assimilationism in mind is clear from ibid., p. 126, where a passage runs: "true universal religion... which we cannot conceive as a culmination in experience, but can merely anticipate, i.e., *prepare for*, in continual progress and *approximation* toward the highest good *possible on earth.*" My emphasis.
333. Ibid., p. 123.
334. Ibid., p. 125. Kant's collectivism (discussed in n.'s 307 and 319 above) is quite apparent here. Cornehl, *Zukunft*, pp. 36–38, has perceptively noted how Kant is using Semler's rendering of accommodationism to finesse Reimarus' understanding of Jesus' use of eschatology.
335. Kant, *RWL*, pp. 126 and 125, respectively. As Despland notes, *Kant*, pp. 260–262, Kant is developing "a systematic theory of symbols" here. That theory, though, raises difficult questions about the "secular–sacred" aspects of Kant's thought. Schiller, too (*AE*, p. 95[14/2]), discusses religion in terms of its symbolic form.
336. Kant, *RWL*, p. 126.
337. Ibid., p. 112. In *TE*, p. 495, Hegel speaks of "the people" being "led to *Vernunftreligion*" and of their becoming "receptive to it." When this happens, he says, God will be worshiped "in spirit" rather than by "cleaving to the letter." Put another way, "fetish faith" will give way to "service" to God, which consists "only in virtue."
338. Kant, *RWL*, p. 112. On p. 126, Kant makes clear that the "all in all" phrase here refers, à la Joachim, to the supercession of the visible church by an "invisible" one. Harris, *HD*, especially pp. 96ff, has stressed the importance of the phrase for the *Stiftler*. Allison, *Lessing*, p. 73, notes Lessing's use of the biblical phrase. I think, though, Harris and Allison both over-emphasize the uniqueness of the Germans' use of the phrase. It is a very old, main-line Protestant conception. As C. Patrides has shown [*The Phoenix and the Ladder* (Berkeley, 1964)], pp. 63ff, it is a central motif in Milton's *Paradise Lost*. In *PH*, p. 345 (n.), Hegel ties the "all in all" expression to a three-stage theology of history. Most apt, I would think, given our argument. Also see n. 58 above.
339. Wacker, *Kant*, p. 16, is clear on the point. Also see Harris, *HD* p. 34.
340. The parallels are so numerous that I shall not list them.
341. My argument would be that Kant's so-called teleological "leap" is directly connected to his increasing interest in accommodationism and assimilationism as eschatological categories. On this "leap" in Kant, see, e.g., Yovel, *Kant*, p. 42. Also see Yovel's summary of what this leap consists in, pp. 271–306, especially p. 298, where Kant is compared to a "religious devotee." Fackenheim, "Kant's," had earlier made much the same argument.
342. Yovel, *Kant*, is most puzzling here. On the one hand (pp. 7, 16, 97, n. 13, p. 215, and 218), he insists that Kant's religious concerns are a "cover" for secular intentions. On that score he denies Kant the status of a "genuine

religious reformer." On the other hand (pp. 210–211), Yovel credits Kant with wishing to prevent the "devaluation" of religion. Thus, Yovel admits that many of Kant's "terms are not meant as [religious] metaphors." It is in this context that Yovel then concedes that Kant wished "to reinstate the sacred within the secular." Surely this latter admission must be construed in terms of religious reform and sacralization rather than secularization.

343. Kant, *CJ*, p. 75.

344. Ibid., pp. 81 and 105. Cassirer, *Rousseau, Kant, and Goethe* (New York, 1963), pp. 52–54, is adamant about this. Kant's is an "ethical" not an "aesthetic religion."

345. In *CJ*, p. 111, a key sentence runs: ". . . moral teleology supplements the deficiency of physical teleology, and for *the first time* establishes a theology." My emphasis.

346. A. Lovejoy, *Essays*, Chapter XVI, especially p. 338, where Tertullian's acceptance of accommodationism and assimilationism is directly related to the themes in Lessing's *Education*.

347. The fragment, *BP*, has been translated by Harris, *HD*, pp. 508–510. Hegel asks the question on p. 509.

348. Hegel, *BP*, p. 508. Again, Löwith's point (*From*, p. 323) about Hegel's conception of man, as always being informed by the "image and likeness of God" idea, is relevant here.

349. Hegel, *BP*, p. 508. It is important to relate this statement not only to Kant but to the political circumstances in Old-Württemberg discussed in Chapter 3. In that context, the legality–morality split would relate to the split within the traditions of the Good Old Law. Also see nn. 7 and 10, above.

350. Hegel, *Brf.*, v. 1, p. 24. With this statement, the tension between the "bourgeoisie" (i.e., law-abiding people) and liberal Protestants (i.e., Hegel) becomes clearest. Hence, the problem of a "bourgeois-Christian" society discussed above in n.'s 145 and 148. There is a good deal of this tension in Schiller, *AE*, in his discussion of the difference between "an individual" and "a person."

351. Hegel, *Brf.*, v. 1, pp. 24 and 16, where orthodox Lutherans are criticized for their political inaction.

352. Ibid., p. 17; I have followed Harris' translation here (*HD*, p. 187). His discussion (pp. 249–250) of Hegel's conception of ethical theology, though, is quite odd in that he reads Hegel as trying to effect, à la Schelling, a "transition from *Ethikotheologie* to *Physikotheologie*." That is not what Hegel is doing here, which Harris seems to admit when he notes that Hegel's "project" here is the "moral salvation of Physics," not the reverse.

353. Hegel, *Brf.*, v. 1: p. 16.

354. Hegel, quoted in Harris, *HD*, p. 510. The emphasis on "from there" is meant to correlate with our earlier argument about secularization and sacralization, n. 342 above.

355. Hegel, quoted in *HD*, pp. 510 and 512, respectively.

356. Ibid., p. 510.

357. Hegel, *Brf.*, v. 1: p. 29. Harris' claim (*HD*, n. 2, p. 204) that the "drawing

near to God" project was "abandoned" by Hegel "in favor" of a more "direct application" of Kant is quite misleading. The Kantian application and that project are both informed by the principles of assimilationism. Nohl (*Jugendschriften*, n. 1, p. 233) has seen this. It is worth observing that the "drawing near to God" theme was a main concern of liberal Protestants in the eighteenth century. The phrase, moreover, has ethical and eschatological roots in the Bible – in the Books of James and Hebrews, respectively.

358. Harris, *HD*, pp. 207 and 234, and Wacker, *Kant*, p. 37, are correct to link the two works.
359. Plant, *Hegel*, p. 43, and Harris, *HD*, pp. xxiii and 207, are clear on this.
360. Brought out well by Harris, *HD*, p. 178.
361. In Hegel's *Jugendschriften*, pp. 75–136.
362. Ibid., p. 75. Also see p. 79.
363. Ibid., p. 75. Compare this with *RWL*, p. 149, where "happiness" is presented as a concern of "clever" rather than "moral" men.
364. Hegel, *Jugendschriften*, p. 79. Also see p. 77.
365. Ibid., p. 79.
366. Ibid., pp. 77 and 79.
367. Ibid., p. 77. See n. 236 above for the religious spin associated with the term *Bestimmung*.
368. Ibid., p. 94. Also see p. 86.
369. Noted by Harris, *HD*, p. 199.
370. Hegel, *Jugendschriften*, p. 81.
371. Haering, *Hegel*, v. 1: p. 189.
372. Lukács, *Young*, p. 110.
373. P. Wernle, *Der Schweizische Protestantismus*, 3 v. (Tübingen, 1923–1925).
374. Ibid., v. 2: p. 12.
375. Ibid., v. 1: pp. 512ff, and v. 2: pp. 206–217 and 398–400. Also for Werenfels, see K. Barth, *Protestant*, pp. 144–147.
376. Wernle, *Protestantismus*, v. 1: p. 512.
377. On Hess, see ibid., v. 2: pp. 17–18, and v. 3: pp. 317ff.
378. Ibid., v. 2: pp. 206–215, 332–339, 390, and 447–458. What follows comes from these sections of Wernle.
379. See, e.g., Kroner, "Hegel's," pp. 4–8; J. Maier, *On Hegel's Critique of Kant* (New York, 1966), pp. 15–19; and Knox, "Attitude," pp. 71–72 and 79.
380. Knox, "Attitude," p. 72.
381. Hegel, *Jugendschriften*, p. 83.
382. This I take to be an appropriate answer to the "paradox" Knox focuses upon in "Attitude," p. 70. For Knox, the paradox turned on the question of how Hegel could declare himself a good Lutheran and a Kantian at one and the same time. As I have tried to show, there is no paradox if we are talking (as we must) about Hegel as a Württemberg Protestant and about Kant as the author of *RWL*, a liberal Protestant tract.
383. The essay has been translated and appears in *ETW*, pp. 67–181. Included in this edition (pp. 167–181) is a later (1800) revision of the essay's

early sections.

384. Hegel, "Positivity," p. 68.
385. Ibid.
386. Ibid., pp. 68–69.
387. Ibid., p. 69.
388. Ibid.
389. Ibid.
390. As was noted in n. 242 above, there is a close approximation between the "letter–spirit" argument and the "contract – covenant" one. In ibid., pp. 69–70, Hegel makes this clear in two ways. First, he dismisses the "blood tie" to Abraham as an appropriate focus for Jewish solidarity. Instead, he singles out the moral principles of the "sacred books" as most deserving of Jewish allegiance. Furthermore, Hegel identifies these principles with the call for perfectionism that is so central, in his reading, to the book of Matthew. Later (pp. 99 and 138) Hegel equates "fulfillment" of these same principles with concerns that lie beyond the letter of the law in a formalist sense. Knox has appreciated the connection. See his nn., pp. 160–161.
391. Ibid., pp. 71, 73, 77, and 83–84.
392. Ibid., p. 84. That this right to self-legislation is collective as well as individual is made clear on p. 145.
393. Ibid., p. 98. Also see pp. 71 and 99.
394. Ibid., p. 99.
395. Ibid., p. 179, for the "reformer" reference. The "immaturity" theme appears on pp. 99 and 178–180.
396. Ibid., p. 71.
397. Ibid; on p. 77 Hegel says such usage was an "indispensable condition of his finding entry into their minds."
398. Ibid., p. 73.
399. Ibid., p. 75. See, e.g., Lessing, *LTW*, p. 106, statement n. 4. The contrast that Hegel draws (p. 81) between Jesus' and Socrates' followers here was quite common among Swiss Protestants in Bern.
400. Hegel, "Positivity," p. 81. Reiterated, p. 169.
401. Ibid., pp. 174 and 181. For parallel views in Lessing, see *LTW*, pp. 53 and 106. In *AE*, p. 179, Schiller does the same. Also see editors' n., *AE*, p. 277.
402. Hegel, "Positivity," p. 138. Thus, Hegel stands to the positivity of orthodoxy as Jesus and Luther stood, initially, to the positivity of Judaism and Catholicism.
403. Ibid., p. 139. As he notes, "Christians [Catholics *and* Protestants] have thus reverted to the position of the Jews."
404. Ibid., p. 152, to wit: what accounts for the "supplanting of paganism by Christianity?"
405. Ibid., where he uses the phrase.
406. Ibid., p. 174, where the "accidental" aspect of the disciples' stress on the person of Jesus is tied to "authority" in a positive sense.
407. Ibid., p. 162. Also see p. 154.

408. Ibid., p. 161.
409. Ibid., p. 163. Also see p. 160.
410. Ibid., p. 158.
411. Ibid.; obviously, the "cooperation" reference is important to the synergism argument of Part I of this study.
412. Ibid., p. 159.
413. Ibid., pp. 159–160.
414. Ibid., p. 160. Cf. Knox's n., p. 160.
415. In n.'s 322–325 above I have discussed this point with regard to Kant. It applies to Hegel as well.
416. See n. 324 above.
417. Hegel, "Positivity," p. 155.
418. Ibid.
419. Ibid., p. 156.
420. Ibid.
421. Ibid.
422. Ibid., p. 157. In Part III, I show how the exchange of political rights for economic ones was, for Hegel, associated with the quest for "bourgeoisie" security.
423. A most revealing Weberian-like passage (ibid., p. 158) runs: "In this situation men were offered a religion which either was already adapted to the needs of the age (since it had arisen in a people characterized by a similar degeneracy and a similar though differently colored emptiness and deficiency) or else was one out of which men could form what their needs demanded and what they could then adhere to."
424. In Part III, I argue that Hegel's strategy for reform becomes one of "indirection."
425. Hence, the origins of the "bad infinity" argument that I discuss in Part III in terms of luxury as a psycho-economic category. E. Voegelin, "On Hegel: A Study in Sorcery," in *Studium Generale*, v. 24, 3 (1971), has a good deal to say about "boredom" in Hegel's thought in the early 1800s. He fails, I think, to relate Hegel's concern with boredom to economics, preferring a more "existential" approach to the problem. I offer a correction in Part III.
426. By dialectic I mean a linguistic effort (of a "tender-minded" sort) that serves the interest of "coy theology." See n. 55 above for details. As Burke has well understood, "dialectics" is another way of talking about "dramatic" and "symbolic" action.
427. On the methodological strategy employed here see the references to Burke in n. 26 to the Preface.
428. See Burke, *A Grammar of Motives*, pp. xviii–xix, on how to exploit such resources.

Part III

The epigraphs come from Goethe, quoted in Kaufmann, *Hegel*, p. xii; from Rousseau, *Émile*, A. Bloom, trans. (New York, 1979), p. 108 (n.); and from Max Weber, *From Max Weber*, p. 280.

1. Hegel, *TE*, p. 482.
2. Ibid.
3. Ibid., p. 495.
4. Ibid., pp. 495–496.
5. I have discussed Kant's views on this at length in Chapter 4, section 2.
6. Hegel, *TE*, p. 508.
7. Ibid.; Harris has translated Hegel's "die Bürgerliche Gesetzgebung" as "the public legal system." Given Hegel's intention, I think that that rendering is too neutral. The term "civil," I think, retains an aspect of neutrality while also pointing beyond to Hegel's sense of the "civil" as deficient in a moral sense. It is clear that as early as 1794 Hegel was attaching different "spins" to the term *"bürgerlich."*
8. Hegel, *Brf.*, v. 1, p. 24. I have followed for the most part Harris' translation, *HD*, p. 184. I believe, though, that my paraphrase captures more of the tension between "legal" and "moral" than Harris' translation expresses.
9. That Hegel uses the phrase "sheer culture" to describe this "gain" speaks to Kant's influence on him at this time. This latter had used a similar formulation to describe that advance in his "Idea for a Universal History." (See *KOH*, p. 21, and *CJ*, pp. 92ff.)
10. As Kant had said (*KOH*, p. 21): "We are...cultured...civilized....But to consider ourselves as having reached morality – for that much is lacking." The "spins" Kant attaches to "culture" here – first as synonymous with "civilization" and then as opposed to it – are revealing.
11. Discussed in Chapter 3, above, esp. nn. 90 and 131. Also see n. 318, Chapter 2.
12. See nn. 242, 268, and 297, Chapter 4, for instances.
13. Hegel, *Brf.*, v. 1, p. 24. Hegel had both the Württemberg and Bern situations before him when he made this statement.
14. Ibid.
15. To wit, their oft-cited claim that Smith was the "Luther of political economy."
16. Hegel, *TE*, p. 496, repeatedly uses the idea of "awakening" man to the higher moral purpose within him to make this point.
17. Burke, *Permanence and Change*, pp. liv–lv and Part II.
18. Ibid.; I take it that this line of argument was assimilated in Burke's later work to the symbolic action argument in general and to the synonymizing and desynonymizing argument in particular (nn. 426–428, Chapter 4).
19. I believe this is close to the methodological point Plant, *Hegel*, p. 112, was making when he juxtaposed (for other purposes) the German and European contexts of Hegel's thought.
20. J. Schmidt, "Recent Hegel Literature," *Telos*, no. 46 (1980–1981), pp. 115 and 123–124, has offered some wise observations here.
21. Schiller, *AE*, pp. 12–13.
22. The brilliance of Löwith's conception of Hegel's relation to a "bourgeois Christian world" is that it articulates the basic problem Hegel confronted here.
23. Because the forces Hegel is trying to reconcile are both relatively progressive

it is difficult to see how the concepts of "transition periods" and "historical backwardness" explain the dynamic of his thought.

24. I am well aware of the literature that questions the usefulness of "laissez-faire" as an historical label for certain aspects of eighteenth-century Scottish thought. I discuss the problem of interpretation in Chapter 5.

25. Putting the problem this way enables us to avoid "telescoping" the steps in Hegel's development as a social and political theorist. I discuss the telescoping tendency below, Chapter 7.

26. In F. Hirsch's terms, Hegel was aware of the problem political economy faced with regard to its "depleting moral legacy." See his *Social Limits to Growth* (Cambridge, MA, 1976).

27. A key theme in two of Hegel's main sources in the 1790s: Schiller's *AE* and Kant's *RWL*.

28. On the conditional mode of discourse see L. Krieger, *An Essay on the Theory of Enlightened Despotism* (Chicago, 1975), pp. 84–85.

29. On "overlaying" as a methodological strategy, note K. Baker's usage with regard to Saint-Simon, in *Condorcet*, p. 374.

30. There has been some debate about this among Hegel scholars. M. Riedel, "Die Rezeption der Nationalökonomie," *SHR*, pp. 84–85, argues for a difference between the writings before 1803–1804 and the *Philosophy of Right*. In this, Riedel means to challenge the views of Rosenkranz, Glockner, and Häring, who all stressed the continuity of development between the two groups of writings. Still, Harris, "Hegel's System of Ethical Life: An Interpretation," in *Ethical*, pp. 86–87, urges us not to "exaggerate the difference" between Hegel's political conceptions at Jena and at Berlin. I agree, moreover, with his reasons for stressing the point.

Chapter 5

1. Pocock, *TMM*, pp. 135–137.

2. Ibid., p. 136.

3. Ibid., p. 137. Cf. Hexter's comment, n. 170, Chapter 3.

4. For evidence using the English case see N. McKendrick et al., *The Birth of a Consumer Society* (Bloomington, Ind., 1982), especially pp. 9–33.

5. There is a large, albeit very uneven, literature on the problem of luxury in eighteenth-century thought. Old, but still very useful for the French case, is J. Spengler, *French Predecessors of Malthus* (New York, 1965). For a more general survey, see J. Sekora, *Luxury: The Concept in Western Thought from Eden to Smollett* (Baltimore, 1977). Most helpful, though, are two un-published Ph. D. dissertations: S. M. Wade, Jr., "The Idea of Luxury in Eighteenth-Century England," Department of History, Harvard University (1968); and Ellen Ross, "The Debate on Luxury in 18th Century France," Department of History, University of Chicago (1975). As Wade has observed (p. 4), the association of "luxury" and "civilization" is very old, going back at least to Tacitus, who explained the convergence in pejorative terms. Many other such links appear in the writings collected by Lovejoy and Boas in *Primitivism*. Since Mandeville is so crucial to the luxury problem in eighteenth-century thought, a good place to begin to study it is

F. B. Kaye's Introduction to Bernard Mandeville's *The Fable of the Bees*, 2 v., F. Kaye, ed. (Oxford, 1924).

6. J. Appleby, "Ideology and Theory: The Tension Between Political and Economic Liberalism in Seventeenth Century England," in *AHR*, v. 81, 3 (1976), especially pp. 504–506, notes how this way of thinking began to be prominent in England in the 1690s. And as McKendrick has observed (*Birth*, p. 18), Mandeville was, for many eighteenth-century thinkers, the main theorist of this way of thinging.

7. See Hume, "Of Refinements in the Arts," in *David Hume: Writings on Economics*, E. Rotwein, ed. (Madison, Wis., 1970), p. 19. Cf. pp. 20 and 30. The original title of this essay was "Of Luxury"; it was changed in 1760 to its present form.

8. Ibid., p. 22. Cf. p. 28, where "liberty" and "progress in the arts" are equated.

9. Note what Hume says, ibid., p. 22: as "the mechanical arts" advance, "they commonly produce some refinements in the liberal; nor can one be carried to perfection, without being accompanied, in some degree, with the other." A very useful survey of some of those who thought this way may be found in L. Febvre's "*Civilisation*: Evolution of a Word and a Group of Related Ideas," in *A New Kind of History*, P. Burke, ed., especially p. 242, where Guizot's "synthesis" is discussed.

10. Hume, "Arts," p. 23.

11. Ibid., p. 22; according to Hume, commerce qua economics creates leisure, which, in turn, creates opportunities for commerce qua conversation. Hence, the association in Hume's mind of commerce, socialization, and civilization. The interplay here has been provocatively discussed by A. O. Hirschman in terms of the idea of "doux-commerce." See his *The Passions and the Interests* (Princeton, 1977), pp. 56–63. Also see J. G. A. Pocock, *Virtue, Commerce and History*. (Cambridge, England, 1985), for fine discussions of the relationship between doux-commerce and "manners."

12. Hume, "Arts," p. 23.

13. Wade, "Luxury," Chapters V–IX, has much of value to say about the context of Brown's "neo-Puritan" moralism in the 1750s. Segora, *Luxury*, does the same for Smollett over roughly the same period.

14. Note A. Hirschman's remarks about "repressing" the passions as the traditional way of dealing with them, in *Passions*, pp. 14ff.

15. Hume uses the phrase in "Arts," p. 26. Cf. pp. 20 and 29.

16. Ibid., p. 20.

17. Ibid.; thus the tendency in much of the literature on luxury to regard Hume as a point of mediation and/or synthesis with regard to hitherto divergent tendencies in the history of luxury. See, e.g., E. A. Johnson, *Predecessors of Adam Smith* (New York, 1965), pp. 161–181 and 281–297; and James Bonar, *Philosophy and Political Economy*, 3rd ed. (New York, 1968), Chapter 6. That there was by Hume's day a "moderate" position on luxury is emphasized by Saint-Lambert in his essay on luxury in *ES*.

18. Hume, "Arts," pp. 32 and 30.

19. Ibid., p. 32.

20. The connection between Hume's view of luxury and that articulated by Saint-Lambert in his essay on luxury in *ES* is that both regard vicious luxury as a consequence of political mismanagement. This view goes back at least to Mandeville.

21. The distinction between "solid" and "vain" is adapted to our purposes here from Montesquieu's *The Spirit of the Laws*. See *PTM*, p. 289. A. Ferguson, in 1767, reiterated the point in *An Essay on the History of Civil Society* (London, 1980), pp. 159–160.

22. Notice that the police action is directed toward *social* excesses, not economic ones per se. As E. Johnson has observed (*Predecessors*, p. 297, "vicious" luxury was for Hume a "non-economic" category!

23. On the "harnessing" of the passions, see Hirschman, *Passions*, pp. 14ff, and N. Keohane, *Philosophy and the State in France* (Princeton, 1980), Chapter V. J. Viner, "The Intellectual History of Laissez-Faire," in *Journal of Law and Economics*, v. 3 (1960), p. 57, links the effort "to harness...selfish energy to a desirable social...set of objectives" with a quasi-liberal form of moderate mercantilism.

24. A very important qualification needs to be introduced here. Not all the Scots were as optimistic as Hume about the relationship between commerce and the advance of civilization. This is most evident in Monboddo and Ferguson, who were troubled by some of the more commercial aspects of civil society. For an especially clear discussion of their position see Tuveson, *Millennium and Utopia*, Chapter V, especially pages 188–197. Also note the entry on commerce in the *Encyclopedia Britannica* (1771).

25. On Ferguson's reception in Germany see the following: K. Aner, *Lessingszeit*, pp. 351–354; H. Leisergang, *Lessings Weltanschauung* (Leipzig, 1931), pp. 117ff; F. Meinecke, *Die Entstehung des Historismus*, C. Hinrich, ed. (Munich, 1965), pp. 263–265; E. Flajole, "Lessing's Retrieval of Lost Truths," in *PMLA*, v. 74, (1959); Allison, *Lessing*, pp. 81–82 and n.'s 2, 7, and 12, pp. 185–195; R. Pascal, "'Bildung' and the Division of Labor," in *German Studies Presented to W.H. Bruford* (London, 1962); G. Lukács, *Goethe and His Age*, R. Anchor, trans. (New York, 1968), pp. 106–107; and B. von Weise, *Schiller*, pp. 78ff.

26. Leisergang, *Lessings*, p. 117, and Flajole, "Lost," p. 62, tell us that Jünger translated the *Essay* in 1768. Plant, *Hegel*, p. 17, among others, believes Garve did the translation. I have looked at the 1768 translation – it does not indicate who did it. There is, though, no doubt about Garve's translation of the *Institutes* in 1772. Harris, *HD*, n. 2, pp. 50–51, is wrong about Garve's translating Ferguson's *Principles* in 1772. He has confused the *Institutes* with the *Principles* of 1792.

27. I have used the second edition of the *Institutes* published in Edinburgh, 1773. See pp. 21–22, 86–90, and 110. The argument referred to here is also clearly made in Ferguson's *Essay*, "Part First." There he used the idea of the "social" in three very different ways.

28. Ferguson, *Institutes*, pp. 110–111. Crucial here is the fact that Garve in *Anmk.*, in his commentary on the *Institutes*, pp. 317–321, and Schiller, in *AE*, p. 181, treat man in this "society" as "an animal endowed with reason."

The point has been appreciated by Schiller's editiors, *AE*, pp. 277–278. In Mandeville's terms, man in this social condition is just a "taught animal." See Mandeville, *Fable*, v. 1: p. 286, where this kind of man is linked to the "comfortable" life of "a civil society."

29. Ferguson, *Institutes*, pp. 73–74. Garve, *Anmk.*, pp. 316ff, applauds this view and equates it with the realization of man's telos qua magnanimity.

30. See n. 242, Chapter 4, for Lessing; n.'s 283–284, Chapter 4, and n. 10 to the Introduction to Part III for Kant; and Chapter 4 for Hegel.

31. C. Garve, *Anmk.*

32. Ibid., pp. 300, 316–319, and 341. According to Tuveson, *Millennium*, p. 197, this was Ferguson's position, too.

33. Garve, *Anmk.*, pp. 291 and 312–314. Surely it is no accident that the excerpts Hegel made from Garve's work contain clear references to the leisure – reflective moment – true telos interplay. See *DHE*, pp. 116–136.

34. Garve, *Anmk.*, pp. 330–332. The German term here is *Einbildungskraft*. For its various uses during this period see the glossary to *AE*, pp. 306ff. More generally see J. Engell, *The Creative Imagination* (Cambridge, Mass., 1981), especially Chapters 8–10 and 16. Here, of course, the idea, so prominent in Garve and Schiller, of "no leaps" in nature, means that the process of liberation will be gradual. I discuss the point in Chapter 8 with regard to Schiller's claims in *AE*. Compare Garve and Schiller here with Monboddo, quoted in Tuveson, *Millennium*, pp. 190–191. On the general connection between "no leaps in nature" and Christian eschatology, see Lovejoy, *The Great Chain of Being*, p. 246, and Hazard, *European Thought*, pp. 370–371. Above all, see A. Funkenstein's essay on Maimonides, who used the phrase, in *Miscellanea Mediaevelia*, v. 11 (1977).

35. See n. 216, Chapter 4, for the Kant reference.

36. For a fuller appreciation of the tension see Engell, *Creative*, pp. 131–135, and E. Tuveson, *The Imagination as a Means of Grace* (New York, 1974), p. 148.

37. Clearly this is what Kant is doing in the essay on "Universal History" in *KOH*, p. 21. But note that Kant's criticism is presented in terms of a forward-looking "philosophical millennianism" rather than a backward looking primitivism."

38. Garve, *Anmk.*, p. 293.

39. Ibid.; clearly the "chain" reference, which was commonly used among the Scots, fits in with the "no leaps" in nature argument mentioned in n. 34 above.

40. Lovejoy discusses the difference between man qua *animal rationale* and man qua *animal rationabile* in the context of Monboddo's evolutionism. See Lovejoy's *Essays*, pp. 54–56. What Lovejoy says there applies to Ferguson and to the Germans, too.

41. See J. Viner, *The Role of Providence in the Social Order*, pp. 26–42; Tuveson, *Millennium*, Chapters IV and V; and R. S. Crane, "Anglican Apologetics and the Idea of Progress, 1699–1745," in *MP*, v. 31 (1933–1934), pp. 273–306 and 349–382.

42. Crane, "Progress," p. 381.

43. Ibid.
44. Taylor, quoted in ibid., pp. 378–379.
45. Discussed in ibid., pp. 349ff, and in Tuveson, *Millennium*, pp. 147ff. Law's main work, a most popular one, was translated into German in 1771. See Crane, n. 2, p. 349.
46. In Crane, "Progress," pp. 366–367, Law is quoted to the effect that "leisure" is vital to the development of "perfect notions of [God's] Nature and Providence."
47. Law, quoted in ibid., p. 367.
48. Ibid.; cf. Law, quoted in Tuveson, *Millennium*, p. 147.
49. Appreciated by Tuveson, *Millennium*, pp. 148–149.
50. Crane, "Progress," p. 368, notes the close connection between the theologies of Law and Lessing.
51. In the literature noted in n. 25 above, only Allison downplays the Ferguson–Lessing connection. Among the others, Flajole, "Lost," pp. 52 and 61–65, is the most insistent about the influence.
52. Ibid., p. 52.
53. Ibid., p. 66. My emphases.
54. Lessing, quoted in ibid., pp. 66. The power referred to here is that of "*sinnlichen Begierden.*" In his commentary on Ferguson's *Institutes*, Garve (*Anmk.*, p. 313) contrasts this power with one that involves human reflection. Schiller is another who develops the idea of reflection in this context.
55. Worthington, quoted in Crane, "Progress," p. 301.
56. Ibid.; I think the reference to "vibrating for a time from one extreme to the other" captures quite well what Löwith meant to express by treating Hegel as a philosopher who faced up to the dilemma of living in a "bourgeois Christian world."
57. Garve, Koselleck has reported, preferred the German word *bürger* to that of the French *bourgeois* precisely because it retained that religio-moral sense of telos. The difference is also important to Hegel. See Chapter 6 below.
58. In their Introduction to Schiller's *AE*, the editors (p. xxxii) note Garve's and Ferguson's "great" influence on Schiller.
59. Schiller, *AE*, p. 167 (23/8). I have a good deal to say about this in Chapter 8. See the crucial note by Schiller's editors, p. 254.
60. Ibid.
61. The quotations come from ibid., pp. 165 (23/7), 165 (23/6), and 169 (23/8).
62. Ibid., p. 163 (23/5). This, we shall see, is Hegel's view also.
63. Here a comment by W. Lehmann, *John Millar of Glasgow 1735–1801* (Cambridge, England, 1960), p. 155, is most illuminating. Referring to a remark Goethe made in 1830, on the occasion of the publication of Carlyle's *Life of Schiller*, Lehmann noted: "Goethe was not only acquainted with the Scottish philosophers but he assures us that they had long been held in high regard by German scholars and recommended them as being intelligible to ordinary understanding and as manifesting a desirable reconciliation of sensationalism (i.e., empiricism) with spiritualism, effecting a union of the real and the ideal, and thus creating a more satisfactory foundation for

human thought and action than was to be found among German
philosophers, whom he accuses of failing to 'lay hold on life'" This
commitment to "lay hold on life" is, I think, crucial to understanding
the Scottish–German connection. For the "laying hold on salvation"
reference, see n. 69 below.

64. Tollinton, *Clement of Alexandria*, v. 1: pp. 307–321, has translated
Clement's "Sermon on Riches." There (p. 311), Clement contrasts "learned
leisure" with the pursuit of "empty fame and reputation."

65. Clement, quoted in ibid., p. 314.

66. Clement, in ibid., p. 312. The point I have made here with reference to
Clement has been made by Lovejoy with reference to Tertullian (*Essays*,
p. 337n.). It is fair, I think, to say that on this matter Clement and Tertullian prefigure a good deal of what Calvin has to say in the *Institutes* about
the use of wealth. Lovejoy explains the tie with reference to the idea of
"moderate hedonism." I do not think that that idea adequately expresses
what is going on here. Calvin, e.g., had said (*Insts.*, Book III) that while
possessions may indeed be "indifferent" things, the true Christian will use
them "indifferently" as well. In saying this, I think Calvin is doing more
than moderating hedonism. He is invoking, as Clement before him had,
the idea of the soul as having passions of its own. These passions are distinct
from those of the body. In the latter case, we have what the Stoics called
"adfectus." They are natural, physical, and unavoidable passions. When,
however, these passions penetrate to the soul they become "morbi" – which
means man has consented to them on a spiritual level. It is, of course, the
passions qua "morbi" that Calvin is addressing in his discussion of wealth
and its relation to a Christian life. On the Stoic conception see A. Levi,
French Moralists (Oxford, 1964) especially pp. 69–72.

67. Clement, in Tollinton, *Clement*, v. 1: 314.

68. Clement in ibid., p. 310; compare with Calvin (*Insts.*, Book III): "Let all
men, in their respective stations . . . live in the remembrance . . . that God
confers his blessings on them for the support of life; not for luxury."

69. Clement, in Tollinton, *Clement*, v. 1: p. 312. Equally revealing (p. 314): it
is not "impossible . . . , to lay hold on salvation, could a man but learn to
use rightly, as a means of eternal life, the riches which intrinsically are
neither good nor bad."

70. By using the word "containment" here I mean to suggest something
similar to what S. R. Sen, *The Economics of Sir James Steuart* (Cambridge,
England, 1957), pp. 130ff, means by an "economics of control." Nevertheless, it is containment in the senses in which S. Kaplan, *Bread, Politics,
and Political Economy in the Reign of Louis XV*, 2 v. (The Hague, 1976), p. 3,
and K. Polanyi, *The Great Transformation* (Boston, 1944), p. 62, use the
term that is more apt in the context of the economic concerns of late
eighteenth-century "police ideology." I think the term more adequately
captures the conditional economic liberalism of the later eighteenth-
century mercantile position.

71. P. Chamley, "Les Origines de la pensée économique de Hegel," in *HS*, v. 3
(1965), p. 226.

72. K. Rosenkranz, *Hegel*, p. 85.

73. Clearly there are other ways to read Locke. Chamley, I gather, is inclined to follow Macpherson, *The Political Theory of Possessive Individualism*. One could just as easily follow J. Dunn, *The Political Thought of John Locke*. The issue, at bottom, comes down to a Marxian versus a Weberian interpretation of Locke. I prefer, for historical reasons, the latter approach.

74. The first two interests are commonly referred to by Hegel scholars. S. Avineri, *Hegel's*, pp. 4–5, and J. Ritter, *Hegel et la Révolution Française* (Paris, 1970), p. 49, make the point about Steuart. H. Harris, *Hegel's Development*, v. 2 (Oxford, 1983), n. 2, p 126, makes the point about Smith.

75. The point has been made by C. Fay, *The World of Adam Smith* (Cambridge, England, 1960), p. 10; and by Petter Stein, *Legal Evolution: The Study of an Idea* (Cambridge, England, 1980), passim.

76. See Rosenkranz, *Hegel*, p. 86. P. Chamley, "Origines," pp. 235ff, discusses the particulars of the translations.

77. Specifically, in *Realphilosophie I*, J. Hoffmeister, ed. (Leipzig, 1932), p. 239.

78. H. S. Harris, *HD*, pp. 46 and 50–1. The source for much of this is Rosenkranz, *Hegel*, p. 14, who relies on Hegel's sister's claim that Ferguson and Garve were the decisive influences on Hegel during the Stuttgart years. For her remarks see *DHE*, pp. 393, 401, and 420–423. B. Teyssèdre, "Hegel à Stuttgart," in *Revue Philosophique*, no. 2 (1960), p. 213, declares Hegel read Ferguson's *Essay* while in Stuttgart. However, I found no other support for this claim. J. Ripalda, *The Divided Nation* (Assen, Netherlands, 1977), p. 205, speculated that Hegel probably had read the *Essay* but offers no evidence.

79. On *Popularphilosophie* in general see B. Wiese, *Schiller*, pp. 76ff. M. Riedel, "Reception," p. 77, ties it into Hegel specifically. Both, moreover, quite rightly emphasize the importance of Garve here. On Garve see the old but sharply focused piece in *Allgemeine deutsche Biographie*, v. 8 (Leipzig, 1878), pp. 385–392. Ripalda has much to say (*Divided*) about the aesthetic influence Garve exercised on the very young Hegel but does little with the sociohistorical aspect of Garve's work. That is what I stress below.

80. Ferguson's influence on Schiller has been discussed by R. Pascal, "'Bildung'"; by B. v. Weise, *Schiller*, pp. 78ff; by G. Lukács, *Goethe*, pp. 106–107; and by Hoffmeister, *DHE*, 407–408. A common source for information about Ferguson was Schiller's and Hegel's teacher, Abel. We need to know more about him.

81. Rosenkanz, *Hegel*, p. 80. Rosenkranz's reading is probably wrong insofar as it fails to distinguish mercantile from neomercantile aspects of late eighteenth-century economic thought. The importance of the distinction should become obvious in the course of this chapter.

82. Lukács, *The Young Hegel*, pp. 170ff, 329, and 353; Hyppolite, *Studies in Marx and Hegel*, pp. 75ff.

83. See Plant, *Hegel*, pp. 57ff and 114ff. For Avineri and Ritter see n. 74 above.

84. See Chamley, "Origines," passim, and Plant, ibid., pp. 64ff. For a criticism of this view see J. Schmidt, "Recent," p. 132. As Schmidt notes, and as Harris and Teyssèdre confirm, Hegel's interest in "pragmatic history" emerges very clearly during the Stuttgart years, long before his reading of Steuart.

85. Häring, *Hegel*, v. 1: pp. 378–379; and P. Vogel, *Hegels Gesellschaftsbegriff* (Berlin, 1925), pp. 115–118.

86. Pascal, "'Bildung'," pp. 15 and 25–26; Plant, *Hegel*, p. 22; and Lukács, *Young*, p. 329. F. Meinecke, *Entstehung*, makes the fine point that it is the concept of the division of labor that permits the convergence of "Enlightenment" and "Romantic" thought in late eighteenth-century Germany. He offers Ferguson and Garve as two of the keys to this development. I agree completely. For more on this see Chapter 8 and n. 99 below.

87. Hoffmeister, *DHE*, p. 420. F. Meinecke, *Entstehung*, pp. 263–265, attributes much of this interest to Garve, who had singled out Ferguson as offering a wholly new conception of *Sittlichkeit*. Garve offered this assessment of Ferguson in *Anmk.*, pp. 330ff.

88. That this influence is beginning to be appreciated should be obvious from Plant's splendid *Hegel* and his "Hegel and Political Economy," in *The New Left Review*, n.'s 103 and 104 (1977).

89. The recent interest in the thinkers of the "Scottish Enlightenment" stems, I think, from four different schools of revisionist scholarship. First, there has been the interest – expressed by R. Pascal and R. Meek – in the ties between the Scottish Historical School and Marxism. One of several fruitful results here has been an appreciation of the many Scottish contributions to the development of historical sociology. See, for example, R. Meek, "The Scottish Contribution to Marxist Sociology," in *Economics and Ideology and Other Essays* (London, 1967). Also of interest: R. Pascal, "Property and Society: The Scottish Historical School of the Eighteenth Century," in *The Modern Quarterly*, v.'s 1 and 2 (1938); A. Swingewood, "Origins of Sociology: The Case of the Scottish Enlightenment," in *British Journal of Sociology*, v. 21 (1970); and A. Skinner, "Economics and History – The Scottish Enlightenment," in *Scottish Journal of Political Economy*, v. 12 (1965). Second, there have been attempts to rehabilitate Smith as a social thinker. Here the application of the concept of laissez-faire to his thought is regarded as a distortion of his thinking. See, for example, J. Viner, "Adam Smith and Laissez-Faire," in *The Long View and the Short* (Glencoe, Ill., 1958); and N. Rosenberg, "Adam Smith and Laissez-Faire Revisited," in *Adam Smith and Modern Political Economy* G. O'Driscoll, ed. (Ames, Iowa, 1979). Third, since Keynes there has been an effort to rehabilitate mercantilism in general and James Steuart in particular. S. R. Sen's *Steuart* was instrumental in triggering this interest. Meek's review of Sen, "The Economics of Control Prefigured by James Steuart," in *Science and Society*, v. 22, 4 (1958), was also pivotal. A. Skinner continued the rehabilitation of Steuart with his "Sir James Steuart: Economics and Politics," in *Scottish Journal of Political Economy*, v. 9, 1 (1962). All this, moreover, was helped considerably by the fine essays collected in *Revisions in Mercantilism*,

D. C. Coleman, ed. (London, 1969). Still more recently, Hirschman, *Passions*, has helped to spark interest in Steuart. Finally, Pocock's *TMM* has done much to draw the Scots into the debate about the continuing relevance of civic humanism to the development of Western political thought and values since the Renaissance. Here D. Forbes' work has also been most illuminating. See, for example, his "Sceptical Whiggism, Commerce, and Liberty," in *Essays on Adam Smith*, A. Skinner et al., eds. (Oxford, 1975).

90. See A. Small, *Adam Smith and Modern Sociology* (Chicago, 1907). Also of interest in this line: A. Salmon, "Adam Smith as Sociologist," in *SR*, v. 12, 1 (1945).

91. One of the more recent statements: A. Coats, "Adam Smith: The Modern Reappraisal," in *Renaissance and Modern Studies*, v. 6 (1962).

92. See R. Meek, "Contribution."

93. See, e.g., my essay, "Historicizing the 'Adam Smith Problem'," *JMH* v. 58 (1986).

94. The phrase "conditional economic liberal" comes from J. Spengler, *Predecessors*, p. 53. He uses it with regard to a main line of French economic thought in the eighteenth century. It is, I think, another way of characterizing neomercantilist thought.

95. See Allison, *Lessing*, p. 63.

96. See n. 26 above.

97. Useful on the particulars of the Smith translation is W. Treue, "Adam Smith in Deutschland," in *Deutschland und Europa*, W. Conze, ed. (Dusseldorf, 1951). Also see C. Hasek, *The Introduction of Adam Smith's Doctrines into Germany* (New York, 1925).

98. On Garve's translation see Hasek and Treue (n. 97 above). Also of interest: R. Van Dusen, *Christian Garve and English Belles-Lettre* (Bern, 1970), pp. 134ff.

99. As I try to show in Chapter 8, the idea of the division of labor is crucial to tying the socioeconomic-historical and aesthetic aspects of Scottish thought together. As Meinecke and Van Dusen have well understood, two of Hegel's key sources – Garve and Schiller – attempted such a synthesis. In following them Hegel found himself at the point of convergence of Enlightenment and Anti-Enlightenment thought. Hegel, however, only "picked up" the aesthetic line between 1803 and 1804, after having first come to terms (between 1796 and 1803) with the socio-economic-historical one. By then, Hegel had developed a disciplined conceptual framework within which aesthetic considerations had a place – *but only a place*. As a consequence, Hegel never felt comfortable with out-and-out aestheticism. G. Kelly, "Social Understanding and Social Therapy in Schiller and Hegel," in *Retreat*, makes the point well.

100. On the school, see L. Whitney, "English Primitivistic Theories of Epic Origins," in *MP*, v. 21, 4 (1924). There Kames and Ferguson are included in the school. One should not be misled here by the term "primitivist." As Lovejoy, *Primitivism*, and Tuveson, *Millennium*, especially p. 201, have noted, very often primitivism has a theory of "progress" built into it.

101. A. Ferguson, *Essay*, pp. 6, 167, 171, 6, 168, and 77, respectively.

102. That this periodization scheme was not unique to Scottish thinkers has been shown by R. Meek, "Smith, Turgot and the Four Stages Theory," in *History of Political Economy*, v. 3, 1 (1971).

103. On the two universities see G. von Selle, *Königsberg* and *Göttingen*. It may be of some interest that D. Schwab's work on Stein's library indicates a considerable Scottish presence. See Schwab's *Die Selbstverwaltungsidee der Freiherrn vom Stein und ihre Geistigen Grundlagen* (Frankfurt, 1971).

104. For the difference between economics as science and as art see E. A. Johnson, *Predecessors*, pp. 259ff; and S. Sen, *Steuart*, pp. 18 and 31. That the difference was obvious to Smith's contemporaries can be seen in D. Stewart's comment (p. 317) on the matter. For Stewart's claim, see n. 119 below.

105. Again, see Johnson, *Predecessors*; A. Small, *The Cameralists* (New York, 1909), pp. 11–12; H. Braun, "Economic Theory and Policy in Germany, 1750–1800," in *Journal of European Economic History*, v. 4, 2 (1978).

106. See K. Polanyi, *Great*, pp. 43–55.

107. Essays by A. Skinner and A. Coats, in *Essays on Adam Smith*, argue that Smith, too, was always "policy" oriented in his thought. In this, they challenge the textbook view.

108. Hasek, *Smith*, pp. 64 and 74–78, is informative on the reviews. So, too, is Treue, "Smith," passim. Given these reviews, I am at a loss to explain what K. Epstein, *Genesis*, p. 182, had in mind when he claimed that "the doctrine of laissez-faire originally carried Germany by storm." For the correct view, see Hasek, *Smith*, p. 65.

109. Hasek, *Smith*, p. 64. Obviously, they had reservations about what Hirschman has called the "doux-commerce" thesis. See his *Passions*, passim.

110. Hasek, *Smith*, p. 78. See also the remarks by Forbonnais, one of Spengler's neomercantilists, in the article on "Commerce" in *ES*, p. 69. What F. Venturi says about Galiani, a neomercantilist, in *Italy and the Enlightenment* (New York, 1972), especially pp. 187–188, shows how common this view was among European economic thinkers.

111. J. G. H. Ferder, quoted in Hasek, *Smith*, p. 64.

112. On the importance of the shift in policy from producing wealth for the prince to producing it for the society, see J. Viner, "Power Versus Plenty as Objectives of Foreign Policy in the Seventeenth and Eighteenth Centuries," in *Revisions in Mercantilism*, D. Coleman, ed. (London, 1969).

113. See, e.g., C. Wilson, "The Other Face of Mercantilism," in *Revisions in Mercantilism*, D. Coleman, ed. (London, 1969), p. 136.

114. Johnson, *Predecessors*, pp. 259–262. Johnson notes the importance of the etymology of the word "fit" for the artistic aspect of economic thought.

115. Kaplan, *Bread* v. 1: pp. 97ff; and Spengler, *Predecessors*, p. vii. F. Crouzet, "England and France in the Eighteenth Century," in *The Causes of the Industrial Revolution in England*, R. Hartwell, ed. (London, 1967), pp. 156–157, likewise stresses the compatibility of the two.

116. G. Sartorius, quoted in Hasek, *Smith*, p. 78.

117. The inadequacy of the mercantilism – laissez-faire dichotomy has recently

been stressed by I. Hont and M. Ignatieff, "Needs and Justice in the *Wealth of Nations*; An Introductory Essay," in *Wealth and Virtue*, Hont and Ignatieff, eds. (Cambridge, England, 1983), pp. 14–20. Also see Kaplan, *Bread*, v. 1: pp. 100, 128, and 689; and N. Rosenberg, "Adam Smith," pp. 25–27. Here I should also note I. Bog's criticism of C. Wilson found in *Revisions in Mercantilism*, Coleman, ed. (London, 1969). Wilson, Bog argues, tends to present social mercantilism in terms that fit in with absolutist models of state buildings. Bog grants that this may have been the case early in the eighteenth century, but he claims that German "mercantilists" toward the end of the century were much more flexible (i.e., open to liberal economic theory) than Wilson's argument allows for. In this Bog follows A. Tauscher, *Staatswirtschaftslehre des Kameralismus* (Bern, 1947). There is some support for Bog's views in Viner's (*Providence*, p. 43) distinction between "moderate" and "extreme mercantilism" (i.e., Bog's "mercantilists" versus "fiscalists"). Of interest also is A. Hirschman's suggestion (*Passions*, p. 86) that later mercantilists (e.g., Steuart) argued for a very different kind of "interventionism" than had earlier ones.

118. Hasek, *Smith*, pp. 84ff, and Treue, "Smith," pp. 111ff.
119. D. Steward, quoted in Adam Smith, *Essays on Philosophical Subject*, W. Wightman, ed. (Oxford, 1980), p. 349.
120. On Steuart in general see A. Skinner's "Biographical Sketch" and "Analytical Introduction" both in Steuart's *An Inquiry into the Principles of Political Economy*, 2 v., A. Skinner, ed. (Edinburgh, 1966); Johnson, *Predecessors*, pp. 209ff; S. Sen, *Steuart*; and Hirschman, *Passions*.
121. A. Skinner, "Economics and Politics," pp. 30ff.
122. Here Skinner, Meek, Sen, and Hirschman take exception to the conventional wisdom that Steuart was *just* a mercantilist; e.g., E. Roll, *A History of Economic Thought*, 3rd ed. (Englewood, N. J., 1954), pp. 125ff. Skinner, "Analytical," p. lxxxii, argues that Steuart was an advocate of "planning within the framework of the exchange economy." Meek, "The Rehabilitation of Sir James Steuart," in *Economics*, p. 7, calls Steuart an "enlightened mercantilist."
123. Sen, *Steuart*, pp. 18–22; Meek, "Rehabilitation," p. 12; Skinner, "Sketch," p. lxiii; idem, "Economics and Politics," p. 19.
124. See Steuart, *Principles*, v. 1: pp. 39, 41, 69, 89, 96, 146, and 151.
125. Ibid., pp. 20 and 142–143.
126. Ibid., pp. 22, 89, 149, and 207–208.
127. Ibid., pp. 8, 17, and 74.
128. Skinner, "Sketch," p. xxiv; and Johnson, *Predecessors*, p. 211.
129. Steuart, *Principles*, v. 1: pp. 3–5 and 10, stresses the point himself.
130. As Skinner, "Analytical," pp. lxxxii and xlvi–xlvii, has noted, though, this line provoked criticism among his English reviewers.
131. Steuart, *Principles*, v. 1: pp. 122, 191–195, 217, and 278–279.
132. Ibid., p. 217. Discussed by Hirschman, *Passions*, p. 86.
133. Steuart, *Principles*, v. 1: pp. 191–195, 217–218, and 281. Again, he was criticized for this by his English reviewers. For Steuart's response see his addition to the 1767 text (noted by Skinner, p. 81). Also see A. Skinner's

remarks, "Sketch," p. xlvi.

134. Steuart, *Principles*, v. 1: pp. 29, 181, 238, and 287. For clarification see Sen, *Steuart*, p. 31.

135. Small, *Cameralists*, pp. 1–20. Also see Sen, *Steuart*, pp. 27 and 181; and Braun, "Economic," passim.

136. G. Parry, "Enlightened Government and Its Critics in 18th Century Germany," in *Historical Journal*, v. 6, 2 (1963), p. 188.

137. Ibid., p. 185.

138. Steuart, *Principles*, v.1: pp. 11–12, 16–17, 25, 96, 122, 189, 201, 217, 238, 257, 259, and 325. This specific passage was a later addition to the manuscript. But there are many similar claims made in the original 1767 edition.

139. See n. 130 above.

140. Insofar as this is true, and I think it is, Skinner's view supports the position of I. Bog versus that of C. Wilson. See n. 117 above.

141. Steuart, *Principles*, v. 1: pp. 217 and 278–279.

142. Ibid., p. 238.

143. Ibid., p. 279. This is a central theme of Hirschman's *Passions*.

144. Steuart, *Principles*, v. 1: p. 217. Forbonnais, "Commerce," in *ES*, p. 75, makes a similar claim.

145. See Nicole, quoted in N. Keohane, *State*, pp. 297–298, and Mandeville, *Fable*, v. 2: p. 270.

146. See, e.g., Seyssel, quoted in Keohane, *State*, pp. 35–38, and Skinner, *Found.*, pp. 260–261.

147. Calvin, quoted in Barker, *Church, State and Education*, p. 84. The theme is discussed by Skinner, Founda., pp. 315–316.

148. See, e.g., *CR*, pp. 116 and 180, respectively.

149. This, obviously, is what Steuart meant when he claimed (*Principles*, v. 1: p. 281), that "modern" luxury was "systematical" rather than "arbitrary."

150. Ibid., pp. 172, 191, 201, 238, 253, 259, and 326.

151. Ibid., p. 122. My emphasis. Cf. pp. 253, 259, and 326. It is interesting that in his essay on the Württemberg Estates Hegel uses a similar description to underline the need for reconstruction in Württemberg. See Hegel, "Recent," in *HPW*, p. 244.

152. See Sen, *Steuart*, pp. 9–10.

153. Steuart, *Principles*, v. 1: pp. 12 and 22–24.

154. Ibid., pp. 17 and 22–29.

155. Ibid., pp. 24–26.

156. Ibid., p. 219.

157. Ibid., p. 27.

158. Ibid., p. 251.

159. Ibid., pp. 231 and 243–244. See, especially, p. 326: "A principal object of [the statesman's] attention must therefore be, to judge when it is proper to encourage consumption, in favor of industry: and when to discourage it, in favor of a reformation upon the growth of luxury."

160. Ibid., pp. 43–47 and 265ff.

161. Steuart uses the phrase in ibid., p. 266.

162. Ibid., p. 224.
163. Ibid., pp. 251 and 263.
164. M. Raeff, "The Well-Ordered Police State," in *AHR*, v. 80, 5 (1975), is an invaluable source here; also Mack Walker, "Rights and Functions: The Social Categories of Eighteenth Century German Jurists and Cameralists," in *JMH*, v. 50, 2 (1978).
165. Raeff, "Police," pp. 1223–1225.
166. Ibid.
167. Ibid., pp. 1223–1224, 1227, and 1231.
168. In this, of course, we begin to move very close to the idea of "civil religion." As S. Wolin, "America's Civil Religion," *Democracy*, v. 2, 2 (1982), has recently noted, though, it is important to remember that traditionally the idea of "civil religion had been shaped by the state and imposed on society." In much of Protestant Germany, and certainly in Old-Württemberg, the reverse was true, at least for a while. Over time, however, the weighting of the political as against the religious shifted away from the religious and toward the political and economic. As a result, the language of the ordinances of the *Polizeistaat* became less religious and more secular in orientation. That is certainly the case in most of Central Europe, but in Old-Württemberg the language remained very religious.
169. Raeff, "Police," pp. 1226.
170. Here I have shifted the emphasis in Raeff's "Police" from a concern with a contradiction *within* the administration of the economy to one between religion and economics. This latter theme was anticipated by Merk, "Besten," p. 500. Much can also be learned about it from J. H. Elliott, "Self-Perception and Decline in Early Seventeenth Century Spain," in *PP*, no. 74 (1977), especially pp. 53–60, where the "moral" vis-à-vis "economic" response to "decline" is discussed.
171. Raeff, "Police," pp. 1224, 1226–1227, 1231, and 1235.
172. Ibid., p. 1231.
173. M. Riedel, *SHR*, pp. 135–166.
174. See Chapter 3 above for the particulars.
175. M. Walker, *Moser*.
176. Cf. n.'s 112, 126, and 152 in Chapter 3.
177. Walker, *Moser*, pp. 196, 200–201, and 211.
178. Ibid., p. 255.
179. Ibid., pp. 285–286.
180. Ibid., p. 287.
181. Ibid., p. 308.
182. By use of the term "government" here I mean to suggest that Moser is finessing a very old problem in political theory. See Keohane, *State*, pp. 76ff, for a brief discussion of the issue.
183. Walker, *Moser*, pp. 198–215, 285, 306–308, and 342–344. Also see Raeff, "Police," p. 1230.
184. See Merk, "Besten," pp. 516ff, and Walker, *Moser*, pp. 199–205 and 213.
185. Merk, "Besten," n. 55, p. 517, and Walker, *Moser*, p. 203. My use of the terms "power" and "plenty" is meant to suggest Viner's hint – pursued by

Bog, "Mercantilism" – that there was a gradual shift in eighteenth-century police ideology from identification with the political power of the state to a concern with the "welfare" of what we today – following Hegel – would call "civil society." Krieger, *Essay*, pp. 49–50, while discussing the shift from "security" to "welfare" cautions against complete endorsement of the "expanding welfare" thesis.

186. Walker, *Moser*, pp. 200, 306–308, and 326.
187. H. Liebel, *Enlightened Bureaucracy Versus Enlightened Despotism in Baden: 1750–1792* (Philadelphia, 1965); Raeff, "Police," sees this as fundamental to the *Polizeistaat* and not, strictly speaking, as an exclusively eighteenth-century problem.
188. Walker, *Moser*, pp. 194 and 215, is useful here.
189. Disinterestedness was a key characteristic of Steuart's "statesman." See his *Principles*, v. 1: pp. 26 and 235.
190. See, e.g., Chapter 3.
191. Here I am following A. Skinner, "Analytical," p. lxxxii. His argument would seem to apply to Moser as well. See, e.g., Walker, *Moser*, pp. 198ff, 204–205, 216–217, and 284–285.
192. Raeff, "Police," pp. 1224, 1227, and 1231.
193. Ibid., pp. 1228–1229.
194. Very clearly stated by Steuart, n. 159 above.
195. Steuart, *Principles*, v. 1: p. 266.

Chapter 6

1. It is an unfortunate truism of Hegelian scholarship that most of the work done on Hegel's concept of *Sittlichkeit* has been based on his discussion of the subject in the *Philosophy of Right*. Recently, however, attempts have been made to show how important *Sittlichkeit* was to Hegel during his years in Jena. Riedel, *SHR*, was one of the first to do this, but since then a number of other studies have offered a more nuanced view of the role *Sittlichkeit* played in the texts of the early Jena period. Among these, I have found the essays of Rameil, Horstmann, and Trede most stimulating. See U. Rameil, "Sittliches Sein und Subjektivität," in *HS*, v. 16 (1981); R. Horstmann, "Über die Rolle der Bürgerlichen Gesellschaft in Hegels Politischen Philosophie," in *HS*, v. 9 (1974); and J. Trede, "Mythologie und Idee," in *HS*, Beiheft 9 (1973). All approach the problem of *Sittlichkeit* from slightly different angles, but none, I think, really works the economic factor into the argument. As a result, none really confronts the full implications of the religious–economic overlay in Hegel's thought. Plant (*Hegel*, Chapter IV) offers, I think, the best brief overview of the period from the point of view of economics. He, too, though, neglects the overlay problem as I have posed it.
2. The point about Württemberg is rather important. It seems to me that Hegel might very well have accepted the Moser–Steuart version of the bureaucratic *Polizeistaat* had the political situation in Württemberg not changed dramatically in 1798. But the reestablishment of princely despotism in that year ruled out that solution to the religious–economic overlay.

3. As will become clear in this and the next two chapters, Hegel's concern with economics was directed more toward its relation to values than toward its formal organizational aspects.

4. Ferguson, *Essay*, p. 14. He develops the argument throughout Part I of the *Essay*, especially in pp. 11–15 and 30–37.

5. Ibid., p. 15.

6. Ibid., pp. 33–38 nd 43–44.

7. Ibid., pp. 15, 36, and 44, respectively. Crucial to our purposes is Ferguson's contention that the root of this problem lies less in the fact of physical indulgence than in "an error in speculation" (p. 4) about what is important for a *human* as distinct from an *animal* being. Schiller reiterates, *AE*, pp. 175–177.

8. The references used here are to statements of Goethe and Schiller cited in Chapter 5.

9. The labels used here are derived from the discussion in Chapter 5.

10. Dumont's discussion of the "economic ideology" is helpful here. See his *From Mandeville to Marx*, passim.

11. Throughout the notes I shall use shortened English titles, *Law* and *Ethical*, to identify the two texts.

12. On the *Critical Journal*, see Riedel, *SHR*, pp. 42–75.

13. Rameil, "Sittliches," reads much of what I see as unique to *Law* into the text on *Faith and Knowledge*. The economic factor, though, does not appear in that text. Hence, my differences with Rameil.

14. By "prescriptive" I mean to suggest that Hegel puts the argument into a "conditional" mode of discourse. By doing this he is able to present his audience (i.e., potential historical actors) with choices between types of actions and fields of values. I explain more fully in Chapter 7.

15. Here I follow Plant, *Hegel*, Chapter IV.

16. I refer, of course, to the titles of this and the next chapter.

17. Riedel, *SHR*, and H. Acton, Introduction to Hegel's *Law*, pp. 12–13 and 43–44, explain why the editors of the *Critical Journal* were concerned with the problem of natural law.

18. The discussion begins in *Law*, pp. 58ff.

19. Ibid., p. 64.

20. Ibid., pp. 62 and 70ff.

21. Ibid., p. 70. I realize, of course, that in Chapter 4 I argued for a Hegel–Kant convergence in the early 1790s. Clearly, something in their relationship changed by the late 1790s. Though Lukács (*Young*) presents Kant in stereotypical Marxist terms, he offers much insight into the Kant–Hegel relationship during these later years.

22. Hegel, *Law* p. 132. Cf. p. 79.

23. Ibid., pp. 68–69.

24. Ibid.

25. Ibid., p. 75.

26. Hegel picks up the Schelling argument in *Law*, pp. 83ff.

27. That *Sittlichkeit* was on the one hand a *problem* for Hegel and on the other the result of an assumed identity between sets of antitheses for Schelling goes far to explain the differences between the two. Hegel – in taking

account of the economic factor – was the more realistic of the two, but that does not mean he was any less idealistic in terms of the aspirations he projected into his philosophy of *Sittlichkeit*.

28. Hegel, *Law*, pp. 68–70.
29. Ibid., p. 68.
30. Ibid.
31. Ibid., pp. 70 and 128. The reference to "animal life" here is suggestive of Steuart and Ferguson. Another source could be Kant, *KOH*, pp. 60–62, or Schiller, *AE*, p. 177 (24/5). For more on "animal life," see n. 28 in Chapter 5 and n. 290 in Chapter 4.
32. Hegel, *Law*, pp. 70–83.
33. Ibid., pp. 79–97.
34. Ibid., pp. 79–80.
35. Ibid.; cf. p. 132.
36. See Chapter 4.
37. Hegel, *Law*, p. 85.
38. Ibid., p. 132.
39. Ibid., pp. 84ff.
40. Clearly, the conditional aspect of the argument is rooted in Hegel's voluntarism and his commitment to self-realizing teleology.
41. Hegel, *Law*, p. 85. I have commented on "leaping" in n. 34, Chapter 5. Of added interest: Rousseau's statement in *Émile*, p. 168 – "Let us transform our sensations into ideas but not leap. . .from objects of sense to intellectual object." Schiller discusses the point too; see Chapter 8.
42. Hegel, *Law*, pp. 85, 85, and 124, respectively.
43. Ibid., pp. 96–97.
44. Ibid., p. 124. Surely it is no accident that Hegel uses the participatory language of the "general will" here (pp. 87–88) to criticize Fichte.
45. Ibid., pp. 88–89.
46. Ibid., pp. 88–89. Cf. p. 85–86.
47. Ibid., pp. 84–85.
48. Ibid., p. 89.
49. Ibid., p. 92.
50. Ibid.
51. Ibid.; I stress the equation here because it is fundamental to an understanding of Hegel's thought. After 1803 he differentiated the absolute from the objective. For my elaboration, see the Epilogue.
52. Ibid., p. 84.
53. Ibid.
54. Ibid.
55. The terms appear, respectively, on pages 133, 114, 98, 104, 62, 132, and 70 of *Law*.
56. Ibid., p. 95.
57. See ibid., pp. 94 and 98, where the phrase is used. Clearly, he means to divide objective experience into two different spheres. See n. 63 below for a clear citation to that effect.
58. Ibid., p. 99.

59. Ibid., p. 104.
60. Ibid., pp. 66 and 98ff. On the importance of the parenthetical statement see n. 51 above.
61. Ibid., p. 109.
62. This is a trope that Hegel, *Law*, pp. 128ff, discusses in terms of Montesquieu. It was, however, also a major concern of Garve, who found it, as we saw in Chapter 5, most explicit in Ferguson.
63. Ibid., p. 104. Here, I think, is a perfect example of why Hegel's language needs to be decoded. Hegel is proposing to "lay hold on life" for the sake of *Sittlichkeit*.
64. Hegel uses the phrase "moments" in ibid., p. 66.
65. Ibid., p. 133.
66. Ibid., p. 104.
67. J. Schumpeter, quoted in L. Dumont, *Mandeville*, p. 33. The conceptual difference between "separate" and "definite" existence comes quite close to Polanyi's differentiation between a "disembedded" and an "embedded" economy.
68. Hegel, *Law*, p. 94.
69. Ibid.
70. Ibid., p. 95.
71. Ibid., pp. 99.
72. Ibid., pp. 128–129. Cf. n. 98, below.
73. Ibid., pp. 86–89.
74. Ibid., p. 108.
75. Ibid.
76. I cannot emphasize enough how important this is. It means that Hegel will have to develop – à la Marx – a critique of civil society from a point within civil society itself. This is not what Fichte and Schelling were doing at the time. The fact that Hegel does do it explains his differences with them and also casts some light on how he might be associated with Marx. The critique he does develop, however, differs significantly from that of Marx and comes close, I think, to anticipating – at least conceptually – Gramsci. For more on the last point, see Chapters 7 and 8.
77. I am referring to *AE*, p. 169, cited earlier. For a similar formulation see Herder, cited in R. Pascal, "Herder and the Scottish Historical Schooll," *Publications of the English Goethe Society*, New Series, v. 14 (1938–1939), pp. 32ff. This is all pertinent, I think, to Hegel's idea of giving "wings" to *Physis* discussed in Chapter 4.
78. Hegel, *Law*, p. 94.
79. In this essay, Hegel stresses the positive benefits of the market system of production and consumption. In the essay on *Ethical Life*, however, he begins to explore the negative aspects of the matter.
80. Note Mandeville (*Fable of the Bees*, v. 2: p. 350): "that every Body is obliged to eat and drink, is the Cement of civil society."
81. Steuart, *Principles of Political Economy*, v. 1: p. 89.
82. Ferguson, *Essay*, p. 43. That Ferguson did not find this a wholly adequate bond is revealed in *Essay*, pp. 19, 43–44 and 144–145.

83. On the role of providence in eighteenth-century social and political theory see Viner, *The Role of Providence in the Social Order*, especially pp. 23, 31–32, 36–38, 41, and 49.

84. Note Hegel's negative comment in *Law*, p. 132.

85. Hegel, *Law*, p. 103. Also see pp. 95, 102, and 123. This is an extremely important concession, for it allows Hegel to argue his case against the bourgeois conception of ethical life on the level of ideology. Also see Hegel, cited n. 104 below.

86. I think W. Kaufman's discussion of the difference between translating *Allgemeinheit* as "universality" and as "generality" is crucial here. For what is at stake see R. Schacht's very useful discussion in *Alienation* (New York, 1970), p. 34. Suffice it to say that the issue turns on the matter of Hegel's understanding of "relative" universals (i.e., closed systems of cultural meaning that really do not have any claim to true universality)

87. Hegel, *Law*, p. 123.

88. Ibid.; cf. p. 102.

89. Ibid., p. 114. I discuss the importance of "courage" (*Tapferkeit*), section 3.

90. Ibid., pp. 114 and 102–103, respectively.

91. Ibid., p. 103. Compare with Mandeville, cited in n. 28, Chapter 5.

92. Ibid., pp. 103 and 102.

93. Ibid., p. 102.

94. Ibid., p. 113.

95. See, e.g., Steuart, *Principles*, v. 1: p. 143; and Ferguson, *Essay*, p. 31.

96. Ferguson, *Essay*, pp. 31–36 and 52–54, is especially clear on this.

97. Ibid., p. 12. Cf. p. 262.

98. Obviously I have Montesquieu in mind here. He uses the phrase in *PTM*, p. 164.

99. Hegel, *Law*, p. 103.

100. Ibid., p. 102. Cf. Ferguson, *Essay*, p. 217, whose phrase I am citing.

101. Hegel, *Law* p, 123.

102. See Chapter 5 for the discussion.

103. Ferguson, *Essay*, p. 112; my emphasis. Cf. p. 247, where Ferguson proposes to use morality to prohibit the economic ethic from becoming the "principal" aim of life.

104. In his essay on the "German Constitution," written around this time, Hegel refers to the need of "the bourgeois spirit" to find an "outer legitimation" for itself. See Hegel, *HPW*, p. 190.

105. Schiller, *AE*, p. 177 (24/5).

106. Ibid., p. 181 (24/8); also see editorial n., pp. 277–278, where they point out that Schiller is playing with the "age-old distinction between intelligence and wisdom." For evidence of this distinction in Rousseau and Kant, see n.'s 215–216, Chapter 4. For Hegel, see Chapter 7.

107. Cf n. 3 above.

108. Ferguson, *Essay*, p. 112.

109. Note Kant here (quoted in Riley, *Kant's Political Philosophy*, p. 173): "Man in the system of nature . . . is a being of little significance. . . . But man as a person . . . is exalted above all price." For more on Kant's idea of person, see

nn. 289–294, Chapter 4.

110. Hegel, *Law*, pp. 101–104 and 112–114.
111. Hegel's fear of the tie between absolutism and state building is obvious here.
112. Ferguson, *Essay*, pp. 221 and 222, respectively.
113. Ibid., p. 220.
114. Ibid., p. 218.
115. Ibid., p. 262.
116. Ibid., p. 247.
117. Ibid.
118. Ibid., p. 221.
119. Ibid., p. 251.
120. Ibid.; Montesquieu, *The Spirit of the Laws*, T. Nugent, trans. (New York, 1966), pp. 317 and 327; and Garve, quoted in Koselleck, *Prussen Zwischen Reform und Revolution*, p. 100.
121. Ferguson, *Essay*, p. 70.
122. Ibid., p. 71. My emphasis to bring out the "ideological" aspect.
123. Hegel, *Law*, pp. 93–94, 102, 104, and 113–114.
124. Ibid., pp. 101–102. Note Gibbon's distinction between "personal valor" and "public courage." Its importance will be clear in section 3.
125. Ibid., pp. 103 and 104.
126. Ferguson, *Essay*, p. 224.
127. Ibid., p. 221, 238, and 238, respectively.
128. Ibid., p. 250. My emphasis to stress the possibility of "redirection." Schiller makes a similar claim, *AE*, p. 141 (20/3): to wit, "to destroy and to maintain" we must confront one determination "with another."
129. Very revealing here is Montesquieu's discussion of how "the principal citizens" should go about moderating "luxury." See Montesquieu, *PTM*, p. 206, where "the spirit of commerce" is the topic
130. Ferguson, *Essay*, p. 259.
131. Ibid.
132. I have recently found confirmation of my own view that *Tapferkeit* is important to Hegel's development at this time in Trede, "Mythologie," pp. 179ff and 190ff.
133. Hegel, *Law* pp. 114 and 103.
134. For Ferguson see *Essay*, pp. 35–36. Also see Schiller, *AE*, p. 177 (24/5), where the phrase "animality striving toward the Absolute" occurs.
135. Montesquieu, *PTM*, pp. 119–120.
136. For the quotation from the *Lectures*, see A. Hirschman, *The Passions and the Interests*, p. 106. also see Smith, *An Inquiry Into the Nature and Causes of the Wealth of Nations*, E. Cannan, ed. (Chicago, 1976), v. 2: pp. 302–304.
137. Smith, quoted in Hirshman, *Passions*, p. 106.
138. Saint-Lambert, *ES*, p. 206.
139. Ibid., p. 214; cf. p. 226.
140. Ibid., pp. 214 and 227, respectively.
141. Ibid., p. 227.
142. References here are to *The First and Second Discourses*, J. Masters, trans., R.

Masters, ed. (New York, 1964); and to the "Discourse on Political Economy," an article Rousseau wrote for the *Encyclopedia*, which appears in *On the Social Contract*, R. Masters, ed. (New York, 1978).

143. Rousseau, "Discourse," p. 219.
144. Ibid., p. 222.
145. Ibid., pp. 222–223. Also see Rousseau, *First*, pp. 54–55.
146. Rousseau, "Discourse," pp. 223–224.
147. Rousseau, *First*, pp. 41 and 54–55.
148. Ibid., p. 54. "True courage," I think, is what Gibbon (n. 124 above) meant by "public courage." It has a clear *political* component. Also see n. 152, below.
149. Discussed by Shklar, *Men and Citizens*, p. 14. Cf. Rousseau, *Émile*, p. 444, where the link is discussed in etymological terms.
150. Rousseau, *First*, pp. 54–56; idem, *Second*, pp. 81–82; idem, "Discourse," pp. 223–224.
151. Before Rousseau, Mandeville, *Fable*, v. 1: pp. 208–211, and v. 2: p. 86, had distinguished between "natural" and "artificial" courage. Although the former was common to men and animals, the latter was political in nature and was a unique quality of human beings.
152. Note Monboddo, quoted in Lovejoy, *Essays*, p. 45: to wit, "There cannot be virtue ... until every man is become a ... political animal; then he shows true courage very different from ... the brute."
153. Rousseau, *First*, p. 56.
154. Ibid.
155. I have borrowed the phrase from J. Geerken, "Machiavelli Studies Since 1969," in *JHI*, v. 37, 2 (1976), pp. 361–362.
156. Here I have found A. Bloom's Introductory Essay to his edition of Plato's *Republic* (New York, 1968), pp. 348–357, helpful.
157. For what follows see. A. Taylor, *Plato* (New York, 1957), p. 284; E. Barker, *Greek Political Thought* (London, 1918), pp. 146–147; W. Jaeger, *Paideia*, v. 3: p. 351; M. Foster, *Political Thought of Plato and Hegel*, Chapters I and II; E. Cassirer, *Myth of the State*, p. 84; H. Marrou, *A History of Education in Antiquity*, p. 78; and R. Cumming, *Human Nature and History*, v. 2: pp. 38–43, and v. 1: p. 286.
158. On *thymos* in Greek political philosophy, see Foster, *Plato*; W. Jaeger, *Theology of the Early Greek Philosophers* (Oxford, 1947), pp. 74–83; and Cumming, *Human*, v. 2: pp. 38–43.
159. These terms, of course, are integral to Rousseau's argument in the *Second Discourse*. Barker sees their relevance for the Greeks and I think they are crucial to the *Natural Law* and *Ethical Life* essays. See n. 192 below also.
160. Bloom, "Introductory," pp. 354 and 356, and Foster, *Plato*, pp. 53–66, are especially good on this.
161. Cumming, *Human*, v. 2: pp. 39–41, makes the key point when he suggests that Plato's notion of *thymos* is fulfilled in Aristotle's idea of the magnanimous man.
162. Again, I have borrowed a phrase from Geerken, "Machiavelli," p. 362.
163. Rousseau, "Discourse," pp. 218–219 and 224.

164. Ibid., pp. 222–223.

165. In *Émile*, p. 443, Rousseau put it this way: "In learning to desire, you have made yourself the slave of your desires." He is speaking here of civilized man.

166. Kant, *RWL*, p. 50, for example. And Schiller, n. 171 below.

167. Rousseau makes the distinction in *Contract*, p. 54. From Rousseau's comment, made with reference to Bodin, it is clear that he wishes to rehabilitate the classical idea of citizenship. Several points need to be made here. First, participation is the key to citizenship for Rousseau – which means he objects to Bodin's attempt to build "subordination" into the idea of citizenship. Second, A. Bloom, in the notes to his translation of *Émile* (n.6, p. 482) claims that the meaning Rousseau assigns to "bourgeois" anticipates Marx's usage of the term. R. Masters, *Contract*, p. 138, rejects this view. I think Masters is right insofar as Rousseau (in *Contract*, p. 54, and in *Émile*, p. 40) is using "bourgeois" to express the ambivalence, not the "one-sidedness," of the values of many eighteenth-century Frenchmen. For a similar usage see Diderot, quoted in Riedel, *SHR*, p. 84. For Hegel's exploitation of this ambiguity see n. 242, Chapter 4, and n. 7 to the Introduction to Part III.

168. For Garve's comment see R. Koselleck, *Prussen*, p. 88. On pp. 120–121, Koselleck wisely notes the close connection between Garve and Hegel.

169. I stress conversion here for the same reason D. Kelley, *The Beginning of Ideology*, pp. 88–89 and 150–151, does: it expresses not just the idea of a "turning" but also the idea of initiation into, and regeneration of, the community on religious grounds. The movement, from "inside out," is important, as was noted in Chapter 4 and in Part I.

170. Schiller, *AE*, p. 167 (n.). In what follows, I try to differentiate Hegel from Schiller. In the next chapter, however, I shall try to show how Hegel uses Schiller more positively. For a brief overview of the different aspects of Hegel's relation to Schiller see G. A. Kelley, *Hegel's Retreat From Eleusis*, pp. 55–89.

171. Schiller, *AE*. As the editors of *AE* point out in their Glossary (pp. 313–314), Schiller occasionally made the term *Gemüt* interchangeable with *Geist*. Also worth observing: the way Schiller in the Eighth Letter runs energy, courage, and spirit together in the textual context of a discussion of "warlike" virtue. See *AE*, p. 51 (8/6).

172. It is variously translated as psyche, mind, heart, or spirit.

173. See Chapter 4, especially n.'s 9, 226, 229–236, 289, and 324.

174. Hegel uses the term, e.g., in *TE*, pp. 485–486 and 500. In the essay on the Württemberg Estates (*HPW*, pp. 243–245) *Gemüt* seems to have a political connotation. Implicit in both, however, is the sense of "sacrifice" for the sake of the ethical well-being of the collectivity. For the tie, see Hegel's letter to Schelling, *Brf.*, v. 1: pp. 24–25.

175. I am relying here on M. B. Foster, *Plato*, p. 127.

176. Schiller, *AE*, p. 167 (n.).

177. See M. Ginsberg, "German Views of the German Mind," in *The German Mind and Outlook* (London, 1945), p. 47. My emphasis to accent the

422 Notes to pp. 224–228

nonspecific character of the aesthetic line.

178. This is something, I think, that Ripalda, "Poesie," in *HS*, v. 8 (1973), neglects to discuss, preferring a wholly aesthetic interpretation of Hegel's writings.

179. See Chapter 4, n.'s 232 and 289, and Introduction, n. 101.

180. Rameil, "Sittliches," pp. 154–155, is one of the few to appreciate the implications of Hegel's reluctance to use a one-sided subjective (i.e., romantic) vocabulary to define virtue.

181. Obviously what I am trying to do here is use Hegel's politicoreligious commitment as a way of separating him from romanticism.

182. Ripalda, "Poesie," implies that Garve's influence on Hegel ceased at Bern.

183. On the translation, see M. Stolleis, *Die Moral in der Politik Bei Christian Garve* (Munich, 1967), pp. 78ff. Garve died in 1798.

184. For the following discussion see Garve, *Ethik*, v. 1: pp. 572–575, 585, 603, 629, 630–631, and 653–654.

185. See Garve's discussion of *Tapferkeit* in *Eigene Betrachtungen über die allgemeinsten Grundsätze der Sittenlehre* (Breslau, 1798), pp. 135ff.

186. Ibid.

187. Ibid., p. 145. Insofar as Garve uses a *political* standard to define "civil society" he is employing the traditional, pre-Hegelian sense of the term.

188. Ibid., p. 137.

189. For this see ibid., pp. 146, 145, and 152.

190. Ibid., pp. 145–146.

191. Ibid., p. 145.

192. Hegel could be following Montesquieu here. Montesquieu had claimed that whereas "animals" were "united by sensation," men – in order to be human – had to be "united by the kind of knowledge" that goes into the formulation of "positive laws." See Montesquieu, *PTM*, p. 174.

193. I have C. Taylor, *Hegel*, in mind here.

194. I explain in Chapters 7 and 8.

195. A key point in separating idealists from romantics. Here Schiller, *AE*, p. 165 (23/7) says "nature" offers us "no directives." And Rousseau (*Émile*, p. 445) says "nature says nothing to us about those [ills] which come from ourselves." For Hegel, see n.'s 48–50, Chapter 4.

196. Hegel, *Law*, p. 104.

197. Specifically, I have in mind those aspects of *TMM* that deal with the Aristotelian and Protestant eschatological convergence. See, especially, pp. ix, 7, 43, 84–85, and 462–463. For an appreciative review of this aspect of Pocock's work, see Hexter, "Review," cited often in Chapter 3.

198. The following summary can be gleaned from Pocock's remarks, *TMM*, pp. viii–ix.

199. Ibid., p. ix.

200. Ibid.

201. See, respectively, J. Elliot, "Self-Perception and Decline," *PP*, no. 74 (1977), p. 46; Hexter, "Review," p. 319; Pocock, "*The Machiavellian Moment* Revisited," in *JMH*, v. 53, 1 (1981), p. 57; Kant, *KOH*, pp. 21–22; N. Hatch, *Sacred Cause of Liberty*. p. 19.

202. Pocock, *TMM*, p. 85; P. Miller, *The New England Mind: The Seventeenth Century*, pp. 420–421, has made the point nicely with regard to America and the dynamics of covenant theology: to wit, God works indirectly through a covenanting people to create the state. For more on the latter point, see the Epilogue.

203. Pocock, *TMM* p. 43.

204. See Gilbert's review, "Corruption and Renewal," in *Times Literary Supplement* (Mar. 19, 1976), pp. 306–308.

205. Pocock, *TMM*, pp. 462–463, is most explicit on this point. The point has been justly appreciated by Hexter, "Review," p. 308. The dovetailing is also noted repeatedly in MacIntyre, *After Virtue*, especially p. 168.

206. If there is a reason for calling Riedel's and Ritter's views on Hegel into question, it is here. They are undoubtedly correct to emphasize the role Aristotle plays in Hegel's thought early in the 1800s. But neither Riedel nor Ritter considers the possibility of Aristotelianized Protestantism.

207. Pocock, *TMM*, pp. 499–505.

208. For Calvin, see n. 66, Chapter 5; for Rousseau, see *Émile*, pp. 443–445; for Ferguson, see *Essay*, p. 261. For all three, the problem is understood in terms of a weakness of the "soul." Schiller reiterates, *AE*, p. 133 (19/7). Also see n. 139, Chapter 7.

209. Rousseau, *Émile*, p. 443; Ferguson, *Essay*, n.'s 4–7, above. Also see Garve's comments, *Anmk.*, pp. 318–321.

210. The distinction Diderot drew between the "real" needs of "nature" and the "imaginary" needs of "society" is important here. See Diderot, in *ES*, n. 3, p. 49.

211. Rousseau, *Émile*, pp. 443–444. I think this is evidence of Rousseau's Calvinism (n. 66, Chapter 5). Looking forward, it is very similar to Hegel's notion of "bad infinity," discussed in Chapters 7 and 8.

Chapter 7

1. The point has been discussed by Harris in his introduction to *Ethical*, pp. 5ff, and by Plant, *Hegel*, Chapter IV, espectially pp. 89 and 95.

2. Compare Hegel with Schiller, *AE*, p. 27 (5/4): "For society, released from its controls, is falling back into the Kingdom of elements, instead of hastening upwards into the realm of organic life."

3. All three texts, I would argue, are concerned with the need to prod the German *Bürger* into action. For a different view, see Plant, *Hegel*, pp. 95–96.

4. Plant, *Hegel*, p. 95.

5. See Harris, "Hegel's *System*," in *Ethical*, pp. 12–20 and n. 28, p. 90.

6. See n.'s 242 and 296, Chapter 4; n. 57, Chapter 5; and n. 167, Chapter 6.

7. Riedel, *SHR*, pp. 135–166.

8. Precisely why Garve and Hegel used the French "bourgeois" in this context.

9. Throughout this study (e.g., in the Preface and in n.'s 426–428, Chapter 4) I have made reference to Burke's idea of "dramatic action." In *A Grammar of Motives*, Introduction and Part Three, he has much to say about

the "dramatic" and "dialectic" aspects of language use. What he says is most relevant to Hegel. H. White, *Metahistory*, p. 94, has seen this clearly. I follow them both in what immediately follows.

10. White, *Metahistory*, p. 205.
11. Ibid., p. 227, refers to this as "mediating historicism." I borrow his formulation here.
12. Nicely put by White, ibid., p. 94. For a less historical, more existential rendering of the dramatic action framework, in which presentation of choice is interpreted as a way of inhibiting choice, see J. Shklar, *Men and Citizens*, pp. 5, 184, and 214; Shklar's subject is Rousseau.
13. Burke, *Grammar*, p. 202.
14. A. Hirschman, *Shifting Involvements* (Princeton, 1982), p. 5, explains the difference between the "push and pull" factors. In this he may have been following Lovejoy's earlier formulation of the same thing. See Lovejoy, *Reflections on Human Nature*, pp. 74–75.
15. See Hegel, *Ethical*, pp. 102ff.
16. The conventional points, I think, are all part of what may be called the naturalist or evolutionist view of the origin of society problem. Mandeville is a key figure here. As he put it (*Fable*, v. 2.: p. 189), "Men become sociable, by living together in Society." For a discussion of the point about Mandeville, see Dumont, *From Mandeville to Marx,* p. 67. For the same theme in Rousseau and in Rousseau and Monboddo see the two essays by Lovejoy in *Essays*. For the Scots see H. Höpfl, "From Savage to Scotsman," in *JBS*, v. 17, 2 (1978).
17. Hegel, *Ethical*, pp. 104–107. Cf. Mandeville, *Fable*, v. 2: pp. 214 and 242; Montesquieu, *PTM*, p. 175; and Schiller, *AE*, p. 175 (24/5).
18. Hegel, *Ethical*; cf. Rousseau, *Émile*, pp. 185–193.
19. Hegel, *Ethical*; for Steuart, who is quite original in this, see his *Principles of Political Oeconomy*, v. 1: pp. 30–43 and 146–151.
20. Ferguson, *Essay*, p. 5, uses the phrase.
21. I discuss this point at length in section 2. Suffice it to say here that the expansion is considered to be limited in that it is only "practical" in nature. In Hegel's terms, the expansion is one that takes place without an increase in "wisdom." Schiller, *AE*, p. 39 (6/10), and Kant, *CJ*, p. 106, say the same thing.
22. What was said earlier (Chapter 5) about Hume's exploitation of the double meaning of "commerce" is relevant here. Commerce qua trade led to commerce qua conversation and civility.
23. Many of Hegel's sources make this point. For Ferguson, see *Essay*, pp. 30–37, and Schiller, *AE*, pp. 175–181; and for Rousseau, see sections 2 and 3.
24. Hegel, *Ethical*, p. 150.
25. Ibid., p. 171.
26. Schiller, *AE*, p. 175 (24/5); my emphasis. Schiller neatly summarizes his argument (p. 181, 24/8) with the claim that the "moral is still at the service of the physical."
27. Hegel, *Ethical*, pp. 112–113.

28. Ibid., pp. 118–124 and 173.
29. Like Montesquieu, then, Hegel refused to make the idea of a social contract the axis of transition between savage and civil society. Both are evolutionists in that regard.
30. See Schiller, *AE*, pp. 11–13, and the editors' comment, pp. xlv–xlvi and lxii (n. 2).
31. Ibid., p. 11 (3/2).
32. Ibid., p. 13 (3/3). A key point because it allows Schiller to regard the *Naturstaat* as having a political dimension and yet to claim that that dimension, however natural, need not be a "norm" for a human being. The point was also made by Ferguson, *Principles of Moral and Political Science*, 2 v. (New York, 1973), v. 1: p. 256.
33. Schiller, *AE*, p. 177 (24/5).
34. Ibid., p. 181 (24/8). The terms here come from Mandeville, who was mentioned earlier in this regard. Schiller's terms are "animal void of reason."
35. Ibid., p. 181 (24/8).
36. Ibid., p. 13 (3/3 and 3/2, respectively).
37. Hegel, *Ethical*, pp. 104–105.
38. See n. 17 above.
39. Fear is stressed by Montesquieu, Mandeville, and Schiller (n. 17 above). Steuart emphasizes the demographic factor (n. 19 above), as does Mandeville, *Fable*, v. 2: p. 230.
40. On the four-stage theory, see R. Meek, "Smith, Turgot and the 'Four Stages' Theory," in *Smith, Marx and After* (London, 1977), and A. Skinner, "Natural History in the Age of Adam Smith," in *Political Studies*, v. 15, 1 (1967).
41. W. Lehmann, *Henry Home* (The Hague, 1971), especially p. 262, notes this tendency in Home and Steuart.
42. Mandeville, *Fable*, v. 2: p. 230, was one of the first to elaborate the point.
43. See Lehmann's discussion of Home, in *Home*, Chapter XII, and Steuart's *Principles*, pp. 146–151.
44. Mandeville, *Fable*, v. 2: p. 180; cf. pp. 180–183.
45. Steuart, *Principles*, v. 1: p. 89.
46. Ibid., p. 150.
47. Hegel, *Ethical*, pp. 104–105: to wit, "Need [belongs] entirely to nature."
48. Clearly the implication à la Ferguson and Schiller is that "society is the physical state of the species." The phrase is Ferguson's, *Principles*, v. 1: p. 24.
49. Schiller, *AE*, p. 11 (3/1).
50. I stress "yet" because Hegel will eventually link the "bad infinity" argument and social artificiality through a discussion of luxury.
51. Very clear in Rousseau, *Émile*, pp. 185–193. For a fine comment on this point see L. Colletti, *From Rousseau to Lenin* (New York, 1972), p. 164 (n. 67).
52. Rousseau, *Émile*, p. 314, summed up the issue well: "We work in

collaboration with nature, and while it forms the physical man (i.e., man in society], we try to form the moral man."

53. The phrase is Duncan Forbes', from his introduction to another edition of Ferguson's *Essay*.

54. Montesquieu, *PTM*, pp. 174–175.

55. Steuart, *Principles*, v. 1: pp. 269ff.

56. Ferguson, *Essay*, Part One.

57. Schiller, *AE*, p. 11 (3/2).

58. Steuart, *Principles*, v. 1: p. 266.

59. Ferguson, *Essay*, p. 237. I stress "accidental" because it is central to the argument in section 2.

60. Ibid., p. 217: "society is made to consist of parts, of which none is animated with the spirit of society itself."

61. Hegel, *Ethical*, p. 171: "The relation of physical dependence is absolute particularization and [yet] dependence on something abstract. [A true] constitution creates a living dependence and a relation of individuals, a different and an inwardly active connection which is not one of physical dependence."

62. Here Hegel is quite in line with some of the Scottish thinkers. See Tuveson's fine discussion, *Millennium and Utopia*, pp. 186–192. As we shall see in section 3, this is Kant's position in *CJ* as well.

63. Fully elaborated in Chapter 8, below.

64. To avoid the charge of anachronism, I should note that Ferguson uses the phrase, with much of its modern conceptual meaning, in *Essay*, p. 188. Cf. Mandeville, *Fable*, v. 2: p. 349.

65. Hegel, *Ethical*, pp. 120–124, 148–150, 154–155, and 167–174.

66. For Ferguson's sense of interest, see chapter 6, above. Hegel uses the phrase "system of need" in *Ethical*, p. 167.

67. Hegel, *Ethical*, p. 167. Cf. p. 123, where Hegel discusses the "spirit" that governs contractual relationships in an exchange society.

68. Hegel, *Ethical*, pp. 122–124, where exchange relations become "a totality" by way of the spirit that informs contracts.

69. There are echoes of this argument in *Ethical*, pp. 148ff.

70. In Rousseau's terms (*Émile*, n. 2, p. 488), Hegel wished to show how "it is possible for the morality of human life to emerge from a purely physical revolution." For Hegel, the revolution is a consequence of the principle of the division of labor, and the morality that is to emerge is that of *Sittlichkeit*.

71. Hegel uses the phrase "totality" frequently in *Ethical*; e.g., p. 124.

72. Ibid., p. 142 ("totality of particularity") and p. 173 ("particular possession...is essentially something universal").

73. Ibid., pp. 117 and 124.

74. Ibid., pp. 118ff and throughout the essay.

75. Ibid., pp. 149 and 118, respectively.

76. The phrase "relative ethical life" occurs throughout the text: ibid., pp. 102, 118, 124, 142, 149, and 173.

77. Rousseau, *Émile*, p. 243; my emphasis. See Bloom's useful note on amour

propre, pp. 483–484.

78. Rousseau, *First and Second Discourses*, Masters, ed., Note O, pp. 221–222.
79. Rousseau, *Émile*, p. 81. Cf. pp. 443ff.
80. Ibid., p. 236.
81. Ibid., p. 443.
82. Ibid., pp. 443–444.
83. Ibid., p. 81. Cf. Kant, *CJ*, p. 97 (n.).
84. Rousseau, *Émile*, p. 79; cf. Rousseau's remarks on "whim," pp. 48, 68, and 86. One should understand "whim" qua false wisdom as *fantaisie*, as misdirected imagination from a moral point of view.
85. Ibid., pp. 215 and 236.
86. Hegel, *Ethical*, p. 113.
87. Ibid., pp. 108, 150, 171, and 176.
88. Ibid., pp. 113 and 143, respectively.
89. Ibid., pp. 150, 171, and 142.
90. Ibid., p. 176.
91. Ibid., p. 120; Schiller, *AE*, p. 39 (6/10). The enjoyment and possession arguments are constant themes in the text.
92. Schiller, *AE*, p. 179 (24/7).
93. Ferguson, *Principles*, v. 1: pp. 134–139.
94. Ibid., compare this with Smith's position in *Wealth of Nations*, Cannan ed., v. 1: p. 17. There Smith claims that contractual cooperation makes participation in an exchange society a nonaccidental occurrence. It is, therefore, a distinctively human action. Ferguson, Schiller, and Hegel all disagree with Smith about this. For them an occurrence based on the dovetailing of material interest is no less "accidental."
95. Hegel, *Ethical*, pp. 148–155.
96. Ibid., pp. 118–124.
97. Ibid., pp. 118.
98. Ibid., p. 124; cf. pp. 142 and 149.
99. Ibid., p. 149.
100. Ibid., pp. 152–154.
101. Ibid., p. 153.
102. Ibid., p. 154. We mentioned earlier (Chapter 4, n.'s 242, 296, and 349) why Hegel as well as Lessing and Kant criticized bourgeois legalism. Hence, Hegel's remark about law acting as "a real physical control" against those who would take exception to "immersion in possession" as a way of life.
103. Ibid., p. 155.
104. Ibid., pp. 150 and 155.
105. Ibid., pp. 149 and 154. Here Hegel links "wisdom" with the translation of thought into action. Hence his comment: "Thus [the] rationality [of honesty for the bourgeois] is to perceive that absolute *Sittlichkeit* must remain a thought."
106. Rousseau, *Émile*, p. 37 (n.).
107. Hegel, *Ethical*, pp. 167–174.
108. Ibid., p. 167.

109. Ibid.
110. Ibid., pp. 169–170.
111. Ibid., p. 171.
112. Ibid., p. 121.
113. Ibid., p. 171.
114. Ibid.
115. Ibid., p. 144.
116. Ibid.
117. Ibid.
118. Ibid., p. 147.
119. I should note here that while the phrase "bad infinity" is Hegel's and comes from the earlier Jena period, it is not used in *Ethical*. Hegel, however, does use the phrase "false infinity," p. 174. There is, moreover, nothing unique about his usage of the infinity concept. It is, e.g., crucial to Schiller's argument, *AE*, p. 145 (21/3).
120. Rousseau, *Émile*, p. 195.
121. Ibid., p. 185.
122. Ibid.
123. Ibid., p. 189.
124. Ibid.
125. Ibid., p. 190.
126. Ibid.
127. Schiller, *AE*, p. 39 (6/10).
128. Rousseau, *Émile*, p. 188. Cf. Veblen's notion of "trained incapacity."
129. See Hegel, *Ethical*, pp. 167–171.
130. For Hegel on money see ibid., pp. 124, 154, and 167–174.
131. Steuart, *Principles*, v. 1: p. 45.
132. Ibid., p. 155.
133. Ibid., p. 44.
134. Hegel, *Ethical*, p. 154.
135. Ibid., pp. 169–171.
136. Ibid., pp. 169–171.
137. Ibid., p. 170.
138. Koselleck, *Preussen Zwischen Reform und Revolution*, pp. 121–122, citing an essay Garve wrote on luxury, tells us that it prefigured Hegel in much of its content. In that context, he cites Garve to the effect that desires that are limitless can only give rise to unhappiness.
139. For the tradition, see Chapter 5 above. According to Ferguson, *Essay*, pp. 243 and 261, and Schiller, *AE*, p. 133 (19/7), the obsession with luxury is "a weakness of the spirit." As Schiller said, "The senses can never set themselves up against man as a power, unless the spirit has of its own free will renounced all desire to prove itself such." Cf. Rousseau, *Émile*, p. 445.
140. See the discussion of Calvin, Chapter 5, for particulars.
141. Schiller, *AE*, p. 175 (24/4). Surely it is no accident that this statement is made in the context of a textual disussion about animality, infinity, and what it means to be a human being.

142. See n. 147 below for the sources.
143. For Hume see Chapter 5 above.
144. Hegel, *Ethical*, p. 170.
145. I borrow this formulation from K. Burke, *Grammar*, p. 92. Burke's discussion, pp. 92–94 and 112–113, addresses the religious–economic overlay problem quite explicitly.
146. Ibid., p. 94; cf. pp. 108–113.
147. Rousseau, "Discourse on Political Economy," in *On the Social Contract*, Masters' ed., p. 222: "to elevate [man's] soul perpetually toward [patriotism]; and thereby to transform into a sublime virtue this dangerous disposition [i.e., amour propre] from which all our vices arise." In *Émile*, p. 219, the disposition toward vice is regarded as an error of "imagination." In both contexts, Rousseau is referring to the pursuit of luxury – "that contemptible activity that absorbs all virtue and constitutes the life of petty souls" ("Economy," p. 223). In *AE*, pp. 175 (24/5) and 177 (24/6), Schiller speaks of the mistaken objects of reason qua aesthetic imagination. And Ferguson, *Essay*, p. 52, says most clearly that avarice and vanity "are not to be charged upon any excess in the care of ourselves, but upon a mere mistake in the choice of our objects." And later (p. 217) he equates the ascendancy of luxury with "profit" and "interest" and claims that all three advance at the expense of a properly directed "imagination." For Hegel, *Ethical*, p. 177, "lack of imagination" is the root cause of "irreligion" in the modern age.
148. Rousseau, "Economy," p. 222.
149. The relevance of this formulation to Löwith's thesis, discussed in Chapter 4, should be noted.
150. Fully appreciated by Lovejoy, *Reflections*, pp. 208ff.
151. Veblen, quoted in Lovejoy, ibid., pp. 209–210.
152. Ibid., p. 210.
153. Ibid.
154. Ferguson, *Essay*, p. 143.
155. Ibid., pp. 161–162.
156. Diderot, quoted in *ES*, n. 3, p. 49.
157. See Chapter 5 above.
158. To wit, Rousseau (*Émile*, p. 445): "It is not within our control to have or not have passions. But it is within our control to reign over them." This, of course, is precisely where Rousseau, Ferguson, Schiller, Kant, and Hegel thought morality began.
159. See n.'s 63–69, Chapter 5 above. The quotations here are from Calvin's *Institutes*.
160. Note H. Deane's discussion of Hobbes and Augustine on this point, *The Political and Social Ideas of St. Augustine* (New York, 1963), pp. 46ff and n. 31, p. 267.
161. Kant, *CJ*, pp. 95–96; my emphases.
162. See Chapter 4 above, especially n. 283.
163. Kant, *CJ*, p. 95.
164. Ibid.; in *Ethical*, pp. 176, Hegel invokes this idea as an alternative to the

bourgeois system of recognition.

165. Kant, *CJ*, p. 93. I have discussed Hegel's similar position on this in Chapter 4. It relates to the Pantheism–Pelagian and Stoic–Platonic tendencies in late eighteenth-century German culture.

166. Ibid., pp. 92ff; in these pages Kant very often associates the end of creation with "freedom" and religion.

167. The point has been discussed at length in Chapter 4.

168. Kant, *CJ*, p. 93. Cf. n. 1, p. 97.

169. Ibid., p. 97.

170. Ibid.

171. Ibid., pp. 97 and 94, respectively. For Kant (p. 106) real existence is associated with the "wisdom" we possess about final ends.

172. Ibid., p. 97.

173. This fits nicely into Kant's theology of history discussed in Chapter 4 above. See, especially, *RWL*, p. 46. He signals the connection in *CJ*, n. 1, pp. 97–98, when he contrasts enjoyment and "doing," a main religious theme in *RWL*.

174. I discuss the notion of Christian pride in the Epilogue. Suffice it to say here that Hegel and Kant (*RWL*, n.'s pp. 172–173) wish to make the practice of piety the instrument of collective reformation and civil pride.

Chapter 8

1. What I wish to stress here is that at a certain point in the text Hegel's handling of the division of labor concept becomes "conditional." It becomes associated with the "work-like" quality of the text – that is, it operates according to a logic internal to the argument of the text itself. Its references, therefore, are not contextual in any obvious sense. For more on the work like quality of the text, see the Epilogue, n.'s 106 and 107.

2. In some respects, Scottish ambivalence about the division of labor lies at the heart of the "paradox of progress" argument that is so often used in discussions of Scottish thinkers. See, e.g., Hirschman's discussion, *Shifting Involvements*, p. 49, and the literature cited therein in n. 6, p. 49.

3. Smith, *The Wealth of Nations*, Cannan, ed., v. 2: p. 302.

4. Ferguson, *An Essay on the History of Civil Society*, p. 183.

5. Ibid.

6. Ibid., p. 218.

7. Smith, *Wealth*, v. 2: pp. 302–303.

8. R. Pascal made the point long ago.

9. The phrases come from Schiller, *AE.*, pp. 39–43.

10. Ibid., p. 33 (6/6).

11. Ibid., p. 35 (6/7).

12. Ibid., p. 35 (6/8). I prefer Snell's translation of *Amt* as "function" here rather than the editors' translation as "office."

13. Ibid., p. 35 (6/7). Cf. Ferguson, *Essay*, pp. 182–183.

14. Schiller, *AE*, p. 35. CF. ed. n. on Hölderlin, p. 232.

15. Ibid., p. 27 (5/4). The "relapsing" phrase is from Snell's translation.

16. See, respectively, ibid., pp. 37 (6/9), 27 (5/5), and 27 (5/5).

17. Ibid., p. 43 (6/14).
18. In ibid., p. 27 (5/5), the phrase "without ever acquiring therefore a heart that is truly sociable, we suffer all the contagions ... of society" is strikingly similar to Ferguson's "spirit of society" phrase in *Essay*, p. 218. Rousseau's "aggregation–association" distinction is relevant here, too.
19. Schiller, *AE*, p. 25 (5/3).
20. Ibid., p. 25 (5/5).
21. Ibid., pp. 63 (10/1) and 27 (5/5), respectively.
22. Ibid., p. 51 (8/6).
23. Ibid.
24. Ibid.; note the opposite conclusion Smith draws in *Wealth*, Book V.
25. Schiller, *AE* p. 27 (5/5); cf. pp. 51–53 (8/6).
26. Ibid., p. 51 (8/6). As we shall see, this is a key passage. It looks back to Kant's so-called "deepening" of Rousseau and ahead to Hegel. My emphasis to stress the voluntarist aspect of man's being a slave of civilization.
27. Ibid., pp. 27 (5/5) and 51 (8/6), respectively.
28. For the phrases, see ibid., pp. 27 (5/5), 51 (8/6), and 27 (5/5).
29. Ibid., pp. 51 (8/4) and 27 (5/5).
30. Ibid., pp. 49 (8/1) and 51 (8/6).
31. For the editors' comments on Schiller's use of "wisdom," see ibid., n. p. 238.
32. Ibid., pp. 51 (8/6) and 55 (9/1).
33. A main theme of Schiller's editors. They base their claim on the text of *AE*, pp. 9 (2/4), 17 (4/1), 25 (5/2), 45 (7/1), and 55 (9/1).
34. Very clear in ibid., pp. 45 (7/1) and 55 (9/1).
35. Ibid., p. 45 (7/1): to wit, "the State as at present constituted has been the cause of the evil...." For the "degradation" phrase, see p. 47 (7/3).
36. Ibid., p. 55 (9/1). As I show in the Epilogue, the idea of "instrument" has a long history in Protestant thought.
37. For many scholars this maneuver constitutes a typically German "sublimation" of politics. I argue against this view in the Epilogue.
38. The phrases come from *AE*, pp. 7 (2/3), 55 (9/2), 69 (10/6), 69 (10/7), and 87 (13/2).
39. Ibid., p. 7 (2/3).
40. Ibid., pp. 57 (9/4) and 147 (21/5).
41. Ibid., p. 57 (9/4). Cf. p. 185 (25/3). Here Schiller quite clearly is forward looking in a millenarian sense. Schiller's editors have quite rightly related this to Lessing (see ed. n., p. 296) and, by implication, to Joachimism. Kant's "philosophical" millenarianism is also relevant here.
42. Ibid., p. 7 (2/3).
43. The idea of "indirection" is discussed by Schiller in 1795 in a letter to Garve. The text, quoted by the editors of *AE*, p. cvii, runs as follows: "from the quite peculiar circumstance that the writer is as it were invisible, and has to work upon his reader from a distance; that he is denied the advantage of affecting the psyche directly through the living expression of speech to the accompaniment of gestures; that he can only address feeling

indirectly, through abstract signs, hence through the medium of the understanding. . . ." Several points warrant comment. First, the editors (pp. lxxxiff) claim that the "doctrine of indirection" is the "kingpin" of the argument in *AE*. They tie the doctrine, moreover, to the notion of "creative regression," which is crucial to Schiller's conception of "indifference." So it is important. Second, Schiller's letter indicates his concern with how the audience will receive his message. As I note in the Epilogue, this makes him more a "pragmatic" than an "expressive" artist. That, in turn, fits in nicely with Schiller's concern with what he called the "ideal of popularization" (*AE*, p. cviii). Finally, it is important to realize, as the editors have (n. 262), that the doctrine of indirection is basically a pedagogic conception that militates against "leaps in nature" – a theme in *AE*, pp. 139 (20/3) and 185 (25/4). And because it is pedagogical, it is "forward looking" in the sense noted above, n. 41. All these concepts, in short, are part of the same "semantic field," and all operate, in one form or another, in Lessing, Kant, Schiller, and Hegel.

44. Schiller, *AE*, p. 9 (2/4).
45. Ibid., p. 9 (2/5).
46. See ibid., pp. 45–61.
47. Ibid., p. 55 (9/1).
48. Ibid., p. 45 (7/1).
49. Ibid., p. 49 (8/1–8/3).
50. Ibid., p. 59 (9/7).
51. Ibid., p. 61 (9/7). I think this formulation suggests that Schiller wished to address a "middle class" audience. Hegel, as we have seen, is even more explicit. It is this group that has, supposedly, experienced what F. Hirsch has recently called the "paradox of affluence." Schiller's concern with the "middle class" is manifest in 1789 – in his inaugural lecture on universal history at Jena.
52. Schiller, *AE*, p. 61; the idea of art triumphing over nature presents a problem for those who wish to see Schiller and Hegel as pantheists. Conversely, it fits in nicely with the Pelagian analysis.
53. Ibid., p. 49 (8/3). And in the letter to Garve (n. 43 above) he says the artist must be "invisible" – a reference, perhaps, to the idea of the "invisible church."
54. Ibid., pp. 51 (8/4) and , above all, 55–59 (9/4–9/6).
55. Ibid., p. 61 (9/7). Cf. p. 57 (9/5), where art's task is to oversee the "union of what is possible with what is necessary."
56. Ibid., p. 61 (9/7). Hegel, we shall see, makes the same appeal.
57. Clearly stated, ibid., p. 147 (21/5).
58. Ibid., pp. 17–19 (4/2).
59. Ibid., p. 21 (4/5). The state here, of course, is an "as if" construction.
60. Ibid., pp. 145–147 (21/3–21/5).
61. Ibid., p. 147 (21/5). The counterweight claim is stated on p. 141 (20/3).
62. Ibid., pp. 147–149 (21/5–21/6).
63. In general, see ibid., pp. 35–43. In particular, see p. 37 (6/8).

64. Ibid., p. 39 (6/10). Schiller's conception of "imagination" is often misunderstood. To get it right, one should consult the ed. n., p. 234, and the entry in the glossary, pp. 306–307. Suffice it to say that Schiller did not countenance the use of imagination for what he called "arbitrary" purposes. Hence his position against "leaps" of imagination.

65. Clear from his n., pp. 141–143 in ibid.; the editors, too, make much of this point, pp. xxix an clxiv.

66. Consult editorial n., pp. 240–241.

67. Schiller, *AE*, p. 59 (9/6).

68. See, respectively, ibid., pp. 57 (9/5), 59 (9/6), and 59 (9/6).

69. Ibid., p. 59 (9/6).

70. Ibid.; I found this most revealing because it fits in so nicely with the axiological versus teleological argument that was discussed earlier (Chapter 1). It is also important in the context of *vitalistic* versus *reformist* approaches to religious renewal. The difference speaks worlds to the idealist–romantic dichotomy.

71. For Schiller's view against sudden leaps of imagination, see ibid., pp. 139 (20/3) and 185 (25/4). I should also note here that there is a clear conceptual relationship between "indirection" and "in-betweenness." On the "in between" (what the Greeks called "the metaxy") see Voegelin, *Order and History*, v. 4: pp. 330–333.

72. W. Jaeger, *Paideia*, v. 3: pp. 280–281, and P. Friedländer, *Plato*, v. 3: p. 121, both trace the idea of the "roundabout way" to Plato. And in both instances Hegel is cited as heir to that idea.

73. I say more about Lessing's view of indirection in the Epilogue.

74. Schiller, *AE*, p. 215 (27/8). As we shall see, Schiller equates this third kingdom with the idea of "indifference" itself.

75. Ibid., pp. 215 (27/9) and 217–219 (27/11).

76. Ibid., p. 217 (27/11). The claim should be read against the pretensions of enthusiasts and in terms of Schiller's pedagogical commitment to popularization.

77. Ibid., p. 219 (27/11). I stress the importance of "assent" in the Epilogue.

78. Ibid.

79. "Indirection," in other words, involves a commitment to realism as well as to a program of pedagogical idealism.

80. See E. R. Curtius, *European Literature and the Latin Middle Ages*, W. Trask, trans. (New York, 1953), especially pp. 397–401; and E. Kantorowicz, "The Sovereignty of the Artist," in *Essays in Honor of Edwin Panofsky*, v. 1, M. Meiss, ed. (New York, 1961), pp. 267–279. Also see Abrams, *Natural Supernaturalism*, pp. 117–122, for specific references to the German context under consideration here.

81. Kantorowicz, "Artist," p. 278, insists that the Renaissance conception of the redemptive power of art did not entail validation by anyone besides the artist. This is neither Schiller's nor Hegel's view.

82. À la Josiah Royce, Abrams makes the point about Hegel in *Natural*, p. 229.

83. Schiller, *AE*, p. 183 (25/2), refers to a "stage of reflection" between time
    and eternity. Earlier, pp. 139–141 (20/3), he had equated this reflective
    moment with indetermination. In both instances, he is talking about the
    moment of indifference and about the preconditions of a "liberal" state of
    mind.
84. Ibid., pp. 123 (18/2) and 161 (23/2). Ed. n., p. 257, and pp. xxxiiif, trace
    the idea of the "middle state" back to an early (1784) Schiller essay. We
    know, moreover, that many Württemberg pietists were using this idea
    during these years.
85. Ibid., p. 161 (23/2).
86. Ibid., pp. 163–165 (23/5).
87. Ibid., pp. 11–15.
88. For the general argument, see ibid., pp. 129–181.
89. Ibid., p. 139 (20/2).
90. Ibid., p. 171 (24/1).
91. Ibid., pp.. 161–165 (23/3–23/5). A key passage [p. 161 (20/3)] says that
    in this middle state the power to think and decide is imparted to man. That
    power, however, does not carry with it any plan for how it is to be used. It
    remains for man to decide that. For that reason, "voluntarism" and
    "liberalism" (n. 83 above) are connected in Schiller's thinking.
92. Ibid., pp. 161–169. Cf. p. 183 (25/2), where the "stage of reflection" is
    said to arise as sensation relaxes its hold upon man. This is a theme that is
    often discussed by liberal Scottish Protestant ministers (e.g., Hugh Blair).
93. Ibid., p. 161 (23/2).
94. Ibid., p. 163 (23/5).
95. Ibid., p. 171 (24/1).
96. Ibid., p. 141 (20/3–20/4). Schiller uses the idea of cancellation to express
    this. The key German term is *aufheben*. Ed. n., p. 257, uses the idea of
    "equilibrium" here.
97. Ibid., p. 167 (23/8); my emphasis. As the editors note (p. 254),
    indifference is not apathy. At the same time, they connect indifference with
    "the notion of *Bestimmbarkeit*," and we know from Chapter 4 that that idea
    is crucial to the telos of *homo religiosus*. From my limited reading in this area
    this connection is only possible if we read indifference in a Calvinist sense.
    Although I do not agree with E. F. Meylon's conclusion, his remark that
    Calvin used the idea of indifference to advance assimilationism is most
    important for our purposes here. See his "The Stoic Doctrine of Indifferent
    Things and the Conception of Christian Liberty in Calvin's *Institutio
    Religionis Christianae*," in *Romanic Review*, v. 28, 2 (1937), pp. 143–144.
98. See Schiller, *AE*, pp. 169 (23/8) and 147 (21/5).
99. Ibid., pp. 139 (20/3) and 183 (25/2).
100. Ibid., p, 141 (20/3).
101. Ibid., pp. 141 (20/4) and 105 (15/5).
102. Ibid., p. 145 (21/4). Cf. p. 89 (13/4).
103. Ibid., pp. 103–105 (15/5). Man, as it were, has in the "aesthetic state" a
    Pelagian-like capacity for "either direction." Like Hegel, though, Schiller
    wishes man to choose one direction rather than another. Schiller also speaks

of man's "mixed nature," n. p. 137.

104. Ibid., p. 147 (21/4).
105. Clear from ibid., pp. 139 (20/3) and 185 (25/4).
106. Ibid., pp. 139 (20/3) and 167 (23/8). In all this, of course, stepping backward leads to a "moment" of reflection. For Schiller, though, reflection does not translate directly into redemption. For a recent, quite unintentional, I am assured, reformulation of Schiller's argument, see A. Hirschman, *Shifting*, pp. 66–76, where the subject is (p. 67) how to "awaken the public citizen who slumbers within the private consumer." The parallels between Schiller and Hirschman (and his sources) are startling indeed.
107. Schiller, *AE*, pp. 123 (18/1) and 185 (25/4).
108. Ibid., Schiller's n., p. 103.
109. Ibid., Schiller's n., p. 209. The editors are quite right in stressing the importance of this idea. They call it "creative regression" (p. lxxxii). In Schiller's terms, it is the aesthetic condition itself – the "liberal" moment of reflection–indifference.
110. Note the quotation, n. 55 above.
111. Schiller, *AE*, p. 139 (20/2). In ed. n., p. 312, the editors cite this as "perhaps the key sentence of the whole treatise."
112. Ibid., pp. 135–137 (19/11), for a full statement.
113. Ibid., p. 137 (19/11).
114. Ibid., pp. 147 (21/4) and 163 (23/5).
115. Ibid., pp. 27 (5/5) and 51 (8/6).
116. Ferguson, *Essay*, p. 183.
117. Ibid.
118. Ibid., p. 185.
119. Ibid., p. 186; my emphasis.
120. Schiller, *AE*, p. 183 (25/2).
121. Another way of putting this would be to say that *Bildung* and *Besitz* were going their separate ways. Or, in Schiller's terms (*AE*, p. 139), "person" and "individual" were going separate ways.
122. Hegel, *Ethical*, pp. 100ff.
123. Ibid., p. 101.
124. Ibid.
125. Ibid., pp. 104–105, where Hegel equates "need" with what is natural.
126. Ibid.; in this sense, "feeling" and "need" are both "natural" but in very different subjective senses. Cf. Schiller, *AE*, p. 177 (24/6).
127. Hegel, *Ethical*, p. 102.
128. Here I have found Plant, *Hegel*, pp. 85ff, helpful.
129. Abrams, *The Mirror and the Lamp*, p. 52.
130. Schelling, quoted in ibid., p. 209. The parallel with Schiller's "by the grace of nature" phrase is important. Yet, as Abrams notes (p. 210), Schiller criticizes Schelling's view for its lack of attention to the "reflective" aspect of artistic creation.
131. Ibid., pp. 209–210.
132. Ibid., pp. 42–44. According to Abrams, it is this turning inward, toward

the intuitive, that defines romantic art.

133. Ibid., pp. 226 and 43–44.

134. Ibid., p. 43.

135. Plant, *Hegel*, p. 86, has seen this clearly.

136. Cassirer, *The Philosophy of the Enlightenment*, p. 327, puts it this way: "Genius has no need to go in quest of nature or truth; it bears them within itself."

137. Schiller, *AE*, p. 171 (24/1).

138. Consult Harris, Introduction to *Ethical*, n. 28, p. 90, for the specifics.

139. Abrams uses the phrase somewhere in *Mirror*. In our terms, Schiller's doctrine of indirection constitutes a corrective to Schelling's "leaping" (i.e., to his automatism).

140. I take up the theme of this paragraph in the Epilogue. For general introductions to the topic see Abrams, *Mirror*; and idem, *Natural*.

141. Plant, *Hegel*, pp. 86–87, is again helpful.

142. Ibid., p. 88. As we have seen, "assent" was crucial to Schiller and would be to Hegel. For both, therefore, the idea of the "audience" was crucial to their conception of art and *Bildung*.

143. Ibid., p. 87.

144. Hegel addresses the issue in *Ethical*, p. 126, in the context of a discussion of lordship and bondage. I discuss the issue fully in the Epilogue, especially n. 115.

145. See Abrams, *Mirror*, pp. 21–26.

146. Hence, both insist on calling spiritual man – the artist whose imagination has run away with him – back to reality. Hence, both make man's *Einbildungskraft* part of the effort to "discipline" civilization by means of culture. They do not see it, therefore, as a vehicle through which to escape from civilization to culture.

147. The point is brought out nicely in the editors' discussion of *Einbildungskraft* in *AE*, pp. 306–307.

148. Hegel, *Ethical*, pp. 166ff. Cf. Schiller, *AE*, p. 177 (24/6).

149. Hegel, *Ethical*, p. 102.

150. Ibid., pp. 115ff.

151. Ibid.

152. Ibid., p. 116.

153. Ibid.

154. Ibid.; as will become obvious, Hegel's aim was to make "speech" the key to public enlightenment. In this, the idea of "assent" is crucial. I discuss this more fully in the Epilogue. Suffice it to say here that there is, as Schiller's editors have well appreciated (*AE*, p. 316), a decided "democratic" aspect to this educational ideal. But it is "democratic" in a religious rather than a secular sense. As Schiller put it, *AE*, p. 217 (27/11), what was once "a monopoly of the schools" must be transformed "into the common possession [*Gemeingut*] of Human Society as a whole." It is this kind of "equality" that Schiller believes will be realized in the third age. Hegel makes this kind of "equality" essential to what he calls "ethical lordship" (*Ethical*, p. 126).

155. Hegel, *Ethical*, p. 105.
156. See, e.g., Hegel's statement of purpose, *Ethical*, p. 104.
157. It must become a *Gemeingut* (as in n. 154 above).
158. Here Hegel's political programming of the terms "voice" and "speech" is evident.
159. Hegel, *Ethical*, pp. 105ff.
160. Ibid., p. 105.
161. Ibid.
162. Ibid.; cf. p. 115, where "specific character" is equated with the "inner" that has acquired an "outer" political focus.
163. Ibid.
164. Ibid.
165. Ibid., p. 110. Cf. pp. 147 and 166.
166. Following Schiller, Hegel uses the terms "nullity" and "complete indeterminacy" in ibid., pp. 164 and 134, respectively.
167. Ibid., p. 109. Cf. n. 154 above.
168. Ibid., pp. 114ff. Here Hegel means to tie "speech" to the emergence of "rational" or "true" as distinct from "practical" intelligence. For the latter idea see Chapter VII, where it is connected with what Hegel called (pejoratively) the bourgeois penchant for "wisdomless" universals.
169. Ibid., pp. 102–103.
170. Ibid., pp. 143 and 153.
171. Ibid., pp. 114–115.
172. Ibid., pp. 143–145.
173. Ibid., pp. 114–115. I stress "persuasion" here to remind the reader of the pedagogical intention of the doctrine of indirection and to prepare the way for the discussion in the Epilogue of the first class as the carrier of an educational ideal.
174. Ibid., p. 152, where Hegel says the task of the first class is to cultivate "in the people" the "organic" (i.e., true *Sittlichkeit*) itself. In the Epilogue I note how this task can be explained in terms of the "creation" of *a people* argument.
175. Ibid., pp. 164–166. There is a "militant" aspect to Hegel's terminology here. But as was the case with Schiller [*AE*, pp. 49 (8/2) and 51 (8/6)], Hegel meant to equip the first class with the divinely inspired weapons of wisdom rather than with real ones. The first class, in short, is a "warrior class" in a very specific *cultural* sense: it preaches courage and pride in order, in Schiller's terms, "to fight a hard battle with the senses, which are loath to be snatched from their sweet repose." Its task is *ideologically* to contest the value orientation of the bourgeoisie – to fight a metaphorical "war of position" against bourgeois values. To read more militarism into Hegel's view than that would be a mistake, I think.
176. Hegel, *Ethical*, p. 143.
177. Ibid., p. 164.
178. Ibid., p. 144. Hegel's strategy, then, is to coordinate the arguments about indifference and the creation of a people with the argument that brings the first class onto the stage of history. Indifference is the precondition for the

first class; the first class is a pre-condition for the creation of a people; and the creation of a people is a precondition for the realization of true *Sittlichkeit* as a religious ideal on earth. Hegel's discourse, in short, is in the "conditional" mode.

179. I develop the religious aspects of this theme in the Epilogue.

180. Hegel, *Ethical*, p. 144.

181. Ibid.

182. Ibid., p. 145.

183. Ibid., pp. 116 and 165–166.

184. Ibid., p. 162. Here, of course, religious language begins to reassert itself *within* Hegel's work. See, especially, pp. 143–145 and 159–162.

185. Abrams, *Natural*, pp. 207–208 and 229–230, has appreciated the religious drive here. And he quite rightly relates it to the idea of *Bildung* in Schiller and Hegel.

186. Again, self-realizing teleology and the voluntarist aspect of Schiller's and Hegel's theologies of history converge at this "moment" in their thought. For them, it is the "moment" of liberal Protestantism.

187. Hegel, *Ethical*, pp. 108–116.

188. Ibid., pp. 110–111.

189. Ibid., pp. 111–112.

190. Ibid., pp. 112–113.

191. Ibid., pp. 112–113 and 117–118.

192. Ibid., pp. 113–114. Cf. n. 168 above.

193. Ibid., pp. 114–115.

194. The decisive argument appears for the first time in ibid., pp. 125–126. There "indifference" is related to the condition of "freedom" and to "what is most ethical" about life. The carrier of "what is most ethical" is, of course, the first class.

195. Ibid., p. 113.

196. Ibid., pp. 113–114. With this statement Hegel *sociologizes* indifference.

197. See Ferguson, *Essay*, pp. 183–186.

198. Ibid., pp. 28–29.

199. Hegel, *Ethical*, p. 130. As Hegel implies, the group gives "the form of unity" to "multiplicity."

200. Ibid., p. 158.

201. Ibid., pp. 152–153.

202. Ibid., p. 131. Cf. pp. 152–153.

203. Ibid., pp. 152ff.

204. Ibid., pp. 152–153.

205. Ibid., p. 152.

206. Ibid.

207. Ibid., p. 153.

208. Ibid.; cf. Hegel's remark (p. 149) that the "rationality [of the bourgeois class] is to perceive that absolute *Sittlichkeit* must remain a thought."

209. Ibid., p. 153. Needless to say, activism was implicit in this effort.

210. Harris, Introduction, p. 63, has this just right. Moreover, he well understands that this "need" is religious.

211. Hegel, *Ethical*, p. 162. Cf. p. 158.
212. I elaborate in the Epilogue.
213. The theme is also elaborated on in the Epilogue.

Epilogue

1. Though I have found J. Passmore's discussion of the different forms of pride – aristocratic, Pelagian, and Socratic – interesting I have "intimate" disagreements with him with regard to his choice of labels. What he calls "Pelagian pride" I would call "romantic" or "expressive." And what he regards as Socratic or "classical" pride, I would call Pelagian. Later, Passmore equates Pelagian pride with romanticism. For all this see Passmore, *The Perfectibility of Man*, pp. 287ff and 322. For the conception of pride in the eighteenth century see Lovejoy's essay on the subject in *Essays*. If the latter's essay on pride is read closely a problem arises. Criticisms of "pride" are directed on the one hand at Stoic intellectualism (i.e., men are gods) and on the other hand at Stoic prudence (i.e., man must humbly conform to nature). Read this way, Christian pride qua assimilationism is a *via media* between the two.
2. Hegel, *Ethical*, p. 158.
3. Schiller, *AE*, especially pp. 165–169 and n. 1, p. 167.
4. J. L. Stocks, "Scolē," in *Classical Quarterly*, v. 30, 3 (1936), is useful on the former; R. D. Cumming, *Human Nature and History*, v. 1, passim, on the latter.
5. L. K. Little, "Pride Goes Before Avarice," in *AHR*, v. 76, 1 (1971), pp. 18–19.
6. Ibid., p. 20; and Deane, *The Political and Social Ideas of St. Augustine*, pp. 16–19, 44–55, and 80–81.
7. Deane, *Ideas*, p. 57.
8. Ibid., p. 20; certainly it is no accident that Augustine regards assimilationism as a manifestation of pride and, conversely, that it is assimilationism that the *Aufklärer* wish to rehabilitate vis-à-vis Augustinianism. See Deane, pp. 16–17 and 49, for specifics.
9. See Chapter 4, above.
10. My reference here is to the "original sin" debate discussed earlier in this study.
11. To wit, our previous discussion of the differences between assimilationism and deification. See, especially, the Introduction, n.'s 70, 81, 190, and 221.
12. I have discussed the ties between Calvinism and Pietism and the idea of "relative" perfection in Chapters 1 and 2. Troeltsch, *ST*, p. 595, is clear on the connection.
13. The overlay here speaks directly to the claim that Smith is the Luther of political economy.
14. The theme of Chapter 8.
15. Two points warrant comment here. First, the point about independence from need is a main theme in Smith and Ferguson. It is not a German creation. Second, the "free-floating" character of the first class should not

necessarily be construed as an anticipation of Mannheim. It is just as easily related – as Walzer has taught us – to the Protestant notion of the pastor as an "instrument" of God. In the same vein, see the quotation from Choisy in Troeltsch, *ST*, n. 371, p. 906, where pastors are presented as "impartial mediators between the social classes."

16. It would not be difficult to twist this argument into one in which technology becomes a mode of salvation. That reading, though, would work against the idea of voluntarism as a "reflective" ethical moment.

17. Recall Crane's argument, discussed in Chapter 5, about the Anglican apologists. For an analysis of the dovetailing of religious and economic language among Calvinists in the sixteenth century, see D. Little, *Order*, Chapters 3 and 4, especially pp. 59–60, 66, and 96.

18. On the Weberian usage here, see n. 63, Introduction.

19. A crucial theme in appreciating Calvinism as a political ideology. See, e.g., Wolin, *Politics and Vision*, Chapter 6; Walzer, *Saints*; and Little, *Order*, Part Two.

20. Wolin, *Politics*, especially pp. 176, 180–181, and 192, is excellent on the distinctively Christian rather than classical aspect of this argument. In Pocock's terms (*TMM*, p. 374), it is when the "'end' of Aristotelian teleology" becomes swallowed up in the "eschatological 'end' of prophetic time."

21. Wolin, *Politics*, p. 19, notes how "architectonics" may be shaped to the needs of Christian theology. P. Riley, *Kant's Political Philosophy*, discusses Kant's "teleological architectonic" in terms that, I think, fit Hegel. My only difference with Riley is that he refuses, as Yovel does, to acknowledge that the German reconsideration of teleology was theologically rooted. I have argued otherwise in Chapter 4.

22. I am, of course, not comfortable with the idea that something can be "strictly" political. But there is a lot of literature on Protestantism as a political ideology that stresses its "antipolitical" or "nonpolitical" character. See, e.g., Skinner, *Founda.*, pp. 211 and 331; Wolin, *Politics*, pp. 166–167; Walzer, *Saints*, pp. 51–57; and Cumming, *Human*, v. 2: p. 3.

23. I rely here on E. Barker, ed., *The Politics of Aristotle*, (London, 1946), pp. lxviiff. Barker notes there that those in the *archē* generally held official positions. When, however, such "initiatives" came from "persons other than magistrates," then the word *demagogue*, he advises, is the relevant term. (See Barker, n. LL, p. 169). While this distinction may be important in the context of a discussion of Aristotle, it loses some of its force when we use *archē* as a term for "first or fundamental source." That is how it should be understood with regard to Hegel's first class. That is to say, leadership that comes from leading citizens need not be construed as coming from demigods because they hold no political office.

24. I borrow J. Shklar's term, *Men and Citizens*, p. 74.

25. In the Introduction to Part I, I made points about the "incipient" action, the formation of a "counterpolity" and civil piety. They become relevant here.

26. Barker, *Aristotle*, n. 1, p. lxvii, and p. lxviii, expresses the difference in two ways: first, in terms of the difference between being in the *archē* and being in the telos; and second, in terms of the requirement that initiatives be submitted to a deliberative body for validation. In our terms that means the first class is not a sovereign authority.

27. It is perhaps important that in Greek the deliberative body was the *ecclesia*: among some groups of Protestants the term acquired a different connotation. It meant the assembly of a religiously minded people in a voluntary social rather than "ecclesiastical" sense. Hence, the importance of Hegel's watchword: "the invisible church."

28. Thus the importance among Protestants from Calvin to Schiller of the claim that those charged with the task of social regeneration were involved in a "Second Creation."

29. The phrase "new order of men" relates back to the discussion of Joachimism in Chapter 1. It is also a constant refrain in the literature on Puritanism.

30. See Chapter 8 for the details.

31. The references here have been discussed in Chapter 1, esp. n. 133.

32. The line of continuity has been discussed in Chapters 1 and 2.

33. M. H. Abrams, *The Mirror and the Lamp*, passim, especially pp. 23 and 226ff, makes the latter point about romanticism. For our purposes it is important to stress that the Protestant conception of leadership was a highly "impersonal" construct. For this, see Wolin, *Politics*, Chapter Six, and Walzer, *Saints*, passim. Hegel's conception of the first class is, clearly, cast in the Protestant, not the romantic, mode. See, e.g., *Ethical*, p. 126, where "ethical lordship" is presented in impersonal terms. For an interesting attempt to run the two conceptions together see R. Williams, *Culture and a Society* (New York, 1958), pp. 44–46.

34. As we noted in Chapter 4, Hegel objected to the "cult of personality" that had grown up around the figure of Jesus for just this reason.

35. The call to "office," of course, is not meant to be a call to *political* office. This is why Barker's distinction (n. 23 above) between *archōn* and *demagogue* does not work in a Protestant context.

36. The "instrument" of God theme has been oft-discussed by students of Puritanism. See, e.g., Walzer, *Saints*, pp. 166–167; Wolin, *Politics*, pp. 177 and 186; and Little, *Order*, pp. 105ff. Also see n. 70, below. Schiller, we saw in Chapter 8, used the idea in *AE*.

37. By this I am referring to my earlier argument about the differences between Plato's *ethical* and the Stoic's *natural* conceptions of teleology.

38. Abrams, *Mirror*, pp. 14–26.

39. To wit, Mornay's remark (quoted in Walzer, *Saints*, p. 85) that the " 'whole body of the people' ...should be considered as 'the office and place of one man'." Calvin, as Little (*Order*, pp. 69–71) has noted, frequently used the idea of " 'the general voice' " to express the result of the communication between a "pastor" and his "pupils."

40. See Lessing, *LTW*, pp. 83–84 (n.'s 2–5 and 17) and 93–97 (n.'s 67–91).

41. Ibid., p. 95, and, more generally, pp. 93–97.

42. As was noted in Chapter 1, Lessing is drawing on pietistic sources here

(e.g., Spener). Schiller, it seems was indebted to Lessing on this point. See *AE*, p. 59 (9/6).

43. Lessing, *LTW*, p. 97.
44. I have found Cumming's discussion of the relationship between nobility and recognition helpful here. See his *Human*, v. 1, especially n. 76, p. 279.
45. Rousseau, *On the Social Contract*, Masters, ed., pp. 68–70.
46. Ferguson, *An Essay on the History of Civil Society*, p. 63.
47. On the Latin term, see Cumming, *Human*, v. 1, n. 12, p. 227. For how it figured in Protestant schools, see Kelley, *The Beginning of Ideology*, pp. 156–157.
48. Rousseau, *Contract*, p. 67, uses the idea of the blind multitude's need for "guides" to set up his introduction of the "Great Legislator."
49. To see the Calvinist roots of this, consult Little, *Order*, pp. 69–71.
50. Ibid., pp. 56, 75, and 129, characterizes this as "the dilemma of earthly power" that "haunts" Calvinism (not to mention many other isms).
51. The point has been made by Kelley, *Ideology*, pp. 150–151 and 157. Exactly where the one becomes the other is a knotty conceptual problem. Walzer (*Saints*, p. 27) resorts to an artificial distinction between "theology" and "ideology" and, as a result (p. 19), is required to study Calvinism as an ideology. Wolin (*Politics*, p. 193) argues that the lines between theology and ideology blur in Calvinism and leaves it at that.
52. A telling point made clearly by Walzer, *Saints*, p. 63. Also see Little, *Order*, pp. 69–75, where to become "all in all" is the telos of the pastor's preaching.
53. I follow Cumming, *Human*, v. 1: pp. 209, 286, 292, and 297. As Cumming notes, there is enormous opportunity for "religious" ingress in this conception of the statesman.
54. The relevant pages in *Contract* are pp. 65–71.
55. Ibid., p. 52. As Masters notes, n. 28, p. 137, this act is best understood as a "covenant" rather than a "contract."
56. See ibid., for the phrase.
57. Rousseau, *Contract*, p. 68.
58. Ibid.
59. Ibid., p. 69
60. On these authorities see ibid., pp. 69–70, and ed. n.'s 53, 55, and 58. I don't agree, however, with what Masters says there about Calvin. See n. 62 below for my reason.
61. Ibid., p. 69.
62. Masters in ibid., n.'s 55 and 58, downplays this point. J. Shklar, *Men*, p. 154, specifically downplays Calvin. She writes: "Calvin is mentioned only once, in a footnote and then as a legislator whose work did not endure too well." Curious, for Rousseau's note runs as follows: "Those who only consider Calvin as a theologian do not understand the extent of his genius. The drawing up of our wise edicts [in Geneva] does him as much honor as his *Institutes*. Whatever revolution time may bring about in our cult . . . the memory of that great man will never cease to be blessed."
63. Rousseau's use of "chiefs" is interesting, as Shklar, *Men*, p. 205,

understands, In the *Second Discourse* men who speak with a "divine voice" and with "celestial" intelligence are called "chiefs." Compare with Calvin, quoted in Walzer, *Saints*, p. 63.

64. Rousseau, *Contract*, p. 70.

65. Ibid., and, as Rousseau also notes here, religion and politics must "have a common object" if a "people" is to be founded.

66. Ibid., p. 70.

67. One should remember here that in Greek the word "belief" (*pistis*) also means "proof" and that the word for "obey" also means "believe."

68. Rousseau uses this formulation in "Discourse on Political Economy," in *Contract*, p. 213. Masters' ed. n. 10, p. 238, is very misleading. It implies that Rousseau was using the "voice of God" phrase as the Romans did and as a criticism of "revealed religion." That is true; but the phrase was also part of covenant theology and resistance theory. Hence, the symmetry among Calvinists with reference to the ideas of the "voice of God," the godly people, and the commitment to making that voice "all in all." Those ideas are not Roman.

69. The argument is clearly related to Protestant activism in general and to the "progressive sanctification" of the world in particular. Calvinism, of course, is the subject matter here. For all the details see Wolin, *Politics*, Chapter 6; Walzer, *Saints*; Little, *Order*, Part Two; and, especially, Troeltsch, *ST*, pp. 576–691.

70. Troeltsch, *ST*, n. 371, p. 906. Also see Walzer, *Saints*, p. 98, and Skinner, *Founda.*, pp. 231 and 238. According to Walzer (p. 99), there is a close correlation between the role the prophet played in Judaism and the role the pastor qua "instrument" of God played in Calvinism. (Cf. n. 36 above.) Troeltsch, n. 332, pp. 887–890, especially p. 890, is most emphatic on the activistic implications of Calvin's repeated references to the Old Testament.

71. Troeltsch, *ST*, p. 586.

72. Ibid., p. 589, for the "instrument" argument.

73. Ibid., pp. 628–629 and n. 271, pp. 905–906.

74. This is consistent with Calvin's wish (Walzer, *Saints*, p. 64) to depersonalize prophecy. It is also, as Little (*Order*, pp. 69–73) notes, crucial to Calvin's sense of the need for a "consensual polity." On both these themes also see Wolin, *Politics*, pp. 177–178, 186, and 191–193. On the presence of this consensual theme in Schiller and Hegel see Chapter 8, especially n. 154.

75. For the concepts used here see Burke, *A Grammar of Motives*, pp. 41–43. McGiffert, "Covenant, Crown, and Commons," in *JBS*, v. 20 (1980), p. 45, put it more succinctly: the first class should be interpreted as "the ecclesiola in ecclesia."

76. Little, *Order*, pp. 69–71, is especially clear on this.

77. Walzer, *Saints*, p. 55, speaks of "the coincidence of believer and citizen" in Calvinism. Cf. Pocock, *TMM*, p. 398, where theocracy and republic are said to converge.

78. I am combining here what was said earlier, in n.'s 37 and 38 above.

79. Troeltsch, *ST* p. 601 and n. 332, pp. 887–888, makes much of the heroic character of Calvinistic activism. He means, of course, to tie it to the "sanctification" argument that is central to his view of Calvinism. As we have seen in Chapter 4, Hegel's *Philosophy of History*, esp. Part IV, is shaped in this image.
80. Wolin, *Politics*, pp. 167, 180–181, and 190, is clear here. Walzer (*Saints*, p. 51) is also helpful. Both argue persuasively for the "two faces" view of Calvinism with regard to political action.
81. Wolin, *Politics*, pp. 180–181.
82. Troeltsch, *ST*, p. 595, discusses the idea of "actual holiness" as an alternative to Lutheran orthodoxy. He also ties it to the idea of "relative" perfectionism.
83. Ibid., p. 632; and Baron, "Calvinist Republicanism," in *CH*, v. 8 (1939), pp. 40–41.
84. I have detected some confusion in Walzer's account of this (*Saints*, pp. 84–85 and 90). His view of Mornay seems to oscillate between covenantal and contractual conceptions. That's fine; but the inconsistency raises questions about his larger thesis – namely, that the Huguenot differed from the Marian exiles on just this issue.
85. Burke, *Grammar*, pp. 196–197, explains the difference between the two processes.
86. Rousseau, *The First and Second Discourses*, Masters, ed., pp. 170 and 202; and idem, *Contract*, passim.
87. As was noted in Chapter 1, this procedural commitment was prominent in Joachim.
88. Rawls, *A Theory of Justice* (Cambridge, MA, 1971), pp. 83ff, has much of importance to say about different types of procedures. Here the procedure is "imperfect" rather than "perfect" or "pure."
89. This, as Troeltsch (*ST*, p. 632) and Walzer (*Saints*, p. 90) have noted, is typical of a certain kind of Calvinism.
90. From Puritanism, through Pietism, to John Stuart Mill there is a tendency that holds that free public debate clarifies truth. Cartwright is cited by Little (*Order*, p. 92) as an example of this line of thought. For the pietists, see Chapters 1 and 2 above.
91. Lovejoy, *Reflections on Human Nature*, pp. 79–80.
92. Two points. First, Shklar, *Men*, pp. 174–175, argues the point with regard to Rousseau. And second, Rawls (*Theory*, p. 256), in a context of "deepening" Rousseau, makes a similar point about Kant. I wish to say it about Hegel.
93. For Hegel, the revolution in France was an "objective" expression of this moment.
94. I borrow the phrase from Beyerhaus, quoted in Little, *Order*, p. 41. As we have seen, for Lessing, Kant, and Hegel this moment is historically specific and contains an implicit criticism of "bourgeois" values. Rawls' interpretation of Kant and his idea of the "original position" does not seem to take this into account.
95. This is a familiar maneuver in Protestant thought. See, e.g., McGiffert,

"Crown." p. 45, and Shklar, *Men*, pp. 177 and 179. Thus, Rousseau's famous distinction between the "general will" and the "will of all."

96. Hegel, *Ethical*, p. 144, makes the distinction. It should be emphasized that Hegel was not drawing the distinction for Burkean reasons. True, for both the idea of a people is a "fiction" and has a "religious" element. But whereas Burke's people is constituted "by nature" (i.e., historically), Hegel's people can only emerge by transcending nature (i.e., by becoming something other that what it was).

97. McGiffert, "Crown," p. 37, speaks of the covenantal conception of a people as a "theo-political fiction." As his work shows, though, it would be more appropriate to speak of a "theo-social fiction" that has very definite political implications.

98. Cf. Chapter 5 for Garve's rendering of "excellence" (*Vollkommenheit*) as the telos of history.

99. See Burke's discussion of the "as if" character of this kind of action in *Grammar*, p. 196. In Riley's terms (*Kant's*, p. 24), it is a conception of moral causality that is "independent of natural causality." It has what Kant called "supersensible purposiveness" built into it. Schiller used a similar phrase, "super-sensuous origin," in *AE*, p. 137 (19/11).

100. This set of ideas is ably discussed by Riley, *Kant's*, pp. 70, 91, and 95. He is quite right to see this (against Rawls) as "reconceived teleology." I differ with him, though, when he says all of this operates independently of theology.

101. I borrow the terms from P. Riley, "How Coherent Is the Social Contract Tradition?" *JHI*, v. 34 (1973), 545.

102. Miller, *The New England Mind*, p. 419.

103. Ibid., p. 420.

104. As Rousseau noted, *Contract*, p. 70, collective action very often *at the start* involves religion and politics serving each other as instruments. Walzer, *Saints*, p. 259, makes the point about Protestant activism in early modern European history. The argument, as my contextual work has shown, is obviously important for understanding Hegel.

105. As Wolin, *Politics*, p. 191, wisely notes, there is no obvious distortion of value in the "transformation" from the one to the other.

106. Lukács, *The Young Hegel*, p. 507, is quite right to say that "absolute Spirit" has nothing to do with "real history." (Whether that makes it an "empty utopia" (p. 505) is another matter.) Where Lukács is mistaken, I think, is in believing that what came before absolute Spirit was "real" history. From the moment the first class comes into existence it is quite clear that Hegel's discussion of its positive tasks is cast in the "as if" form. If that is true, then absolute Spirit was developed not so much to deal with (i.e., escape from) a real historical situation in the present as to anticipate and confront a theoretical problem that had developed *within* the text itself. Absolute Spirit, in short, is a discovery–creation that grows out of the "work-like" quality of the text itself. E. Voegelin, "On Hegel: A Study in Sorcery," in *Studium Generale*, v. 24 (1971), pp. 355–356, has seen this clearly. I elaborate in n. 107, below.

107. Because the problem of absolute Spirit arises *within* the text we need to distinguish between two different aspects of Hegel's thought. First, *in context*, Hegel's preferences for the values of what we have called liberal Protestant humanism are clearly manifest in his antibourgeois, pro-*Sittlichkeit* mode of discourse. *In the text*, however, institutionalization of those values themselves creates a theoretical problem for Hegel that he tries to solve with the conception of absolute Spirit. In this mode liberal Protestant humanism acquires a very different meaning, for insofar as absolute Spirit is connected with it, it would seem now to contain a religio-cultural criticism of itself as a political form. That's not exactly what we mean by escapism. And it is precisely because Hegel develops the idea of absolute Spirit in this *textual* context that I think Voegelin, "Sorcery," is wrong to argue that Hegel wished to destroy the *metaxy*.

108. Wolin, *Politics*, pp. 187–188, has some interesting things to say about the politics of conscience in Calvinism. Much of what he says can be used to illuminate Hegel.

109. Williams, *Culture*, pp. 33–34 and 44–46, collapses the two together.

110. J. Schmidt, "Recent Hegel Literature: The Jena Period and the Phenomenon of Spirit," in *Telos*, v. 48 (1981), pp. 140ff, offers a nicely focused overview of the main lines of interpretation (e.g., Shklar, Hyppolite, Rosenkranz, et al.) of Hegel's conception of absolute Spirit.

111. It might be better to think here of the two faces of absolute Spirit as affirming a "sect–church" dichotomy rather than an "individual–collectivist" one. Little, *Order*, n. 173, p. 76, makes the point via Troeltsch about Calvinism. I think it would be wise to apply it to Hegel, too, especially since voluntarism and coercion are at issue.

112. Note the discussions of Wolin, *Politics*, pp. 193–194, and Walzer, *Saints*, p. 27, on the problem of "believing" and "knowing" in Protestant thought. For both these theorists, the relationship between the two is vital to the distinction between theology and ideology.

113. The curious aspect of this circularity argument is that by "closing" the circle Hegel means to keep it perpetually open.

114. Voegelin makes the point in many places. See, e.g., *Order and History*, v. 4: pp. 262ff, and "Sorcery," passim.

115. The real issue here is whether a teacher–pupil relationship can be rendered in terms of a ruler–ruled relationship. Both, obviously, involve authority; but one is quite clearly political, the other nonpolitical. My sense is that in a relationship where authority is spiritual and is meant to confer dignity on the person who accepts it, we are dealing with education rather than indoctrination, with what Hegel called "ethical lordship."

116. J. Talmon, *Political Messianism* (London, 1960), is a good example. The problem, as Wolin has noted (*Politics*, pp. 433–434) is that not every call for collective action need be "totalitarian." How to draw the line becomes the issue.

117. B. Schwartz, "The Religion of Politics," *Dissent*, v. 17, 2 (1970), tends to make these kinds of arguments with regard to late eighteenth-century German thought.

118. Tocqueville, *Democracy in America*, Mayer, ed., p. 547.
119. Ibid., pp. 547–548.
120. Ibid., p. 548.
121. Ibid.
122. Ibid.
123. Ibid., pp. 548–549. "Seeing from afar" was, as we saw in Chapter 4, a main idea of Lessing, Kant, and Hegel. It was, moreover, religious for all three in the sense Tocqueville is talking about here.
124. Ibid., p. 549; Montesquieu (quoted in Hirschman, *The Passions and the Interests*, p. 77) once used a very similar formulation in expressing his preference for indirection.
125. Tocqueville, *Democracy*, p. 632.
126. Ibid.; he is being facetious about the "vice" of pride.
127. Ibid., p. 12; he wished for what he called an "educated democracy."
128. A major theme in Wolin's, Walzer's, and McGiffert's studies of Puritanism.
129. My "two faces" argument from Part I is relevant here.
130. As before, the reference is to Löwith's *From Hegel to Nietzsche*, p. 47, and Part Two.

Index

Abraham, 99–103, 354n176, n182, n187, 361n285, 362n304; and covenant theology, 102ff, 349n106; and resistance theory, 107ff

Abrams, M. H., 266, 268, 283

absolute spirit, 445n106, 446n107, n111; among German idealists, 209–13; and first class, 276; and objective experience, 416n51; and point of indifference, 266, 268; as pre- and postpolitical idea, 290ff

accommodationism, religious, 12–17, 305n67, 310n92, 348–9n105, 352n150, 355n197, 393–4n318; and teleology, 383n127, 387n214; in Bengel, 96; in Calvinism, 92, 347n89; in Christianity, 12ff; in Clement, 15, 92; in covenant theology, 103; in Hegel, 387n211, n214; in Kant, 391n275, 395n341; in Protestantism, 15; its economies, 190–1. *See also* covenant theology; divine economy

Alexandrian Fathers, 27–9, 47, 54, 74, 306n70, 307n71, 308n79, 310n89, n92, n96, 313n142; and synergism, 55, 308–9n82; theology of, 13–6. *See also* Clement; Origen

Alte Recht (*Altrechtlern*), ix, 7–11, 37–9, 112–37 passim. *See also* Good Old Law

Ancient Constitution, 118–23 passim, 366n44; and Moser, 128–30; religious aspect of, 121ff

Andreae, J. V., 61–9 passim, 75, 78–80, 84, 85, 121; and civil piety, 67–8; and *praxis pietatis*, 66–7; and Second Reformation, 69, 332n182; as critic of orthodox Lutheranism, 66–8; *Christianoplis*, 66–8, 73. *See also* Pietism

animal life, 403–4n28, 416n31; and

Gemüter, 392n289, n90; in Ferguson, 415n7; in Hegel, 210, 236; in Rousseau, 221–3; in Schiller, 218, 236, 237, 261

approximationism, religious, 317n221, 334n209; as distinct from deification, 14; in Kant, 169–70. *See also* assimilation to God; deification

Aristotelianized Protestantism, 227–30 passim, 314n162, 423n206

Arndt, J., 62–6, 69, 74, 75, 79, 92, 94, 333n191, n199, n200; as critic of orthodox Lutheranism, 62–3; doctrine of assimilationism in, 62–3, 333n202; opposed to deification, 63; *True Christianity* by, 62–3, 66. *See also* Pietism

assimilation to God (*homoiosis*), 13–6 passim, 27–9, 44, 47, 50–1, 62, 63, 306n69, n70, 307n71, 333n202, 338n288, 350n123, n127, 384n144; among Alexandrians, 13–16, 147; among *Aufklärer*, 135, 146–7; among German Protestants, 74–5, 100, 104, 126; and *Gemüt*, 163; and Kingdom of God, 164; eschatology of, 16, 93, 149; in Hegel, 160, 279; in Joachim, 54; in Kant, 166–7, 169–70, 172, 279; in Pelagius, 27–9; Platonic aspect of, 62. *See also* drawing near to God; Genesis 1:26; *homoiosis*; self-realizing teleology

Aufklärung (*Aufklärer*), 12–32 passim, 135, 314n170; Pelagianizing tendencies in, 17–34 passim; theology of, 12, 22–7, 135

Augustine (Augustinianism): and sacramentalism, 42, 51–2; and theocentric religion, 17–27 passim, 30;

449

cunning, 387n216; in Ferguson, 205; in Hegel, 236, 244–5, 275, 427n105; in Kant, 430n171; in Rousseau, 243, 247, 286; in Schiller, 256–8, 418n106. *See also* civilization; luxury

Yates, F., 63–6
young Hegel: as concept distinct from old man, 140–52 passim, 155, 183, 245; Lukács on, 151f; Taylor on, 152ff